The Dynamics of Full Employment

LABOUR MARKETS AND EMPLOYMENT POLICY

General Editor: Günther Schmid, *Director of the Research Unit on Labour Market Policy and Employment, the Social Science Research Center (WZB) and Professor of Political Economics, Free University of Berlin, Germany*

This volume is part of a series arising from an international research network on 'Social Integration Through Transitional Labour Markets' that was funded under the European Commission's Fourth Framework Programme of Targeted Socio-Economic Research (TSER) 1996–9. This project focused on the potential of a new regulatory idea – 'transitional labour markets' – for building institutional bridges which support individual transitions between various employment statuses (unpaid and voluntary civil work, part-time and full-time work, continuous education or training, dependent employment and self-employment). A basic premise of the series is that 'making transitions pay' enhances the employment intensity of growth and avoids the dilemma of growing segmentation of the labour market into 'insiders' and 'outsiders' thereby fostering social integration in a world of rapid structural change.

Titles in the series include:

Working-Time Changes
Social Integration Through Transitional Labour Markets
Edited by Jacqueline O'Reilly, Inmaculada Cebrián and Michel Lallement

Labour Market Policy and Unemployment
Impact and Process Evaluations in Selected European Countries
Edited by Jaap de Koning and Hugh Mosley

Education, Training and Employment Dynamics
Transitional Labour Markets in the European Union
Edited by Klaus Schömann and Philip J. O'Connell

The Dynamics of Full Employment

Social Integration Through Transitional Labour Markets

Edited by

Günther Schmid

Director of the Research Unit on Labour Market Policy and Employment, the Social Science Research Center Berlin (WZB) and Professor of Political Economics, Free University of Berlin, Germany

Bernard Gazier

Professor of Economics at the University of Paris 1 and member of MATISSE (Modélisations Appliquées, Trajectoires Institutionnelles et Stratégies Socio-économiques), University of Paris 1 and CNRS, France

LABOUR MARKETS AND EMPLOYMENT POLICY

Edward Elgar
Cheltenham, UK • Northampton, MA, USA

Published by
Edward Elgar Publishing Limited
Glensanda House
Montpellier Parade
Cheltenham
Glos GL50 1UA
UK

Edward Elgar Publishing, Inc.
136 West Street
Suite 202
Northampton
Massachusetts 01060
USA

A catalogue record for this book
is available from the British Library

Library of Congress Cataloguing in Publication Data

The dynamics of full employment: social integration through transitional labour markets/edited by Günther Schmid, Bernard Gazier.
    p. cm.—(Labour markets and employment policy)
  Includes bibliographical references and index.
  1. Full employment policies. 2. International cooperation. I. Schmid, Günther, 1942– II. Gazier, Bernard. III. Series.

HD5706.D96 2002
339.5—dc21   2001040969

ISBN 1 84064 281 5

Typeset by Cambrian Typesetters, Frimley, Surrey
Printed and bound in Great Britain by MPG Books Ltd, Bodmin, Cornwall

Contents

Tables

Figures

Preface

The reasons to look for new institutional arrangements to cope with structural change are straightforward. Unemployment in most post-industrial societies has risen to levels unprecedented in post-war history. In countries that face this phenomenon, rising levels of unemployment have led to persistent long-term unemployment. The economic and social problems related to this development are clear: the longer the exclusion from gainful employment, the higher the risk of being also excluded from full participation in social and political life; this especially holds true for women and for young people with low skills. This threat to social integration may even undermine the trust in the basic institutions of our democratic societies. An *underlying assumption* of this series is that a return to full employment in the traditional sense is highly unlikely or only at unacceptable social costs. If some countries have succeeded in recent years in reaching levels of unemployment similar to those in the 1960s, it has been at the cost either of high income differentials and increasing numbers of working poor or of many precarious employment relationships, especially for women, and more or less involuntary massive early retirement for many older workers. The objective of this project, therefore, is to seek alternatives to such ill-conceived responses to 'globalization' and 'individualization' which in different ways can generate forms of social exclusion.

It is not only structural unemployment that is of concern, although this is the most visible change. More importantly, the underlying forces of balancing supply and demand on the labour market seem to be quite different from the past. The aim of our common effort was, therefore, also to understand these new dynamics and to ask which institutional arrangements would be able to prevent or to alleviate the high flows into unemployment and to mitigate the concomitant adverse selection mechanisms during the subsequent difficult processes of reintegration, which often result in the unemployed also becoming victims of social exclusion. Social exclusion is the counterpart of social integration which erodes the 'cement of societies'. Social integration in modern societies, therefore, does not just mean having a permanent job and being protected by social rights such as unemployment benefits. It also means having the perspective of evolutionary job careers, having access to the means of ensuring employability by lifelong learning, and being able to participate fully in all relevant areas of social life. The risk of unemployment is always a risk of reducing substantially the freedom of choice for a significant minority of people concerned, as well as the range of social participation.

The project was subdivided into three modules around the following topics: social integration through working time transitions, social integration through training and human capital investment and social integration through active labour market policy. Outside the formal contractual support, a fourth module was set up to work on a larger theoretical and empirical framework of employment systems. The common underlying argument of the four modules is based on the *concept of transitional labour markets*. Transitional labour markets (TLMs), as an *analytical concept*, refer to the observation that the borderlines between gainful employment and other productive activities are becoming increasingly blurred. The 'standard labour contract' is eroding, but we do not know yet which new standards will develop. People transit more and more between different employment statuses, for instance between different working time regimes, between unemployment and employment, between education or training and employment, between unpaid family work and gainful labour market work, and between work and retirement. Thus, as an analytical concept, TLMs emphasize the dynamics of labour markets, which means focusing the analysis on flows rather than purely on stocks, and applying methodologies that find out and explain patterns in the many transitions during the life cycles of individuals or groups in different societies.

Some of these transitions are critical in the sense that they may lead to downward spirals of job careers (exclusionary transitions), ending in recurrent unemployment or (finally) in long-term unemployment, poverty, discouraged inactivity or violent protest. We identified five major critical transitions during a life cycle: (1) the transition from school to work, (2) the transition from part-time to full-time work or vice versa, (3) the transition between family work and labour market work, (4) the transition between employment and unemployment, and (5) the transition to retirement. As a *normative concept*, TLMs envisage new kinds of institutional arrangements to prevent those transitions from becoming gates to social exclusion and to transform them into gates to a wider range of opportunities for the employed (maintenance transitions) as well as for the inactive or unemployed people (integrative transitions). 'Making transitions pay' requires institutions that realize in one way or the other the following principles: work organizations which enable people to combine wages or salaries with other income sources such as transfers, equity shares or savings; entitlements or social rights which allow choices to be made between different employment statuses according to shifting preferences and circumstances during the life cycle; and policy provisions which support multiple use of insurance funds, especially the use of income (unemployment) insurance for financing measures that enhance employability.

The following research institutions were involved in the joint venture to search for solutions to these problems: Economic and Social Research Institute (ESRI), Dublin; Hugo Sinzheimer Institute at the University of Amsterdam; Economic Faculty of the Universidad de Alcalá, Madrid; Institute for Employment Studies (IES), University of Sussex, Brighton; Manchester School of Management (UMIST); Netherlands Economic Institute (NEI), Rotterdam; the Centre for European Labour Market Studies (CELMS), Gothenburg, in cooperation with the University of Växjö; Modélisations Appliquées, Trajectoires Institutionnelles et Stratégies Socioeconomiques) (MATISSE), Centre National de la Recherche Scientifiques (CNRS) Université de Paris 1; Sociological Faculty at Tilburg University; and, as co-ordinating institution, the Labour Market Policy and Employment Research Unit at the Social Science Research Center Berlin (WZB).

BERNARD GAZIER
GÜNTHER SCHMID

Acknowledgments

The three-year project on which the contributions to this book are based has benefited from the support and help of a number of persons and institutions. We would like to thank, first of all, Jacqueline O'Reilly for her enthusiastic and energetic partnership in coordinating the 'TRANSLAM-project'. Her function included not only a key role in the project application and moderation but also a continuous stimulation of often frustrated or confused collaborators with their many diverse European idiosyncrasies. Jackie's language capabilities, her intellectual inspiration and Irish humour were indispensable in keeping the crowd together and chasing their members to perform what they promised, even when the result sometimes turned out to be a bit distant from the objective or at least different from what was expected, the present authors not being entirely guiltless.

We would like to thank Anders Hingel, Nicole Dewandre and Fadila Boughanemi at DGXII of the European Commission who managed the Fourth Framework of the Targeted Socio-Economic Research Programme (TSER) through which this project was funded. We are extremely grateful to Karin Reinsch, Christoph Albrecht and Hannelore Minzlaff at WZB who have provided excellent administrative support for the financial management and coordination of the project, as always. Special thanks go to Silke Kull for her able assistance in the final phase of editing, and, last but not least, to Andrew Wilson, who as an excellent copy editor greatly improved our English and style. However, we as editors and all the authors of course remain responsible for any errors and weaknesses.

Finally, we would like to thank our publisher Edward Elgar as well as his friendly and most effective crew for continuous support and interest in publishing our research. A number of authors have received feedback on their work from outside the research network and they have personally expressed their thanks in the individual chapters.

This book represents a collection of chapters which bring together economists, sociologists, political scientists and lawyers who use both quantitative and qualitative methods from a comparative perspective to develop and apply the concept of transitional labour markets and to derive their implications for social integration in different societies. In many ways we as authors and researchers have benefited immensely from this period of collaboration, and we hope that some of these benefits will be passed on to our readers.

xiv

Contributors

Dominique Anxo is co-director of the Centre of European Labour Market Studies and associate professor at the Department of Economics, University of Gothenburg, Sweden. His research interests fall broadly into the areas of labour economics and industrial relations, gender and time-use studies and evaluation of labour market policy.

Peter Auer studied economics and political science in Paris, Vienna and Bremen. He is a former senior research fellow at the Wissenschaftszentrum Berlin für Sozialforschung (Social Science Research Center Berlin, WZB), and former scientific director of the Institute for Applied Socioeconomics and has been programme manager of the European Employment Observatory. At present he is head of the labour market policy team in the Employment Strategy department of the ILO in Geneva.

Peter Bates, an economist, is a research officer at the Institute for Employment Studies. He has been involved in several research projects evaluating active labour market policies. He is currently engaged in a three-year panel study of the impact of the financial support given to young people moving into self-employment in the UK.

Patrick Detzel was a Marie-Curie research fellow attached to the European Work and Employment Research Centre, Manchester School of Management, UMIST, from 1998 to 2000, investigating the transitions from school to work of young people in Germany, France and the UK. He had previously completed at the University of Geneva his doctorate on the career trajectories of male and female banking employees, and is now employed as a financial consultant in Switzerland.

Bernard Gazier is professor of economics at the Université Paris 1 (Panthéon – Sorbonne) and member of the MATISSE laboratory (CNRS/Université Paris 1) specializing in statistical modelling, labour economics and industrial economics. He has worked mainly on labour market policies, and also on economic history, poverty and theories of justice. Recent publications bear on transitional labour markets, employability and employment in the services sector.

Jaap de Koning is professor of labour market policy, director of the Foundation for Labour Market Policy Research and co-director of the Social Economic Research Institute Rotterdam, Erasmus University Rotterdam. His main fields of interest are labour economics, the economics of education and training and policy evaluation.

Thomas Kruppe is a research fellow at the Institute for Employment Research (IAB), which is part of the Federal Employment Service (Bundesanstalt für Arbeit), Nuremberg. Formerly he was a researcher at the Wissenschaftszentrum Berlin für Sozialforschung (Social Science Research Center Berlin, WZB) and the Institute of Advanced Socio-Economics (IAS), Berlin. He is a sociologist currently working on comparative labour market analysis, mainly in the field of the evaluation of active labour market policies.

Nigel Meager, a labour economist by training, has worked at the Institute for Employment Studies (where he is associate director) since 1984, following research posts at the universities of Bath and Glasgow. His research interests include labour market disadvantage and the evaluation of active labour market policies, and he has recently undertaken several research projects evaluating the impact of measures to integrate disabled people in the labour market. Another major area of his work focuses on the labour market implications of self-employment growth. He is currently leading a longitudinal evaluation of public support for self-employment start-ups among young people in the UK.

Hugh Mosley is a senior research fellow in the labour market and employment research unit at the Wissenschaftszentrum Berlin für Sozialforschung (Social Science Research Center Berlin, WZB). He is a political scientist specializing in comparative research on labour market policies, especially working-time issues and labour market regulation.

Jacqueline O'Reilly is a senior research fellow in the labour market and employment research unit at the Wissenschaftszentrum Berlin für Sozialforschung (Social Science Research Center Berlin, WZB). Her research has focused on working-time flexibility in Britain, France and Germany. She is currently working on a new book, *Changing the Gender Contract*.

Ralf Rogowski is reader in law and director of the law and sociology programme at the School of Law of the University of Warwick. He has formerly taught at the Free University in Berlin and at Lancaster University, and has been a visiting fellow at the University of Wisconsin at Madison, at the University of Limburg at Maastricht and at the Wissenschaftszentrum Berlin. His areas of teaching are European law, labour law, comparative law and social theory of law.

Jill Rubery is professor of comparative employment systems at the Manchester School of Management, UMIST. Her research focuses on the comparative study of labour market organization, women's employment, payment systems, working-time arrangements and internal labour markets. She has coordinated the European Commission's network of experts on women's employment and acted as a consultant for the International Labour Office and the OECD.

Günther Schmid is director of the research unit on labour market policy and employment at the Wissenschaftszentrum Berlin für Sozialforschung (Social Science Research Center Berlin, WZB). He is also professor of political economics at the Free University of Berlin. His main research is on equity and efficiency in labour market policy.

Ton C.J.M. Wilthagen studied sociology, with an emphasis on sociology of law and criminology at Tilburg University and the University of Amsterdam. From 1985 he has been affiliated to several interdisciplinary research groups on labour law, industrial relations and social security, located within the Faculty of Law of the University of Amsterdam. Currently he is working as a senior researcher at the Hugo Sinzheimer Institute for Socio-legal Research on Labour and Social Security. He is also a member of the Amsterdam Institute for Advanced Labour Studies (AIAS). His current research interests include reflexive regulation of employment and industrial relations, flexicurity strategies and transitional labour markets.

E24
J68

1. The dynamics of full employment: an introductory overview

Bernard Gazier and Günther Schmid

The principal aim of this book is twofold. It seeks, first, to enhance understanding of the dynamics of modern labour markets and, second, to determine which institutional arrangements might best be able to prevent structural unemployment, one of the main causes of social exclusion. The various contributions share the assumption that social integration means more than having a decent and stable income stream from permanent employment. The network labour market that characterizes the knowledge society and gender relations that aspire to equality between men and women require an environment that is sufficiently flexible to allow workers real scope to make choices about what work they do and when and where they do it over the course of their lives. Thus social integration also means flexible careers that evolve over the life course, access to resources that ensure employability at critical points of transition and the ability to participate fully in all relevant spheres of social life.

The main question this book seeks to address, therefore, is how to achieve social integration through participation in the labour market without excluding productive activities in other spheres of social life. The main argument developed in this volume is that transitional labour markets – defined as legitimate, negotiated and politically supported sets of mobility options – are becoming an essential ingredient of successful employment policies.

In this introductory chapter we provide an overview of the key features discussed in this book. First, we briefly outline the notion of full employment as it applies to the modern labour market. Second, various approaches to studying the nature of and changes in employment systems are examined. Third, some theoretical and normative issues associated with transitional labour markets are briefly discussed. Finally, some empirical applications of transitional labour markets, and the associated policy strategies, are summarized.

1 FULL EMPLOYMENT RECONSIDERED

In the last 30 years, most of the developed industrial countries have been far from achieving the goal of 'full employment' as originally defined by Lord

1

Beveridge: 'Full employment means that unemployment is reduced to short intervals of standing by, with the certainty that very soon one will be wanted in one's old job again or will be wanted in a new job that is within one's powers' (Beveridge, 1945: 18). This definition made it very clear that full employment is far more than the absence of unemployment. On the contrary, 'frictional unemployment' is seen as a consequence of a progressive society in which workers retain the civil liberty to move between jobs. However, the definition also expresses very clearly the association of full employment with social integration or inclusion. Whereas Beveridge's first report on 'Social Insurance and Allied Services' (Beveridge, 1995 [1942]) took 'freedom from Want' to be the central aim of social insurance, he declared 'freedom from Idleness' as the ultimate aim of a policy for full employment. Labour markets should be organized in such a way that participation in productive and meaningful employment should be possible for all who wanted it. 'Idleness even on an income corrupts; the feeling of not being wanted demoralizes' (Beveridge, 1945: 19).

Thus, although Beveridge did not use the words 'social integration', active participation or inclusion in productive work and awareness of being an accepted part of a collective identity were an essential element in his definition of 'full employment'. As a consequence, the labour market should always be a seller's rather than a buyer's market. Full employment

> means having always more vacant jobs than unemployed men, not slightly fewer jobs. It means that the jobs are at fair wages, of such kind, and so located that the unemployed men can reasonably be expected to take them; it means, by consequence, that the normal lag between losing one job and finding another will be very short. (Ibid.: 18)

Beveridge was also bold enough to set the full employment level of unemployment at 3 per cent. What is more,

> this 3 per cent should be unemployed only because there is industrial friction, and not because there are no vacant jobs. For men to have value and a sense of value there must always be useful things waiting to be done, with money to pay for doing them. Jobs, rather than men, should wait. (Ibid.: 21)

There are also other reasons – 'only slightly less important' – why full employment should be given a broader and participatory meaning. First, if there is work for all, there is greater readiness to cooperate. Second, there is less resistance to progress. Third, a shortage of labour gives rise to technical advance (ibid.: 19)

As progressive as it was for the time of writing, neither the definition nor the policy menu proposed by the famous Beveridge Report can be taken for granted today. Certainly, the emphasis on 'freedom from Idleness' – that is, social integration – remains an important if not essential guideline for modern employment policy. However, the underlying premises as to the kind of jobs that should be available and the assumption that men or male breadwinners should be the sole target group for full employment policy are rather outmoded. The main causes of unemployment were quite simple for Beveridge: lack of effective demand, industrial change and the ensuing need to relocate. The policy menu, accordingly, was also simple: the lack of effective demand was to be compensated for by public expenditure and mobility incentives, or even by controlling firms' locational policies, with the emphasis on bringing jobs to men and not vice versa.

In the meantime, both the economy and society have changed fundamentally. The causes of unemployment, especially of persistent long-term unemployment, are much more complex, and the policies favoured by Beveridge turned out to be ineffective, politically unfeasible or simply inadequate. Thus both Beveridge's diagnosis and the course of action he advocated have to be updated. Of course, a myriad of studies have already done precisely this. At a very abstract, but also political, level, the key issue is the nature of the link between work and social protection that society wishes to put in place. The range of existing proposals can be illustrated by two important reforms recently advocated: the universal basic income and the employment subsidy.

As regards the *universal basic income* (van Parijs, 1996), the basic traits of such a reform are as follows. The core public intervention is to give everyone a minimum income regardless of situation or work effort. The introduction of such an income involves acceptance of the notion that labour and income should be disconnected in order to promote citizenship and 'real freedom' for all. The focus is on developing a non-profit-oriented lifestyle. The basic income, funded out of taxation, would substitute for welfare payments and labour market regulations. It would be left up to individuals to find work, to decide whether or not to accept flexible wages and to negotiate social protection arrangements. The approach is individualistic and egalitarian, with a strong concern for women and part-timers.

This contrasts sharply with the employment subsidy proposal (Phelps, 1997). Here what is suggested is that low-skill, full-time work should be subsidized in order to bring every full-time worker's wage closer to the level of the median wage.[1] Like Beveridge's prescriptions, it focuses on traditional breadwinners and deliberately excludes part-timers. The main objective of the reform is to reinforce the ties between work and social protection. This 'new social wage' is expected to 'shrink welfare market share' and to limit the costs of criminality. Financed by a payroll tax, the scheme is intended to replace other institutions (in the US case the Earned Income Tax Credit) and to be self-financing. The strategy is to narrow pay differentials for full-time workers while maintaining them for firms. Thus the philosophy is one of 'rewarding work' and 'earning one's way out of poverty': a radical way of 'activating' income protection, of pushing people towards work. The proposal converges with most of the official OECD proposals centred on the motto of 'making work pay' (OECD, 1996).

What is being proposed, therefore, is, on the one hand, a complete disconnection between paid work and basic social protection and, on the other hand, a reinforcing of the link between the two. The two proposals can be seen as the two polar doctrines for a post-Beveridge era. There is no space in this introductory chapter for a thorough discussion of these approaches. In essence, however, they both have significant drawbacks. As far as the basic income is concerned, the hope is that richer interpersonal relations, non-profit initiatives and altruistic behaviour will develop. However, the uncontrolled development of free market relations could lead to low effort, low protection and low wages for some groups and could undermine solidarity between people of different capabilities or capacities. The objective of the employment subsidy proposal is to build a relatively high-wage economy by explicitly subsidizing low-productivity workers. However, non-full-time workers are deliberately excluded, and this could generate poverty and strong gender tensions. It also seems contradictory to advocate the old American dream of self-sufficiency so strongly while permanently subsidizing low-skill labour. In both cases, the aim of social integration might not be fulfilled and a more unequal and segmented society could result.

This book goes back to the spirit of Beveridge and seeks to develop further the contribution of social reformers like Gösta Rehn. Considered one of the founding fathers of the Swedish model so often praised during the 1980s, Rehn was a pioneer in developing not only an active labour market policy but also life-long learning and the negotiated flexibilization of working time (Rehn, 1977). Whereas many studies have rather neglected Beveridge's emphasis on social integration, this book aims to refocus the analysis on the participatory aspect of full employment. It seeks, therefore, to understand the dynamics of modern labour markets and to develop institutional arrangements capable of preventing structural unemployment and its concomitant of 'idleness', which today might better be labelled 'social exclusion'. Following in Beveridge's footsteps, we take 'social exclusion' to mean more than simply the lack of a permanent job and exclusion from social entitlements such as unemployment benefits. It also means not having the prospect of a career that evolves over time, not having access to the resources needed to ensure employability and not being able fully to participate in all spheres of social life because of a lack of secure employment prospects. As Beveridge noted, social exclusion means 'not being wanted', being unable to use one's own productive capacities. Thus we use the term 'social exclusion' not in the narrow sense of selective discrimination or to denote cultural 'outcasts' but in a broader sense, to denote universal tendencies towards inequality of opportunity related to changes in the labour market (Silver, 1994).

The main question this book seeks to answer, therefore, is how to achieve social integration through labour market and employment policies. However, the question goes beyond Beveridge's target of achieving 'freedom from Idleness' mainly for 'male breadwinners'. For Beveridge, it was self-evident that the counterpart to this freedom from long-term unemployment or unpaid work was full-time employment with a wage sufficient to enable a whole family to live decently. Today, the question of participation in productive activities cannot be restricted to full-time paid work. Social integration or inclusion in the labour market now means more than simply 'making work pay'; it also means 'making transitions pay' in such a way as to extend the opportunity set available to individuals as they move between various productive activities, and particularly those seeking to achieve an equal balance between family life and paid work.

The second deviation from the Beveridge approach is a different view of the functioning of labour markets. The shift in work organization from the hierarchical bureaucracy of medium-sized or large enterprises to network labour markets renders obsolete the clear distinction between the market and the state. Thus a policy for full employment can no longer be confined solely to market intervention but must involve more subtle interaction between public and private capabilities and resources. Labour market and employment policy is becoming increasingly reliant on negotiated management, in particular at local level, that is at the level of the firm, community, region or industrial sector, which in many cases now transcend national borders.

The first key hypothesis that unifies the authors of this book is that the new dynamics of the labour market and the causes of structural unemployment can only be understood in the broad analytical perspective of employment systems. Employment systems are defined as the set of institutions and of policies affecting these institutions that simultaneously determine the level of production and employment. It is the interaction between production systems and labour market systems that determines quality and quantity of employment. And it is institutions that determine the outcome of this interaction (Schmid, 1994). These institutions act as filters, explicitly or implicitly suggesting to the actors certain reactions and excluding other possible reactions to external challenges from globalization or the new economy and to internal challenges from demographic changes or individualization. Thus the book addresses the question of how employment systems react to these challenges and whether good practices or transferable strategies can be identified that might foster mutual learning processes within the European Union.

The second key hypothesis around which the book is organized is that transitional labour markets are beginning to emerge. Transitional labour markets are both a theoretical and a policy-oriented concept. They are based on the observation that the boundaries between labour markets and other social systems (such as the educational system or private household economics) are becoming increasingly blurred and on the assumption that these boundaries have to become more open to transitions between gainful employment and productive non-market activities if 'insider–outsider' distinctions are to be broken down, long-term unemployment is to be prevented and segmentation or occupational segregation in the labour market reduced. This part of the book identifies the economic and institutional conditions for 'good' labour market transitions likely to enhance employability, prevent downward spirals into precarious employment statuses and increase social integration. In transitional labour market theory, employment acquires a new meaning. Traditionally, employment has been defined as the act of employing a person, the state of being employed or a person's regular occupation or business. In its new meaning, employment denotes a temporary state or the current manifestation of long-term employability (Arthur and Rousseau, 1996; Gazier, 1999; Moss Kanter, 1989). Whereas the prototype of the old employment relationship was the internal labour market, with its predefined entries and exits and robust and inflexible career ladders, the prototype of the new employment relationship is the network labour market, with its flexible entries and exits contingent on opportunities and professional expertise and discontinuous and flexible paths of accumulating work experience.

Transitional labour markets foresee the end of purely dependent labour, the individual's release from the bonds of the firm and the beginning of a new form of self-employment, in which the 'self' does not mean an independent self but rather an interdependent self, in which psychological identity flows from social integration, that is from the individual's relations with others. In this sense, social integration means participating in various productive social networks related not only to paid work but also to family work, cultural activities and voluntary work. And just as the world of work is changing, so the meaning of the term 'transition' is changing as well. It used to denote simply the movement between employment statuses. In its new meaning, however, transition stands for flexible employment careers, including the stages of preparation, encounter, adjustment, stabilization and renewed preparation for a new job or task (Arthur and Rousseau, 1996: 378). This redefinition clearly shifts the emphasis towards evolution. From this perspective, all apparently uncomplicated, one-dimensional measures intended to solve long-term or structural unemployment, such as providing a basic minimum income for everybody or the negative income tax, begin to look doubtful. Transitional labour markets provide a much richer and realistic concept of a proactive and cooperative labour market policy, which is the third key issue addressed in this book.

2 THE PERFORMANCE OF EMPLOYMENT SYSTEMS IN A TIME OF CHANGE

In Part I of the book, various approaches to the changing nature of modern labour markets are presented. The concept of 'employment systems' is developed as an analytical framework for international comparative studies of the relationship between employment regime and employment performance. This approach is then applied to an examination of the success of four small countries, Austria, Denmark, Ireland and the Netherlands. Finally, the youth labour markets in Germany, France and the United Kingdom are compared.

Chapter 2 (Schmid) begins by clarifying the terms 'globalization' and 'individualization' and discusses their possible effects within the employment systems framework. The central hypotheses guiding the subsequent empirical analysis are the concepts of 'requisite variety' (only institutional variety 'destroys' external variety); 'institutional complementarity' (the functional harmonization of institutions influencing a particular target variable) and 'institutional congruency' (correspondence of decision-making autonomy and financial responsibility for the decisions taken).

The chapter goes on to assess employment performance at different levels from 1971 to 1997. The European Union (EU15) is compared with the competing Japanese and American employment regimes and selected EU member states (Austria, Denmark, France, Germany, the Netherlands, Sweden and the United Kingdom) are compared with one another. Employment elasticities are estimated, since the more slowly employment reacts to economic growth, the greater the risk of segmentation in employment and unemployment becomes. High employment elasticity can be achieved through two different strategies: on the one hand, high wage flexibility, on the other, high working time and skill flexibility. Which countries follow which strategy can be ascertained by breaking down the change in employment into its individual components. A simple but effective method of decomposition reveals the contribution of demographic, behaviour-specific and policy-related factors to the dynamic of employment. The results of this decomposition serve as a basis for typologies of 'employment regimes'. The next concern is to ascertain whether these regimes also have identifiably different effects on economic well-being in various dimensions. By examining the combined effect on 10 performance measures, the chapter demonstrates the existence of important trade-offs. Good performance in one dimension (for example, employment growth or declining unemployment) might diminish performance in other dimensions (income distribution or productivity, for example). It also emerges from this exercise that no single country can be held up as a model of successful employment policy, and that countries can make, and have to make, choices regarding the employment regime they prefer.

Nevertheless, there are signs that those employment systems that have adjusted well to 'globalization' and 'individualization' share certain characteristics. Developments in Denmark and the Netherlands in particular, and to some extent in the United Kingdom as well, seem to offer some guidance for the less successful employment systems, and the European Union as a whole, in drawing up an effective employment strategy. Such a strategy requires four elements if it is to succeed. First, it should offer a broad opportunity set of mobility between various forms of employment relationships. Second, multiple risk management institutions should be established to protect workers not only against loss of earnings through unemployment but also against fluctuations in earnings as a result of changes in their employment relationships. Third, wage systems should be put in place that are increasingly independent of formal employment status and more closely linked to performance; these systems should be supported by an employment-friendly system of taxation and social security contributions. Fourth, and finally, employability needs to be maintained and extended through the institutionalization of lifelong learning, both at individual and at company level.

Chapter 3 (Auer) analyses more specifically the contribution of labour market policies and their delivery institutions to the employment success of Austria, Denmark, Ireland and the Netherlands. While the 'generosity' of the unemployment benefit system is often blamed today for the persistence of long-term unemployment, this chapter provides evidence that it might be the use of the unemployment benefit system as a temporary lay-off system rather than any lack of 'generosity' that explains to some extent the relatively low levels of long-term unemployment in these countries. The lay-off system,[2] which is especially highly developed in Austria and Denmark, can be seen as institutional support for 'maintenance transitions';[3] such transitions allow firms to adjust employment levels while at the same time providing income and employment security for workers. The study also demonstrates the extensive use of the unemployment insurance system for transitions between work and early retirement. Although early retirement schemes are costly and run counter to the trend towards longer productive lives, the chapter argues in favour of keeping this labour market policy instrument as a countercyclical buffer. However, it would be sensible to make this instrument reversible[4] and to develop institutional devices for transforming exclusionary transitions into integrative transitions for older workers, for instance by introducing phased retirement programmes. Special training courses for the elderly, work place adjustment, part-time work or wage subsidies would be further options.

Finally, the chapter argues strongly for the development within active labour market policies of institutionalized bridges that can be used in critical transitions between public and private labour markets or between gainful employment and other useful activities. In this sense, active labour market policy would be a permanent feature of modern employment systems. For individuals, however, such 'bridges' should be regarded only as transit zones. Modern labour market policy should be 'activating' rather than 'active' in order to prevent workers being trapped in publicly subsidized 'secondary labour markets'.

Chapter 4 (Detzel and Rubery) turns to the crucial role of the youth labour market in organizing the transition from school to work.[5] The authors choose three quite different employment regimes to demonstrate the impact of basic structural differences on employment opportunities and trajectories over the life course. The first of these regimes is the French one, which is still largely characterized by internal labour markets and central state legislation. The second is the German system, which still revolves around the three pillars of the dual vocational training system, the corresponding occupational labour markets and corporate forms of regulation. The third is the UK, a 'Balkanized', company-led employment system with little central intervention and regulation. Each system has specific strengths and weaknesses. The French system is particularly exclusive, offering few points of entry into protected internal labour markets and forcing young people into long sequences of transitions. This leads to a highly competitive labour market, especially for highly-skilled workers. This in turn gives rise to displacement processes affecting the less skilled or to an increase in the time spent in formal education. The German system is the only one that keeps the level of youth unemployment down to the average level, albeit at the expense of those hard-core, especially ethnic, minorities who fail to enter the occupational labour market and therefore suffer social exclusion. The British system leads young people to enter the regular labour market much earlier than their French and German counterparts. This gives them an opportunity to acquire more practical experience through the various employment transitions they undergo, although they have little incentive to acquire formal qualifications beyond the standard school-leaving certificates. This leads to some degree of career immobility. On the basis of these findings, the chapter argues strongly against a universal concept of employment systems and emphasizes the need for context-specific institutional arrangements to foster the mobility that is one of the most important characteristics of transitional labour markets.

Four conclusions are derived from this analysis. First, universal labour market policy prescriptions must be avoided. Second, lifetime trajectories have to be considered in evaluating proposals for transitional labour market policies. Third, the principles of institutional congruency and complementarity (see also Chapter 3) require that path dependency be considered in all policy proposals. Fourth, policies aimed at one group, young people for instance, have always to be assessed in terms of their side-effects on other target groups. Finally, in order to avoid zero-sum games among target groups, in which young people's gains might be achieved at the expense of low-skill women or older workers, transitional labour market policies also require an appropriate macro-level employment policy, a conclusion which is strongly corroborated by Chapter 2.

3   THEORETICAL AND NORMATIVE DEVELOPMENTS

The second part of the book tackles specific analytical and normative issues of transitional labour markets, starting with a presentation of the overall framework of the concept and continuing with in-depth studies of particular aspects. The theory of transitional labour markets is examined against the background of possible criticisms and the discourses of segmentation and transaction cost theory. A third chapter deals with legal barriers and opportunities and new legal issues arising from the concept of 'flexicurity'.

Chapter 5 (Schmid) starts with a critical consideration of the 'standard employment relationship', whose end is frequently announced as a proven fact. On closer examination, however, it becomes clear that the majority of workers are still in permanent, dependent, full-time employment relationships. 'Atypical employment relationships' (part-time working, self-employment, fixed-term contracts and agency work) are on the increase, but mainly at either end of the working life, where they serve as 'bridge jobs' for those entering or leaving the labour market. One exception is the substantial minority (in the Netherlands even a majority) of married women with children who traditionally use (or are confined in) non-standard employment forms. However, the gender gap in employment forms is closing, and what hitherto has been regarded as the standard employment relationship is also changing in nature, too, and increasingly includes elements of risk sharing, such as performance-related pay, and flexible working-time arrangements.

Globalization, information technologies, rising female participation rates and demographic changes, however, can only partly explain the change in forms of labour market participation. A theoretical model that distinguishes between sales contracts and employment contracts reveals that 'employees' (including women) and 'employers' will continue to have a strong interest in permanent employment contracts. However, such contracts will increasingly contain elements derived from sales contracts, such as explicit agreements on specified targets, the sharing of both profits and training costs and flexible work organization. Examination of the labour market for artists and journalists sheds further light on the world of work of the future, and especially on the opportunities and dangers of a new risk culture in employment. Here we find strategies – such as maintaining and enhancing employability through continuous training, multiple employment relationships, combinations of dependent employment and self-employment and public–private mixes of insurance systems – that can be considered as important elements in the re-engineering of the modern welfare state.

However, most people are unable to cope by themselves with the increasing risks associated with such flexible labour markets. This is especially true of the majority of families with children who have to struggle to combine unpaid care work (done mostly by women) with the need to earn a decent income through their labour services. Care work has to be recognized more explicitly as a productive social resource and institutional arrangements are required to enable people to cope with transitions between various forms of productive activities during the life course, especially those critical events related to the transition from school to work, from labour market to family work, from unemployment to re-employment, from dependent to self-employed work and (gradual) transitions into retirement. Both the new 'gender contract' and the new 'generation contract' require a new concept of 'full employment', for which the chapter provides guidelines and principles. It is suggested that 'full employment' be understood as a 'fluid equilibrium' around an average 30-hour working week over the life course, from which there could be substantial upward or downward variations (transitional employment, unemployment or 'inactivity') according to family needs, the need for adjustment to economic or technological change or simply changes in individual preferences. In order to support men and women in their attempts to cope with these critical transitions, reliable 'bridges' are required. These 'bridges' would take the form of legitimized and socially protected options to take, or to negotiate on, career breaks, amounting, in effect, to the institutionalization of transitional labour markets (for applications, see Chapter 12).

In Chapter 6, Bernard Gazier considers the problems of justifying, implementing and evaluating transitional labour markets as reforms of the labour market. He does so by linking this new concept to basic theories of the functioning of the labour market. Two main criticisms based on differing views of adjustment processes are discussed. The first, centred on classical labour market adjustments and flexibility, argues that transitional labour markets are unduly complicated arrangements and that mobility or leave arrangements are best managed through free negotiations between the actors who can choose from the available 'contractual variety.' This contrasts with segmentation theory, which suggests that transitional labour markets could become traps from which, for the disadvantaged elements of the workforce, it would be difficult to escape. By answering both criticisms, Gazier shows that transitional labour markets could be a realistic and effective means of reforming the labour market. He goes on to discuss implementation and evaluation problems stemming from complexity and control issues.

In response to the free market argument, transitional labour markets can be presented as a device for multiplying the number and interaction of adjustment variables in a field in which traditional variables such as prices, quantities and qualities (in other words wages, jobs, hours and workers) are strongly constrained and perform many functions. As far as the segmentation argument is concerned, it is shown that transitional labour markets, if properly managed, could confer greater bargaining power on 'outsiders' and disadvantaged sections of the employed workforce, thereby fostering social integration. The chapter investigates the complexity and control issues in some detail, examining the possible drawbacks of a locally managed negotiation process on 'transitions', chief among them the problems of moral hazard and adverse selection. The suggested solutions include the introduction of competition between employment agencies, a transfer policy allowing poor regions to finance 'transitions' and the introduction of homogeneous and relevant evaluation criteria. 'Employability' and 'profiling' are briefly discussed, and finally, transitional labour markets are presented as a specific learning and political process.

Chapter 7 (Wilthagen and Rogowski) deals with some of the legal aspects of the emergence, operation and efficacy of transitional labour markets. It starts with a discussion of the legal boundaries of labour market policies, which include legal complexity, regulation thresholds and the costs of transitions and transactions that arise as a result of legal regulation. It then explores a number of legal and social strategies and reforms that provide opportunities for a legal design attuned to the dynamics of transitional labour markets. First, a strategy based on the reflexive deregulation of legal barriers to transitions is discussed, with particular reference to a reregulation strategy involving the introduction of vouchers. The main thrust of these schemes is that workers are granted rights to transitions (for instance, training leaves or temporary short-time work) which are exercised within a legally determined framework but are brought into effect by means of an individual decision, freely taken, rather than as the result of risk. For this reason, these rights are also referred to as 'social drawing rights' (Supiot, 1999). The chapter carefully discusses historical experiences, the range of possibilities and the conditions under which transaction costs might be contained and collective and individual interests balanced within the context of voucher schemes, for instance through the introduction of so-called 'default terms'.

Second, the authors analyse some examples of reflexive regulation, and in particular equal treatment law, as a strategy for overcoming discrimination thresholds, with particular reference to the regulation of part-time work, 'flexicurity' and the regulation of training for agency workers. The chapter provides examples of good practice, with special emphasis on Dutch experiences, and stresses the need for intermediary job services or transition agencies to implement transitional labour markets effectively. The authors refer especially to the 'flexibility versus training paradox' and to the possible role of temporary work agencies (already widespread in the Netherlands) in providing a solution. It appears that this innovative institution is increasingly serving as a transition agency, channelling new entrants (young people) or re-entrants (women or men coming off extended parental leave) into the regular labour market. To some extent, they even provide permanent employment, albeit in the form of a sequence of jobs with different employers. Finally, the chapter explores the possibility of introducing a constitutionally protected right to transitional employment at the European level, even going so far as to propose a concrete formulation.

4   APPLICATIONS AND POLICY STRATEGIES

The third and final part of the book opens with an examination of the employment dynamics of EU member states that draws on the transition matrix of flows in and out of various labour force statuses. This matrix not only demonstrates the high level of mobility in the labour force in any one year but also reveals a diversity of country-specific dynamics requiring explanation and further research. This is followed by an investigation of transitions into and out of self-employment in Europe. Empirically, the emphasis is on the UK, and the investigation seeks to ascertain the extent to which new forms of self-employment enhance social integration. These empirical chapters are followed by discussions of three key policy issues related to the promotion of transitional labour markets. The first focuses on policies and institutional arrangements for working-time flexibility as a means of promoting integration and helping to maintain employability. The second examines the potential for transforming 'active' labour market policy into 'proactive' policies, emphasizing interaction and cooperation at the local level. The third considers the possible shift of social policy towards risk management, in which the transformation of unemployment insurance into a comprehensive system of employment or income insurance could play a crucial role.

Chapter 8 (Kruppe) develops a systematic framework – the transition matrix – for investigating the interrelated complexity of transitions between various labour force statuses. It provides for the first time descriptive evidence on the size and composition of transitions for 10 EU member states. Using the annual survey of the European Community Household Panel (ECHP) with monthly calendar information from waves 2 and 3 (1994/5), it demonstrates, for instance, that on average in Europe 16 per cent of the population over 15 change labour force status at least once a year. As expected, women have a higher propensity to undertake such transitions, which explains to some extent the fact that only about 28 per cent of all transitions are related to dependent employment. More than two-thirds of the transitions are related to unemploy-ment (about 20 per cent), self-employment or to various forms of 'inactivity' such as education or training, household activities or (early) retirement.

Special emphasis is given to transitions out of education or training and unemployment. The quality of these transitions is a decisive element in the proper functioning of labour markets. The study finds great variations in both sets of transitions. Only in Ireland, Germany, Denmark and the United Kingdom do more than half of all those leaving education or training end up with an 'active' labour force status (dependent employment, self-employment, family work, apprenticeship, community or military service), suggesting that the other countries (Belgium, Greece, France, Italy, Spain and Portugal) have severe transition problems. The level of transitions out of unemployment varies even more. In some countries, a substantial share of the unemployed (as high as 43 per cent in Germany) does not enter dependent employment im-mediately, passing first through other intermediate stages, inactivity or retire-ment. This too is indicative of precarious transition patterns.

The chapter ends by suggesting a range of possible future applications if more waves of the ECHP become available. The utility of dynamic employ-ment studies based on the transition matrix could be much improved if the data were structured in greater detail according to performance measures related to the European employment strategy.

Chapter 9 (Meager and Bates) enquires into the role that might be played by self-employment and by transitions between self-employment and other labour market statuses. It starts by briefly considering some of the evidence on the labour market significance of self-employment, looking at trends in stocks and flows in European countries. While growth in non-agricultural self-employment is less dramatic than often claimed, there is nevertheless a clear upward trend. A growing proportion of the workforce, including social groups among whom self-employment has traditionally been low, will experience one or more spells of self-employment during their lifetime. The implications for income, employment opportunities and social security, especially in old age, are still largely unknown.

This chapter provides a sophisticated and thorough analysis of these ques-tions. It draws basically on the British Household Panel Survey (BHPS), which makes it possible to study to some extent the employment history of people transiting in and out of self-employment. The results, backed up by detailed descriptive material and logit models determining the individual char-acteristics related to transition patterns, are at first glance rather pessimistic. It appears that being self-employed increases the risk of being poor, especially in old age. Clearly, neither the social security nor the tax system is adapted to the needs of the growing group of people in precarious self-employment, and especially not to the high share of people in 'pseudo' self-employment.

Although governments, not only in the UK but also in most other European member states, have begun to tackle the issue, it is not straightforward to design a regulatory regime that provides both social security and incentives for self-employment.[6]

On the other hand, the study provides more encouraging evidence showing that positive transition routes can be identified in some segments at least of the new self-employed population. This applies in particular to more highly qualified people, who have a high propensity both to move into self-employment and to transit back into better paid dependent work. In this group, in which women are well represented, successful combinations of part-time self-employment and home activities or dependent work can also be found (see also Chapter 5). In addition, recent studies show that transitions into and out of self-employment enhance employability through the acquisition of human and social capital and that the long-term unemployed who enter self-employment tend to be more stable in their work than those who go into wage employment. Finally, the study emphasizes the importance of identifying in future research those structures that will best enable the new self-employed to develop and update their vocational skills.

Chapter 10 (Anxo and O'Reilly) deals with time flexibility over the life course and the institutional arrangements that favour such flexibility. It concentrates on three major aspects, namely different approaches to regulating working time within a range of European Union countries, trends towards a general reduction of full-time working hours and the development of non-standard employment. The authors argue, first, that there has been a general trend since the 1980s towards the diversification, decentralization and individualization of working time. However, at least three different types of flexibility strategies have to be acknowledged: state-regulated flexibility (France and Spain), negotiated flexibility (Finland, Denmark, Germany, the Netherlands and Sweden) and individualized/market-regulated flexibility (United Kingdom, Ireland). These marked differences are reflected in great variations in working-time patterns and require policies to be differentiated accordingly.

Second, the chapter provides a comparative overview of working-time reductions linked to attempts to develop universal solutions to working-time adjustment that cover all employees, or large sections of the workforce in a particular sector. Evaluations of these policies, both at macro and at microeconomic level, conclude, somewhat pessimistically, that the conditions required for a collective reduction in working time to have a long-term impact on employment or unemployment are very restrictive. In contrast to general, undifferentiated, across-the-board reductions in working time, negotiated and decentralized reductions providing incentives for continuing training and education or the use of time accounts (accumulation of overtime work on an individual account to be exchanged later for times not worked) promise better results.

Third, non-standard forms of employment are often seen as solutions for individuals seeking to adapt to particular circumstances and resolve competing demands on their time. However, individuals' ability to make use of such options is highly contingent on the general regulation of working time in a given country and on the way employers use working-time flexibility. The authors synthesize their own studies of this issue,[7] and show that the contribution of non-standard employment forms to social integration has been rather disappointing to date. Part-time work clearly acts as a form of integration for those outside the labour market and for a tiny minority of the unemployed. It is rarely part of a maintenance transition and seldom leads to full integration into the labour market. For low-skill women in particular, part-time work and other non-standard employment forms often lead to social exclusion. In order to extend the range of positive trajectories, which in the past have mostly involved more highly skilled people, a thorough rearrangement of the benefit and tax system is required as well as provisions for the decentralized negotiation of flexibility. The European employment strategy has still a long way to go to reach this goal.

Chapter 11 (de Koning and Mosley) investigates how active labour market policy can be made more effective and contribute to the establishment of successful transitional labour markets. Emphasis is given to the increasing need for flexibility and continuing training. While workers have a strong preference for a stable income reflecting their activity rate over time rather than at a specific point in time, firms prefer payment for actual performance and tend to reduce their human capital investment if employment relations become less stable. No straightforward solution to this flexibility–training paradox is in sight.[8] Although workers could in principle transfer income over the course of their working lives by alternately borrowing and saving money, this seems feasible only for relatively few individuals. Imperfections in the capital market make it unlikely that, for instance, an adult person without much education could borrow the money needed to finance training. Thus there is a (possibly growing) need for government to share the risks associated with the modern labour market (see also Chapter 12).

In principle, active labour market policy can help to solve this paradox by increasing labour mobility through transitional labour markets. However, the evaluation literature on active policies reviewed in this chapter is rather pessimistic about the effectiveness of conventional measures.[9] In fact, a majority of these measures are directed not towards mobility but towards exclusionary transitions (early retirement) or maintenance transitions not designed to enhance employability. The authors argue, however, that it is failures in targeting policies towards the most needy problem groups but also, if not principally, in implementation that are responsible for the poor results of active labour market policy. They therefore examine in detail implementation designs and put forward various proposals for enhancing policy effectiveness. In particular, they recommend the introduction of competition into the implementation process, with the proviso that governments should set quality standards and carefully monitor and evaluate the outcomes. They also stress the need to exploit more effectively the possibilities offered by the new information technology. Finally, they recommend the establishment of closer links between active labour market policy and social security, the design of which should provide much stronger incentives for both workers and employers to avoid claiming benefits at all or, if this proves impossible, to limit the benefit duration by involving people with as little delay as possible in measures intended to enhance their employability.

Chapter 12 (Schmid) begins by attacking the present trend in European social policy towards a selective welfare state and argues for the maintenance of a universal system of mutually supportive social protection and employment policy. What is required is not a shrinking of the welfare state to a social protection system of last resort for the 'needy', but a comprehensive system of public–private risk management. A central element of joint risk management must be the extension of conventional unemployment insurance into a broader system of employment insurance which encourages people to assume the income risks of flexible employment relationships. By making transitions pay, a strategy of establishing institutionalized 'bridges' between various employment states would provide a set of mobility opportunities for all categories of workers. In contrast to the incipient fiscal crisis that threatens to engulf the traditional welfare state, transitional labour markets are self-containing since they require negotiation, cofinancing and individual participation in the provision of social protection. They emphasize the ex ante promotion of mobility rather than ex post redistribution through transfers. The aim of risk management, therefore, is not to minimize risks but to make risk taking acceptable through the provision of new forms of intertemporal, intergenerational and interregional forms of solidarity.

The second (and longer) part of this chapter seeks to ascertain what might constitute good practice in transitional labour markets. Quality criteria for 'good transitions' are developed. These criteria include freedom of choice through empowerment, solidarity through joint risk sharing, effectiveness through a combination of cooperation and competition ('co-epitition'), efficiency through decentralization and monitoring or evaluation of quality standards. The five main types of transitions in the labour market are then scrutinized. The type of risk inherent in each one is defined more precisely and interesting innovations in risk management susceptible of generalization within EU member states are described. Policy recommendations for activating these transitions are then advanced. For transitions between training and work, leave schemes supported by training vouchers are proposed (see also

Chapter 9). For those between various working-time regimes or employment statuses, flexible income security schemes are recommended, together with an extension of wage policy to include such transitions (concession bargaining). For transitions between private household and labour market work, income support schemes are proposed (in-work subsidies, for example), together with the inclusion of care leave into the extended employment insurance system. For those between employment and unemployment, one proposal among many other possibilities is that professionalized job services should be set up in the form of various transition agencies (for example, temporary work agencies). Finally, for transitions between work and retirement, various forms of phased retirement are proposed, especially those that use entitlements to unemployment benefits as cofinancing instruments for in-work subsidies and job creation.

The third part of the chapter concludes by framing the elements of a new European employment compact, a term that denotes a new regime of formal and informal agreements between the state (at transnational, national and local level), the social partners, employers and employees. The new roles these actors would have to play are described. These roles have three key features: the assumption of more entrepreneurial functions, together with the corresponding responsibilities and risks, the continuous promotion of sustainable employability through lifelong learning and acceptance of responsibility for the disadvantaged through the provision of meaningful jobs for all.

It is not clear whether national perceptions and constraints will lead to generalized compliance with this new European labour compact. However, even if compliance is obtained, there is still the question of what should be done next to help solve old and, especially, new structural problems in the labour market. Unemployment is still high in many countries and long-term unemployment still leads to social exclusion. Many people are still disadvantaged by inadequate education and recurrent precarious employment relationships, while poverty linked to precarious or discontinuous employment careers is on the increase. Inequality of employment opportunities persists, and family-friendly work organization systems have yet to be fully implemented. Last but not least, skill mismatches are continuing to increase.

A realistic next step from the European perspective would probably be to increase transfers of good practices ('bench-learning'), as suggested in this book and the other volumes in this series.[10] Such a process of convergence through learning will no doubt be important. One beneficial side-effect would be the avoidance of 'social dumping' as borders open up and competition within the European zone increases. However, the disaster of long-term unemployment and the new risks inherent in the modern labour market call for wider and more visible initiatives. Some of these could be directed towards the monetary and budgetary spheres, while others could focus on labour market policies and the link between labour market regulation and social protection that this volume has sought to develop.

Clearly, it would be impossible and probably counterproductive at present to propose an integrated, all-encompassing strategy in such an enormous and heterogeneous field. The diversity of member states' policy choices and social protection arrangements is even greater than the diversity of their labour market policies. However, such unified proposals are not what is needed. What is needed – and what is currently lacking – is persuasive regulatory ideas. In this volume, we have suggested that a number of different experiences all point to a need to open up greater opportunities for mobility in and around the labour market. It may be possible to meet this common need in different ways in different countries. In order to systematize this perspective, we propose the concept of transitional labour markets as one of the regulatory ideas required for reform of the labour market. Such ideas obviously need to be combined with other approaches to social solidarity and reciprocity. In the field of employment policy, their contribution may be to provide not an integrated but a systematic framework for improving the coherence and efficiency of programmes intended to enhance employability. They would open up the prospect of a new full employment equilibrium compatible with equal opportunity and a non-segmented world of diverse employment relationships.

NOTES

1. In the USA (the only country considered by the author), the median hourly wage is $10. The proposed subsidy begins with a $3 boost for an hourly wage of $4, thereby raising the hourly rate to $7, and gradually decreases to zero for basic wage rates in excess of $12 per hour (Phelps, 1997: 113).
2. In such a system, the unemployed can be recalled to the workplace if demand rises.
3. For the useful distinction between integrative, maintenance and exclusionary transitions, see O'Reilly *et al.* (2000: 3–4).
4. As the Dutch case shows, the shortage of skilled workers recently led to the introduction of special programmes to bring older people (those who had taken early retirement, or the partially disabled) back to the labour market. It is obviously easier to implement such schemes in a flexible employment regime with many part-time or temporary jobs than in a rigid full-time regime in which the only instrument available is wage flexibility.
5. As a complement to this chapter, see the collection of contributions in Schömann and O'Connell (2001).
6. See also Chapter 5, and Chapter 7 on the detection threshold that causes this hybrid employment relationship to be systematically neglected.
7. See the collection of contributions in O'Reilly *et al.* (2000).
8. See also Chapter 9 in this volume and the concluding theoretical chapter by Schömann in Schömann and O'Connell (2002).
9. This conclusion is reinforced by a number of recent impact assessments collected in de Koning and Mosley (2001).
10. O'Reilly *et al.* (2000); de Koning and Mosley (2001); Schömann and O'Connell (2002).

BIBLIOGRAPHY

Arthur M.B. and D.M. Rousseau (1996), *The Boundaryless Career – A New Employment Principle for a New Organizational Era*, Oxford: Oxford University Press.

Beveridge, W.H. (1945), *Full Employment in a Free Society*, New York: W.W. Norton & Company.

Beveridge, W.H. (1995 [1942]), *Social Insurance and Allied Services*, London: Reprint.

Gazier, B. (ed.) (1999), *Employability: Concepts and Policies*, Berlin: Institute for Advanced Studies (IAS); 1998 Report of the Employment Observatory Research Network of the European Commission.

de Koning, J. and H. Mosley (eds) (2001), *Labour Market Policy and Unemployment. Impact and Process Evaluations in Selected European Countries*, Cheltenham, UK and Northampton, US: Edward Elgar.

Moss Kanter, R. (1989), *When Giants Learn to Dance: Mastering the Challenge of Strategy, Management and Careers in the 1990s*, New York: Simon & Schuster.

OECD (1996), *Making Work Pay. A Thematic Review of Taxes, Benefits, Employment and Unemployment*, DEELSA/ELSA WP1 and DAFFE/CFA WP2.

O'Reilly, J., I. Cebrián and M. Lallement (eds) (2000), *Working-Time Changes. Social Integration Through Transitional Labour Markets*, Cheltenham, UK and Northampton, US: Edward Elgar.

Phelps, E.S. (1997), *Rewarding Work. How to Restore Participation and Self-Support to Free Enterprise*, Cambridge, MA: Harvard University Press.

Rehn, G. (1977), 'Towards a Society of Free Choice', in R. Wiaburg (ed.), *Comparing Public Policies*: Woclaw.

Schmid, G. (ed.) (1994), *Labor Market Institutions in Europe. A Socioeconomic Evaluation of Performance*, Armonk, NY: M.E. Sharpe.

Schömann, K. and P. O'Connell (eds) (2002), *Education, Training and Employment Dynamics: Transitional Labour Markets in the European Union*, Cheltenham, UK and Northampton, US: Edward Elgar.

Silver, H. (1994), 'Social Exclusion and Social Solidarity: Three Paradigms', *International Labour Review*, 133(5–6), 531–78.

Supiot, A. (1999), 'The Transformation of Work and the Future of Labour Law in Europe: A Multidisciplinary Perspective', *International Labour Review*, 138(1), 31–46.

Van Parijs, P. (1996), *Real Freedom for All*, Oxford: Oxford University Press.

PART I

Change and Performance of
Employment Systems

2. Employment systems in transition: explaining performance differentials of post-industrial economies

Günther Schmid[1]

Employment systems in mature industrialized societies face a dual challenge. Firstly, digital information and communications technologies seem to have burst the remaining spatial boundaries of human interaction to encompass the entire globe, thereby opening up hitherto unsuspected opportunities for rationalization, creating new products and services and further intensifying competition. This economic globalization seems to be calling into question the established institutions of national welfare states and changing the rules governing labour markets. Secondly, changes in values seem to be reconfiguring social relationships, destroying traditional ties and opening up new possibilities for the gender division of labour and the diversification of life styles. Furthermore, the continuing increase in average life expectancy seems to be extending the scope for activities. This individualization is often assumed to be threatening established social structures, particularly the family, and to require new intergenerational and, especially, gender contracts.

These challenges are much debated, although their consequences are not yet well understood. What hidden meanings do the slogans 'globalization' and 'individualization' actually harbour? What adjustment problems are they causing for established labour market institutions? How are other countries dealing with these trends? How are their employment systems performing and what explanations can be adduced for the differences between them? What can we learn from these differences? These are the questions this chapter will seek to answer.

The chapter begins by clarifying the terms 'globalization' and 'individualization' (section 1). The question of their possible effects on employment requires an analytical framework within which the relationship between employment policy institutions and exogenous trends can be systematized. The hypotheses developed within this analytical framework will then be used to explain how and why employment systems in some OECD countries and, in particular, in some EU member states have clearly adapted more quickly and more successfully than others to these broad trends (section 2). These hypotheses have to be tested very carefully, since employment policy has multiple goals with possible trade-offs and negative side-effects. Section 3, therefore, assesses performance at different levels. It begins with a comparison of employment elasticities, since the more slowly employment reacts to economic growth, the greater the risk of segmentation in employment and unemployment becomes. This examination reveals that high employment elasticity can be achieved through two different strategies: high wage flexibility, on the one hand, or highly flexible working times and skills, on the other. Which countries follow which strategy can be ascertained by breaking down the evolution of employment into its individual components. A simple but effective method of decomposition reveals the contribution of demographic, behaviour-specific and policy-related factors to the employment dynamic. The results of this decomposition serve as a basis for developing typologies of 'employment regimes'. Our next concern is to ascertain whether these regimes also have identifiably different effects on the various dimensions of economic well-being (section 4). The final, summarizing section examines the combined effect on 10 performance measures. It emerges from this examination that no single country can be held up as a model of successful employment policy. Nevertheless, there are signs that the outlines of a new, forward-looking employment system can be discerned more clearly in some countries than in others. Developments in Denmark, the United Kingdom and the Netherlands, in particular, seem to offer the less successful employment systems some ideas for reform and the European Union some guidance for a coordinated employment strategy.

1 EMPLOYMENT SYSTEMS IN THE MODERNIZATION PROCESS

One of the effects of globalization is to subject a growing share of the world's population to the same conditions. Individual and collective actors are increasingly being exposed to developments that take place 'somewhere', over which they have no control and to which they can merely adapt. In this sense, globalization is certainly nothing new. Since the 16th century at least, when the trade in colonial commodities began to develop, economies have been operating on a worldwide basis and, as early as the turn of the 19th century, the share of international trade in world market output was at approximately the same level as today. This share fell sharply subsequently. At its peak, the industrial period was a predominantly national phenomenon.

What is new about globalization today, however, is the development of institutional structures superordinate to the national level. Integration and interdependence are increasing, not only in economic and financial systems but also in the scientific, technological, spatial and logistical dimensions.[2] In earlier times, states traded with each other in nationally produced goods ('made in X-land'), English woollen cloth in exchange for Portuguese wine, for example. However, the British did not produce grapes, presses or barrels for the Portuguese wine industry, nor did the Portuguese produce wool, iron or machinery for the English textile industry. Upstream activities, or inputs, were not integrated to any significant extent. National production was geared to the domestic market and was largely unexposed to outside influences. As a result, the international division of labour was *macrostructural* in nature; that is, it was based on the manufacture and trade of end products (Huber, 1998: 37).

Globalization today is changing the leverage ratio between domestic and foreign markets. Domestic markets are extending beyond the boundaries of individual nation states. The European economic and currency union is a particularly striking example of this phenomenon. Trade is increasingly trade in intermediate products. Activities upstream of the end product or service are becoming increasingly integrated, whether between firms, regions or nation states. This *microstructural* international division of labour is driven mainly by multinational groups, although medium-sized firms have long been involved as well, all of them global players engaged in coproduction throughout the world and helping to coordinate transnational manufacturing and service systems ('made by X-company'). This trend is even affecting basic research in economics and the other social sciences, while those more dedicated to the gratification of the senses will not ignore the trend towards 'global cuisine', that is the mutual influence exerted on each other by different culinary cultures.[3]

This process finds tangible expression in, among other things, the rise in direct foreign investment and in the above-average growth in foreign trade volumes and currency flows. Optimists forecast that international trade volumes will reach a value of around 11 billion US dollars by 2005, equivalent to 28 per cent of global economic output. In 1998, the share was 24.3 per cent; in 1968, it was still less than 10 per cent. Transnational cooperation is reflected in spectacular mergers of large manufacturing and service companies, as well as in the globalization of research and development.[4] The organizational principle underpinning globalization is the intensification of vertical and horizontal *networking* beyond national boundaries. The driving force behind the 'new globalization' is the digital revolution in information and communication technologies which, following mass motorization and the transport revolution, have once again broken through the 'sound barrier' of *factor mobility*. This applies particularly to capital and information; that is, labour services that can now be digitized. One manifestation of this revolution is 'teleworking', which is rapidly spreading around European countries, especially in the sparsely populated areas of Scandinavia.[5]

The extent to which globalization is pressurizing industrial employment systems to adapt will be discussed later in this chapter. Prior to this, however, it is necessary to consider another broad trend that is often neglected in the debate currently dominated by special interest or pressure groups concerned only with competitiveness. This is the growing trend towards social differentiation, which may even constitute a new phase in the process of individualization. The social revolution in gender relations, combined with a lasting change in demographic structures, means that employment systems in modern industrial societies face new challenges that are at least as dramatic as the changes in the global economy context. Individualization has added a new element of modernization to the historical phases of civilization, rationalization and differentiation.

Civilization denotes both the process whereby physical force is increasingly centralized as the state gradually monopolizes power and the process of increasing self-control. Unless fears of external encroachments on the lives of individuals and of inadequate protection in old age or in the event of illness can be minimized, a highly sophisticated society based on a complex division of labour is scarcely conceivable. The same is true of the essential function of controlling a strong superego. Without the 'inner fears', for example of losing one's reputation, that are inculcated over many years, it would be virtually impossible for trust in professional competences to develop (Elias, 1976 [1936]).

The process of *rationalization*, on the other hand, has demystified the world. According to Max Weber, this denotes less the increase in general knowledge of the conditions under which individuals live than the realization or belief 'that, in theory at least, *one could control all things if only one wanted to*' (Weber, 1946 [1917]). Thus the rationalization of society involves a belief in the increasing intellectual mastery of living conditions and the concomitant trust in or reliance on the appropriate experts. According to Max Weber, rationalization also denotes the pluralization of value systems and the scientific search for the means to put them into practice.

One of the consequences of rationalization has been an accelerating process of *social differentiation*. Even at a very early stage of its development, Adam Smith saw the basis of this differentiation, namely a division of labour based on specialization, as ambivalent. If the division of labour does indeed lead to greater rationalization, is it not achieved at the expense of human beings, who increasingly become merely small cogs in a giant wheel, condemned to dull and repetitive routine activities? Emile Durkheim saw things differently. For him, the division of labour was a process that constituted the main source of social stability:

In fact, besides this, we may observe that labor becomes more continuous as it is more divided. . . . As we go forward, however, work becomes a permanent occupation, a habit, and indeed, if this habit is sufficiently strengthened, a need. But it would not have been set up and the corresponding need would not have arisen, if work had remained irregular and intermittent as heretofore. We are thus led to the recognition of a new reason why the division of labor is a source of social cohesion. It makes individuals solitary, . . ., not only because it limits the activity of each, but also because it enhances it. It adds to the unity of the organism, solely through adding to it life. At least, in its normal state, it does not produce one of these effects without the other. (Durkheim, 1933: 394–5).

Durkheim even spoke of a duty to specialize, 'instead of trying to make ourselves a sort of creative masterpiece, quite complete, which contains its worth in itself and not in the services that it renders' (ibid.: 401). However, this specialization was not to be taken too far. There was also an obligation 'to realize in ourselves the collective type as it exists. There are common sentiments, common ideas, without which, as has been said, one is not a man. The rule which orders us to specialize remains limited by the contrary rule' (ibid.). A division of labour could not foster solidarity unless at the same time it produced law and moral principles. Economists' notion of a diminishing importance of law (deregulation) was absurd, since the division of labour brought not individuals but social functions into confrontation with each other.

And society is interested in the play of the latter; in so far as they regularly concur, it will be healthy or ill. Its existence thus depends upon them, and the more they are divided the greater its dependence. That is why it cannot leave them in a state of indetermination. In addition to this, they are determined by themselves. Thus are formed those rules whose number grows as labor is divided, and whose absence make organic solidarity either impossible or imperfect. But it is not enough that there be rules; they must be just, and for that it is necessary for the external conditions of competition to be equal. (Ibid.: 407)

What is genuinely new about current developments? Whereas Durkheim took the view that the development of individual personalities should remain confined to the autonomous mastering of a function within the division of labour located within a vague collective whole, the individualization argument starts from the assumption that individuals are increasingly seeing themselves as the creators of their own, non-collective life plans. Taken to its logical conclusion, this means that the principle of constant renewal or innovation can be applied universally, with the only limits to its diffusion being a lack of resources or thoughtfulness. These limits are variable and random. At one extreme, individuality can be a niche phenomenon without consequences for others, while at the other it can trigger a fashion craze that carries the whole world along with it in next to no time. This phenomenon has always existed in individual cases and in the higher social strata. However, the early 1970s saw a significant shift in this direction. Since then it has been possible to speak of a phase of individualization in which a critical mass of separate individual interests, not only of men but also of women and children, is defined and put into practice, in the face not only of the state and the church, of local communities and kin, but even of individuals' families.[6]

The consequences can only be intimated with the aid of a few key terms: an endogenous trend towards increasing female participation in the labour market, rising divorce rates, increasing numbers of single parents and declining birth rates. The trend towards individualization is further reinforced by demographic changes. The period of independent living between retirement and death is now longer than it used to be. Thus individualization also means a society in which longevity, with increasingly long periods of free time, is now the norm. The consequence is a change in the age structure, which in turn affects the conditions under which the labour market operates. To date, for every 100 people aged between 20 and 60 (that is, those who are, for the most part, economically active), there have been about 35 pensioners; in the not very distant future, that figure will rise to 70 or more.[7]

The new phases in the development of globalization and individualization pose challenges to the basic institutions of the employment systems in modern industrial societies that can be regarded not simply as problems but also as opportunities for renewal. Firstly, the interface between the private household economy and the labour market is affected. Fixed or predetermined role allocations in the social division of labour are no longer compatible with the spread of individualization. This applies particularly to the gender division of labour. The single male breadwinner model, in which the man is in continuous full-time employment and earns a wage that is sufficient to support a dependent wife and children, corresponds less and less to reality. This development, which has been evident for a long time, has not, however, led to the emergence of a new model for the institutional rules governing the gender-specific division of labour. Thus individualization means that a new *gender contract* is required. For its part, globalization is calling into question the traditional notion of full employment in its temporal, spatial and social dimensions. In the information age, working for an employer at a fixed location and producing goods or services for an anonymous market is becoming increasingly obsolete. Thus the model of work organization characterized by continuous, full-time, dependent employment in one and the same firm, at one and the same place and in one and the same occupation will soon be a thing of the past. Thought through rigorously, therefore, globalization brings with it the need for a *restructuring of the employment relationship* or *employment contract*. Both of these trends, individualization and globalization, are eroding the traditional notion of full employment, making it necessary to develop a new notion of what a 'fully employed' society might be.[8]

Secondly, social security systems are also being called into question on two fronts. In particular, the march of individualization is raising the question of independent social security for women. This applies to both the risks of old age and those of sickness and unemployment. Poverty in old age affects women in particular and, despite a certain degree of flexibilization, unemployment insurance is still not geared to discontinuous patterns of labour market participation (which are increasingly affecting young males, incidentally). Globalization, for its part, is increasingly placing the pressure of competition directly on labour as a productive factor, that is on wage and non-wage labour costs. This raises the question of whether, in future, social protection for old age and against the increasing risk of fluctuating or lost earnings can still be financed primarily out of contributions and income tax or whether it is necessary to institutionalize alternative sources of finance or subsistence, either to supplement or to replace the current funding arrangements. The changes in the age structure and the increasing length of retirement are making these problems ever more acute and are fuelling demands for a new *intergenerational contract*. Both individualization and globalization obviously require a system of risk management that can react more flexibly than the traditional social security system to the increasing diversity of income risks.

Thirdly, the institutions of wage formation are also facing challenges on two fronts. Individualization means that the more or less implicit notion of the family wage, that is a full-time wage that is supposed to be sufficient to support a family, or of a full-time wage that also recognizes status (for example, age), is no longer in tune with the times. Nor is the still observable practice of discriminating between men's and women's pay, which also contradicts any attempts to put in place a rigorous equality norm. This individualization means that *new remuneration principles* will have to be developed. They will also have to be adapted to the demands of globalization and information technology, as well as to the new modes of work organization that have emerged in their wake. Apart from wage discrimination, this applies in particular to the notion of a solidaristic wages policy and to pay by seniority. The individual incentive functions of wages will presumably have to become more evident than hitherto. Furthermore, globalization means an intensification of wage pressure that affects (and this is nothing new) not only low-skill workers but also intermediate and high-skill workers. In the coming age of the global, integrated labour market, German computer specialists, for example, will compete on wages with their Polish or Indian counterparts, and in the near future this will even apply to German professors of economics, land use planners or urban sociologists, who will increasingly have to compete with colleagues from abroad.

Fourthly and finally, individualization and globalization are also calling into question the traditional institutions of general and vocational education. Because of the 'ageing' of the potential labour force, on the one hand, and the technological revolution, on the other, adult education or *lifelong learning* will have to be developed as the 'fourth pillar' of the education system. At the same time, this raises the question of a redistribution or redefinition of the roles of the three established 'pillars' of the German education and training system: general education, initial vocational training and higher education. The large, bureaucratically regulated internal labour markets that provided systematic opportunities for further training and advancement are being eroded in the same way as labour markets structured around lifelong 'occupations'. New forms of professionalization, or at least a growing willingness to cooperate in project-based working practices, are required.

In sum, the challenges of globalization and individualization can be said to have put an end to the antagonistic contradiction between 'capital and labour' that characterized the era of the industrial society. The new fault lines are increasingly running at right angles to these categories. The global integration of productive systems and the constant change that now characterizes so many aspects of modern societies (individuality and innovation) are intensifying the conflicts: between global and local enterprises, between highly-skilled specialists with key competences in demand in the global market place and less skilled workers with more circumscribed horizons, between men and women with equally strong aspirations to independent careers, between career women and traditional housewives or marginal female workers, and – last but not least – between younger workers under pressure to take responsibility for protecting themselves against risk and older workers expecting to be protected by solidaristic standards. Clearly, these conflicts are by no means any less socially inflammatory than the old class conflicts. For this reason, the advantage in future will lie with employment systems that can also develop new rules for conflict resolution.

In any event, employment systems have to adapt to the challenges posed by the broad trends of globalization and individualization. The mass unemployment that still plagues most European and OECD countries can be seen as the expression of an inadequate capacity for adjustment to these trends. However, what does this capacity for adjustment consist of? How are the various national employment systems reacting to the new challenges? Do the various patterns of adjustment clearly distinguish successful from less successful systems? What is the essence of this distinction? These questions, typical of any system comparison, will be investigated in what follows. We begin with a brief outline of our analytical framework.

2   AN ANALYTICAL FRAMEWORK FOR COMPARING EMPLOYMENT SYSTEMS

Le réel est étroit, le possible est immense. (Lamartine)

Employment systems are constituted of institutions and policies acting upon them that determine, simultaneously, the level of unemployment and employment. Institutions act here as filters, making certain reactions to external shocks or challenges probable, while at the same time, as the quotation from Alphonse de Lamartine suggests, virtually excluding others that are theoretically possible.[9] In what follows, the relevant institutions will first be ordered systematically before consideration is given to the links between system performance and institutional arrangements.

The Interaction between Productive and Labour Market Systems

Employment systems are characterized by the interaction of two subsystems, namely the production system and the labour market system (Figure 2.1). It is in the production system that decisions on production are taken. Those decisions are influenced by the following institutions:

- the capital market, which determines interest and exchange rates, and therefore the costs of capital formation and the terms of trade;
- the research and development system, which either encourages or inhibits innovation;
- taxes and contributions, which affect the cost of production factors and profits;
- the regulatory system which, depending on its constitution, gives rise to or reduces transaction costs.

Changes in these parameters are determined by actors whose decisions are, in turn, made within a framework of institutionalized rules: by central banks, (Schumpeterian) entrepreneurs, private households, treasury officials and bodies representing various interests. *From this point of view, unemployment can be seen as the result of foregone or uncompetitive production.*

Viewed from this angle, the long-term upward trend in unemployment can be readily explained. In the 1970s and 1980s, growth rates fell by half in virtually all industrialized countries, with the exception of Japan. Industries with the highest productivity increase are no longer those in which employment is expanding, as was the case in the 1950s and 1960s. On the contrary, in many industries in which employment levels have hitherto been high, the price elasticity of demand is declining because saturation points have been reached. In

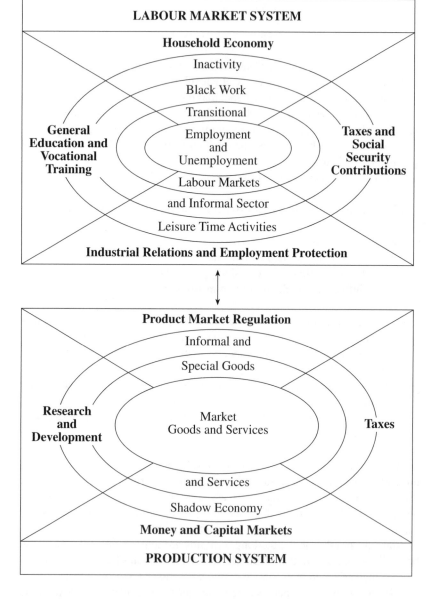

Figure 2.1   Analytical framework for the comparison of employment systems

consequence, investment to serve larger markets is not worthwhile and large numbers of jobs are lost. International price competition worsens the situation, and there is not yet any sign of an economic upturn sustained over a long period (Kondratieff cycle) by information and communications technologies (ICTs).[10]

One way out of this dilemma might be to strengthen the innovation drive and improve the basic conditions for research and development. However, such measures cannot be expected to make a substantial contribution to solving the employment problem unless they are focused on the service sector. In many service industries, demand still reacts strongly to productivity increases and the consequent price reductions, making it possible to open up new markets or extend existing ones.[11] However, even with the use of ICTs, productivity increases are very difficult to achieve in many areas of the service sector (for example in education, health care, craft services or the caring professions) and it will be necessary to put in place a finance and wages policy that seeks to structure costs in a way likely to foster employment. In the case of these services, this applies first and foremost to direct and indirect wage costs and to sales taxes.

But why has Europe's position worsened dramatically relative to that of competitors subject to the same trend? The first suspicion must be that Europe has lost ground in the international 'trade war'. However, comparison of growth rates shows that, at best, this can be only a partial explanation. It is true that Japan had consistently higher growth rates until the early 1990s, but a large part of this difference is attributable to the 'latecomer' effect. The subsequent sharp drop in growth rates was an early sign of a fundamental structural crisis in the Japanese employment system that cannot be analysed in any greater detail here.[12] On the other hand, growth rates for actual GDP in North America (USA) and Europe (EU15) have been broadly comparable since the mid-1970s. However, it is significant that the economic data for the USA following the three recessions of 1974/5, 1980/81 and 1992/3 are consistently more positive than for EU member states. Since the link between economic growth and employment, contrary to a widely held view, is again becoming closer rather than looser, as will be shown later, the key to explaining the desperate European employment situation lies, in part at least, in the determinants of the regressive growth dynamic and in the structuring effects, such as segmentation, hysteresis and insider–outsider divisions, that are familiar from institutional labour market theory. The argument, repeatedly confirmed in many empirical studies, that the negative selection effects in favour of weaker groups in the labour market are stronger in periods of economic upturn than during downturns applies as strongly as ever: the weaker and more hesitant the upturn, the more strongly the negative selection effects make themselves felt (Schmid, 1980).

However, there are indications that Europe has a qualitative growth problem. European production regimes seem to be less innovative than the American one. There is more than enough evidence to show that overregulation of the product market delays reactions to new market segments. Even in traditional product markets, such as the construction and food industries, Europe does indeed seem to be suffering from regulatory sclerosis compared with its main competitors.[13] There are also signs that the countries with the best growth rates in recent years (for example, the USA, the UK, Australia and Canada) have benefited from massive investment in information technology and the deregulation or appropriate reregulation of this product market (Motohashi and Nezu, 1997). In any event, Europe is lagging behind in several new growth areas, and in Germany, in particular, 'employment opportunities (have) undoubtedly been squandered' as a result of blockages in the innovation system (Zukunftskommission, 1998: 174). Furthermore, there are signs that monetary and financial policies are not sufficiently well coordinated. In particular, rigid adherence to the Maastricht criteria as a condition of entry into the European Currency Union has brought (countercyclical) public investment activity virtually to its knees and unduly reined in actual demand. These brief observations will have to be sufficient to counter the current tendency to focus solely on labour market institutions or regulation in the search for a scapegoat for the desperate employment situation in Europe.[14]

We turn now to the other side of employment systems, since decisions to produce are not necessarily followed by decisions to create new jobs and hire additional workers. These decisions are made in the labour market. The rules and incentives that lead to decisions on labour supply and demand constitute what we term the *labour market system*. From this perspective, unemployment can be seen as the result of inadequate incentives for (formal) gainful employment and of unrealized or misplaced employment. At least four institutions play a role in such decisions.

- The first is private households, the '*household economy*', which offers alternatives to paid work, shapes individual attitudes to gainful employment and reduces or extends the volume of time available for paid work.
- The second is the *tax and social security system*, which affects individual employment decisions in two ways. First, the state as employer can provide alternative employment (funded out of taxation or charges) in social spheres outside the market. Second, the largely state-regulated benefit system can offer alternatives to earned income for workers in certain risk situations (unemployment, sickness, old age).
- The third is the *industrial relations system*, which regulates the conflicting interests of labour market actors, whether through self-organization (for example, collective agreements that determine both the level and

the structure of wages, as well as employment conditions) or through statutory regulations (such as dismissal protection, or rules on the duration and scheduling of working time), or a combination of the two.

- The fourth is the *general and vocational education system*, which produces general knowledge, learning skills and vocational competencies and determines the limits of vocational mobility and flexibility.

Labour market policy can influence employment decisions through all four of these institutional pathways: by providing systematic information and advice (job placement) and by taking measures that favour disadvantaged groups in the labour market, by changing the level and duration of benefit payments, by subsidizing wage costs and by promoting further training and retraining programmes. Labour market policy can also influence the demand side, for example by deregulating or reregulating employment relationships or by boosting public-sector employment (the state as employer).

The Link between Performance and Institutions

As the formal analytical framework has made clear, employment systems are very complex institutional arrangements. Their very complexity rules out one-dimensional theories of unemployment; equally, however, they cannot be regarded as an arbitrary conglomeration of institutional factors. In reality, fairly stable patterns can be observed, that is employment policy configurations that have developed over time and have regional and national characteristics. As with the observations made in chaos theory, institutional centres of attraction grow up in the course of time that give a characteristic coherence to the multitude of everyday interactions between individual members of society. Such configurations are denoted by the term 'employment regime'. One such configuration is referred to as 'competitive capitalism', which denotes the predominance of market mechanisms in decisions on production and employment, as exemplified by the USA. Another is known as 'coordinated capitalism', which refers to the close coordination between state and business in decisions on production and employment that characterizes Japan, for example. A third configuration is commonly referred to as 'welfare capitalism', a term that alludes to the important role played by social security systems in decisions on production and employment in most European countries.

The end of the struggle between capitalism and socialism seems to have unleashed competition between various capitalist regimes, the outcome of which cannot yet be foreseen. There are considerable differences in this respect within the European Union. Even Esping-Andersen's oft-quoted distinction by between liberal, conservative and social-democratic welfare states is not sufficiently differentiated to capture the variety of institutional arrangements in Europe.[15] Not only does the competition between the various regimes make the differences more visible, but those differences are also relevant to the question of whether a new, independent and successful European model will emerge from this competition. Nor are employment regimes in any sense free from internal tensions and contradictions. Even if, at a certain point in time, they take on the appearance of a coherent whole by virtue of their historical development, they are also constantly changing as they adjust to or even imitate their environment (Rubery, 1994). This is why individual employment regimes have to be regarded as open systems which, in accordance with general systems theory, have characteristics such as integrating norms, functional differentiation, equifinality and evolutionary development (Morgan, 1997: 39–43).

For the purposes of system comparison, and particularly when it comes to the question of institutional transferability, the theory of *institutional equivalence* is of some significance. The suggestion here is that, in principle, a choice can be made not only between individual elements but also between entire sets of institutional arrangements. Flexible working time arrangements (in respect of short-time working, for example) may be as effective in facilitating the adjustment of employment to changes in demand as flexible wages. It is open to the state to put in place a highly developed regulatory framework as a means of exerting influence over employment, but to restrict its role as a direct employer. Japan and Switzerland are examples of countries where the state has followed this path. Conversely, the state can itself create jobs and restrict regulation of the private sector to a minimum. Denmark and Sweden come close to this model.

Ultimately, even a systems-theoretic approach is not complex enough to capture the increasing interdependence of national employment systems and their embeddedness in various transnational employment systems. Contingency and game theory (among others) have to be called upon in order to keep pace with the growing complexity.[16] Nevertheless, even within the tradition of the institutional choice approach, three general *hypotheses* on the effectiveness of employment systems can be advanced (Schmid and Schömann, 1994: 20–22).

1. The *requisite variety* hypothesis suggests that, as the system environment becomes increasingly complex, so the number of coordinating instruments within the system must also increase. As a result, simple 'paths to full employment' (to say nothing of a single path) become increasingly improbable and the ability of societies to learn is likely to become increasingly dependent on their openness to experimentation.
2. *Institutional complementarity* denotes the functional harmonization of institutions influencing a particular target variable. For example, if handicapped

people are to enjoy special protection against dismissal, in order to shield them from the open labour market in recognition of their disadvantage, institutions have to be created to provide compensation for the additional costs incurred. In the absence of such institutions, these costs would work against the recruitment of these target groups. Or if, in the future, the standard wage relationship is to decline in favour of greater autonomy and self-employment, measures have to be taken to ensure that productive capacities are shared out as widely as possible and that the average level of human capital embodied in individual workers is raised considerably. In this way, 'self-exploitation' in small and very small enterprises can be avoided and the ability to adjust to structural change increased. Institutional complementarity also denotes a preference for rapid learning and the transmission of tacit knowledge, two important preconditions for an innovative economy.

3. *Institutional congruence* means that autonomy in decision making and financial responsibility for the effects of the decisions taken are given equal weight. This criterion of effective institutional arrangements applies independently of the level of aggregation. At the individual level, the reverse of institutional congruence is an arrangement that increases the temptation to exploit entitlements by making unjustified use of the triggering condition ('moral hazard'). At the organizational level, institutional incongruence means, for example, separate consideration of the financial charges and reliefs associated with labour-market policy measures (Schmid, Reissert and Bruche, 1992).

These systems-theoretical hypotheses can give comparisons of employment systems a general direction; in order to produce specific explanations, however, they need to be broken down further. By also taking into account the four systemic problems or challenges triggered by the onward march of globalization and individualization, as outlined in section 1, and the ideal-typical employment regimes (system configurations) described earlier in this section, frameworks can be drawn up for theories of intermediate scope that can then be empirically tested.[17] Thus the following hypotheses are oriented for the most part towards the conditions prevailing in the corporatist systems that predominate in Western Europe and that also, in accordance with the notion of path dependency, will also play a large part in determining the mode of adjustment to the trends outlined above and the challenges they pose.

Hypothesis 1
As far as the challenge of producing a new gender contract is concerned, the requisite variety hypothesis means offering young men and women opportunities structured in such a way that they are not confined to certain role

models. Thus employment systems will adapt all the more successfully to the challenges of globalization and individualization if they offer men and women a range of institutionalized options rather than prescribing a fixed gender division of labour. One of the preconditions for this is that the institutions of social security, education, wage determination and family law do not give undue preference to the single (male) breadwinner model of the family and that the objective of full-time employment is predicated not on the notion of the standard employment relationship (continuous full-time employment) but rather on a range of different employment relationships over the course of a working life. As female participation rates continue to rise and working time over the life cycle increases (again), the average time devoted to paid work can be further reduced if at the same time high productivity gains can be achieved in the service sector.

Hypothesis 2

In an open society that offers its members opportunities to choose or to combine various productive activities over the course of their lives, the risk of lost or fluctuating earnings will increase. Thus employment systems will be all the more successful if they are able to establish flexible risk management institutions, in accordance with the notion of requisite variety and complementarity. In such employment systems, it is to be expected that social protection, both during the working life and in retirement, will in part be independent of the requirement of a continuous work history. Flexible eligibility periods independent of paid employment (for child raising, education or voluntary activities, for example) or a basic level of insurance cover independent of actual work histories will have to be introduced in order to ensure that women, in particular, but also the increasing number of men taking on the roles (previously) ascribed to women, have adequate insurance cover in old age.

Hypothesis 3

Globalization, and in particular the burgeoning system of transnational, multi-level governance, combined with individualization, is increasingly exposing employment conditions in national systems to the pressure of competition. As a result, the growth required to raise employment levels can be achieved only if labour market institutions as a whole develop greater capacity to adjust. In accordance with the notion of institutional congruence, therefore, collective (corporatist) wage bargaining systems will not be successful unless they combine industry-wide collective agreements with measures to ensure employability (training, for example) and working-time flexibility and unless they open up scope at a decentralized level for the negotiation of employment contracts (company agreements, individual agreements on annualized working hours and so on). In order to be accepted, this increased flexibility, as required by the notion of institutional complementarity, must be offset by greater security. However, this security cannot apply to each individual job but rather to employment prospects. This security can be achieved either systemically, through generally high levels of mobility, or individually, by maintaining individual employment relationships while varying the form or content of the employment contract. For this reason, employment systems will be successful if the incentives offered by their taxation and social security systems are aimed at achieving a high level of labour market inclusiveness, that is high labour force participation, combined with a high level of variability in employment forms.

Hypothesis 4

Internal and occupational labour markets are one of the strongest characteristics of corporatist employment systems. Such systems will be all the more successful the more they institutionalize functioning network labour markets that can take the place of traditional hierarchical labour markets. In network labour markets, access to 'occupations' (where formal qualifications are the barrier to entry) is reorganized, in accordance with the notion of requisite variety, through the introduction of high, self-regulated quality standards (where performance and reputation are the barriers to entry). However, access to these occupational labour markets can be obtained at any phase of the life cycle by acquiring the necessary additional qualifications (modular certificates). Under certain circumstances, the qualification or occupational 'club membership' could be withdrawn if it is not regularly renewed. In such systems, the link between original status (parents' income and educational level) and achieved status becomes increasingly loosened. Lifelong learning gains in importance relative to initial education. Since knowledge in the information age is increasingly becoming a public good, well-developed public infrastructures and pooled funding systems are required, as the notion of institutional complementarity and congruence would suggest.

To sum up, successful employment systems are characterized, in terms of performance, by

- a high degree of integration into the labour market for adult men and women; indicators of this would include high employment rates, high or rising female participation rates and low unemployment (particularly low long-term unemployment);
- high variability in employment relationships; indicators would include a high share of skilled part-time employment,[18] a high share of self-employment outside agriculture (possibly combined with dependent employment);

- wide distribution for the employment and income effects of growth; indicators would include a low employment threshold and low income disparities;[19]
- high labour market efficiency through the professionalization and net-working of production; indicators would include high labour productivity and per capita income increases.

In theory, there is a range of institutional arrangements through which employment systems can achieve good performance. However, as already set forth above in the three systems-theoretic principles, we would expect to see employment policy configurations in which indicators of requisite variety, institutional complementarity and institutional congruence accumulate. In brief, the four hypotheses outlined above imply that employment systems will have high social integrative effects if they (1) institutionalize employment policy arrangements offering opportunities such as secure transitions between various forms of employment relationship, (2) establish multiple risk management institutions that protect workers not only against loss of earnings through unemployment but also against fluctuations in earnings as a result of changes in their employment relationship, (3) establish wage systems that are, on the one hand, increasingly independent of status and linked to performance and, on the other, unencumbered by taxes and contributions, and (4) maintain and extend employability through the institutionalization of lifelong learning, at both individual and company or institutional level.

We can now turn to the question of the actual patterns of reaction that can be observed in selected employment systems and the extent to which these correspond to our hypotheses.

3   PERFORMANCE INDICATORS FOR EMPLOYMENT SYSTEMS

The question of the link between growth and employment can be answered initially by calculating the employment elasticity. I begin with this point because the main cause of the European employment crisis is often said to lie in the fact that growth is not sufficiently employment-intensive. So how are decisions on employment linked to decisions on production (quantitative and qualitative growth)? Is there any truth in the notion of jobless growth? And if the link between employment and growth is slackening, how is this to be assessed both in theoretical terms and in the light of our initial hypotheses?

Employment Elasticities

Since employment consists of three components, namely of hours worked per employee, the number of employees and the number of unemployed people, a comprehensive analysis would require that the elasticities for all three components be calculated, in order to obtain a complete picture of the dynamic of employment systems. These elasticities can be expressed approximately by simple regression equations:[20]

$$\Delta E = a + b\Delta GDP, \tag{2.1}$$

$$\Delta U = a + b\Delta GDP, \tag{2.2}$$

$$\Delta h^*E = a + b\Delta GDP. \tag{2.3}$$

ΔE is the rate of change in the number of employees, ΔGDP the rate of change in GDP, ΔU the rate of change in the size of the unemployed population and Δh^*E the rate of change in actual average annual working time. In what follows, regressions will be calculated only for employment as the dependent variable (equation 2.1). There are two reasons for this restriction. The first is that the change in unemployment is generally strongly correlated with the change in employment, so that little additional information would be obtained from equation 2.2.[21] Secondly, working-time data are still very unreliable from the international comparative point of view. Two coefficients are of interest in investigating the link between employment and growth:

$$El_0 = -a/b_{\Delta GDP} \tag{2.4}$$

The *employment threshold* El_0 indicates the (zero) point of economic growth at which employment remains constant (thus $a + b\Delta GDP = 0$) and after which each additional positive change in economic growth is also reflected in an increase in employment. In the light of our hypotheses, the employment threshold is to be judged all the more positively the lower it is: all others things being equal, a low threshold indicates a high level of labour market inclusiveness.

$$El_1 = 1/b_{\Delta GDP} \tag{2.5}$$

Employment intensity El_1 measures the closeness of the link between economic growth and employment; it indicates the number of percentage points by which the economy has to grow in order for employment to rise by one percentage point. Elasticity thus defined is the reciprocal value of the regression coefficient: the lower the value, the more employment-intensive economic growth is. However, this indicator cannot be evaluated without additional information. High employment intensity may reflect not only low productivity but also the absence of regulatory barriers in the labour market; that is, numerical or external flexibility. Conversely, low employment intensity may be an expression of high functional or internal flexibility, which productively cushions fluctuations in demand by putting in place the appropriate institutional buffers, thereby guaranteeing continuity of labour market participation in the form of variable employment relationships.

The countries to be compared were chosen with the following considerations in mind. We begin by comparing the countries of the so-called 'triad', that is the three countries or regional blocs that have developed historically and by virtue of their size into the three major competing regimes: the European Union, the United States and Japan. There follows a direct comparison of two neighbouring countries, Germany and the Netherlands, in which, if the sole criterion adopted is the evolution of employment and unemployment over the past 10 years, the latter can be regarded as the 'winner' and the former as the 'loser'.[22] The next stage of the comparison involves a block of three countries (Austria, Denmark and the UK) which, by the same criterion, can also be regarded as successful countries. The final block, in contrast, includes two countries, France and Sweden, that are regarded as the two big losers in the competition between rival systems during the 1980s and 1990s. The following analysis is intended to show whether, and why, these classifications are justified.

How does theory depict the link between growth and employment? It should be noted at the outset that growth measured in terms of the change in (real) GDP is not an exogenous value; it is endogenous and therefore also dependent on the change in employment. As a result, the following calculations of employment elasticities, in which GDP is formally regarded as the independent variable, are not fully satisfactory. They must be supplemented by further analyses or interpreted qualitatively with the appropriate care and caution.

So why is to be expected that employment in the various countries will react differently to economic growth? First, the employment intensity of growth can vary because the connection between growth and labour productivity can take various forms. In countries in which the service sector accounts for a high and rising share of economic activity, productivity will rise less quickly than in countries in which manufacturing is the engine of growth. In the first case, all things being equal, employment intensity will be high, and in the second case relatively low. Thus if productivity growth declines, employment intensity will rise. Second, in a labour market with high wage flexibility and low dismissal protection, the link between employment and growth, all things being equal again, will also be greater than in a labour market with low external flexibility or mobility. Third, in an insider labour market with high efficiency wages and highly reactive working times (overtime, short time), the employment level will react less quickly than in a deregulated, flexible labour market. If inadequate wage flexibility is compensated for by excluding highly-paid older workers, then both the employment threshold and employment intensity will rise. Fourth and finally, in a labour market regime with declining average working time per person employed (as a result of a concerted work-sharing policy, for example) the employment threshold will fall while the effects on employment intensity will be asymmetrical. As demand rises (economic growth), so employment intensity will rise, but it all depends on how the reduction in working time is compensated for through higher labour productivity and work intensity; as demand falls, so employment intensity declines, because declining working times ease the pressure on employers to dismiss workers (all things being equal, of course).

Figure 2.2 shows three stylized links between employment and growth, with the corresponding employment thresholds and employment intensities. In the first case (A), the employment threshold is actually negative, meaning that employment rises even with zero growth in GDP; such a case is conceivable as a consequence either of a strategy of massive work redistribution or of an externally induced increase in population. As the gently rising straight line in

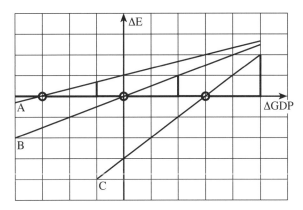

Key:
A, B, C   = Stylized Examples for Employment Intensity of Growth
ΔE   = Change of Employment
ΔGDP   = Change of Gross Domestic Product
⊸⌋   = Employment Threshold
⌐⌋   = Employment Intensity

Figure 2.2   Stylized employment thresholds and employment intensities

Change and performance of employment systems

case (A) shows, employment intensity is relatively weak, for example because of available employment buffers or sharply rising labour productivity. In the second case (B), the employment threshold lies at the zero point; that is, any positive economic growth is reflected immediately in an increase in employment, with employment intensity being greater than in case A but weaker than in case C. In the third case (C), the employment threshold is very high, for example because of a marked division between insiders and outsiders or a large-scale exclusion strategy, while the employment intensity is equal to one, as is evident from the steep slope of the straight line; in other words, each percentage point of growth is reflected in a one percentage point increase in employment.

Table 2.1 shows the employment threshold and employment intensity for the chosen countries (cf. also Figure 2.3). The first observation to be noted is that the link between growth and employment varies in strength. Over the period as a whole, only the USA and France show a strong linear connection. Employment in these countries reacts quickly to economic growth. It is hardly surprising, given our theoretical deliberations, that such a link is to be found in a deregulated (USA) and highly regulated (France) labour market. In a

Table 2.1   *Employment threshold and employment intensity for selected OECD countries and periods*

	Employment threshold $El_0 = -a/b_{\Delta GDP}$			Employment intensity $El_1 = 1/b_{\Delta GDP}$		
	1971–97	1971–85	1986–97	1971–97	1971–85	1986–97
USA	−1.18**	−1.93**	0.02**	2.04**	2.17**	1.64**
Japan	−2.19	−1.62	−0.93*	6.25	6.67	3.70*
EU	1.90*	2.28*	1.85**	2.56*	4.00*	1.23**
D[a]	2.29*	2.60	2.18*	2.04*	2.94	1.39*
NL	−0.40	2.39	−3.68	3.33	4.35	3.23
A	1.62	2.73	1.38*	3.85	4.55	1.89*
DK	1.37*	1.28*	1.51	2.33*	2.27*	2.56
UK	1.54*	2.03	1.57**	2.00*	3.03	1.27**
F	1.81**	2.23**	1.40**	3.23**	3.33**	2.38**
S	1.58*	−0.54	2.01**	1.35**	3.85	0.95**

Notes:
[a]until 1991, only West Germany.
*=moderate linear coherence ($R^2 \geq 0.30$); **=strong linear coherence ($R^2 \geq 0.60$); own calculations; the values are not standardized to maintain consistency with the country-specific figures.

Source: OECD, *Economic Outlook* (1985, 1991, 1993, 1998).

Figure 2.3 Growth rates for GDP and employment in selected OECD countries, 1971 to 1997

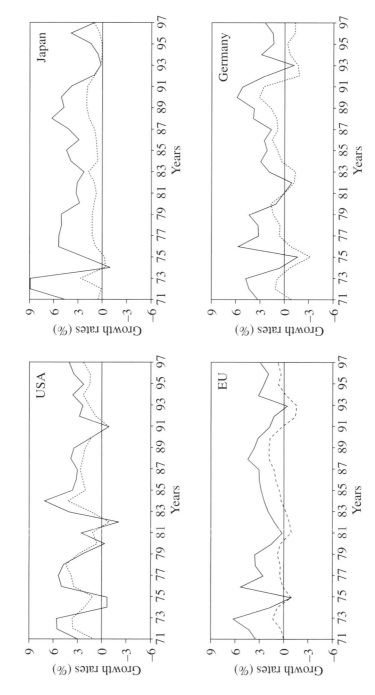

continued overleaf

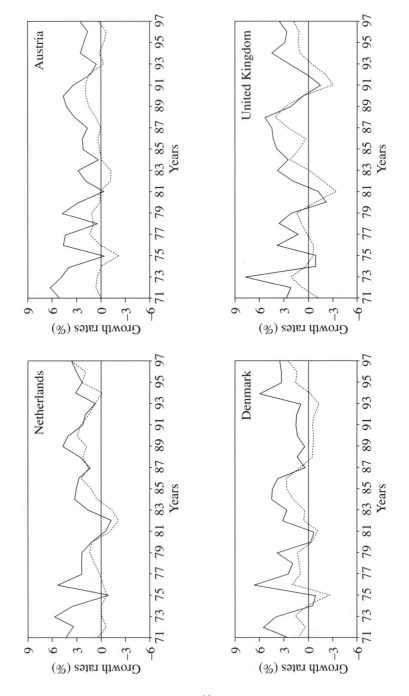

46

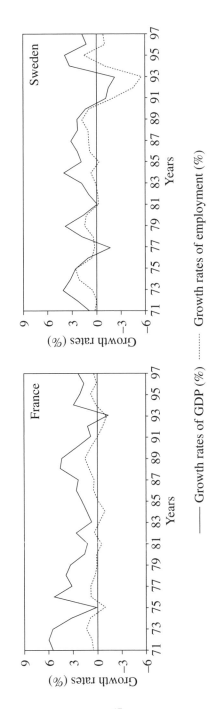

highly regulated labour market that has little internal flexibility (in other words, one that has no employment buffers), employment will react more strongly to fluctuations in demand than in a strongly regulated labour market with high internal flexibility. In marked contrast to these two counties are those that have employment systems in which the link is weak (Japan, Austria and, particularly, the Netherlands). Here there must be institutional filters that considerably loosen, or even eliminate altogether, the link between production and employment decisions. Labour hoarding or the variation of working time are the most familiar mechanisms for loosening this connection. In between these two groups are those countries in which the link is significant but not particularly marked. This group includes Germany, Denmark, the UK, Sweden and the EU as a whole. In some of these countries, however, the link did not manifest itself until more recently, which would seem to reflect the effect of deregulatory measures taken in Germany, the UK and Sweden, for example. In France and in the EU as a whole, the link between growth and employment strengthened further in the 1970s and 1980s. Only in Denmark has the link between employment and growth weakened, which may be attributable to the most recent work redistribution measures (leave programmes).

We turn next to the *employment threshold*. For three countries (the USA, Japan and the Netherlands) the values are negative for the entire period, that is employment rose even when GDP growth rates were negative. Such a link is possible only if the economically active population is increasing considerably in size, if there is high wage flexibility or if the available volume of work is being redistributed. All the other countries needed economic growth of about 1.5 per cent in order just to maintain a constant level of employment; it was not until growth exceeded this level that employment also began to rise. In some countries (the USA, Japan and Sweden), the employment threshold deteriorated, while in others it improved (France, Austria and, particularly, the Netherlands). On the other hand, in the EU as a whole and in Germany, a growth rate of around 2 per cent is still required in order to keep the employment level stable, let alone to push it upwards. These developments are presumably the basis for the widely accepted notion of jobless growth.

However, the jobless growth argument cannot be sustained if we consider *employment* intensity and ask: how much growth is required to increase employment by one percentage point? In this case, the calculations produce a baffling picture. Over the period as a whole, the (non-standardized) employment elasticities fluctuate between 6.3 (Japan) and 1.4 per cent (Sweden). In other words, economic growth of 6.3 per cent on average was required in Japan over the period between 1971 and 1997 in order to raise the employment level by one percentage point. In Sweden, on the other hand, growth of only 1.4 per cent was required, while in the other countries two to three percentage points of economic growth were required in order to raise employment by one percentage point, irrespective of the employment threshold. In addition to Japan, France, Austria and the Netherlands have the lowest levels of employment intensity, while Germany, with its allegedly high level of regulation, has values that are just as good as those in the deregulated USA and UK.

Dividing the period as a whole into two subperiods reveals a clear trend towards convergence. In virtually all the counties (with the exception of Denmark, where the statistics have little explanatory power), employment intensity clearly improved in the more recent period, and in some cases very considerably so (European Union, Sweden, Japan, Germany, Austria). Over the period 1971–85, economic growth of about 3.7 per cent was required in the selected OECD countries in order to raise employment by one percentage point (all things being equal); between 1986 and 1997, however, the growth required was only 2.1 per cent. From this perspective, the European Union has an even higher level of employment intensity than the USA. Once the employment threshold has been exceeded, economic growth of 1.2 per cent is sufficient to raise employment by one percentage point. Thus the European plight lies in an (excessively) high employment threshold and not in a low level of employment intensity. In the light of the theory outlined above, the only explanation for this astonishing finding is that Europe as a whole tried to deal with the employment crisis of the 1970s and 1980s primarily through numerical flexibility (unemployment, early retirement, quantitative expansion of training and education) rather than functional flexibility (wage flexibility, variation of working time, qualitative expansion of training and education).

In any event, the link between growth and unemployment has become stronger rather than weaker, contrary to popular opinion. It can only be concluded from this that it is nowadays worthwhile boosting (qualitative) growth by taking the appropriate monetary, financial and pay policy measures. This applies irrespective of the nature of the national employment systems. Put even more strongly, the current preoccupation, not only in the European Commission but also in virtually all governments, with so-called 'structural causes' and the corresponding supply-side measures is not plausible. What is needed, in fact, is measures to boost demand, without thereby calling into question the need for structural adjustments. The dualism of supply and demand is an ideological construct and not useful, either in theory or in practice.

Further consideration of Table 2.1, however, suggests there may be important differences in the reactions of individual EU member states. We would draw attention in particular to the Netherlands, where a particularly striking pattern can be observed, or rather a change in the pattern of reactions over time. The link between economic growth and employment is weaker in the Netherlands than in all the other countries in our sample. Two striking features become immediately obvious on examination of the time series (cf. Figure

2.3). In the earlier period, despite occasional spurts of strong economic growth, there was no increase at all in employment, and the employment threshold was accordingly one of the highest, after Japan and Austria. In the later period, the employment threshold improved considerably and the sign was even reversed. Employment intensity also improved, but remained relatively low, and the employment dynamic lagged behind economic growth. Nevertheless, the Netherlands succeeded in raising the employment level considerably through work redistribution, a moderate pay policy and further development of the service sector.[23] Otherwise only Japan stands out for its consistently low level of employment intensity, while the low employment intensity in Austria improved significantly in the second half of the period as a whole, an observation that tallies with the findings of another study (Pichelmann and Hofer, 1999).

Can any other explanations be found for the differing national patterns of reaction, as reflected in the link between employment and growth? As intimated in the outline of the analytical framework at the beginning of this chapter, the link between production and employment decisions is determined to a large extent by the industrial relations system, and in particular the institutions involved in wage formation. The current theory has it that that the less employment reacts to growth, the more rigid the wage structures must be. What has this argument to offer?

This is a difficult and, in terms of economic theory, controversial question to answer. The reason for this lies in the complexity of the linkages: wages are not only costs but also incentives for productive work habits and the basis of a demand with the necessary purchasing power. Moreover, since considerable labour turnover occurs every year, either through the termination and beginning of employment relationships or as a result of demographic exits and entries, wage flexibility can be achieved even if wage structures remain rigid. This latter seems to be a particularly characteristic feature of European employment systems. Thus many European countries reacted to the intensification of international competition by excluding older workers, some of whom were highly skilled.[24] As the institutional filter theory would suggest, this form of wage cost reduction is encouraged by two specific characteristics of European labour markets: relatively inflexible wage structures, and in particular seniority pay, on the one hand, and a highly developed social security system, on the other.

As is known from efficiency wage theory, such wage structures are not necessarily harmful (Akerloff and Yellen, 1986). Skill flexibility, for example, can be a functional equivalent for inadequate wage flexibility. And in fact, as will be shown later, differences in performance within the European employment regime are attributable to differences in the performance of education and training systems. Moreover, wage flexibility can also be achieved by exchanging older workers for more highly skilled younger workers who are lower down the seniority pay scale. However, a strategy of this kind is risky in the long term, since it leads to an irreversible loss of productive potential and gives rise to high non-wage labour costs, particularly when social security funding is closely linked to earned income.

The result of this exclusion strategy is clearly reflected in the evolution of labour market participation, which has stagnated or even fallen in most European countries, while it has risen in Japan and, particularly, in the USA (cf. Figure 2.4). As the differentiation by gender shows, the increased participation rate in America is due largely to rising female participation (cf. Figure 2.5). This change in women's labour market behaviour certainly reflects a shift in women's preferences towards increased economic independence; at the same time, however, it is certainly reasonable to assume that the change is also driven in part by economic considerations, namely the need to compensate for declining real male wages in the lower and intermediate wage brackets.

The effect of the exclusion strategy is even more clearly visible in the falling employment rate (cf. Figure 2.6). This decline in the employment rate is problematical not only because it excludes an increasing number of people from active cooperation within the community but also because it reduces the available (and distributable) national product. Not even higher productivity

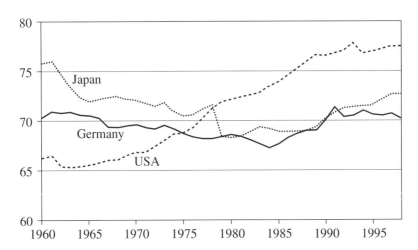

Note: Data for Japan since 1990 have been retrospectively revised in OECD Labour Force Statistics (1978–98).

Source: OECD Labour Force Statistics; OECD *Employment Outlook*, various volumes.

Figure 2.4   Participation rates in Japan, USA and Germany, 1960 to 1998

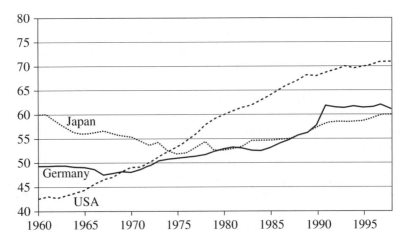

Note: Data for Japan since 1979 have been retrospectively revised in OECD Labour Force Statistics (1978–98).

Source: OECD Labour Force Statistics; OECD *Employment Outlook*, various volumes.

Figure 2.5   Female participation rates in USA, Japan and Germany, 1960 to 1998

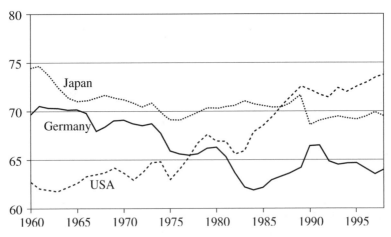

Note: Data for Japan since 1990 have been retrospectively revised in OECD Employment Outlook 1999.

Source: OECD Labour Force Statistics; OECD *Employment Outlook*, various volumes.

Figure 2.6   Employment rates in Japan, USA and Germany, 1960 to 1998

can really compensate for this loss, particularly if it is the result more of the exclusion strategy than of improved capital resources, whether in the form of capital funds or of human resources. The trend towards higher levels of employment intensity already alluded to above indicates, however, that the potential of this exclusion strategy is now largely exhausted in continental Europe; as a result, the employment level is again reacting more sensitively to the stimulus of economic growth.[25]

However, we do not yet have a wholly satisfactory explanation for the varying employment elasticities. In particular, it is still not clear what contribution differing conditions on the supply side of national labour markets make to explaining these differences. It may very well be that high employment intensity and high employment growth are also the product of a sharp increase in the potential labour force or, as already intimated in the case of the USA, of a change in labour market behaviour. This question will be examined in the next section.

Decomposing Employment Growth

As we have just seen, growth and employment are much more closely linked in the USA than in most EU member states, and at the same time the employment threshold is very low, even negative.[26] As a result, any positive economic growth in the USA is immediately reflected in increased employment. However, Japan and the Netherlands also have low employment thresholds, although employment intensity is weaker. Is the US 'jobs miracle' a model to be emulated? If it is, what institutional arrangements in the US labour market are responsible for it? Which of them can be transferred to Europe? What institutional alternatives are there, if such a transfer is either not possible or not desirable? Do Japan and, in particular, the Netherlands (whose culture and institutions are closer to ours) offer alternatives?

In order to answer these questions, it is necessary first of all to decompose the 'jobs miracle', that is to break it down into the various components which, taken together, determine the evolution of employment. The following identity can be used for this purpose:[27]

$$E = POP_L * LFP * (1 - U), \qquad (2.6)$$

in which E is employment, POP_L the population of working age (15–64), LFP the labour force participation rate and U the unemployment rate; $(1 - U)$ is the share of the total labour force in employment.[28] The growth in employment is the sum of the rate of growth in the working-age population, the rate of growth in the labour force participation rate and the rate of growth in the share of the total labour force in employment. This can be expressed in the following equation:

$$\Delta \ln E = \Delta \ln POP_L + \Delta \ln LFP + \Delta \ln(1 - U).^{29} \qquad (2.7)$$

The change in the working-age population ($\Delta \ln POP_L$) is an indicator of increase or decrease in the structural labour force potential. Interpretation of this indicator is context-dependent. Any increase unaccompanied by a change in the total population means that the labour market is being 'burdened' with an increased labour supply. However, if the increase is merely running parallel to an increase in the population as a whole, which also goes hand in hand with an increase in potential demand, then it is synonymous with extensive economic growth and has little to do with institutional or policy changes. The latter applies particularly to the USA, as Table 2.2 shows.

Table 2.2 reveals, firstly, the little-known fact that the total population is still rising, even in the developed industrialized countries. In the USA, the annual increase in the population between 1970 and 1990 was almost 1 per cent; that is, in just one year the North American population grew by about 2.5 million and in 20 years by about 50 million. The growth dynamic weakened somewhat in the 1990s. The population of Japan also grew sharply during this period, by 0.84 per cent per annum. The Dutch and French populations also grew relatively rapidly over the period as a whole, while even the German, Austrian, Danish, UK and Swedish growth rates have risen of late.

The second striking fact to emerge from Table 2.2 is the shift in the ratio of the working-age population (15–64) to the total population. In the 1970s and 1980s, virtually all the countries, with the exception of Sweden, recorded a disproportionate increase in the working-age population, a rise that was particularly

Table 2.2   Annual rates of growth in the working-age population (POP$_L$) relative to total population (POP)

	1970–1990			1991–1997		
	POP	POP$_L$	Difference	POP	POP$_L$	Difference
USA	0.99	1.30	0.31	0.91	0.94	0.03
Japan	0.84	0.89	0.06	0.28	0.09	–0.18
EU	0.38	0.68	0.30	0.36	0.29	–0.07
D	0.21	0.65	0.44	0.43	0.26	–0.17
NL	0.69	1.18	0.49	0.58	0.51	–0.07
A	0.17	0.62	0.46	0.55	0.32	–0.22
DK	0.21	0.43	0.22	0.42	0.23	–0.19
UK	0.17	0.36	0.19	0.34	0.24	–0.10
F	0.56	0.84	0.28	0.45	0.37	–0.08
S	0.33	0.23	–0.10	0.44	0.64	0.20

Sources: OECD, *Annual Labour Force Statistics; Employment in Europe* (1998).

marked in Germany, the Netherlands and Austria. In the 1990s, on the other hand, the ratio was reversed, again with the exception of Sweden, while in the USA the two growth rates evened out. Assuming no change in labour market behaviour, this means that, in the 1970s and 1980s, national labour markets had to deal with (in some cases considerable) increases in the labour supply, while in the 1990s they were relieved of some of that burden. The differences between the individual countries in this respect are very striking and should be taken into account in interpreting the results of the following decomposition.

Let us return again to equation (2.7). The change in the participation rate ($\Delta\ln LFP$) is an indicator of the change in labour market behaviour. It shows the endogenous growth or decline in the labour supply, while the decomposition of employment reveals the extent to which the expansion of employment and the increase in labour market participation run in tandem. The change in the participation rate ($\Delta\ln(1{-}U)$) shows the extent to which the active potential labour supply is being utilized; decomposition of employment growth can indicate the extent to which the expansion of employment and unemployment run counter to each other, as is normally to be expected.

Table 2.3 shows employment growth and its decomposition into the shares attributable to changes in the working-age population, in labour force participation and in the share of the total labour force in employment. The choice of

Table 2.3   Decomposition of employment growth, 1970–90 and 1991–7

				Average annual growth						
		1970–1990				1991–1997				
	E	= *POP* +	*LFP* +	(1–*U*)		*E* =	*POP* +	*LFP* +	(1–*U*)
USA	1.98	= 1.32 +	0.68 +	–0.03		1.51 =	0.94 +	0.24 +	0.34
Japan	1.03	= 0.93 +	0.15 +	–0.05		0.49 =	0.09 +	0.62 +	–0.22
EU	0.44	= 0.71 +	0.05 +	–0.32		–0.22 =	0.23 +	–0.02 +	–0.51
D[a]	0.33	= 0.66 +	–0.05 +	–0.29		–0.76 =	0.13 +	–0.14 +	–0.87
NL[b]	1.42	= 1.19 +	0.58 +	–0.34		1.48 =	0.51 +	1.00 +	–0.01
A	0.99	= 0.69 +	0.39 +	–0.10		1.11 =	0.53 +	0.71 +	–0.22
DK	0.61	= 0.43 +	0.58 +	–0.40		0.22 =	0.34 +	–0.66 +	0.47
UK	0.42	= 0.35 +	0.23 +	–0.17		0.24 =	0.08 +	0.02 +	0.24
F	0.31	= 0.81 +	–0.14 +	–0.34		–0.13 =	0.35 +	0.09 +	–0.55
S	0.79	= 0.22 +	0.57 +	0.00		–1.84 =	0.01 +	–0.96 +	–0.89

Notes:
[a]Germany since 1991 including former GDR.
[b]Netherlands: date from *Employment in Europe*.
E = employed persons; *POP* = working-age population; *LFP* = labour force participation rate; *U* = unemployment rate.

Sources: OECD, *Annual Labour Force Statistics*; OECD, *Annual Economic Outlook*.

countries is the same as in the analysis of employment elasticities; the available data meant that the period selected had to be changed slightly.

The first thing to be noted is that Table 2.3 once again makes the American 'jobs miracle' graphically clear. With average annual employment growth of almost 2 per cent in the 1970 and 1980s, the American employment system stands out a long way from the other countries or regions. In other words, in the period from 1970 to 1990, the number of people employed in the USA rose from a good 80 million to virtually 120 million, or by almost 50 per cent! Only in the Netherlands, where the average annual growth rate was 1.42 per cent, did employment grow at anything like the same pace. France and Germany are in the lower part of the range, although the balance is still positive, with an average annual increase in employment of about 0.3 per cent. In the case of (Western) Germany, this means, in concrete terms, that the employment level in 1990 was around 1.8 million higher than in 1970, which at any rate is almost 7 per cent more than the initial level of 26.7 million.

The picture did not change significantly in the 1990s. True, the US jobs machine lost some of its dynamism, but it remained very vigorous, with an annual average increase in employment of 1.51 per cent. The Netherlands even kept pace with the American employment dynamic. The European Union, on the other hand, suffered from negative employment growth of 0.22 per cent per annum on average, which translated into the loss of almost 2 million employees over seven years. Among the countries in our sample, Germany and, in particular, Sweden, recorded heavy job losses, which can, however, be explained by certain exceptional circumstances: unification in the case of Germany and the collapse of Eastern European markets in the case of Eastern Germany and Sweden.[30]

Decomposition of the evolution of employment reveals some surprising details. It is clear from Table 2.3 that the description of developments in the USA as a 'jobs miracle' seems somewhat exaggerated. Almost 70 per cent of the growth in employment in the 1970s and 1980s is attributable to the growth in the working-age population, and the same applies to the 1990s. The next most important component is the change in labour market behaviour, which manifests itself in the rising participation rate, particularly among women, as already noted above. However, the extremely positive evolution of employment in the USA did virtually nothing to improve utilization of the potential labour force in the 1970s and 1980s, as can be seen from the continuing slight rise in unemployment. It was not until the 1990s that the growth in employment began to make an obvious contribution to the decline in unemployment.

In Japan, the expansion of employment in the 1970s and 1980s ran more or less parallel with that of the working-age population, while employment growth in the 1990s was based almost wholly on the rising participation rate, although it was not sufficient to prevent unemployment from rising.

In the European countries, on the other hand, employment growth in the earlier part of the period was typically not sufficient to absorb the expansion of the potential labour force. On the contrary, a high proportion of the unemployment of the 1970s and 1980s is attributable to the disproportionate increase in the potential labour force. This interpretation is further reinforced by the disproportionate growth in the working-age population relative to the population as a whole (cf. Table 2.2). This demographic factor also came into play in Western Germany and, particularly, in France. Between 1991 and 1997, the UK and Denmark were the only countries in which the evolution of employment was linked to a reduction in unemployment.[31] In Denmark, however, this success was marred by a sharp decline in the participation rate, clearly the result of a vigorous early retirement policy, while the participation rate in the UK stagnated. In all the other countries, and particularly in Germany, France and Sweden, the decline in employment levels was associated with a sharp rise in unemployment.

Thus Table 2.3 reveals at least one competitor to the 'American jobs machine' whose pattern of growth in respect of social integration into the labour market seems to be much more interesting. Although the increase in the working-age population explains part of the growth in employment in the Netherlands as well (84 per cent in the 1970s and 1980s, and 34 per cent in the 1990s), the major share in the growth in employment is attributable to the increase in the participation rate: a good 40 per cent in the 1980s and 68 per cent in the 1990s. To what extent this high inclusiveness is due to increased part-time employment, and how this should be judged in employment policy terms, is the subject of the next section.

Decomposing Part-time Employment

Increased part-time employment seems to be a general trend in employment relations in late capitalist employment systems. However, it is clear just from a descriptive comparison that this phenomenon has developed very differently in the countries in our sample and has also spread at different rates (Table 2.4). A quick glance at the table shows, first, that the share of part-time work in total employment varies considerably. In 1998, the shares in the countries investigated here ranged from 11.5 per cent in Austria to 30 per cent in the Netherlands. Second, the part-time rate has risen in all countries, but again to widely differing extents; the rates of increase between 1973 and 1991 ranged from 2.4 percentage points in Austria to 30.1 percentage points in the Netherlands. The third thing to note, however, is the change of trend in some countries (USA, Netherlands, Denmark, Sweden) towards declining part-time rates in the 1990s. Fourth, part-time work is concentrated among women.[32] And fifth, a trend towards convergence at the international level can be observed.[33]

Table 2.4   Part-time work in the various employment regimes, 1973, 1991 and 1998

	Part-time employed (per cent)								
	Total			Men			Women		
	1973	1991	1998	1973	1991	1998	1973	1991	1998
USA	13.9	17.4	13.4	7.2	10.5	8.2	24.8	25.6	19.1
Japan	7.9	20.5	23.6	4.8	10.1	12.9	17.3	34.3	39.0
EU	12.5	15.3	15.9	3.3	5.2	5.9	4.8	29.4	29.8
D^a	7.7	15.5	16.6	1.0	2.7	4.6	20.0	34.3	32.4
NL	4.4	34.5	30.0	1.1	16.7	12.4	15.5	62.2	54.8
A	6.4	8.8	11.5	1.4	1.5	2.7	15.6	20.1	22.8
DK	17.0	23.1	17.0	1.9	10.5	9.8	40.3	37.8	25.4
UK	15.3	22.2	23.0	1.8	5.5	8.2	38.8	43.7	41.2
F	5.1	12.0	14.8	1.4	3.4	5.8	11.2	23.5	25.0
S	18.0	23.7	13.5	3.7	7.6	5.6	38.8	41.0	22.0

Notes:
The definitions of part-time work vary considerably across OECD countries, which affects the international comparability and the comparability within countries themselves.
For further definitions, see OECD, Labour Market and Social Occasional Papers no. 22, 'The Definition of Part-time work for the Purpose of International Comparisons', which is available on the internet (*http://www.oecd.org/els/papers/papers.htm*).
^{a}until 1991, only West Germany.

Source: OECD, *Annual Employment Outlook*.

Two different schools of thought dominate the debate on part-time work. One regards part-time work as the ideal means of reconciling working-time preferences on the supply and demand sides of the labour market. Since women are entering the labour market in increasing numbers, there is a need to reorganize domestic work and paid work, for example by making working times more flexible for both men and women. At the same time, the structural change from manufacturing to services is increasing the need for flexible forms of work organization. Since these needs for flexibility are not necessarily compatible with each other, there is a continuous and differentiated need for coordination and negotiation. Part-time work that is managed in such a way as to be flexible in both scheduling and duration is probably the outcome of such coordination processes. The other school of thought regards the spread of part-time work as part of an unfortunate trend towards segmentation, that is towards the creation of inferior jobs with low rates of pay, few opportunities for promotion and poor social protection, while the core workforce, or 'insiders', are offered job guarantees and enhanced status. From this point of view, moreover, firms are making increased use of part-time work in order to reduce labour costs in the face of increased international competition.

It is the institutional conditions under which the first variant operates that interest us here. This leads us to pose the following question: is part-time work merely an expression of increased female labour market participation or may it also be an indication of a more equal distribution of work between the sexes? In order to answer this question, the following decomposition can be used:[34]

$$PT = PTm*Em + PTf*Ef, \quad\quad\quad (2.8)$$

in which *PT* is the part-time rate, that is the share of part-timers in total employment, *PTm* the male part-time rate, *PTf* the female part-time rate, *Em* the share of men in total employment and *Ef* the share of women in total employment. This identity can be disaggregated into the following components that make up the growth in full-time employment:

$$\Delta PT = \Delta PTm*Em_0 + \Delta PTf*Ef_0 + (PTf_0 - PTm_0)*\Delta Ef$$
$$+ [\Delta PTm*\Delta Em + \Delta PTf*\Delta Ef]. \quad\quad (2.9)$$

$\Delta PTm*Em_0$ and $\Delta PTf*Ef_0$ represent those components of the growth in part-time work that are attributable to the change in male and female part-time work; $(PTf_0 - PTm_0)*\Delta Ef$ is the component attributable to the shift in the employment structure in favour of women; $[\Delta PTm*\Delta Em + \Delta PTf*\Delta Ef]$ is an interaction value representing the influence of interactions in the component dynamic. Table 2.5 shows the result of the decomposition procedure for the rates of growth in part-time employment from 1983 to 1996.[35]

Initial comparison of employment regimes in the USA/Japan/Europe triad reveals some interesting differences. In the USA, part-time employment declined between 1983 and 1996, with women's labour market behaviour making the biggest contribution to the fall; if the employment structure had not shifted in favour of women, the part-time rate would have declined even further. In Japan, part-time employment rose by about six percentage points, with men responsible for almost half of this increase. In Europe, part-time employment rose by 2.7 percentage points; about a third of the increase is attributable to the shift in employment structures in favour of women, but much of it is due to changes in men's labour market behaviour.

As expected, the part-time dynamic in Europe varies considerably from country to country, which points to significant institutional differences. In Germany, the growth in part-time employment was much weaker than in the 1970s. The change in the employment structures in favour of women accounted for about half of the increase, with the other half being attributable to increased part-time work among men. A good third of the sharp rise in part-time work in

Table 2.5   Decomposition of the increase in part-time work from 1983 to 1996

	ΔPT	=	$\Delta PTm \times Em_0$	+	$\Delta PTf \times Ef_0$	+	$(PTf_0 - PTm_0) \times \Delta Ef$	+	$\Delta PTm \times \Delta Em + \Delta PTf \times \Delta Ef$
USA	−4.51	=	−1.35	+	−3.45	+	0.43	+	−0.14
Japan	5.90	=	2.72	+	2.92	+	0.23	+	0.03
EU	2.71	=	1.24	+	0.57	+	0.92	+	−0.02
D	2.05	=	1.21	+	−0.04	+	0.95	+	−0.07
NL	8.26	=	2.99	+	1.95	+	3.23	+	0.10
A	2.21	=	0.68	+	0.65	+	0.85	+	0.03
DK	−6.86	=	2.01	+	−8.88	+	0.02	+	−0.01
UK	3.86	=	2.58	+	0.04	+	1.40	+	−0.16
F	4.23	=	1.90	+	1.63	+	0.67	+	0.03
S	−9.90	=	0.27	+	−10.43	+	0.61	+	−0.35

Notes:
PT = part-time rate (share of part-timers in total employment).
PTm = male part-time rate; PTf = female part-time rate.
Em = share of men in total employment; Ef = share of women in total employment.

Sources: OECD, *Employment Outlook* (1997, 1999), OECD, *Labour Force Statistics* (1977–97).

the Netherlands is attributable to the change in women's share in total employment, while the rise in part-time employment among men accounts for just about another third, more than the rise in part-time work among women: in terms of the dynamic at least, an almost equal division of labour between the sexes! About one-third of the rise in part-time employment in Austria, however weak it may have been overall, was due to a change in men's labour market behaviour. The sharp increase in the United Kingdom is largely attributable to the rise in part-time employment among men, and men are catching up in France in relative terms as well. In the Scandinavian EU member states, however, the trend towards a redistribution of work between the sexes through part-time work has clearly been reversed, with part-time rates declining rapidly. If men, and particularly those in Denmark, were not still making a positive contribution to the expansion of part-time work, part-time work would have declined even further in importance; the change in employment structures in favour of women is now contributing virtually nothing to the (originally) positive dynamic of part-time work.

In sum, it can be said, not without some degree of surprise, that the trend towards the expansion of part-time work seems to have come to a halt; where it is continuing, it is increasingly men who are contributing to the expansion. In view of these contradictory trends, we will investigate in the next section the frequently expressed conjecture that strategies of work and income redistribution, as practised in the Netherlands, are damaging to economic well-being and the dynamic of its development.

4 ON THE ECONOMIC EFFICIENCY OF EMPLOYMENT SYSTEMS

Might the differences between the USA and Europe also lie in the fact that their respective productive systems are organized differently, with the output of the production process being distributed according to different principles? This question begs the even more fundamental one of differing notions of fairness. If the prevailing view in a society is that every person should receive what he or she contributes to the social 'cake', this principle leads both to minimal redistribution and to pressure on individuals to take part in the 'baking of the cake' under all possible circumstances. Countries dominated by a performance principle of this kind can be expected to have both a high participation rate and marked wage differentiation in accordance with individual market value (productivity).

This has an even further-reaching consequence. Because of the high participation rate, average hourly productivity will be lower than in a regime in which the notion of fairness based on contribution or performance is combined with a notion of fairness based on need. In regimes of this kind, factors that have little or nothing to do with work done in the market will be taken into account in the distribution process; these might include, for example, family allowances or tax breaks for unpaid child raising or care of the elderly. In such a regime, there are incentives to ensure that it is primarily highly productive workers who take part in the 'baking of the market cake', while those who are less productive in the market fulfil 'alternative roles' that are more or less socially legitimated. If these alternative roles, such as those in the traditional gender division of labour, are also allocated institutionally (by means of religious norms or even legal regulations), competitiveness in the labour market is, conversely, restricted by the obligation to fulfil these alternative roles. In a regime of this kind, labour market integration will be low but hourly productivity will be high.

Thus there seems to be a trade-off between high labour market integration and efficiency as reflected in high hourly productivity. However, there is no conflict between social well-being and high labour market integration, since the lower hourly productivity can be offset by higher participation rates and longer individual working times. Conversely, a low average individual working time can be compensated for by high hourly productivity and high participation rates. Thus there are institutional alternatives (or functionally equivalent institutional arrangements) for the organization of economic well-being, and employment regimes can be characterized or typologized on the basis of these alternatives. I will again use the decomposition method below in order to point out such empirical alternatives.

Decomposition of per capita GDP

Economic well-being at the aggregate level of national societies is generally measured in terms of GDP per capita. This indicator will be the subject of a critical assessment later in the chapter. The following identity will serve as a formal representation of the composition of per capita GDP:

$$GDP/POP = GDP/h * h/E * E/WAP * WAP/POP. \qquad (2.10)$$

GDP/POP represents gross domestic product per capita (*POP* = total production), which serves as a *measure of economic well-being*, measured in purchasing power parity and dollars. *GDP/h* represents productivity per hour worked and can be taken as a measure of economic efficiency. The term *h/E* denotes the average number of hours worked by the labour force per year; the lower the number of hours worked, the more equal work sharing is likely to be and the more flexible autonomous time management and work organization are likely to be. This indicator is of great interest because of the numerous different ways in which it can be interpreted. Correct interpretation requires a more thorough analysis, since the average working time per economically active individual may be based on a very high standard deviation (polarized work sharing) or a very low standard deviation (equal work sharing). *E/WAP* is the employment rate, that is the share of employees in the working-age population; it can be considered as a measure of social integration into the labour market. *WAP/POP* denotes the share of the working-age population (15–64-year-olds) in the population as a whole and reflects the population structure, which can vary over time or relative to other countries and influence performance and output.

Let us turn now to the left-hand side of the equation, that is the overall measurement of the economic efficiency of employment systems. Table 2.6 shows that, in 1997, the USA had the highest level of economic well-being as measured in terms of per capita GDP and internationally comparative prices, followed by Denmark and Japan. Of the countries in our sample, Sweden and the United Kingdom have the lowest values. After lagging a long way behind as recently as 1994 (Schmid, 1998), the Netherlands had overtaken Germany by 1997.

It can of course be questioned whether per capita GDP is in fact an appropriate indicator of economic well-being.[36] The inventors of national accounting did not in fact intend to develop such an indicator: they were merely

Table 2.6   *Decomposition of per capita GDP (GDP/POP) into indicators of efficiency, work sharing, labour market integration and population structure in 1997 (in US$)*

	GDP/POP	=	GDP/h	×	h/E	×	E/WAP	×	WAP/POP
USA	29 326	=	30.49	×	1 966	×	0.74	×	0.66
Japan	24 574	=	24.89	×	1 900	×	0.75	×	0.69
EU15	20 609	=	29.64	×	1 706	×	0.61	×	0.67
D	22 047	=	32.24	×	1 570	×	0.64	×	0.68
NL	22 622	=	34.94	×	1 365	×	0.69	×	0.69
A	23 080	=	28.67	×	1 747	×	0.68	×	0.67
DK	25 511	=	31.56	×	1 593	×	0.76	×	0.67
UK	20 802	=	26.09	×	1 736	×	0.71	×	0.65
F	21 291	=	33.93	×	1 634	×	0.59	×	0.65
S	20 434	=	29.70	×	1 552	×	0.71	×	0.63

Notes:
GDP = gross domestic product (prices, exchange rates and purchasing power parity of 1999);
POP = resident population; WAP = working-age population; E = employed persons; h = hours worked.

Sources: OECD, *Annual Labour Force Statistics*; OECD, *National Accounts*; OECD, *Annual Employment Outlook* (1999); own calculations

seeking to make available an instrument for measuring market-mediated transactions. Two main criteria were used. The first was that only legal transactions should be measured. Thus the proceeds of the drugs trade, now measured in billions of dollars, of gambling dens, of prostitution and of clandestine work are not included in GDP. Secondly, only end products should be measured, in order to avoid double counting. In practice, this principle can lead to peculiarities or to very differing practices from country to country.[37]

One of the problems with the notion of GDP is the measurement and inclusion of government services. In many cases, what is measured is not output, that is, for example, the economic value of education services, but input, that is teachers' wages. However, there would be good reasons for assessing the real economic value of many government services and including it in GDP. There would also be good reasons for taking out certain services, such as police services or even defence, that can be regarded as intermediate products rather than 'consumable' values.

As far as private business is concerned, there has to be a question mark over the inclusion of transactions that merely compensate for damage (such as environmental pollution or storm damage) without creating any additional prosperity. Irreparable environmental damage, which is put at up to 6 per cent of

GDP in Germany (Leipert, 1997; Simonis and Leipert, 1995), is not measured (and therefore not entered as a negative value either). On the other hand, as already indicated, GDP does not measure the additional economic prosperity produced without market-mediated transactions. Examples include not only do-it-yourself work in the house or garden but also, and in particular, child raising and other care activities and housework, most of which is still 'contributed' by women, who remain unpaid for their efforts.

The informal economy, which is not quantified and included in GDP, is also of significance for the future of work. The value of the output of the informal economy is put at 13.9 per cent of GDP in the Netherlands, 13.1 in Germany (and the trend is upwards) but only 8.6 in the USA (Schneider, 1994, 1996). The available evidence suggests that, here too, earnings are unequally distributed, with the lion's share falling to employees who are already successful in the market. In future, however, as the standard employment relationship inevitably breaks up, more attention than hitherto must be paid to this area outside the market, in which additional income is earned. One important precondition for productive independent work in the informal economy is the availability of own capital or assets to supplement current income when it is reduced as a result of part-time work, whether enforced or not, or early retirement.

Furthermore, the part that policy on wealth distribution might play in employment policy has not yet even been properly recognized, let alone acted on. However, for any given level of technology (which can be assumed to be relatively equal in the industrialized countries), the opportunities for productive independent work are all the greater the shorter working time in the official labour market is and the greater the assets available to individuals are. In that sense, a country with low per capita GDP can be economically wealthier than one with high per capita GDP. This is particularly true if hourly productivity is very high, as it is in the Netherlands, quite apart from the fact that there are other aspects to well-being in addition to the purely economic ones. Free time, for example, can also be used for cultural, entertainment or sporting activities that may be only partly mediated through the market, if at all.[38] In other words, and with reference to the interface between the *private household system and the labour market* alluded to at the outset, a broad and egalitarian distribution of wealth encourages a redistribution of work that will have a positive employment effect.

Before seeking further to elucidate the decomposition of GDP, we can sum up by pointing once again to the limited meaningfulness of this indicator: depending on what is included and what is not, how the measurements are made and what price basis is selected, alternative calculations of GDP produce widely differing results. For example, alternative estimates for 1966 in the USA produce values for GDP that range between 122 and 468 per cent of the officially recorded value (Eisner, 1988: 1668).

We turn now to the classificatory components of GDP. As far as the *efficiency indicator* is concerned, that is hourly productivity, the rank order is quite different. The Dutch head the table, with a GDP per hour of $34.94, while the Japanese bring up the rear with 'only' $24.89 per hour. This is probably connected to the fact that Japan is a latecomer in terms of industrial development and still permits itself the luxury of having a lot of jobs with very low productivity (and pay), particularly in personal services. The Netherlands are followed by France, Germany, Denmark and then, trailing by some distance, the USA.

When it comes to the *indicator of work sharing* and autonomous time management, the Netherlands again leads the pack with the lowest average working time per person employed. (Dependent) employees in the Netherlands work on average only 1365 hours per year, while the USA, with 1966 hours per year, surprisingly brings up the rear once again, trailing behind Japan. Average annual working times are relatively high in Austria and the United Kingdom as well, while Sweden and Germany, with relatively low average annual working times per employee, are positioned just behind the Netherlands.

It will be no great surprise that the rank order for the employment rate as an indicator of *labour market integration* is different again. This time, Denmark heads the table with an employment rate of 76 per cent; that is, a good three-quarters of the working-age population are integrated in some way into the labour market. Japan and the USA are hard on the heels of Denmark, with rates of 75 and 74 per cent, respectively. At the other end of the range, only 59 per cent of the working-age population in France is gainfully employed, and in Germany the employment rate, at 64 per cent, is now lower than in the Netherlands, where it stands at 69 per cent; a few years ago, both countries had similarly low rates, around the European average of 61 per cent.[39]

We conclude with a brief look at the influence of the population structure. The share of the working-age population in total population fluctuates in the advanced industrial and service societies within a narrow range, from 63 per cent in Sweden to 69 per cent in Japan and the Netherlands. In order to get some idea of the strength of the influence, two examples will be simulated. If Sweden had the same population structure as the Netherlands, it would advance to virtually the same level of economic performance as the Netherlands; conversely, if Japan had the same population structure as Sweden, it would still not match the Netherlands.

The results of the decomposition analysis confirm the theoretical expectation that there is a trade-off between efficiency and labour market integration. The extent to which such a trade-off is actually realized depends crucially on the interposing variable, namely the number of working hours per economically active individual. A country with a highly productive employment system will be unable to achieve a high degree of integration unless average working time is low and unemployment is successfully combated. The Netherlands seems to be heading in this direction, as the latest successes in combating unemployment would seem to suggest. The example that counters that of the Netherlands is France, where hourly productivity is almost as high as in the Netherlands while the number of working hours per economically active individual is relatively high, resulting in a low level of integration and correspondingly high levels of unemployment. The high hourly productivity means that a work-sharing strategy intended to achieve a higher level of integration would be a realistic option for France, and one that would not seriously jeopardize economic prosperity.

However, such a strategy seems less well-suited to solving the unemployment problem in the United Kingdom, because efficiency there is low; any work-sharing strategy would have to be accompanied by a massive training campaign in order to raise hourly productivity. An alternative, or complementary, option for the Anglo-Saxon employment regime would be that adopted in America, where the level of integration has been raised by increased wage differentiation and reductions in real wages, which serve to offset relatively low labour productivity. It is interesting to note that the strategy adopted by the current Blair government since December 1997 is heading in precisely this direction.

The Decomposition of Economic Growth

Up to this point, we have confined ourselves to static analysis of the links between employment regimes and economic well-being. However, the dynamic aspect is even more interesting: to what extent have the factors used above to characterize employment regimes, albeit sketchily, contributed to economic growth? Is it possible, from these various models, to glean further clues as to why many European countries have such a poor record on employment compared with the USA and Japan?

Following on from our previous analysis, our initial hypothesis will be that a nation's employment performance is all the poorer the lower the increase in efficiency (labour productivity) and the lower the extent of social integration (through work sharing, for instance). In order to examine this argument, we will again adopt the decomposition method. Economic growth measured in terms of per capita GDP can be expressed, in a modification of identity (2.10), as the sum of the increase in hourly productivity, the rise in hours worked per economically active individual and the increase in labour market participation (E/POP):

$$\Delta \ln GDP/POP = \Delta \ln GDP/h + \Delta \ln h/E + \Delta \ln E/WAP + \Delta \ln WAP/POP.$$

$$(2.11)$$

A few observations on data quality are appropriate before we proceed to interpret the results. The measurement of economic performance can be compared, without exaggeration, to walking through a minefield. The risk of being metaphorically blown to smithereens is high. Sources of errors abound, so the results can vary considerably depending on how the time period, price index, exchange rate, purchasing power parity and reference countries are selected. An excellent illustrative example is the dispute between the Swedish sociologist, Walter Korpi, and various, mainly Swedish, economists.[40]

It is not our intention to arbitrate in this dispute. However, it is apposite to note that comparisons of performance in respect of economic growth are sensitive in particular to the choice of time period, exchange rate and purchasing power parity. As Henrekson (1996: 1754) shows quite clearly, rank orders can be reversed according to the parameters chosen, and Agell (1996: 1763) demonstrates effectively how bivariate regressions between economic growth and social expenditure can reverse their sign when additional determinants, such as the initial level of GDP (base effect) or employment structure are introduced. Because of the sensitivity of the results to the parameters listed above, the following two tables compare economic growth per capita in two relatively short time periods, 1983–90 and 1991–7, on the basis of standardized prices and exchange rates in both instances. In addition, the values are adjusted for the purchasing power parity prevailing in the base year in each case.[41] Because of the problems already alluded to above, however, the findings should be regarded merely as indicators of a trend and not as accurate comparisons of performance.

First, comparison of Tables 2.7 and 2.8 clearly shows once again the effects of the recession of 1992/3. With the exception of the USA and Denmark, growth rates in national income per capita were much lower in the 1990s than in the 1980s. Second, it is immediately evident that Japan's economic dynamic slackened off considerably and declined to the level of the European Union. Thirdly, and this is hardly surprising after the analysis of employment elasticities, all countries with a successful employment policy record also have an above-average growth dynamic, particularly Denmark and the Netherlands. Those whose record in this respect is less impressive – Germany, France and Sweden – have only a slight increase in per capita GDP to report. Thus both tables confirm the close relationship between employment and growth.

Decomposition of the increase in national income per capita in the 1990s reveals an astonishing picture. The difference between the American and European employment regimes catches the eye immediately. Whereas economic growth in the USA has been based largely on the increase in actual working time per economically active individual and in labour market participation, in Europe it is virtually labour productivity alone that has maintained economic growth. And if average hourly productivity hardly improved at all

Table 2.7   Decomposition of economic growth, 1983–90, into indicators of efficiency, work sharing, labour market integration and population structure

	GDP/POP	=	GDP/h	+	h/E	+	E/WAP	+	WAP/POP
			Average annual growth rates of						
USA	2.7	=	0.8	+	0.5	+	1.5	+	−0.1
Japan	4.3	=	4.0	+	−0.4	+	0.3	+	0.4
EU	2.7	=		+		+		+	
D[a]	2.3	=	2.7	+	−1.0	+	0.8	+	−0.2
NL[b]	2.7	=	0.9	+	−0.9	+	2.6	+	0.1
A	2.4	=		+		+		+	
DK	2.3	=		+		+		+	
UK	2.8	=	0.9	+	0.4	+	1.7	+	−0.2
F	2.1	=	2.5	+	−0.4	+	0.5	+	−0.5
S	2.0	=	1.2	+	0.3	+	0.8	+	−0.3

Notes:
[a]only West Germany.
[b]Netherlands only dependent employees.
Because of missing work time data, it was not possible to do the decomposition for the EU, Austria and Denmark.
GDP = gross domestic product (prices, exchange rates and ppp of 1999); *POP* = resident population; *WAP* = working-age population; *E* = employed persons; *h* = hours worked.

Sources: Main economic indicators, December 1985, January 1990; OECD, *Annual Labour Force Statistics*; *Employment Outlook* (1997).

in the USA in the 1990s, it has continued to rise sharply in all European countries (and in Japan), particularly in Germany.

However, this indicator can be assessed from an employment policy perspective only in conjunction with the two other components of growth. If the level of employment (*E/WAP*) declines at the same time, then it can reasonably be assumed that the increasing efficiency is being achieved largely by excluding less productive workers and it is therefore a statistical artefact. This interpretation seems to suggest itself for Germany, France and Sweden in the 1990s. In the 1980s, efficiency and participation increased in parallel in all the countries in our sample. The decline in the number of hours worked indicates that in Japan and, particularly, Germany and the Netherlands this was achieved with the aid of some degree of work and income redistribution. In the 1990s, this still applied only to the Netherlands and Japan, while working-time reductions could by now only alleviate the drastic decline in labour market integration in the united Germany. The main reason for this was, of course, the transformation of the East German command economy and its rapid integration into the Federal Republic; in particular, the high participation rate among women in the former GDR could

Table 2.8   Decomposition of economic growth, 1991–7, into indicators
of efficiency, work sharing, labour market integration and
population structure

	GDP/POP	=	GDP/h	+	h/E	+	E/WAP	+	WAP/POP
			Average annual growth rates of						
USA	2.72	=	0.35	+	1.76	+	0.57	+	0.03
Japan	1.06	=	1.99	+	−1.12	+	0.39	+	−0.18
EU	1.10	=		+		+		+	
D[a]	0.96	=	3.06	+	−0.41	+	−1.47	+	−0.17
NL[b]	1.91	=	1.62	+	−0.61	+	0.97	+	−0.07
A	1.43	=		+		+		+	
DK	3.04	=		+		+		+	
UK	2.02	=	2.00	+	0.11	+	0.02	+	−0.10
F	0.92	=	1.63	+	−0.11	+	−0.52	+	−0.08
S	0.64	=	2.07	+	0.93	+	−2.50	+	0.19

Notes:
[a]only West Germany.
[b]Netherlands only dependent employees.
Because of missing work time data, it was not possible to do the decomposition for the EU,
Austria and Denmark.
GDP = gross domestic product (prices, exchange rates and ppp of 1999); *POP* = resident population; *WAP* = working-age population; *E* = employed persons; *h* = hours worked.

Sources: Main economic indicators, December 1985, January 1990; OECD, *Annual Labour*
Force Statistics; *Employment Outlook* (1997); *Employment in Europe* (1998).

not be maintained. Particularly worthy of mention is the 'Americanization' of
the working-time regimes in the United Kingdom and Sweden, where working time per economically active individual has been rising since the 1980s,
particularly in Sweden during the 1990s, in contrast to continental European
countries.

It is also clear from this analysis that the weaknesses of the Swedish and
French employment regimes were already perceptible in the 1980s. The two
countries had the lowest rates of growth in national income, which can be
explained in part by low rates of increase in labour market participation
(although, in the case of Sweden, the high initial participation rate should be
taken into account). France, it is true, has one of the highest rates of increase
in labour productivity (that is, the efficiency indicator), but the contribution
of work redistribution to the increase or maintenance of labour market integration is very modest in comparison with the Netherlands and Germany. In
contrast to the Netherlands, the reduction in individual working time was not
converted into a higher labour market participation rate. The reasons for this
difference are still unclear. Since France has the lowest level of labour
market integration of all the countries investigated here, and also the lowest

part-time rate apart from Austria, the answer to the puzzle may lie in the underdevelopment of part-time working. In this account, it is the Swedish employment regime that comes off worst, particularly in the more recent period. True, the productivity increase is respectable, but the level of labour market integration fell dramatically, which certainly reflects the drastic increase in unemployment and the relatively high initial level of labour market integration.

Japan emerges from this analysis as the high-productivity regime par excellence. Labour productivity rose in the 1980s far more sharply than in the other countries, and this increase was accompanied by a relatively large reduction in working time (albeit from an extremely high level), which contributed to the further rise in employment intensity or labour market participation. Japan is also the only country where the demographic component (the rising share of the working-age population in total population) made a significant positive contribution to growth in the 1980s. In most of the other countries, and particularly in France, the demographic factor (relative decline in the working-age population) depressed economic growth. The same applies to the 1990s, with the exception of the USA and Sweden.

Both Germany and the Netherlands (and presumably Denmark as well) are employment regimes in which the evolution of average working time per capita made a strongly negative contribution to economic growth. This reduced the level of growth that was possible, but in both cases it was obviously converted during the 1980s into higher employment intensity. However, only the Netherlands succeeded in both periods in fully compensating for the negative contribution of working-time reductions through an even higher increase in the employment level.

Comparison of the two periods reveals a surprising change in the United Kingdom in the contributions of the various components of economic growth. In the 1980s, the distribution pattern of the various components almost exactly matched that in the USA: increasing labour market participation and working times explain two thirds of economic growth per capita, with only the remaining third being accounted for by improved labour productivity. In the 1990s, the United Kingdom more closely resembled its continental European partners, except in one respect: virtually all growth was attributable to rising labour productivity rather than rising participation. The only point in common with the USA was the (weak) upward trend in working time.

5   SUMMARY: THE ILLUSION OF BEST PRACTICES

We are now in a position to summarize the comparison of employment regimes. At least three types of employment regimes can be identified: the liberal, the state and the social market regimes. These are all ideal types that usually occur in reality in various combinations.

The USA comes closest to the *liberal market* regime (competitive capitalism), that is a competitive employment regime uncoordinated by the state; the European country that most closely resembles this regime is the United Kingdom, since the Thatcher government at least. In this regime, adjustment to the major trends of globalization and individualization has been mediated largely through wage flexibility, that is through widening wage differentials. This was made possible by the trade unions' dramatic loss of power, in part a deliberate result of government policy. The general increase in pay flexibility has been accompanied by falling real wages, particularly among male middle-income earners. The ensuing fall in household incomes has been clearly offset in part by rising female labour market participation and in part by longer individual working times. The level of part-time work is moderate but stagnating, and the trend among women is even declining. Apart from the increase in female labour market participation, employment growth is driven largely by the increase in the working-age population. Thus what we are dealing with here is an extensive growth regime, since at least half of economic growth per capita is explained by extensive growth factors, that is the increases in working time and participation rates. Official unemployment has been kept under control, and has even fallen considerably in recent years. However, the negative consequences include rising income inequality and poverty, as well as hidden unemployment (some of it in the form of criminality).

The *state market economy* regime (coordinated capitalism) is characterized by close cooperation between the political class, state elites and large companies. Japan comes closest to this model, but some of its most important elements can also be found in France, Austria and even the Netherlands.[42] If it is not the major companies it is the employers' associations that, in this regime, have the upper hand over the bodies representing employees' interests. As a result, adjustment to globalization and individualization has been characterized by moderate wage policies and widening wage differentials, combined with Keynesian demand management and/or active industrial policies. Employment growth is average to high and driven largely by the increases in female labour market participation and part-time work. The largest share of the relatively strong economic growth is explained by 'intensive' growth factors, that is by rising labour productivity and declining actual working time. The rise in official unemployment is modest, and long-term unemployment is low.

The third and dominant type of employment regime in Europe is the *social market economy* (welfare capitalism). The fundamental characteristics of this type are low wage differentials and comprehensive social protection in the event of sickness, old age and unemployment. Wage-related and, in certain cases, generous income guarantees for the unemployed and the elderly are a particularly typical feature. Germany and the Scandinavian countries come closest to this type, although France and the Netherlands also have many of its characteristics. With the major exception of the Netherlands, employment growth in these countries in the last decade was slight or even negative; in those countries where it was positive, the increase was driven largely by work redistribution or an increase in the size of the working-age population. Economic growth is driven principally by rising labour productivity, and is therefore intensive rather than extensive, particularly since actual working time per employee fell considerably in this employment regime. This also reflects the power of the trade unions which, by virtue of their involvement in corporatist arrangements, is very considerable and has enabled them to fight successfully for working time reductions in exchange for more jobs. Part-time work is high or rising. However, in those countries where part-time work is already very high, as in Denmark or Sweden, the trend among women is in the opposite direction, while part-time work is on the increase among men.

In this variant of the regime, men's and women's working time is apparently beginning to converge, but a prominent characteristic of most representatives of the social market economy type is declining or stagnating employment rates or high unemployment, together with a high share of long-term unemployment and the threat of social exclusion for those affected. Only countries with an explicit work redistribution strategy (Denmark and the Netherlands) have been able to reverse the trend towards rising unemployment or social exclusion. However, these countries also seem to have succeeded in occupying new market niches through the flexibilization of product and labour markets, thereby stimulating employment-intensive economic growth.

As already assumed theoretically, even a simple performance comparison shows how illusory the search for cases of 'best practice' is. Table 2.9 compares the countries in our sample on the basis of 10 performance criteria, although the indicators do not fulfil the ideal requirements in every case.[43] The narrow range of the average rank order (between 3.6 and 6.9) is quite astonishing, as is the clustering of cases around the middle of the ranking. This means that good rankings on one target indicator must obviously be bought at the expense of poor rankings in respect of other targets.[44] Nevertheless, the groups of more and less successful countries in the 1990s can be discerned clearly enough. The more successful group includes the USA, UK, the Netherlands and (still) Japan, while the less successful group includes Germany, France and, contrary to our expectations, Austria. On the other hand, the cumulative performance of Sweden is better than expected, and this surprising finding is confirmed by the latest positive developments.

Overall, Denmark comes out best. However, Denmark is a small, homogeneous country, with intensive trading relations with its direct neighbours, and

Table 2.9 Comparison of the performance of employment systems

	Employment rate		Labour force participation rate of women		Unemployment rate		Share of long-term unemployed		Part-time rate		Self-employment rate		Employment threshold		Income inequality		ΔLabour productivity		ΔGDP per capita		Average rank
	1	r	2	r	3	r	4	r	5	r	6	r	7	r	8	r	9	r	10	r	Ør
United States	73	2	71 (+)	3	4.5 (–)	3	8	1	13	8	11	2	0.0	3	2.1 (+)	9	0.4	9	2.7	2	4.2
Japan	69	5	60 (+)	9	4.1 (+)	2	20	2	24	2	9	4.5	0.9 (–)	2	>1.6	5	2.0	5	1.1	6	4.3
EU15	61		58 (+)		10.0 (–)		50		16		13		1.9		no data		2.0		1.1		
Germany	65 (–)	8	61 (+)	7.5	9.4	8	52	9	17	4.5	8	7	2.2	9	>1.4	3	3.1	1	1.0	7	6.4
Netherlands	65 (+)	7	63 (+)	5.5	4.0 (–)	1	48	8	30	1	9	4.5	3.7 (–)	1	<1.6	4	1.2	8	1.9	4	4.4
Austria	68 (–)	6	63 (+)	5.5	4.7 (+)	4	30	4	12	9	7	8.5	1.4	4.5	2.0	8	1.9	6	1.4	5	6.1
Denmark	75	1	75 (–)	2	5.1 (–)	5	29	3	17	4.5	7	8.5	1.5	6	<1.4	2	2.3	3	3.0	1	3.6
United Kingdom	70	4	68 (+)	4	6.3 (–)	6	33	5	23	3	12	1	1.6	7	1.8 (+)	7	2.2	4	2.0	3	4.4
France	60	9	61 (+)	7.5	11.7 (–)	9	44	7	15	6	9	4.5	1.4	4.5	<1.7	6	1.5	7	0.9	8	6.9
Sweden	71	3	76 (–)	1	8.2 (–)	7	34	6	14	7	9	4.5	2.0	8	>1.3	1	2.5	2	0.7	9	4.9

Notes:

1 Employees as a percentage of resident population able to work, average 1990/98 (OECD, *Employment Outlook* 1999, p. 225).

2 Labour force participation rate of women in 1998 (+ increasing trend, – decreasing trend since 1990) (OECD, *Employment Outlook*, 1999, p. 227).

3 OECD – standardized unemployment rate in 1998 (OECD, *Employment Outlook*, 1999, p. 224).

4 Share of survey-based unemployed, who were jobless for more than 12 months, as a percentage of total unemployment in 1998 (OECD, *Employment Outlook*, 1999, p. 242).

5 Share of employees who work less than 35 hours per week, as a percentage of total unemployment in 1998 (OECD, *Employment Outlook*, 1999, p. 240).

6 Share of self-employed, apart from agriculture, as a percentage of total employment (*InfoMISEP*, no. 64, p. 38); estimated data for USA and Japan.

7 Percentage of GDP growth required to generate employment (see text, section 4), 1986–97.

8 Relation of the fifth to the first deciles of earnings in the mid-1990s (OECD, *Employment Outlook*, 1996, p. 61–2).

9 Annual change of hourly productivity 1990–98 (for USA and Japan, 1991–7) (*Employment in Europe*, 1999, p. 127f).

10 Annual change of gross domestic product per capita, 1991–7, per cent (see text, Table 2.8).

r = Rank (without EU); (+) = increasing trend; (–) = decreasing trend.

can hardly be held up as a model for the large EU member states. Nevertheless, Denmark does contradict the prevalent notion that the only way of responding to globalization and individualization is radically to reduce the role of the state, to cut benefits and to introduce greater wage differentiation. And one thing that Denmark does share with other comparatively successful countries, and particularly the Netherlands, is a lively approach to institutional reforms, which have been proceeding along the same lines as our analytical framework: the institutionalization of leave arrangements and mobility, multiple risk insurance through the activation of wage replacement benefits and the introduction of additional income sources, moderate wage policy and some easing of the burden of taxation on earned incomes, and the establishment of a high-level education and training culture in networked and decentralized labour markets.[45]

However, this comparison based on performance indicators also shows that different employment regimes can achieve similar results or weight the portfolio of target indicators in different ways. The good news for the less successful employment systems is that their institutional path dependency (or their regime type) does not prevent them from pursuing a successful strategy; the bad news is that successful strategies require, first, the abandonment of old habits, second, the elimination of the privileges of status and, third, patience and persistence.

NOTES

1. I thank Christian Brzinsky and Alev Deniz for invaluable technical assistance.
2. See, for instance, Sassen (1994); in the extensive literature in this area, Rodrik (1997) and Lee (1997) take account of the interface between social protection, labour markets and globalization.
3. 'Fusion cookery merges the best of the West with an Eastern edge. The new style blends food, ingredients and techniques from many different cultures . . . eclectic cosmopolitanism that was unthinkable just 20 years ago' (*Newsweek*, Dec. 1997/Jan. 1998, pp. 72–3).
4. To take just one example, expenditure on foreign R&D by Hoechst (a German chemical giant) was just 5 per cent in 1970, compared with almost 50 per cent in 1995. One-quarter of R&D expenditure by US subsidiaries abroad is located in Germany (Gerybadze *et al.*, 1997).
5. Teleworking increased in Germany, for example, by 34 per cent from 1994 to 1999. Six per cent of the jobs here are now classified as 'telejobs', compared, for instance, with 2.9 per cent in France (obviously a laggard in this respect), 7.6 in the UK, 10.8 in Denmark, 14.5 in the Netherlands, 15.2 in Sweden and, at the top, 16.8 per cent in Finland (source: empirica, Institut der deutschen Wirtschaft, 1999).
6. Cf., among others, Beck (1986), Friedrichs (1998), Huinink (1995), van de Loo and van Reijen (1992), Miegel and Wahl (1993), Mayer (1996).
7. Cf., among others, Baltes and Mantada (1996), Deutsche Gesellschaft für die Vereinten Nationen (1994), Enquête-Kommission (1994), Harrison (1994), Hof (1993), Klose (1996).
8. Cf. Chapter 5 for a more detailed exposition.
9. On the significance of institutions cf., among others, Garrett and Lange (1995), North (1991), Schmid, Reissert and Bruche (1992), Schmid (1994).

10. Freeman and Soete (1994), on the other hand, are more optimistic and see digital information technologies as heralding a new 'long wave'.
11. Thus this point of view, which combines insights made by Schumpeter and Keynes, demands that any 'innovation offensive' be concentrated on the service sector if the employment crisis is to be solved; a more detailed theoretical justification can be found in Appelbaum and Schettkat (1993) and Schettkat (1996).
12. On the Japanese employment system, cf. among others, Takanashi *et al.* (1999).
13. Cf. several short articles, with usefully extensive bibliographical references, in *OECD Observer*, no. 206, June/July 1997. European standards on cucumbers, which are unfortunately all too real, are rigid to the point of parody. According to the regulations, this vegetable cannot be designated a 'cucumber' unless it is crooked. According to press reports, a Swedish grower was prevented from exporting or selling his 'straight' cucumbers.
14. Boyer and Drache (1996), Naschold *et al.* (1997), Zukunftskommission (1998: 159–223) are all recommended as further reading on the comparison of production regimes.
15. See, among others, Albert (1992), Crouch and Streeck (1995), Esping-Andersen (1990, 1996), O'Reilly and Spee (1998).
16. I will not, of course, be able to meet all these demands here, but at best merely mention them briefly.
17. Work on developing these theoretical frameworks has not yet advanced very far, so the following observations can only give a 'flavour' of the direction that comparative systems research might take.
18. That is, part-time employment involving between 20 and 35 hours' work per week for skilled workers.
19. This advocacy of low income disparities is based on a value judgment that can, nevertheless, be justified in economic terms: low income disparities can, on the one hand, increase willingness to engage in teamwork and in constant further training and, on the other, encourage firms to innovate.
20. The following model would provide an alternative method of calculating employment elasticities: $(\Delta \ln E_t - \text{mean value } (\Delta \ln E)) = a + b_1 (\Delta \ln GDP_t - \text{mean value } (\Delta \ln GDP)) + b_2 (\Delta \ln GDP_{t-1} - \text{mean value } (\Delta \ln GDP))$, with $b_1 + b_2$ as the measure of elasticity (cf. Schettkat 1999). However, I prefer the simple regression procedure because it permits the important distinction to be made between the employment threshold (point of intersection on the x axis) and employment intensity (gradient of the straight lines). Moreover, it can be depicted diagrammatically.
21. Cf. Schettkat (1999), who finds very high correlations (around –0.9), except in the case of Austria; this exception is explained by a very strong reaction on the part of the labour supply to changes in employment; however, this explanation itself requires further clarification (cf. Pichelmann and Hofer, 1999).
22. For a differentiated comparison, see Schmid (1998).
23. See Auer in this volume and Auer (2000); Schmid (1998); Visser and Hemerijck (1997).
24. Cf., among others, Freeman and Soete (1994), Jürgens and Naschold (1994), Delsen and Reday-Mulvey (1995).
25. The weakening employment intensity in Denmark (the only exception among our sample of countries) can be attributed to the decline in part-time employment and to the introduction of various kinds of leave programmes; by controlling statistically for the resultant wide fluctuations in actual working time, a higher level of employment intensity would undoubtedly be obtained for Denmark as well.
26. In contrast to France, where the linkage between economic growth and employment is also strong, but with a high positive employment threshold (cf. Figure 2.3).
27. The inspiration for this kind of decomposition comes from Houseman (1995).
28. Not to be confused with the employment rate, which denotes the share of the working-age population in employment; the share of the total labour force in employment denotes the proportion of the economically active population (employed + unemployed) in employment.
29. This equation can be reformulated via the following step: $Et_1/Et_0 = POPt_1/POPt_0 * LFPt_1/LFPt_0 * (1-U)t_1/(1-U)t_0$; the cumulative composition of the annual growth rates can then be calculated, e.g., via $\Delta Et_i/Et_j = x^{1/t}$.

30. Moreover, international comparative employment statistics are anything but reliable and valid. For example, if the values for marginal part-timers computed by the DIW 1977 are included, the decline in employment in Germany does not seem so drastic, and the component structure changes accordingly to -0.49 $(\Delta E) = 0.35$ $(\Delta POP) - 0.20$ (ΔLFP) $- 0.64$ $(\Delta(1-U))$.

31. The finding for the Netherlands, where a decline in unemployment was also to be expected, can be explained by the low cyclical level of unemployment in 1991, which rose considerably afterwards, until the Dutch 'jobs miracle' manifested itself in a drastic decline in unemployment, which was maintained in 1998/9.

32. In 1998, women's shares in total part-time employment ranged from 67.6 per cent in Japan to 84.1 per cent in Germany.

33. What is suspected at first sight can be listed precisely in statistical terms: across the OECD countries as a whole, the variation coefficient for the total part-time rate fell between 1973 and 1998 from 0.50 to 0.37; the variation coefficient for the male part-time rate fell from 0.71 to 0.46, while that for the female part-time rate fell from 0.45 to 0.37 (own calculations based on (unweighted) OECD data). The variations between OECD countries in the share of women in part-time work also fell slightly, from 0.13 to 0.10; however, the low variation coefficient clearly shows that international variations in the gender-specific structure of part-time work are considerably smaller than the variations in the overall level of part-time work.

34. The inspiration for this decomposition procedure came from Houseman and Osawa (1996), where it is used for the USA and Japan.

35. The data for 1997/98 required for the decomposition were not available.

36. The following statements on the meaningfulness of GDP are based on the excellent survey by Eisner (1988); Eisner also discusses and outlines several alternative methods of measuring GDP.

37. Thus private companies' security services are treated as intermediate products that at best are included in GDP indirectly through higher costs. State police or security services, on the other hand, are treated as consumable end products and appear as such in GDP. For the same reason, television programmes financed by private advertising are not included in GDP, whereas every publicly funded programme is included. The arbitrary treatment of household services is evident from the (no longer politically correct) joke: if a university professor marries his maid, then GDP falls by the amount of the wage she used to receive, although economic well-being clearly does not suffer.

38. Without undermining our essentially academic approach, we can allow ourselves the indulgence of injecting a romantic note into the proceedings at this point by thinking, for example, of the (not virtual, but real) experience of catching crayfish in a remote Swedish lake, cooking them with mushrooms one has gathered oneself and washing them down with a bottle of Chardonnay. This whole event takes up time, of course, but gives (not for every character type of course) more pleasure than an expensive meal in one of the so-called 'international metropolises'. Of course, the employment effect of such experiences is weak. Eisner (1988) points to approaches, such as those developed by the highly reputed economists James Tobin and William Nordhaus, that seek to estimate the economic value of leisure time and include it in GDP.

39. The employment rate in the EU as a whole is affected by the low employment rates in the still largely agrarian southern member states (Italy, Spain, Greece).

40. Korpi (1996) finds that, in comparison with other OECD countries, the Swedish economy (and hence the Swedish welfare state as well) is still efficient and productive. He takes his economist colleagues to task for being insufficiently careful with their empirical evidence and sees no reason to call into question the foundations of the Swedish welfare state. For their part, the economists have brought all their guns to bear on Korpi in order to press home the message that Sweden's economic performance has declined sharply relative to the OECD average. While Lindbeck (1997) and Henrekson (1996) also conclude that the Swedish welfare state is the cause of the decline and that it is therefore in need of fundamental reform, two other authors (Agell, 1996; Dowrick, 1996) have taken a somewhat more differentiated and cautious line.

41. In a global economy with free movement of goods and services, price levels should actually grow closer together, so that the exchange rates obtaining at a given time would also be considered the real exchange rates or purchasing power parities (PPP). As is well known, there are barriers to national and, in particular, international price adjustments, and exchange rates do not always reflect the real exchange relationships. This is why the PPP procedure was developed, in order approximately to calculate real exchange rates. The theory and method of this procedure are still controversial. One of the difficulties is that it requires a standard basket of goods; however, that basket would have to be weighted differently from country to country and from period to period in accordance with customs and cultural preferences. The PPP relationships calculated and published by the OECD are, nevertheless, the best alternative currently available for comparisons of economic performance, since exchange rate relationships fluctuate wildly over time (one has only to think of the ups and downs of the US dollar over the last 15 years). Dornbusch (1987) provides an excellent historical and methodological survey of PPP.
42. Switzerland, which is not included in this comparison, also belongs to this type of regime.
43. Some, such as the inclusion of a distribution indicator (income inequality) or the self-employment rate, may even be controversial.
44. Thus, for example, the rank order correlation coefficient between labour productivity and the employment threshold is –0.84; productivity and unemployment level also correlate negatively (–0.53), whereas the rank orders for the unemployment rate and the employment threshold correlate at 0.80.
45. Cf. in greater detail Auer in this volume and Auer (2000), Madsen (1998), Döhrn *et al.* (1998), Schrader (1999).

BIBLIOGRAPHY

Agell, J. (1996), 'Why Sweden's Welfare State Needed Reform', *The Journal of Economic Literature*, 106 (November), 1760–71.

Akerloff, G.A. and J.L. Yellen (eds) (1986), *Efficiency Wage Models of the Labour Market*, Cambridge: Cambridge University Press.

Albert, M. (1992), *Kapitalismus contra Kapitalismus*, Frankfurt a. M.: Campus-Verlag.

Appelbaum, E. and R. Schettkat (1993), 'Employment Developments in Industrialized Economies: Explaining Common and Diverging Trends', WZB discussion paper FS I 93–313, WZB, Berlin.

Auer, P. (2000), *Employment Revival in Europe. Labour Market Success in Austria, Denmark, Ireland and the Netherlands*, Geneva: International Labour Office.

Baltes, M.M. and L. Mantada (eds) (1996), *Produktives Leben im Alter*, Frankfurt a. M.: Campus-Verlag.

Beck, U. (1986), *Risikogesellschaft: Auf dem Weg in eine andere Moderne*, Frankfurt a. M.: Suhrkamp.

Boyer, R. and D. Drache (eds) (1996), *States Against Markets. The Limits of Globalization*, London and New York: Routledge.

Crouch, C. and W. Streeck (eds) (1995), *Modern Capitalism or Modern Capitalisms?*, London: Sage.

Delsen, L. and G. Reday-Mulvey (1995), *Gradual Retirement in the OECD Countries. Macro and Micro Issues and Policies*, Aldershot: Dartmouth.

Deutsche Gesellschaft für die Vereinten Nationen und Deutsche Stiftung Weltbevölkerung (ed.) (1994), *Weltbevölkerung und Entwicklung – Die Herausforderung des globalen Bevölkerungswachstums*, Bonn: Deutsche Gesellschaft für die Verein Nationen; Bonn: Deutsche Stiftung Weltbevölkerung.

DIW (Deutsches Institut für Wirtschaftsforschung) (1997), 'Erwerbsstatistik unterschätzt Beschäftigung um 2 Millionen', *DIW-Wochenschrift*, 64 (38), 689–94.

Döhrn, R., U. Heilemann and G. Schäfer (1998), 'Ein dänisches Beschäftigungswunder?', *Mitteilungen aus der Arbeitsmarkt- und Berufsforschung*, 2, 312–33.

Dornbusch, R. (1987), 'Purchasing Power Parity', in P. Newman, J. Eatwell and M. Milgate (eds), *The New Palgrave: A Dictionary of Economics*, London: Macmillan, pp. 1075–85.

Dowrick, S. (1996), 'Swedish Economic Performance and Swedish Economic Debate: A View from Outside', *Economic Journal*, 106 (November), 1772–9.

Durkheim, E. (1933), *The Division of Labor in Society*, translated by George Simpson, New York: The Free Press.

Eisner, R. (1988), 'Extended Accounts for National Income and Product', *Journal of Economic Literature*, XXVI (December), 1611–84.

Elias, N. (1976 [1936]), *Über den Prozeß der Zivilisation. Soziogenetische und psychogenetische Untersuchungen*, (2 vols), Frankfurt a. M.: Suhrkamp.

Enquête-Kommission Demographischer Wandel (1994), '*Herausforderungen unserer älter werdenden Gesellschaft an den Einzelnen und die Politik*', Zwischenbericht, Deutscher Bundestag, 12. Wahlperiode, 12/7876, Bonn.

Esping-Andersen, G. (1990), *The three worlds of welfare capitalism*, Cambridge: Polity Press.

Esping-Andersen, G. (1996), *Welfare states in transition. National adaptation in global economies*, London: Sage.

Freeman, C. and L. Soete (1994), *Work for all or Mass Unemployment? Computerised Technical Change into the 21st Century*, London: Pinter Publishers.

Friedrichs, J. (1998), *Die Individualisierungs-These*, Opladen: Leske+Budrich.

Garrett, G. and P. Lange (1995), 'Internationalization, Institutions and Political Change', *International Organization*, 49(4), 627–55.

Gerybadze, A., F. Meyer-Krahmer and G. Reger (1997), *Globales Management von Forschung und Innovation*, Stuttgart: Schäffer-Poeschel Verlag.

Harrison, P. (1994), *Die dritte Revolution – Antworten auf Bevölkerungsexplosion und Umweltzerstörung*, Heidelberg: Spektrum Akad. Verlag.

Henrekson, M. (1996), 'Sweden's Relative Economic Performance: Lagging Behind or Staying on Top?', *Economic Journal*, 106 (November), 1747–59.

Hof, B. (1993), *Europa im Zeichen der Migration – Bevölkerungs- und Arbeitsmarktentwicklung in der Europäischen Gemeinschaft*, Cologne: Deutscher Instituts-Verlag.

Houseman, S.N. (1995), 'Job Growth and the Quality of Jobs in the U.S. Economy', *Labour* (IIRA), 93–124.

Houseman, S.N. and M. Osawa (1996), 'Part-Time Employment in the United States and Japan', paper prepared for the Workshop on Part-time Paradoxes, September 1996, Wissenschaftszentrum Berlin für Sozialforschung.

Huber, J. (1998), *Vollgeld. Beschäftigung, Grundsicherung und weniger Staatsquote durch eine modernisierte Geldordnung*, Berlin: Duncker & Humblot.

Huebner, M., A. Krafft, H. Thormeyer, G. Ulrich and K. Ziegler (1990), *ABM in der Politikarena*, Berlin: edition sigma.

Huinink, J. (1995), *Warum noch Familie? Zur Attraktivität von Partnerschaft und Elternschaft in unserer Gesellschaft*, Frankfurt a. M: Campus-Verlag.

Jürgens, U. and F. Naschold (1994), 'Arbeits- und industriepolitische Entwicklungsengpässe der deutschen Industrie in den neunziger Jahren', in W. Zapf and M. Dierkes (eds), *Institutionenvergleich und Institutionendynamik*, Berlin: Sigma Verlag (WZB Jahrbuch 1994), pp. 239–70.

Klose, H.-U. (1996), *Revolution auf leisen Sohlen. Politische Schlußfolgerungen aus dem demographischen Wandel*, Bonn: forum demographie und politik.

Korpi, W. (1996), 'Eurosclerosis and the Sclerosis of Objectivity: On the Role of Values Among Economic Policy Experts', *Economic Journal*, 106 (November), 1727–46.

Lee, E. (1997), 'Globalization and labour standards. A review of issues', *International Labour Review*, 136(2), 173–89.

Leipert, C. (1997), 'Theoretische und methodische Grundfragen bei der Berechnung eines Öko-Inlandsprodukts', in F. Biermann, S. Büttner and C. Helm (eds), *Zukunftsfähige Entwicklung. Herausforderungen an Wissenschaft und Politik*, Festschrift für Udo E. Simonis zum 60. Geburtstag, Berlin: edition sigma, pp. 99–113.

Lindbeck, A. (1997), 'The Swedish experiment', *Journal of Economic Literature*, XXXV (September), 1273–1319.

Loo, van de. H. and W. van Reijen (1992), *Modernisierung. Projekt und Paradox*, Munich: Deutscher Taschenbuch-Verlag.

Madsen, P.K. (1998), 'A Transitional Labour Market: The Danish Paid Leave Arrangements', in *European Academy of the Urban Environment, New Institutional Arrangements in the Labour Market*, Berlin: Publications of European Academy of the Urban Environment, pp. 68–73.

Mayer, K.-U. (1996), 'Erklärung und Folgen der Bevölkerungsentwicklung. Anmerkungen zu dem Buch von Meinhard Miegel und Stefanie Wahl' in "Das Ende des Individualismus" in Friedrich Ebert Stiftung (ed.), *Gesellschaft des langen Lebens: Sozialgeschichte und Gesellschaftspolitik* (Gesprächskreis Arbeit und Soziales Nr. 68), Bonn: Friedrich-Ebert-Stiftung, pp. 57–75.

Miegel, M. and S. Wahl (1993), *Das Ende des Individualismus*, Munich and Landsberg: Aktuell.

Morgan, G. (1997), *Images of Organization*, London and New Delhi: Sage Publications.

Motohashi, K. and R. Nezu (1997), 'Why Do Countries Perform Differently?', *OECD Observer*, 206, June/July, 19–22.

Naschold, F., D. Soskice, B. Hancké and U. Jürgens (eds) (1997), *Ökonomische Leistungsfähigkeit und institutionelle Innovation. Das deutsche Produktions- und Politikregime im globalen Wettbewerb* (WZB-Jahrbuch 1997), Berlin: edition sigma.

North, D.C. (1991), 'Institutions', *Journal of Economic Perspectives*, 5(1), 97–112.

O'Reilly, J. and C. Spee (1998), 'The Future Regulating of Work and Welfare: Time for a Revised Social and Gender Contract?', *European Journal of Industrial Relations*, 4 (3), 259–81.

Pichelmann, K. and H. Hofer (1999), *ILO Country Policy Review*, Geneva: ILO.

Rodrik, D. (1997), *Has Globalization Gone Too Far?*, Washington, DC: Institute for International Economics.

Rubery, J. (1994), 'The British Production Regime: A Societal-Specific System?', *Economy and Society*, 23 (3), 335–54.

Sassen, S. (1994), *The mobility of labour and capital*, Cambridge: Cambridge University Press.

Schettkat, R. (1996), 'Das Beschäftigungsproblem der Industriegesellschaften', *Aus Politik und Zeitgeschichte*, 26 (96), 25–35.

Schettkat, R. (1999), 'Macroeconomic Policy', in P. Auer (ed.), *Labour Market Institutions for Decent Work*, Geneva: ILO.

Schmid, A., S. Krömmelbein, W. Klems, G. Gaß and S. Angerhausen (1992), 'Neue Wege der Arbeitsmarktpolitik für Langzeitarbeitslose – Sonderprogramm und Modellvorhaben', *Mitteilungen aus der Arbeitsmarkt- und Berufsforschung*, 3, 323–32.

Schmid, G. (1980), *Strukturierte Arbeitslosigkeit und Arbeitsmarktpolitik*, Königstein im Taunus: Athenäum.

Schmid, G. (ed.) (1994), *Labor Market Institutions in Europe. A Socioeconomic Evaluation of Performance*, Armonk, NY: M.E. Sharpe.

Schmid, G. (1998), 'The Dutch Employment Miracle? A Comparison of Employment Systems in the Netherlands and Germany', in L. Delsen and E. de Jong (eds), *The German and Dutch Economies. Who Follows Whom?*, Heidelberg: Physica Verlag, pp. 52–85.

Schmid, G. and K. Schömann (1994), 'Institutional Choice and Labour Market Performance', in G. Schmid (ed.), *Labor Market Institutions in Europe. A Socio-Economic Evaluation of Performance*, Armonk, NY: M.E. Sharpe, pp. 9–57.

Schmid, G., B. Reissert and G. Bruche (1992), *Unemployment Insurance and Active Labour Market Policy. An International Comparison of Financing Systems*, Detroit: Wayne State University Press.

Schneider, F. (1994), 'Determinanten der Steuerhinterziehung der Schwarzarbeit im internationalen Vergleich', in Ch. Smekal and E. Theurl (eds), *Stand und Entwicklung der Finanzpsychologie*, Baden-Baden: Nomos, pp. 247–88.

Schneider, F. (1996), 'Aktuelle Ergebnisse über die Schattenwirtschaft (Pfusch) in Österreich', manuscript, Institut für Volkswirtschaftslehre, Johannes Kepler Universität Linz.

Schrader, K. (1999), 'Dänemarks Weg aus der Arbeitslosigkeit. Vorbild für andere?', *Die Weltwirtschaft*, 2, 207–33.

Simonis, U.E. and C. Leipert (1995), 'Environmental Protection Expenditures in Germany', WZB discussion paper FS II 95–404, WZB, Berlin.

Takanashi, A. *et al.* (1999), *Japanese Employment Practices*, Japanese Economy & Labour Series, No. 4, Tokyo: The Japan Institute of Labour.

Visser, J. and A. Hemerijck (1997), *A Dutch Miracle – Job Growth, Welfare Reform and Corporatism in the Netherlands*, Amsterdam: Amsterdam University Press.

Weber, M. (1946 [1917]). *Essays in Sociology*, trans. and ed. by H.H. Gerth and C. Wright Mills, New York: Oxford University Press, pp. 129–56.

Zukunftskommission der Friedrich-Ebert-Stiftung (1998), *Wirtschaftliche Leistungsfähigkeit, sozialer Zusammenhalt, ökologische Nachhaltigkeit. Drei Ziele – ein Weg*, Bonn: Dietz.

3. Flexibility and security: labour market J6 5 policy in Austria, Denmark, Ireland and the Netherlands

Peter Auer

This contribution is part of a broader ILO study of the reasons for labour market success in four smaller European countries. It analyses one particular aspect: the contribution of both passive and active labour market policies and of the delivery institutions to the employment success in four countries. In the broader study other policy fields were investigated, such as macroeconomic policy (including tax issues) and industrial relations, as well as equal opportunity and working-time policies.

After a short statistical description of the relative labour market success of the countries, selected issues in both passive and active labour market policy are discussed. While the 'generosity' of the unemployment benefit system is today often blamed for the persistence of long-term unemployment, this chapter advances the hypothesis that it might be the use of the unemployment benefit system as a temporary lay-off system, rather than a relative lack of generosity, that could be one of the factors explaining low levels of long-term unemployment. The lay-off system is one institutional feature that provides 'numerical' workforce adjustment for firms and income and employment security for workers. In addition, another 'passive' policy is presented as also providing both flexibility and security, namely the transition between work and retirement through early retirement schemes. More generally, the chapter asks whether there is a general trade-off between employment protection and social protection. We then go on to discuss the contribution of active labour market policy to employment success and find that the results vary widely. However, in all the countries, both active and passive policies are a permanent feature of the labour market and have thus to be included in any new notion of full employment, which has to be redefined not in stock but in flow terms.

1 RELATIVE EMPLOYMENT SUCCESS

Some of the smaller European countries have had success in their labour markets lately: this is particularly the case in Ireland and the Netherlands with

Table 3.1   Recent employment growth (average annual growth rates)

	1987–97	1998	1999	2000
Austria	0.7	0.9	1.4	1.0
Denmark	−0.1	2.1	0.8	0.8
Ireland	2.4	10.2	5.8	4.7
Netherlands	2.0	3.3	3.0	2.5
US	1.4	1.5	1.5	1.3
EU15	1.0	1.5	1.6	2.0

Source: OECD, *Employment Outlook*, (June 2000).

Table 3.2   Unemployment change, July 1998 to July 2000, seasonally adjusted (%)

	Total			Male			Female			Gender gap
	July 1998	July 2000	% Change	July 1998	July 2000	% Change	July 1998	July 2000	% Change	July 2000
Austria	4.6	3.2	−1.4	3.9	2.7	−1.2	5.5	3.8	−1.7	1.1
Denmark	5.2	4.8	−0.4	4.0	4.2	0.2	6.7	5.6	−1.1	1.4
Ireland	7.6	4.5	−3.1	7.8	4.5	−3.3	7.2	4.4	−2.8	0.1
Netherlands	3.9	2.6	−1.3	3.1	1.9	−1.2	5.0	3.6	−1.4	1.7
USA	4.5	4.0	−0.5	4.5	3.8	−0.7	4.5	4.3	−0.2	0.5
EU15	9.9	8.3	−1.6	8.6	7.2	−1.4	11.7	9.9	−1.8	2.7

Source: Eurostat; for Denmark and Netherlands the data refer to June 2000.

respect to employment (Table 3.1). In Denmark as well, unemployment has been halved since 1993, while Austria has always had one of the lowest unemployment rates in Europe (Table 3.2).

Very recently, however, some of the bigger European countries have also recorded decreasing unemployment, and labour market improvement has spilled over to more countries. Unemployment reduction is attributable in part to economic and associated employment growth. For example, the employment content of economic growth has lately risen in Ireland, Denmark and the Netherlands, the three countries with the most remarkable success. The Okun coefficients, which measure the impact of economic growth on unemployment, have also improved. This shows that the impact of economic growth not only on employment creation but also on unemployment reduction has increased in recent years (Schettkat, 2001).

Net employment growth is occurring almost exclusively in the service sector (except for Ireland, where employment in manufacturing is also rising) and women's employment has been growing more than men's. Part-time shares have risen (except for Denmark, where they have declined), but in Ireland, for example, many full-time jobs have been created as well. Between 1980 and 1996 in Austria it was only in the public sector that there was net job creation, while employment in the private sector declined. In Denmark, there was net job creation in both the public and private sectors, while in the Netherlands and, to a somewhat lesser extent, in Ireland job creation occurred mostly in the private sector. Self-employment in the non-agricultural sector has been growing in Ireland and the Netherlands, but less so in Austria and Denmark. In stock terms, fixed-term contracts still account for only around 10 per cent of all dependent jobs, although they are more significant in flow terms. Given an almost stable distribution of employment by company size over the last 10 years, the pattern of employment growth by firm size has not dramatically altered: in Ireland around 50 per cent of all net job creation has been concentrated in small and medium-sized firms, but this figure is as high as 70 per cent in Denmark and over 60 per cent in both Austria (64.5 per cent) and the Netherlands (60.4 per cent).

Relative labour market success has also to do with the institutional features of the labour market. Several such factors can be singled out (Auer, 2000): social dialogue (industrial relations), education and training and working-time policies, among others. While labour market policy is only one of these features, it is a prominent one. In the remainder of this chapter we will discuss mainly labour market policy issues. For a more thorough account of the relative labour market success in the four countries, see Auer (2000), Hartog (1999), Madsen (1999), O'Connell (1999) and Pichelmann and Hofer (1999), as well as the 2001 publications of Bosch, Schettkat, Rubery and Visser.

2 LABOUR MARKET POLICIES

In order to influence unemployment and employment more directly, the governments and social partners of all four countries have used labour market policy. Indeed, passive and active labour market policies are some of the few instruments in policy makers' tool kits that enable them to influence the labour market directly, as they allow for job search and job matches, for supply enhancement and reduction and the creation of additional jobs, while generally providing replacement income. In passive labour market policies, claimants are generally not required to be involved in any activity, whether employment or an active labour market measure, but must be available and actively searching for work. Active policies, on the other hand, always require those receiving benefits to participate in either work or training activities.[1] While 'passive' income replacement programmes include unemployment insurance (UI) benefits and all other benefits paid on the condition of not being active, such as early retirement benefits, active policies comprise a wide range of measures acting on both the supply and the demand side of the labour market.

Passive Labour Market Policy

In the 1970s, unemployment was still considered to be the product of temporary mismatches in the labour market and temporary periods of insufficient demand. Thus the basic function of unemployment benefit systems was temporary income provision to allow job search or to weather cyclical troughs. Since the 1980s, this has changed. Unemployment benefit systems have had to face increased structural change as a consequence of shifts in the sectoral distribution of employment, technological and organizational change and globalization, which together had led to continuous 'downsizing' in traditional parts of the economy and rising employment in new sectors. This has resulted in prolonged periods of insufficient labour demand and mismatches of supply and demand, that is structural demand deficiencies. Supply-side restrictions, such as inappropriate or outdated skills and disincentives for labour mobility, also play a role. In economic theory, however, structural features are considered to be relevant no longer to labour demand, but almost exclusively to labour supply. For example, as far as unemployment benefit systems are concerned, the 'generosity' of income replacement and the duration of benefit payment (see Table 3.3) came to be seen, not as protecting workers against prolonged periods of income losses, but as a major cause of unemployment, and particularly of long-term unemployment.

The evidence suggests that the benefit system has an effect on the persistence of unemployment, and that duration of benefits, rather than benefit levels, accounts for most of this effect (Graafland, 1996). Such results seem plausible and draw attention to a simple fact: if it were legally possible to draw benefits for a long period, this should result in a longer (registered) duration of unemployment, as long as the cause of unemployment (for example, insufficient acceptable job offers) persists. Clearly, in unemployment systems that offer benefits only for a short period (six months, for example), registered long-term unemployment cannot occur by definition.[2] It is hard to prove this with the available information on replacement rates and unemployment duration in the four countries. However, it is possible in all four to draw benefits, or at least unemployment assistance, for a long period.

It cannot be denied that there is a (usually) unknown percentage of abuse in the system and that generous systems alleviate the pressures immediately to accept work of any kind. In fact, such systems were established and/or

Table 3.3   Replacement rates and duration of benefits, 1997

Replacement rate		Duration
Austria		
1.	58/74	Depending on insured employment and age: 20 weeks to 52 weeks.
2.	57/70	Assistance: unlimited subject to means test
3.	63/79	
4.	60/76	
Denmark		
1.	67/77	4 years (activation measures after 1 year)
2.	67/97	
3.	94/95	
4.	94/92	
Ireland		
1.	48/62	390 days
2.	48/62	Assistance: unlimited subject to means test
3.	65/73	
4.	65/73	
Netherlands		
1.	83/85	General benefits: 6 months
2.	76/79	Extended: depending on age and duration of insured employment:
3.	89/90	From 9 months to 5 years
4.	93/94	Follow-up benefits: 2 years

Notes:
Net replacement rates for single earner households, 1997:
1. = for couple no children/2 children, 1 month of unemployment, as a percentage of average production worker (APW) income.
2. = couple no children/2 children 60 months of unemployment, average APW.
3. = same as 1 but at two-thirds of APW and including social assistance.
4. = as for 2 but two-thirds of APW and including social assistance.

Source: OECD (1999).

reformed in order – among other things – to allow better job matching, which is always more difficult in periods of high unemployment. The litmus test for assumptions that the 'generosity' of the UI system is a more than marginal cause of long-duration unemployment is a sustained recovery in the job market without a corresponding improvement in, for example, the Beveridge (or unemployment vacancy) curve.

On the basis of the evidence from our four countries, the assumed generosity of the benefit system does not easily provide empirical evidence for a more than marginal impact on unemployment in the longer term. In the cases of Austria and Ireland, the Austrian system is clearly more generous for most categories than the Irish, while benefits can be drawn indefinitely in both systems (subject to means testing). Despite this, Ireland has much higher long-term unemployment rates. And comparison of the Netherlands and Denmark, where replacement rates for the long-term unemployed are about the same, produces another starkly contrasting picture: Denmark has low long-term unemployment rates, but the Netherlands still has high rates. This argument could be extended to different regions in one country: here at least it can be assumed that national replacement and duration rates do not vary by region and can therefore not be held responsible for any differences in long-term unemployment rates. However, these rates do differ by region, suggesting that other explanations, such as the extent of structural change, are important. It also has to be borne in mind that women usually have less entitlement to benefits than men (for example, they experience greater difficulty in gaining access to benefits because of their typically more heterogeneous career paths) and only in Denmark do women reach a high coverage share (Rubery, 2001).

Nevertheless, many smaller (administrative) reforms have been introduced into the unemployment protection systems in almost all of the countries under review, some of which have also produced the intended effect. One or more of the following changes have been enacted: either the duration of benefits and/or the level of wage replacement rates has been cut and/or eligibility restricted. In addition, all countries have resorted to much stricter enforcement of job search and suitable work provisions. That is to say, in different ways in different countries, access to, and duration of, benefits have been restricted and sanctions tightened. Some of these restrictions have had an impact on the decline in unemployment, albeit one that is difficult to measure. In Denmark, for example, restricting access to benefits for young people with low qualificational levels by linking benefit payment to compulsory participation in education had a tangible effect on youth unemployment. However, this is much more an activation policy (as it offsets restrictions on the passive side with offers on the active side) and it would seem, in the light of our earlier observations, that in general activation policies are more promising than administrative changes alone.

Flexibility and security in unemployment benefit systems
One explanation for differences in the scale of long-term unemployment (LTU) beyond the traditional generosity/duration argument could be the high rate of turnover among the unemployed in Austria and Denmark, both countries with

low rates and shares of long-term unemployment. In Austria, for example, around 700 000 people register as unemployed each year, but the stock remains around the 200 000 level. The ratio of stocks to flows into unemployment over the course of a year is about 1:3.5 in Austria and 1:2 in Denmark, but is about 1:1 in the Netherlands (at least for registered unemployment in 1994) (no data for Ireland; data from OECD, 1996). This might change over time, but high shares of LTU and a concentration of the unemployed in the longer duration brackets (see Table 3.4) suggest a much lower level of mobility among the unemployed in the Netherlands and in Ireland.

This is explained to some extent by high seasonal unemployment in Austria and by the fact that Denmark traditionally runs a sort of lay-off system, combining low employment protection with high social protection. In Austria, such lay-off behaviour, with frequent recalls, also seems to spread beyond the seasonal sectors. It is estimated that around 30 per cent of the unemployed have a promise of a job with the same employer after their unemployment spell (Frühstück *et al.*, 1998). In lay-off systems (and unemployment systems with a large seasonal component) there is a sort of implicit contract between employers, their workers and unemployment compensation institutions, which allows companies to shift their labour costs onto the unemployment compensation systems during slack periods or temporary declines in demand. Laid-off workers are rehired once demand picks up again or the busy season begins. Such mutually advantageous use of the unemployment benefit system supports labour market flexibility while providing a safety net for workers, albeit at a certain cost to the unemployment protection system. It might also enable firms to retain an experienced workforce, thereby enhancing productivity. This depends not least on how recurrent unemployment is. In Austria, for example, individuals experience on average 1.3 spells of unemployment per year, suggesting that a certain degree of recurrence in associated with this particular system. However, other job openings also seem to be available in these systems, as not all of those laid off return to the employer who laid them off. In Denmark, to a greater extent than in Austria, labour market policy has contributed to this labour market flexibility and security arrangement.

Flexible use of the UI system seems to have positive effects on the employment rate as well, since both Denmark and Austria have higher employment to population ratios than the two other countries and a larger share of the unemployed had held a job before becoming unemployed.[3] Thus lay-off procedures that amount, in effect, to a 'joint venture' involving all the parties concerned could be another possible explanation for relatively good labour market performance, that is a high labour turnover, combined with high participation rates and low-duration unemployment. In Austria, for example, the high turnover in the unemployment system is mirrored by high turnover in the

Table 3.4 Duration of unemployment (percentage)

Duration	Austria		Denmark		Ireland		Netherlands		EUR 15	
	1992	1996	1992	1996	1992	1996	1992	1996	1992	1996
Less than 6 months	–	57.5	50.1	55.6	22.6	24.3	23.1	18.6	–	33.2
men	–	61.8	51.2	55.8	20.1	20.8	25.2	18.8	–	35.3
women	–	51.9	49.0	55.4	27.2	29.9	21.6	18.5	–	31.0
of which less than 3 months	–	29.2	31.7	37.2	11.1	14.3	11.0	9.4	–	
men		30.9	31.8	36.0	9.5	10.5	14.7	8.9		
women		28.6	31.7	39.8	14.0	15.4	10.5	9.9		
6 to 11 months	–	16.8	22.9	17.9	18.5	16.2	32.9	32.4	–	18.6
men	–	15.0	23.4	16.1	16.8	14.6	27.8	27.7	–	18.4
women	–	19.3	22.5	19.3	21.5	18.9	36.8	36.6	–	18.8
12 months and more	–	25.6	27.0	26.5	58.9	59.5	44.0	49.0	–	48.2
men	–	23.2	25.3	28.1	63.1	64.6	47.0	53.5	–	46.3
women	–	28.8	28.5	25.3	51.3	51.2	41.6	45.0	–	50.2
24 months and more	–	13.4	8.8	11.6	39.2	41.1	27.7	33.7	–	30.0
men	–	13.1	6.9	12.3	44.9	47.4	31.7	37.9	–	28.7
women	–	13.7	10.6	11.0	29.0	31.0	24.6	29.9	–	31.5

Source: ILO CEPR data bank based on Eurostat (LFS) data.

88

employment system, with around one million entries and one million exits each year among a labour force of 3.8 million.

More traditional use of the unemployment compensation system prevails in Ireland and the Netherlands. In such systems, the seasonal and temporary lay-off component is smaller, while long-term unemployment is higher. Here, lower employment rates go hand in hand with higher unemployment among labour market entrants (young people, for example) and lower turnover among those in employment. However, while the social partners might find a lay-off system satisfactory (especially in small firms), there are also critics of the system who point to the costs for others. Heavy use of unemployment funds by certain sectors, such as agriculture, construction and hotels and catering, leads to cross-subsidization, especially in UI systems funded by contributions. Seasonal unemployment is made more viable, and the OECD has pointed out that high seasonal unemployment is indeed a problem in Austria (OECD, 1998).

The problem of cross-subsidization could be addressed by introducing experience rating, although this would have a bearing on labour costs that might negatively affect hiring decisions, especially in low-wage sectors. Alternative sources of employment might also be developed for slack seasons. Working-time flexibility could also be an alternative. In Austria, for example, the social partners have recently agreed on the introduction of a working-time pattern that has the effect of prolonging the season in the construction industry by annualizing working time. Overtime is rewarded by the granting of time off in lieu and workers are obliged to take part of their holiday entitlement during the 'dead' season. However, while these changes might prevent the development of extreme forms of distorted use of the UI system, the core of the systems should be maintained as they provide firms with flexibility and workers with flexibility and security.

It can be concluded from this that 'passive labour market policy' is indeed conceived not only to provide income protection for workers but also to allow flexibility, especially for small companies. Thus any substantial changes to the system, such as tightening access, restricting 'generosity' (replacement rates, introducing waiting periods, and so on), might have drawbacks for labour market flexibility. For example, a recent Danish report indicates that a reduction in overall generosity (that is, in replacement rates) could lead to demands for more dismissal protection. This raises the question of whether there is a basic trade-off between dismissal protection at the firm level and social protection at the macro level and how changes in one system might affect the other. The evidence that such a trade-off exists is clearly outlined in a recent paper by the 'forward studies unit' of the European Commission (Buti *et al.*, 1998), which shows that there is a tendency for weaker social protection to go hand in hand with tighter dismissal protection, at least in European countries. The authors assume different 'indifference curves' for the Anglo-Saxon countries (which generally have lower replacement rates and less employment protection) than for continental European countries, with higher values for both.

Such a trade-off is important for policy, as it implies a need for complex policy making which considers both sides of the trade-off. It is also necessary to disentangle the purely legal dimension from what actually happens in practice. For example, despite Austria's tighter dismissal protection and the lower generosity of its benefit system, the actual trade-off between employment protection at firm level and social protection at macro level seems to work just as well as in Denmark.[4]

Exit measures for the older workforce: early retirement and invalidity pensions

Another strand of passive policies has been heavily used in order to reduce supply-side pressure in the labour markets of all the countries under review, and has therefore helped to keep unemployment below the level it would have reached in the absence of such policies. Early retirement schemes, and to a certain extent invalidity pensions as well when granted on labour market grounds, have been important tools in allowing older workers to leave the labour market, despite particularly strong dismissal protection for older workers and/or the particular social responsibility firms have towards their long-term staff. Here there is clearly a trade-off between dismissal protection and social protection of a different kind; the better the protection against dismissal is, the more exit measures there are to help firms adjust their employment levels to the needs of structural change.

Early retirement has played an important role in reducing the labour supply in all four countries (see Table 3.5). Invalidity pensions have also been used increasingly for labour market reasons. Both have contributed especially to the decline in employment rates among older men and have lowered the actual average retirement age.

Table 3.5   Employment rates for the 55–64 age group

	Total		Male		Female	
	1990	2000	1990	2000	1990	2000
Austria	28.4*	29.2	39.7*	41.4	18.0*	17.8
Demark	53.6	54.6	65.6	61.9	42.4	46.2
Ireland	38.6	45.2	59.5	63.0	18.2	27.1
Netherlands	29.7	37.9	44.5	49.9	15.8	25.8
EU	38.4	38.5	53.1	48.9	24.7	28.4

*Data refers to 1994.

Source: OECD, *Employment Outlook, (July 1997, June 2001).*

Table 3.6   Statutory and actual retirement age

	Statutory retirement age		Actual retirement age			
			1970		1990	
	Male	Female	Male	Female	Male	Female
Austria	65	60*	62.2	60.0	58.5	56.4
Denmark	67	67	66.8	61.5	62.9	59.5
Ireland**	65/66	65/66	69.5	72.6	63.7	61.2
Netherlands	65	65	64.0	62.1	59.0	55.7

Notes:
*   After 2024, gradual increase to 65.
** 65 for retirement pension, 66 for old-age pension.

Source: Missoc (1998), Latulippe (1996).

While early retirement has been an important tool in alleviating supply-side pressures in the labour market, it has also been increasingly criticized as a very costly alternative. The ageing of the workforce, combined with pressures on public budgets, has made it necessary to restrict access to these kinds of 'easy exit' options that have generally met with approval from the social partners, employees and firms. Several changes have been introduced in the countries under review.

Austria restricted access to early retirement in 1996 by abolishing the *Sonderunterstützung*, or special support arrangements, a combination of early retirement and unemployment benefits, and is further reducing the attractiveness of all early retirement possibilities (by cutting the reference wages, for example) with the aim of closing the gap between the actual and statutory retirement ages (see Table 3.6).

Denmark has abolished all opportunities to take early retirement between the ages of 50 and 59 but has retained certain options for those aged between 60 and 66. Attempts have also been made to curb early retirement in the Netherlands. Dutch labour market exits are collectively agreed at sectoral level and wage replacement for early retirees aged over 55 is financed by topping up unemployment benefits. Until 1994, this practice was encouraged by the government, but it has since been restricted by the legislation on administrative penalties introduced in 1996, which makes 'voluntary' unemployment unlawful (OECD, 1998). While Ireland also makes provision for early retirement for labour market reasons (mainly for the long-term unemployed), it is much less widely used than in the other three countries.

The disability pension system has also been used for labour market reasons and as an alternative to other forms of early retirement, most particularly in the Netherlands, but also in Denmark and Austria. Recent attempts to tighten access (through stricter medical checks) have increased outflows from the system and at least temporarily reduced the number of benefit claimants, for example in the Netherlands. A sort of experience rating has also been introduced, penalizing those firms that make frequent use of the system. The various options for early exit (for example, via unemployment, early retirement or invalidity pensions) seem to act – in the absence of job opportunities for the elderly – as functional equivalents for each other. If the inflow into one system is restricted, inflow into the other systems increases, albeit not in a 1:1 relation. In Austria, such a substitution occurred between the various invalidity pension systems (Pichelmann and Hofer, 1999; OECD, 1998). In the Netherlands, the decrease in invalidity pensions has led to an increase in unemployment among older people. Reforms have, therefore, to take account of the possibilities of substitution between several regimes. Since their aim is to allow older workers to remain in employment or to find new jobs, they have also to offer incentives and provide the organizational assistance required to make such policies successful. Austria is experimenting with a bonus–malus system, penalizing firms that dismiss older workers and offering incentives to firms employing them.

Largely because of the existence of functional equivalents for early retirement and the limited opportunities for older workers to take up new jobs, the ending of schemes that have considerably alleviated supply-side pressures in the labour market, and are popular among firms and workers, should be accompanied by the provision of 'activation' alternatives. Otherwise, the abolition of these schemes will lead to greater poverty and uncertainty at the end of the working life and result in greater adjustment rigidity for firms. The careful analysis that is required before major changes are made to the schemes is further justified by the fact that these schemes have been overwhelmingly dominated by men and that their abolition coincides with increasing numbers of women becoming potentially eligible for them. In any event, cuts in passive benefit schemes have to be balanced by the provision of real alternatives if the potential beneficiaries of these systems are not to become unemployed or enter another scheme providing for basic subsistence that has a degrading effect on status. Incentives and/or active labour market policies should be put in place in order to maintain older workers in jobs and to facilitate access to jobs for older workers. Phased retirement systems are one of the possible measures that could be implemented or extended.

Active Labour Market Policies
The activation of labour market policy (LMP) is currently the most important area of reform in European labour markets and is the cornerstone of the

Table 3.7   Labour market policy expenditure and the share of active labour market policies in total LMP

	Total LMP spending	Active LMP*	Passive LMP*	Share of active LMP**, 1994–7	Share of active LMP**, 1999
Austria	1.81	0.39	1.42	21.5	30
Denmark	6.40	1.88	4.59	29.4	36
Ireland***	4.32	1.64	2.68	38.0	41
Netherlands	4.85	1.40	3.45	28.9	39

Notes:
*   As per cent of GDP: average values for the years 1994–7.
**   Share of active LMP in total LMP.
***   Ireland 1994–6 and 1996.

Source: OECD, *Employment Outlook*, 1998.

European employment strategy,[5] which is expected ultimately to lead to an increase in employment rates. All the countries under review have subscribed to this goal. Reducing the share of passive LMP and increasing the share of active policies is very much at the top of the agenda. A new social contract between the unemployed and the labour market administration is about to be established. The terms of this contract are that, after a certain time spent on unemployment benefit, individuals have to be offered a regular job or a place on an active labour market scheme. From that moment on (as a rule before six months have been spent on benefit, in the case of young people, and 12 months for adults), benefits are available only in exchange for active participation in work or training. This should be seen both as a right to 'activation' and a duty on the unemployed to participate in active labour market policy measures.

Countries differ in terms both of overall spending and of their shares of active and passive LMP. Denmark spends the most and Austria the least (see Table 3.7). In general, active labour market policy increased as a share of total LMP (with some fluctuations), confirming a slight move towards activation and reflecting both a relative decline of passive LMP (except in the Netherlands) and an absolute increase in active LMP (ALMP) (except in Denmark).

Changing policy mixes
While the level of ALMP in the four countries is generally increasing, the composition of measures within ALMP has changed over time, sometimes

dramatically. All countries offer a range of measures that can be classified either as supply-side measures, such as training for youth and adults, or demand-side measures, such as employment subsidies and temporary (public) job creation schemes. In Denmark, for example, labour market training now accounts for almost 50 per cent of active labour market policies – largely as a consequence of training leave schemes – while youth measures have declined in importance, as has subsidized employment. In Ireland, by contrast, subsidized employment now accounts for more than 50 per cent of total ALMP expenditure, while training measures as well as youth measures have declined relatively in importance. Subsidized employment has also increased quite considerably in the Netherlands with the introduction of so-called 'Melkert jobs' (subsidized public-sector jobs for the long-term unemployed), while labour market training and measures for the disabled have declined. In Austria, the composition has remained fairly stable over time. Those countries with high long-term unemployment (the Netherlands and Ireland) are also the countries that have recently expanded subsidized employment, which can be seen as an appropriate measure for those hard to place in regular jobs.[6] The two other countries make greater use of training measures, which might be more appropriate for an unemployed population that experiences shorter spells of unemployment. In Denmark, a high proportion of labour market training funds is allocated to the employed. Ireland also runs active training measures for the employed, but public labour market training activities in Austria and the Netherlands are geared almost exclusively towards the unemployed.

Has ALMP contributed to employment success?
It appears that, in the absence of ALMP measures, unemployment would have been considerably higher, especially in Denmark and Ireland, which have the highest ALMP enrolment figures.[7] Data on outflows from the unemployment register into ALMP measures confirm this. In Denmark in 1994, for example, entries into ALMP represented around 30 per cent of outflows from the register; figures for Austria and the Netherlands show a rate of outflow of 10 and 17 per cent, respectively, confirming the lesser quantitative importance of ALMP in the two countries. No data were available for Ireland. In Denmark, outflow into ALMP has recently increased dramatically: in 1995, 60 per cent of participants in the various leave schemes were formerly unemployed. It is estimated, for example, that the total fall in unemployment from 1994 to 1996 is attributable to those enrolled in leave schemes (which, because of their job rotation and training aspects are considered as active measures) and early retirement schemes (Döhrn *et al.*, 1998). For Denmark at least, labour market policy is a crucial factor in explaining the decrease in unemployment. The question remains whether this is a sustainable solution, however, as those leaving unemployment temporarily for a leave scheme might return to unemployment after

their leave period. Recent data (Madsen, 1999) show that this has so far applied only to a minority and that the majority of those on leave schemes have tended either to leave for employment, to continue training or to leave the labour force altogether.

Table 3.8 shows changes in unemployment, employment and participation in measures between 1994 and 1995 (the only years for which we have consistent data). Several observations can be made. In Austria, where the share of ALMP is relatively low and has remained almost stable, with only slight reduction in the numbers of participants, it evidently made no contribution to reducing unemployment, but it is striking that the increase in the number of unemployed went hand in hand with a reduction in the number of those in demand-side labour market policy schemes (job creation). However, as later increases in unemployment were accompanied by a rise in the number of those participating in schemes, this could be mere coincidence. Measured in the same way, the contribution of ALMP measures to the reduction in unemployment in Denmark between 1994 and 1995 was around 40 per cent. Within the ALMP measures, the 'training for the unemployed and those at risk' category has expanded. And in Ireland, ALMP seems to have made a marginal contribution to the lowering of unemployment and also to employment growth, as demand-side measures (subsidies and public job creation schemes) have increased. Even in the Dutch case, some effect on the (small) decrease in unemployment and on employment cannot be precluded, as demand-side measures have increased slightly despite a small overall reduction in the numbers participating in ALMP measures.

Table 3.8   Changes in unemployment, employment and ALMP participation[1]

	Unemployment (%)	Employment (%)	ALMP entries[2]
Austria	+0.1	+0.6	0
Denmark	−1.0	+1.7	+0.37
Ireland	−2.0	+4.7	+0.15
Netherlands	−0.2	+2.7	−0.07

Notes:
1. Changes for 1994/5 expressed as % of labour force.
2. In full-time equivalents (here, for reasons of simplicity, the Danish average – a mean average duration of 4.4 months for all measures – was taken, corresponding to a correction coefficient of 0.37).

Source: European Commission, *Employment in Europe*, 1997; OECD, *Employment Outlook*, 1998, CEPR data base.

Table 3.9   Participants per 1 per cent of GDP in 1995 as percentage of labour force

	Gross (inflows)[1]	Net (stock)[2]
Austria[3]	4.6	1.66
Denmark	9.8	2.70
Ireland	7.1	2.36
Netherlands	1.8	0.90

Notes:
1. OECD, *Employment Outlook*, 1998.
2. Gross inflows controlled for estimated duration for Ireland, Netherlands and Denmark on the basis of Danish data, corrected for distribution of measures. Duration multiplier of 0.40 for Denmark but 0.50 for Ireland and the Netherlands (subsidized jobs usually last longer than training measures). Actual duration for Austria. As percentage of labour force for 1% of GDP spending. Only unemployed participants.
3. For Austria, hypothetical, as only 0.36% of GDP was spent. Actual spending was 1.97 in Denmark, 1.68 in Ireland and 1.28 in the Netherlands.

Sources: OECD, *Employment Outlook*, 1998; Arbeitsmarkt service (Austria), 1998; Madsen, 1999, own calculations.

Another indicator of the impact of ALMP is the percentage of the labour force covered by ALMP measures for a given level of expenditure. While we were concerned above with the effect of changes over time, the focus here is on the overall impact on unemployment. The rates should be interpreted as the estimated gross effect of ALMP on unemployment; they take no account of deadweight or other effects that would reduce gross results to a greater or lesser extent, depending on their magnitude.

Table 3.9 gives information on the number of unemployed persons entering measures in 1995 per 1 per cent of GDP spent on active labour market policies. Gross rates control neither for employed participants in labour market policies (of whom there are many in Ireland and in Denmark) nor for duration of measures, but net rates (stocks) do. Net values are estimates of how much unemployment is avoided per 1 per cent of ALMP spending in 1995. If these estimates are also correct for those countries for which we do not have actual duration data (Ireland, Netherlands), the table shows two things. Firstly, the overall impact of ALMP is significant and, secondly, there is a wide variation between countries in the effectiveness of ALMP spending, which might depend on the nature and cost efficiency of measures and forms of implementation used.

Whereas ALMP has made a considerable contribution in Denmark and Ireland to the reduction in unemployment, it is quantitatively less important in both Austria and the Netherlands, both of which, however, have recently experienced an increase in ALMP, as is evident from national sources.[8] While the question of how much ALMP contributed to employment success can be only partially answered in quantitative terms, there is a lot of evidence that it is indeed one of the important qualitative elements in European employment systems and has at least prevented unemployment from rocketing during the years of the employment crisis, at the same time contributing to human resource development.

Most importantly, any definition of full employment today has to take into account active labour market policy, which has become an important element in many employment systems.[9] Its importance will be increased in future under the European Employment Strategy, which for the first time has established quantitative targets. If the targets are reached (each unemployed young person must be given a place on an ALMP measure before the sixth month of unemployment and each adult before the twelfth), long-term unemployment could decline to low levels. In our four countries, an equivalent of between 3 and almost 20 per cent of the labour force flow into such measures each year, and without them unemployment would be considerably higher. While ALMP remains a 'second-best solution' after regular employment, it would seem to be a necessary solution in today's labour markets.

This is not to say that all measures perform perfectly well. Various evaluation results using different evaluation methods (see OECD, 1996; Meager, 1999) show that there are sometimes high deadweight, substitution and displacement effects linked to the measures. This suggests that some of the unemployed would have found work even in the absence of measures, that some measures lead to the replacement of employed persons by (subsidized) unemployed persons and that some subsidized activities displace unsubsidized activities. Various evaluation studies have shown that active measures are more successful in integrating the unemployed into the regular market if the measures are close to regular business activities (that is, if they prepare participants for marketable jobs or private enterprises are involved in the implementation). O'Connell and McGinnity (1998) show that schemes that are close to such market activities contribute to higher programme effectiveness, especially for women. Programmes also seem to be more effective if they address the needs of the unemployed and take account of local conditions (Meager, 1999). It follows from this latter requirement that smaller, more specific programmes need to be designed and implemented as a replacement for broader, more general programmes (see also OECD, 1996). We have not addressed the issue of equal opportunities in labour market policies, mainly because of a lack of data. Rubery (2001) presents some evidence indicating that women are underrepresented in programmes and that programmes may even tend to encourage and reinforce the 'development of labour market conditions that have proved disadvantageous to women in the labour market'.

3 REFORMS OF IMPLEMENTATION STRUCTURES

In all four countries, the public employment service (PES), as the main deliverer of measures, has seen its structures changing quite dramatically in a move towards decentralization and the development of tripartism, with scope also being created for private placement. In the Netherlands and Austria, the PES has been removed from the Ministry of Labour's sphere of competence and is now run by the social partners on a tripartite basis. The changes also included a move towards decentralization to regional levels.[10]

In Ireland, a trend towards more local involvement can be seen in the creation of 'local employment services' (LES), which come under the authority not of the FAS (the national employment service) but of the Department of Enterprise and Trade. LES are mainly responsible for tackling the problem of the long-term unemployed, and their brief involves collaboration with local FAS offices (Employment Services Offices: EOS) and other actors at the local level. In Denmark, in conjunction with an activation approach, responsibility for designing and implementing active labour market policy has been devolved to tripartite regional labour market councils on which local authorities, employers and unions are represented.

There has been some evaluation of the working of the new structures. After only four years under the new structure, an evaluation of the Dutch PES reorganization found that the changes introduced had not produced the expected results. According to an evaluation report compiled by a committee of independent experts (Dercksen and de Koning, 1996), the social partners have neither interacted efficiently nor adequately monitored their decentralized offices, especially at central boards (CBA) level. Cooperation between the various actors seems to have been much better in the local offices. The government was criticized for having too many conflicting roles as partner, supervisor and funder. As a result of the report, changes have been proposed that would give the Ministry greater authority over planning and monitoring. The Ministry will not, however, participate directly at CBA level, the state being represented by independent members nominated by the crown. Local and provincial governments will be represented on the regional/local boards (RBA), while the PES is to concentrate on the hard to place. Incentives (payment by results) will also be introduced. Despite the unfavourable evaluation, the role of the social partners has not yet been fundamentally changed but a new reform will see their role declining.

There has been no evaluation of the Irish reforms. While some see an overlapping of functions between LES and EOS, the Department of Enterprise and Trade sees LES as an additional element in its drive to curb long-term unemployment, with a clear focus on specific local conditions. Danish evaluations show that the potential risks of decentralization, such as a clash of interest between national and regional targets, seem to be outweighed by the gains, particularly improved adaptation of measures to local conditions and stronger involvement on the part of local partners. In Austria, too, it was found that the PES works efficiently under the new organizational framework.

While it is difficult to draw definite conclusions on a reorganization that is still in progress, it appears that, in general, policies have been better adapted to disparate local conditions and that the involvement of the social partners and the municipalities (which have become important actors in the delivery of ALMP) has produced encouraging effects. Some problems remain, however. The division of labour between the central and the decentralized units needs to be better coordinated, as do the activities of the various partners at local level. Central organizations require information on the dealings of their decentralized units, while decentralized units need clear goals but also enough autonomy. The bottom-up definition of targets, consideration of disparate local conditions and needs and an efficient system for monitoring target attainment are some of the conditions for the efficient decentralization of PES (Auer and Kruppe 1996). Institutional reforms also need a certain time to bed down before they work properly. While it is advisable to put in place a monitoring process at the same time as introducing reforms, it seems to be counterproductive to enact too many fundamental changes in too short a time. There needs to be a balance between change and stability if efficient outcomes are to be produced.

One interesting development is the increasing share of private placements in some of the countries. In the Netherlands, in particular, temporary agencies have increased their placement activities, thereby contributing, together with an increase in part-time employment, to the 'jobs miracle'. The present policies of 'flexicurity' are intended to introduce greater job security in this area without impairing flexibility.[11] Another point often raised is whether it is advisable to integrate benefit payment and placement. The conventional wisdom (see, for example, various OECD country economic surveys) is that such integration is preferable, since it creates opportunities for better follow-up of the unemployed, provides them with a quicker service (as regards placement in active measures, for example) and makes it easier to control job search and fraud. 'One-stop shops', providing all labour market services such as information, counselling, placement, benefit administration and active labour market programmes, are seen as an efficient answer to the coordination problems that arise between different agencies.

In our sample, all the countries except Austria have kept their benefit payment agencies separate from the other functions of the employment service. While there have been attempts to improve coordination between the various services (for example, through the introduction in the Netherlands of a single personal file for each unemployed person, even though he or she may be a client of different services), the basic distinctions still remain. It is interesting to note that coverage rates (both insurance and assistance benefits) are higher in the three countries with separated services than in Austria, with its integrated services.[12] This might be due to other reasons, such as the existence of unemployed individuals not subject to the job search obligation (older workers, for example). On the the other hand, there may be a contradiction between the 'welfare' principle underpinning the operation of benefit payment agencies and the 'activation' principle on which the work of placement services is based that works against the trend towards the activation of LMP. The effects of this contradiction could be mitigated by integrating the systems.

4   CONCLUSIONS

Both active and passive labour market policies are important tools for the regulation of employment and unemployment. Properly coordinated, they can be mutually supportive. We have shown how unemployment benefit schemes may act as efficiently functioning 'flexicurity' devices in certain sectors of the labour market, especially for those small firms that use a lay-off system. In addition, while an increase in actual retirement age is desirable, matching the statutory and actual age of retirement will be a difficult task as firms are reluctant to retain older workers. This can be proved by the fact that older workers are generally the category best protected by dismissal regulations but are usually a priority target for redundancies. It may be concluded from this that some early retirement schemes will have to be maintained, while greater efforts will have to be made to ensure that firms retain their older workers, at least on a part-time basis within the framework of part-time retirement schemes. Different funding instruments have to be found (such as 'self-financing' schemes, in which a certain proportion of wage increases are allocated to collectively negotiated funds), and support for changes in work organization, for training adapted to the needs of the older workforce and, possibly, wage subsidies could be part of an incentives package designed to encourage employers to retain their older workers.

Unless there is a general and sustained recovery on the labour market, and possibly even if such a recovery were to occur, active labour market policy will play a role in any new definition of full employment. In all developed countries, a certain percentage of the labour force is always involved in ALMP measures at any one time. This percentage is bound to increase under the European Employment Strategy. In order to prevent the development of secondary labour markets in which a marginalized group of workers would remain permanently trapped, ALMP should be used to offer only temporary assistance for individuals in their transitions to and from the regular labour market. Labour market policies have to be screened to ensure compliance with that objective, and some, such as the leave schemes in Denmark and the employment companies (*Stahlstiftungen*) in Austria, have produced encouraging results.

The timing of policies is also important, as the example of Denmark indicates. The implementation of the leave schemes coincided with a period of labour market recovery. Thus there were net outflows from the schemes into employment. Such procyclical intervention seems to be particularly effective in the case of training schemes. However, it is also crucial to maintain countercyclical labour market policy interventions, as policies are most needed when the economy enters a recession. Although the short-term effectiveness of LMP is reduced at such times, such interventions should help to maintain employment and incomes until the next upswing. In this way, they contribute to the long-term efficiency of the labour market.

Along with many other labour market institutions, such as employment protection, unemployment benefits, early retirement and education and training, active labour market policies provide a sort of buffer zone around the regular labour market and as such are an indispensable element of the European socioeconomic system. While active (and passive) labour market policies are by no means the only element of 'transitional labour markets' (Gazier, 1998; Schmid, 1995), they are an important part of them. As a 'second-best solution', they provide an organizational framework for those transitions that require some assistance. They are usually aimed at the harder to place, and there is no need to assist in those transitions that are effected spontaneously through the market. They might intervene at particularly important points in an individual's career, for example when moving from school to work, from a (lost) job to a new job or from work to retirement.

In some cases, 'transitional labour markets' might be created by providing labour market regulations and (financial) incentives only.[13] This would apply to transitional periods such as training or parental leave. In these cases, providing a set of collective rights and financial aids is usually sufficient to induce a demand for such 'transitions'. In some cases, however, transitions not only have to be encouraged by providing incentives and rights but also require an organizational framework. In such situations, active labour market policy can play a role; it can be used, for example, to deliver active assistance for young people who are difficult to place in the labour market by providing an infrastructure (such as an intermediary organization or a project) that might serve as a bridge into the labour market. It is also important in cases where the market spontaneously discriminates against older workers but demographic change and the financing of pensions make it necessary to extend the working life. Thus the active labour market policy element in 'transitional labour markets' could become a permanent feature of modern employment systems (at least as long as there are people experiencing difficult transitions) and provide bridges into and out of the regular public or private labour market. In order to be effective, these bridges, or institutions, would have to be permanent rather than temporary; for individuals, however, they should be regarded only as transit zones. In other words, the institutions might have to be permanent to be effective, while every effort must be made to ensure that people remain within them only temporarily. The difficulty here is that the flow of people in transit is also dependent on the business cycle and thus fluctuates. This may well represent the most important challenge for policy makers, who will have to decide how to put in place something more than ad hoc measures responding to cyclical crises while at the same time establishing permanent structures that are flexible enough to cope with fluctuations.

NOTES

1. This should not be misinterpreted as suggesting that the unemployed are passive, or that unemployment renders them passive. It is true that there is some controversy about the distinction between active and passive labour market policy. Schwanse (1997) has suggested that some active measures might in fact provide only income replacement rather than any chance of employment in the regular market, while passive income replacement schemes that place a strict obligation on beneficiaries actively to seek work sometimes lead to recipients finding such jobs. The definition used here is based not on the outcomes of policies but on the regulatory level. Another reason for adopting it is that, otherwise, the notion of policy 'activation', a major policy issue in the countries under review, not least as a result of the European Employment Strategy, would become somewhat meaningless.
2. This institutional effect on unemployment duration affects registered unemployment and Labour Force Surveys (LFS) unemployment differently. In the latter, unemployed individuals exhausting their benefit entitlement should still be classified as unemployed, provided they fulfil the ILO criteria of being out of work, available and actively searching for jobs. It is probable, but cannot be proved here, that there is some relation between the benefit system (affecting mostly registration) and unemployment as measured by surveys, as those receiving benefits and/or registered as unemployed might more easily classify themselves as unemployed than those unable to draw benefits. The relationships between surveyed unemployment and registered unemployed are complex, however: for example, in Europe older people who registered as unemployed are often exempt from job search and will not be counted as unemployed in LFS. Indeed, LFS unemployment is usually lower than registered unemployment.
3. In Austria 79.5 per cent of the unemployed held a job before becoming unemployed. Comparative figures are 63.5 per cent for Denmark, 53.8 per cent for the Netherlands and only 25.7 per cent for Ireland. There are marked differences in these figures for men and women (Austria m: 90 per cent/f: 65.5 per cent; Denmark m: 68.3 per cent/f: 59.7 per cent; Ireland: m: 30.6 per cent/f: 18.0 per cent; Netherlands m: 54.1 per cent/f: 53.6 per cent).
4. On this point, and for a critical discussion of employment protection indicators, see Bertola *et al.* (2000).
5. Since the publication of the White Paper on Growth, Competitiveness and Employment in 1993, the European Employment Strategy has been gradually developed through many European council resolutions. Employment was finally integrated as a title in the Amsterdam Treaty of 1997. The extraordinary job summit in Luxembourg at the end of 1997 laid the basis for the implementation of the strategy. The Commission enacts guidelines, which are implemented and monitored by the member states through national action plans. Four policy areas are covered: employability, entrepreneurship, adaptability and equal opportunities.

6. There seems also to be some relationship between youth unemployment and the share of youth measures within a country: countries with high youth unemployment (Denmark, Ireland) usually allocate a larger share of ALMP expenditure to young people than those with low youth unemployment (Austria). The Netherlands is an exception: until recently, high youth unemployment was accompanied by low relative spending.

7. Our figures are estimated as follows: for Denmark, for example, the gross effects for certain years are estimated on the basis of entries and duration of measures. In estimated gross terms, around 200 000 people (full-time equivalents) out of 550 000 participated in active labour market policy measures in 1995. Of these, an estimated 95 000 were already employed participants in labour market training. A first gross estimate, then, shows that unemployment would have been 105 000 higher without measures; that is, the unemployment rate would have been roughly 11 per cent instead of 7.2 per cent in 1995. For the other countries, similar estimates result in unemployment reduction rates of 3.3 percentage points for Ireland, 0.7 for Austria and 1 for the Netherlands.

8. In Austria, inflows into schemes almost doubled between 1993 and 1997, reaching 112 280 people in 1997, corresponding to an annual average of around 38 000 people (around 2.9 per cent of the labour force in flow and 1 per cent in stock terms). The Netherlands have also increased their ALMP, but the most important measure now in terms of participants is a reduction in labour tax for those employed on low wages, with some 780 000 participants in 1996. However, jobs have also been created in the public sector specifically for the long-term unemployed (so-called 'Melkert jobs'). Interestingly, spending has not been increased, which might indicate that the tax cut is not included in the spending figures.

9. In 1999, Denmark, Ireland, the Netherlands and Sweden spent more than 1.5 per cent of their GDP on active measures, while Belgium, Finland, France, Germany and Italy spent between 1 and 1.5 per cent. Austria, Greece, Spain, Portugal and the UK spent less than 1 per cent, with the UK, however, recording a large increase, albeit from a low level, because of the 'New Deal'.

10. See also the contribution by de Koning and Mosley in this volume.

11. See also the contribution by Wilthagen and Rogowski in this volume.

12. In 1955 these coverage rates were 149 per cent in Ireland, 127 per cent in the Netherlands, 100 per cent in Denmark and 90 per cent in Austria (OECD, 1997). Coverage rates are defined as the number of registered unemployed who received benefits relative to the number of unemployed (labour force survey definition). However, other definitions (for example, benefit recipients as a share of LFS/ILO defined unemployed) produce much lower figures: Ireland 82 per cent, Austria 74.6 per cent, Denmark 68.2 per cent and Netherlands 62.2 per cent (Rubery, 2001).

13. See the contributions by Gazier and Schmid in this volume.

REFERENCES

Auer, P. (2000), *Employment Revival in Europe: Labour Market Success in Austria, Denmark, Ireland and the Netherlands*, Geneva: ILO.

Auer, P. (2001), Changing labour markets in Europe: The role of institutions and policies, Geneva: ILO.

Auer, P. and T. Kruppe (1996), 'Monitoring of Labour Market Policy in EU member States' in G. Schmid and J. O'Reilly (eds), *International Handbook of Labour Market Policy and Evaluation*, Cheltenham, UK and Brookfield, US: Edward Elgar.

Bertola, G., T. Boeri and S. Cazes (2000), 'Employment protection in industrialized countries: the case for new indicators', *International Labour Review*, 139 (1), 57–72.

Bosch, G. (2001), 'From the Redistribution to the Modernisation of Working Time', in P. Auer (ed.), *Changing labour markets in Europe: The role of institutions and policies*, Geneva: ILO.

Buti, M., L.R. Pench and P. Sesito (1998), 'European Unemployment: Contending Theories and Institutional Complexities', document 11/81/98, European Commission DG II and Forward Studies Unit, Brussels.

Dercksen, H.J. and J. de Koning (1996), 'The New Public Employment Service in the Netherlands', WZB Discussion Paper, FS-I-, 96–201, WZB, Berlin.

Döhrn, R., Heilmann and G. Schäfer (1998), 'Ein dänisches Beschäftigungswunder?', *Mitteilungen aus der Arbeitsmarkt- und Berufsforschung*, 2, 312–23.

Europäische Komission (1998), 'MISSOC: *Soziale Sicherheit in den Mitgliedsstaten der Europäischen Union*', Luxemburg: Amt für amtliche Veröffentlichungen der Europäischen Gemeinschaften.

Frühstück, E., P. Gregoritsch, R. Löffler and M. Wagner-Pinter (1998), *Die Rückkehr in ein vorübergehend aufgelöstes Beschäftigungsverhältnis*, synthesis, Vienna: AMS.

Gazier, B. (1998), 'Ce que sont les marchés transitionnels', in J.-C. Barbier and J. Gautié (eds), *Les politiques de l'emploi en Europe et aux Etats-Unis*, Paris: Presses Universitaires de France, pp. 339–55.

Graafland, J. (1996), 'Unemployment Benefits and Employment: a Review of Empirical Evidence', in W. Van Ginneken (ed.), *Finding the Balance: Financing and Coverage of Social Protection in Europe*, Geneva: International Social Security Association.

Hartog, J. (1999), 'The Netherlands: so what's so special about the Dutch Model?', Employment and training paper 54, ILO, Geneva.

Latullipe, D. (1996), 'Effective retirement age and duration of retirement in the industrial countries between 1990', Issues in Social Protection discussion paper 2, ILO, Geneva.

Madsen, P.K. (1999), 'Denmark: Flexibility, security and labour market success', Employment and training paper 53, ILO, Geneva.

Meager, N. and C. Evans (1999) 'The evaluation of active labour market measures for the long-term unemployed', Employment and training paper 16, ILO, Geneva.

O'Connell, P. (1999), 'Astonishing Success: Economic growth and the labour market in Ireland', Employment and training paper 44, ILO, Geneva.

O'Connell, P. and F. McGinnity (1998), 'What works, who works? The impact of labour market programmes on the employment prospects of young people in Ireland', *Working schemes? Active labour market policy in Ireland*, Aldershot: Avebury Press.

OECD (1996), *Jobs Study, Implementing the Strategy*, OECD, Paris.

OECD (1997, 1998), *Economic Surveys: Austria, Denmark, Ireland, the Netherlands*, OECD, Paris.

OECD (1999), *Benefit Systems and Work Incentives*, OECD, Paris.

Pichelmann, K. and H. Hofer (1999), 'Austria: Longterm success through social partnership', Employment and training paper 52, ILO, Geneva.

Rubery, J. (2001), 'Equal Opportunities and Employment Policy', in P. Auer (ed.), *Changing labour markets in Europe: The role of institutions and policies*, Geneva: ILO.

Schettkat, R. (2001), 'Small Economy Macroeconomics', in P. Auer (ed.), *Changing labour markets in Europe: The role of institutions and policies*, Geneva: ILO.

Schmid, G. (1995), 'Is Full Employment still Possible? Transitional Labour Markets as a New Strategy of Labour Market Policy', *Economic and Industrial Policy*, 11, 429–56.

Schwanse, P. (1997), 'Activation of LMPs: The position of the OECD', in Joint

Employment Observatory Conference (JEOC), *Activation of labour market policies in the European Union: Proceedings of the Joint Employment Observatory Conference (JEOC)*, Stockholm 26th and 27th of June 1997, Berlin: IAS.

Visser, J. (2001), 'Industrial Relations and Social Dialogue', in P. Auer (ed.) *Changing labour markets in Europe: The role of institutions and policies*, Geneva: ILO.

4. Employment systems and transitional labour markets: a comparison of youth labour markets in Germany, France and the UK

Patrick Detzel and Jill Rubery

Transitional labour markets have been proposed as a means of reducing the extent of social exclusion associated with current labour market trends and conditions. There are two elements to the notion of transitional labour markets. Firstly, there is an emphasis on developing transitions both for those in work and for those outside the labour market. For the former, such transitions will offer opportunities to combine work with other meaningful activities or to take a break from the constraints of work, while the latter will be able to participate in work, if only for short periods of time, and thereby maintain and enhance their work skills. Secondly, there is an emphasis on the regularization of activities, such as training, childcare and informal, casual and part-time work, that fall outside the conventional labour market. The objective here is for these activities to become part of a transition process, that is a pathway back to the labour market or into the labour market for the first time, and not simply a means of filling in time or enforced alternatives to labour market participation (for example, childcare not undertaken under the auspices of parental leave schemes).

Young people are a particular target group for transitional labour market policy, for two reasons. Firstly, they are by definition involved in a transition from school or other forms of higher education to work, and one aim of transitional labour market policy must be to ensure that this is a good transition. Thus training schemes for young people should not be a way simply of filling in time but should provide an effective pathway into more regular work. Similarly, informal, casual or part-time work should provide stepping stones or bridges into the regular labour market and not be simply part of a cycle of informal work followed by unemployment, particularly if participation in such a cycle eventually becomes a barrier to entry to the regular labour market as young people become stigmatized as unstable workers without the appropriate work discipline. Young people may also be expected to benefit particularly from the opportunities for short-term labour market participation offered by leave schemes and other transitional policies for those in regular jobs. Older unemployed workers may not be willing to enter a job which is very short-term just to improve their work skills, but young people who have never had the experience of working, and perhaps need the opportunity to try out different forms of work, may be more amenable to short-term job offers. The role of young people in transitional labour markets is thus critical.

However, while youth labour markets are central to the overall objectives of transitional labour markets, such markets are also very diverse and take different forms and shapes across European countries. This diversity is a product not only (or even mainly) of the overall level of labour demand but rather of the institutional arrangements or societal systems that create different paths or transitions for young people seeking to enter the labour market. All European countries are experiencing certain difficulties with the established or traditional systems of transitions for young people into the labour market, and thus attention needs to be paid in policy debate to the reform and development of these transitions. However, the exact nature of the problem varies considerably between countries and so the appropriate policy prescriptions will differ accordingly. Yet the transitional labour market approach, as currently developed, tends to stress general principles that might be expected to be applicable across all countries. There is, of course, no suggestion that all countries have adopted or should adopt the same form of transitional labour market model, but equally there has been limited analysis of what might be an appropriate transitional labour market policy in one country but an inappropriate or even possibly dangerous policy in another context.

Recognition of the dangers or disadvantages inherent in a specific transitional labour market approach arises from the application of a more global or holistic analysis of labour market systems than is often used to evaluate specific transitional labour market policies. For example, evaluations of policies intended to facilitate the transition from unemployment into wage work do take into account problems such as deadweight effects (that is, the share of the unemployed who would have been likely to find work without the policy), but the prioritization of the registered unemployed over, for example, the inactive who wish to work is assumed to be an objective of the policy. In countries with low female participation rates, such an approach tends to hide the continued gender discrimination within the labour market. Similarly, evaluations of the youth labour market tend to be confined to policy objectives aimed specifically at young people, and the possible displacement effects on other groups are not directly considered. For example, much of the attention paid to the impact of the minimum wage has focused on whether it reduces the incentive to hire young people, without consideration of its effect on the labour market position of adult women, a tendency pointed out by Dolado *et al.* (1996).

Indeed, we need to consider the possibility that good transitions for young people might take place at the expense of other groups in society. If this is found to be the case empirically, we would have to ask whether there is a strong ethical or political basis for favouring young people. As with all policy approaches, there is the risk of creating losers as well as winners. While the basis for the transitional labour market approach is that policies should be devised which, taking all things into account, have overall beneficial or positive impacts, the possibility of negative outcomes for some groups needs to be taken into account directly. The actual effects will depend on the specific contexts in which policies are implemented, and the outcomes of specific policies in one context cannot be assumed to have general applicability in others. However, we also need to avoid the equally deterministic but pessimistic approach that all positive advances for some groups are necessarily equally balanced out by losses for others. Good transitions can improve efficiency and equality in the labour market and establish the basis for a general expansion of good employment opportunities, provided macroeconomic conditions are favourable. Thus there is a need to consider the specific conditions for young people in actual employment systems. This chapter attempts to do so with respect to the employment regimes in France, Germany and the UK.

1   DESCRIPTION OF THE THREE EMPLOYMENT REGIMES

It is broadly accepted that the way different labour markets work is profoundly influenced by the institutional settings in which they are embedded (Granovetter, 1985). Any investigation of the nature of a specific country's employment system requires an interpretation both of the current form and level of social exclusion and of the role transitional labour markets can play in reducing such problems. This applies even when the main focus is on young people, since it is necessary to understand how youth labour markets fit into the overall employment regime. In order to elucidate the institutional configuration and its dynamics, as well as the characteristics of the different labour markets, a conceptual framework is required. The framework adopted here is that developed by the French *régulation* school (Boyer, 1986).

The Employment Regimes in France, Germany and the UK

Each national labour market and its institutional setting constitute the national employment regime. This term reflects the notion of sets of relatively stable structures defined at specific times and in specific spaces. It is, therefore, a heuristic instrument that can be used to capture the differing institutional configurations and the varying trajectories of national labour markets (Boyer, 1994a). For example, according to Crouch (1994), two variables can be used to analyse the wage policies adopted by different economies. The first reflects the extent to which wage policy is institutionalized and the form that it takes, the second the extent to which the institutional arrangements actually prevailing in a specific labour market match those of an 'ideal-type' labour market. Despite its reductionist bias, this type of framework provides a means of positioning, heuristically, the various employment regimes and can be used to identify the different trajectories of the countries under consideration.

The *French* labour market, despite the recent profound transformation of the French economy, is still characterized by the presence of stable internal labour markets (Boyer, 1994b). This explains why, once entry to internal labour markets is achieved, individuals tend to remain in employment. Those who do not integrate fully into the labour market through stable employment are at risk of being locked into an erratic employment path, characterized by short employment durations and frequent transitions between unemployment and various labour market and employment policy measures (OECD, 1996: 167).

One has to be aware, however, that such employment relations do not characterize the various sectors of the economy in the same way (Moncel, 1997; Louzeau, 1997). One of the effects of internal labour markets is to generate job queues among entrants, the length of which has been further increased recently by the job-cutting programmes instituted by the large employers. The internal labour market system explains the slow but steady promotion patterns of large sections of the low-skill male core labour force,[1] and the long hierarchical chains could explain the high wage dispersion between the top and median earnings deciles.

Another specificity of the French labour market is the central role of the state (Boyer, 1994b; Penard and Sollongoub, 1995).[2] This affects the labour market institutions on different levels and through different channels. The active role of the state in the shaping of the employment system contrasts sharply with the weak positions of the other actors involved in workplace relations (employees' representatives and employers) (Boyer, 1987a; Petit, 1987; Boyer and Dore, 1994). The state regulates labour markets through the minimum wage, which reduces the incentives to employ cheap labour. It shapes the employability of low-status workers such as young people and older, less highly skilled workers through employment schemes and early retirement programmes and facilitates female employment through various family support measures and the provision of an extensive childcare infrastructure. It has, however, a very limited impact on the policies of organizations. There has been a recent shift in the form of state intervention towards increased decentralization of the administrative authorities. The regional dimension of state activities, such as regional training systems involving local employers (Hildebrandt, 1996; Mansuy, 1995), should ideally also be taken into account if regional labour market differences are to be properly understood (Agullo and Skourias, 1995). The importance of public expenditure in shaping the labour market can be illustrated both by measures of public expenditure as a percentage of GDP and by the participant inflows into state employment and training schemes. In 1994, participant inflows as a percentage of the labour force stood at 11.9 per cent compared with 4.2 per cent for the unified Germany and 2.5 per cent for the UK (cf. Tables 4A.1, 4A.2 and 4A.3).

The *German* labour market has been profoundly influenced by the economic and social consequences of unification. Eastern and Western Germany differ quite markedly in terms of labour market outcomes but have become very similar in institutional arrangements as a consequence of the extension of almost all West German institutions to the former East Germany. Despite the very high unemployment figures, almost all young people are integrated into employment through the dual system of vocational training as well as the school-based education system (Franz and Soskice, 1995). However, for those who have not been able to gain access to one of the various educational pathways, the probability of being fully integrated into the skilled labour force is considered to be very low (Blossfeld, 1990; Blossfeld *et al.*, 1993). The reduced employment opportunities open to low-skilled individuals can be explained both by the very small numbers of such jobs in the high-wage German economy and by the important role of occupational labour markets. Access to vocational labour markets in high-skill areas of manufacturing industry and the role of the welfare system in shaping the German labour market are illustrated in the studies of Esping-Andersen (1990). The employability of low-skilled individuals has been further limited by the slow expansion of the service sector in the German economy and by the very small number of low-level service sector jobs. In contrast to the French model, the state plays a fairly limited role in the regulation of the labour market (Leithäuser, 1987). Early retirement programmes and other measures have been used in specific sectors (such as mining), and more extensively in East Germany, in order to reduce employment, but their use has not been as widespread as in France. After reaching a peak of 0.59 per cent of GDP, expenditure on early retirement programmes fell to a low of 0.06 per cent (see Table 4A.2). Consequently, unemployment among older people has risen more rapidly than in all other age groups in Germany.

In that sense, the German labour market can be defined as neocorporatist (Buttler *et al.*, 1992; Soskice, 1993; Streeck, 1994). The lower skill differentials revealed by Maurice *et al.* (1984), Steedman (1987) and Steedman *et al.* (1991) at the corporate level, as well as the maintenance of the vocational training system and its extension to the service sector, are the outcomes of policies pursued by a strong cooperative network of companies aimed at avoiding state intervention and maintaining high skill levels among the labour force.

This neocorporatist employment system has, however, been placed under strain by the very high costs of reunification, which manifested themselves in very considerable direct transfers, increased tax burdens and rising social costs (to say nothing of the indirect costs associated with the relatively high interest rates needed to attract foreign capital). One consequence could therefore be increased marginalization among already weak groups, such as those without vocational qualifications, female returners and other women with little in the way of skills or qualifications, the low-skill unemployed in Eastern Germany and immigrants.

The *UK* employment regime is commonly described as a 'Balkanized' labour market with inflationary pressures coming not from trade unions but from employers, as a result of company-level wage agreements and skill shortages (Brown and Walsh, 1991; Boyer, 1994a, Brown, 1994).[3] It is moving towards a company-led model, with a very low level of state and trade union intervention. It is the employment regime closest to the 'ideal type' of the flexible firm model proposed by Atkinson (1987). The UK employment system is therefore fragmented, characterized by considerable flows of individuals between employment and unemployment and wage levels determined more by organizations' ability to pay than by the labour market, which generates wide and increasing wage differentials between groups and organizations. Despite its tradition of apprenticeship, the UK is characterized by a considerable discrepancy between the high level of education offered to the elite and the relatively low emphasis on employer-led training and by a recent move towards school-based full-time education (Soskice, 1993), away from the vocational training models emphasized in the Youth Training Scheme (YTS) programmes (Finegold and Soskice, 1988).

Tables 4A.1 to 4A.3 show that the UK has the lowest level of public expenditure on labour market programmes of the three countries examined here (1.94 per cent of GDP in 1995). It is especially in the area of active employment measures that expenditure is low, at 0.53 per cent, covering only 2.5 per cent of the labour force (compared with 11.9 per cent in France and 4.2 per cent in Germany). As a result of the increased importance attached to the 'enterprise culture', the influence of trade unions and of collective bargaining is increasingly confined to particular sectors and organizations.

To illustrate the different configurations of the national labour markets, account needs to be taken of the nature and length of labour market transitions as well as of the composition of the various labour market queues.

The Nature and Length of Transitions in the Three Countries

The three countries studied here are quite distinct in terms of the dynamics of labour flows. In contrast to general belief, it is in Germany that labour turnover is highest[4] (Schettkat, 1996a): despite the neocorporatist labour market, the labour turnover rate reached 25 per cent during the 1980s. The British labour market, which is regarded as flexible and company-led, had a turnover rate of 20 per cent, whereas the corresponding figure for the highly regulated French labour market was 15 per cent (ibid.). The labour turnover rate includes three forms of transition into employment as well as three forms of transitions out of employment from the following three labour market statuses: inactivity, unemployment and employment. The labour turnover rates differ in terms not only of level but also of composition.

Examination of the flows into and out of unemployment shows that they are relatively low in France and relatively high in the UK (Table 4.1). However, the reduced flows between the three states in France are the result of different dynamics. Fougère (1996) has shown that transitions out of inactivity have been stable for the last 23 years. Movements out of unemployment into employment or inactivity, on the other hand, have declined steadily to only 57 per cent of their 1969 level, whereas transitions from employment have been rerouted towards unemployment instead of inactivity. In the light of these flows, it can be hypothesized that there is a gradual trend in France towards a more 'absorbing' unemployment status. The rising unemployment rate in Germany over the last 15 years, despite the relative high flows out of unemployment and the relative slow rise of the inflows, is explained by Schettkat (1996b) by the large increase in the duration of unemployment (from 15.9 weeks in 1985 to 25.9 weeks in 1993).

Thus labour market transitions in these three countries seem to be quite different in both form and nature. Germany has the highest rate of labour market turnover, but these transitions take place mainly within the employed population; that is, they involve transfers between jobs. These findings may

Table 4.1   Flows into and out of unemployment, 1990

	Inflows in 1990 (% of working population)	Outflows in 1990 (as % of unemployed population)
France (1991)	0.3	5.5
Germany	0.2	8.0
UK	0.6	13.4

Source: OECD (1993: Table 3.3).

reflect the German vocational training and labour market system, which tends to promote job-to-job mobility. Once individuals enter unemployment or inactivity, the risk of staying may be quite high.

In the UK, the turnover rate of 20 per cent seems to be composed of different transitions between the various states. The increased use of a flexible labour force and the radical reshaping of the welfare system have led to increased movements between the different employment statuses.

France is characterized by low levels of transitions in general and 'absorbing' states in particular. Three striking aspects of labour market transitions in France are highlighted by the findings of Lollivier (1994) and Fougère (1996). Prime-age workers have higher transition rates between temporary jobs and stable jobs than young people. Once they become unemployed, prime-age workers have a higher propensity to move back into stable jobs than temporary jobs, whereas young people are more likely to gain access to jobs through temporary contracts. The gendered dimension of these transitions also seems to reinforce the differences between prime-age workers and young people. On the basis of these limited indicators, it would seem that internal labour markets continue to prevail in France, favouring those individuals who are already part of the labour market.

Even these limited flow data reveal the considerable differences in labour market transitions in Europe. In Germany, transitions seem to take place within the employed population. In the UK, on the other hand, transitions involve movements between different employment statuses (see Table 4A.4). France has a generally low rate of transitions.

The analysis as presented thus far has been based mainly on the hypothesis of a homogeneous population. All labour market studies show, however, that the risk of being in a specific labour market status is not evenly spread across the population but is related to age cohort, education, gender and occupational status. We will now draw on stock data from cross-sectional sources in order further to differentiate the nature of the labour market regimes.

The Different Labour Queues

The first step in understanding the structure of labour queues is to analyse access to the labour market according to labour market status, gender, age and educational level. 'Low-skilled and less-experienced workers have been particularly hit by these adverse labour market developments' (OECD, 1997: 1). Because of the large gap between the old and the new *Länder* in Germany, we have tried to differentiate as much as possible between conditions in Eastern and Western Germany (Schwarze *et al.*, 1994a).

In 1996, Eastern Germany had by far the highest unemployment figures in the three countries in the over-24 age groups, and unemployment there was significantly above the average European level (see Table 4A.5). The high levels of inactivity among male and female, low-skilled and highly educated individuals in Eastern Germany are the result of the massive use of early retirement programmes in the years following reunification (Bellman and Buttler, 1994; Licht and Steiner, 1994; Parmentier and Tessaring, 1994). In Eastern Germany, only 27.7 per cent of low-skilled men and 13.8 per cent of low-skilled women in the 50–64 age bracket are active in the labour market. Eastern Germans seem clearly to be located in unfavourable labour market queues as a result of the profound restructuring of the East German economy, which has destroyed almost 40 per cent of the jobs that existed before unification (Licht and Steiner, 1994; Bellmann and Buttler, 1994).

The same kind of early retirement programmes have been introduced in France and Western Germany, but they were less extensively used during the first half of the 1990s. In France, the inactivity rate among men aged over 50 declines sharply as educational level rises, from 52.5 per cent for men with low educational levels to 21 per cent for the highly educated. This can be explained by the fact that early retirement programmes are aimed at reducing employment in traditional industrial sectors in which the workforce is made up predominantly of low-skilled male workers. The inactivity rate among women aged between 50 and 64 is also high but does not differ significantly from European levels.

The second category of individuals in a precarious state in France is young people. Irrespective of educational level, levels of youth unemployment in France were higher in 1996 than in Germany and the UK, and the shares of young people in full-time employment lower (especially among women, and particularly those of low educational attainment). In the light of these first results and of those relating to the transition intensities, France seems to have a large population of predominantly young and older men excluded from the labour market.

Measured by employment rates, the UK seems to fare relatively well, as has been emphasized by different labour market studies (OECD, 1996, 1997). It should be kept in mind that these performance measures are offset to some extent by an increased wage dispersion and greater job instability (see the flow analysis above). In terms of employment status, young men of low educational attainment seem to underperform compared with their European counterparts. Since young people in Britain tend to leave the school system early (Bynner and Roberts, 1991; Bates and Riseborough, 1993; Banks, 1994; Ashton *et al.*, 1990; Furlong and Cartmel, 1997), the inactivity rate is quite low. The percentages of the young who are unemployed or in part-time work are, however, quite high, indicating that a large proportion of young people in the UK face a choice between part-time work or unemployment.

Employment status can be considered a rough proxy for position in the labour market queues but cannot reveal much about the degree of integration into the labour market. Once individuals are in the labour market the question about the degree of participation remains.

Table 4A.6 shows the number of hours worked in the three countries as well as in Europe. Despite the clear gendered distribution of work in Germany (East as well as West), the distribution of hours in that country is a traditional one, centred around the 36–40-hour mark. France is characterized by higher numbers of hours worked by core-age men and women. The UK, on the contrary, has a multimodal distribution of hours. The proportion of young people working only a few hours is relatively high, indicating the presence of a large group of individuals only marginally integrated into the labour market.

Large internal labour markets in France and increased wage flexibility in the UK should in theory give rise to differences in the trends and structures of wage dispersion in the three countries, although trends in wage dispersion are also affected by sectoral shifts and changing life-course trajectories throughout the countries. Figure 4.1 illustrates such structures and trends by plotting the ratio of the highest earning deciles (D9) to the median earning deciles (D5) and the ratio of the lowest earning deciles (D1) to the median earning deciles (D5). With its strong internal labour markets and extensive hierarchies, France is expected to have the largest difference between the deciles, whereas the UK is expected to show an increase in wage dispersion throughout the observed period. No specific hypotheses can be made about Germany, besides the fact

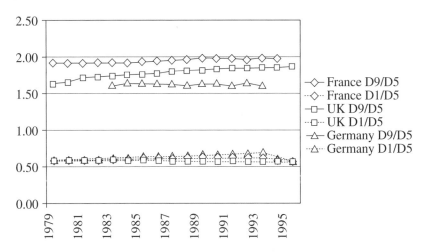

Source: OECD (1996: 61).

Figure 4.1   Structures and trends in wage dispersion, D9/D5 and D1/D5, 1979–95

that many specialists have described German wage policies of the 1980s and 1990s as having been characterized by wage moderation as a result of trade union intervention and the tight fiscal policies adopted by the Bundesbank (Streeck, 1994; Crouch, 1994).

France has the highest dispersion between the top and median deciles but a relatively narrow wage dispersion between the median and the bottom deciles, which can be explained by the presence of a minimum wage. The degree of wage dispersion was, however, quite stable throughout the period, underlining the fact that the adverse supply shocks did not lead to increased wage inequality. The British labour market, in contrast, experienced increasing wage dispersion throughout the working population. Germany is characterized not only by a low level of wage dispersion (as expected by Buttler *et al.*, 1992) but also by a decreasing wage dispersion throughout the 1983–93 period.

Drawing on the notion of employment regimes and on the limited data illustrating the different employment queues, we can distinguish three forms of labour markets. With its internal labour market structure and the increased educational achievement of its population, France is characterized by long employment queues, with educational level determining the position of individuals in those queues. The opening up in the 1990s of certain managerial positions in the public and private sectors to young, highly-educated people has increased the attractiveness of the elite *grandes écoles* but has at the same time reduced promotion opportunities for workers in internal labour markets (Verdier, 1995, 1996). However, the massive public intervention in youth labour markets through the introduction of training and work schemes does not seem to have increased young people's employability. There continues to be a major shortage of openings for young people such that employment remains rationed. In practice, the various public schemes act as a sort of signalling device for entry into the private sector. These programmes play a dual role, with certain programmes working as screening advice for the employers and others functioning more as a form of 'warehousing', providing only limited possibilities of access to a full-time employment position (Charpail *et al.*, 1997; Martinez and Vanheerswynghels, 1997; Werquin, 1997). Despite their relatively good positions in certain industries such as banking (O'Reilly, 1992, 1994), women also find it difficult to gain access to internal labour markets and in consequence account for a large share of the casual labour markets. Older semi-skilled men in manufacturing and heavy industries have also been locked out of the labour market through extensive early retirement programmes. As a result, activity rates among the over-55s are very low.

The German labour market can be broadly categorized as an occupational labour market based on a skilled labour force. Unskilled jobs are relatively few in number and have even declined over the last 15 years, despite the slow movement towards service sector-led growth (Esping-Andersen, 1990; Blossfeld *et al.*, 1993). Low-skilled service sector jobs are also considered merely as stopgap employment or even as labour market traps that do little to increase employability. Thus the creation of unskilled, low-paid jobs is seen as a way of integrating women who have left the labour market for domestic reasons but not seen as a means of facilitating labour market access for young people.

The UK labour market, despite its occupational labour market history (Marsden and Ryan, 1995), is evolving towards company-led labour market (Brown, 1994; Crouch, 1994) with only limited development of broadly-based, labour market-level training programmes. The restructuring of the various training institutions has led to an increased movement towards internal labour markets (Green, 1995). The recent large increase in participation in full-time education, combined with the poor image of the vocational training system, is indicative of a shift towards school-based routes into internal labour markets.

We can postulate that the transitions between the various employment statuses (unemployment, employment and out of labour force) are not only nationally and regionally specific but also dissimilar for different groups. The UK has been described as the most flexible labour market, but this seems to apply more to transitions into and out of the labour force than to job-to-job mobility. Thus marginalized workers seem to have no place in the unemployment queues, unlike young people and lower-skilled men in France or large parts of the population in Eastern Germany. In the UK, they alternate rather between low-paid, insecure jobs and unemployment.

Thus the experience of unemployment has different consequences. For more highly educated young people in all three countries it postpones the transition into employment. In the UK, the frequent transitions between the different labour market statuses could be interpreted as the result of a large number of stopgap jobs in the service sector. France, with its strong job rationing, is facing a major problem with the disrupting effect of unemployment for young people with lower and intermediate levels of education (Werquin, 1997). In Germany the disrupting effect of unemployment seems to have an impact mainly on individuals without vocational qualifications as well as on large parts of the Eastern German population. It has only a marginal impact on school-to-work transitions (Detzel, 1998). The high level of unemployment in France and Germany and the high level of insecure jobs in the UK can be interpreted as a breakdown of the traditional systems of transition. However, since these traditional systems differ in scope, their breakdown is likely to lead to the increased marginalization of different groups within the population.

2   THE NATURE OF YOUTH TRANSITIONS

We saw in section 1 that the employment regimes in the three countries differ in important ways and that these differences have led to distinct employment trajectories and different forms of labour queues. The notion of transitional labour markets has therefore to take into account the different patterns of transition between employment statuses and the different signals that these transitions generate in the labour markets. We would like, however, to explore this argument further by looking at a specific segment of the labour market, namely the youth labour market. Young people in modern societies can be considered to be in a state of transition between various labour market and domestic statuses (Chisholm, 1995). The transitional spells of young people are indeed lengthening with the increasing socio-economic instability of Western societies (Cavalli and Galland, 1995). We do not postulate, in contrast to Ashton *et al.* (1990), that youth labour markets are autonomous segments of the broader labour market, or that youth employment is simply more subject to volatile movements than the overall labour market. Indeed, youth employment patterns have to be understood in relation to national labour markets and to general labour market institutions. Thus, before analysing the nature of the youth-specific employment regimes, we will describe the nature of the employment statuses of young people in the three countries under investigation here.

The Employment Statuses of Young People

With the exception of Germany, young people throughout Europe are more vulnerable to the business cycle than the rest of the adult population and have higher rates of unemployment than adults. No age group appears to have benefited more from the upturn of economic activity between 1987 and 1990 (European Commission, 1997). Germany is the only country in Europe to have similar unemployment rates among young and adult workers (see Table 4.2).

Although young people in all countries are vulnerable, there are large differences between countries in the employment ratios of young people, a finding that supports the hypothesis of separate labour markets. The ratios presented in Table 4.3 show that the routes into employment for the 15–19 age

Table 4.2   Unemployment rates, 1997

	EU15	France	Germany	UK
15–29	18.7%	23.5%	9.7%	12.8%
30–59	9.4%	11.0%	9.9%	6.0%

Source: European labour force survey, 1997.

Table 4.3 *Employment ratios by age and gender, selected years (%)*

	1979			1983			1989			1994			1997		
	15–19	20–24	35–54	15–19	20–24	35–54	15–19	20–24	35–54	15–19	20–24	35–54	15–19	20–24	35–54
France															
Men	22.8	73.8	93.3	18.0	68.9	91.9	12.9	59.0	89.8	6.8	42.2	85.9	9.7	45.4	87.3
Women	13.5	59.0	59.5	8.7	52.4	61.9	7.0	45.5	64.0	3.1	32.8	66.6	4.6	38.5	68.6
Germany															
Men	46.9	76.8	93.0	40.4	69.3	88.4	39.7	73.3	87.1	35.0	67.7	83.0	30.4	64.9	87.0
Women	42.2	67.7	53.3	34.6	62.7	53.7	34.3	68.3	57.7	30.6	65.7	63.7	24.9	60.3	67.2
UK															
Men	–	–	–	54.9	72.8	86.4	65.8	81.6	89.2	48.9	68.6	83.9	42.1	73.2	85.0
Women	–	–	–	52.1	60.1	60.2	64.3	69.2	67.3	48.6	62.4	69.3	42.0	64.8	72.6

Source: OECD (1996: 112) and European labour forces survey, 1997.

Change and performance of employment systems

Table 4.4   Status of young people at different ages, 1995 (%)

Age	Status	EU	F	G	UK
15	In education and inactive	93.5	100.0	97.2	99.9
	In education and active	2.9	–	2.8	–
	Not in education and active	2.2	–	–	–
	Not in education and inactive	1.4	–	–	0.1
18	In education and inactive	59.0	84.0	47.5	27.3
	In education and active	17.1	6.8	38.5	29.4
	Not in education and active	19.3	7.2	11.3	37.5
	Not in education and inactive	4.5	2.0	2.7	5.8
24	In education and inactive	14.3	12.7	17.3	3.5
	In education and active	8.8	7.7	9.8	9.9
	Not in education and active	66.8	72.7	63.8	74.1
	Not in education and inactive	10.2	6.9	9.0	12.4

Source: Eurostat (1997).

group differ markedly between countries. Young adults in France are increasingly choosing full-time education as a pathway into the labour market. Young adults in Germany are relatively more likely to choose full-time education or to delay starting an apprenticeship until after they have obtained the *Abitur* (Buchtemann *et al.*, 1993, 1994; Sanders and Becker, 1994). Despite the large increase in the number of individuals staying in full-time education (Brown, 1994), young adults in Britain start looking for jobs very early in their life (Bynner and Roberts, 1991; Roberts, 1993, 1995).

These differences are further illustrated by the distribution of young people across the different statuses (see Table 4.4). France has the largest share of young adults in full-time education at age of 18, whereas the UK has the largest share of young people who are economically active on a full-time basis. The two routes into employment in Germany (dual system and school-based education) are reflected in the high shares of young people in the 'education and active' and 'education and inactive' categories.

These figures reflect the different Vocational Education and Training (VET) systems in the three countries. We saw in the preceding section that the three countries differ quite markedly in their labour markets, employment systems and socio-economic evolution. Young people do not gain access to the labour market through the same occupations (European Commission, 1997) and industries as the adult population. These transitions are dependent upon educational background and the national vocational system as well as on the economic evolution of specific sectors (White and McRae, 1989; Ashton *et al.*, 1990).

Table 4.5 shows that the concentration of young adults in the different industries is not the same in the three countries. Germany has the lowest ratio of young people in so-called 'young people's' service-sector industries such as hotels and catering and wholesale and retail (personal consumer services). The UK, in contrast, has the highest ratio, especially among young male adults, who tend to be located in industries with low promotion prospects and low pay. In France, personal consumer services are characterized by a relatively high concentration of young females, reflecting the difficulty young women experience in gaining access to traditional internal labour markets.

Despite its high youth unemployment rate, France still has a large concentration of young men working in manufacturing industry. This could be explained by the extensive use of state-led work schemes and part-time employment in these industries and by the existence of internal labour markets.

These ratios show that the 'points of entry' into the labour force are quite different in the three countries. They reflect the extensive influence of personal consumer services in the UK and the 'stopgap' function of such jobs (Esping-Andersen, 1993). These ratios do not, however, take into account the role of public work schemes, the quality of the jobs offered or the opportunities they provide for integration and mobility over the life course. Such questions can be addressed only with longitudinal data.

The extent to which young people can be considered to be in a precarious position depends not only on their position in the labour market but also on their degree of autonomy[5] and family background. Family support is even more important for young people than for adults, particularly since the length of time between inactivity and employment is increasing. Indeed, throughout Europe, there is an increased concentration of unemployment within households, leading to a growing number of households without any earners (OECD, 1998). This trend also applies to young people, as Table 4.6 shows.

The Role of the Employment Regimes and of the State

The institutional configurations of the employment regimes play a similar role in youth employment. The role of the state is stronger in the two countries with the highest youth unemployment rates, that is France and the UK. The importance of French state institutions in youth employment can be understood as part of a long history of rationalistic state intervention in the education system. In the UK, in contrast, the massive intervention of the state during the Thatcher years is quite counterintuitive and appears to contradict the *laissez-faire* attitude of the Conservative Government (Green, 1995; Almond and Rubery, 2000; Deakin, 1996). 'A new Conservative Government was elected in 1979, and soon adopted a *laissez-faire*, free-market approach to economic policy.

Table 4.5 Ratio of shares of employment for those aged 15–24 relative to those aged 25 and over for selected industries, 1996

	Men					Women			
	Manufacturing	Electricity	Construction	Wholesale	Hotels & rest.	Private households	Wholesale & retail	Hotels & rest.	Health & social work	Community	Private households
W.Ger.	0.88	0.61	1.57	1.60	2.09	1.34	1.12	1.69	1.27	1.10	0.42
E.Ger.	0.77	0.56	1.59	1.35	2.57	NA	1.20	2.25	1.28	1.15	0.00
France	1.05	0.26	1.53	1.51	3.25	0.60	1.86	3.42	0.76	1.90	0.66
UK	0.79	0.43	1.04	2.25	4.57	0.65	1.69	2.54	0.59	1.45	2.81
EU15	0.99	0.40	1.41	1.87	2.97	0.40	1.69	2.41	0.74	1.46	0.88

Source: European labour force survey, 1996.

122

Table 4.6   Proportion of unemployed youth in households where no other person is employed, 1985 and 1993

	1985 (%)	1993 (%)
France	15	28
Germany	27	34
UK	32	34

Source: OECD (1996: 116).

However, with the youth labour market in massive disequilibrium, supply being far in excess of demand, the interventionist policies adopted by the Labour Government in the late 1970s had to be continued' (Deakin, 1996: 82).

The costs of these programmes and the flows of young people involved are very high, although once again there are major differences among the three countries (see Tables 4A.1, 4A.2 and 4A.3). In France, the costs of youth employment measures represent 0.27 per cent of GDP, compared with 0.06 per cent in Germany and 0.13 per cent in the UK. The numbers of individuals involved in such programmes differ considerably from one country to the next but are in line with the youth unemployment figures. In France, the number of young people taking part in these programmes amounts to 3.2 per cent of the working population. Two-thirds of these participate in training schemes. Despite the relatively low expenditures in Germany, the proportion of young people involved in these programmes as a share of the working population is similar to that in the UK.[6] The nature of these programmes is, however, very different. In Germany most expenditure goes on unemployment benefits, whereas in the UK youth schemes are principally aimed at providing training positions in the private and public sectors. More recently, the state in Germany has extended its role both by subsidizing apprenticeships on a large scale and organizing school-based apprenticeship places in East Germany. Furthermore, it has approved a large 'billion DM' programme for disadvantaged groups (Presse- und Informationsdienst der Bundesregierung, 1999b).

Despite the central role of the state as a provider of funds, the emphasis of the different programmes is consonant with the animating principles that underpin the various employment regimes. The statements issued by the various national representatives within the EU, summarized below, reflect the differing roles of the social partners in vocational training.[7]

France: The social partners are involved in the development of vocational training policy at the national, industry and firm levels. They manage the organizations which collect the contributions that fund the training of young people and continuing training.

Germany: The social partners' role in training policy is institutionalized through committee participation at federal, *Land* and regional level, works councils, consultation at firm level and through industry-level collective agreements. Their role at all levels is to advise on:

- the preparation and the implementation of policy in order to ensure quality;
- the content and duration of training;
- the organization of courses; and
- examination requirements.

Some trade associations and trade unions are also training providers.
United Kingdom: The government encourages employers to take responsibility for the training and development of their workforce. While collective bargaining is not common at industry level, unions are often involved in industry-level working parties set up to develop standards and competencies, particularly in the case of Modern Apprenticeships. The scope of bargaining and consultation at firm level is variable. Electronic Retrieval System on Employment Policies (ERSEP) on Employment Policies, produced by ECOTEC for the European Commission

The relative lack of involvement on the part of the social partners in the UK and France led to intervention by various actors in an attempt to address the problem of growing youth unemployment during the 1980s. At the risk of reductionism, the intervention of the different partners can be illustrated by means of the same elements used to characterize the labour market as a whole.

In France, it was mainly the state that tried to tackle the problem of growing youth unemployment. This started with the introduction of measures to reduce the costs of youth employment by paying subsidies to employers or reducing the social costs of employing young workers. These programmes had a significant impact on youth labour markets (Le Goff, 1995a) but did not reduce unemployment because of substitution effects. In 1994, no fewer than 900 000 young people, or more than an entire age cohort, were employed on subsidized contracts (Chastand and Gelot, 1996). Every second young individual without the *baccalauréat* has participated in a youth scheme at least once (Werquin, 1997). The question of whether such schemes enhance participants' employability has been widely analysed and discussed and is also addressed in the next section. The rapid extension of youth measures was not, however, the only measure used by the government. The problem of job rationing and job substitution led the government to involve the social partners more extensively by increasing the local and regional autonomy of the VET system and by trying to improve the image of the apprenticeship. Despite the increased subsidiarity, it is still the state that plays the largest role in both funding and setting the agenda.

The politics of youth employment programmes in the UK are more erratic. They are characterized by quite strong state intervention, albeit in favour of company-led education and training. The main scheme over the last 15 years was the Youth Training Scheme, which used to take up to 25 per cent of the young people leaving the school system (Deakin, 1996; Andrews and Bradley, 1997). It is mainly seen as a beneficial scheme, not so much for the young people it is aimed at but for the companies taking advantage of the subsidies. The further development of the YTS towards a credit system was followed by the introduction of the Modern Apprenticeship in 1994 (in operation in September 1995 and endorsed in 1997 by the new government) and the introduction of competency-based training modules, National Vocational Qualifications (NVQs).

Further devolution was accompanied by further liberalization of labour market processes, which conferred greater market freedom upon new trainees, and by the introduction of output-related funding. The government continued to fund youth training services but ceased to provide such services itself. However, the relatively low commitment of employers to standardized vocational qualifications has led to a weakening of broad vocational standards and to very tightly defined, job-related qualifications. The broader Modern Apprenticeship scheme is mainly used by very small companies in the service sector. Over a third of participating companies have fewer than 10 employees and a further quarter between 10 and 24 employees. Nearly two-thirds of Modern Apprenticeship employers have only one apprentice, with most of the rest having between two and five. Only 4 per cent have more than 10 employees (Howarth and Stone, 1999).

The policy shift towards the establishment of a quasi-market in youth training services is reflected in the scheme introduced by the new Labour government and known as the New Deal. The New Deal for young unemployed people is aimed at those aged 18–24 who have been claiming jobseeker's allowance (JSA) continuously for six months. Participation is mandatory. Those joining New Deal first enter a so-called 'gateway period' lasting up to four months. This period includes career advice and guidance and help with job-seeking skills. The aim of the gateway period is to help as many people as possible find unsubsidized employment (Hall and Reid, 1998). Individuals who have not secured employment at the end of the gateway period have to choose between the following options: employment with training and subsidy to the employer, work experience with a voluntary organization with training, work experience on an environment task force with training or full-time education. Up to the end of 1998, over 214 000 young people had started on the New Deal and 140 100 had left the gateway. Table 4.7 illustrates the immediate destinations of leavers from the gateway between January and December 1998. The long-term effects of this policy are of course as yet unknown.

The German VET system is a complex system of cooperation between *Länder*, employers and employees, dominated by the dual system, which sets the qualifications needed for a specific job status. Major investments in the

Change and performance of employment systems

Table 4.7   Immediate destination of leavers from Gateway (per cent)

Not known	Unsubsidized jobs	Employer option	Education	Voluntary and environment option	Other
18.80	26.70	9.90	20.40	11.00	13.20

Source: Daly and Bently (1999: 201).

VET system and the considerable contributions made by employers in the form of stable offers of apprenticeship positions compensate for the low level of state funding of youth employment measures (Franz and Soskice, 1995). However, the system is facing some major challenges, which are related not to the increased number of unemployed young people or to a mismatch problem (Witte and Kalleberg, 1995) but rather to the relative rigidity of the system, the low involvement of employers in Eastern Germany and the increased attractiveness of school-based education. The German VET has also to take into account the small but stable share of young people leaving the VET without minimum qualifications (Banks, 1994) and who are at risk of being trapped in low-level jobs with poor career prospects. In 1999, according to new research by the German Ministry of Education, 11.6 per cent of young people were without qualifications. Among non-German young people this figure reaches 32.7 per cent (Presse- und Informationsdienst der Bundesregierung, 1999a).

Forms of Transitions among Young People in Germany, France and the UK

It is difficult, for a variety of reasons, to compare the role and effectiveness of the various national VET systems. The first difficulty concerns the criterion to be used to measure effectiveness. Cross-sectional data provide the most extensive information but do not allow individual trajectories to be taken into account. Labour force survey indicators, such as the stocks of unemployed, part-time employed or the share of young people in school, are the dynamic result of different economic outcomes and cannot be used to measure the effectiveness of VET systems. The use of indicators of labour market flexibility relative to transitions is also of limited value for similar reasons. A measure of the degree of matching between the VET system and the labour market would certainly be an appropriate indicator but would be strongly related to the institutional context.

A second level of difficulty is related to the scarcity of international studies. Research also reflects national specific interests and methodologies. The available UK studies are concerned mainly with the school-to-work transition and the role of the YTS and draw on panel data and cross-sectional data. French studies are concerned primarily with the school-to-work transitions of specific cohorts based on retrospective interviews and on administrative data from the unemployment office. German studies are even more difficult to find and are mainly based on an institutionalist approach (Büchtemann *et al.*, 1994; Helberger *et al.*, 1994; Sanders and Becker, 1994). We can, however, use the different national and international studies of employment trajectories to highlight the role of the different institutions in the young people's transitions.

Employment trajectories and the role of the VET systems

The rates of youth unemployment in France and the importance attached to the role of the school system have led to the gathering of rich and detailed data and to a very large number of longitudinal studies. Some studies of the transition rates between the different employment statuses have also been made with the intention of describing the evolution of flexibility in the labour market. Lollivier's study (1994), based on Markov chains, examined the stability of the transitions between 1981 and 1989. His estimation of separate transition models for each year led to a rejection of the hypothesis of time homogeneity in the underlying Markovian transition process over this period. The rejection is very strong for young workers (Fougère, 1996: 160). This means that the transition patterns of young people were not stable throughout the period. If account is taken of the decline in the mean duration of regular employment spells over the period and the rise in transition rates from stable employment to temporary work and from temporary work to unemployment, the role of temporary jobs in the integration of young people into the labour force is called into question. Longitudinal retrospective data for France, Germany and the UK confirm these cross-sectional data.

A further element in the link between education and employment is the role of educational or qualification level. In France, the educational level attained does not seem to have the large impact on promotion patterns after integration into the labour market that has been found in Germany (Scherer, 1998). Employment opportunities seem to be more related to initial job and to accumulated work experience.[8] However, education plays a part in determining the probability of obtaining a job in the first place (Le Goff, 1995a, 1995b). An individual's educational level determines his or her place in the job queue (Verdier, 1996). The deterioration of the labour market, together with the increased level of educational attainment among young people (Beduwé *et al.*, 1995; Verdier, 1995), has led to a decline in the value of educational qualifications and to increased unemployment rates among the highly educated[9] (Le Goff, 1995a, 1995b). The education system in France seems to have an important signalling function for the labour market and future employers (Espinasse and Giret, 1997) although it is not coordinated with the labour market

(Moebius and Verdier, 1997; Lefresne, 1996). The loose coupling between education and labour markets has led to increased competition not only among young people within the same cohort but also with slightly older cohorts who have some work experience acquired through work schemes or temporary jobs (Cahuzac *et al.*, 1997).

Studies by Blossfeld *et al.* (1993) and Esping-Andersen (1990) show two, at first glance conflicting, trends in Germany. They are based on the same theoretical background, which emphasizes the emergence of a new post-Fordist system throughout industrialized countries and the simultaneous maintenance of country-specific employment trajectories related to stratification. The first trend has been highlighted by Esping-Andersen (1990), who draws on cross-sectional data. It shows a rapid reduction in the unskilled, post-Fordist service-sector proletariat: 'the post-industrial hierarchy emerging in each country is quite distinct. The German, as we expected, is not only much smaller than elsewhere, but also much more skilled. Its unskilled service proletarians have declined sharply, so that their share is less than half of that elsewhere' (Esping-Andersen, 1993).

The second trend, revealed by examination of the life-course movements of individuals within the occupational hierarchy, is the lack of upward mobility among the unskilled. The transitions between unskilled service jobs and unskilled Fordist jobs are important, but they are not leading to access to skilled jobs. Those individuals in Germany who enter the labour market for the first time in unskilled jobs have a fairly high probability of staying in such positions. In other words, they act as labour market traps rather than as stop-gap jobs for those queuing to enter skilled work. This reinforces the argument that the vocational labour market in Germany and its dual system tend to generate a strong skill-based segmentation. It reduces the chances of young individuals without formal qualifications compensating for these deficits once they have left the VET system. Indeed, the majority of the workers without vocational training enter the unskilled labour market and stay there (Blossfield, 1994).

The study of the UK in Esping-Andersen's research reveals a surprisingly similar profile in terms of the distribution of individuals within the Fordist and post-Fordist ocupations. However, unlike the case of Germany, there is a heavy bias towards unskilled workers in both the Fordist and the post-Fordist hierarchy (Esping-Andersen, 1993; Gershuny, 1993). These unskilled jobs have not traditionally been a labour market trap, unlike the situation in Germany, as they have functioned as an entry point to the labour market for young people (Kerckhoff, 1996). However, Gershuny (1993) has demonstrated that there is increased career immobility among individuals in Britain. In his view, this is related to the weakness of the 'institutional support for the acquisition of formal qualifications that goes well beyond the standard educational provisions for children and young adults. This support is, to judge from the evidence we have considered, lacking in Britain' (Gershuny, 1993: 169). Thus these entry-level jobs are also becoming labour market traps in the UK.

Training opportunities provided by the state

We have seen that the breakdown of the school-to-work transitions in France and the UK (and to a much lower extent in Germany) has led to a large increase in training opportunities provided by the state. Although such programmes may delay youth unemployment, the question is whether they improve young people's employability and increase their probability of embarking on a relatively stable employment trajectory. Do training programmes provide a means of transition or do they lead to further stigmatization of young participants?

The large volume of econometric and economic research on their effectiveness reflects the scale of the French and British programmes in terms of the financial and organizational resources deployed. The German training programmes – owing to the great importance of the dual system – are not as developed, although they were extended in Eastern Germany to deal with the lack of training opportunities.[10] The major programme introduced by the new German government, despite its positive impact on the number of young individuals without a training position (29 403 in 1999 compared to 35 675 in 1998), has not yet been systematically analysed and evaluated (Presse- und Informationdienst der Bundesregierung, 1999a).

The majority of the studies in the UK show a relatively low or even negative impact of YTS in generating secure employment paths for young people (Bradley and Taylor, 1991; Dolton *et al.*, 1991; Main and Shelly, 1990; Main, 1992; Dolton, 1993; O'Higgins, 1994; Lindey, 1996; Andrews and Bradley, 1997). This seems to be particularly so in the case of medium-term job stability. It is generally argued that the evaluation of training schemes in the UK has to be differentiated according to the nature of the schemes. The training schemes based on apprenticeships in private industry tend to have positive effects, whereas those taking place in the public sector or within the educational system are stigmatized and attract only young people with very poor prospects As White and McRae (1989) have shown, the relative effectivesess of the first type of programmes has to be further analysed. Individuals who fail to finish these programmes or who do not embark on an employment trajectory soon after the first training spell tend to fare very badly in terms of employment stability. This is partly explained by the dual function of the training schemes. They are both a relatively cheap screening device for employers and a form of stigmatization for those who have not achieved the expected results.

The French studies show somewhat similar results but emphasize the complexity of drawing conclusions from such results (Werquin, 1997). The study by Bonnal *et al.* (1994), which is based on longitudinal data on unemployed people, shows that the 'youth' employment programmes and subsidized jobs have different impacts on the trajectories of young people, depending on educational background, individual employment histories and the type of programmes they were involved in. Young people employed in subsidized jobs that combine employment with part-time education have a higher probability of gaining access to stable jobs than those taking part in training schemes. However, this result is dependent on the level of education. Training schemes appear to reduce the risk of unemployment as they raise participants' qualification levels (Charpail *et al.*, 1997). This is due to the intense job competition in France. Young people leaving the school system are competing with older cohorts, most of whom have already acquired some form of work experience. This helps to explain the heavy use of such programmes by those who have recently left the educational system (Werquin, 1997).

The second aspect, described in France as well as the UK, is the high selectivity of the training programmes. The better the scheme is, the better the young people applying for it are. In this respect, such schemes differ little from the selection processes already in place in the labour market. A third aspect is the risk associated with failing to reach the required standards of the training schemes. As in the UK, young people who fail the examinations or drop out have a much lower probability of obtaining a first job, irrespective of the nature of the job (Sollogoub and Ulrich, 1997).

Thus these various studies show that training programmes have different impacts that are dependent not only on their content and participants' employment history but also, and perhaps mainly, on the tightness of youth labour markets (White and McRae, 1989; Werquin, 1997). Overall, they do not profoundly reshape the matching process between the educational system and the labour markets; rather, they play the dual role of simultaneously screening and stigmatizing participants.

The role of short-term jobs
Human capital theorists argue that the development of short-term and/or part-time jobs should increase the employability of young people by giving them opportunities to acquire work experience. However, the human capital approach ignores the existence of specific segments in the labour markets and the different types of jobs on offer in the various segments. These jobs have also to be located in specific institutional contexts. A lot of short-term jobs for young people in Germany are an integral part of the dual system and should therefore lead to stable full-time employment, whereas in France they are generally subsidized jobs characterized by relatively low transitions to full-time employment.[11]

Thus the role of short-term jobs in determining access to more stable employment is difficult to assess. There are almost no German or British studies of this aspect of labour markets, so we can report only on French studies. Le Goff (1995a, 1995b) has shown, using duration models, that the probability of entering full-time employment is reduced once individuals have experienced short-term employment. Thus indirect access to full-time employment is riskier than direct access. This is, however, dependent on gender and educational and family background, as well as on industry and size of firm. The embeddedness of these jobs in certain sectors and labour market segments may explain these results.

Short-term employment contracts do not assist entry to more stable employment in France. This could again be the result of either rationing or signalling, or of a combination of the two. These findings cannot be applied to the UK or Germany because of the different nature of such contracts and the different labour market conditions.

3 EMPLOYMENT REGIMES, YOUTH LABOUR MARKETS AND TRANSITIONAL LABOUR MARKETS

This chapter has revealed the specificity of young people's role in employment regimes, on the one hand, and social exclusion, on the other, and illustrated the problems of 'learning' or 'borrowing' from 'best practices' in other countries.

Section 1 showed that the three countries are characterized by different labour market outcomes as well as different institutional settings. The excluded and marginalized groups are not the same in the three countries. Section 2 showed that youth employment markets in the three countries are very different. They are differently configured and the principles driving the various transition processes are by no means the same. The German school-to-work transitions are the most stable ones and are the result of an employer-led, decentralized vocational system (Büchtemann *et al.*, 1994). However, these good and stable labour market transitions are achieved at the expense of stigmatizing those young people who fail to obtain access to the recognized pathways into employment. The UK and France, on the other hand, are characterized by a lack of coordination between the education and training system and the labour market, which in part explains the high mobility of young people between the different labour market statuses. The introduction of transitional statuses such as training scheme places, part-time jobs and subsidized employment contracts has probably not been as successful as expected. Indeed, we would argue that they have not significantly improved young people's labour market situation. Because of the shortage of employment opportunities for young people, the effects of these transitional statuses have not proved to be markedly different from those of the selection processes already taking place in labour markets; that is, screening, on the one hand, and stigmatization, on the other. The different research results in France show, however, that it is not so much the individual experience of marginal employment statuses that is stigmatizing but rather a sequence of such statuses (Balsan *et al.*, 1996).

This specific analysis of youth labour markets in three countries has also provided food for thought as to how the concept of transitional labour markets might best be mobilized and applied in specific institutional environments. There are four conclusions that can be derived from this analysis. First, and most obviously, universal labour market policy prescriptions must be avoided. We have identified differences not only in the extent of the problem of youth labour markets but also in the nature of the problem of integration. For example, in Germany it is a small group of young people without formally validated skills who bear most of the burden of exclusion, but policies borrowed from elsewhere, such as expanding the number of low-skilled jobs, might be counterproductive in the German context. All policies, even good ones, have costs: identifying the 'losers' from a good transition policy does not mean that there are any better policies on offer. In the UK, the problem is not so much establishing access to the labour market but how to transform low-paid and unstable jobs into the first rungs of a ladder to more stable and higher-paid employment. However, this is a general problem for the UK labour market and young people are only one of several groups in the unstable segment of the labour market. In France, the problem of concentration in low-skilled and unstable jobs is more specifically a youth problem and here, therefore, the focus needs to be on preventing involvement in state training or wage subsidy schemes and the associated risk of permanent stigmatization. All countries need transitional labour market policies even if they take different forms and often address different problems.

The second, related conclusion is that the evaluation of transitional labour market policies needs to take into account their impact on lifetime trajectories and not simply the impact on current employment levels. For example, the creation of more low-skilled jobs in Germany might alleviate the apparent problems of social exclusion among unskilled young people in the short term, but could create more problems of social stigmatization in the longer term if such jobs lead to the erection of further barriers blocking access to jobs that provide training opportunities. Such outcomes are not inevitable, but the role of transitional labour market programmes in stigmatization as well as in screening and selection neeeds to be recognized and further researched.

Thirdly, the interlocking nature of labour market institutions needs to be taken into account in the formulation of transitional labour market policies. This follows from the recognition that the form and the extent of social exclusion differ from country to country and that differentiated policies are therefore required. However, we would go further and suggest that even transitional labour market policies which appear to be appropriate for a particular country and a particular labour force category may have unanticipated impacts on other aspects of a societal system or on other labour force groups unless the interlocking nature of a society's institutional arrangements are fully taken into account. Schmid and Schömann (1994) have argued that transitional labour market policies need to meet the criteria of institutional congruency. In Germany, it may be more appropriate to extend the apprenticeship scheme to the adult unemployed than to provide reduced training opportunities for lower-skilled young people, which might encourage employers to opt out of the traditional dual labour market system, thereby putting further pressure on the successful but costly dual training system in Germany.

Fourthly, policies for reducing social exclusion among particular labour force categories, such as young people, have to be considered against the over-all pattern of labour market organization and opportunities for all groups. A good transition for one group might, in part at least, be achieved at the expense of excluding other groups (for example prime-age women in Germany). Similarly, policies for alleviating 'bad transitions' among young people, for example in France, could result in a destabilization of internal labour markets for prime-age workers of both sexes, with potential consequences for the share of households without wage earners as older workers are displaced from the labour market. However, there are also opportunities for groups within the labour market to recognize a common level of interest and to combine to improve the conditions for all marginalized groups. Such an opportunity existed in the UK with the introduction of the minimum wage, which should in principle have benefited both prime-age women and young people, the two main sources of low-paid labour. However, the decision to set a significantly lower minimum wage of £3 per hour for young people up to age 22, compared with the higher rate of £3.60 per hour, opens up once again the possibility and likelihood of competition and substitution between these two groups. This was to some extent the objective of a government seeking to safeguard the New Deal for young people by ensuring that the wages employers had to pay would remain low. Thus it was implicitly accepted that the success of the New Deal might be achieved at the expense of other, more highly-paid adult groups in the labour market.

The transitional labour market approach accords with the view that it is possible to develop and improve labour market institutions in such a way as to generate more employment opportunities and to distribute them more equi-tably. The extent to which such objectives can be achieved through supply-side reforms, without the appropriate macro-level conditions, is a matter for debate at the heart of Europe's current employment strategy. However, it is also clear that, without new forms of labour market organization, favourable macroeconomic conditions will not necessarily bring about good transitions into employment and a reduction in social exclusion. Thus the development of better transitional labour markets and favourable demand conditions may perhaps best be regarded as complements and not competitors in the policy arena. Yet the transitional labour market approach still has to confront the issue of how to deal with different interests in the labour market.

It has been argued that the solution to these problems lies in ensuring that transitional labour market programmes reflect negotiated or collectively agreed systems for the distribution of income and job opportunities (Schmid, 1998). However, many of the groups facing social exclusion are not adequately represented in collective arrangements, even where these exist at national or industry level. Ultimately, therefore, the form taken by transitional labour market policies will depend on governments' judgments as to the political priority to be accorded to the varying groups competing for a scarce supply of jobs in the labour market and also on the priority they attach to employment objectives over the potentially conflicting objectives of fair wage remuneration and prospects for transition into stable and satisfying jobs. Analyses of transitional labour market policies can point to the areas of mutual gain as well as to areas of competing interests between labour force groups. They can also identify trade-offs and complementarities between policies of maximizing the share in employment, on the one hand, and policies intended to create good employment transitions, on the other. However, the priorities to be attached to these objectives are and will continue to be a matter of political decision.

NOTES

1. It is generally assumed that individuals trying to enter the labour market constitute a very heterogeneous population and that work experience has some impact on individuals' employability. These two dimensions are commonly associated with distinct employment trajectories. Espinasse and Vincens (1997), however, use a simulation to show that job rationing, even in the case of a homogeneous population with no work experience affecting employability, can generate a variety of different employment trajectories.
2. 'There is in France a long tradition of conflictive relations between capital and labour, with a few explicit compromises and even less of a consensus. Thus the state has been a key actor in wage and price formation, frequently imposing norms and rules on weak employers' associations and reluctant trade unions' (Boyer, 1994b: 53).
3. 'De ce fait, le salaire d'un employé tient davantage que par le passé à la nature de l'entreprise dans laquell il travaille et à son secteur d'activité, qu'à sa compétence et au lieu géographique où elle s'exerce. Il y a donc accélération d'une orientation, depuis longtemps évidente: que la salaire dépend davantage des facteurs liés au marché des produits qu' à ceux du travail' (Brown, 1994: 43).
4. Labour market turnover rate is defined as (new contracts + terminated contracts)/employment. It is measured continuously over a certain time period. Job flows, on the contrary, are

defined as the gross change in the number of jobs within an industry or in the economy. The job turnover rate is defined as (gross job gains + gross job loses)/employment and is based on a time-discrete measurement (Schettkat, 1996a). Flows of workers are therefore measured by the labour turnover rate and job flows by the job turnover rate.

5. Dufour and Werquin (1997) use longitudinal data to show that the domestic and employment thresholds are closely related. It is young individuals in full-time employment who tend to leave their families first, independently of the fact that women leave their families earlier.

6. These patterns may be explained by relatively short unemployment spells in Germany compared to longer training programmes in the UK.

7. These statements have been retrieved from the ERSEP CD-ROM.

8. However, Balsan *et al.* (1996) show that educational level tends to retain a certain influence even after five years' labour market experience.

9. Another trend in the French labour market is the opening up of closed labour markets in large firms and organizations in response to the increased number of highly educated people entering the external labour market. The filling of these positions by young individuals could lead to a profound reshaping of the promotion patterns of low-skilled workers as managerial positions are filled from outside and for longer periods (because of the relative youth of the new workforce).

10. 'Regional imbalances are most obviously observed between West and East Germany. While in the first half of 1993 in West Germany each applicant could choose between two positions supplied, in April 1993 two thirds of all East German applicants had not yet found a training position. As of November 1993, some 146 000 applicants in East Germany had been offered 84 000 apprenticeship positions in the private sector in 1993. About 50 000 had found a position in West Germany and more than 5 000 youths received training in public training centres' (Franz and Soskice, 1995: 212).

11. A preliminary study by one of the present authors has indeed shown that short-term employment contracts tend to lead to full-time employment contracts (Detzel, 1998). This can be explained by the fact that young people in the dual system (which is characterized by good transition functions to full-time employment) are linked to the labour market through short-term contracts.

BIBLIOGRAPHY

Agullo, M.H. and N. Skourias (1995), 'Processus d'appariement sur le marché du travail: une analyse économétrique des disparités régionales sur données de panel', in A. Degenne, M. Mansuy and P. Werquin (eds), *Trajectoires et insertions professionnelles*, Marseilles: Céreq, pp. 275–94.

Almond, P. and J. Rubery (2000), 'Deregulation and societal systems', in M. Maurice and A. Sorge (eds), *Embedding Organizations*, Amsterdam: John Benjamins.

Andrews, M. and S. Bradley (1997), 'Modelling the transition from school and the demand for training in the UK', *Economica*, 64, 387–413.

Ashton, D., M. Maguire and M. Spilsbury (1990), *Restructuring the labour market: the implications for youth*, London: Macmillan.

Atkinson, T. (1987), 'Flexibility or fragmentation? The United Kingdom labour market in the eighties', *Labour and Society*, 12, 88–105.

Balson, D., S. Hanchane and P. Werquin (1996), 'Mobilité professionnelle initiale: éducation contre expérience professionnelle. Un modèle provit à effets aléatoires', *Economie et statistique*, 299, 95–106.

Banks, J. (1994), *Strategies to improve young people's access to, and their progression within, initial vocational training*, Brussels: European Commission.

Bates, I. and G. Riseborough (1993), *Youth and Inequality*, Buckingham: Open University Press.

Beduwé, C., F. Dauty and J.M. Espinasse (1995), 'Trajectoires types d'insertion professionnelle. Application au cas des bacheliers professionnels', in A. Degenne, M. Mansuy and P. Werquin (eds), *Trajectoires et insertions professionnelles*, Marseilles: Céreq, pp. 7–26.

Béret, P. (1994), 'Investissement et interactions d'emploi: le temps du longitudinal', in M. Ourteau and P. Werquin (eds), *L'analyse longitudinal du marché du travail*, Marseilles: Céreq, pp. 51–62.

Bellmann, L. and F. Buttler (1994), 'The transition process in Eastern Germany: an inflow–outflow analysis', in J. Schwarze, F. Buttler and G. Wagner (eds), *Labour Market Dynamics in Present Day Germany*, New York and Frankfurt: Campus Westview, pp. 17–39.

Blossfeld, H.P. (1990), 'Berufsverlaufe und Arbeitsmarktprozesse. Ergebnisse sozialstruktureller Längtschnittuntersuchungen', *Koelner Zeitschrift fuer Soziologie*, Sonderheft 31, 118–45.

Blossfeld, H.P. (1991), 'Changes in educational opportunities in the FRG. A longitudinal study of cohorts born between 1916 and 1965', in Y. Shavit and H.P. Blossfeld (eds), *Persisting Inequality*, Boulder, CO: Westview Press, pp. 51–74.

Blossfeld, H.P. (1994), 'Different systems of vocational training and transition from school to career: The German dual system in cross-national comparison', in CEDEFOP (ed.), *The Determinants of Transitions in Youth*, Berlin: CEDEFOP.

Blossfeld, H.P., G. Giannelli and K.U. Mayer (1993), 'Is there a new service proletariat? The tertiary sector and social inequality in Germany', in G. Esping-Andersen (ed.), *Changing Classes*, London: Sage, pp. 109–35.

Bonnal, L., D. Fougère and A. Sérandon (1994), 'Une évaluation de l'impact des politiques d'emploi françaises sur les transitions individuelles sur le marché du travail', in M. Ourteau and P. Werquin (eds), *L'analyse longitudinale du marché du travail*, Marseilles: Céreq, pp. 133–74.

Boyer, R. (1986), *La théorie de la régulation. Une analyse critique*, Paris: La découverte.

Boyer, R. (1987a), 'L'évolution du rapport salarial dans sept pays européens', in R. Boyer (ed.), *La flexibilité du travail en Europe*, Paris: La découverte, pp. 11–34.

Boyer, R. (1987b), 'Convergences et spécificités nationales' in R. Boyer (ed.), *La flexibilité du travail en Europe*, Paris: La découverte, pp. 207–34.

Boyer, R. (1994a), 'Introduction: retour de la politique des revenus?', in R. Boyer and R. Dore (eds), *Les politiques des revenus en Europe*, Paris: La découverte, pp. 7–32.

Boyer, R. (1994b), 'Des réformes salariales impulsées par l'Etat: trois paradoxes de la politique des revenus en France', in R. Boyer and R. Dore (eds), *Les politiques des revenus en Europe*, Paris: La découverte, pp. 50–74.

Boyer, R. and R. Dore (eds) (1994), *Les politiques des revenus en Europe*, Paris: La découverte.

Bradley, S. and J. Taylor (1991), 'An empirical analysis of unemployment duration of school-leavers', *Applied Economics*, 24, 89–101.

Brown, W. (1994), 'Du pouvoir syndical aux stratégies des firmes: l'expérience britannique', in R. Boyer and R. Dore (eds), *Les politiques des revenus en Europe*, Paris: La découverte, pp. 35–49.

Brown, W.A. and J. Walsh (1991), 'Pay determination in Britain in the 1980s: the anatomy of decentralisation', *Oxford Review of Economic Policy*, 7.

Büchtemann, C.F., J. Schupp and D. Soloff. (1993), 'Roads to work: school-to-work transition patterns in Germany and the US', *Industrial Relations Journal*, 24, 97–111.

Büchtemann, C., J. Schupp and D. Soloff (1994), 'From school to work: patterns in Germany and the United States', in J. Schwarze, F. Buttler and G. Wagner (eds), *Labour Market Dynamics in Present Day Germany*, Frankfurt am Main: Campus Westview, pp. 112–41.

Buttler, F., W. Franz, R. Schettkat and D. Soskice (eds) (1995), *Institutional Frameworks and Labor Market Performance: Comparative Views on the US and German Economies*, London and New York: Routledge.

Buttler, F., W. Franz, R. Schettkat and D. Soskice (1995), 'Institutional frameworks and labour market performance', in F. Buttler, W. Franz, R. Schettkat and D. Soskice (eds), *Institutional Frameworks and Labor Market Performance: Comparative Views on the US and German Economies*, London and New York: Routledge, pp. 1–19.

Bynner, J. and K. Roberts (1991), *Youth and Work: Transition to Employment in England and Germany*, London: Anglo-German Foundation.

Cahuzac, E., D. Martinelli and F. Stoeffler-Kern (1997), 'Cursus de formation dans l'enseignement supérieur et trajectoires d'insertion', in A. Degenne, Y. Grelet, J.F. Lochet, M. Mansuy and P. Werquin (eds), *L'analyse longitidinale du marché du travail: les politiques d'emploi*, Marseilles: Céreq, pp. 345–72.

Cavalli, A. and O. Galland (1993), *L'allongement de la jeunesse. Changement social en Europe*, Paris: Actes sud.

Cavalli, A. and O. Galland (eds) (1995), *Youth in Europe: Social Change in Western Europe*, London: Pinter.

Charpail, C., F. Piot and S. Zilberman (1997), 'Panel de bénéficiaires des politiques d'emploi et évaluation', in A. Degenne, Y. Grelet, J.F. Lochet, M. Mansuy and P. Werquin (eds), *L'analyse longitudinale du marché du travail: les politiques d'emploi*, Marseilles: Céreq, pp. 17–34.

Chastand, A. and D. Gelot (1996), 'Eléments de réflexion pour une analyse longitudinale des modes de gestion des mesures de politique d'emploi par les entreprises utilisatrices', in A. Degenne, M. Mansuy, G. Podevin and P. Werquin (eds), *Typologie des marchés du travail. Suivi et parcours*, Marseilles: Céreq, pp. 157–68.

Chisholm, L. (1995) 'Conclusion', in A. Cavalli and O. Galland (eds), *Youth in Europe: Social Change in Western Europe*, London: Pinter.

Couppié, T. and P. Werquin (1994), 'Les itinéraires des jeunes dans les dispositifs publics d'aide a l'insertion', in M. Ourteau and P. Werquin (eds), *L'analyse longitudinale du marché du travail*, Marseilles: Céreq, pp. 407–36.

Crouch, C. (1994), 'Politiques des revenus, institutions et marchés: présentation des récentes évolutions', in R. Boyer and R. Dore (eds), *Les politiques des revenus en Europe*, Paris: La découverte, pp. 186–207.

Daly, M. and R. Bently (1999), 'New deals statistics and the New Deal Evaluation database', *Labour Market Trends*, April, 197–206.

Deakin, B.M. (1996), *The Youth Labour Market in Britain. The Role of Intervention*, Cambridge: Cambridge University Press

Detzel, P. (1998), 'Youth economic activity patterns in the perspective of changing socioeconomic institutions', CES conference, Dublin.

Dolado, J., F. Kramarz, S. Machin, A. Manning, D. Margolis and C. Teulings (1996), 'The economic impact of minimum wages in Europe', *Economic Policy*, 23, October, 317–72.

Dolton, P.J. (1993), 'The economics of youth training in Britain', *Economic Journal*, 420, 1261–78.

Dolton, P.J., G.G. Makepeace and J. Treble (1991), 'The Youth Training Scheme and the school-to-work transition', *Oxford Economic Papers*, 46, 629–57.

Dufour, S. and P. Werquin (1997), 'Trajectoires professionnelles et familiales: une insertion professionnelle difficile retarde-t-elle l'autonomie des jeunes?', in A. Degenne, M. Mansuy, G. Podevin and P. Werquin (eds), *Typologie des marchés du travail. Suivi et parcours*, Marseilles: Céreq, pp. 299–322.

Espinasse, J.M. and J.F. Giret (1997), 'Trajectoires d'insertion et modélisation des parcours: quelques remarques', in P. Werquin, R. Breen and J. Planas (eds), *Youth Transitions in Europe: Theories and Evidence*, Marseilles: Céreq, pp. 177–204.

Espinasse, J.M. and J. Vincens (1997), 'Rationnement de l'emploi et trajectoires d'insertion', in A. Degenne, Y. Grelet, J.F. Lochet, M. Mansuy and P. Werquin (eds), *L'analyse longitudinale du marché du travail: les politiques d'emploi*, Marseilles: Céreq, pp. 87–100.

Esping-Andersen, G. (1990), *The Three Worlds of Welfare Capitalism*, Cambridge: Cambridge University Press.

Esping-Andersen, G. (1993), *Changing Classes*, London: Sage.

European Commission (1997), *Key data on education in the European Union*, Luxembourg: Office for Official Publications of the European Communities.

Eurostat (1997), *Youth in Europe: From Education to Working Life*, Office for Official Publications of the European Communities, Luxembourg.

Finegold, D. and S. Soskice (1988), 'The failure of training in Britain: analysis and prescription', *Oxford Bulletin of Economics and Statistics*, 4, 21–53.

Florens, J.P. and D. Fougère (1992), 'Point processes', in L. Matyas and P. Sevestre (eds), *The econometrics of panel data*, Dordrecht: Kluwer Academic Press, pp. 316–52.

Florens, J.P. and T. Kamionka (1994), 'Analyse des biographies individuelles: éléments de modélisation et exemples de résultats', in F. Bouchayer (ed.), *Trajectoires sociales et inégalités*, Ramonville: Erés, pp. 273–96.

Florens, J.P., D. Fougère and P. Werquin (1990), 'Durées de chômage et transitions sur le marché du travail', *Sociologie du travail*, 4, 439–68.

Florens, J.P., D. Fougère, T. Kamionka and M. Mouchart (1994), 'La modélisation économétrique des transitions individuelles sur le marché du travail', *Economie et prévision*, 116.

Fougère, D. (1996), 'Aspects of labour force dynamics in France', in R. Schettkat (ed.), *The Flow Analysis of Labour Markets*, London: Routledge, pp. 152–68.

Franz, W. and D. Soskice (1995), 'The German apprenticeship system', in F. Buttler, W. Franz, R. Schettkat and D. Soskice (eds), *Institutional Frameworks and Labour Market Performance*, London: Routledge, pp. 208–34.

Furlong, A. and F. Cartmel (1997), *Young People and Social Change. Individualization and Risk in Late Modernity*, Buckingham: Open University Press.

Gershuny, J. (1993), 'Post-industrial career structures in Britain', in G. Esping-Andersen (ed.), *Changing Classes*, London: Sage, pp. 136–70.

Granovetter, M. (1985), 'Economic action and social structure: the problem of embeddedness', *American Journal of Sociology*, 91, 481–510.

Green, A. (1995), 'The role of the state and social partners in VET systems', in L. Bash and A. Green (eds), *Youth, Education and Work*, London: Kogan Page, pp. 80–91.

Hall, J. and K. Reid (1998), 'New Deal for the young unemployed: monitoring and evaluation', *Labour Market Trends*, November, 549–53.

Helberger, C., U. Rendtel and J. Schwarze (1994), 'Labour market entry of young people analysed by a double threshold model', in J. Schwarze, F. Buttler and G. Wagner (eds), *Labour Market Dynamics in Present Day Germany*, Frankfurt am Main: Campus Westview, pp. 142–64.

Hildebrandt, S. (1996), 'Berufsausbildung in Frankreich zwischen Staat, Region und Unternehmen', WZB Discussion paper, FS I 96–101, WZB, Berlin.

Howard, S. and S. Stone (1999), 'Modern apprenticeships: four years on', *Labour Market Trends*, February, 75–81.

Kerckhoff, A.C. (1990), *Getting Started: Transition to Adulthood in Great Britain*, Boulder, CO: Westview Press.

Kerckhoff, A.C. (1993), *Diverging Pathways*, Cambridge: Cambridge University Press.

Kerckhoff, A.C. (1996), *Generating Social Stratification*, Boulder, CO: Westview Press.

Lefresne, F. (1996), 'Jeunes et dispositifs d'insertion dans six pays européens', *Agora débats jeunesse*, 3, 23–36.

Le Goff, J.M. (1995a), 'Les processus d'entrée dans la vie active: caractéristiques individuelles et marché du travail', doctoral thesis, Université de Paris I.

Le Goff, J.M. (1995b), 'Processus d'accès à un emploi sur contrat à durée indéterminée des jeunes sortis de terminale en 1983', in A. Degenne, M. Mansuy and P. Werquin (eds), *Trajectoires et insertions professionnelles*, Marseilles: Céreq, pp. 313–30.

Leithaüser, G. (1987), 'Des flexibilités . . . et pourtant une crise: la république fédérale d'Allemagne', in R. Boyer (eds), *La flexibilité du travail en Europe*, Paris: La découverte, pp. 181–206.

Licht, G. and V. Steiner (1994), 'Where have all the workers gone? Employment termination in East Germany after Unification', in J. Schwarze, F. Buttler and G. Wagner (eds), *Labour Market Dynamics in Present Day Germany,* Frankfurt am Main: Campus Westview, pp. 40–66.

Lindey, A. (1996) 'The school to work transition in the UK', *International Labour Review*, 135.

Lollivier, S. (1994), 'L'évolution du marche du travail dans les années quatre-vingt', *Revu Économique*, 43, 429–41.

Louzeau, O. (1997), 'Segmentation et mouvements intersectoriels de la main d'œuvre dans une approche du marché du travail', in A. Degenne, M. Mansuy, G. Podevin and P. Werquin (eds), *Typologie des marchés du travail. Suivi et parcours*, Marseilles: Céreq, pp. 181–96.

Main, B. (1992), 'The effect of the Youth Training Scheme on the employment probability', *Applied Economics*, 23, 367–72.

Main, B. and M. Shelly (1990), 'The effectiveness of the Youth Training Scheme as a manpower policy', *Economica*, 57, 495–514.

Mansuy, M. (1995), 'L'observatoire national des entrées dans la vie active du Céreq', in A. Degenne, M. Mansuy and P. Werquin (eds), *Trajectoires et insertions professionnelles*, Marseilles: Céreq, pp. 353–60.

Marsden, D. and P. Ryan (1995), 'Work, labour markets and vocational preparation: Anglo-German comparisons of training in intermediate skills', in L. Bash and A. Green (eds), *Youth, Education and Work*, London: Kogan Page, pp. 67–79.

Martinez, E. and A. Vanheerswynghels (1997), 'Contribution des enquêtes longitudinales à l'évaluation des politiques de l'emploi', in A. Degenne, Y. Grelet, J.F. Lochet, M. Mansuy and P. Werquin (eds), *L'analyse longitudinale du marché du travail: les politiques d'emploi*, Marseilles: Céreq, pp. 35–46.

Maurice, M., F. Sellier and J-J. Sivester (1986), *The Social Foundations of Industrial Power*: Cambridge, MA: MIT Press.

Moebius, M. and E. Verdier (1997), 'La construction des diplômes professionnels en Allemagne et en France', *Bref*, 130.

Moncel, N. (1997), 'Profils sectoriels de gestion de la main-dœuvre: quelles conséquences pour l'emploi des jeunes', in P. Werquin, R. Breen and J. Planas (eds), *Youth Transitions in Europe: Theories and Evidence*, Marseilles: Céreq, pp. 135–62.

OECD (1993), *Employment Outlook*, Paris: OECD.

OECD (1996), *Employment Outlook*, Paris: OECD.

OECD (1997), *Employment Outlook*, Paris: OECD.

OECD (1998), *Employment Outlook*, Paris: OECD.

O'Higgins, N. (1994), 'YTS, employment and sample selection bias', *Oxford Economic Papers*, 46, 605–28.

O'Reilly, J. (1992), 'Comparaison des stratégies d'emploi flexible dans le secteur bancaire en Grande-Bretagne et en France', *Sociologie du travail*, 3, 55–80.

O'Reilly, J. (1994), *Banking on Flexibility*, Aldershot: Avebury.

Parmentier, K. and M. Tessaring (1994), 'The dynamics of transitions in East Germany: stocks and flows by level of qualification between 1989 and 1991' in J. Schwarze, F. Buttler, and G. Wagner (eds), *Labour Market Dynamics in Present Day Germany*, Frankfurt am Main: Campus Westview, pp. 67–90.

Penard, T. and M. Solongoub (1995), 'Les politiques françaises d'emploi en faveur des jeunes', *Revue Économique*, 46.

Petit, P. (1987), 'Heurs et malheurs de l'Etat face au rapport salarial: la France', in R. Boyer (ed.), *La flexibilité du travail en Europe*, Paris: La découverte, pp. 35–64.

Presse- und Informationsdienst der Bundesregierung (1999a), 'Besserung am Lehrstellenmarkt', *Sozialpolitische Umschau*, 329.

Presse- und Informationsdienst der Bundesregierung (1999b), 'Jugendliche ohne abgeschlossene Berufsbildung', *Sozialpolitische Umschau*, 331.

Roberts, K. (1993), 'Career trajectories and the mirage of increased social mobility', in I. Bates and G. Riseborough (eds), *Youth and Inequality*, Buckingham: Open University Press, pp. 229–45.

Roberts, K. (1995), *Youth and Employment in Modern Britain*, Oxford: Oxford University Press.

Rubery, J., C. Fagan, D. Grimshaw and M. Smith (1998), *Women and European Employment*, London: Routledge.

Sanders, K. and H. Becker (1994), 'The transition from education to work and social independence: a comparison between the United States, the Netherlands, West Germany and the United Kingdom; *European Sociological Review*, 10, 135–54.

Scherer, S. (1998), 'Early career patterns: a comparison of the United Kingdom and Germany', in D. Raffe, R. Van der Velden and P. Werquin (eds), *Education, the Labour Market and Transitions in Youth: Cross-National Perspectives*, Edinburgh: CES.

Schettkat, R. (1995), 'The macroeconomic performance of the German labour market', in F. Buttler, W. Franz, R. Schettkat and D. Soskice (eds), *Institutional Frameworks and Labour Market Performance*, London: Routledge, pp. 316–43.

Schettkat, R. (1996a), 'The flow approach to labour market analysis. Introduction', in R. Schettkat (ed.), *The Flow Analysis of Labour Markets*, London: Routledge, pp. 1–13.

Schettkat, R. (1996b), 'Flows in labour markets. Concepts and international comparative results', in R. Schettkat (ed.), *The Flow Analysis of Labour Markets*, London: Routledge, pp. 14–36.

Schettkat, R. (1996c), 'Labour market dynamics in Germany', in R. Schettkat (ed.), *The Flow Analysis of Labour Markets*, London: Routledge, pp. 256–71.

Schmid, G. (1998), 'Transitional labour markets: a new European employment strategy', WZB Discussion Paper FS I 98–206, WZB, Berlin.

Schmid, G. and K. Schömann (1994), 'Institutional Choice and Flexible Coordination: A Socioeconomic Evaluation of Labor Market Policy in Europe', in G. Schmid (ed.), *Labor Market Policy in Europe: A Socioeconomic Evaluation of Performance*, London and New York: M.E. Sharpe, pp. 9–57.

Schulze, E. and E. Kirner (1994), 'The importance of discontinuous female employment for the labour market in West Germany', in J. Schwarze, F. Buttler and G. Wagner (eds), *Labour Market Dynamics in Present Day Germany*, Frankfurt am Main: Campus Westview, pp. 165–86.

Schwarze, J., F. Buttler and G. Wagner (eds) (1994a), *Labour Market Dynamics in Present Day Germany*, Frankfurt am Main: Campus Westview.

Schwarze, J., F. Buttler and G. Wagner (1994b), 'Labour market dynamics in present day Germany: scope, data and overview', in J. Schwarze, F. Buttler and G. Wagner (eds), *Labour Market Dynamics in Present Day Germany*, Frankfurt: Campus Westview, pp. 8–16.

Sollogoub, M. and V. Ulrich (1997), 'L'entrée dans la vie active: la rôle de l'apprentissage', in A. Degenne, Y. Grelet, J.F. Lochet, M. Mansuy and P. Werquin (eds), *L'analyse longitudinale du marché du travail: les politiques d'emploi*, Marseilles: Céreq, pp. 299–322.

Soskice, D. (1993), 'Social skills from mass higher education: rethinking the company-based initial training paradigm', *Oxford Bulletin of Economics and Statistics*, 9, 101–13.

Steedman, H. (1987), 'Vocational training in France and Britain: office work', *National Institute Economic Review*, 58–70.

Steedman, H., G. Mason and K. Wagner (1991), 'The deployment of skills in manufacturing in three European member states', in L. Hantrais, M. O'Brien and S. Mangen (eds), *Education, Training and Labour Markets in Europe*, Birmingham: Cross-national Research Group, pp. 35–43.

Streeck, W. (1994), 'Modérations salariales sans politiques des revenus: institutionnalisation du monétarisme et du syndicalisme en Allemagne', in R. Boyer and R. Dore (eds), *Les politiques des revenus en Europe*, Paris: La découverte, pp. 147–64.

Verdier, E. (1995), 'Politiques de formation des jeunes et marché du travail', *Formation Emploi*, 50, 19–40.

Verdier, E. (1996), 'L'insertion de jeunes "à la française": vers un ajustement structurel?', *Travail et emploi*, 4.

Werquin, P. (1996), 'Les dispositifs d'aide à l'insertion des jeunes: différer l'âge d'accès a l'emploi?', *Céreq-Bref*, 119.

Werquin, P. (1997), 'Les dispositifs d'aide a l'insertion des jeunes a partir des trois panels téléphoniques du Cereq (1986–1996)', in A. Degenne, Y. Grelet, J.F. Lochet, M. Mansuy and P. Werquin (eds), *L'analyse longitudinale du marché du travail: les politiques d'emploi*, Marseilles: Céreq, pp. 63–86.

White, M. and S. McRae (1989), *Young Adults and Long-term Unemployment*, London: Policy Study Institute.

Witte, J. and A. Kalleberg (1995), 'Matching training and jobs: the fit between vocational education and employment in the German Labour market', *European Sociological Review*, 11, 293–317.

APPENDIX

Table 4A.1 Public expenditure and participant inflows in labour market programmes in France

	Public expenditures as % of GDP				Participants inflows as % of the labour force			
	1991	1992	1993	1994	1991	1992	1993	1994
1. Public employment services and administration	0.13	0.14	0.15	0.16				
2. Labour market training	0.35	0.39	0.45	0.44	5.7	5.6	5.6	5.4
Unemployed adults	0.29	0.32	0.39	0.39	3.8	3.9	4.0	4.0
Employed adults	0.06	0.06	0.05	0.06	1.9	1.7	1.6	1.4
3. Youth measures	0.23	0.26	0.29	0.27	3.1	3.4	3.1	3.2
Unemployed, disadvantaged	0.09	0.08	0.10	0.08	1.3	1.3	1.3	1.1
Apprenticeship, training	0.14	0.17	0.19	0.18	1.8	2.1	1.9	2.1
4. Subsidized employment	0.11	0.13	0.20	0.21	1.2	1.8	2.4	2.9
Regular employment	0.05	0.04	0.04	0.05	0.4	0.4	0.5	0.8
Self-employment	0.02	0.02	0.02	0.03	0.2	0.2	0.2	0.3
Direct job creation	0.04	0.07	0.13	0.13	0.6	1.2	1.6	1.8
5. Measures for disabled	0.06	0.08	0.09	0.08	0.1	0.2	0.3	0.4
6. Unemploy. compensation	1.47	1.61	1.73	1.57				
7. Early retirement	0.47	0.40	0.39	0.38				
TOTAL	2.82	3.00	3.28	3.12				
Active measures (1–5)	0.89	1.00	1.17	1.17	10.2	11.1	11.4	11.9
Passive measures (6–7)	1.94	2.01	2.11	1.95				

Source: OECD (1996: 207).

Table 4A.2 Public expenditure and participant inflows in labour market programmes in Germany

	Public expenditures as % of GDP				Participants inflows as % of the labour force			
	1992	1993	1994	1995	1992	1993	1994	1995
1. Public employment services and administration	0.24	0.25	0.24	0.23				
2. Labour market training	0.65	0.56	0.42	0.38	4.1	1.9	1.8	2.0
Unemployed adults	0.62	0.53	0.40	0.38	3.6	1.6	1.7	1.9
Employed adults	0.03	0.03	0.02	–	0.5	0.3	0.1	–
3. Youth measures	0.06	0.07	0.06	0.06	0.6	0.6	0.6	0.7
Unemployed, disadvantaged	0.05	0.06	0.06	0.05	0.4	0.4	0.4	0.4
Apprenticeship, training	0.01	0.01	0.01	0.01	0.2	0.2	0.2	0.2
4. Subsidized employment	0.51	0.47	0.20	0.21	1.2	1.1	1.3	1.3
Regular employment	0.07	0.07	0.06	0.07	0.2	0.1	0.1	0.2
Self-employment	–	–	0.01	0.02	–	0.1	0.1	0.2
Direct job creation	0.43	0.40	0.31	0.31	1.0	1.0	1.1	0.9
5. Measures for disabled	0.25	0.28	0.26	0.26	0.3	0.2	0.2	0.3
6. Unemploy. compensation	1.48	2.00	2.03	2.08				
7. Early retirement	0.47	0.59	0.27	0.06				
TOTAL	3.65	4.21	3.66	3.47	6.3	3.9	4.0	4.2
Active measures (1–5)	1.69	1.62	1.35	1.33				
Passive measures (6–7)	1.96	2.59	2.31	2.14				

Source: OECD (1996: 207).

143

Table 4A.3 Public expenditure and participant inflows in labour market programmes in the UK

	Public expenditures as % of GDP				Participants inflows as % of the labour force			
	1992	1993	1994	1995	1992	1993	1994	1995
1. Public employment services and administration	0.20	0.22	0.24	0.21				
2. Labour market training	0.15	0.13	0.15	0.13	1.0	1.1	1.3	1.2
Unemployed adults	0.15	0.13	0.14	0.12	0.9	1.1	1.2	1.2
Employed adults	–	–	0.01	0.01	–	–	–	0.1
3. Youth measures	0.17	0.15	0.14	0.13	0.7	0.7	0.8	0.9
Unemployed, disadvantaged	–	–	–	–	–	–	–	–
Apprenticeship, training	0.17	0.15	0.14	0.13	0.7	0.6	0.8	0.8
4. Subsidized employment	0.02	0.04	0.02	0.03	0.2	0.1	0.2	0.3
Regular employment	–	–	–	–	–	–	–	–
Self-employment	0.02	0.01	0.02	0.01	0.2	0.1	0.1	0.1
Direct job creation	–	0.03	–	0.01	–	–	–	0.2
5. Measures for disabled	0.02	0.03	0.03	0.03	0.1	0.1	0.1	0.2
6. Unemployment compensation	1.41	1.59	1.60	1.41				
7. Early retirement	–	–	–	–				
TOTAL	1.98	2.15	2.17	1.94				
Active measures (1–5)	0.57	0.56	0.57	0.53	1.9	2.0	2.4	2.5
Passive measures (6–7)	1.41	1.59	1.60	1.41				

Source: OECD (1996: 207).

Table 4A.4   *Share of employed and unemployed who were inactive one year previously, 1992*

	Share of employed men (%)	Share of employed women (%)	Share of unemployed men (%)	Share of unemployed women (%)
France	4.4	7.2	19	26
Germany				
(United)	3.5	6.2	17	18
UK	8.1	12.2	14	26

Source: Rubery *et al.* (1998: 127 and 141).

Table 4A.5   Activity rates by age groups, gender, educational level, 1996 (per cent)

		15–24				25–49				50–64			
		FT	PT	Unempl.	Inactiv.	FT	PT	Unempl.	Inactiv.	FT	PT	Unempl.	Inactiv.
Low education													
Male	W. Germany	33.2	1.9	5.0	59.9	74.5	2.3	13.0	10.2	46.4	2.0	8.9	42.7
	E. Germany	39.5	0.5	2.6	57.4	65.4	2.2	20.5	11.9	25.6	2.1	10.4	62.0
	France	17.4	3.3	9.4	69.9	77.0	3.8	12.9	6.3	39.6	3.3	4.6	52.5
	UK	32.7	13.6	13.0	40.7	74.7	2.9	11.1	11.3	55.6	4.6	6.7	33.1
	EC15	28.4	5.6	10.3	55.7	77.8	2.6	11.0	8.6	49.2	2.8	5.4	42.6
Female	W. Germany	23.5	3.0	3.1	70.4	30.1	22.7	7.1	40.2	13.8	14.7	3.9	67.7
	E. Germany	27.7	1.1	2.3	68.9	35.0	14.2	18.1	32.7	8.3	5.5	10.1	76.1
	France	6.8	5.2	7.5	80.6	37.4	19.2	13.3	30.0	20.8	11.3	3.3	64.5
	UK	23.6	19.7	6.9	49.9	30.4	31.4	5.0	33.2	24.1	35.1	2.6	38.3
	EC15	17.2	7.7	8.4	66.7	32.2	16.9	9.1	41.8	17.2	11.2	2.7	69.0
Medium education													
Male	W. Germany	62.7	4.0	6.3	27.0	83.3	3.1	5.9	7.7	57.9	1.8	5.8	34.5
	E. Germany	68.4	0.9	11.8	18.8	83.5	0.9	10.3	5.2	44.1	1.1	11.3	43.5
	France	33.6	4.2	10.1	52.1	86.7	2.6	7.8	2.9	51.9	3.5	4.6	40.0
	UK	56.1	12.0	11.3	20.6	85.8	1.9	6.6	5.7	63.5	4.6	6.1	25.7
	EC15	41.0	5.6	10.5	42.8	84.4	2.7	6.7	6.3	57.8	3.0	5.3	33.9
Female	W. Germany	58.1	7.5	4.8	29.6	43.2	26.7	4.9	25.1	23.7	20.7	4.9	50.8
	E. Germany	53.5	7.5	10.8	28.1	53.2	16.3	18.8	11.7	26.3	9.6	15.2	48.9
	France	18.1	12.3	12.7	56.9	52.0	20.2	10.6	17.2	33.2	11.6	4.2	51.0
	UK	42.0	21.8	7.1	29.1	42.4	32.7	4.7	20.3	34.5	36.8	2.6	26.2
	EC15	30.3	10.4	11.3	48.0	47.2	21.8	8.0	23.0	27.9	17.6	4.8	49.7

High education

Male	W. Germany	56.6	2.3	7.1	34.0	90.3	2.8	3.6	3.3	72.8	2.8	4.7	19.7
	E. Germany	65.4	4.2	18.0	12.3	90.7	2.1	5.0	2.2	58.8	2.2	8.8	30.2
	France	34.1	6.3	10.8	48.8	87.3	3.9	5.5	3.3	71.3	3.7	4.0	21.0
	UK	62.8	9.6	11.3	16.3	90.5	2.8	3.7	3.1	64.5	10.9	4.7	19.9
	EC15	45.9	8.1	12.9	33.1	87.9	3.6	4.8	3.8	70.4	4.8	4.2	20.6
Female	W. Germany	64.1	7.6	3.9	24.4	57.4	22.9	4.3	15.4	43.1	19.5	3.8	33.5
	E. Germany	69.7	11.4	5.1	13.9	71.6	14.4	7.7	6.2	48.0	10.3	10.0	31.7
	France	36.8	9.5	12.4	41.3	63.2	18.2	6.8	11.8	48.2	12.2	2.5	37.2
	UK	68.3	12.8	5.7	13.2	59.9	25.8	2.5	11.8	42.7	32.6	1.8	23.0
	EC15	44.7	10.7	14.5	30.1	61.6	19.5	6.3	12.6	46.4	17.8	3.0	32.8

Source: European labour force survey, 1996.

Table 4A.6 Marginal employment by age categories and gender, 1996 (per cent)

		1–10 hrs	11–20 hrs	21–30 hrs	31–35 hrs	36–40 hrs	41–50 hrs	51+ hrs
15–24								
Male	West Germany	3.0	2.1	1.0	5.8	80.8	5.3	2.0
	East Germany	0.9	0.4	0.1	1.5	90.2	4.9	2.0
	France	1.3	6.3	4.4	1.8	72.3	10.3	3.4
	UK	10.4	8.8	4.6	6.4	30.3	28.5	11.0
	EC15	6.1	5.0	3.1	3.9	60.5	16.0	5.5
Female	West Germany	4.5	4.6	3.0	4.2	79.6	3.3	0.9
	East Germany	1.9	2.8	4.7	1.9	85.1	3.0	0.5
	France	4.1	16.1	14.7	4.2	52.8	7.2	0.8
	UK	16.6	13.3	7.1	10.3	34.4	15.4	2.9
	EC15	9.7	9.9	7.1	5.6	55.3	10.4	2.1
25–49								
Male	West Germany	0.8	1.7	1.7	6.9	67.9	10.6	10.4
	East Germany	0.3	0.6	0.7	1.5	81.7	8.0	7.2
	France	0.4	2.6	2.2	2.5	65.6	17.4	9.3
	UK	0.5	1.3	2.0	3.4	27.4	41.0	24.4
	EC15	0.6	1.8	2.1	3.5	60.4	19.8	11.8
Female	West Germany	7.0	18.1	12.8	5.4	49.2	4.2	3.4
	East Germany	2.0	7.5	12.8	5.5	65.3	3.9	3.1
	France	2.6	11.9	12.6	8.7	53.1	8.4	2.8
	UK	8.3	18.4	16.1	8.5	26.9	16.6	5.2
	EC15	4.8	14.2	13.4	6.8	47.4	9.7	3.7
50–64								
Male	West Germany	1.0	1.5	1.5	6.7	64.0	11.6	13.7
	East Germany	0.9	1.4	1.0	2.0	77.4	8.3	9.0
	France	0.9	5.3	3.0	2.0	59.1	17.1	12.6
	UK	1.8	3.8	4.0	4.4	29.2	35.1	21.6
	EC15	1.1	2.8	2.9	3.9	55.3	19.9	14.0
Female	West Germany	8.9	20.9	17.0	5.4	37.7	4.9	5.2
	East Germany	3.3	8.5	14.4	4.9	60.9	4.3	3.6
	France	5.1	14.9	11.4	5.9	48.1	9.6	5.1
	UK	12.1	22.6	20.1	7.8	22.3	10.7	4.5
	EC15	7.1	17.2	15.9	6.1	38.1	10.0	5.6

Source: European labour force survey, 1996.

PART II

Theoretical and Normative Developments

5.   Towards a theory of transitional labour markets

Günther Schmid

Sustained economic growth achieved through innovation and investment is a necessary, but not sufficient, condition for resolving the employment crisis.[1] Even in those countries that have had success in tackling at least mass unemployment, for some groups the thread of exclusionary long-term unemployment or flexibility in the form of continuous precarious employment remains. Increasing inequalities in income distribution or employment opportunities are further indications of the inappropriate organization of work and welfare through the established institutions of labour market regulation and social security. The consequences of the new labour market flexibility is not only unemployment but also the erosion of social cohesion. In searching for remedies, however, neither Japan nor the USA constitutes an appropriate model for the reorganization of work and welfare in Europe; nor can any single country in the European Union claim to provide a genuinely European solution which other countries can adopt, as the preceding chapters have shown. Different traditions and values of the social market economy in member states have to be reflected in meeting the new challenges of economic, social and political changes. How, then, can labour market flexibility be established or increased without damaging the need for social security and justice? Are there any possibilities of organizing social security in such a way as actually to increase flexibility and economic efficiency? Is there a labour market model of social cohesion in which individuals enjoy as much freedom and autonomy in employment as possible without denying solidarity in case of income risks that go far beyond the classical situation of unemployment?

In the attempt to answer these difficult questions, this chapter starts with a critical consideration of the argument that the 'standard employment relationship' is eroding and with it, therefore, social security depending on it (section 1). Since the empirical evidence is inconclusive, a theoretical model on the basis of Herbert Simon's distinction between 'employment contracts' and 'sales contracts' is developed in order to speculate in a more informed way about the future of work. I find reasons for a continuing high interest in employment contracts, so that visions of an entrepreneurial society based on sales contracts are misleading. However, employment contracts will increasingly contain elements derived from sales contracts pushing entrepreneurial risks more and more onto the shoulders of 'employees' (section 2). Since the cultural and media sector represents in embryo many forms of these hybrid employment relationships, the labour market for artists and journalists is scrutinized. Although successes and failures of individual strategies to cope with the new risks provide important hints for 're-engineering' the modern welfare state, they cannot be universally applied (section 3). New collective arrangements are required in order to allow not only a minority but also the majority of people to take over more employment risks. This leads to the theory of transitional labour markets which conceptualizes the way to institutionalize a broad opportunity set of mobility for both women and men in order to maintain employability in critical phases over the life cycle (section 4). The summary concludes with a brief sketch of five transitional labour markets as an institutionalized solution of flexibility and security (section 5).

1   THE END OF THE 'STANDARD EMPLOYMENT RELATIONSHIP'

The employment relationship in European industrial societies has, over time, taken on a particular configuration that is known as the 'standard employment contract'. It contains four elements: first, dependent, full-time and permanent employment contracts for men as family breadwinners; second, a stable system of remuneration based on working time, occupational status and family situation; third, a firm-based system of work organization and, in many cases, lifelong employment in one and the same firm; and, fourth, a high level of permanency combined with generous levels of social security in the event of redundancy or early retirement.

The fact that this ideal type of the standard employment relationship corresponds only partially and to varying extents to historical reality is another matter.[2] Nevertheless, this model long exerted a decisive influence on the regulation of employment relationships in manufacturing industry. Since the beginning of the 1970s, however, the break-up of this standard employment relationship has gathered momentum, and the current debate on part-time work, temporary agency employment, teleworking, marginal part-time jobs, fixed-term employment contracts, pseudo self-employment and the 'new self-employed' or 'worker entrepreneurs' sometimes gives the impression that the situation has already changed completely. What was previously regarded as an 'atypical employment relationship' is now being seen as the 'standard employment relationship' of the 21st century. Thus the first question that has to be answered is: how far has the erosion of the 'standard employment relationship' already advanced?

The German case, on which we now concentrate for a moment, is certainly not representative of all OECD countries. However, other studies on contingent or 'atypical' work find similar patterns for other developed industrialized countries.[3] If the standard employment relationship can be said to cover, first, *manual and white-collar workers* (excluding trainees, civil servants, military personnel, the self-employed and family workers) who, second, *are employed full-time* (that is, whose normal weekly working time is 36 hours or more) and who, third, are on *permanent contracts* (excluding temporary workers supplied by employment agencies), then, in 1985, 54.4 per cent of employees in the Federal Republic of Germany were in such employment relationships; the corresponding figure for 1999 was 50 per cent, precisely half of all employees (Table 5.1). As is to be expected, there is a considerable difference in this respect between men and women. Despite a slightly downward trend, virtually 60 per cent of male employees are in the standard employment relationship, compared with only 40 per cent of women. If civil

Table 5.1   Change of employment relationships in Germany, 1985 to 1999

Women and men	1985	1997	1999	Tendency
1 'Standard relationship'	54.4	51.2	50.0	–
2 Civil servants and soldiers	7.6	4.5	4.3	–
3 Apprenticeships	5.3	3.7	3.9	–/+
4 Fixed-term contracts	2.9	3.4	4.8	++
5 Temporary work	0.1	0.5	0.7	++
6 Part-time work (> 15 h/week)	8.2	11.3	9.8	+/–
7 Part-time work (< 15 h/week)	2.2	4.2	5.6	++
8 Self-employed (full-time)	7.4	7.6	7.9	+
9 Self-employed (part-time)	3.4	0.9	1.5	–/+
10 Participants in LMP[1]	0.4	2.0	1.5	+/–
11 Unemployed	7.9	10.7	10.0	+/–
Total	100	100	100	
Broad LF-Participation Rate[2]	68.0	73.0	73.4	+/?

Notes:
1. Participants in labour market measures do not include those who are counted in other categories of employment relationships, for instance subsidized employees in private enterprises or participants in temporary public job creation.
2. Employed, unemployed and participants in labour market policy measures as a percentage of the working age population (15–65 years).

Source: Microcensus and own calculations.

servants and military personnel are also included, two-thirds of all male employees can be said to be in standard employment relationships.

Atypical employment relationships have become more numerous and more diverse. It should be noted, however, that labour force participation as a whole has risen. Thus, in absolute terms, the number of 'standard employment relationships' has remained more or less constant. The oft-repeated refrain of the 'end of work' is therefore completely misleading. If the standard employment relationship is being eroded, it is the new employment relationships that are affected rather than the old ones. This is reflected primarily in the increase in part-time employment. The share of part-timers who regularly work more than 15 hours per week rose from 8.2 per cent in 1985 to 9.8 per cent in 1999. This employment form is becoming particularly widespread among women, almost a quarter of whom come into this category. However, part-time work is becoming polarized.[4] The number of people in marginal part-time jobs involving fewer than 15 hours' work per week is increasing rapidly, although the precise number of people employed in such jobs in Germany is unknown.[5] Until 1999, these jobs were exempt from social security contributions.[6]

In most EU member states, the share of marginal part-time employees (less than 20 hours) in the total part-time population has scarcely changed and is on average around two-thirds (Table 5.2). On the other hand, the number of part-timers whose working times are just under the 'full-time threshold' is increasing,[7] while the number of full-timers who actually work shorter hours than the standard 'full-time' week (that is, fewer than 35 hours) is also rising (Table 5.3).[8] Consequently, the distinction between 'full-time' and 'part-time' becomes increasingly blurred.

Thus the erosion of the standard employment relationship is reflected not only in the increasing diversity of working times but also in the increasing variability of employment relationships. The distinction between dependent wage work and self-employment as well as the boundaries between dependent employment and self-employment are becoming increasingly blurred. The share of self-employed people in the part-time population has fallen sharply (particularly among women), while the share of full-time self-employed (particularly among men) is rising slightly. The decreases are attributable mainly to the current structural change in agriculture, while the increases are taking place largely outside the agricultural sector. There has been a particularly sharp increase in the share of self-employed people who themselves have no employees. However, their status is often unclear and combines elements characteristic of a normal dependent employment relationship (tasks subject to directions) with features typical of self-employment (pay related to results, no social security). In Germany, the term 'pseudo self-employment', and in the UK the term 'dependent self-employed' have been coined to denote such workers.[9]

Table 5.2 Employees with 'part-time' status according to average actual working time per week, 1985 and 1997 (per cent)

	EU10/15		DK		D		F		NL		UK	
	1985	1997	1985	1997	1985	1997	1985	1997	1985	1997	1985	1997
< 20	61.7	61.2	59.5	55.3	60.8	68.8	55.4	50.7	66.5	61.0	68.2	65.0
21–30	29.7	29.7	33.5	32.7	34.8	31.0	30.9	31.4	26.0	21.4	26.0	28.9
> 30	8.6	9.1	7.0	12.0	4.4	0.2	13.7	17.9	7.5	17.6	5.8	6.1
Total	100	100	100	100	100	100	100	100	100	100	100	100

Source: European Labour Force Survey (1985, Table 51); European Labour Force Survey (1997, Table 078).

Table 5.3 Employees with 'full-time' status according to average actual working time per week, 1985 and 1997 (per cent)

	EU10/15		DK		D		F		NL		UK	
	1985	1997	1985	1997	1985	1997	1985	1997	1985	1997	1985	1997
< 35	6.2	8.1	3.4	5.5	1.2	8.2	7.9	7.6	2.6	1.2	9.0	9.1
36–9	25.1	31.4	4.6	69.4	11.7	38.9	55.8	61.5	15.9	35.4	25.8	21.9
>40	68.8	60.5	92.0	25.1	87.1	52.9	36.3	30.9	81.5	63.3	65.2	69.0
Total	100	100	100	100	100	100	100	100	100	100	100	100

Source: European Labour Force Survey (1985, Table 49); European Labour Force Survey (1997, Table 076).

The rise of temporary workers in private employment services is a new phenomenon in Germany (Rudolph and Schröder, 1997). The number of such agency workers is low in international comparison but has been growing recently at rates of up to 20 per cent. This booming area of employment again is dominated by men (who account for two-thirds of agency workers), but increasing numbers of women are becoming involved in this form of employment. According to figures supplied by the Federal Association of Temporary Employment Agencies in 1998, 575 000 people (flows) were hired as temporary agency workers, corresponding to 253 000 on a daily average, about 0.7 per cent of the economically active population;[10] in 1975, only 11 000 were counted in West Germany. In the Netherlands, increasingly regarded as a trendsetter, 4.6 per cent of all employees work already for temporary employment agencies.[11] These companies are increasingly operating on an international or, indeed, global basis.[12] The employees of these private employment services are usually hired on permanent contracts, are paid a fixed salary and receive the usual social benefits and holiday entitlement. What distinguishes them in formal terms from workers in standard employment relationships, therefore, is simply the fact that their place of work is not fixed and that they share some of the risk if demand for work dries up. They are paid a guaranteed wage that is some 15 to 20 per cent lower than 'regular' employees in similar positions would earn.

However, many agency workers seem prepared to accept this disadvantage, or else they are in a transitional phase in which such an arrangement acts as a sensible and practical bridge to another phase of their lives. They are usually younger people who want to acquire work experience. Another third use agency work as a means of getting through a particular period in their lives, such as a spell of unemployment. Others have just been through periods of retraining, have left temporary jobs or fall into the 'difficult to place' category. Students may also use agency work as a means of finding jobs. The main areas of employment for agency workers are in clerical and other office jobs. Market niches have recently been identified in more highly-skilled segments of the labour market: in outplacement, in the organization of rescue companies, for well-qualified secretaries with foreign language skills and in the IT and marketing areas. Approximately one-third of agency workers are eventually offered permanent jobs at the client firms of temp agencies; in clerical jobs, the figure may be as high as 40 per cent. The trade unions, which initially took a very hard line against this form of employment relationship, are now beginning to come to terms with it.[13]

Fixed-term full-time employment contracts are to some extent interchangeable with agency or temporary work. In countries where there are strict rules governing periods of notice, as in the Netherlands or Spain, employers are making increased use of fixed-term employment contracts or agency workers;

in those countries where the rules governing dismissals are more liberal, or non-existent, as in Denmark, fixed-term contracts are virtually unknown and agency work is less widespread (Schömann, Rogowsky and Kruppe, 1998). The USA seems to be of particular interest, since it is always cited as a model for Europe.

Advocates of flexibility might expect clear signs of a severe erosion of the standard employment relationship. However, the evidence does not meet this expectation (Table 5.4). Even though the various occupational categories are not fully comparable with the reported German data, and although the 'regular full-time employees' category in the USA also includes trainees, civil servants and full-time employees on fixed-term contracts, it cannot be said that the erosion of the standard employment relationship is further advanced in the USA than in Germany; if anything, the data show that the opposite is the case. However, it cannot be denied that, in the USA as in Germany, the trend is heading away from the standard employment relationship, albeit at a slower pace than is often assumed. In the USA, the share of temporary agency workers rose from 0.9 per cent of all employed in 1990 and 1.0 per cent in 1997 to 2.3 per cent in June 1999 (Eberts and Erickcek, 2000).

It is time for *a first provisional appraisal*: however the 'standard employment relationship' is defined, it is clear that the boundaries between the various employment statuses have become more fluid. It is becoming increasingly difficult to know what the 'standard employment relationship' is and what employment forms are associated with what opportunities *and* risks, both for

Table 5.4   Distribution of employment by work arrangement in the USA, 1997

Arrangement and definition	Per cent
Agency temporaries (paid by a temporary-help agency)	1.0
On-call or day labourers (self-indication as such)	1.6
Independent contractors (consultants or freelancers)	6.7
Contract company workers (primarily work for one client)[1]	0.6
Other direct-hire temporaries (other fixed-term contracts)	2.6
Other self-employed (other non-independent contractors)	5.1
Regular part-time employees (work fewer than 35 hours per week)	13.6
Regular full-time employees (work 35 hours or more)	68.8
Total	100.0

Note: [1]So-called 'feint self-employment'.

Source: Houseman (1999).

individuals and society as a whole. On the one hand, atypical employment forms have less legal protection and provide less social security than the standard employment relationship; on the other hand, they may be primitive forms of a new standard employment relationship, acting as links between the old and the new economy. The erosion of the standard employment relationship may be a product of an increasing propensity to seek paid work, or it may merely reflect a persistently bad labour market situation. The trend might reverse, or at least slow down, if the labour market situation were to improve. Since the empirical evidence about the future of work is inconclusive, it is worthwhile to think about the employment relationship in theoretical terms.

2   ON THE THEORY OF CHANGING EMPLOYMENT FORMS

The literature of employment protection and social legislation provides a good deal of rational arguments for the standard employment relationship. From this point of view, the main reasons for the persistence of this contracting form are the close link between social security and economic activity and the fact that it is in the interest of employees and employers alike to secure the return to specific investments in the long term.[14] However, since labour and social legislation is ultimately only a reflection of the balance of interests and power, we need to dig a bit deeper and to examine carefully why it is that people enter into employment relationships at all. How is it that a relationship of dependency or authority enshrined in an employment relationship is accepted when self-determined exchanges between independent individuals could equally well be regulated by sales contracts? Why is a labour market not organized like a commodity market, and what has this to do with the change in employment forms?

   1   The distinction between an employment contract and a sales contract in economic theory goes back to early studies published by the Nobel Prize winner Herbert A. Simon (1951). The fundamental characteristic of an employment contract is that the 'employee' accepts that the 'employer' exercises authority. The employee has a set of potential labour services from which the employer selects according to circumstances. In an employment contract, the scope of these labour services is negotiated and laid down and a (specific) price or wage for the (as yet not fully specified) services is set. In a sales contract, the vendor demands a certain price for a specified product, while the purchaser promises to pay the price stipulated for the product. The vendor has no further interest in what the purchaser does with the product, whereas in an employment contract the 'vendor' is most definitely interested in what services the 'purchaser' might demand. How is it that the employee is willing

to submit to the employer's authority and at the same time make out a blank cheque that the employer can use to demand whatever services he wishes (within the limits laid down in the contract)? Why does the employee not sell his or her labour services in the market? Under what circumstances does the employer choose a sales contract rather than an employment contract, which grants him or her the prerogative of deciding how the labour he or she has purchased is to be deployed but takes control over the results more or less out of his or her hands?

Simon's concern was to model these questions formally within a bounded rationality framework. In consequence, his model amounts to a very tightly constrained decision-making model under conditions of uncertainty. Its fundamental discovery is that an employment contract is rational from the purchaser's point of view when the required information as to the nature of the desired services will not be available until some point in the future, but reliable access to it is required immediately. Simon compared this deferment of a decision with the liquidity preference of a capital investor seeking to optimize his portfolio. Such an investor ties up only part of his capital in long-term investments, in order to reap the benefits of moderate but certain interest rates; the rest of his capital is placed in short-term investments in order for him to be able to react quickly to fluctuating profit-making opportunities. Conversely, vendors of labour services are concerned to secure a continuous flow of income, so they surrender their decision-making sovereignty in favour of a guaranteed income, or they trade off unpleasant work, for example, against high wages. Furthermore, a dependent employment relationship offers some degree of protection against competition for the duration of the contract.[15]

2   This finding is certainly not a new one, and has been further developed and given more differentiated expression in recent contract theory.[16] The framework has also to be extended by the possibility of collective bargaining or standard regulation by the state. In particular, job-specific demands[17] that can scarcely be covered by contracts and which, if explicitly incorporated into contracts, would give rise to high transaction costs indicate that the two contractual forms in Simon's model should be regarded, not as alternatives, but rather as the two extremes on a continuum of possible contractual forms. Furthermore, collective agreements make it possible to lay down minimum standards and objectified rule systems, through which wages can be allocated to jobs rather than to individuals and through which transparent career paths are established. This not only restricts the objects of negotiation, and the associated costs, but also protects the weaker party from exploitation and acts as a check on the opportunism of the stronger party. Nevertheless, even Simon's simple model contains parameters and keys that have hitherto been ignored in the debate on changing employment forms. In particular, very little attention has been paid to date to the importance of changes of context for the interests

Table 5.5   Interests in employment or sales contracts

Interest of 'employee' in employment contract	Interest of 'employer' in employment contract
Income security	Authority ('liquidity preference')
Exclusion of competition	Quick and reliable labour services
Accumulation of experience/knowledge	Use of experience/knowledge

and strategies of possible contracting partners. This can be illustrated by a simple 'interests chart', supplemented by the most significant findings of institutional theory. The interests in the extreme form of the employment contract are to be understood simultaneously as disinterests in the extreme form of commercial contract (Table 5.5).

3   Let us consider the individual parameters and ask which of the strategic contextual conditions (technology, market size, uncertainty), that might influence the basic decision between employment contracts and sales contracts, have changed. The interest in *income security* through a traditional dependent employment relationship might have reduced for potential employees, for example, because they increasingly have access to other sources of income (apart from social security benefits). If this were the case, the interest in binding long-term employment contracts would decline accordingly. Unfortunately, comparable data in this area are a scarce commodity.[18] Some information is provided by the share of income from assets in average disposable income by household categories and/or in average annual income; this figure can be regarded as a reference value for the dependency on regular earnings from gainful employment. A corresponding analysis for Germany shows, first, that the share of income from assets in disposable household income does not exceed 8 per cent, and is particularly low in the households of manual workers and the unemployed. Second, the share of income from assets in the reference income varies between 2.1 and 18.1 per cent and, as expected, gives the households of the self-employed and some white-collar and civil servant households a certain degree of independence from earned income. Third, with the exception of white-collar households, the share of income from assets fell in the 1990s, so that – measured in terms of the selected indicators – dependency on regular earned wage income rose rather than fell. Thus the evolution of the most important parameter, namely income security, suggests that interest in employment relationships is as great as ever.

4   The interest in the *exclusion of competition* may be less strong now among increasing numbers of skilled workers than it was when the labour supply was relatively homogeneous. Increasing specialization creates a natural monopoly, as it were, leading to a decline in the advantages of the standard

employment contract and increasing interest in sales contracts, or at least in the incorporation of certain elements of such contracts into employment contracts. Interest in the acquisition of *specific skills and experience knowledge* (and the corresponding interest in their utilization) was the central argument for the emergence and persistence of internal labour markets. As already noted above, more recent studies have revealed a slight tendency towards the erosion of internal labour markets in favour of network labour markets, as well as a renaissance of occupational labour markets, in which it is not length of tenure but experience of a wide range of projects and various forms of cooperation that gives workers the edge in terms of knowledge accumulation.[19] In sum, it would seem that interest in limiting competition and in firm-specific knowledge is tending to decline, in contrast to interest in security of income. Nevertheless, the evidence would suggest that this trend applies only to certain groups of workers, mainly highly skilled ones, and that we should not be too hasty in generalizing it to all workers. It is reasonable to assume that the majority of (potential) workers will continue for the foreseeable future to have a strong interest in excluding competition and accumulating specific skills or knowledge derived from experience; however, the second condition seems to be less and less linked to permanent jobs with the same employer.

5   What constitutes a strategic advantage for (potential) employees is generally a disadvantage for (potential) employers. The weaker the interest in a continuous income flow, the higher the transaction costs involved in fixing the content and scope of the tasks over which an employer would like to have control; the stronger the monopoly, the less certain the delivery of labour services becomes, either because of inadequate opportunities for control or because of opportunism; and the weaker the interest in job-specific knowledge and experience, the greater the risk of a lack of motivation, unwillingness to cooperate and exit. In other words, those factors that, for employees, constitute positive incentives in favour of sales contracts are regarded by employers as negative incentives in favour of employment contracts. Consequently, small positive incentives in favour of sales contracts can quickly cause employers to turn away from employment contracts (at least of the traditional kind). The authority or liquidity preferences of potential employers may be reduced, for example, by the considerably quicker and cheaper access to information afforded by the digital technology revolution, which may in turn lead to reduced interest in lengthy or permanent employment contracts. At the same time, the technological revolution reduces the half-life of knowledge, so there is no longer any guarantee that the services provided by employees will be of the quality that was explicitly or implicitly agreed. Furthermore, informatization makes it possible quickly and cheaply to buy in complex labour services from outside the sphere of the employment contract, that is the firm. The

reduction of transport and communications costs encourages virtual organizational forms and 'fractal' factories, in which the ties that find expression in long-term employment contracts lose their significance.

6   Viewed in their totality, these trends – a slightly reduced interest in a secure income from paid work and, to a somewhat greater extent, in protection from competition and in the accumulation of job-specific knowledge, on the one hand, and reduced uncertainty, a lower level of dependency on spatially constrained labour services and more rapid, technologically mediated access to specific services, on the other – would lead us to expect, first, that sales contracts will increasingly be preferred to employment contracts, or, second, that elements of sales contracts will increasingly be incorporated into employment contracts or, third, that elements of employment contracts will increasingly be built into sales contracts.

In the first case, we would observe an increase in self-employment outside agriculture, and particularly in self-employment without dependent employees. From an international comparative perspective, however, it is not possible to discern a clear, let alone a marked, trend towards self-employment.[20] Here, however, and in the following cases, we need to take account of the extent to which strategic power relations, particularly the labour market situation, influence preferences for particular contractual forms. The decision to go self-employed, for example, may be born simply of the need to escape unemployment when there is little prospect of obtaining a regular job. On the other hand, the preference for self-employment, that is for autonomy and independence from an authority relationship, may be suppressed by the unequal distribution of income and assets or because of inadequacies in the capital market.[21] Recent surveys suggest that the number of people aspiring to self-employment is rising and is greater than the number who actually achieve their goal.[22]

In the second case, it is to be expected that a higher share of employment contracts will be fixed-term or that permanent contracts will increasingly specify and quantify employees' performance, for example through target setting, profit sharing and contributions to costs (of training programmes, for example). We would expect to find such contracts particularly in high-level service activities, which increasingly depend, on the one hand, on customer-specific services (an argument in favour of sales contracts) and, on the other, on the ability to react flexibly and reliably to rapidly changing customer demands (an argument for liquidity preference). The new collective agreement on service activities concluded at Debis (the service group at Daimler-Chrysler in Germany), for example, is designed in this way. Among other things, it contains a payment system linked to the market and to performance, in which individual annual target salaries can vary by up to 60 per cent and are paid on top of the collectively agreed annual target salary. Furthermore, the individual annual target salary consists of a fixed element (80–90 per cent) and a variable element (10–20 per cent), with the latter being subdivided into two further elements, one determined by individual performance and one by corporate results (Debis, 1999).

In the third case, implicit arrangements are to be expected, whereby contracts for services are tied to a long-lasting partnership which nevertheless allows both contracting parties to select opportunistically other partners if the circumstances are favourable. The use of sales service to outsource work to self-employed workers would correspond to this model. We can also, on the basis of this model, forecast an increase in the supply of workers by temporary employment services, that is an ingenious combination of sales and employment contracts. In temporary or agency work, the temporary worker and the agency conclude an employment contract, the employer and the agency conclude a sales contract, and the employer and the employee act as if they had concluded a fixed-term employment contract. In the case of agency work, with the sales contract between agency and the employer – in contrast to regular sales contracts – the vendor retains an interest in the way in which his product or services are utilized in order to maintain their value. In consequence, 'value maintenance clauses' will be incorporated into contracts. If the employer, who was seeking to maintain his liquidity by renting products or services, discovers that the value of the service from the temporary worker meets or even exceeds expectations, the combination of the commercial contract between the agency and the employer and the fixed-term employment contract between the temporary worker and the agency will be converted into a standard employment contract between the temporary worker and the employer.

7   Of course, labour, social security and tax legislation impinge on the strategic contextual conditions, colouring individual choices among the three alternatives and also differentiating them from country to country (even though the contextual conditions remain subject to the same trends). Thus permanent marginal part-time employment relationships would be an interesting option for employers if social security and tax legislation offered the appropriate incentives. It is now well known that this was very much the case for a long time in Germany (Dingeldey, 2000). Another example of such impingement is the notorious one of pseudo self-employment, already discussed above, in which a sales contract is used to avoid the payment of social security contributions and taxes, although a *de facto* authority relationship is maintained (Dietrich, 1999).

Even when changes in contextual conditions might lead us to expect a more pronounced trend towards the use of sales contracts or increasing commercialization of employment contracts, there are clear limits to such developments. Theory would suggest that the strategic interests in employment contracts on

both sides – (potential) employees and (potential) employers – remain as powerful as ever. Good reasons can also be adduced to explain why such interests
remain decisive in many sectors of the economy, or may even possibly be
becoming more important. In activities in which service reliability and quality
are achieved only after lengthy processes of professionalization or in which
close cooperation and precise coordination are required, permanent employment
contracts will be more efficient than sales contracts. Even in those activities in
which professionalism is dependent on a willingness to engage in continuous
learning and to transmit knowledge derived from experience,[23] competitive,
uncertain employment relationships are more harmful than useful.[24]
Consequently, professionally institutionalized and secure permanent employment relationships will continue to be the norm in many occupations in future as
well. However, because of rapid technological change or customer-specific
requirements, even these employment relationships will have to incorporate
flexible organizational elements, that is elements derived from sales contracts.

Let us take stock once again. Even if it is much too early to announce the
end of wage work, one trend seems set to gain strength over the long term. The
significance of dependent wage work involving authority relationships will
decline in favour of employed workers who will have to 'sell' their services in
the form of target agreements with related performance pay, or in favour of
self-employed who sell their services through sales contracts not just to one
buyer, that is their 'employer', but to a number of different customers or the
same customers with changing demands. In each case, such changes of position will go hand in hand with critical transitions in which skills will have to
be enhanced or networks reconstructed, which will take time and may also
cause earnings to be lost. This poses the problem of how people will deal with
these new freedoms and related uncertainties, which leads us to the next question: is a new standard employment relationship now taking shape, and what
institutions are providing support for those attempting to deal successfully
with the new risks?

3   THE LABOUR MARKET FOR ARTISTS AND JOURNALISTS

> The job of the future is not car mechanic, but to be famous once in a lifetime. (Andy
> Warhol)

In the expanding culture and media sector, there is a high probability of finding not only artists but also experts in the art of living who have found ways
of coping with high levels of economic or social risk that lie outside the well-
worn tracks of the traditional welfare state. Thus social scientists inquisitive

about social innovations that might be transferred to other areas of life might find food for thought here. On the other hand, it is highly likely that they will also stumble across massive unresolved social problems that demand new institutional solutions. Many of these new jobs are related to persistently low pay or a sudden loss of economic or social status. Failure to cope with the new risks leads to poverty and income inequalities, or at least to *de facto* dependency and susceptibility to extortion despite formal self-employment. A final consequence may be social isolation of the 'lone combatant', leading ultimately to the threat of social exclusion.

It is not unreasonable to suppose that problems similar to those that have long been evident in creative and media labour markets will crop up in future in other occupations or activities. In particular, we are highly likely to find in this area hints for broader solutions of re-engineering the modern welfare state. Thus the question is whether artist and media labour markets provide sufficient material to flesh out the contours of the 'fashioned flexibility' that could avert the catastrophic consequences of the 'natural flexibilization' to which much admired cultural critics such as Richard Sennett (1998) have given so much publicity. Although this segment of the labour market is (as yet) very small in size, there are, in addition to its high growth rate, important theoretical arguments in support of the view that it may well provide evidence on the future of work that is susceptible of generalization.

'Culture' may be a more likely institution than the 'market' to be regarded as a 'prototype of the economic logic', since an innovative dynamic is an inherent part of its constitution, leading to constant re-evaluations of existing values (Groys, 1999: 15). Furthermore, celebrity – as the quotation from Andy Warhol at the beginning of this section indicates, albeit exaggeratedly – has an important guidance function in the creative world. In speculative but thoroughly serious mood, Paul Krugman even forecasts the advent of the 'celebrity economy'. By this he means an economy which, because of the digital information revolution, that is the virtually cost-free and instantaneous reproduction of new creations, creativity and innovation can be made to pay off only by being sold indirectly through advertising media. 'In short, instead of becoming a knowledge economy, we are becoming a celebrity economy' (Krugman, 1999: 203). Finally, the cultural sphere is also the prototype par excellence of the 'cost disease' (Baumol and Bowen, 1993)[25] which is one of the fundamental challenges for labour market policy in the modern service society.

The Development and Characteristics of the Artist and Media Labour Market[26]

In the recent past, the creative and media industries have experienced the highest rates of employment growth, and are likely to continue to do so in future.

In addition, international reports and statistics show that, in virtually all EU member states, the trend in the creative and media sectors is towards more self-employment and part-time work (Benhamou, 1996). A substantial share of artists and journalists are self-employed,[27] or combine dependent part-time work with self-employment, and the majority of this labour market segment is concentrated in large urban areas.

Creative and media workers are exposed to considerable uncertainty and risk in employment. In 1995 in Germany, only 45.1 per cent of such workers were in 'standard' employment relationships, and apart from the high share in self-employment they are more prone to fixed-term contracts than in the economically active population as a whole. A further peculiarity is the above-average level of formal qualifications, on the one hand, and the indeterminacy or diversity of the content of those qualifications, on the other. Whereas the share of graduates in the economically active population in Germany is only 15 per cent, the share of working artists with university degrees is almost 35 per cent. Among women artists, the share of university graduates is even higher than among their male counterparts. The tendency towards self-employment rises with educational level.

Work in the creative and media industries is knowledge-intensive, and in many areas of the cultural sector it is no longer possible to speak of occupations in the established sense of the term. Skills are often acquired through practical training, whether through spells of work experience or on the job, and lifelong training is becoming increasingly important. Even within the established creative occupations, a standard occupational title, such as 'performing artist', is problematic, since many creative occupations now involve a combination of different activities. Thus the occupational profile of many artists is characterized by a diversity of activities. The typical artist deploys his or her basic musical, dramatic or pictorial abilities in various areas, sometimes simultaneously, sometimes over the course of his or her working life. This kind of mobility within the general field of the arts takes place particularly between adjoining spheres of activity. A musician, for example, may work as a conductor on a dependent or self-employed basis, and may combine conducting engagements with teaching or composing.

Over and above occupational mobility, artistic professions require a high degree of flexibility in terms of the breadth of activities. These activities are generally grouped around a core professionalism, frequently the outcome of a specific training course. In many artistic occupations, however, there is no standard course or place of training. Training for actors is not subject to normative legislation, and as a result no occupational profile for actors has yet been drawn up. However, it is particularly in the so-called 'secondary' cultural occupations – upstream and downstream of the artistic process itself – that there are not yet any specific vocational training programmes. Thus occupations such as publisher's reader or adviser, reader/literary editor to a theatre company, producer, artists' agent, critic or presenter are not based on any specific courses of training or study.

A further peculiarity of artist and media labour markets is the relatively low and uncertain average income. Many creative and media workers in dependent employment are paid less than employees with comparable formal qualifications. In the case of freelancers, both very high and very low incomes are typical. One obvious explanation for this is the decline in public subsidies for the arts. Comparison of the evolution of public spending in this area with the actual and forecast evolution of the labour market for artists points to a discrepancy that is indicative of the 'cost disease' syndrome. The stagnating of the publicly subsidized cultural sector contrasts with the very positive dynamic in the labour market for artists, which suggests funding and income problems.

Consequently, the process of wage formation and risk management are of particular interest in the light of growing income uncertainties. The higher educational level already referred to above can be interpreted as a key strategy for insuring individuals against income uncertainties, a strategy that does not, however, always meet with success. Theoretical and empirical studies have revealed that market clearing in creative occupations in fact takes place in part through a higher than normal level of wage differentiation (Menger and Gurgand, 1996). By way of compensation for uncertainties, artists who are employed only periodically are paid higher fees than their colleagues in permanent jobs. However, these mechanisms function only selectively. Labour markets for artists are characterized by a paradoxical situation: there is a constant oversupply of labour while at the same time there is a permanent shortage of talents or (contingent) specialists. One important reason for this is that demand is uncertain. Since searching for talents is time-consuming, if a particular need arises suddenly because of the dictates of fashion, it is in the interest of purchasers to be able to draw on as large a pool as possible of (potential) talents. If an opportunity presents itself, the talent that has been sought out or the specialist who has already been used may enjoy a monopoly for a time, putting them in a position to negotiate monopoly premiums. Labour markets for artists frequently turn into 'winner-takes-all' markets, with winners taking everything and losers going away empty-handed (Frank and Cook, 1995). The obverse of such monopoly gains, however, are high losses, because losers have to write off considerable investments as sunk costs. At the very least, all participants in such labour markets have to reckon with considerable fluctuations in income.

Thus a rational strategy for artists and media workers is to acquire a monopoly position through specialization or closed networks. Individually, monopoly can be achieved by adopting niche strategies or by accepting as many 'engagements' as possible – to echo the pithy expression used by artists. The more engagements an artist accepts, the more his or her reputation grows, bringing more offers of engagements in its wake. In this way, a positive feedback circuit develops, which may lead either to rapid fame (cf. the Warhol quotation) or to rapid oblivion, since the converse also applies of course: the fewer engagements artists are offered, the less experience they acquire, the further their reputation declines and the fewer engagements they are offered.

Individualistic strategies are extremely risky and probably only rational for exceptional performers. Residual income from active marketing and commercialization, supported and protected by (closed) professional networks, is therefore another strategy to deal with volatile income from project-related work organization. A good example is the Hollywood labour market, aptly described in Paul and Kleingartner (1994) and Marsden (2000). Creative work often generates income that goes beyond simple box office receipts, notably through the income from residual obligations, analogous to copyright, and deriving from further use made of the work: for example, from using a film's name or the reputation of a famous orchestra in advertisements for other products. For the Screen Actors' Guild members in 1988, about 45 per cent of total income came from residuals, compared with 55 per cent from initial compensation. Essential for the Hollywood case is the strong union organization, which administers the all-important 'residual obligations' which are distributed on the basis of film credits. The union functions as an information pool and sanctions opportunism on both sides, the producers (trying to exploit the artists and to hide information about profits) and the artists (trying to exaggerate their individual contribution to the teamwork). In the absence of formal qualifications, the information network is a very important vehicle for reputation, and membership of the network is crucial for the spreading and protecting of reputation.

Insurance, finally, is another form of (artistic) risk management. Since many creative and media workers hover between self-employment and wage dependency, special social security arrangements have developed in some countries. Two examples will be outlined here. Since 1 January 1983, under the terms of the Artists' Social Security Act, self-employed artists and media workers in Germany have been integrated as compulsory contributors into the statutory health, old age and (since January 1995) nursing care insurance schemes.[28] The basic stipulation of the Act is that half of the health and old-age insurance contributions are paid by the insured. Until 1999, a quarter was paid by representatives of the arts and culture industries (including arts enterprises, gallery owners, theatre managements, newspaper book publishers, advertising agencies, record companies and radio stations) and a quarter by the federal state. Since the year 2000, the federal government's contribution has been reduced to only 20 per cent, so that the arts and culture industries now have to pay a contribution of 4 per cent of their expenditures on fees into the artists' social security fund to make up the other 30 per cent of the whole tax bill. The reason for the reduction in the federal government's contribution was the unexpectedly sharp increase in the number of people insured. For example, music schools are increasingly going over to using self-employed teachers, who are then insured through the artists' social security fund, rather than permanent staff.

Controlling such a moral hazard is increasingly becoming a problem. The financing arrangements for the artists' social security fund constitute a significant departure from the equivalence principle adopted by the other social security agencies. Only after a series of heated arguments did the government accept that participation in the management of risk in the artist and media labour markets was in the public interest.[29] This means that self-employed artists and media workers are treated as employees in social policy terms (except for unemployment insurance). In other words, they are treated considerably more favourably than other self-employed workers who, should they wish to join a compulsory insurance scheme, have to pay the full contributions themselves. However, the real innovation lies in making consumers contribute to risk management.

Like other dependent employees, artists and media workers on permanent employment contracts enjoy the normal social protection, including unemployment insurance. However, in the case of artists whose employment is marginal or irregular, there has to date been no opportunity for building up entitlements to unemployment benefits. In France, on the other hand, an insurance scheme for artists has been developed that takes account of the precarious situation of this particular occupational group. Income substitution benefits enable artists to bridge periods of non-employment (what actors call 'resting'); this French system is very heavily subsidized by the general unemployment insurance scheme. Studies have also shown that this method of risk management is problematic, since it encourages moral hazard. Since the system was introduced, both the number of people employed in this segment of the labour market and the number of short-term engagements and/or temporary spells of non-employment have increased. It has even been estimated that half of the income of artists in this group is derived from transfer payments made under the terms of the unemployment insurance scheme (Menger and Gurgand, 1996).

Germany and other countries are still a long way from establishing a scheme like the one that exists in France. Furthermore, experience suggests that it would be extremely problematic simply to adopt the French scheme in its entirety. Other ways will have to be found, but discussion of them will be deferred to a later stage (cf. Chapter 12). In the concluding part of this section, we will turn instead to the question of how far the artist and media labour markets can be said to offer a glimpse of the future world of work and the conclusions that can be drawn for labour market policy.

Artist and Media Labour Markets: Harbingers of the Future?

The production structures in the expanding artist and media labour markets confirm the trend towards network labour markets. Long-established corporate structures are disappearing and production processes are broken down into modules and networks. These networks are characterized by flat hierarchies. Teams of professional 'lone wolves' are being put together, the composition of which changes according to the nature of the task in hand, so that close personal relationships do not develop. On the contrary, the 'strength of weak ties' is becoming a strategy for success (Granovetter 1973). In so far as such organizational principles are becoming established, national labour market and social policies are losing firms and employees as sources of funding but have to shoulder the consequences of virtual entrepreneurship, such as higher unemployment or discontinuous work histories, that bring with them a correspondingly higher risk of earnings fluctuations.

The functioning of the networks that are now emerging in the artistic and cultural sphere is supported by high skill levels and willingness to undergo training. Anyone who knows how to make use of these networks will also be able to sustain their own employability. The stability and permanence of existing employment relationships are based, not solely on acquired rights and separation costs that serve as a deterrent to employers, but also on employees' continuing employability. Since many artists and media workers are not in permanent dependent employment relationships, mobility and the willingness to undergo training are crucial for sustaining the market. Payment structures in creative and media labour markets are also specific. The seniority principle plays only a subordinate role in determining pay levels, and payment by hours worked or by family or occupational status are also much less important than in the standard employment relationship; performance-related pay and remuneration by market value including residual profits are gaining much greater prominence.

In artist and media labour markets, the choice of occupation seems to be motivated increasingly not by a desire to go into any particular profession but rather by reputation (and, in extreme cases, fame).[30] Even the economic logic of art alluded to at the beginning of this section, namely the constant re-evaluation of values, is increasingly permeating 'normal' product markets. The demand for novelty and originality seems to be inexhaustible, and customers' quality requirements are helping to drive this process even further forward. Whereas the traditional notion of occupation denoted a specific and constant (where necessary improving) ability or skill that was exercised within the framework of a dependent employment relationship and in an enterprise with a clearly defined local market, the new professionalism seems to denote a professional activity that is pursued on a self-employed basis or at least – in the case of employment relationships that are formally dependent – in a manner characterized by greater independence and personal responsibility, in changeable markets and with more frequent changes of firm or of teams within the same firms.[31]

Of course, the striving for recognition results in fame[32] only in extreme cases. Esteem of this kind can be acquired by sharpening occupational skills. However, since this process takes place in competition with other individuals following the same strategy, the outcome is very uncertain, to say the least. In other words, the future of work seems to be linked to objectives and technological conditions that are themselves associated with two new kinds of risk.[33] The first of these is what might be termed the 'reputation risk', which arises because the social esteem is not subject to fixed rules but is heavily dependent on fashion (constant re-evaluation of values) or other contingent factors. The second is a higher risk of income fluctuations, which arises because competition is increasing and markets are becoming more changeable. It is true that 'fame' is often associated with considerable gains, in accordance with the 'winner-takes-all' principle. Conversely, however, it may also be associated with considerable losses occasioned by fruitless investment. Attention is a scarce resource (Franck, 1998), so that the 'fame game' often turns into a zero-sum game: the attention one artist gains will be the loss of attention for another artist. At the very least, considerable fluctuations in income have to be reckoned with. Moreover, the 'winner-takes-all' principle may lead to the abandonment of vocational training or even of occupations with secure incomes, because the horizon is constantly shimmering with new opportunities that seem to offer a quicker route to fame and fortune. If this principle gains greater prominence, then – as Robert Frank and Philip Cook (1995) have shown – there is a high probability that the associated incentive structures will lead, economically, to considerable waste of resources and, socially, to greater inequality. The 'celebrity economy' that Paul Krugman (rightly) speculated about also has its costs.

Certainly, it would be an exaggeration to conclude that the future of the labour market lies only in the artist and media labour markets. Taken in conjunction with the trend outlined above, however, it does not seem too bold to suggest that the jobs of the future will increasingly take on some of the characteristics of jobs in the arts and media. They are likely to involve more self-determination and competition, to be more fluid in terms of the nature and scope of the employment relationship and more project or team-oriented, to be increasingly integrated into networks and less into firms and to entail a variety of different tasks whose very diversity over the course of the working life will encourage lifelong learning. On the other hand, however, earnings will fluctuate and be combined with other sources of income or unpaid do-it-yourself work.

In two important respects, the characteristics of artist and media labour markets are not representative of the jobs of the future, or certainly should not be. Reputation as a control mechanism breaks down, or should be restricted, in those activities in which work quality must meet objectifiable functional standards. In the case of dentists, heart surgeons, engineers or educators (to name just a few examples), who may indeed have a reputation but are in reality nothing but quacks or unable to keep pace with the development of professional standards, inadequacies in the relevant professionalism would cause serious and irreparable damage.[34] Since professionalism is also dependent on a willingness constantly to update one's knowledge and skill and on the transmission to team workers of knowledge derived from experience, competitive and uncertain employment relationships in professional labour markets are more damaging than useful. For this reason, a high share of occupations will in future continue to be carried on within the framework of institutionalized employment relationships that are secured over the long term. Thus our investigation of the artist and media labour markets confirms the findings of our theoretical deliberations on the strategic advantages and disadvantages of employment contracts and sales contracts. What are the implications of this for labour market policy?

Implications for Labour Market Policy

Artist and media labour markets show how the 'cost disease' that afflicts the service sector can be cured, at least in some service activities, by tapping unused productivity potential. In core areas of these labour markets, the new logic of labour utilization clearly contrasts with the Taylorist principles governing traditional work organization in manufacturing. Management of the functional transformation of capacity for work into labour services is increasingly being devolved to workers themselves; that is, it is being internalized. As a result, reserves of productivity are being tapped through the implementation of three principles: first, increased self-control of workers, that is increasing self-responsibility even in formally heteronomous structures;[35] second, increased self-promotion, that is the strategic marketing by individual workers of their own human capital; third, self-rationalization and a blurring of the boundaries between private life and work, to the point where it is difficult to distinguish the two (Voß and Pongratz, 1998).

These trends have ambivalent consequences. On the one hand, they set free creative and innovative forces and the potential for rationalization already alluded to, leading to greater independence and personal responsibility. On the other hand, they bring about increasing isolation, new inequalities or permanent self-exploitation, an increased risk of a loss of social status and the erosion of solidarity as success and performance norms take on the character of ideology. In order to cushion or prevent these negative consequences, new arrangements for the collective representation of interests are required, as are new institutional arrangements designed to enhance solidarity.

Undoubtedly, successful individual risk-management strategies also exist. As we have shown, educational levels and the willingness to undergo training are higher than average in the creative and media industries and are becoming increasingly important. However, this strategy is clearly not sufficient in itself. Our empirical analysis of low average earnings and high wage dispersion suggests that there is a high risk of fluctuating earnings in this sector. This risk was mitigated to some extent in Germany by the 1983 Artists' Social Security Act, which was in its time an almost revolutionary innovation. Since then, however, there have been no further developments of any substance. It is true that self-employed artists and journalists have been placed on an equal footing with salaried employees with respect to social insurance, yet this insurance system does not provide adequate protection. Artists continue to bear considerable residual risks. There has not to date been any opportunity for the self-employed to claim unemployment insurance and to take advantage of the associated employment promotion measures. It would be worth considering, therefore, whether artists and media workers, as well as the 'new self-employed' in similar situations, could be given access to an (extended) employment insurance scheme. By analogy with the contributions currently made to the artists' social insurance fund, this would mean that honoraria for works contracts (a kind of sales contract), for example, would become liable for contributions. This would also help the growing number of young academics for whom a succession of works contracts has now become almost the normal route into the profession.

Network structures, which are a key element, both socially and professionally, in the functioning of artistic and cultural labour markets, play an important role in risk reduction. These networks provide support during the critical transitions between individual sequences of discontinuous employment. We know too little about their function in equalizing earnings risks, but we assume they play an important role and might well provide some interesting illustrations of innovative approaches to risk management. The Hollywood labour market can be interpreted as the renaissance of the occupational labour market (Marsden, 2000) regulating and protecting reputation in professional labour markets where qualifications can hardly be formalized. Such networks also seem important in administering the residual incomes from service-product chains (Schmid, 2000), residual engagements, royalties, copyrights and other fringe benefits. Finally, private artists' agencies, alongside stage, TV and film actors' unions, play a central role in organizing these network labour markets. Since such networks tend to close against outsiders, new forms of segmentation will arise. Thus there is also a role to be played by state institutions, as already established public artists' agencies show. The coexistence of private and public placement agencies, or the public–private mix of placement services that characterizes the artistic and cultural labour market, will in future play a greater role in other subsegments of the employment system as well.

High unemployment that still prevails in many EU member states, or cumulating precarious employment relationships, seem to be merely a concentrated reflection of the unresolved problems related to the future of work touched upon here. The final section of this chapter will address the question of how labour market policy might help to meet these new challenges more effectively. What institutional arrangements might be capable of regulating the uncertainties and risks increasingly associated with the new employment relationships in such a way that they do not lead to new forms of social exclusion? Is there a new form of solidarity that guarantees greater mobility and freedom of choice while at the same time meeting the undoubted need for financial and contractual certainty? How might we heed the insistent warnings of cultural critics and channel the risks inherent in labour market flexibilization in more productive directions? How can the apparently contradictory demands for flexibility and social security be reconciled? The final section will attempt to answer these questions.

4   PRINCIPLES AND FORMS OF TRANSITIONAL LABOUR MARKETS

One conclusion can be drawn from the analysis to date: full employment in the sense of 'life-long, full-time employment for all' is no longer a realistic goal. Indeed, any attempts to achieve such a goal would be to embrace a backward-looking Utopia based on a model of the family in which the man was the sole breadwinner and the woman an unpaid domestic worker and occasional secondary earner. What would constitute a realistic objective and a forward-looking Utopia, however, would be a notion of full employment that gave everyone – men and women alike – the opportunity to find forms of employment that varied to suit the particular situation and aspirations during their life course.[36]

Thus defined, full employment would be possible but only under two conditions. First, monetary, financial and wages policy must be better coordinated in order to stimulate sustainable, that is qualitative, economic growth. Second, labour market and social policy must be more thoroughly reformed than hitherto in order to guarantee everybody an appropriate share in earned income and the social esteem associated with it. To put it crudely: without growth, everything will come to nothing, but growth is not everything. A situation in which, in accordance with the Pareto principle, there are only winners and no losers is highly improbable. The evolution of social market economies has always been characterized by institutional arrangements that gave losers a fair chance of a share in national wealth and to become winners themselves (Schmid and Schömann, 1994: 50). Economic and social innovations have to go hand in hand. Simply to rely on growth will lead to the exclusion of many members of society, and merely to call for a redistribution of work is not sufficient. Only by implementing a dual strategy can 'social integration', that is universal participation in the economy and society, be ensured.

One possible misunderstanding must be cleared up from the outset. The demand for a redistribution of work is not based on the assumption that we are running out of work. True, the notion of technologically-driven unemployment has enjoyed periodic spells of social acceptability ever since the introduction of steam power. However, it has never withstood close scrutiny. The demand for a redistribution of work is derived rather from the judgment that the current distribution of employment opportunities, and in particular the high and unevenly distributed risk of unemployment or volatile labour income, is not only economically unreasonable but also unfair and no longer chimes with contemporary notions of a society free of discrimination. The question of how such a redistribution of work might be organized without affecting economic efficiency and consigning many people to lengthy periods of unemployment will now be addressed.

The Goal of Full Employment Redefined

Changed economic conditions and social structures, together with the associated changes in values, make the goal of full employment as formulated by Lord Beveridge in 1944 seem outmoded. Today, the idea of creating permanent, full-time jobs for all (at that time, of course, male) heads of household, that is jobs requiring eight hours' work a day, five or six days a week, 48 to 50 weeks a year over a working life lasting 45 to 50 years, would be not only unrealistic but also backward-looking. It would be more in keeping with the spirit of the times to make the boundaries between paid work and other meaningful activities more fluid, and it would not be utopian to set our sights in the long term on the 'flexible 30-hour week' as a target value for the time devoted to paid work by men and women alike.[37] Even today, a 32-hour week would equate to the level of productivity required to produce the current national income if all those who wanted to work were in employment.

Under today's conditions, however, average weekly working time can no longer be fixed; rather – in accordance with the cybernetic notion of 'flowing equilibrium' – it has to be variable in length. The 'flexible 30-hour week' would equate to an average working time over the life course, from which there could be divergences according to the phase of the life course, economic need and individual preference. In other words, the forms of working-time reduction will have to adapt to changing preferences during the individual life course as well as to the new operational requirements of the economy. The universal, standardized reduction in weekly working time is an increasingly improbable, if not actually declining, model.[38] Significant divergences from the 'flowing equilibrium' of the 30-hour week for life course or economic reasons are denoted by the term *transitional employment* or, in the event of temporary unemployment, *transitional unemployment*, while the institutional arrangements by which such transitions are instituted, regulated and promoted are denoted by the term *transitional labour markets*.

There are good reasons for accelerating the rate of reduction in actual working time rather than slowing it down. Some of these reasons are environmental: work mediated through the market is generally more damaging to the environment than non-market work, such as that involved in many care or educational activities. Others have more to do with fairness: at least some of the paid overtime regularly worked by 'insiders' could be converted into jobs for 'outsiders'. Yet others have to do with equality of opportunities for men and women: if men were to take on more of the (unpaid) domestic work, then their (frequently more highly educated) wives would have more time for higher-status jobs.

However, there are also good reasons for leaving questions of working time to social policy decisions. This is because working-time preferences are culturally diverse, and the decision to opt for more free time (and consequently more time for do-it-yourself work) is dependent on, among other things, the state of economic prosperity already achieved (cf. also the fourth section of Chapter 2). What is important about the redefined notion of full employment is less the trend towards a further reduction in actual working time than the greater diversity of employment relationships and the opportunities for choosing freely between them. Thus transitional labour market theory is not dependent on the paradigm of the 'flexible 30-hour week'; it would also be valid if a national economy were to align itself to the 'flexible 35-hour week' or even to the 'flexible 40-hour week'. Ultimately, the essence of the argument can be reduced to the notion that the employment level rises (and hence unemployment falls) if the range of potential employment relationships is extended. The institutionalization of transitional labour markets is one hitherto neglected way of extending that range.

A way to illustrate the consequences of the proposed new concept of full employment is to look at the frequency distribution of working times by gender when they follow particular patterns or 'regimes'. Figure 5.1 depicts

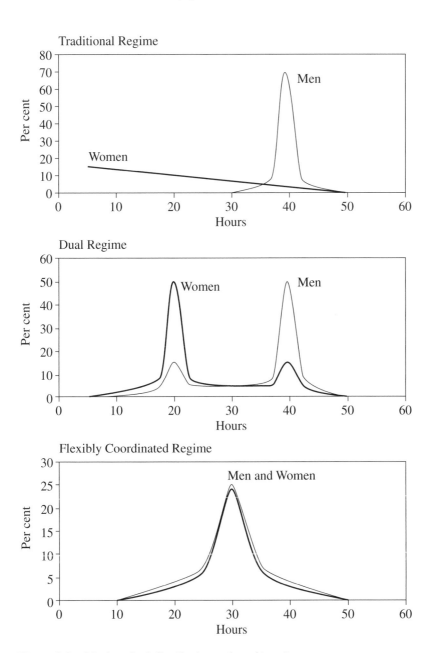

Figure 5.1   Ideal-typical distributions of working time

three ideal-typical working-time regimes that can be compared with real patterns of distribution in actual employment systems (Figure 5.2).[39]

1   The *traditional working-time regime* is characterized by a highly standardized pattern of working time for men and a completely unstandardized one for women. Virtually all male jobs involve a fixed number of hours' work that equates to the historically contingent standard of 'full-time employment', while there is a virtual absence of 'atypical' employment relationships above or below that standard. The jobs taken by women in their capacity as occasional secondary earners, on the other hand, are not standardized at all; in their case, the expectation is that frequency declines continuously as working time rises. The current structure of working-time distribution among men in France corresponds almost exactly to this ideal type. The full-employment standard in France has long been stable at 39 hours, while male distribution structures in Germany[40] and Denmark[41] come very close to this standard. As far as women are concerned, the (actual) pattern of distribution in the Netherlands and UK largely corresponds to the expectations of this ideal type. However, the other distribution patterns reveal a completely 'untypical' structure among men in UK, which acts as a sort of counter-pattern, as it were, to the (expected) female distribution, with frequencies rising as weekly working time rises. The obvious explanation lies in the fact that working time in the neoliberal regime in England is scarcely regulated at all. Women in France and Denmark, whose working time, like that of men, has a maximum of 39 or (in Denmark) 37 hours, also confound the expectations of the traditional pattern.

2   In the *dual working-time regime*, weekly working times among men cluster around a historically contingent 'full-time standard', as in the traditional regime, with some men adjusting to the female pattern of conventional part-time work. The majority of women are in a standardized form of part-time employment, which means that their average working time goes up to about 20 hours, that is about half of the 'standard' working time; some women adjust to the men's pattern. The Netherlands comes closest to this ideal type, and the distribution patterns of women in France and Germany have elements of this regime, in so far as the peaks equate roughly to traditional part-time jobs.

3   In the *flexibly coordinated working-time regime* which, in its ideal-typical form would correspond to the principles of transitional labour markets, both men's and women's jobs would cluster around the 30-hour week, for example, but working times above and below this level would occur with declining frequency, so that the distribution structure would resemble a normal distribution and be gender-neutral. Few would work below 15 hours, but some, as in the other regimes, would work more than 40 hours at some time in their life course. Even if none of the countries under investigation here (or any other, come to that) currently has a distribution structure of this kind, some of the elements of such a distribution structure can already be discerned, albeit to

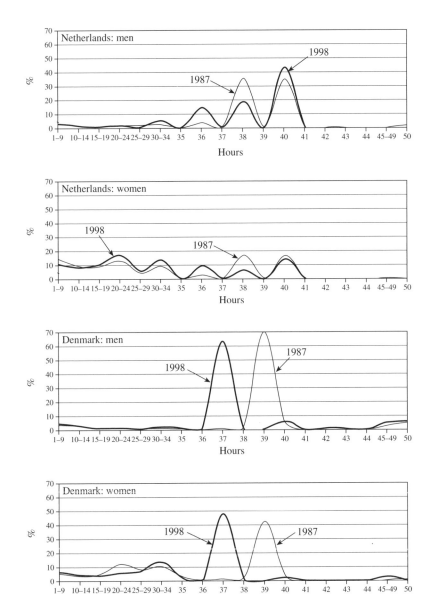

Source: Eurostat.

Figure 5.2   Actual patterns of weekly working time distribution in selected EU member states

varying degrees, in all countries. This applies in particular to the United Kingdom, the Netherlands and Denmark (also, incidentally, the most success-ful countries in employment policy terms; cf. Chapter 2), as well as to women in Germany and France.

One further observation has important implications for the transitional labour market argument. In the area of the knowledge or information society, actual and preferred patterns of working-time distribution – controlled for wage preferences – seem to drift apart. The typical pattern that emerges from this is that, in the lower half of the intermediate working-time segment, particu-larly between 15 and 33 hours, workers express a preference for longer hours than are contractually stipulated. On the other hand, in the upper half of the intermediate working-time segment, between 34 and 40 hours, that is, where transitional labour market theory locates the steady state or equilibrium point, workers express a preference for shorter working hours (European Commission, 1995). Also more recent surveys on actual and desired (regular) working times in EU member states suggest that the range of the preferred steady state is moving further downwards. The majority of those surveyed would in future prefer standard working times between 30 and 35 hours, as well as opportunities for varying working time by agreement without adversely affecting job security (Atkinson *et al.*, 1999).

The reasons for the discrepancies between actual and preferred working time lie especially in the increasing preferences to combine family or individ-ual non-market work with gainful employment. The new concept of full employment, therefore, has explicitly to take into account equality of oppor-tunity in labour markets for men and women. It has to extend the notion of work to include non-market activities that are, nevertheless, productive on either the individual or the wider social level. In consequence, the new full employment norm is to be understood as a point of equilibrium around which the majority of employment relationships cluster. This 'steady state' might lie in the near future at around 30 hours per week, although in theory it could be higher or lower. At the same time, however, there are many other employment relationships with considerably lower working times, which are usually combined with other productive activities, as well as others with considerably longer working times, which make full use of phases of high individual market productivity. However, these divergences from the new 'standard working time' are time-limited transitions. The risks associated with undertaking such transitions can be offset by institutionalizing transitional labour markets.

In essence, transitional labour markets are forums for the negotiation or agreement of variable employment relationships. As such they contrast sharply with the paradigm of the 'standard employment contract' which left little room for varieties adjusted to local circumstances or changing individual needs through the life cycle. What justifies the talk of such a new paradigm?

Short-time Working as a Model for Transitional Labour Markets

I would like to usher in the transitional labour market 'paradigm' with a personal anecdote. During an interview in the 1970s, the manager of an employment office in what was then still a rural region of Baden-Württemberg explained the principle of the short-time allowance to me in the following terms:

> The people here accept a temporary cut in working time with only partial wage compensation as a legitimate form of adjustment to cyclical drops in demand. They prefer this form of adjustment to layoffs or dismissals for part of the workforce, and they use their free time to work on their smallholdings, in their gardens or on their houses. They even feel exasperated if the period of short-time working does not coincide with the workload on their small farms, and they regard short-time working almost as a right. For their part, employers are able to retain skilled workers and can count on their employees to be especially loyal and ready for work when required.

It is immediately understandable that a socially legitimated and economically efficient institution such as short-time working will be associated with a level of employment that is higher (and an unemployment level that is lower) than it would be in the absence of such an arrangement, which spreads cyclical risks more evenly between employers and employees. The example of the short-time allowance (Mosley and Kruppe, 1996) contains three further lessons that could well be applied more widely.

First, labour markets are constantly exposed to shocks to which firms and their employees have to adjust. These shocks may be external ones: market changes, technological change, labour migrations, birth cycles and so on. However, they may also be internally generated: catastrophic management errors on the employer's side or, on the employees' side, health catastrophes or life crises, such as one of a married (two earners) couple commuting to another region, divorce, chronic illness, a sudden aversion to one's occupation or the arrival of a first child. One characteristic of modern service societies is 'burnout'; that is, psychological exhaustion and diminished efficiency resulting from overwork or prolonged exposure to stress, particularly in pressurized service occupations. People working in education and in the caring professions and, in my view, politicians as well, seem to be particularly susceptible to burnout. Victims of burnout may be forced to change occupation, or at least to take time out, and bridges have to be created in order to enable them to do so. Thus one fundamental characteristic of the information and communication society is the increasing incidence of self-produced 'internal' or 'manufactured risks'.[42] Although practicable remedies or compensations are available for the 'external risks', the existing set of labour market and social policy instruments still takes little account of such internal risks.

Such internal risks are the cause of discontinuous employment trajectories and, increasingly, of unemployment as well. What is involved here usually is short periods of unemployment that act as a 'bridge' in the event of a planned change of job, a return to education or a change of occupation or family circumstances. In certain cases, such periods of unemployment may also be longer, for example when they constitute a phase of preparation prior to (early) retirement or a withdrawal into family activities. Such endogenous spells of unemployment differ from traditional unemployment in so far as they are not closely related to traditional causes of unemployment such as cyclical ups and downs or technological change. They may even lead to better working conditions or higher salaries; however, they may also (especially for women and for the few men taking over family responsibilities) be the starting point of a social and economic downward spiral. Thus in addition to frictional, structural and cyclical unemployment, a new and separate type of unemployment is emerging, denoted by the term 'transitional unemployment', for which new solutions are required.

The second lesson to be drawn from our little anecdote is that labour markets are not product markets but social institutions.[43] Consequently, their capacity to adjust to internal or external shocks through variations in wages is limited. What is more, the greater the need for adjustment, the less likely it is that the required adjustment can be achieved solely by means of wage flexibility. One only has to think, for example, of the process of transition in Eastern Germany which, in the absence of any social buffering for the majority of the population, would have led to catastrophe.[44] Similarly critical, though not quite so dramatic transitional processes still await us with the completion of European monetary union. To leave adjustment solely to the markets would be to permanently damage many individuals or groups. In particular, the notion of fairness restricts the capacity of wages to effect the adjustment required. Social status, solidarity and basic rights prohibit wages from following the ups and downs of the markets and falling below a certain threshold.

However, it is not only a sense of justice but also a readiness to cooperate and retrain that is encouraged through due consideration of differences in performance and security of income. Moreover, stable wage structures require firms to demonstrate a constant willingness to innovate; if such innovation is successful, the increased ability to pay is not immediately swallowed up by wage demands. In this way, a risk community can develop that is both socially just and economically efficient. Thus labour markets require not only social legitimated institutions to manage adjustment to internal or external shocks. The structural limitation on the capacity of wages to effect the adjustment required also follows from the fact that wages fulfil a multiplicity of functions.[45]

Third, the anecdote teaches us that planned or even unplanned or enforced spells of unemployment should not necessarily be a negative experience. Provided the appropriate precautions are in place, the time freed by unemployment can be used for activities of the person's own choosing, which may contribute to personal development, encourage do-it-yourself work or help to improve individuals' productive capacities in preparation for a return to regular work. In the 'golden age of manufacturing industry', it was agriculture, small-scale artisanal trades or the extended family that provided, as it were, natural institutional buffers and a social space for productive but not market-determined activities. These 'natural' buffers are either long gone or in the process of disappearing. New, 'artificial' or socially constructed buffers must be created in order to cushion the internal and external risks to which the labour market is exposed.

However paradoxical it might sound, *new institutional arrangements are required to regulate discontinuous employment trajectories.* In other words, and to retain the metaphor used in the anecdote, we need a *functional equivalent* for the 'hinterland' that, during the transition from the agrarian to the industrial society, helped many people to bridge periods of economic uncertainty and risk. Thus, at the turn of the 19th century, for example, cows, goats and pigs, which formed part of the subsistence economy of many families, were a common sight on the streets of Manhattan (Smuts, 1971). During the 1930s, the French unemployment rate was never more than 6 per cent despite the Great Depression and sluggish economy afterwards. Gazier (1995) connected this fact with the strong rural roots retained by French workers who went back into their families in the agricultural zones. In the first two decades after the Second World War, this subsistence economy was still an important additional source of income in rural regions of Germany. In industrial towns, it was workers' housing estates, with their allotments, that provided some of this 'hinterland'.[46]

Such subsistence economies actually seem to be going through something of a renaissance at the moment. By way of example, I would like to quote an extract from a report from France that is certainly representative of most European countries. On 3 September 1997, *Le Monde* published an article on 'The cancer of employment in Andelys', a small town on the Seine.

> The allotments flourished for a time after the Second World War, but by the 1970s they had almost disappeared. They are now flourishing again. Since 1990, these modest enclaves have been mushrooming and their owners are far from being just pensioners. 'A lot of unemployed workers have really made their allotments an instrument of economic survival,' said Francis, a hairdresser in the centre of the small town. He has been running a salon in the Place Nicolas Poussin for 15 years, and his customers often talk to him in confidence. 'It's much worse today than it used to be. Almost everybody's affected by it.' His customers talk of the 'pressure'

at work … where everybody has the feeling that 'everything might collapse overnight'. And he added bluntly: 'I see a lot of people without a livelihood, and my custom is declining. More and more people are getting their friends to cut their hair.'

However, this state of affairs must be regarded as a retrograde step for developed market economies, one to which people have resorted out of sheer necessity.[47] These newly revived allotments are not the functional equivalent of the 'hinterland' that I would like to support. We know that the functional equivalent of the 'hinterland' of the Industrial Revolution was the development of social security systems. However, what is the institutional solution best suited to the risks of the information society? What needs to be done is not to recreate a subsistence economy of the past but rather to establish a lasting, modern solution. Such a solution will certainly involve a further development of tried and tested social security instruments, but it must be complemented by innovative elements.

Such innovations, transitional labour markets indeed, will have to concentrate on three aspects. The first is the development of institutional solutions that accord greater financial recognition to social useful activities that are not rewarded in the market place (particularly childcare and care of the elderly). The second is the establishment of a mode of work organization that allows more scope for freely chosen activities, either ones that are intrinsically beneficial, such as sporting, musical or artistic activities, or entrepreneurial activities that create additional sources of income. The third is the creation of additional sources of income independent of paid employment, such as shareholdings, other forms of holdings in companies or real estate.

The Need for Transitional Labour Markets

As has already been suggested on various occasions, differentiation and discontinuity of employment trajectories are the fundamental characteristics that will increasingly shape the labour market of the future. These characteristics are also consistent with new findings in psychology and sociology, according to which it can no longer be assumed that the pattern of individual lives will be socially or biologically predetermined (Erikson, 1979). Rather, we will have to be prepared for 'contingent', that is chaotically determined, life events. Coping with such contingent events will require the acquisition of skills that have to be permanently renewed and an infrastructure on which individuals can count if required. By analogy with the theory of life transitions in psychology (Schlossberg, 1984), labour market transitions can be regarded as 'critical events' that bring with them both risks and opportunities. This is why life event histories have become so important in empirical labour market research as a means of ascertaining the conditions required for the successful management of such critical events as the school/work transition, a change of employer or of occupation, a change from one working-time regime to another (for family reasons, for example) or retirement.[48]

However, such critical transitions are also, so to speak, doors closing behind us while there is still considerable uncertainty as to the doors that might open up for us in future. Thus each critical labour market transition brings with it a high risk of social exclusion. 'Social exclusion', in the strict sense of the term, does not necessarily refer solely to the fact of being disadvantaged in the labour market or even being unemployed. It denotes in particular the personal reaction of those who, in the face of all the difficulties that can pile up during a critical transition, withdraw discouraged from the labour market. The probability of such a reaction rises as the period of time spent out of work increases. Ultimately, discouraged workers might end up even not as part of the 'reserve army of labour' of which Karl Marx spoke. They may become 'disposable' or even 'superfluous', people who are no longer needed in society. And there is hardly anything that can cause greater damage to personal identity and self-confidence than being disposable or superfluous. The damage caused by such a process of exclusion is all the greater the fewer 'alternative roles' (such as 'housewife', 'house-husband' or 'pensioner') society offers. This is the reason why social exclusion is most fraught with danger for young people, because they have scarcely had an opportunity to prove their capabilities. Moreover, social exclusion in one sphere, in this case the labour market, often gives rise to processes of exclusion in other spheres, in cultural life, for example, in access to a reasonable level of prosperity or in the political arena.[49]

Success in coping with discontinuous employment trajectories depends on several factors. Psychological research on transitions highlights three in particular: first, the way in which individuals perceive sudden radical change; second, individual characteristics and abilities; and third, the social environment. In the case of the first factor, that is individuals' perception of sudden change, psychological research shows that what is decisive is whether the uncertainty generated by the shock is regarded as permanent or as an event that can be overcome by drawing on their own self-confidence and the support they can expect from others. The greater the certainty that things will improve in the foreseeable future, the easier it is to mobilize individual resources. If, on the other hand, the situation is perceived as a 'never-ending nightmare', the ability to resist can become paralysed, making it much more difficult for individuals to accept the need for change. The decisive factor in coping with crisis is the attitude that it is all part of life's rich tapestry and may even be an opportunity. This in turn generates the kind of optimism and confidence that can 'move mountains'.

While it is true that such optimism and confidence cannot be institutional-ized, it is, nevertheless, worth inquiring into the conditions that encourage such optimism and confidence. Strengthening the personal resources on which individuals can draw (*empowerment*), through lifelong learning for example, would be one such condition; the provision of a *material infrastructure* in the form of competent information services, for example, would be another; the establishment of a *procedural infrastructure* by providing support for local networks, for example, would be a third; and the creation of a reliable *legal infrastructure* through the introduction of new civil rights, for example, would be a fourth condition. Finally, it is not only tangible resources, such as mon-etary assets, capital, property and land, but also free time that is critically important for the accumulation of the resources required to cope with critical transitions. 'Ample time for all' may well be the slogan for the coming millen-nium; time was, after all, a luxury that was once available only to the 'leisure classes'.[50]

5   SUMMARY AND CONCLUSIONS

We can now sum up. The end of the 'standard employment relationship' is frequently advanced as a proven fact. On closer examination, however, it becomes clear that the majority of employment contracts still consist of perma-nent, dependent, full-time employment relationships. True, such employment relationships are on the decline, because new contracts are increasingly becom-ing more variable; at the same time, however, the propensity to work is also increasing because more and more women now want to be economically inde-pendent. Flexibilization seems to be a better description of the current evolu-tion than the talk about the erosion of the standard employment relationship. Since the precise nature of this flexibilization is still unclear, we have been trying to shed light through a theoretical model that distinguishes between sales contracts, and employment contracts provided further clues for future develop-ment. Both forms of contract have characteristic advantages and disadvantages. The choice of contract type depends on how concerned the contracting parties are, on the one hand, with security of income, restriction of competition and skill formation and, on the other hand, with freely available labour services ('liquidity'), reliable performance and experience knowledge that cannot be purchased in the market. Changes in basic conditions may lead to a decline in interest in standard employment contracts in favour of sales contracts, or to the emergence of hybrid forms that combine elements of the two contract types. This would explain the increase in flexible employment relationships. However, discussion of this model reveals that 'employees' and 'employers' will continue to have a strong interest in permanent employment contracts, but that such contracts will increasingly contain elements derived from sales contracts, such as agreed targets or cost and profit sharing.

What form might the 'standard employment relationship' take in future? In order to answer this question, we have been casting a more searching eye over those segments of the labour market in which early forms of the labour markets of the future may already be developing. We suspected that such forward-looking employment relationships are already present in embryo in the labour market for artists and journalists. At the same time, however, these labour markets reveal the limits of those bold visions in which wage workers cease to exist and are replaced by 'worker entrepreneurs' whose only product is their own labour. These labour markets have long contained features that can no longer be located simply in the grey area between self-employment and dependent employment. We are dealing here with separate forms of economic activity which are precarious only because the associated risks are very difficult to manage successfully. Nevertheless, it would appear that such employment relationships are increasingly being preferred to dependent wage work.

The ways in which individuals and society manage the risks inherent in such employment relationships provided some ideas that could be applied more generally: Maintaining and enhancing employability through continuous training, multiple employment relationships ('engagements'), profit sharing, basic income security through negative income taxes and broadening the tax base of social security contributions to all kinds of income are such elements to be considered in re-engineering the modern welfare state. However, most people are not able to cope alone with the increasing risks related to flexible labour markets. We identified the need for collectively organized and negotiated arrangements to cope with critical transitions between various forms of productive activities during the life cycle, especially those transitions related to family work. This led us to consider possibilities to establish a broader set of opportunities for mobility related to critical transitions typical during an average life course.

'Internal', home-made risks in particular are increasing in labour markets. It is in the critical phases of the adult working life that the risk of unemployment, loss of income or even social exclusion is particularly high. In order to support individuals in their attempts to cope with these transitions, reliable bridges are required that provide properly institutionalized, that is calculable and socially legitimated, options for negotiating in the critical phases. Five labour market transitions that should be promoted through enduring bridges into and out of employment can be systematically identified: (1) transitions between education/training and employment; (2) transitions between part-time and full-time dependent employment, or between dependent employment and self-employment, or combinations of the two; (3) transitions between (usually unpaid) private or family-based activities and paid work; (4) transitions

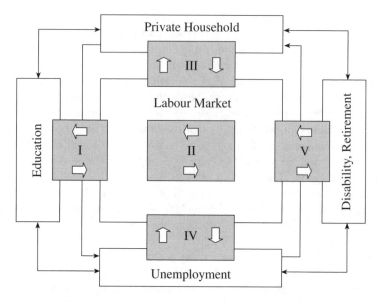

Figure 5.3   The transitional labour markets framework

between unemployment and employment; and (5) transitions between periodic incapacity for work and employment, as well as flexible transitions from work into retirement (Figure 5.3).

The theory of transitional labour markets draws attention to the fact that all labour market flows are interacting and can occur in both directions (see Chapter 8). Transitional labour market theory indicates that these interdependencies in the design of the new labour market policy should be taken into account. Further, it points to the risks of social exclusion associated with critical transitions and to starting points for attempts to cope successfully with these unavoidable crises. The institutionalization of 'transitional labour markets' establishes stable 'bridges' linking all forms of productive activity and facilitating movement in one direction or the other: paid work with variable employment relationships or working times, lifelong learning, unpaid family or do-it-yourself work, other recognized forms of social work, such as voluntary work or neighbourhood schemes, as well as time for creative leisure (sabbaticals), during which new abilities can be tested without any requirement to be successful. The institutions of labour market policy should be designed in such a way as to create incentives for the transition between these various forms of productive work, to make possible combinations of various forms of work and to provide social protection for the ensuing risks. The more options for transitions are institutionalized, the more employment opportunities could be created and a significant contribution to the reduction of unemployment could be made. Further consideration of these thoughts, together with examples from EU member states, will be the object of the final chapter in this volume.)

NOTES

1. I am very grateful for comments by Bernard Gazier, Jacqueline O'Reilly and Donald Storrie, and for the translation by Andrew Wilson; remaining errors and weaknesses are my responsibility.
2. In reality, this ideal type was characteristic, for instance, of Germany (and even then only of Western Germany) for only about three decades after the Second World War. For a historical survey, see Bertram (2000) who points out that at no time since 1950 have more than 50 per cent of children up to the age of 15 in the USA or in Germany grown up in the conventional family model.
3. For discussion of the erosion of the 'standard employment relationship' and international comparative evidence (although scattered) see Delsen (1995), Felstead and Jewson (1999), Mangan (2000), Rubery (1998), Tálos (1999).
4. See also Blossfeld and Hakim (1997) and O'Reilly and Fagan (1998) for a comparative perspective.
5. According to the official statistics, there were 2.15 million in 1998 (5 per cent of the economically active population), while specialist studies put the figure at 5.6 million, a figure reached in part by the inclusion of second jobs (Buch, 1999). Thus, before the German national accounts were revised in April 1999, the number of people in marginal part-time jobs was considerably underestimated; following the revision, the number of economically active individuals rose by 2 million, almost 6 per cent of the 34 million economically active people identified in 1997. In consequence, and again because of the adjustment of the German statistics to the European system of national accounts, productivity increase per economically active person fell from 2.7 to 1.9 (1998) – a figure with significant implications for pay policy, for example.
6. Since 1999, employers have to pay a flat-rate contribution of 12 per cent to the statutory pension insurance scheme and a 10 per cent contribution to the health insurance scheme if these jobs are regular; employees holding such jobs, however, are only entitled to health and pension insurance if they contribute in addition 7.5 per cent of their wages into the respective insurance funds.
7. Germany is an inexplicable exception in this respect.
8. In the European Union (EU 15) in 1997, 4.8 per cent of men with 'full-time status' actually worked between 21 and 35 hours per week only (7.4 per cent in Germany); the figure for women was 11.4 per cent (10 per cent in Germany). The reasons for this have not been clarified in detail, but the main factors are likely to include cyclical short-time working and the temporary absence of employees on parental or training leave.
9. The number of 'pseudo self-employed' in Germany is estimated at between 179 000 and 431 000, or between 0.5 and 1.1 per cent of the economically active population (cf. Hoffmann and Walwei, 1998; Buch, 1999; Dietrich, 1999).
10. More than half of them were working in the engineering and electrical industries. Of the agency workers registered in the first six months of 1998, 27 per cent were unskilled workers or had not declared their occupations, 20 per cent were fitters and mechanics or similar and 11.1 per cent were in organizational, administrative and clerical occupations.
11. UK (3.7 per cent), USA (2.3 per cent), France (2.2 per cent) and Belgium (1.6 per cent) were other countries with relatively extensive use of temporary work; on the other hand, this employment relationship is not yet widely distributed in the Scandinavian countries: Norway (0.7 per cent), Finland (0.5 per cent), Sweden (0.3 per cent) and Denmark (0.3 per cent); see Klös (2000) and Weltverband Zeitarbeit (CIETT) (1999).
12. For example, Manpower, Adecco and Randstad; Adecco, with 3 000 branches in 49 countries, employs 300 000 workers.

13. In June 1999, at a time when preparations were being made in Germany for EXPO, a major international exhibition where agency work is particularly prevalent, the Hanover branch of the engineering workers' union IG Metall, after a hard-fought battle that lasted a year, concluded a collective agreement on behalf of six trade unions affiliated to the German TUC that provided for new hourly wage rates of between 13.84 and 25.08 DM. Under the terms of the collective agreement, Adecco undertakes to give preference in recruitment to the long-term unemployed and to give priority to insurable employment relationships and to training programmes, particularly in the area of unskilled activities.

14. Cf. the surveys in Büchtemann (1993), Büchtemann and Walwei (1996). For a summary of arguments and empirical evidence about the impact of employment protection regulation on employment, cf. Bertola *et al.* (2000).

15. We should not allow ourselves to be blinded by formal regulations: even in employment relationships subject to little formal regulation, there is in practice a multiplicity of implicit contracts that give dependent employees a monopoly position.

16. Cf. in particular Williamson *et al.* (1975) and Williamson (1985).

17. Sociological/institutional labour market theory denotes these demands with the term 'job specificity' (Doeringer and Piore, 1971: 15ff), while the institutionalist economic school uses the term 'idiosyncratic tasks' (Williamson *et al.* 1975: 256ff). We take the term 'job-specific demands' to denote both specific, non-standardizable skills or knowledge derived from experience and the capacity for job-specific cooperation.

18. Issues around the structure, dynamic and distribution of income are extremely complex, and the data situation is very unsatisfactory. Moreover, we know of no differentiated analysis of the link between income portfolios and labour market behaviour or employment forms. In consequence, the following observations are to be regarded as extremely provisional.

19. Cf. Gazier in this volume.

20. Cf. Meager and Bates in this volume.

21. Statutory regulations may also make it difficult to become self-employed. Thus the German legislation regulating the conduct of craft trades (*Handwerksordnung*), for example, restricts access to certain occupations.

22. A recent survey conducted in the EU member states (plus Norway) found that 25 per cent of those surveyed wanted to become self-employed in the near future (Atkinson *et al.* 1999); the self-employment rate (the self-employed population outside agriculture as a percentage of the population of working age) is about 9 per cent in the EU (Schömann, Kruppe and Oschmiansky, 1998: 38).

23. This means context-specific, local knowledge, frequently also referred to in theoretical writings as 'tacit knowledge', that cannot be standardized and therefore cannot (and should not) be marketed.

24. This is why the insights of efficiency wage theory should not be thrown overboard; cf., among others, Akerloff and Yellen (1986).

25. The first edition of this book appeared in 1966. This would seem to confirm this position that the culture economy rather than the urban economy had a decisive influence on the development of Baumol's theory of costs disease.

26. This and the following sections are distilled from an essay co-authored with Carroll Haak; cf. Haak and Schmid (2001).

27. According to the German microcensus, 35 per cent of artists and journalists were *self-employed* in 1995, a considerably higher share than the general average of 9 per cent. Women have been the main beneficiaries of the positive growth, and may even account for 38 per cent of the self-employed.

28. Those engaged in artistic or media work as dependent employees are not affected by the Artists' Social Security Act.

29. The Artists' Social Security Bill was hotly disputed, and another product of the SPD/FDP coalition that lost power in 1982; without the active support of celebrities in the world of the arts (including Günter Grass), the Bill would not have become law. When it came to power, the CDU/FDP coalition was careful not to disrupt the compromise that had been reached with such difficulty.

30. This is not to deny the great importance of 'calling', natural talent or intrinsic motivations in creative professions.
31. The notion that average tenure changed little during the last decades is, therefore, not contradicting this argument.
32. To adapt Stephen Hawkins' words freely, fame is when more people know oneself than one knows other people.
33. Without the old risks, such as the obsolescence of skills, the distortion of demographic structures or cyclical economic risks, disappearing.
34. Reputation may have the effect of creating a monopoly, that is erecting barriers to entry, restricting competition and reducing the pressure for continuing learning; with the passage of time, it can give rise to alarming incompetence even among professionals who started out competent.
35. Control through self-control is known to be particularly effective, as Elias's theory of civilization (1976) impressively demonstrates.
36. See Chapters 1, 7 and 8.
37. By way of a reminder: in 1856, the 70-hour week was introduced in the German printing industry; in 1900, the trade unions were fighting for the 60-hour week; in 1950, the average length of the working week was 48 hours, in 1980, 40 hours and in 1993, 38 hours. Between 1983 and 1995, the average number of hours worked in the European Union (EU12) declined by just over 1.5 hours, from around 40 a week to 38.5. There are signs, however, that the overall historical trend of weekly working time reduction is slowing down and being replaced by increasing variability of working time (European Commission, 1996: 77–87).
38. Cf., among other publications, the report by a French committee on the future of work entitled 'Work in 20 years' time' (Boissonat, 1995). The French experiences on the basis of a universal weekly working time reduction contradict only at first glance this argument. The implementation of the '35-hour week' stipulated by the two Aubry laws in fact shows a rather flexible adjustment of the firms, and – even more important in our context – a stimulation of local negotiations to adjust for the specific needs of firms and individuals.
39. For Germany, France and the UK see Figure 10.1 in this volume.
40. The bimodal and the recent trimodal distribution in Germany is a specific characteristic of the corporatist system that has introduced the (flexible) 35-hour week in some collective bargaining areas, notably the engineering industry, and the 38-hour week particularly in the public sector.
41. With their working time maximum at 37 hours, however, Danish men are considerably below the 'standard working time'.
42. Cf. the sociologists Ulrich Beck (1986) and Anthony Giddens (1996).
43. Cf., among others, Solow (1990); Schmid and Schömann (1994).
44. To illustrate the size of the 'social buffer' provided by active labour market policy in East Germany: at the height of the employment crises in 1991, 1.9 million persons were in labour market measures, about 23 per cent of the active labour force. Without it, the unemployment rate would have been 35 per cent instead of 'only' 12 per cent officially reported (Schmid and Wiebe 1999: 381).
45. Malcom Sawyer's (1993) fundamental considerations on the function of prices in markets can be extended to wages. Sawyer distinguishes five functions: the allocative, the conductive, the positional, the strategic and the financial functions of prices or of wages; a sixth function can be added referring to incentives for cooperation.
46. An interesting historical account of how people at the beginning of capitalism dealt with unemployment through risk spreading is provided by Piore (1987).
47. The 'agricultural hinterland' as a buffer providing some degree of social security might rightly be judged differently in the case of the so-called 'transition economies' (for example, Genov, 2000). The relatively low level of unemployment in some of these countries in transformation is attributable, among other things, to the fact that many unemployed people, usually older men, retire to three or four hectares of land that they have acquired in the course of privatization and grow products on it for their own consumption. True, they continue to look for jobs, but with little prospect of success, and they do not usually count as unemployed.

48. Cf. Mayer (1997), Schömann (1996); Blossfeld and Rohwer (1995).
49. On questions of 'social exclusion' or 'social inclusion', cf., among others, Kronauer (1997), Morris (1994) and Silver (1994).
50. Cf. Veblen (1971), who coined the term 'leisure class' and whose work remains as illuminating as it ever was.

BIBLIOGRAPHY

Akerloff, G.A. and J.L. Yellen (eds) (1986), *Efficiency Wage Models of the Labour Market*, Cambridge: Cambridge University Press.
Atkinson, J., H. Bielenski, G. Gasparini, J. Hartmann and F. Huijgen (1999), *Employment Options of the Future. First Analyses of a Representative Survey in all 15 EU Member States and in Norway*, Munich: Infratest Burke Sozialforschung (on behalf of the European Foundation for the Improvement of Living and Working Conditions, Dublin).
Baumol, W.J. and W.G. Bowen (1993), *Performing Arts – The Economic Dilemma. A Study of Problems common to Theater, Opera, Music and Dance*, Aldershot: Gregg Revivals.
Beck, U. (1986), *Risikogesellschaft. Auf dem Weg in eine andere Moderne*, Frankfurt a. M.: Suhrkamp.
Benhamou, F. (1996), *L'économie de la culture*, Paris: Éditions La Découverte.
Bertola, G., T. Boeri and S. Cazes (2000), 'Employment protection in Industrialized Countries. The Case for New Indicators', *International Labour Review*, 139(1), 57–72.
Bertram, H. (2000), 'Arbeit, Familie und Bindungen', in J. Kocka and C. Offe (eds), *Geschichte und Zukunft der Arbeit*, Frankfurt a. M.: Suhrkamp, pp. 308–42.
Beveridge, W.H. (1945 [1944]), *Full Employment in a Free Society*, New York: W.W. Norton & Company.
Blossfeld, H.-P. and C. Hakim (1997), *Between Equalization and Marginalization. Women Working Part-Time in Europe and the United States of America*, Oxford: Oxford University Press.
Blossfeld, H.-P. and G. Rohwer (1995), *Techniques of Event History Modeling. New Approaches to Causal Analysis*, Mahwah, NJ: Lawrence Earlbaum Associates.
Boissonat, J. (1995), *Le travail dans vingt ans*, Paris: Editions Odile Jacob, La Documentation française.
Buch, H. (1999), *Ungeschützte Beschäftigungsverhältnisse. Scheinselbständigkeit und geringfügige Beschäftigung auf dem deutschen Arbeitsmarkt*, Frankfurt a. M.: Peter Lang.
Büchtemann, C.F. (ed.) (1993), *Employment Security and Labor Market Behavior*, Ithaca, NY: ILR Press.
Büchtemann, Ch. and U. Walwei (1996), 'Employment Security and Dismissal Protection', in G. Schmid, J. O'Reilly and K. Schömann (eds), *International Handbook of Labour Market Policy and Evaluation*, Cheltenham, UK and Lyme, US: Edward Elgar, 652–93.
Debis (1999), Dienstleistungstarifvertrag. Kongress mit Fachtagung, 'Partnerschaftlich die Arbeitsbedingungen des 21. Jahrhunderts gestalten. Neue Wege in der Tarifpolitik', 14.–15. October.
Delsen, L. (1995), *Atypical Employment: An International Perspective. Causes, Consequences and Policy*, Groningen: Woltersgroep.

Dietrich, H. (1999), 'Empirische Befunde zur selbständigen Erwerbstätigkeit unter besonderer Berücksichtigung scheinselbständiger Erwerbsverhältnisse', *Mitteilungen aus der Arbeitsmarkt- und Berufsforschung*, 1, S. 85–101.

Dingeldey, I. (2000), *Erwerbstätigkeit und Familie in Steuer- und Sozialversicherungssystemen. Begünstigungen und Belastungen verschiedener familialer Erwerbsmuster im Ländervergleich*, Opladen: Leske + Budrich.

Doeringer, P. and M. Piore (1971), *Internal Labour Markets and Manpower Analysis*, Lexington, MA: D.C. Heath and Company.

Eberts, R. and G. Erickcek (2000), 'The Nature and Determinants of Service Sector Growth in the United States', in D. Anxo and D. Storrie (eds), *The Job Creation Potential of the Service in Europe*, Gothenburg: Centre for European Labour Market Studies (Final Report of the Employment Observatory Research Network), pp. 130–82.

Elias, N. (1976 [1936]), *Über den Prozeß der Zivilisation. Soziogenetische und psychogenetische Untersuchungen* (2 vols), Frankfurt a. M.: Suhrkamp.

Erikson, E. H. (1979), *Identität und Lebenszyklus. Drei Aufsätze*, Franfurt a. M.: Suhrkamp.

European Commission (1995), 'Performance of the European Labour Market. Results of an ad hoc Labour Market Survey Covering Employers and Employees', *European Economy. Reports and Studies*, no. 3.

European Commission (1996), *Employment in Europe 1996*, Luxembourg.

Felstead, A. and N. Jewson (eds) (1999), *Global Trends in Flexible Labour*, Houndmills and London: Macmillan Press.

Franck, G. (1998), *Ökonomie der Aufmerksamkeit. Ein Entwurf*, Munich and Vienna: Carl Hanser Verlag.

Frank, R.H. and P.J. Cook (1995), *The Winner-Take-All Society*, New York: The Free Press.

Gazier, B. (1995 [1983]), *La crise de 1929*, 4th corrected edn, Paris: Presses Universitaires de France (Que Sais-Je 2126).

Genov, N. (ed.) (2000), *Labour Markets and Unemployment in South-Eastern Europe*, Berlin: Wissenschaftszentrum Berlin für Sozialforschung.

Giddens, A. (1996), *Beyond Left and Right. The Future of Radical Politics*, Cambridge: Polity Press (first print 1994).

Granovetter, M. (1973), 'The Strength of Weak Ties', *The American Journal of Sociology*, 78(6), 1360–80.

Groys, B. (1999), *Über das Neue. Versuch einer Kulturökonomie*, Frankfurt a. M.: Fischer Taschenbuch Verlag.

Haak, C. and G. Schmid (2001), 'Arbeitsmärkte für Künstler und Publizisten. Modelle einer künftigen Arbeitswelt?', *Leviathan*, 29(1), 156–78.

Hoffmann, E. and U. Walwei (1998), 'Normalarbeitsverhältnis: ein Auslaufmodell? Überlegungen zu einem Erklärungsmodell für den Wandel der Beschäftigungsformen', *Mitteilungen aus der Arbeitsmarkt- und Berufsforschung*, H. 3, 409–25.

Houseman, S. (1999), 'Flexible Staffing Arrangements: A Report on Temporary Help, On-Call, Direct-Hire Temporary, Leased Contract Company and Independent Contractor Employment in the United States', Report to the US Department of Labor, Kalamazoo, MI: W.E. Upjohn Institute for Employment Research.

Klös, H.-P. (2000), 'Zeitarbeit – Entwicklungstrends und arbeitsmarktpolitische Bedeutung', *IW-Trends*, 27(1), 5–21.

Kronauer, M. (1997), ' "Soziale Ausgrenzung" und "Underclass": Über neue Formen der gesellschaftlichen Spaltung', *Leviathan*, 25(1), 28–49.

Krugman, P. (1999), *The Accidental Theorist. And Other Dispatches from the Dismal Science*, Harmondsworth: Penguin.

Leisering, L. and R. Walker (eds) (1998), *The Dynamics of Modern Society. Poverty, Policy and Welfare*, Bristol: Polity Press.

Mangan, J. (2000), *Labour Markets in Transition. An International study of Non-standard Employment*, Cheltenham, UK and Northampton, US: Edward Elgar.

Marsden, D. (2000), 'Adapting European Labour Institutions to Global Economic and Technical Change', paper delivered to the first conference of the St. Gobain Foundation of Economic Research in Paris, 8 and 9 November, mimeo.

Mayer, K.-U. (1997), 'Notes on a Comparative Political Economy of Life Courses', *Comparative Social Research*, 16, 204–26.

Menger, P.-M. and M. Gurgand (1996), 'Work and Compensated Unemployment in the Performing Arts. Exogenous and Endogenous Uncertainty in Artistic Labour Markets', in V.A. Ginsburgh and P.-M. Menger (eds), Economics of Arts – Selected Essays, Amsterdam: Elsevier, pp. 347–81.

Morris, L. (1994), *Dangerous Classes. The Underclass and Social Citizenship*, London: Routledge.

Mosley, H.G. and Th. Kruppe (1996), 'Employment Stabilization through Short-time Work', in G. Schmid, J. O'Reilly and K. Schömann (eds), *International Handbook of Labour Market Policy and Evaluation*, Cheltenham, UK and Brookfield, US: Edward Elgar, pp. 594–622.

O'Reilly, J. and C. Fagan (eds) (1998), *Part-time Prospects – An International Comparison of Part-time Work in Europe, North-America and the Pacific Rim*, London and New York: Routledge.

O'Reilly, J., I. Cebrián and M. Lallement (eds) (2000), *Working-time Changes. Social Integration Through Transitional Labour Markets*, Cheltenham, UK and Northampton, US: Edward Elgar.

Paul, A. and A. Kleingartner (1994), 'Flexible Production and the Transformation of Industrial Relations in the Motion Picture and Television Industry', *Industrial and Labor Relations Review*, 47(4), July, 663–78.

Piore, M. (1987), 'Historical Perspectives and the Interpretation of Unemployment', *Journal of Economic Literature*, 25(4), 1834–50.

Rubery, J. (1998), 'Part-time Work. A Threat to Labour Standards?', in J. O'Reilly and C. Fagan (eds), *Part-time Prospects – An International Comparison of Part-time Work in Europe, North-America and the Pacific Rim*, London and New York: Routledge, pp. 137–55.

Rubery, J., M. Smith and C. Fagan (1996), *Trends and Prospects for Women's Employment in the European Union in the 1990s*, Brussels: European Commission, DGV [V/2002/96-EN].

Rubery, J., M. Smith, C. Fagan and D. Grimshaw (1998), *Women and European Employment*, London and New York: Routledge.

Rudolph, H. and E. Schröder (1997), 'Arbeitnehmerüberlassung: Trends und Einsatzlogik', *Mitteilungen aus der Arbeitsmarkt- und Berufsforschung*, H.1, 102–26.

Sawyer, M.C. (1993), 'The Nature and Role of the Market', in Ch. Pitelis (ed.), *Transaction Costs, Markets and Hierarchies*, Oxford: Basic Blackwell, pp. 20–40.

Schlossberg, N.K. (1984), *Counseling Adults in Transition. Linking Practice with Theory*, New York: Springer.

Schmid, G. (2000), 'Beyond Conventional Service Economics. Utility Services,

Service-Product Chains and Job Services', in D. Anxo and D. Storrie (eds), *The Job Creation Potential of the Service in Europe*, Gothenburg: Centre for European Labour Market Studies (Final Report of the Employment Observatory Research Network), pp. 290–305.

Schmid, G. and K. Schömann (1994), 'Institutional Choice and Labour Market Performance', in G. Schmid (ed.), *Labor Market Institutions in Europe. A Socio-Economic Evaluation of Performance*, Armonk, NY: M.E. Sharpe, pp. 9–57.

Schmid, G. and N. Wiebe (1999), 'Die Politik der Vollbeschäftigung im Wandel. Von der passiven zur interaktiven Arbeitsmarktpolitik', in M. Kaase and G. Schmid (eds), *Eine lernende Demokratie. 50 Jahre Bundesrepublik Deutschland*, Berlin: edition sigma, pp. 357–96.

Schömann, K. (1996), Longitudinal Design and Evaluation Studies', in G. Schmid, J. O'Reilly, K. Schömann (eds), *International Handbook for Labour Market Policy and Evaluation*, Cheltenham, UK and Brookfield, US: Edward Elgar, pp. 115–42.

Schömann, K., T. Kruppe and H. Oschmiansky (1998), 'Beschäftigungsdynamik und Arbeitslosigkeit in der Europäischen Union', WZB Discussion Paper FS I 98–203, Wissenschaftszentrum Berlin für Sozialforschung, Berlin.

Schömann, K., R. Rogowski and T. Kruppe (1998), *Labour Market Efficiency in the European Union. A Legal and Economic Evaluation of Employment Protection and Fixed-Term Contracts*, London: Routledge.

Sennett, R. (1998), *The Corrosion of Character. The Personal Consequences of Work in the New Capitalism*, New York: W.W. Norton.

Silver, H. (1994), 'Social Exclusion and Social Solidarity: Three Paradigms', *International Labour Review*, 133(5–6), 531–78.

Simon, H.A. (1951), 'A Formal Theory of the Employment Relationship', *Econometrica*, 19, 293–305.

Smuts, R.W. (1971 [1959]), *Women and Work in America* (Paperback edn), New York: Schocken Books.

Solow, R.M. (1990), *The Labour Market as a Social Institution*, Oxford: Basil Blackwell.

Tálos, E. (ed.) (1999), *Atypische Beschäftigung. Internationale Trends und sozialstaatliche Regelungen*, Vienna: Manzsche Verlags- und Universitätsbuchhandlung.

Veblen, T. (1971 [1899]), *Theorie der feinen Leute. Eine ökonomische Untersuchung der Institutionen*, Munich: Deutscher Taschenbuchverlag (Original title: The Theory of the Leisure Class).

Voß, G.G. and H.J. Pongratz (1998), 'Der Arbeitskraftunternehmer. Eine neue Grundform der Ware Arbeitskraft?', *Kölner Zeitschrift für Soziologie und Sozialpsychologie*, Jg. 50, H. 1, 131–58.

Weltverband Zeitarbeit (CIETT) (1999), *Report of Activities 1998*, Brussels.

Williamson, O.E. (1985), *The Economic Institutions of Capitalism. Firms, Markets, Relational Contracting*, New York and London: The Free Press, Collier Macmillan.

Williamson, O.E., M.L. Wachter and J.E. Harris (1975), 'Understanding the Employment Relation: The Analysis of Idiosyncratic Exchange', *Bell Journal of Economics*, 6(1), 250–80.

6. Transitional labour markets: from positive analysis to policy proposals

Bernard Gazier

At first glance, the idea of systematically organizing the negotiated management of transitions in and around the labour market is a patently obvious one. It would appear to be a Pareto-improving process: there are transitions, good or bad, in the labour market and the general policy prescription arising out of transitional labour market (TLM) theory is that the whole network of transitions available to the workforce at large should be extended and improved.

However, there are costs involved of course, and this raises basic questions about efficiency. Direct evaluation is not necessarily appropriate given the present state of the TLM debate. TLM is more an approach than a specific programme, more a procedural tool than a policy device. Before any direct evaluations can be carried out, country-specific applications will have to be formulated and implemented.[1] The purpose of this chapter is to prepare the ground for the evaluation process by assessing the scope and potential of TLMs as a regulatory idea and to discuss the ways in which TLMs may affect labour market functioning and performance in developed countries.

The TLM approach focuses on the development of relatively new objects of negotiation and coordination, namely legally structured rights to mobility. Two main criticisms are currently levelled against the TLM approach. First, it is suggested that TLMs may be ineffective and/or too costly coordinating devices: it is often said that almost all conceivable kinds of transitions have been tried in the labour market (either by firms or as part of state-led labour market programmes) and any attempt to extend them must be left to private actors since they might otherwise be perceived as an unjustified extension of collective intervention. The second criticism is that TLMs may lead to the development of a second-class labour market, with dead-end, low-paid jobs.

Obviously, these two criticisms are based on two very different approaches to the functioning of the labour market. The first stresses the market process, which must, it is argued, be left as free as possible, while the other is based on the segmentation approach and emphasizes the considerable differences in constraints and opportunities in the various segments of the labour market. It is not the purpose of this chapter to discuss such a fundamental divide as that between market homogeneity and heterogeneity. Our starting point, rather, will be the particular nature of the labour market, characterized by Solow as a 'social institution' (Solow, 1991). We will adopt both points of view in turn, leaving open the question of whether they might complement or contradict each other.

A useful framework for our task is provided by the notion of 'remediableness' developed by Oliver Williamson in the context of transaction costs analysis (Williamson, 1996). In any discussion of the deficiencies and failures of complex arrangements involving markets, organizations and institutions, the practicable aim is not to present first-best or even second-best options but rather to assess whether some workable alternative (reform) might remedy some of the deficiencies, thereby providing a net gain. Here we set out the case for TLMs by examining how they might help to solve or mitigate certain familiar labour market adjustment problems and at the same time seeking to identify any possible shortcomings.

Accordingly, the main methodological choice made in this chapter is to strike a balance between abstraction, on the one hand, and excessively narrow or specific issues, on the other. We begin by briefly gathering some simple stylized facts on current labour market arrangements and functioning, before setting these broad facts and trends alongside the TLM perspective. For a more detailed description and assessment of labour market performance in developed countries, the reader is referred to the first part of the present volume.

In sections 1 and 2 we outline, for both approaches, the possible contribution of TLMs to labour market regulation. Section 3 examines some of the problems of complexity, incentives and control that would arise if the active management of labour market transitions were to be put forward as a workable reform.[2]

1 TLMS AND THE LABOUR MARKET: FROM COMMAND VARIABLES TO EMPLOYMENT REGIMES

For the sake of simplicity, it is expedient to identify three categories of variables that interact in labour market adjustments: prices (relative and absolute wage levels), quantities (that is, number of persons employed or of jobs, numbers of hours worked) and quality (individual skill levels, skill requirements and opportunities and job attractiveness). Adjustments can be left mainly to private actors but always involve some public intervention (basic education, labour law, unemployment insurance, minimum wages and so on).

Two different sets of basic stylized facts will be gathered and organized here. The first relates to the major and persistent difficulties arising from adjustment processes and variables in the labour market. The second relates to the various forms of path-dependent adjustment processes that emerged in different countries during the 1980s and the 1990s. A first approach to TLMs is then proposed, which locates them in the context of constrained and path-dependent labour market adjustments.

Stylized Facts Set 1: Adjustment Variables that are Difficult to Manage

The prices–quantities–qualities triptych generates a considerable number of labour market variables.[3] For example, in order to balance supply and demand, changes might occur in overall wage levels (through nominal wages, inflation or monetary adjustments such as devaluation) and/or in wage dispersion (as a result of different bargaining outcomes in different sectors, firms or labour market groups, increased premiums, the elimination of some categories of job slots, the introduction of a minimum wage and so on). Quantities on the supply and the demand side can be affected by, for example, creating public-sector jobs, encouraging or discouraging certain categories of workers, or introducing a legal limit on daily or weekly working time. Finally, training policies are one obvious way of affecting the quality of workers. Furthermore, there is some possible substitution between these variables. For example, raising the skill level of the workforce while leaving wage levels unchanged can – in theory – be equivalent to lowering real wages.[4]

However, it is well known that, for many different reasons, these variables are neither very flexible nor very effective. Leaving aside normative issues, wages are a variable whose movements are restricted by the various functions they fulfil: remunerating work, encouraging and rewarding performance, establishing hierarchical distinctions, financing social security, giving shape to career structures, and so on.[5] If wages are adjusted for one reason or another, adjustments in other functions may be disrupted. Thus tampering with wages is always a tricky matter. Employment subsidies, although not ineffective, are now notorious for the deadweight effects they induce. As for quantities, few people now advocate the expansion of public-sector employment.[6] Policies aimed at reducing the number of people in the labour market ('parking' schemes, large-scale early retirement programmes, grants to encourage immigrants to return to their country of origin, and so on) have serious drawbacks. They lead to the growth of 'passive' expenditures, with production losses. If early retirement policies are combined with the hiring of young workers, they may to some extent be the functional equivalent of wage adjustment and training policies. However, there is international evidence that the trade-off between early retirement and youth unemployment is not working. In any case, in years to come, the prospect of an ageing workforce and the need to fund ever larger numbers of pensioners will make it necessary to have more, not fewer, older workers active in the labour market. It also seems quite costly to place direct constraints on the hours worked (as with statutory limits on weekly working time). Finally, as regards quality and training measures, their impact on employment levels is difficult to measure and seems diffuse and gradual.

The variety of labour adjustment devices deployed in firms, including job rotation, shift work, overtime, extra pay, delayed or accelerated promotions, recruitments and lay-offs, seem largely to overcome these limitations. However, these practices depend on a variety of different employment statuses and levels of job security: a complicated picture emerges here, connected to a set of legal prohibitions and rules and to the various institutions and conventions that structure the labour market. It would be very difficult to disentangle the market failures, the interventions intended to remedy them and the policy failures that lead in turn to further compensatory measures. Operating with a greater or lesser degree of coherence, these sets of rules and institutions are intended to protect workers as well as to allow or encourage certain behaviours; there is always a problem when one rule has to be changed, because it is part of a balanced system in which each rule compensates or reinforces the others.

Thus the 'command variables' in the labour market may be seen as intertwined variables, with a significant change in one leading to major compensating reactions. Traditional allusions to 'wage stickiness' emphasize the social role of wages and the key influence of workers' and unions' perceptions in that area. It must be added that, from an explicitly normative point of view, there are limits to wage adjustment. However, it does seem justifiable to speak of a more general 'variable stickiness' in the labour market, owing to the number and variety of points at issue, rules and institutions that contribute to its regulation. This is probably why Ehrenberg (1994), in his comparative overview of the functioning of labour markets in North America and Europe, presents a sceptical analysis of the alleged need for convergence through the harmonization of labour standards and the introduction of greater flexibility. He observes that the continuing processes of integration allow national specificities to remain and that there are no irresistible or desirable pressures towards the convergence of labour market standards. He stresses the possible perverse effects of certain forms of flexibility, such as migration or increased mobility resulting from reduced job security.

However, various overall adjustments do take place in the labour markets. Do these adjustments follow certain specific national patterns?

Stylized Facts Set 2: 'Employment Regimes' in the 1980s

The 'employment regime' hypothesis furthers the previous observations by giving a content to national specificities in labour market adjustments. In its minimalist version, it follows on Solow's analysis of wage paths (Solow, 1991). A broader and more ambitious version would draw on the work of Günther Schmid (Schmid, 1994), which introduces institutional networks together with efficiency and equity standards and seek to characterize and explain employment and wage paths in the context of productive systems.

We will assume that the notion of an 'employment and employment policies regime' combines various forms of labour force mobility with a dominant mode of wage setting and wage adjustment (cf. Gazier, 1998). What is meant by this notion is actually quite simple. Given the various forms of institutional structuration and intervention mentioned above, average and relative wages may 'stick' at various levels. The extent to which they fluctuate will depend on the possible interaction between other regulatory and adaptive mechanisms that will produce relatively consistent ranges of variation of a greater or lesser magnitude.

If this hypothesis is applied to the evolution of the developed countries during the 1980s, some rather stable patterns emerge.[7] Two well-known polar cases give some idea of the diversity of employment regimes during this period. At one extreme is the USA, which tended to favour wage adjustments – wage flexibility – and intervened only ex post on incomes through EITC (earned income tax credit), a complex mechanism designed to supplement the very low wages earned by the 'working poor'. At the other extreme is the pre-1993 Swedish model, which sought to minimize the extent and role of wage differential adjustments as far as possible in order to develop an ambitious and expensive 'ex ante' employment policy based on the development of public jobs, inter-firm mobility grants and massive subsidies intended to encourage the recruitment of specific disadvantaged groups.[8]

Two other countries are quite close to each of the two extremes but also tend to implement mainly training policies. Germany is close to the Swedish model and proactive in its employment policies, having developed an integrative form of education and training policy, notably through the celebrated dual system of apprenticeship. In the United Kingdom, on the other hand, the Conservative governments from 1979 onwards sought to establish wage flexibility while stressing the importance of education and training and help for young people.

Finally, there are several countries in what might be termed 'intermediate' positions between the two poles represented by the USA and Sweden, in which the employment regime is less obviously polarized and the main target of ex post interventions is not wage differentials. Policy in Belgium and the Netherlands tends to focus on influencing the volume of jobs by acting on working hours, seeking to develop part-time work and introducing such measures as early retirement schemes and employment subsidies. France and Canada are also in this intermediate group. The French are making notable efforts in continuing education,[9] but have also intervened on a massive scale in order to influence job volumes by encouraging young people to delay their first entry into the labour market and making extensive use of early retirement schemes. In Canada, the minimum wage is much higher than it is in the USA and unemployment benefits are more generous. Moreover, Canadian expenditure on the public employment services is biased towards active measures and is comparable in this respect only to that in Sweden and Germany.

The Japanese trajectory is located somewhere between the German ex ante qualification adjustments and the French ex post ones. The constant internal mobility in large Japanese firms is intended to produce renewal within the company without resort to the external labour market.

Stylized facts set 2 (continued): the Exploration of New Adjustments during the 1990s

This elementary comparative distribution has undergone considerable change since the beginning of the 1990s. These changes first affected the 'integrative' European models, that is to say those of Germany and Sweden.

Let us start with the Swedish case. When the country entered the EU and became subject to international pressure to balance its budget, Sweden could no longer boost employment levels by increasing public-sector employment or use devaluation as an adjustment mechanism. (Sweden used to devalue periodically in order to reconcile wage fluctuations with the demands of world competition.) As a result, there was a sharp increase in unemployment to around the European average, a development that was sometimes interpreted as signalling the end of the Swedish model. Expenditure on unemployment benefit has increased massively. The Swedish have, however, increased expenditure on active employment policies, investing heavily in training for the unemployed. Thus Sweden is moving towards an intermediate position and, since the productive system and the education system are only weakly linked, such an evolution calls into question the ex ante adjustments. In the event, Sweden's efforts and redeployments in the late 1990s produced remarkable results. By 1999, the unemployment rate, after six years at between 8 and 9 per cent, had fallen to 6.4 per cent. At the beginning of the 21st century, the Swedish model is developing a stronger training focus and looking to become fashionably lean.

In Germany, the favourable prospects faded away after unification. However, it would be misleading to focus solely on the problems arising out of that momentous but unique event, for two reasons. The first has to do with the dynamics of a fundamental institution, namely apprenticeship. Géhin and Méhaut (1993) studied the adaptive capacities of the German dual system and compared them with the intensive use in France of continuing education and training. They observed two symmetrical shifts or processes of reorientation, brought about largely by the pressures and the challenges of mass unemployment and the need to accelerate labour force adaptation. The French general education system had traditionally produced a labour force with good basic skills that was adaptable because workers were able to rely on firms' commitment to training or retraining and because these skills were officially recognized. This prevented the system from leading to careers based on non-transferable skills limited to a single firm. At the same time, in Germany, the existence of trade unions representing homogeneous groups of workers with high levels of occupational skills had encouraged the development of codetermination and collegiality. However, this also restricted the promotion prospects of those categories excluded from the process, namely the unskilled. Here attempts to develop functional flexibility had to depend on expanding the general education component of the apprenticeship system and on greater job mobility within firms. The changes of the 1990s were to result in a kind of swap. Germany now needs to place greater emphasis on general training and to introduce more systematic retraining for the unskilled elements of its labour force, while France is endeavouring to develop an apprenticeship system. In France, progress is slow and apprenticeships are still stigmatized as low-level training. In Germany, the changes are not easy to implement because they give rise to disputes between the different levels of the occupational categories, since their identities and trajectories are based on initial training.[10]

The second element that has to be considered is the comparative evolution of industrial relations in both countries (Lallement, 1996, 1999). Let us look firstly at the well-known French weaknesses. These include the developing tendency towards decentralization and the rise in the number of company agreements in a context where wage earners are at a disadvantage in terms of the balance of power. Mention can also be made of the fragmented trade union movement, excessive state involvement and, in many cases, anomy in industrial relations. However, the German collective bargaining system has also reached its limits and been decentralized to some extent. It is widely circumvented in the new Länder, so much so in fact that regional fragmentation is becoming an important concern in both Eastern Germany and Western Germany. From this point of view, innovations such as the negotiations on working hours, which are often commented on, if not praised, seem heterogeneous and far from generalizable.

For Sweden and, later, Germany, the turn of the century brought good news with a return to growth in Europe and a clear drop in unemployment figures. In both countries, the long-established model had been disrupted. They adapted, slowly, by introducing a new emphasis on previously less used or neglected adjustment variables.

The French employment revival since 1998 (the unemployment rate, persistently around 12 per cent, was less than 10 per cent in May 2000 and the trend is expected to continue) is largely attributable to economic growth, but was fostered also by the state-led drive to reduce weekly working time, by measures to reduce the cost of low-skill work and by large-scale subsidies for part-time work. The UK, which has been quite successful since the mid-1990s, has introduced both a minimum wage and specific 'active' labour market policies, with the jobseeker's allowance and the New Deal giving opportunities to the young unemployed and putting pressure on them to seek employment. However, these developments, which combine training and concerns about employability, have been accompanied by growing polarization and inequality.

The USA, finally, seems to have been an unqualified success story during the 1990s, reaching very low levels of unemployment through rapid and sustained growth and exploiting the job creation potential of the 'new economy'. Very high levels of income inequality are persistent. Recent research has identified the existence of 'high-performance work systems' in manufacturing, with more autonomy and opportunities for participation being given to frontline workers, although it remains to be seen how far they will spread over the economy as a whole (see Appelbaum *et al.*, 2000).

The success of the Netherlands in the late 1990s offers an alternative way. Against a background of cuts in its welfare system and a general policy of wage moderation, the country's 'employment and employment policy regime' seems stable, with its main planks still income sharing and a massive extension of part-time work (in 1995, it accounted for 35 per cent of total employment and no less than 65 per cent of women's employment). Some recent comparative work on national employment performance and adjustment patterns (cf. Auer, 2000) shows that other ways are being explored. In their small open country success story, the Netherlands are not isolated and do not represent the only possible adjustment pattern. Despite enormous differences, Ireland, Austria and Denmark, for example, all achieved considerable reductions in their unemployment rates during the 1990s, often as a result of negotiated wage moderation policies and strong social protection.

Thus the 1990s did not see the end of strong societal specialization but rather the end of simple adjustment patterns based on a single dominant sphere of adjustment. A brief overview of this kind leaves some scope for proposing other combinations of the variables and other policy options for management in and around the labour market.

TLM as a Systematization of New Labour Market Adjustments

At least four arguments can be advanced for introducing TLMs as a practicable set of alternatives or supplements to current employment and employment policy regimes. One of their main guiding principles is to limit adjustments brought about by widening wage differentials because they lead to increasing social inequality, among other things. Negotiating on 'transitions' within a structured framework can foster better and faster labour market adjustments through various mechanisms.

The first of these is preventive flexibility. Once implemented, TLMs would consist essentially of a set of negotiated mobility rights, which could be extended or deferred by the social partners and policy makers in accordance with the changing needs of the labour market. The classic example, which currently exists in isolation, is the dual apprenticeship system in Germany, which, among its other virtues, allows the social partners to create more training places during slumps. In this way, it plays a modest anticyclical role. However, if such a system remains isolated, there are risks of crowding out, or spillover, or bad quality training providing little more than 'parking schemes'. The idea of TLMs is to develop a broader set of transitions and to put in place various forms of cofinanced cooperation between a broader range of partners. TLM decisions can be easily adapted to different labour market contexts. When a large number of jobs is being created in the private sector, the need for such 'bridging' activities will decrease and the social partners can agree to reduce the number of places or to concentrate on specified social needs. Thus the implementation of mobility rights introduces or strengthens negotiated and preventive controls of labour market imbalances.

The second mechanism is improved interplay between the three categories of adjustment variables, mainly at local level. It has been observed that the employment regimes mentioned above follow diverse adjustment patterns, each emphasizing a preferred set of variables. If wage differentials are the preferred adjustment mechanism, there is no need, within certain limits and in a specified context, to develop homogeneous or ambitious training policies. On the other hand, if the preferred option is to create a huge number of public-sector jobs and to establish inter-firm mobility rights (the Swedish approach during the 1980s), the same conclusion holds, again within certain limits and in a specified context, but there is also little use of wage differentials. It may be argued that the pressures of the 1990s increased the need for adaptation in the labour force and that the challenge now is to combine quantity and quality adjustments more effectively within a socially acceptable wages policy. The fact that TLMs would, ideally, be developed largely as local bargaining processes means that they could well make a valuable contribution in this regard. 'Local' here means firm, sectoral or regional level, that is levels at which the actors involved may more easily identify needs and possible cofunders, as well as the potential supply and demand. TLM rights would depend, to a very significant extent, on national transfers (especially from the funds devoted to public employment policies, which can be decentralized and remitted to local agencies and local partners).

So TLMs can be presented as better coordinating devices, with the potential to achieve bargained solutions. Traditional public employment policies, on the other hand, are unilaterally managed, while firms' employment policies depend on the goodwill and financial resources of individual employers.

The third mechanism is the introduction of important endogenizing processes (externalities and financing feedbacks). TLMs could also be a set of incentives for all actors involved in the labour market – firms and institutions, as well as individuals. It is often argued that 'making work pay', together with the 'activation' of labour market policies, are the essential slogans of today. However, such incentives are aimed solely at the labour force. While recognizing that in some cases there is a clear need to stimulate individual initiatives towards work, the TLM approach pinpoints the need to provide incentives for firms as well as for collective actors and organizations in the labour market. As regards firms, the main question is the externalities arising from their employment decisions: demand failures, exclusion costs, human capital losses and underinvestment, and excessive or insufficient mobility. TLMs may be viewed as a way to make explicit the costs and rewards of labour market decisions on a broader basis. The same holds for employment agencies: when some 'active' expenditures make it possible to save on 'passive' outlays, it is important that those funding both activities benefit from the savings, since the 'active' measures could be more easily and efficiently developed in a context where their positive implications (falling unemployment) can be quickly and practically perceived.

The fourth mechanism is the plasticity of TLMs. This plasticity means that they can be adapted to different adjustment paths and different challenges. Of course, TLMs are of particular relevance in the European context of unemployment. They can be interpreted as flexible work sharing, affecting the whole working life. But they are more generally designed for combating polarization in the labour market and its outcomes such as bad careers and the persistent poverty of the 'working poor'. The TLM approach does not rely on a single policy agenda. Rather, each nation or region can adopt its own sets of transitions and its own set of institutions and bargaining arrangements. Clearly, in countries such as Germany or Sweden, where unions are strong and well organized, TLMs may rely mainly on collective agreements. In other countries, such as France, where the unions are fragmented and weak, different partners, such as the state, non-profit federations or networks or municipalities, could take the lead.

Ultimately, at least two different types of TLM could gradually emerge. The first would be one that sought to anticipate or combat the undesirable effects of adjustment processes and to systematize the training effort. In essence, this would be an update of the Anglo-Saxon model. The second, highly structured and negotiated, would seek to increase the 'ex ante' scope for action. It would extend the German model and become, in its various guises, the continental European model. All in all, in contrast to the pressures that characterized the 1990s, there could be a return to preliminary consultations and early interventions.

To sum up in Williamsonian terms: in the labour market and in employment relationships, various transaction costs are incurred, which give rise to significant externalities, whether static or dynamic. These include turnover costs, placement costs, income maintenance costs and the cost of combating exclusion. This leads typically to hybrid arrangements, intermediate between markets and hierarchies. TLMs could be part of these arrangements. Their originality lies in the fact that they have the potential to make explicit and generalize certain transactions and processes that are implicitly present but not fully taken into account in conventional labour market arrangements, namely mobility options and lifelong career management.

2   TLMS AND LABOUR MARKET SEGMENTATION

One of the most frequent arguments against TLMs has its roots in labour market segmentation. Since the labour markets of developed countries are segmented, disadvantaged workers are trapped either in unstable and low-paid jobs in the lower segment or in mass unemployment. Under these conditions, it is argued, developing TLMs as a policy tool for combating unemployment and poverty would be illusory: simply multiplying the 'transitions' between standard employment, socially useful activities such as training, voluntary work and, especially, part-time work, would lead to second-class arrangements for disadvantaged workers and losers.

More specifically, the common fear is that two more or less separate networks of transition opportunities could appear. The first one would be for core workers and would provide 'good transitions', well-designed training programmes and childcare opportunities that would allow participants to maintain a good level of income and social protection and good labour market status. The second, on the other hand, would be for peripheral workers; income would be lower, the programmes would have less legitimacy and participants would have less commitment to regular work. Under these circumstances, TLMs would be a way of hiding and maybe even rationalizing a triple and ugly reality: rotation among dead-end and low-paying part-time jobs in the most successful case, the 'active' combination of some income maintenance and more or less enforced work as an intermediate case and, in the worst scenario, sorting devices pointing losers towards exit options such as retirement, last resort minimum income or discouragement.

In other words, TLMs would make a virtue of a necessity by building bridges between privately paid work, public income maintenance programmes and publicly subsidized, socially useful activities. Despite their work-sharing effects, they would merely spread the persisting job scarcity among already disadvantaged sections of the labour force. They would amount, it is argued, to a rationalization of rationing, with the channelling effects of public policy and the differentiated treatment of the secondary labour force serving merely to reinforce the existing segmentation.

In order to provide a basis for discussing this important reservation which, if left unchallenged, could generate considerable scepticism as to the central function and potential of TLMs, we will present two further sets of stylized facts as a prelude to introducing the TLM perspective.

Stylized Facts Set 1: Endogenous Labour Market Heterogeneity and the development of Internal Labour Markets during the 1960s and 1970s

The literature on segmented labour markets being very rich, and the topic hotly debated in labour economics, no attempt will be made here to summarize the whole debate, even less to propose a unified point of view. After briefly outlining some of the basic characteristics of the dual/segmentation approach and some of the paths along which it has developed since its beginnings, we will focus on employment integration, starting with the 'spontaneous' integration produced by the functioning of the primary and secondary segments, before going on to introduce public policies into the argument. This section draws heavily on Doeringer and Piore's seminal work (Doeringer and Piore, 1971).

The classic basic presentation of dual labour market theory refers to the American situation at the end of the 1960s and starts with the concept of the internal labour market (ILM), which is defined as 'an administrative unit, such as a manufacturing plant, within which the pricing and the allocation of labor is governed by a set of administrative rules and procedures' (ibid.: 1–2). It is then customary to identify two different kinds of external labour market: the primary market (or segment), structured by firms with internal labour markets, and the secondary market (or segment), in which firms without internal labour markets operate.

Furthermore, Doeringer and Piore noted that internal labour markets are also of two different kinds: the majority are plant or enterprise ILMs, as described above, but some are craft or occupational ILMs, organized around the local union.

The differences between the ways in which primary and secondary labour markets function are clearly revealed by an examination of admission and promotion procedures. To enter an ILM, workers have to be recruited at a limited number of low hierarchical levels, called 'ports of entry'. Promotion is governed by impersonal rules, often seniority, so workers move upwards in 'mobility clusters'. In a secondary labour market, on the other hand, entry can occur at any level, and the scarce promotion opportunities do not obey a structured pattern.

The distinction between primary and secondary labour markets is mirrored in the distinction between two groups of workers: 'primary workers' who are strongly committed to regular work and hold 'good jobs', and 'secondary workers' who are less attached to regular work habits and accustomed to unstable, low-paid jobs. A final contrast emerges here between the vast majority of protected, often unionized, workers with good-quality jobs and a minority of disadvantaged groups with 'bad jobs'.

The initial typology of 1971 remained to be tested empirically and firmly grounded in theory. However, it met with considerable success and was frequently used and reinterpreted. On the empirical level, numerous studies in many different countries sought to verify the heterogeneity of the labour market, on a local, regional or national basis, and to apply the primary/secondary duality. Some of the principal findings of these studies will be briefly outlined here. Firstly, it was found that the labour market could be more realistically split into four segments, with Doeringer and Piore's primary and secondary segments sandwiched between the 'irregular economy' at the bottom and, at the top, a 'primary–superior' segment for executives, in which promotion is conditioned by external mobility. Secondly, a number of national variations were identified, with some countries having primary segment firms simultaneously managing a periphery of disadvantaged and less protected workers, while others corresponded more closely to the initial description based on the American situation. Thirdly, there was a shift from the observation and discussion of strongly discontinuous situations to more continuous, though still polarized, situations. Fourthly, and finally, the good job/bad job dichotomy was observed in all countries, with some workers being trapped in the latter.

Against this background, what can be said about integration into and exclusion from the labour market? Clearly, the internal labour market is both an integrative and exclusionary device. It is integrative because it recruits a considerable number of workers at relatively lowly ports of entry and provides them with on-the-job training and promotion ladders. On the other hand, it is also exclusionary, whether directly, as when secondary workers are rejected at the ports of entry (because they are considered unreliable or 'outsiders') or indirectly, as when those secondary workers who are admitted are unable to adapt quickly to work practices and constraints within the firm, or when potential candidates from the secondary labour force are discouraged from applying for jobs in the primary segment.

The integration/exclusion process can also be seen at work in the secondary 'queue'. Thus people without a work history, such as newly arrived immigrants or married women looking for jobs after bringing up a family, begin by taking the least well protected and lowest paid jobs and then seek to progress within the secondary segment to relatively more stable jobs even if they remain low-paid and without promotion and training prospects.

However, this is only the optimistic side of the coin. The dynamics of employment and mobility cause job opportunities and employee behaviour and expectations to interact in vicious circles. The stable jobs may be rationed and secondary workers, having acquired unstable habits in their family and social environments and seen their behaviour confirmed in their work situation, are unable to find and keep a stable job and may remain trapped in unstable jobs. In order to become integrated into the more stable segment, such groups would have to be offered new opportunities and to unlearn the habits acquired in the secondary segment.

Thus social integration in a dual labour market emerges as a rather complex process, linked to the social structure and other institutions such as welfare policy and unions, including mobility inside the secondary segment as well as access to the primary segment.

In short, and despite some caveats, the most important lesson to be derived from the dual labour market approach is that the job security provided by ILMs should be extended and generalized through a range of programmes and in-depth reform of the labour market.

Stylized Facts Set 2: Internal Labour Markets under Pressure during the 1980s and 1990s

Formulated in the rather optimistic period of the 1960s and early 1970s, labour market segmentation theory emphasized the persistence of poverty and bad jobs in the midst of prosperity. When mass employment appeared, especially in Europe, such an approach appeared well suited to analysing the situation and its consequences. Some observers even proposed the term 'dualization' to characterize the problems arising from the coexistence of high-income groups and the socially excluded.

However, things are not that simple and there are pronounced differences between 'dualism' and 'dualization'. 'Dualism' refers to the structuring power of ILMs and primary markets. The more recent developments characterized by the term 'dualization' are connected to a complex picture dominated by the growing pressures exerted by external markets and the consequent contraction and reshaping of internal labour markets. Moreover, mass unemployment was not predicted by the initial dual approach. The only expected consequence for unemployment was high structural/frictional unemployment in the secondary market, where turnover is high. It was even suggested in some studies that the secondary market functioned in a way akin to a competitive market, relying on wage flexibility for adjustments and thereby avoiding mass unemployment.

Even if there is broad agreement on the weakening of primary workers' employment prospects, the corresponding stylized facts come in a number of very different versions. In what follows, we will draw on three well-developed national analyses: Peter Cappelli's for the USA, Jill Rubery's for the UK and that of Freyssinet (and others) for France.[11]

Cappelli's[12] main thesis is a simple one. He adheres to the standard representation outlined above, denoting ILMs with the term 'internalized employment systems' and accepting that they insulate some workers from the external labour market. He presents three main characteristics of such systems: work organization (allowing low-level recruitment and promotion by seniority), job security (jobs for life for managers, and temporary lay-offs and recalls for production workers) and wages largely unrelated to company performance.

During the 1980s, according to Cappelli, 'several important developments combined to create an environment that substantially reduced the benefits derived from internalized employment systems. The most important of these were changes that increased the burdens of fixed costs' (Cappelli 1995: 566–7). These changes included increased competition, changing product markets, which made fixed costs vulnerable and led to the development of cross-functional teams, external sourcing and subcontracting and made it more risky to develop skills and competences inside organizations, and new management techniques that linked executives' compensation to shareholder value and created 'profit centres', thereby giving rise to a preference for contingent workers, contingent pay and contracting out. At the same time, these new management techniques directly affected production workers' employment relationships, reducing the role of middle management, empowering employees (giving them more responsibility but less direct control and increasing the pressures on them) and paving the way for a continuous restructuring of core competences. The last area of change was linked to a form of 'social learning': union and government pressure to internalize declined, stock markets reacted positively to 'downsizing' and one of the main thrusts of public policy was to create incentives to unravel internalized arrangements.

In work organization, Cappelli pinpoints greater autonomy for production workers and, with the tendency to broaden skill requirements for a given job, the shrinking of promotion opportunities and a reduced commitment to train low-skill workers. At the same time, employment security was declining. Downsizing was affecting not only newcomers but also the traditional beneficiaries of the system, such as white-collar staff and senior manual workers. Job tenure was also declining,[13] at least for the less educated and older workers, while contracting out and temporary employment agencies developed. Finally, wages were affected by trends towards greater sensitivity to market perfor-mance. As a result, inequality in the workplace increased to the benefit of professional and managerial staff, returns to seniority collapsed and the vari-able, performance-related component of pay increased as a share of total pay.

The analysis proposed by Jill Rubery (1994) and extended by Grimshaw and Rubery (1998) adopts another approach. She prefers to emphasize the numerous conflictive aspects of what she calls the 'internalizing process', that is the permanent interaction between internal and external dynamics and the fundamental heterogeneity of firms operating in different segments, in product markets as well as in factor markets.

The main tenet of such an analysis is that job security and earnings/promo-tion guarantees always depend on changing conditions in the external labour market. If in a given area there are no opportunities in the external labour market for a certain segment of the workforce employed by certain firms, employers can stabilize and even motivate workers with low-cost policies: they do not need to offer full employment security, high pay or even many promotion opportunities. They may do so on occasions, however, depending on union pressure and the availability of financial resources, for example.

Thus the diagnosis becomes less simple: different countries and different sectors may experience different internalizing and externalizing pressures at different times. In the case of the UK, Jill Rubery identifies a long-lasting 'destructuring' process, now affected by a 'reinstitutionalization process', whose significance remains to be seen.

For France, Freyssinet's (1982) analysis focused on the evolution in the late 1970s of the employment policies of large firms with correspondingly exten-sive internal labour markets. Freyssinet identified a number of trends, among which was the development of diversified employment policies within an inte-grated framework. These policies made it possible to segment employees into subgroups and led to an increased variety of employment and compensation practices, following a general trend of decentralizing business decision-making units. So the evidence shows the erosion of previous solidarities and guarantees, even for the remaining 'core' workers who came under increased pressure, with the protections previously acquired being more or less circum-vented by the differentiating process.

This analysis was later confirmed by other studies, including the present author's book on human resources strategies and their changing priorities (Gazier, 1993) and an important empirical study by Galtier (1996). This latter may be seen as a confirmation of the previous analyses. In her analysis of the employment practices of a large sample of French firms, Galtier showed that, in addition to those firms that had retained a traditional stabilized workforce, on the one hand, and the traditionally unstable sector, on the other, there was a third group of firms that were adopting weaker stabilization practices while at the same time investing heavily in training for a skilled workforce. Such a combination, which the various earlier versions of ILM theory did not antici-pate, is interesting because it is an indication of persistent attempts to restruc-ture and flexibilize skilled workers in the internal labour market.[14] There may be a link here with the extensive regulatory framework in France, which was widely accepted during the 1960s and the 1970s but has been under growing pressure from employers ever since.[15]

There are two possible and complementary explanations of the differences between countries and analyses. First, the studies cited depend on different methodological choices, and build different perspectives on different periods. However, the differences in the stylized facts can also be easily attributed to basic differences in national versions of the earlier 'internalizing process': the erosion of the classic ILM in the USA, the destructuring of 'professional markets' combined with a process of 're-institutionalization' in the UK (Grimshaw and Rubery 1998: 202) and the emergence of a 'stratified' internal model in France.

Having identified and explained the differences, we can now highlight the essential point, namely the strong consensus among these authors as to the increased importance of external aspects of the labour market. For Rubery, the significance of the external labour market is a permanent (albeit sometimes hidden) phenomenon, while for Cappelli and other authors it is now dominant. The internal 'organizational' determinants of employment systems still exist, but they must be permanently weighed against external pressures and oppor-tunities, either because it was always so, as Rubery suggests, or because it is so now, as Cappelli and others conclude. In short, one author emphasizes external conditions for methodological reasons, while others do the same from a historical point of view.

In consequence, all these authors directly or indirectly reject the so-called 'core/periphery model' that is well established in Europe and according to which firms today manage two different groups of workers: a core of perma-nent insiders, for whom functional flexibility is the adjustment mechanism, and a periphery of unstable employees, for whom numerical flexibility is the adjustment mechanism. They show that insiders are no longer protected, even if they remain stabilized. And using a provocative and perhaps metaphorical formulation, Grimshaw and Rubery (1998) speak of an external labour market 'embedded' in the internal labour market (ibid.: 217).

The main result of these arguments is simple: the job security traditionally provided by ILMs is no longer the reference point. It may remain so for civil servants, but, for the bulk of workers, segmentation of the workforce is now more an option for employers, combined with subcontracting and contingent work, than the result of a stable division of the labour market. Insiders are permanently under threat from external comparisons.

However, such a situation does not help to create a new norm that would determine what constitutes a 'good' job. Misleading it may have been, but 'traditional' ILM job security was a social focus point, and it has not been replaced.

TLMs: Reforming the Labour Market and Facilitating Integration

How could TLMs affect both internal employment systems and external labour markets? On the face of it, their influence would extend mainly to behaviour and income outside firms, and it was for this reason that some doubt arose about their ability to combat the segmented mobility and exclusion patterns of existing labour markets. Managing TLMs in isolation would, it was argued, lead merely to the development of 'closed loops' for unemployed and disadvantaged workers, albeit with a few exceptions.

However, this is not true of all elementary TLMs, established either by firms or by public policies. We can point first to new versions of the internal labour market that attempt to combine a certain degree of flexibility with workforce stabilization. The so-called 'Volkswagen model' could be seen as one of these.[16] It was created by a specific agreement concluded in 1993 between the German car maker and IG Metall, the engineering workers' union. The core of the agreement is a reduction of weekly working time, which is normally distributed over four working days, with the possibility of variations. VW agreed to call a halt to redundancies during the term of the agreement in exchange for a 20 per cent wage reduction (additional measures limited the wage loss to employees to 16 per cent) and some time flexibility. We can point, secondly, to phased early retirement schemes as another example of an integrating mechanism, even though they may be difficult to implement and are not accepted by all the workers affected by them.

However, there are two more general reasons why TLMs as a whole could affect 'insiders' and function as new institutions influencing and changing employers' strategies. Firstly, they would, once established, be part of a new local bargaining process, involving unions, insiders and new partners such as local authorities and non-profit-making organizations. Collective bargaining on new forms of career, with periods of retraining and reorientation, is today a necessity, and all workers are expected periodically to update their competences and even to change occupation. TLMs provide structured opportunities to do so. Secondly, considered in the round, from the perspective of state as well as company employment policy, TLMs could expand the range of opportunities available to workers facing critical events in their life: having children, looking for a new job or training place, going part-time, and so on.

In principle, therefore, TLMs could give more choice and more power to workers, to 'insiders' as well as to 'outsiders', and especially the latter, because not only would they be offered more opportunities but 'insiders' would also be likely to be more mobile rather than sticking to one job and their now limited job security. In the absence of a single agreed analysis of segmentation, one way of examining more precisely the potential of TLMs is to consider successively the varying perspectives, outlined above, on the current destabilization of ILMs and the main problems they highlight.

We start with the destabilization of traditional ILMs as analysed by Cappelli with reference to the USA. He highlighted the growing difficulties affecting the integration and training process of low-skilled workers and the concomitant risk of producing large groups of demotivated workers. He identified four contradictions.

1. How can teamwork be developed, with firm-specific skills requiring training and being hard to replace, at a time when the overall commitment to the firm is weakening?
2. If the traditional 'job ladders' are collapsing, how can newcomers be integrated into teamwork?
3. How can a decline in commitment to individual employers be reconciled with increasing commitment to occupations? The contradiction is particularly evident in the increasing demand for training from workers and the decline in employer-provided training.
4. How can declining employment commitment be reconciled with increasing long-term pressure on performance? Possible solutions include team empowerment (with peer pressure), short-term 'projects' and a new culture of risk taking for young workers. However, these are short-term solutions, or limited to certain groups.

TLMs may provide some answers to these dilemmas. Firstly, they could foster new teamwork and limit skills shortages because TLMs would provide a mechanism for cofunding some of the training and integration costs even if workers are less attached to individual firms. TLMs could be a way of subsidizing on-the-job training and, through the incentives they provide, persuading reluctant firms to reconsider their restrictive attitudes towards low-skilled newcomers.

Secondly, by increasing mobility opportunities in the external labour market, TLMs could help to limit the problems arising from the integration of low-skilled workers into the internal labour market, with its dearth of promotion opportunities. Furthermore, they could also mitigate the problem of more highly skilled workers crowding out the less advantaged, while some socially useful activities could be tailored to disadvantaged groups.

Thirdly, if people are more individualistic and less attached to a specific firm than to their occupation, TLMs may help by creating sources of joint funding for training programmes and training leave. The local network arrangements alluded to above could help to solve the contradiction by providing a forum for bargaining that would enable training to be combined with external mobility. In so-called 'industrial districts' (cf. Gazier, 1993), there has long been a collective training policy and a highly mobile workforce moving between the large number of small, specialist firms operating within the confines of a given area. TLMs could be seen as a way of expanding such arrangements beyond narrow product specialization by introducing other sources of funding and expanding career opportunities.

Fourthly, TLMs are not intended to address directly the final contradiction between decreasing employee commitment and the increasing long-term pressure on performance. This issue has more to do with the problem of power and control inside organizations. However, TLMs could help to establish a new culture of risk taking inside firms and in the labour market: not the current individualized risk, with winners and losers trapped in their failures, but a socialized risk. TLMs would encourage self-employment and career initiatives while at the same providing a real safety net and laying the foundations for a culture of permanent adaptation.

Finally, it is interesting to note that Capelli, at the end of his article (1995: 594), mentions the old-fashioned craft unions as they developed in the USA as a relevant adjustment tool. They operated in a way very similar to ILMs, and indeed there existed, as we saw, 'craft ILMs'. Such organizations were able to provide greater security in situations where attachment to individual employers was weak or non-existent. Today, this seems to be the case again, and some human resource managers and commentators see in craft unions the future of unions in highly developed countries. However, they have now to be developed for jobs and workers that are integrated into sophisticated and diversified firms, and it is unclear whether they can be adapted to meet such a challenge. However this may be, there is no doubting the complementarity between this argument and the TLM approach. TLMs could help such unions to develop; furthermore, they open up new areas of coordination and bargaining, thereby introducing different actors and creating regional mobility incentives.

We turn now to Rubery's main thesis, namely that there are in our economies 'internalizing' processes that are heterogeneous, reversible and dependent on the restricted capacity of employers' strategies for adaptation to changing internal and external conditions. Thus the emphasis here shifts away from a supposed social contract to changing balances of power and to the existence of trapped groups, whether inside or outside firms. It can be argued that, in such a context, TLMs could fulfil two main functions. Since they depend essentially on institutional changes affecting external as well as internal labour markets, they could, firstly, provide the impetus for the breaking down of segmentation among disadvantaged groups and, secondly, help to reinternal-ize the workforce on a broader basis.

Among the various disadvantaged groups, Rubery highlights one particular group, namely those apparent 'insiders' who are exploited, trapped in low-quality, low-paid jobs, without promotion prospects or training opportunities, in which they remain because the only alternative is unemployment. In their case, the role of TLMs would be, first, to encourage human resource managers in low-paying firms to adopt a longer-term perspective by alleviating some of the financial constraints on training provision and opening up mobility oppor-tunities. They could also help to keep the labour market tight, thereby limiting the pressure of the 'reserve army' and making it more difficult to exploit a segmented and disadvantaged labour force. Of course, employer opportunism must be considered here: employers may simply take the subsidies and go on offering low-quality jobs to second-class workers. However, once in place, TLMs would be part of a bargaining process and it would be possible, against a background of falling unemployment, to establish certain standards. This leads us to the second role of TLMs whose very existence could help to restore some power to employees, the unemployed and unions.

As far as the process of reinternalization is concerned, the implementation of TLMs could affect the whole process of integration in the labour market. From Rubery's perspective, there is no single previous model, even though low-skill ports of entry into internal labour markets clearly led to career paths combining integration and exploitation and are now increasingly less reward-ing. Furthermore, the integration of some groups can be realized at the expense of others. By seeking to effect a shift in existing public employment policies, TLMs could combine centralized initiatives and funding with decen-tralized initiatives, funding and implementation. They would have to be linked to minimum income guarantees and to employment subsidies, but their imple-mentation at local level would vary in accordance with the actors involved, their preferences and local conditions. Thus they fit neatly with two important characteristics of current labour market adjustments: the pressure to decen-tralize and the strong influence of dynamic externalities. This last term is intended to denote the collective needs and opportunities arising from the permanent adaptation and retraining of the labour force that are not taken into account by individual employers or by pricing adjustments. Since workers' mobility decisions are conditional on actual mobility levels among other workers, TLMs could help to solve a problem much akin to a prisoner's dilemma.

The main institutional effect of TLMs would be to create local networks for the local management of labour market mobility, notably by creating linkages between part-time jobs and training or other socially useful activities. As suggested above, they would operate like labour markets in industrial districts, where a number of independent and flexible specialist firms collectively fund training and high-skill workers go from firm to firm, creating subcontracting units during downturns and rejoining the main firms during upturns. However, TLMs would not be dependent on a specific productive specialization, and in this respect would be more flexible than 'districts': depending on needs, they can adopt different structures and priorities.

Such networks could provide a new basis for the 'internalization' process. We noted above the possible limitations of the employment security provided by classic ILMs: in many cases, they provided only a weak and narrow basis for promotion, training and staff allocation, even if employers were willing to offer such career opportunities and had at their disposal the financial resources to put them in place. This brings us close to the 'craft' or 'occupational' ILM, but without the strongly specialized and union-dominated aspects. Here again, comparison with existing arrangements highlights the flexible and integrative way in which TLMs could operate once in place.

These same arguments can be applied to segmentation in France, and especially those firms that once operated in the primary sector and now place 'insiders' under increasing pressures. By giving more opportunities to both insiders and outsiders, TLMs could help to reduce the pressure while making it easier for employees to adapt to increased training and flexibility requirements. However, there is an obvious problem here, namely the risk of reinforced segmentation arising out of the interplay of public employment policies and firms' strategies. One well-known perverse effect of large-scale state interventions in France (and in other European countries) is the creation of a subsidized secondary labour market for temporary and low-paid occupations that hold out little hope of integration into the primary sector. The challenge is compounded when account is taken of the fact that public policies, in anticipation of firms' reactions, act as a sorting device, ranking the unemployed in terms of their perceived employability and channelling them into different programmes with segmented outcomes. The most employable are given access to good-quality placement and training programmes and may be successful in embarking upon normal, albeit delayed, careers. The less employable are put on benefits and diverted away from the labour market (early retirement, disability allowance and so on). The intermediate category are accepted onto short-term job experience programmes but often suffer from the 'revolving door' effect, moving from temporary jobs into training, then back to temporary employment, via occasional spells of unemployment.

It is not our purpose here to discuss the shortcomings of public employment policies, whether in general or with reference to France in particular (for more evaluations and discussion, see Schmid *et al.*, 1996; Barbier and Gautié, 1998; De Koning and Mosley, 2001). Rather, it seems more valuable briefly to examine TLMs as a possible means of fostering greater equity and efficiency in public employment policies. These policies are not automatically condemned to becoming unjust and inefficient. Even if they are no panacea, and have to be evaluated and integrated with other policies, widely accepted analyses have identified at least three general factors required for positive outcomes. These are the existence of, first, an extensive infrastructure of employment services and expert agencies; second, long-term dialogue between the social partners; and third, a range of opportunities in or around the labour market. TLMs could be one way of fulfilling these conditions: once in place, they would constitute precisely such a range of opportunities in and around the labour market, be the result of bargaining and be dependent on the public (and private) employment service infrastructure. TLMs are intended as a means of reforming the labour market with a view to introducing a jointly funded and negotiated element into public employment policy that might help to rehomogenize the labour market.

They would also introduce another element into general employment policies that would supplement established 'passive' and 'active' programmes.[17] In addition to the income maintenance insurance component and employability insurance, TLMs introduce a largely preventive 'mobility' insurance giving mobility rights to insiders and outsiders.

To sum up, it is inaccurate to present TLMs simply as a way of tampering with or reorganizing the job queue. Such a characterization would cast them as nothing more than an expansion of the existing set of public employment policies in a zero-sum game where what is gained by some groups is lost by others. They are intended to bring about the reform and reorganization of public employment policies by providing integration incentives for firms and labour market institutions as well as for individuals.

In this section we have departed somewhat from a strictly Williamsonian point of view by introducing additional distribution issues. Over and above transaction costs and externalities, the question of who bears the costs and who is able to transfer their cost burden to other categories emerged as a key issue. Some costs may be considerable and end up not being minimized if some groups are able to shift them onto others. Then the costs of integrating the unemployed and 'exploited' secondary workers came under the spotlight. TLMs emerged here as a device for shifting the balance of power, either by lowering the barriers to integration or by expanding the range of choices available to workers, whether in employment or not.

So far we have made the case in favour of TLMs in a context of homogeneous (section 1) or heterogeneous (section 2) labour market adjustments. It may be concluded, provisionally, that the development of TLMs can be seen as a conceivable reform of the present state of affairs in developed countries, plagued as they are by high unemployment or by strong and polarized inequalities in their labour markets. We have now to examine more directly the possible problems stemming from the implementation of TLMs. How feasible are TLMs in practice and what would their distributive impact be?

3 INCENTIVES AND COORDINATION IN THE LABOUR MARKET: THE TLM CONTRIBUTION

As specified by O. Williamson, the 'remediableness' test for a policy intervention is whether '(1) an alternative can be described that (2) can be implemented with (3) expected net gains' (1996: 210). Williamson goes on to set down the conditions for a legitimate public intervention: it is necessary that '(i) the public sector is better informed about externalities, (ii) the requisite collective action is easier to orchestrate through the public sector (possibly by fiat), and/or (iii) the social net benefit calculus differs from the private in sufficient degree to warrant a different result' (ibid.: 241). As numerous authors have remarked, such a clear-cut analysis is of course difficult to develop, because it would be necessary to identify and measure the transaction costs and externalities involved. This is especially true of labour markets and TLMs. The important externalities arising in labour markets have already been alluded to above, in particular the benefits stemming from a homogeneous, adaptable and skilled workforce and the social losses resulting from long-term unemployment. It is not difficult to draw up a list of the main transaction costs that arise in the same markets: job and worker search, screening, placement, matching, as well as integration costs and so on. However, from the dynamic perspective of transitions, the list is somewhat longer and also includes skill losses, recruitment errors and career reorientation.

Williamson rightly puts the emphasis on the practical challenges of implementation, which demand at least plausible answers, and on the likely net gains for society. As a consequence, when costs and responsibilities cannot be easily identified, and when the optimal combination cannot be found, he advocates reversible arrangements.

We will not try here to draw up a complete inventory of the externalities and transaction costs involved, nor to measure them. However, we will apply a somewhat similar and pragmatic methodology to TLMs. In this third section, therefore, we will begin by briefly locating the TLM approach within the wider set of policy interventions affecting the labour market. We will then go on to deal with the implementation of TLMs and the three main problems it raises: complexity, incentives and control. We end with a discussion of two complementary views on TLMs: TLMs as a learning process and TLMs as a political process and part of a new social contract.

TLMs as Embedded, Flexible Risk-sharing Arrangements in a Changing Labour Market

TLMs may be conceived of as 'mobility insurance', supplementing and combining with other risk-spreading or risk-mitigating devices in the labour market. When it comes to protecting against the various risks of income loss in the labour market, institutions such as unemployment insurance or minimum wages are 'second-best tools' for sharing labour income losses. Determinedly radical first-best policies include Meade and Weitzman's well-known work-sharing proposals.[19]

Without entering here into the debate on the virtues and drawbacks of different approaches to labour market reform, it is interesting to note that the TLM approach actually occupies the middle ground. TLMs would not really be 'futures' markets, directly insuring workers against income variations; nor are they reforms directed at firms with a view to securing a permanently high level of labour demand. However, they do seek to influence firms' and workers' behaviour in a preventive way, by regulating working time over the whole life cycle. In this sense, they go beyond traditional interventions: both those, such as the minimum wage and the legal structuring of the employment relationship, that have an impact on firms' internal workings and those, such as unemployment insurance, whose impact is felt outside firms.

The contribution of TLMs emerges more clearly when considered against the background of today's changing labour markets, which are tending to become increasingly risky.[20] As a result, neither unemployment insurance, minimum wages nor social insurance protection, with their positive and perverse effects, are adequate instruments for dealing with the new situation. The distribution of mobility rights (through vouchers, for example) and the diversification of employment and other opportunities that would flow from the development of TLMs are ways of sharing the risks. Other aspects of TLMs are more preventive, providing more and better training opportunities, improved career guidance and more appropriate family arrangements.

Against this background, we can briefly bring together here the two strands of the argument in favour of the TLM approach outlined separately in the previous two sections. TLMs can be viewed as a strategy for reducing segmentation (cf. section 2 above) with a view to increasing or restoring competition in the labour market (cf. section 1 above) and thereby increasing efficiency as well as equity. They have the potential to achieve these objectives because they would encourage neither hire and fire policies nor pure wage flexibility. Rather, they are designed to cope with the complexity of the new, network-type transactions now developing in today's labour markets. They take full account of the incipient sequentiality of labour markets: individual careers now tend to be more discontinuous, constructed as they are out of sequences of projects interspersed with periodic spells of retraining and reorientation. In such a context, employability depends more on the quality and diversity of individual work histories, on reputation, social capital and on adaptability than on traditional skills and qualifications. The changing nature of the employment relationship presents a challenge because it relies simultaneously on trust and mobility.

Viewed in the context of our initial 'triptych', it can be seen that TLMs would function as submarkets for temporary employment and other activities, offering specific combinations of prices, quantities and qualities for negotiated transitional slots. Because they would be collectively organized and introduce new sources of funding and new positions and guarantees, they would supplement the established stabilizing devices found in internal or occupational labour markets. And because they would rely on individual choices and offer tailor-made career paths, they would foster individual initiatives and projects.

This said, however, it must be noted that TLMs, despite their broad scope, would be only partial and 'embedded' devices. They could not exist in isolation from other policy interventions affecting the level and distribution of risks in the labour market, particularly job creation and overall economic growth. They must also be considered in conjunction with current reforms of labour law and the employment relationship that seek to extend the basis of work-related rights (for a European perspective, see Rogowski and Schmid, 1997; Supiot, 1999).

Thus TLMs are labour market reforms that create new markets or develop existing ones within the current framework of labour market institutions and industrial relations (even though they may contribute to their evolution: see below). TLMs could be created by the social partners, could involve private entrepreneurs (notably in training and placement activities) and could be subsidized and/or regulated by governments. From a pragmatic perspective, therefore, they are flexible tools, located midway between private and state intervention. It may be added that TLMs mark a shift away from unilateral state intervention towards a mix of private (profit-making and non-profit-making) and public interactions.

Complexity, Incentives and Control

The implementation of TLMs raises at least two challenges.[21] The first is their complexity. If income security is the main concern, it has already been noted that labour market constraints and outcomes are becoming increasingly multidimensional. Some of the key issues for individuals are skill development, self-discovery among young workers seeking to specialize, reorientation, the balance between private and family life and career development and the social policy components; for firms, they include continuous adaptation of the workforce, the management of effort and organizational choices. Thus very different situations arise for different people at different times and it would be difficult to assess the legitimacy, success or failure of TLM arrangements if choices and evaluations refer to multidimensional and changing criteria. This first problem leads to a second, even more intractable one, namely the incentives and control problem. Classical agency problems raise their heads here, particularly moral hazard and adverse selection. Will TLMs subsidize idleness among the workforce or choosiness among firms (moral hazard) and will the heterogeneity of labour market actors impede the development of a workable system of mobility insurance (adverse selection)?

It is often argued that the main target is to build incentives for individuals trapped in discouragement or dependency and that the corresponding motto should be 'making work pay'. Our contention is that such incentives may be useful and even necessary, but we have also to consider the incentives for firms and labour market institutions to provide real opportunities for workers and the unemployed. Thus the proposed slogan is 'making transitions pay'. This said, how can the dual challenge of complexity and incentives be met?

The first point to be made is that the local nature of the transitional markets being advocated here can be seen as an aid in the management of complexity. When people know each other, it is easier to make complex choices and to adapt policy tools to changing situations. Complex transitions are already fairly well managed by large firms putting in place labour pools and career development paths for their employees. Local actors have an informational advantage when the stabilizing process shifts away from traditional internal markets. This is the fundamental argument in favour of local negotiations on TLMs, and leads to the idea of a local diversity of transitional arrangements. Arrangements may also differ from country to country in accordance with national situations.

However, in order to encourage local negotiations involving a range of different actors (and specific transaction costs as well), two conditions need to be met. The first concerns the public partners, who must have some room for manoeuvre in deciding on the share of budget they can allocate to specific transitions. The second concerns the issues at stake in the bargaining process, which must be consistent enough to involve local actors. Thus the idea here is to base the bargaining on a rich diversity of choices, not on separate decisions on training, placement or leave arrangements, and to provide a significant budget to be allocated collectively.

TLMs imply local bargaining and decisions taken by the social partners on a wide set of labour market policy measures in order to select the portfolio of measures best suited to local needs and preferences on both the supply and the demand side. Thus the TLM approach is simultaneously local and globalized, but how can agency problems, which may affect all those involved, be avoided or mitigated? The solution may lie in a number of partial answers, both substantive and procedural. We consider, first, four general arguments before introducing the theme of criteria and evaluation. We conclude by summing up the incentives available for the three main categories of actors: employers, workers and labour market organizations and institutions.

The overall incentive and control structure

Firstly, a *free choice* for those seeking to put together a transition portfolio and *competition* among agencies (either public or a mix of public and private) may ensure that the opportunities on offer are defined in response to social demand and with an emphasis on cost minimization.

Secondly, *cofinancing* offers another solution to moral hazard problems, as well as leverage for developing transitions. As the example of apprenticeship shows, cofinancing by firms and apprentices, who temporarily accept low pay in exchange for training, may help to solve such problems. Both partners have an interest in achieving a good transition because they are paying for it. The same argument applies to tripartite arrangements involving older workers, their original employers and new part-time employers put in place to fund semi-retirement programmes with a half-time job funded by a non-profit-making organization or local authorities. Top-up or matching grants (a long-established tool of labour market policy) are an essential feature of the TLM approach.

Thirdly, the objects of the bargaining process are *sequential* positions, which are to be periodically re-examined. Once again, we are close to the notion of non-irreversibility advocated by Oliver Williamson.

Fourthly, the possible transition set would be as equal as possible for every worker: TLMs are *structured and nationwide* rights, not particular arrangements for certain groups, whether favourable or otherwise. This implies a public transfer policy, in order to compensate disadvantaged regions or local areas. Thus a corrective and redistributive intervention is needed from government.

Criteria and evaluation

There is no simple criterion or universally accepted set of criteria for evaluating transition needs and transition performances in the labour market, for the reason alluded to above, namely the multidimensional nature of both needs and outcomes. This difficulty is compounded by the problems stemming from the challenges inherent in the long-term evaluation of labour markets. Assessment of the actual effects of certain transitions is anything but easy and sometimes requires lengthy periods of observation. Thus it may take time to identify 'bad' transitions. However, the general concerns of the TLM approach are with long-term self-sufficiency and independence in normal full-time jobs.

So the answer may be twofold. In procedural terms, the idea would be to develop independent local employment observatories charged with the task of identifying 'good' transitions and good practices. In substantive terms, multi-dimensional criteria could be developed, together with benchmarking practices (cf. Schmid, 1994; Tronti, 1998).

A rather interesting recent development should be mentioned and briefly discussed here. A synthetic criterion is now available to public actors and local employment services, namely the long-term capacity of an individual to earn his or her living and escape poverty through work. Such a criterion is one of the numerous definitions of employability.[22] Employability may be conceived and operationalized, for example, as the probability of being employed (during a specified period) multiplied by the probable length of working time and the expected hourly earnings. In this sense, it reflects earning capacity, that is the ability to extract meaningful earnings from the labour market.

Another interesting definition of employability is that based on profiling.[23] Developed in the USA during the 1990s, profiling consists of ranking the unemployed as they enter unemployment by their probability of coming off unemployment benefits before their entitlement expires. The ranking is based on a statistical model that includes personal as well as contextual characteristics and produces a continuum of individuals ranging from the least to the most employable. The least advantaged are then referred, in order of priority, to the placement and training services of public employment agencies. These agencies use their own experience and knowledge to draw up an individualized programme for each client.

As implemented here, profiling is a rationalizing, rationing and coordinating mechanism. It has a rationalizing function because it serves to identify those most in need and avoids creaming and the definition of target groups on the basis of less general criteria. It is also a rationing tool, because those above a certain cut-off point are not considered and benefit only from the general, basic assistance for the unemployed. The available cost–benefit evaluations show that profiling pays for itself by shortening the time spent on unemployment benefit.

However, extending the tool beyond the US unemployment insurance context is still a topic of debate, especially in the European context of high unemployment. Some of the reservations expressed are cultural or political in nature, since the unidimensional ranking of the unemployed runs counter to the culture of equality among citizens. Another important argument, however, is statistical and operational in nature. When the odds on re-employment are low and more or less the same for huge numbers of people, it may be misleading to rely too heavily on a single early identification tool. Under such circumstances, periodical evaluation of the relative position of various unemployed populations in a process combining statistical appraisal and expert assessments may be a more suitable tool.

Profiling also functions as a coordinating mechanism, because it encourages inter-agency cooperation. When training, placement and subsidizing institutions operate in isolation, for historical or management reasons, they may serve different clienteles and find it difficult to identify the priority groups. A common definition of employability and shared concerns may help to establish priorities.

It can be argued that, from the public point of view, various definitions of employability may become a focal point for establishing the priorities and evaluating the performance of active labour market policies and TLMs.

The Incentives and Control Set for each Category of Labour Market Actors

Since the overall objective is to improve individuals' long-term capacity to secure their income and manage their careers, the incentive and control mechanisms for employees could consist of a set of rights and related obligations, including the right to be trained and retrained, the right to paid leave in certain circumstances and the right to select from a range of opportunities when unemployed. The countervailing obligation is to choose a sequence of transitions and to undertake adaptation when needed. In order to avoid unilateral pressure on individuals, it may be necessary to establish users' committees and to involve them in the definition and control of the opportunity sets.

As regards labour market institutions, the main incentive, over and above the competition mentioned above, could be the implementation of systematic financial feedbacks (cf. section 1): if costly active measures succeed in reducing the burden of unemployment insurance, the active and passive funding arrangements will have to be linked in order to foster the long-term efficiency of such policies.

Finally, firms may also be persuaded to put in place long-term arrangements for the development of a high-quality workforce. This can be done, not by securing lifelong employment relationships, but by ensuring that firms feel the long-term consequences of some of their decisions. For example, this would be the case with a bonus/malus scheme for unemployment insurance (experience rating). The insider workforce could also be given greater control over the flexibilizing process, with overtime being offset by additional time off and wage premia paid through a regularizing fund. At most, firms could be persuaded to conclude local agreements on training and re-employment opportunities through the introduction of spending targets and/or tax breaks.

TLM as a Learning and Political Process

Finally, adopting a (moderate) evolutionary perspective, we will attempt to locate TLMs in the context of developments currently affecting contemporary labour markets. It seems clear that labour markets are not conducive to collective learning. Labour market innovations are few and, while different models, such as the Swedish one, have been developed, successes in one country seem difficult to replicate in other countries. Another striking example is early retirement. This labour market policy option has been strongly criticized for being too expensive and irreversible and for distorting firms' behaviour. In the general context of an ageing labour force, early retirement may also produce considerable inequalities, since it causes different age groups to be treated differently, and inefficiencies, because it amounts to a waste of labour. Nevertheless, a number of countries are proceeding with huge programmes and others are considering introducing them. There is a general tendency in labour markets towards 'overshooting'. Firms facing increased uncertainty as to the quantity and quality of their future labour requirements may react by taking the 'precaution principle' (cf. Petit, 1999) to extremes, recruiting only highly skilled and adaptable workers while trying to obtain the widest possible range of short-term flexibility options. Once again, segmentation processes are at work here, further reinforced by the overall uncertainty and some of the labour market policies adopted by the state.

Of course a segmentation dynamic exists in all labour markets, and may be more or less durable, more or less damaging and more or less socially acceptable. TLMs could provide an opportunity to examine and negotiate on the social control of occupational trajectories, not only the opportunity for some workers to be integrated into an internal labour market but also, and more generally, the career path of every individual worker. The gender dimension is a key example here. TLMs could make it possible for men's and women's careers to be considered and regulated in conjunction and could be used to introduce greater gender equality into the labour market. TLMs are not, of course, a substitute for a policy directly aimed at narrowing the gap between men and women in the labour market. However, they could usefully supplement such a policy.

Thus the specific approach to learning to be derived from transitional markets is one based on networks and local negotiations. However, this approach goes beyond mere adaptation to local needs. It encourages reinternalization on a wider scale because it sets in train a more systematic process: it is designed to capture externalities to a much greater extent and to promote a more homogeneous labour market.

The learning process includes TLM failures. As we have already seen, the transaction costs associated with specific transitions are not easy to identify and measure and the relative share of externalities may appear only after a process of trial and error. There is plenty of scope for inadequate provision of transitional arrangements, as well as for gradual learning. The TLM approach takes as its starting point firms' new concerns in respect of mobility and the blurring of the boundaries between employment and other activities. The development of TLMs works with the grain of these trends and may lead to revelation of the preferences of labour market actors and of responsibilities for labour market externalities. This brings us back once again to the need for benchmarking and the exchange of good practices.

This learning process focuses on the intended and unintended economic and social consequences of transitions and on the collective control of them. Thus TLMs may be presented as an essential part of a new social contract.

There is also a political dimension to the development of TLMs. The expected long-term result is less inequality in an adaptable labour market. From a TLM perspective, labour market homogeneity could be presented as a collective good. The choices may lead to the withdrawal of some public subsidies for favoured groups and to the introduction of selective assistance for other, less advantaged groups: in other words, to positive discrimination. However, the possible distributional impacts of TLMs remain a topic for further exploration.

The implicit expectations of both workers and employers were traditionally organized around stable career prospects within firms, and collective arrangements were structured accordingly. Within internal labour markets, the management of stable and homogeneous careers for employees with different levels of productivity and commitment functioned as an implicit subsidizing process. Such a balancing act is becoming increasingly difficult to sustain, as we saw in the first two sections of this chapter. The objective of the TLM approach is to identify a new and enlarged basis for workforce stabilization in order to minimize the increasing distance between highly-skilled and lower-skilled workers. TLMs could be the functional equivalent of the old social guarantees based on internal labour markets and may act as new property rights. However, these rights, given to individuals, are essentially collective.

The TLM response to the problems of managing an ageing workforce should also be given prominence. The current tendency in labour markets is to reject older workers, for reasons of declining individual productivity and adaptability. The TLM approach here is to encourage negotiated arrangements combining subsidies with organizational adaptation. In this way, it would be possible to keep such groups in 'soft' positions and/or in half-time jobs.[24] Such collective arrangements have already been put in place, either within firms or within networks of firms, but to date only on a limited scale. Such arrangements link up with our earlier observations on employability. Employability is meaningless if it is not related to a specified economic and institutional context: this leads to the idea of collective employability and the social construction of employability.

Thus TLMs can be understood as a means of combining the individualizing tendencies in our societies with collective solidarities.

4 CONCLUSION

The main objective of this chapter was to forge closer and more explicit links between positive analysis of the functioning of labour markets and the policy proposals derived from the TLM approach. This goal was achieved in three steps. We began by considering interactions in the context of a more or less homogeneous market before proceeding to a lengthy discussion of segmentation dynamics. We concluded with a discussion of some of the issues raised by the possible implementation of TLMs.

The main finding from the first two sections is that the TLM approach offers a range of possible reforms which, if implemented, would facilitate labour market adjustments and make them less unequal and more efficient.

TLMs would foster continuity of employment and earnings through the negotiation of flexible arrangements. They emerged in section 1 as a new co-ordinating tool, capable of reducing certain transaction costs and offering more coherent incentives to firms and collective actors alike. They would be able to capture externalities, whether static or dynamic, mainly by systematically expanding and enlarging local bargaining processes. Thus it was argued that the flexible and reversible work sharing they offer would create new opportunities for the ex ante regulation of the labour market.

In the light of the segmentation dynamic affecting labour markets (see section 2), the potential of TLMs as a rehomogenizing tool was discussed. The risk of producing bad transitions and reinforcing segmentation was considered. The segregational bias of some existing public employment policies may be attributable to the fact that they are implemented in isolation and on a limited scale. By extending the choices available to less advantaged groups in the labour force and influencing firms' behaviour both internally and in the external environment, TLMs may prevent the exploitation of some segments and lower barriers to the integration of low-skill workers.

However, these virtues are not unmixed blessings, as was shown in section 3, devoted to incentives and controls. If TLMs represent the emergence of a new commodity in the labour market, it must be acknowledged that they are only the beginning of a complex learning and political process. They must be seen as a set of promising but still evolving coordinating mechanisms and policy tools for use in changing and polarized labour markets.

NOTES

1. For a useful discussion on the various issues at stake and the methodologies of labour market policy evaluation, see Schmid *et al.* (1996).
2. This chapter is largely a synthesis of three papers presented at the 1998 and 1999 Berlin conferences of the TRANSLAM programme. The author thanks the programme participants, and especially Jill Rubery and Günther Schmid, for useful comments. He remains, however, responsible for any possible mistakes and omissions.
3. For an overview covering the North American trading zone (ALENA) as well as the European Union, see Ehrenberg (1994).
4. A good concrete example is given by K. Abraham and S. Houseman in Blank (1994): the adjustment speeds of employment to demand in the manufacturing sector in Europe and the USA differ substantially (Europe being much slower), but are equalized when allowance is made for adjustments in hours worked and short-time working.
5. We cannot present or discuss wage rigidity theories here (efficiency wages, implicit contracts, insiders/outsiders). They differ widely in their causal orientation and policy prescriptions, but all focus on the built-in mechanisms that limit market wage adjustments.
6. However, it should be noted that enormous differences persist amongst countries, at the turn of the century, in the size of the public sector. For example, Denmark, a small open economy, seems able to reconcile a huge public sector (30 per cent of total employment) with a rather good overall employment performance.
7. Cf. Gazier (1998). The main indicators are the interdecile ratio for wages, the unemployment level and the expenditure level on active and passive labour market policies.
8. Such subsidies compensate for productivity deficiencies but leave the existing limited (egalitarian) wage differential unchanged. The role of these compensating subsidies is the complete opposite of that of some UK subsidies during the same period, which were intended to encourage wage cuts. For more details, see Gautié *et al.* (1994).
9. An elementary statistical comparison may be helpful here: in 1993 further training expenditure per employee was 3944FF in France, 2365FF in Germany and 1470FF in Belgium (FORCE report, Eurostat). The 1999 OECD *Employment Outlook* (OECD, 1999) gives an overview of developments in 24 developed countries in the 1990s based on several different comparative studies. It examines participation rates and training volumes, and gives a ranking for both. France is first for volume and fifth for participation; Germany is 10th for volume and 16th for participation. The USA is in a median position (12th on both scores), the UK is 6th for volumes and 3rd for participation; Italy is 23rd for volume and 21st for participation and Belgium 20th and 17th. Interestingly enough, Sweden is 18th for volume and 2nd for participation, suggesting that for most of the 1990s continuous training here was more a social policy than a labour market policy tool.
10. For a complementary analysis of the future of the 'high-skill equilibrium' in Germany, see Culpepper (1999).
11. These selected references and national cases remain subjective to some extent. A related general overview is proposed by Marsden (1996), while another useful reference for the United States is Appelbaum and Batt (1994). A recent study of the German case is summarized in Baden and Schmid (1998).
12. Our references are taken from Cappelli (1995). See also his more detailed collective book, Capelli (1996).
13. Capelli himself notes that hard general evidence on shortening job tenure and diminishing job security is difficult to find in the USA (as elsewhere). In any event, decreasing job security may cause incumbents to remain in their jobs, thereby offsetting the tendency towards shorter job tenure.
14. The French automotive sector, which once offered generous stabilization policies, provided in the late 1990s a spectacular illustration of these tendencies. Cf. Gorgeu and Matthieu (1998).
15. A recent study by Beffa *et al.* (1999) puts forward a converging typology and identifies three forms of the employment relationship that were emerging at the end of the 1990s. The first

is the classic internal labour market, adapted to incorporate functional flexibility; the second is a (dominant) secondary market, unstable and poorly qualified, and the third is a new 'professional' labour market for highly skilled workers.

16. Cf. Thoemmes and Labit (1995) and Rosdücher (1997).
17. For more details, see Schmid *et al.* (1999) and G. Schmid's last chapter in the present book.
18. Cf. Schmid *et al.* (1999) for a discussion of the connection between TLMs and passive/active labour market policies.
19. For a recent synthesis and discussion, see Putterman *et al.* (1998).
20. For a general discussion of this question, see also Gazier (1999b).
21. For a discussion of these two challenges starting from a 'local justice' point of view, see Gazier (2000).
22. A general appraisal and more detailed discussion of employability can be found in Gazier (1999c).
23. For more details, see Eberts (1999).
24. For other TLM arrangements within firms, including working-time accounts and premium funds, see Rogowski and Schmid (1997).

BIBLIOGRAPHY

Appelbaum, E. and R. Batt (1994), *The new American workplace: transforming work systems in the United States*, Ithaca, NY: Cornell University Press.

Appelbaum, E., T. Bailey, P. Berg and A.L. Kalleberg (2000), *Manufacturing advantage. Why high-performance work systems pay off*, Ithaca, NY: Cornell University Press.

Auer, P. (2000), *Employment revival in Europe. Labour market success in Austria, Denmark, Ireland and the Netherlands*, Geneva: ILO.

Auer, P. and G. Schmid (1997), 'Transitional Labour Markets. Concepts and Examples in Europe', paper prepared for the conference on 'New Institutional Arrangements in the Labour Market', European Academy of the Urban Environment, Berlin, April.

Baden, C. and A. Schmid (1998), 'Arbeitmarktsegmentation und Informationstechnologien: Zu den Auswirkungen von CIM-Technologien auf Struktur und Funktionsweise von Teilarbeitmarkten – Zusammengefasste Ergebnisse eines Forschungprojekts', *Mitteilungen aus der Arbeitsmarkt und Berufsforschung*, 31(1), 143–54, J.W. Goethe Universität.

Barbier, J.C. and J. Gautié (eds) (1999), *Les politiques de l'emploi en Europe et aux Etats-Unis*, Paris: PUF.

Beffa, J.L., R. Boyer and J.P. Touffut (1999), 'Les relations salariales en France: Etat, entreprise, marchés financiers', *Notes de la Fondation Saint-Simon*, Paris.

Blank, R. (ed.) (1994), *Social Protection versus Economic Flexibility. Is there a Trade-off?*, National Bureau of Economic Research, Chicago and London: The University of Chicago Press.

Cappelli, P. (1995), 'Rethinking Employment', *British Journal of Industrial Relations*, 33(4), December, 563–602.

Cappelli, P. (ed.) (1996), *Change at Work*, Cambridge: Cambridge University Press.

Culpepper, P.D. (1999), 'The future of the high-skill equilibrium in Germany', *Oxford Review of Economic Policy*, 15(1), Spring, 43–59.

De Koning, J. and Mosley, H. (eds) (2001), *Labour Market Policy and Unemployment: Impact and Process Evaluations in Selected European Countries*, Cheltenham, UK and Northampton, US: Edward Elgar.

Doeringer, P. and M. Piore (1971), *Internal Labor Markets and Manpower Analysis*, Armonk, NY: M.E. Sharpe (reprinted with a new introduction in 1985).

Eberts, R. (1999), 'The Use of Profiling in the United States for Early Identification and Referral of less Employable Unemployment Insurance Recipients', in B. Gazier (ed.), *Employability. Concepts and Policies*, Berlin: IAS.

Ehrenberg, R. (1994), *Labor Markets and Integrating National Economies*, Washington, DC: The Brookings Institution.

Freyssinet, J. (1982), *Politiques d'emploi des grands groupes en France*, Grenoble: Presses Universitaires de Grenoble.

Galtier, B. (1996), 'Gérer la main-d'œuvre dans la durée: des pratiques différenciées en renouvellement', *Economie et Statistique*, 298, 45–70.

Gautié, J., B. Gazier and R. Silvera (1994), *Les subventions à l'emploi: analyses et expériences européennes*, Paris: La Documentation française.

Gazier, B. (1993), *Les stratégies des ressources humaines*, Paris: La Découverte.

Gazier, B. (1998) 'Plein emploi, régimes d'emploi et marchés transitionnels: une approche comparative', in D.G. Tremblay (ed.), *Objectif plein emploi. Le marché, la social-démocratie ou l'économie sociale?*, Etudes d'Economie Politique, Montréal: Presses de l'Université du Québec, pp. 57–83.

Gazier, B. (1999a), 'Ce que sont les marchés transitionnels', in J.C. Barbier and J. Gautié (eds), *Les politiques de l'emploi en Europe et aux Etat-Unis*, Paris: PUF.

Gazier, B. (1999b) 'Assurance chômage, employabilité et Marchés Transitionnels du Travail', working paper, *Cahiers de la Maison des Sciences Economiques*, 9903, Paris.

Gazier, B. (ed.) (1999c), *Employability. Concepts and Policies*, Berlin: IAS.

Gazier, B. (2000), 'L'articulation justice locale–justice globale. Le cas des "marchés transitionnels du travail" ', *Revue Economique*, May, 571–81.

Géhin, J.C. and P. Méhaut (1993), *Apprentissage ou formation continue? Stratégies éducatives des entreprises en France et en Allemagne*, Paris: L'Harmattan.

Gorgeu, A. and R. Matthieu (1998), 'L'emploi dans la filière automobile', *La lettre du Centre d'Etudes de l'Emploi*, December, 1–10.

Grimshaw, D. and J. Rubery (1998), 'Integrating the internal and external labour markets', *Cambridge Journal of Economics*, 22, 199–220.

Lallement, M. (1996), 'Le système de relations professionnelles allemand à l'épreuve de la réunification', *Relations Industrielles*, 51(3), 443–67.

Lallement, M. (1999), *Les gouvernances de l'emploi*, Paris: Desclée de Brouwer.

Madsen, P.K. (1997), 'Lifelong Learning and Paid Leave Arrangements: Some General Arguments and an Illustration Using the Danish Experience in the 1990s', in OECD (ed.), *Creativity, Innovation and Job Creation*, OECD Proceedings), Paris: OECD, pp. 113–29.

Marsden, D. (1996), 'Employment policy implications of new management systems', *Labour*, 10(1), Spring, 17–62.

Petit, P. (1999), 'Les aléas de la croissance dans une économie fondée sur le savoir', *Revue d'Economie Industrielle*, 88(2).

Putterman, L., J.E. Roemer and J. Silvestre (1998), 'Does Egalitarianism Have a Future?', *Journal of Economic Literature*, XXXVI (June), 861–902.

Rogowski, R. and G. Schmid (1997), 'Reflexive deregulation. International experiences and proposals for labour market reforms', *WZB Working Paper*, FS I 97–206a WZB, Berlin.

Rosdücher, J. (1997), *Arbeitsplatzsicherheit durch Tarifvertrag. Strategie, Konzepte, Vereinbarungen*, Munich and Mering: Rainer Hampp Verlag.

Rubery, J. (1994), 'Internal and External Labour Markets: Towards an Integrated Analysis', in J. Rubery and F. Wilkinson (eds), *Employer Strategy and the Labour Market*, Oxford: Oxford University Press, pp. 37–68.

Schmid, G. (ed.) (1994), *Labour Market Institutions in Europe. A Socio-Economic Evaluation of Performance*, Armonk, NY: M.E. Sharpe.

Schmid, G. (1995) 'A New Approach to Labour Market Policy: a Contribution to the Current Debate on Efficient Employment Policies. Is Full Employment Still Possible? Transitional Labour Markets as a New Strategy of Labour Market Policy', *Economic and Industrial Democracy*, SAGE, 16, 429–56.

Schmid, G., B. Gazier and S. Flechtner (1999), 'Transitional Labour Markets, Employability and Unemployment Insurance', in B. Gazier (ed.) *Employability. Concepts and Policies*, Berlin: IAS.

Schmid, G., J. O'Reilly and K. Schömann (eds) (1996), *International Handbook of Labour Market Policy and Evaluation*, Cheltenham, UK and Brookfield, US: Edward Elgar.

Siebert, W.S. and J.T. Addison (1991), 'Internal Labour Markets: causes and consequences', *Oxford Review of Economic Policy*, 7(1), 76–92.

Solow, R. (1991), *The labour market as a social institution*, Oxford: Blackwell.

Supiot, A. (ed.) (1999), *Au-delà de l'emploi*, Paris: Flammarion.

Thoemmes, J. and A. Labit (1995), 'La "semaine de 4 jours" chez Volkswagen: un scénario original de sortie de crise?', *Travail et emploi*, 64, 5–22.

Tronti, L. (ed.) (1998), 'Benchmarking European Labour Market Policies', IAS Report, Berlin.

Williamson, O. (1996), *The Mechanisms of Governance*, Oxford: Oxford University Press.

7. The legal regulation of transitional labour markets

Ton Wilthagen and Ralf Rogowski[1]

This chapter investigates the relationship between transitional labour markets (TLMs) and legal regulation. The legal regulation of policies generally has two functions. Firstly, it marks out boundaries for policy making, boundaries derived from general normative principles and basic individual rights. Secondly, it provides opportunities for developing policies aimed at flexibilizing institutional structures. This second function requires law to reflect on its own limitations and to strike a balance between concerns derived from established legal structures and those arising out of new legal demands.

A major aspect of the first function of law is to protect individuals from the negative effects of markets. Law does so by conferring rights. In labour law these are employment rights and other measures protecting workers. TLMs can be both hampered and promoted by labour law measures. Without security, workers will be reluctant and lack the motivation to engage in transitions, as they will fear that changing status will bear significant risks and might become a change for the worse. These risks include the loss of a job (or a loss of employment in general), a deterioration of the terms of employment (in particular a decrease in income or in future incomes such as pensions), diminished career opportunities, exclusion from the workplace or from other important spheres of life, interference with social responsibilities and activities beyond the realm of work and an invasion of privacy and civic autonomy as a result of dependency on social benefits. Confronted with such prospects, people tend to stick to the status quo.

However, there is also the risk of long-term unemployment and other forms and causes of exclusion from the labour market. Indeed, at the centre of the concept of the TLM lies a political concern with the structural unemployment that plagues modern society. In its focus on transitory states between gainful employment and productive, non-market activities, the TLM concept is policy-oriented. It is conceived as a vehicle, instrument or method for fighting high structural unemployment or, more optimistically, obtaining full employment in terms of flexible, though substantial and enduring, labour market participation for all (Schmid, 'Towards a Theory of Transitional Labour Markets', in this volume).

By conferring rights and establishing legal structures, law imposes certain boundaries on TLMs. It defines the scope and form of transitions. However, it also provides opportunities to explore new forms of transitions. Thus in some cases legal protection prevents workers from making transitions involving a change of employment status, while in others legal provisions trigger and warrant transitions. It depends to a large extent on the form of legal protection – social security as well as job and employment protection – that legal systems offer workers. Indeed, a legal system that is optimally geared to a TLM requires from most national employment systems substantial reforms of legislation and other legal regulation.

The chapter is divided into two parts. First, three legal boundaries are identified: legal complexity, regulation thresholds and the costs of transitions and transactions related to law. Second, we discuss the legal opportunities for TLMs, with particular reference to deregulation policies, to legislation and other forms of regulation of part-time work and paid leave, to the concept of flexicurity, to training policies, to transition agencies and, finally, to the possibility of constitutionalizing rights to transitional employment at the European level.

1   LEGAL BOUNDARIES FOR TRANSITIONAL LABOUR MARKET POLICIES

Legal boundaries for labour market policies derive from the nature and purpose of law. We can identify internal factors that either limit the capacity of legal regulation, such as legal complexity and the detection threshold, or that relate to normative criteria of legal regulation, such as the discrimination and evaluation thresholds. In addition, there are various costs that occur as a result of legal regulations.

Legal Complexity

In accordance with recent sociological systems theory, we conceive the modern society as consisting of function systems governed by distinct codes and programmes. The modern society is rapidly becoming a world society, in which demarcations by national boundaries are losing their significance. This also holds true for the world legal system, in which regional normative orders like the law of the European Union, in conjunction with international law, are gaining in importance (on the world legal system, see Teubner, 1996; Luhmann, 1993, in particular pp. 571–86). The legal system, like other function systems, is differentiated into subsystems. These include legal fields such as contract law, company law, administrative law, social security law, tax law and labour law. In addition, modern law is characterized by a diversity of legal sources located 'below' the legislation adopted at nation state level. These sources include collective agreements and customary law as well as standard setting, informal agreements and norms created by private bodies.

Each function system and its subsystems require autonomy to fulfil their societal function. Furthermore, each legal subsystem develops its specific internal model of the external world and evolves along trajectories dominated by self-created norms and principles. The result is an enormous increase in complexity in the modern society at the level of the function system and of its subsystems.

Like other social systems, modern labour law is characterized by the need to reduce self-generated complexity. However, in comparison to other legal subsystems, labour law has to cope with particular problems of external complexity related to its regulatory object, namely industrial relations and employment relations in companies (see Rogowski and Wilthagen, 1994). In addition, the normative premises and institutional orders of labour law tend to clash with other legal subsystems and orders. This can be demonstrated with respect to traditional labour law, whose specific normative perspective is centred upon the rights of employees and of trade unions. These labour law regulations have a tendency to clash with other normative legal premises, in particular when the social and industrial basis on which employment rights and collective bargaining rests ceases to exist (see Supiot, 1999). For example, workers' rights to educational, parental or unpaid leave can clash with social security laws that link entitlements to continuous work careers. Another example is pension rights that are lost if a worker switches jobs or moves across sectors and branches of business and industry. Furthermore, informal company or workplace codes can also obstruct legal rights to leave or to work part-time, as availability to work full-time is often considered a prerequisite for promotion.

A legal design attuned to TLMs has to take account of the different animating principles that underpin the various legal subsystems. The modern legal system is increasingly confronted with problems caused by its self-generated complexity and there have been many attempts to tackle the problem of legal complexity. One prominent strategy for reducing complexity is deregulation. However, deregulation is path-dependent. Its goals are shaped by national legal, industrial relations and political systems and accordingly vary widely among countries (Rogowski and Schmid, 1998). Furthermore, deregulation is ineffective or detrimental if it is not perceived as a solution within the various legal subsystems.

Thus a policy that seeks successfully to regulate TLMs must embark on a strategy of coordination of legal subsystems that acknowledges each order's major presuppositions. This approach combines the reduction of legal complexity with flexibilization policies that support parallel trajectories in different subsystems. Such reduction of legal complexity becomes a form of reflexive deregulation when it recognizes the limits of deregulation and leaves scope for reregulation (see below, under 'Reflexive Deregulation').

Regulation Thresholds

Any policy of regulation and/or deregulation has to reckon with regulation thresholds. The concept of thresholds can serve as a method of analysing legal boundaries. A regulation threshold describes the capacity of the legal subsystem to determine its scale of legality. Three types of thresholds can be distinguished: the detection threshold, the discrimination threshold and the evaluation threshold.[2]

The *detection* threshold refers to those aspects of the social object that require regulation; it distinguishes between relevant and irrelevant issues. Some issues are simply not (yet) taken up by the legal system. A legal design for TLMs has to tackle the detection threshold by indicating the legal relevance of unregulated or insufficiently regulated areas. For example, in labour law the legal (de jure) or contractual dependency of one person (employee) on another person (employer) is a decisive criterion, whereas the actual (de facto) dependency is relevant only in cases of doubt about the legal relationship, for example when there is no written employment contract. This means that the situation of persons who are quasi-self-employed, that is strongly dependent on one client (often the former employer, particularly in cases when a job is outsourced and the former jobholder is rehired as a formally self-employed person), is largely neglected in law (see also van der Heijden, 1997).

The *discrimination* threshold concerns differences in the description of the social object that may justify qualitative differences in regulation; it distinguishes between the same – that deserves equal treatment – and the different – that allows unequal treatment. A particular problem is created by legal thresholds that exclude certain employees or non-employees from social benefits or social security schemes.[3] Furthermore, in quite a few countries (Germany and the Netherlands, for example) social protection and employment laws have traditionally been based on the male breadwinner model. This kind of bias does create a barrier for transitional labour markets as it creates a distinction between insiders and outsiders. Moreover, legal complexity will be increased if, in line with a TLM strategy, socially excluded groups begin to (re-)enter the labour market. In the case of interruption of employment there are concerns with the continuation of social protection.[4] However, there is also the issue of reverse discrimination. New rights and opportunities can undermine existing benefits and thus lead to new discrimination against those protected by previous regulation.

The *evaluation* threshold relates to the rights granted to individuals and to the principles that underlie legal structures; it distinguishes between the legal and the illegal. This threshold is highly relevant to TLMs. In most cases, the existing system of rights and institutions provides the framework for new regulation. In addition, there are specific rules derived from non-statutory collective agreements and custom and practice at firm level that limit arbitrary choices. For example, an employer might deny certain career opportunities to an employee who has been on leave, contending that he or she has not shown sufficient commitment and loyalty to the company. In most current legal orders, it is difficult to argue that such a decision is 'illegal'.

Legal Transition Costs

The legal regulation of TLMs can present a barrier to transitions by raising the costs of transitions for the worker and/or the employer or by failing to lower the costs of transitions and transactions where deemed appropriate.

In general, the costs of labour market transitions as defined in the TLM model are comparable to mobility costs, as discussed by Ehrenberg and Smith (1997: 652). These costs are monetary, psychological and legal in nature. They can be labelled *transition costs*. Workers that engage in transitions are threatened with the loss of employee benefits, such as pensions and health insurance, or access to the 'inside track' for future promotions. They might even risk the loss of their job. For employers, transition costs consist of loss of productivity, loss of income, lost investments in firm-specific training and extra hiring and training costs for replacements. From an economic point of view, transitions are only likely to take place once the benefits of a transition are higher than the costs incurred. In that case it is optimal for the employee and the employer to transact or to reach an agreement on the transition.[5]

A specific type of costs that might prevent the transition from taking place are so-called *transaction costs*. Transaction costs are associated with the cost of acquiring information about exchanges; in fact, any exchange, including those in the labour market, has a 'price'. Transaction costs theory suggests that at times it can pay to use the market as a coordination mechanism, while at others it is less expensive to use hierarchical organizations such as firms to coordinate actions (Williamson, 1994). A firm represents a set of long-term contracts between owners of labour and entrepreneurs which, once these contracts have been established, no longer responds to price signals. Instead, the employee transfers certain user rights over his labour resource to the entrepreneur. Long-term/standard employment contracts reduce transaction costs because they relieve employers of spot-market exchanges: that is, repeatedly having to hire and fire employees to perform single tasks. A standard employment contract, which is to a certain extent 'unspecified' in respect of the tasks to be performed and working conditions (this is where the concept of hierarchy comes in), could, in this way, be cheaper and more efficient. In the case of transitions, transaction costs are information production costs.

Managing transitions within a company or in the labour market as a whole causes specific transaction costs. In general, these costs comprise information production costs, drafting costs, communication costs, negotiation costs, agency costs, litigation costs, enforcement costs and costs of opportunistic behaviour. Legal transition costs occur both before and after an agreement is concluded. Typical post-agreement costs are those caused by the maladaptation and adjustment that arise when contract execution is misaligned as a result of gaps, errors, omissions and unanticipated disturbances. Furthermore, there are costs stemming from new legal requirements that actually seek to stimulate transitions. For employers, customized employment contracts and individual fiscal and social security arrangements increase administrative costs, particularly in relation to US-style contractualism.[6] A voucher system or the introduction of default terms, which will be discussed in the next section of this chapter, are possible solutions to this problem.

Finally, even if the legal intention is to reduce transition costs, the law is limited in this respect. Some costs or barriers for workers are related to employers' internal human resource management policies, for example those on promotion and career opportunities within the company. In these areas, law, at present can have little if any effect on the employer's prerogative. In other areas, the legal norms tend to be too general, since they rely on notions such as 'the reasonable employer' or 'good faith' and their implementation depends on the interpretation by case law or collective agreement. Other instruments and strategies, such as education or informal agreements with trade unions and works councils, are often more appropriate than the law.

2   LEGAL OPPORTUNITIES FOR TRANSITIONAL LABOUR MARKETS

In applying general principles, law not only establishes boundaries for policy making but also creates opportunities and steers politics into pursuing certain avenues. Established legal principles, such as discrimination or proportionality, can be used to rethink existing policies, start policy making in new fields and/or design innovative regulatory strategies. Furthermore, the law's structural coupling to the political system is a continuous source of irritations that set in motion both legal and political dynamics.

Our purpose in the following is to discuss examples of legal opportunities for designing TLM regulations that are the result of legal innovations. These opportunities mirror to some extent the boundaries outlined in the previous section.

Reflexive Deregulation

Deregulation is an attractive option for policies that focus on TLMs. Where regulations create obstacles to transitions, and their removal incurs no unbearable costs, a policy of deregulation seems feasible. Such a strategy becomes a form of reflexive deregulation if it involves coordinating the various regulatory principles that govern labour markets (Rogowski and Wilthagen, 1994). Furthermore, reflexive deregulation is usually accompanied by attempts to reregulate the labour market. In the following, we shall discuss general aspects of deregulation from the point of view of reducing complexity and examine a specific example of reregulation, namely voucher systems.

Reducing legal complexity

A general strategy for creating legal opportunities that ease transitions is directly related to the reduction of legal complexity. Modern labour law systems, like other social systems, are continually forced to manage and reduce complexity. When labour law systems realize that the complexity is at least partly self-generated, they become reflexive. In developing system-specific strategies for reducing complexity, deregulation is a widely applied solution.

However, there is no single blueprint for deregulation but rather a variety of deregulation policies. Analyses of the deregulation of Western labour law systems reveal a diversity of approaches. In the United Kingdom, for example, deregulation focused in the 1980s and 1990s on some reduction of employee protection, combined with severe legal restrictions on trade union activities (Dickens, 1994). In Germany, deregulation involved adaptation of the complex structure of the autonomous labour law system in order to achieve certain necessary reforms, particularly in the use of fixed-term contracts. In France, the main purpose of deregulation in the 1980s was to reduce the powers of the labour inspectorate while at the same time strengthening the representation of employee interests at establishment level and making employment relationships more flexible, particularly through new or atypical forms of employment contract. And in the USA, deregulation meant the de facto loss of employee rights because of the decline in trade union membership and the consequent decline in protection provided by collective agreements (Rogowski and Schmid, 1998).

Despite this diversity, there are some common patterns in the deregulation of labour law. One example is the debate on atypical employment contracts. A number of deregulation policies have sought in similar ways to flexibilize the available forms of employment and to support atypical employment contracts, in particular by overcoming the so-called 'legal discrimination' against fixed-term contracts of labour (see Schömann *et al.*, 1998). However, it has to be said that each of these deregulation policies is path-dependent; that is, the form and the actual process of deregulation are determined by the specific character of national labour law systems and their relationships to national industrial relations systems.

The varied experiences with deregulation make it impossible to speak of a uniform trend. The objectives range from radical free-market approaches involving the abolition of employment protection to piecemeal reforms of existing labour laws. However, it is important that deregulation policies are always conducted within the framework of existing legal and other normative structures.

Alongside deregulation, there have been attempts to reregulate the labour market. These are legal strategies that combine the reduction of complexity with the enhancement of individual preferences. Such strategies become reflexive regulation when linked to self-regulation (see Collins, 1999: 62–9 on reflexive regulation). In the following we shall discuss an example of such reflexive reregulation, that is the market-driven but collectively controlled strategy called the voucher system. So far as we know, no country has yet implemented this concept in its labour law or social security practice. However, experimental voucher systems have been introduced in the area of education and training (see Levin, 1980, 1983, 1991).

An example of reregulation: the voucher system and social drawing rights

A voucher system (also referred to as a quasi-market) can be defined as a system that enhances (or restores) the (free) market as well as the freedom and preferences of individual persons (workers) within the regulatory framework of the labour market. At the same time, a voucher system serves to allocate (public and/or private) resources.[7] Voucher systems can be seen as solutions for collective failure (in the case of public or quasi-public goods). However, in our view, they are a means of complementing, supplementing, endorsing or implementing public regulation.

The basic function of a voucher system within a transitional labour market would be to enable workers – financially, but also in other respects – to engage in transitions and to *manage* their own transitions adequately. A voucher system grants legal entitlements. Supiot *et al.* (2001: 56–7) argue that the entitlement of the worker to switch from one work status or situation to another has already emerged as a new legal figure that reconciles freedom and security. They mention special leave schemes, time-saving schemes and training vouchers. The main thrust of these schemes is that workers are granted rights that are exercised within the bounds of a previously established claim but brought into effect voluntarily rather than as the (enforced) result of risk. These rights are denoted by the term 'social drawing rights'.

Vouchers or social drawing rights apply to the following aspects of transitional employment:

1. entitlements to (a certain amount of) training and education (defined, for example, in hours, days or qualification levels);
2. entitlements to the reduction and extension of individual working time over the course of the working life (enabling individuals to switch from full-time to part-time work);
3. entitlements to certain fiscal subsidies, advantages or benefits enabling individuals to switch between employment and self-employment, for example;
4. entitlements to pre-retirement schemes that allow individuals to (partially) retire while at the same retaining their jobs (within certain limits);
5. entitlements to a variety of forms of leave (parental leave, special leave, calamity leave, unpaid leave);
6. entitlements to childcare arrangements (stipulating a certain number of hours, days or years per child, for example);
7. entitlements to holidays and to (a certain amount of) leisure time, for example in the form of a leisure-time account (comparable to a bank account).

Social drawing rights impinge on fundamental aspects of the employment relationship and the relationship between law and the labour market. These include the following issues.

Empowerment and dynamic efficiency   A voucher system contributes to workers' empowerment, which is a precondition for 'good' transitions (Schmid, 'Towards a Theory of Transitional Labour Markets', in this volume). Furthermore, allowing for an exchange of vouchers (within a company or perhaps at an exchange market) enhances individual preferences. Moreover, by using workers' vouchers as a basis for allocating funding to labour market institutions such as training and education services, public employment agencies and childcare centres, a voucher system contributes to another precondition for good transitions, namely dynamic efficiency.

Social purposes and degree of freedom   A voucher system allows individuals to exercise rights not in reaction to risk but rather as a result of their own free decisions. It thus differs fundamentally from a social security scheme based on the payment of premiums (Supiot *et al.*, 2001: 56–7). Social drawing rights can be used for specific social purposes and enable 'drawers' (collectively or individually) to build up reserves that cover the use of the drawing rights. However, the question remains as to the extent to which it is efficient and fair to have individuals freely choose both the time at which their rights are to be exercised and the purpose to which they are to be put. Voucher systems will have to find ways to balance and reconcile collective and individual interests since not all (individual) purposes are necessarily socially gainful activities.

Although the time at which the rights are exercised will generally be decided by the individual, there will be social and organizational constraints that need to be acknowledged. Furthermore, certain times will be attractive from an economic and social point of view. For example, workers might have to use their drawing rights to education during a period of recession rather than at times of economic boom. The decision could be linked to social security benefits. It could also enhance the value of (social security) regulations on temporary unemployment, such as those that exist in Belgium or the short-time working scheme in Germany, because such schemes would be used more actively for the purpose of innovation than is currently the case (Sels and van Hootegem, 1999). One possible way of reducing transaction costs in general and of enhancing the social efficiency of voucher systems in particular (without limiting individual freedom) would be to introduce so-called 'default terms'. Default terms stipulate the way or the time that entitlements are to be used, unless the user indicates that he or she wants to decide otherwise.

Financing and allocation of budgets   A major question in setting up a voucher system is the financing. It is likely that some government funding will be needed, but employers and perhaps trade unions will probably have to contribute as well. In any case the time during which workers exercise such rights will have to count as 'working time' for labour law and social security purposes (Supiot *et al.*, 2001: 57). One important issue is the time limit of entitlements. According to the general concept, the use of vouchers should not be limited in time, and age limits on beneficiaries are an idea at odds with the concept of transitional labour markets. However, the absence of time limits makes it very difficult for organizations and institutions, particularly in the field of education and training, to estimate the demand for their services and hence to allocate budgets. Moreover, if individuals are allowed to save up their entitlements for a long period of time and if the entitlements are based on units such as hours, days, months, training courses or similar quantities, it should be noticed that the actual price and worth of these units could change over time. This also has an impact on budgets and reserves. Pension schemes (both state and company schemes) are a comparable example here. And finally, there is the question of whether organizations and institutions should be allowed to select the persons who decide to exercise their voucher rights or have to admit everyone without selection.

Feasibility; collective bargaining as a starting-point   The practical advantages and feasibility of voucher systems can be demonstrated by reference to a 'natural experiment'. This is the so-called 'GI Bill', which was originally introduced in 1944 to support American war veterans. It entitles veterans to a maximum of 45 months of training in the first 10 years following active service. A person who participates in a training programme is given a monthly allowance (for Vietnam veterans this was $311). A great number of training and education organizations have been accredited for the GI Bill scheme, including colleges and universities. Evaluations show that the participation of veterans in post-mandatory education is higher than among non-veterans. Furthermore, a third of the veterans would not have participated in any training programme if it were not for the GI Bill. Finally, participation rates among black veterans are higher than among white veterans, whereas the opposite is true for non-veteran populations. In that sense, the GI Bill scheme has had a positive impact on the promotion of equal opportunities in education (on the GI Bill see Oosterbeek, 1994).

An important aspect of voucher or social drawing rights schemes is their capacity to enhance the collective bargaining of labour agreements. Many existing collective agreements already allow for differentiation and individual choice.[8] Regulating voucher systems by collective agreements, combined with statutory minimum standards, makes it easier to take collective interest into account and to adapt such systems to the peculiarities and established practices of particular industries and firms. A good example of a collectively agreed labour market measure is the Saar Community Initiative (*Saar-Gemeinschaftsinitiative*) in the German state of the Saarland. Formerly unemployed persons are granted a reduction in social security premiums if they accept a job; this premium is 'paid' in the form of rights to training. [9]

Juridification   Finally, if successfully implemented, voucher systems can help to reverse the juridification of the labour market, to reduce legal complexity and to lower transition and transaction costs. They can also enhance labour market flexibility and help to establish a sound form of deregulation.

Reflexive Regulation of TLMs

It would, of course, be wrong to assume that all new regulation is linked to deregulation efforts. There are a number of new approaches to regulation, well-suited to TLMs, that deal in particular with the problem of regulation thresholds and the lack of individual and collective rights. In the following, we present some examples of reflexive regulation, including attempts to reform existing regulations and to regulate self-regulatory systems, many of which are characterized by sophisticated and successful efforts to strike a balance between a diversity of social and economic interests. In general, a legal reform that seeks to remove the types of legal boundaries or thresholds identified in the section on Regulation Thresholds is carried out at national level by focusing on specific areas. At this level the opportunities for legal change are not confined to legislation but can also be realized through collective bargaining, since collective agreements (whether declared generally applicable or not) are another major source of labour law.

Collective bargaining and industrial relations systems, which are, like labour markets, self-referential systems and constrained by their autopoietic needs (Rogowski, 2000), are rather limited in their 'social responsiveness'. It has been noted that many collective agreements still focus on traditional 'bread and butter' issues and are biased towards the interests of insiders in the labour market (for the Dutch situation, see Rojer, 1995; van den Toren, 1996; van Heertum and Wilthagen, 1996). The opportunities collective bargaining offers for negotiating trade-offs represent both barriers and opportunities for TLMs. Some current collective agreements, for example those in the Dutch banking and printing industries, have been considerably modernized and are reasonably 'enlightened'. Other collective agreements in the Netherlands have also established interesting trade-offs between competitiveness and employment objectives (see van der Meer, 2000). Even European-level collective bargaining is no longer a remote possibility.[10]

There are a number of ways to enhance the social responsibility or cognitive openness of collective bargaining (Heertum and Wilthagen, 1996: 234ff).

1. Social partners at the central level could issue recommendations and agreements to the sectoral level. This is indeed a basic feature of the so-called Dutch 'Poldermodel' and a policy whose adoption is being considered in Germany (in the form of the *Bündnis für Arbeit* or Employment Alliance, a central-level, tripartite negotiating process introduced by the SPD/Green coalition government). Strictly speaking, however, the effect of central recommendations on collective bargaining is limited to economic and financial issues; the parties to collective bargaining tend to be much less concerned with social policy issues. An alternative approach would be to negotiate national collective agreements, as happens in Belgium.
2. A more radical method would be for the government to refuse to declare certain collective agreements generally binding if they are not receptive to so-called 'good causes'.
3. Economic and financial issues could be inextricably bound up with social issues and presented as a take-it-or-leave-it package deal. The Dutch Foundation of Labour's 1993 'new course' agreement (*Een Nieuwe Koers*) in industrial relations represents a good example of such a package (for further information on the Foundation, see p. 254).

4. Attempts can be made to represent the interests of outsiders and single-issue movements at the bargaining table, thereby broadening the agenda. This has been labelled 'post-modern corporatism'.[11]
5. Collective agreements could be more strongly linked to professional standards, best practices and other norms commonly applied at company level (see Arthurs, 1998).

Levelling out discrimination thresholds

This section outlines some Dutch and Scandinavian attempts to level out discrimination. Legal and social reforms in the Netherlands have been concerned primarily with the promotion of part-time employment with a view to enabling men and women to balance paid work and (family) care. In fact, part-time work has facilitated the successful shift that has taken place in the Netherlands from an industrial economy to a (flexible) service economy based in part on female labour (Bruijn and Verhaar, 1999). It has also contributed to a major growth in employment. Scandinavian policies, in contrast, have favoured paid leave schemes.

The regulation and promotion of part-time work in the Netherlands Part-time work provides a good example of the levelling out of concrete discrimination thresholds. In the Netherlands most discrimination thresholds in this area have now been removed. The basic principle of the government's policy is that of equal treatment, laid down in article 7:648 of the Civil Code, which makes it illegal to discriminate against workers in respect of the terms of agreement, renewal or termination of an employment contract on the grounds of their working hours alone, unless such discrimination can be objectively justified. On 1 July 2000, the Adjustment of Working Hours Act came into force.[12] It confers on workers (in companies and services that employ 10 or more workers) the right to adjust their contractual working-time by working either more or fewer hours. Employers can deny workers an adjustment of working time only if 'major corporate or organizational interests' are likely to be adversely affected.

The new law is expected further to promote part-time work, especially among men, and to facilitate the balancing of work and care commitments. Even before the new law came into force, part-time rates in the Netherlands were unparalleled in Europe. In 1995, 37 per cent of all employees worked part-time, a fact that has significantly contributed to the increase in employment. Equal opportunities and labour market policies in the Netherlands are increasingly based on the assumption that each household has 1.5 jobs in total. This is called the 'combination scenario', in which men and women both have a (substantial) part-time job and share work and care responsibilities (see SCP, 2000). Eighty per cent of the Dutch men working part-time and 93 per cent of the women state as their reason that they 'do not want a full-time job' (see Ministry of Social Affairs and Employment, 1997). Box 7.1 gives a short overview of the legal terms of employment and social security for part-time workers in the Netherlands.

BOX 7.1　LEGAL TERMS OF EMPLOYMENT AND SOCIAL SECURITY FOR PART-TIME WORK IN THE NETHERLANDS[13]

Salary
Persons who do the same kind of work should receive the same (gross) hourly wage regardless of working time. As from 1 January 1993, all employees are entitled to a salary based (proportionally) on the legal minimum wage regardless of working time.

Holidays
A part-time worker is entitled to the same number of days off as full-time workers, in proportion to the hours he or she works. For example, if somebody working full-time gets 20 full free days a year, somebody working half time gets 20 half free days a year. (According to the law, 20 days is the minimum; collective agreements generally grant approximately 25 days a year.)

Probationary period
The maximum is two months for permanent contracts and possibly shorter for fixed-term contracts, but this is regardless of working time.

Dismissal law
This is exactly the same for all workers regardless of working time.

Special leave
In principle a part-time worker is entitled to special leave in the same cases as for full-time workers. Divergence from this principle could be justified if the activities could also be fitted in during the part-timer's free time. If a bank holiday falls in the time that a part-time worker is not working, he/she cannot claim a free day at some other time.

Parental leave
Under the terms of the Parental Leave Act, persons employed by the same employer for a year or more are entitled to unpaid part-time leave. In 1997 this Act was changed to include employees working 20 hours or less (up to then this category of employees had been excluded from this possibility). Moreover, parental leave can now be taken in a more flexible manner.

Overtime
Most collective agreements contain clauses on overtime and over-time pay. It is not considered unequal treatment if, on the basis of these clauses, overtime pay is only granted if full-time working hours are exceeded. Nevertheless, social partners may have good reasons for granting overtime pay as soon as working time exceeds the contractually agreed level (whether full-time or part-time).

Pensions
Under the National Old Age Pension Act, every person is provided with a monthly pension. On top of that, employees can, as a rule, build up additional pension rights through company pension schemes. There are some 1000 private pension schemes. As from 1994, an employee can no longer be excluded from participation in a pension fund because of working time. If a wage limit is applied in pension schemes, part-timers' wages have to be converted to the full-time level. A part-time employee acquires pension rights in proportion to the volume of his/her working hours.

Social security
Every employee who has an employment contract with a private employer is insured against unemployment and disablement, regardless of the length of working time. Neither the number of working hours nor the amount of pay exerts any influence on this. In the case of sickness an employer is legally obliged to pay 70 per cent of the employee's salary for a maximum of 52 weeks.

Social security contributions are usually calculated on the basis of a fixed percentage of pay or income. Working time does not enter into the calculation.

Unemployment
Part-time employees receive unemployment benefit for the same period of time and under the same conditions as a full-time employee; the benefit is based on 70 per cent of previous gross pay.

Sickness
Both part-time and full-time employees (whether on permanent or fixed-term contracts) receive at least 70 per cent of their gross salary in the event of illness (but not less than the minimum wage, calculated proportionally for part-timers) paid by the employer for a period of one year.

Disability
Part-time employees receive disability allowance for the same duration of time and under the same conditions as a full-time employee; the benefit is based on 70 per cent of previous income (in the event of complete incapacity) and varies in accordance with the age at which it is first paid.

Health insurance
Up to a certain salary limit (in 2001: 65 700 guilders a year) all employees are insured under the terms of a Compulsory Health Insurance Scheme which provides medical and dental care, hospital, nursing and other services. Above this limit employees have to insure themselves privately. There is no difference in the conditions that apply to part-time and full-time employees. They pay the same percentage of their income plus the same nominal contribution.

Working conditions
Employers are legally obliged to apply the same safety regulations and measures at work for both part-time and full-time workers.

Working hours
The Working Hours Act, which came into effect on 1 January 1996, includes a clause obliging employers to take account of employees' care responsibilities. This means that employers have to give reasonable consideration to individual preferences when planning and allocating working times and schedules.

Taxes
There are no specific or special measures in the tax system to encourage part-time work. As the tax system is based on progressive taxation for higher incomes, the net income losses in the case of part-time jobs are smaller than the gross reduction of income.

An alternative strategy: Scandinavian leave schemes   In Scandinavian countries men and women prefer to work full-time; legal and social reforms
accordingly tend to concentrate on paid leave schemes (and childcare). This
indicates that national social, economic and (last but not least) cultural traditions determine the nature and direction of sociolegal reform (see Pfau-
Effinger, 1998), a realization which, incidentally, constitutes an important
starting point in designing a legal strategy for TLMs. In the following, we shall
briefly discuss two more or less alternative Scandinavian solutions: the Danish
paid leave schemes and the Norwegian parental leave scheme.

The introduction of paid leave arrangements (PLA) in 1994 was a measure
designed to fight unemployment in Denmark. The PLA allow a wage earner to
leave work for a certain amount of time (usually less than 26 weeks but up to
a maximum 52 weeks) in order to pursue other activities.[14] Currently, three
main types of PLAs exist in Denmark: educational leave, sabbatical leave and
childcare leave. Both educational leave and childcare leave are available to the
self-employed and the unemployed. There are, however, several conditions
that need to be considered, such as whether or not applicants have a legal right
to PLA (only in the case of childcare leave) and whether or not employees
on leave have to be replaced (only in the case of sabbatical leave). Other
factors such as eligibility for unemployment benefits, minimum age (25) and
minimum number of years of labour market participation (three) are also
important.

Madsen rightfully argues that both employers and employees can have
economic and non-economic arguments for requesting or, in the case of
employers, granting a PLA. It should come as no surprise that educational
PLAs are the most beneficial type for both parties, although all sorts of leaves
have their pros and cons. As well as their advantages and disadvantages, these
PLAs may also have short- and long-term effects. Exaggerating for the
purposes of simplification, they can be summarized as follows. On the one
hand, PLA programmes run the risk of creating bottlenecks and wage pressures if uptake is confined to a certain segment of the labour market. On the
other hand, PLAs can have positive effects on skill and qualification levels in
the labour force. The short-term effects are rather difficult to quantify because
of the different conditions under which PLAs can take place. In addition to
their macroeconomic effects, PLAs can have a potentially beneficial macro-
social effect in terms of relations and mobility. In particular, work sharing
seems to be very important to people, but PLAs also appear to satisfy certain
needs shared by large sections of the population in Denmark (and most likely
everywhere else).

In Norway, legal reforms have concentrated on parental leave. In 1993,
young parents were granted the right to take, together, up to 42 weeks of fully
paid parental leave, or 52 weeks at 80 per cent of their wages. If the man does

not take a minimum of four weeks' leave, this forgone leave will be deducted from the 42 weeks' paid leave to which the parents are jointly entitled (leaving 38 weeks for the female parent). According to recent figures, 70 per cent of the men eligible to do so make use of this leave scheme. In Norway, 80 per cent of women have a paid job; parents of young children tend to work a combined total of 70 hours per week on average; 60 per cent of children under the age of six attend a childcare centre for 41 hours or more per week.[15]

The flexicurity strategy

The political and social feasibility of legal reform, and its subsequent success, often depend on the extent to which new measures serve the interests of the most prominent parties involved. Legal reform that aspires to trigger, facilitate and safeguard transitions within the labour market will be in need of support from employers and their representatives.[16] In other words, not only workers but employers as well will definitely wish to gain something from transitional employment. For both parties, the benefits of transitions should outweigh the costs. Given that this is so, it may be interesting to have a look at recent initiatives in the Netherlands that seek to create new links and balances between, on the one hand, labour market flexibilization, which is strongly advocated by employers, and, on the other, increased employment and social security for (atypical) workers.

The flexibility and security, or *flexicurity*, strategy is a typical example of legal and social reform within a corporatist system, since the social partners play a leading role at both central and decentralized level. Moreover, this strategy can be characterized as the pursuit of win–win outcomes.[17] It could also be typified as a strategy of reflexive deregulation and reregulation. Indeed, it could be seen as a strategy for implementing transitional labour markets. We define flexicurity as a policy strategy that attempts, synchronically and in a coordinated way, to enhance, on the one hand, the flexibility of labour markets and the organization of work and labour relations and, on the other, employment security and social protection, notably for vulnerable groups inside and outside the labour market.

As in other countries, the Dutch debates on flexible labour and atypical employment relations have concentrated on the limits to labour market flexibilization. A particular issue at stake has been the legal system of dismissal. In the Netherlands there exists a so-called 'dual system' of dismissal law which is, moreover, of a 'preventive' nature. Employers have to address either the Director of the Regional Public Employment Service (*Regionaal Directeur voor de Arbeidsvorziening*: RDA) to ask for a permit *before* any notice to terminate the employment contract can be given, or they have to file a request at the lower courts, requiring rescission of the employment contract on the grounds of 'serious cause'. This system is very unusual in Europe.

A new approach was adopted at the end of 1995 when the Dutch Minister of Social Affairs and Employment, Ad Melkert (Labour Party), deliberately attempted, in a memorandum called 'Flexibility and Security' (*Flexibiliteit en Zekerheid*, December 1995), to strike a balance between flexibility and (social) security. This memorandum contains an interrelated set of starting points and proposals for modifying the dismissal protection enjoyed by employees in standard employment relationships (shorter probationary period, shorter notice periods, greater scope for extending temporary employment contracts without the obligation to give notice and apply for a permit), abolishing the permit system for temporary work agencies (TWAs) in respect of their placement activities and enhancing the legal position of temporary agency workers, whose relationship with the agency is to be defined as far as possible as a standard employment contract (so-called 'presumptions of law'). The minister suggests that existing proposals to reform the dismissal law system be withdrawn.

In essence, these proposals resemble the strategies discussed by Simitis (1994b). In his analysis, he stresses the negative consequences of 'protective' labour laws for particular groups in the labour market (women, in particular). Simitis, following Mückenberger, criticizes the concept of standard employment relationship in labour law and suggests strategies of 'flexible intervention'.

An official at the Ministry of Social Affairs and Employment characterizes the distinctive mix of flexibility and security proposals as a form of 'reallocation of rights between the haves and the have-nots'. Moreover, this official attributes the very fact that flexibility and security issues came to be linked together to the Dutch dismissal system, which employers are thought to try and circumvent by using flexible employment. He states: 'We were fortunate to have some rigidities!'[18] This statement is reminiscent of Dore's (1986) concept of 'flexible rigidities': rigidities in one policy field may inspire or even be a precondition for flexibilization or appropriate adjustments in other policy domains.

It is important to note that the flexibility and security measures put forward by the Dutch government pertain first and foremost to the legal position of employees. The English concept of *flexicurity* as such has not been adopted by the Ministry. However, it was during this same period, in the autumn of 1995, that the very concept of flexicurity did take root in policy circles. The sociologist and member of the Dutch Scientific Council for Government Policy, Hans Adriaansens, launched the concept in speeches and interviews. Adriaansens defines it as a shift from job security towards employment security and makes the case for a different attitude towards flexibility (among workers) and for a flexible and activating social security system.[19]

In the former Dutch coalition government, nowadays referred to as the first 'purple coalition', since a new coalition of Labour, Liberals and Social Liberals is now in power, no agreement on the flexibility and security proposals could be reached. Subsequently, the Foundation of Labour was asked for its advice on this matter. The Foundation of Labour is a consultation and advisory body at central level, which was established at the end of the Second World War (1945). Its members constitute the largest confederations of employers' and workers' organizations. Unlike the Socio-Economic Council, the Foundation of Labour has no members or representatives from the government (see Windmuller, 1969).

The Foundation of Labour used to be a key actor in the government's wage control policy, which set wages up to the 1970s. Now it issues a fair number of recommendations and gives advice on social and economic policy to the actors engaged in collective bargaining and companies, on the one hand, and to government, particularly the Ministry of Social Affairs and Employment, on the other. In addition, the Foundation frequently brokers bipartite agreements between the participating confederations of employers' and employees' organizations and/or tripartite agreements involving the government, especially following the so-called 'spring and autumn' consultations between the Foundation and the government. It is safe to argue that both the bipartite and tripartite agreements are used either to supplement legislation or to avoid statutory regulation in the field of industrial relations and labour law. The relationship between the social partners and the government is perhaps best characterized as 'bargaining in the shadow of hierarchy'.

The Foundation of Labour is central to the Dutch 'consultation' economy, or the 'Polder Model', as it is called nowadays (Visser and Hemerijck, 1997). It is an institution that is remarkable for its strategies of positive sum bargaining. The pursuit of so-called 'win–win' strategies and results, as perceived from the point of view of both workers and employers, is at the core of the Foundation. Despite the fact that it deals mainly with part-time work and business efficiency and performance, the 1993 recommendation on the 'Promotion of Part-Time Work and Differentiation of Working-Time Patterns', already mentioned above (in note 12), is now seen as one of the pioneering agreements leading to an agreement on a bill on flexibility and security.

Under the umbrella of the Foundation, which in the early 1990s was recovering from a period in the doldrums (van Bottenburg, 1995), employees' and employers' confederations managed to hammer out a detailed agreement on flexibility and security that was published in a memorandum of the same name on 3 April 1996 (publication no. 2/96). Moreover, on 2 April 1993, the employers' organizations, the trade unions and the non-profit-making employment agency START had reached agreement on regulating the legal position of temporary agency workers after the new laws came into force. They had decided on a collective agreement that was to run for five years. The main provision of this agreement is that, once workers have completed 26 weeks with the agency, they will be offered a fixed-term employment contract. After 18 or 24 months, this contract will be converted into a permanent contract.

The initiatives of the social partners were very much welcomed by the government. Nearly all the recommendations were taken up in a set of proposals for new bills. The Foundation was much gratified by this renewed recognition and appreciation of its position, as politicians had not long before been making calls for a return to the 'primacy of politics'.

On 7 March 1997, the Flexibility and Security Bill was submitted to the lower house of the Dutch parliament, together with the Allocation of Workers via Intermediaries Bill, which provided for the abrogation of TWA permits. The following rationale for the new proposals was advanced:

> there is a quite high level of protection for workers employed under a traditional contract of employment, while people in flexible employment are faced with a high level of insecurity. The government has therefore sought to fundamentally review and update Dutch labour law. In doing so it worked on the basis of the opinion that employment relationships which are well-balanced, steady and flexible, should be the core of an economically competitive and socially sound labour system.[20]

According to the Ministry of Social Affairs and Employment, these proposals should also be considered in the context of other recent legislation and initiatives, such as the Working Hours Act that came into force on 1 January 1996,[21] and addresses such issues as flexibility and workers' codetermination and the reform of holiday provisions (the accrual of holiday entitlements and more flexible holiday arrangements), the initiatives on 'Work and Care', which deal with several forms of paid and unpaid leave,[22] and the adjustments of social insurance regulations that enable employees to go on unpaid leave without negative consequences for their social security entitlements.[23] One might add the reform of the pension system, which is still a notorious barrier to flexibility and security.

Finally, it is worth mentioning the recommendations published in November 1996 by the Foundation of Labour on the importance of training and education to workers, companies and sectors ('Working on your job'). These recommendations and subsequent initiatives will be discussed shortly.

On 18 November 1997, the lower house of the Dutch parliament accepted the new flexibility and security proposals. As the trade unions, the employers' confederations and the government were very much committed to the proposals that were the outcome of successful negotiations, no fundamental changes had been made.[24] This can be regarded as a typical example of corporatist coordination. Nevertheless, in addition to widespread enthusiasm and euphoria, there was also some criticism regarding the balance between flexibility and security. Some commentators went as far as to conclude that greater emphasis was being placed on flexibility than on security. In particular, the proposal to allow fixed-term employment contracts to be extended three times without any obligation to apply for a permit to give notice was seen as a significant weakening of dismissal protection (Pennings, 1996). Besides, it had become clear that the trade unions' and employers' organizations were putting very different interpretations on the accord on a new collective agreement in the TWA business. The negotiations on the proposed collective agreement did not proceed as smoothly as assumed. However, after some debate the new legislation came into force on 1 January 1999. The main aspects of the new legislation are summarized in Table 7.1. So far there is limited evidence on the effects of the new legislation. A first 'scan' has revealed 'mixed feelings' among employers, workers and their representatives, which are largely the result of the need to think through and implement the consequences of the new legislation and to reorganize administrative procedures (Grijpstra *et al.*, 1999). A second evaluation has revealed that, following the introduction of the Flexibility and Security Act, there has been a shift from temporary to permanent employment contracts (Klaver *et al.*, 2000). About 145 000 existing temporary contracts have been converted into new temporary contracts and nearly 72 000 temporary contracts have been converted into permanent contracts. A total of 86 000 temporary contracts were not renewed. The contracts of 25 000 on-call workers were not renewed, and a further 93 000 on-call workers became either temporary agency workers or changed to fixed-hours or fixed-term contracts.

In comparison with the first evaluation, positive experiences among both employers (including TWAs) and flexible workers now generally outweigh negative experiences. Half of the employers involved in the second evaluation had a favourable opinion of the Act (compared to a third in 1999). However, the views of those running TWAs are less favourable, with only a third expressing positive opinions (in 1999, a quarter of these employers had been positive about the Act). Flexible workers are less likely to attribute negative developments in their employment relationship to the Act. The researchers conclude that firms and workers are getting used to the new rules. Knowledge of the law is fairly widespread, though it is still important to provide information for those engaged in collective bargaining as well as to individuals (Klaver *et al.*, 2000). The Minister of Social Affairs and Employment has stated that he agrees with the researchers that the results of the study are influenced by the current favourable economic conditions, but he also concludes that the legislation on flexibility and security does not represent a barrier to favourable developments in the labour market.

In the meantime, 'flexibility' and 'security' have also become key concepts in European policy making, as documented in the 1997 Green Paper, 'Partnership for a New Organization of Work', which states that 'the key issue

Table 7.1   Central aspects of the Dutch law on flexibility and security

Flexibility	Security
Adjustment of the regulation of fixed term employment contracts: after three consecutive contracts or when the total length of consecutive contracts totals three years or more, a permanent contract exists (this used to apply to fixed-term contracts that have been extended once).	Introduction of two so-called 'presumptions of law' which strengthen the position of atypical workers (regarding the existence of an employment contract and the number of working hours agreed in that contract); the existence of an employment contract is more easily presumed.
The obligation for TWAs to be in possession of a permit has been withdrawn. The maximum term for this type of employment (formerly six months) is abolished as well.	A minimum entitlement to three hours' pay for on-call workers each time they are called in to work.
The notice period is in principle 1 month and 4 months at maximum (used to be 6 months at maximum).	Regulation of the risk of non-payment of wages in the event of there being no work for an on-call worker: the period over which employers may claim that they need not pay out wages for hours not worked has been reduced to six months.
The Public Employment Service (PES) dismissal notification procedure has been shortened and employees are no longer required to file a pro forma notice of objection to the regional director of the PES in the event of dismissal on economic or financial grounds in order to substantiate a claim for employment benefit.	A worker's contract with a TWA is considered a regular employment contract; only in the first 26 weeks are the agency worker allowed a certain degree of freedom with respect to starting and ending the employment relationship.
	Special dismissal protection has been introduced for employees engaged in trade union activities.
	Dismissal cases at the district court (so-called rescission cases): the judge must check whether or not it is prohibited to terminate the employment contract with an employee, for example in the case of employees on sick leave; in the latter case the employer has to produce a reintegration plan for the employee to enable the judge to assess the feasibility of reinstatement.

for workers, management, the social partners and policy makers alike is to strike the right balance between flexibility and security.' The concept of flexicurity was recently taken up in the German debate on labour market flexibilization and the regulation thereof.[26]

Dutch labour market initiatives and practices are heavily influenced by the strategy of flexicurity. This strategy is not limited to legal reform in the area of atypical work, dismissal law and social security. Trade unions and employers are involved in promising experiments under the slogan 'from job security to employment security'. The experiments concern combinations of internal and external flexibility, in so-called 'job pools' or 'flex pools' and other hybrid forms of employment organization that seek to increase the employability of current workers and prevent redundancies.

In the Netherlands, a distinction has to be made between two phenomena which are less similar than one might expect. First, there is the *banenpool*, translated into English as 'labour pool', which is a type of additional employment. The labour pool is a measure (*Rijksbijdrageregeling Banenpool*, 1990) that seeks to create additional jobs for the unemployed who are hard to place. The measure, which has now been incorporated in a new legal scheme on the deployment of jobseekers, is aimed at people who have been unemployed for three years or more. Implementation is entrusted to a municipal or province-level organization. Funding is provided by national government and the Public Employment Service (PES). About 20 000 people are involved in the labour pools.

Second, there is the *arbeidspool*, translated into English as 'job pool', 'employment pool' or 'flex pool'. This is a private or public–private organization (or joint venture involving several organizations) that allocates workers to a company or to a network of several companies within a certain region or sector, depending on the actual demand for labour. Job pools may merely serve companies' internal labour markets, but can also be used to provide temporary workers (external or numerical flexibilization) and as a vehicle for active labour market strategies for the deployment of formerly unemployed persons. The number of job pools is increasing, especially in manufacturing and services. In many cases, TWAs are taking on the role of coordinating these pools, for example in the Dutch distribution sector. Those recruited to these pools are offered training and education facilities if they were previously unemployed.

Job pools should not simply be considered as a second-best option, that is as a form of secondary employment. At Stork Industries, for example, the trade unions have agreed extra pay for the workers at Stork Mobile, an internal flex pool which employs permanent and temporary workers. The permanent workers in this pool get NLG 125 more per month than their 'regular' colleagues at Stork Industries. This is a type of 'mobility allowance'; they also have five paid working days set aside for training and opportunities to accumulate additional spare time or additional holidays (see van Velzen, 2000).

Older forms of job pools can be found in the Amsterdam and Rotterdam ports. These pools had been facing major difficulties and were at risk (owing to declining employment in the ports because of automation) but have now been reorganized with some success. In France similar initiatives involving company networks have been launched (Supiot *et al.*, 2001: 44–5).

Another example of flexicurity is the case of the Heineken Brewery in the Netherlands, where the trade unions have agreed so-called 'investment contracts' regarding job security and training. The Dutch branch of Heineken is seeking to speed up its investments in the application of new technology, while at the same time reshaping its organization through the introduction of teamwork. The new form of organization will demand higher skills and competences from its production workers, notably from low-skilled workers. For that reason, Heineken in 1996 initiated negotiations with the trade unions on the restructuring process and its consequences. The negotiations resulted in an agreement on the deployment of employees, signed on 12 June 1997, including a five-year guarantee of employment and training for all 2000 workers (average age of 41) at the breweries in Den Bosch and Zoeterwoude. All current employees will continue to work within the new organization and will be trained, individually or by functional group, for their new responsibilities. The potential of each employee will be tested by an external agency. If it is thought that an individual worker may not be able to achieve the necessary qualifications, management will ensure that suitable work is found.[27]

Regulating the transition from employment to training: the case of flexible workforces

The transition from employment to training and education can be regarded as typical and illustrative of the dilemmas, paradoxes and problems of modern labour markets, including TLMs. These labour markets, referred to as 'high velocity labour markets' (Hyde, 1998), include a growing population of workers who are not likely to work permanently or be actually present in one particular company or workplace. Of course, the reasons for this will vary and can be judged either negatively or positively. On the one hand, a high proportion of so-called 'contingent workers' are doomed to remain without a permanent job and a decent career, regardless of their own preferences. They are the peripheral workers in a bifurcated labour market. Workers who engage in transitions as envisaged in the TLM model, on the other hand, are constantly on the move, of their own free will and for good individual and social causes. Nevertheless, the existence of both groups does raise similar problems when it comes to investing in training and education.

The paradox at work here can be termed the 'flexibilization versus training' paradox. Modern societies are increasingly being viewed as 'knowledge-driven economies', and training and education are very much on the political and economic agenda.[28] As Crouch (1997: 367) puts it: 'The acquisition of knowledge and skills is increasingly seen as both the main challenge and the central opportunity for achieving a return to full employment.' However, at the same time further flexibilization of the labour market is being pursued vigorously in many countries. Thus the problem addressed in Becker's celebrated human capital theory (Becker, 1964) becomes manifest: why should firms or individuals invest in the production of knowledge and skills if they cannot exclude others from the final gains of these investments? More specifically, it is argued that employers are not likely to invest in general, transferable training.[29] And indeed, empirical studies show that in the Netherlands workers employed on flexible contracts receive about half as much training as workers on permanent contracts. About 40 per cent of this difference is accounted for by the fact that employers are more inclined to invest in the human capital of permanent workers.

This raises the question of how the paradox can be solved and, more specifically, whether and how legal regulation can contribute to the solution. A starting point would be simply to make it mandatory for employers to invest in training for the flexible and 'transitory' workforces they deploy. This strategy is not likely to get strong support: collective agreements stipulating training provision for flexible workforces are thin on the ground. This is undoubtedly further evidence of collective bargaining's bias towards insiders.

A second strategy would be to grant flexible workers or workers in transition certain entitlements to training and education, more or less independently of the companies that hire or deploy them. These kinds of entitlements could also be based on collective agreements or result from the efforts of sectoral partnerships or trade unions. An example is the partnerships for training that are active in the USA, for example in the San Francisco Bay Area. Alternatively, such entitlements could be state-funded, for example through fiscal measures or a voucher system, as discussed in the section on Legal Transition Costs.

In the case of flexible and contingent workers, a third way out would be to turn to so-called 'third parties', such as the TWAs that provide workers for jobs that have been outsourced by regular companies. Osterman (1994) argues that the flexibilization of labour does not necessarily result in a deterioration of working conditions. TWAs could, for example, establish stable relations with the workers they send out to firms. Furthermore, such jobs could be filled primarily by new entrants to the labour market.[30] In that case, Osterman contends, temporary work is merely functioning as a transitory phase from non-employment to regular employment for persons that would be confronted with less stable employment conditions under any circumstances. In both cases, but certainly in the first case, one might expect that TWAs would be more willing to invest in training for flexible workers, as the employment relationship between worker and agency became more or less normalized.

This normalization of contingent work could also be prompted and regulated by law and collective agreements. This is the direction Dutch labour market policies took within the framework of the flexicurity regulation described above in the section on The Flexicurity Strategy. As mentioned there, the new legislation on flexibilty and security, in force as of 1 January 1999, stipulates that the relationship between a TWA and a temporary agency worker is to be considered a normal employment contract, with normal entitlements to social security, although the first 26 weeks allow for more freedom in hiring and firing. Once the temporary agency worker has worked for 18 months at the same client firm or for different client firms for three years, he or she gets a permanent employment contract with the agency, including the kind of dismissal protection that goes with these contracts. The law also stipulates that TWAs no longer need a permit to operate in the labour market and it abolished the maximum period, formerly six months, during which temporary agency workers could be deployed.

The new law did not grant temporary agency workers any rights to training. However, at the same time as the social partners operating under the umbrella of the Foundation of Labour reached agreement on the outline of a law on flexibility and security, the employers (represented by the *Algemene Bond Uitzendondernemingen* (ABU), an association covering 90 per cent of all TWAs) and trade unions in the temporary agency work sector concluded a collective agreement for the years 1999–2003 to deal with the consequences of the new law. The most important innovation in this collective agreement, which is binding at firm level for ABU members, is the introduction of a four-phase model in which temporary agency workers gradually acquire more rights, including rights to training, as the length of the employment relationship increases. The four-phase model is summarized in Table 7.2.

In addition, the collective agreement for the TWA sector stipulates that TWAs have to spend a gradually increasing percentage of the total (gross) wages bill paid to temporary agency workers in a particular year on training for those workers: 0.58 per cent for 1999, rising to 0.92 per cent in 2002. The collective agreement also establishes a training institution for the sector, the Training Foundation for Temporary Employees. This foundation monitors TWAs' training efforts, including the training volume and the kind of training provided. If the training expenditure target is not met in any one year, the foundation can require additional provision to be made in the next year; conversely, if it is exceeded, less provision needs to be made in the following year.

The four-phase model came into effect in June 1999. Trade unions feared that TWAs would not continue to deploy large numbers of agency workers or

*Table 7.2   The four-phase model as laid down in the Dutch collective
agreement on temporary agency work*

Phase	When	Rights for agency worker
I	First 26 weeks of tempoary work	None in particular; parties may agree that the employment relationship ends without notice if the client firm runs out of work
II	Next six months	Entitlements to pensions and training, that is: the agency must discuss the worker's training needs. If training is offered, this has to be laid down in writing and the training goals and amount of training have to be specified
III	At further continuation of the employment relationship or when entering a new one within one year	The worker gets fixed-term contracts for one or more three-month periods
IV	After a total of 18 months at the same client firm or after 36 months of working in different client firms	Worker gets a permanent contract

that they would delegate those workers to agencies not covered by the collective agreement in order to prevent them from getting a permanent contract. This scenario did not in fact transpire, with no more than 1200 agency workers having their employment relationships terminated. At the beginning of 2000, it was estimated that about 20 per cent of all temporary agency workers had a fixed-term (phase 3) or permanent (phase 4) contract with the agency itself.[31]

Towards transition agencies?
The above example does not, of course, provide a general solution for the problem of investment in training in TLMs. However, the example does show that third parties can perform a vital role. It also shows how law and collective agreements can complement each other. Moreover, in the light of the new role

being played by TWAs in job or flex pools (as discussed in the section on The Flexicurity Strategy), a new market could be envisaged for professional and specialist job services, which could be provided through what might be termed *transition agencies*.[32]

TWAs such as the Dutch Randstad, one of the largest in the world, and START are rapidly moving away from their narrowly focused activities in the lower segments of the labour market. Another case is Randstad's operation in Berlin. Unemployment in Berlin is a structural problem. The government of the *Land* of Berlin has decided to start a pilot project to create 120 new jobs and will be making subsidies available. *Randstad Zeit-Arbeit* has been selected to implement the project. GSUB (*Gesellschaft für soziale Unternehmensberatung*), a body of the Berlin government, will be responsible for the initial selection of candidates. Randstad's task is then to look for a job that suits each candidate's knowledge and experience. Once a job has been found, a personal plan will be formulated in consultation with the candidate. The plan will cover up to 600 hours' training, to be provided at well-known institutes such as TÜV (*Technischer Überwachungsverein* or technical inspectorate) or in the workplace.

Apart from becoming increasingly involved in training and active labour market/reintegration policy, Randstad has also become involved in the provision of childcare arrangements, thereby facilitating work–care transitions. Randstad signed an agreement with the major Dutch financial institution ING to cooperate in the provision of childcare. The agreement will lead to the creation of an extensive chain of daycare centres throughout the Netherlands, which will serve ING and Randstad employees (flexiworkers and staff) and be made available to their clients. This new facility will be part of both organizations' employee benefits package. The initiative by ING and Randstad is a response to the strong growth in demand for childcare. Current developments in many areas in the Netherlands mean demand is outpacing supply. At the same time, people are increasingly seeking different types of childcare that are more broadly based and flexible and possibly combined with additional services.

One task for a legal design geared to TLMs could be to create and regulate a market for transition agencies. If these agencies assume substantial responsibilities in the areas of employability enhancement and human resource management (cf. CIETT, 2000: 33ff), then some sort of (state) cofunding arrangement may have to be put in place.

A European Strategy for Regulating Transitional Employment

Probably the most advanced, although abstract, form of TLM regulation would be to introduce a constitutionally protected right to transitional employment. It would create a legal basis for 'entitlements to transitional employment' (Gazier, 'Transitional Labour Markets: From Positive Analysis to Policy

Proposals' in this volume). This legal innovation could be added to the funda-mental social rights[33] protected in European treaties, social charters and inter-national conventions (see Weiss, 1996). The European Social Charter of 1963, which was revised on 3 May 1996, seems an obvious starting point. However, the Charter does not guarantee a job for everyone, it only puts states under an obligation to aim to achieve full employment. Most of the Charter's provisions are of a rather general character. None of the rights can be used easily to construct a TLM right.[34] Moreover, flexible or part-time retirement schemes that seek to facilitate transitions between employment and retirement are not included.[35] There is also, of course, the issue of national legal culture and heritage (Blanpain, 1997).[36]

Atypical employment is regulated in the 1994 ILO Convention 175 and Recommendation 1982. These international documents not only contain several rights for part-time workers and anti-discrimination clauses, but also demand that, where relevant, states should facilitate changes in working hours, that is transitions from part-time employment to full-time employment and vice versa. Important European measures are directives 97/81/EC on part-time work and 99/70/EC on fixed-term work.

Many countries have experimented with interesting legal initiatives (including provisions in collective agreements) intended to adjust the wage-earning status that has traditionally been the central reference point in labour law but has become problematic now that the transitions within a working life are no longer 'linear'. However, no country yet seems able to offer a clear-cut alternative to the traditional wage-earner status (Supiot *et al.*, 2001: 28). In any case, an all-encompassing design capable of promoting atypical employment and transitions requires a new legal and social interpretation of the concepts of 'standard employment'. Such a design should adopt a life cycle perspective, already discussed in the social sciences (Lyon-Caen, 1996).

By way of conclusion, following the comparative analysis, Supiot *et al.* (2001) propose a strategy they describe as 're-institutionalising the employ-ment relationship', which would be achieved by setting rules, allocating nego-tiating forums for these rules and enabling collective actors to intervene effectively. They argue that the basic outline for reinstitutionalization is already present in national legislation. The new employment status should be 'based on a comprehensive approach to work, capable of reconciling the need for freedom and the need for security' (ibid.: 45). The prime aim should be 'to protect workers during transition phases between jobs'. New legal instruments must be developed 'to guarantee the continuity of status above and beyond different and non-working cycles. The worker should be in favour of aban-doning the linear career model. Career interruptions and occupational reorien-tation should come to be considered normal incidents in ongoing employment status. Such continuity may be ensured by law or collective agreement' (ibid.:

183–4). One of the concrete legal forms that is discussed by the authors is the idea of so-called 'drawing rights'. We have already taken up this point in the section on An Example of Reregulation: The Voucher System and Social Drawing Rights, above.

One crucial point in Supiot *et al.*'s analysis is that we should move away from the traditional concept of employment to a notion of work that includes non-market forms of work, continuing training and socially beneficial activities. This redefined concept of work better meets gender equality requirements and extends individual choice over career patterns. Work is distinguished from 'activity' in that it stems from an obligation, whether imposed or voluntarily agreed. Thus domestic work, for example, is rightly considered work. Law should thus apply in all cases of work, but the protection may vary. To this end, four spheres of law pertaining to social protection are proposed. The first sphere would cover universal rights that apply to anyone irrespective of the type of work being done (cf. health insurance). The second comprises rights based on unpaid work and/or socially useful activities (such as retirement benefits and accident insurance for voluntary work), while the third sphere would pertain to the common law of occupational activity, the basis for which can be found in Community law (such as that on equal treatment). The fourth and final sphere covers rights related to dependent employment. The authors contend that this typology would replace the current employment paradigm with one based on occupational status that would cover all the various forms of work a person may undertake over the life course.

A similar analysis, but based on a different, somewhat confusing conceptualization, is presented in a recent report by the Belgian Committee on Work and Non-Work (*Commissie Arbeid en Niet-Arbeid*, 1999). The definition of 'social non-work' that is adopted resembles the concept of 'gainful non-market activities' used in TLM theory. Social non-work comprises domestic work, family care, job seeking, voluntary activities, education and training, and so on. The Committee argues for a reappraisal of social non-work in the light of the importance of these activities for social cohesion. The right to work is therefore broadened to a 'right to social participation'. The Committee sees the central aim as follows:

> To draw up a social charter that takes as its starting point a comprehensive approach to work and gainful non-work. This charter should cover the various forms of social participation and respond to the imperatives of freedom, security and responsibility. The final aim is a cycle of social participation in which various forms of work and non-work alternate in accordance with the social interest and provide entitlements to an agreed income and to social protection (Ibid.: 90, our translation)

The Committee suggests adding a provision to the Belgian Basic Law that states: 'a right to social participation, within the framework of social policy, which attempts to enable, as far as possible, a fair reallocation of work and other gainful activities and a fair remuneration in all circumstances' (ibid.: 131, our translation).

Along the lines of these examples we propose that a general right to transitional employment be introduced at the European level. It could be formulated as follows. Every person aged 15 and over has a right to encouragement, support and protection previous to, during and after transition phases between different employment statuses, including employment, self-employment, unemployment, training, (flexible and part-time) retirement and socially gainful activities in the private and public sphere. The fact that a person considers making such transitions or actually undertakes them shall not, as such, constitute a valid reason for termination of employment, a deterioration of the terms of employment or an unfair limitation of future employment, career prospects or entitlements to social security.

Admittedly, such a provision could cause some legal problems in the member states of the European Union. One particular problem relates to the transition from employment to unemployment or (unpaid) socially gainful activities. If a person currently undertakes such a transition voluntarily this is likely to affect his or her entitlement to social security benefits. This consequence raises the familiar question about the need for a basic income or perhaps a transitional income. Anyway, this kind of right to transitional employment will require extensive reforms of existing systems of social security and labour law.

An alternative, more concise formulation could simply declare it illegal to discriminate against a person who is or has been engaged in making transitions in the labour market. That kind of provision could be directly added to the non-discrimination/equal treatment law that has been developed at the European level and that has proved of paramount importance in fighting discrimination thresholds (see Simitis, 1994a).[37]

However, for the macro-level European strategy of a social right to transitional employment to have an impact it must be accompanied by strategies at the micro level of specific legal regulations. Indeed, the fine-tuning of existing laws in the area of labour law, social policy and social security in order to remove concrete and overt barriers to transitions is already a regular operation in many countries (these laws are called 'organizational laws' or coordination laws[38]). Probably the greatest challenge in this context will be the coordination of different legal orders located at different levels of regulation. An increase in complexity within the legal system and subsequent strategies for reducing complexity are unavoidable consequences of introducing a right to transitional employment that is protected throughout the European Union.

3 CONCLUDING REMARKS

It cannot be denied that there are still major legal barriers to TLMs. Labour markets are located at the point of intersection between several normative (sub)systems, which are characterized by their own distinctive rationale and a high degree of complexity, entail a variety of regulatory thresholds and are still poorly linked and inadequately adapted to the notion of transitional employment. Moreover, legal regulations do generate or increase certain transition costs. However, it has to be stressed that many of the restrictions labour law places on policy innovations derive from general normative principles and basic individual rights that are intended to protect individuals from the negative effects of markets.

Nevertheless, law can contribute in many ways to the creation of opportunities for policies aimed at flexibilizing institutional structures and facilitating transitions in the labour market. Though national social and cultural traditions are of paramount importance and do have to be taken into account, a number of promising legal strategies can be identified. Firstly, there is the strategy of reflexive deregulation, the aim of which is to create opportunities that ease transitions. One promising proposal for reducing legal complexity and lowering the costs of transitions is the introduction of a system of vouchers or social drawing rights that grants people entitlements to transitional employment. Secondly, combating discrimination thresholds, particularly through the application of equal treatment law, has proved to be fairly successful to date. And thirdly, recent developments in the Netherlands (and Scandinavia) show that innovative legal and social strategies are feasible. Some of these strategies could actually produce 'win–win' outcomes in terms of enhancing both labour market flexibility and employment and social security. We have termed these strategies 'reflexive regulation'.

A 'grand' legal design for transitional employment does not yet exist and will not be easy to construct. However, in our view a European strategy of regulating transitional employment that combines a rights-based approach with specific measures to adapt existing regulations seems feasible.

Finally, creating legal opportunities for the establishment of TLMs also requires some sort of intellectual transition. It seems impossible to benefit fully from the potential of legal strategies without involving legal scholars and legal professionals (lawyers, judges and other practitioners) in concrete debates. In analysing the legal regulation of TLMs, we propose to adopt a combined sociolegal and socioeconomic approach. In our understanding, law is an essential part of the institutional structure of labour markets (see also Solow, 1990) and is almost as dynamic in nature as markets themselves. These characteristics are vital for a legal design suited to TLMs. Indeed, transitions and exchanges between the legal discipline, on the one hand, and labour economics and industrial sociology, on the other hand, are another essential prerequisite for the establishment and implementation of transitional labour markets.

ADDENDUM: SELECTED LIST OF RIGHTS CONTAINED IN THE EUROPEAN SOCIAL CHARTER ADOPTED BY THE COUNCIL OF EUROPE

The Parties undertake . . .

Article 1 – The right to work
1. to accept as one of their primary aims and responsibilities the achievement and maintenance of as high and stable a level of employment as possible, with a view to the attainment of full employment;
4. to provide or promote appropriate vocational guidance, training and rehabilitation;

Article 2 – The right to just conditions of work
1. to provide for reasonable daily and weekly working hours, the working week to be progressively reduced to the extent that the increase of productivity and other relevant factors permit;

Article 4 – The right to a fair remuneration
3. to recognise the right of men and women workers to equal pay for work of equal value;

Article 8 – The right of employed women to protection of maternity
1. to provide either by paid leave, by adequate social security benefits or by benefits from public funds for employed women to take leave before and after childbirth up to a total of at least fourteen weeks;

Article 9 – The right to vocational guidance
to provide or promote, as necessary, a service which will assist all persons, including the handicapped, to solve problems related to occupational choice and progress, with due regard to the individual's characteristics and their relation to occupational opportunity: this assistance should be available free of charge, both to young persons, including schoolchildren, and to adults;

Article 10 – The right to vocational training
3. to provide or promote, as necessary:
    a. adequate and readily available training facilities for adult workers;
    b. special facilities for the retraining of adult workers needed as a result of technological development or new trends in employment;
4. to provide or promote, as necessary, special measures for the retraining and re-integration of the long-term unemployed;
5. to encourage the full utilisation of the facilities provided by appropriate measures such as:
    a. reducing or abolishing any fees or charges;
    b. granting financial assistance in appropriate cases;
    c. including in the normal working hours time spent on supplementary training taken by the worker, at the request of his employer, during employment;

Article 12 – The right to social security
3. to endeavour to raise progressively the system of social security to a higher level;

Article 20 – The right to equal opportunities and equal treatment in matters of employment and occupation without discrimination on the grounds of sex
to ensure or promote the application of this right in the following fields:

  a. access to employment, protection against dismissal and occupational reintegration;
  b. vocational guidance, training, retraining and rehabilitation;
  c. terms of employment and working conditions, including remuneration;
  d. career development, including promotion;

Article 22 – The right to take part in the determination and improvement of the working conditions and working environment
the right to contribute:
  c. to the organisation of social and socio-cultural services and facilities within the undertaking;

Article 23 – The right of elderly persons to social protection
to adopt or encourage, either directly or in cooperation with public or private organisations, appropriate measures designed in particular to enable elderly persons to remain full members of society for as long as possible, by means of:
  a. adequate resources enabling them to lead a decent life and play an active part in public, social and cultural life;

Article 27 – The right of workers with family responsibilities to equal opportunities and equal treatment
1. to take appropriate measures:
  a. to enable workers with family responsibilities to enter and remain in employment, as well as to re-enter employment after an absence due to those responsibilities, including measures in the field of vocational guidance and training;
  b. to take account of their needs in terms of conditions of employment and social security;
  c. to develop or promote services, public or private, in particular child daycare services and other childcare arrangements;
2. to provide a possibility for either parent to obtain, during a period after maternity leave, parental leave to take care of a child, the duration and conditions of which should be determined by national legislation, collective agreements or practice;
3. to ensure that family responsibilities shall not, as such, constitute a valid reason for termination of employment;

Article 30 – The right to protection against poverty and social exclusion
  a. to take measures within the framework of an overall and co-ordinated approach to promote the effective access of persons who live or risk living in a situation of social exclusion or poverty, as well as their families, to, in particular, employment, housing, training, education, culture and social and medical assistance;
  b. to review these measures with a view to their adaptation if necessary.

NOTES

1. The authors would like to thank Bernard Gazier, Günther Schmid, Ann-Sophie Vandenberghe and Stephen Vousden for their comments on previous versions of the chapter.
2. The idea of regulation thresholds is borrowed from Sousa Santos (1995: 466–7). We have modified his approach and definitions to suit our purposes.
3. This does not hold merely for legislation, but also for collective agreements and 'soft law'.
4. This became evident when a draft framework agreement on parental leave was being

concluded between ETUC, UNICE (Union of Industrial and Employers' Confederations of Europe) and CEEP (European Centre of Enterprises with Public Participation and of Enterprises of General Economic Interest) in November 1995; the ETUC (European Trade Union Confederation) stressed the need to secure continuity of social protection for workers to cover for all risks (for example, sickness, unemployment, pension, dismissal) during parental leave (see also Barnard, 2000: 94–6).

5. In general, there is no need to assume a structural conflict between corporate and individual interests in transitions: 'If organizations' strategic activity can be described as a series of transitions, so also can individuals' careers. Rather than a strategically planned set of building blocks completing a final imposing career edifice, careers, like organizational strategies, are emergent in an ever-changing context (. . .) As with organizational transitions, so career transitions can be seen as proactive and one's own decision; as proactive and anticipating someone else's decision or the inevitable' (Herriot *et al.*, 1998: 66–7). See also Eggertsson (1990).

6. For an interesting attempt to develop a social contract theory of organizations that emphasizes the importance of the rights and interests of individuals, families and communities, see Keeley (1988).

7. This definition is based on van Gendt (1980), who deals with the voucher concept and the 'publicness of basic education'.

8. In the Netherlands, these collective agreements are called 'à la carte' or 'cafeteria' agreements.

9. The newly hired employee gets a reduction on the social security benefit that is to be paid by him or her (as opposed to that part of the social security benefits that are paid by the employer). These premiums are deducted from the gross wage of the employee. In this particular case, however, the employee does not get an actual reduction (that is, a higher wage because of lower deduction) but he or she is allowed to spend the particular amount of money on trainimg for herself or himself).

10. Compare van den Toren (1996).

11. Vries and Carasso, cited in Heertum and Wilthagen (1996).

12. It was drafted by the Secretary of State for Social Affairs and Employment and is part of the larger Framework Act on Work and Care. The new legislation is also in line with a recommendation issued to the parties to collective bargaining by the Dutch Foundation of Labour in 1993 under the title 'Promotion of Part-Time Work and Differentiation of Working-Time Patterns'. A study by the Dutch Labour Inspectorate (Arbeidsinspectie, 1999) reveals that 19 per cent of the 118 collective agreements studied (covering 3.8 million workers) contain substantial provisions on part-time work. Sixty-four per cent of the collective agreements stipulate than an employee may request his or her employer to adjust his or her working hours. None of the collective agreements contains all of the core elements of the 1993 recommendation issued by the Foundation of Labour. Nineteen agreements make a distinction between long and short-hours part-time jobs (the latter usually involving 12 or 13 hours a week). The question is whether this is against the law. The Secretary of State has asked the Foundation of Labour for its opinion on this matter. It is important that part-time workers should be granted positive rights to vocational training, promotion and career structures, especially when part-time work is considered an employment strategy. Neither the Proposal for a Council Directive on Voluntary Part-time Work (OJ C 62/7, 12 March 1982) nor the 1994 ILO Convention Concerning Part-time Work (Convention No. 175) and the Council Directive 97/81/EC on Part-time Work have gone so far. See Murray (1999).

13. Taken from Ministry of Social Affairs and Employment (1997: 17–20) and slightly adapted by the authors.

14. This section is predominantly based on Madsen (1998a, 1998b); see also Schmid, Chapter 12 in this volume.

15. Source: *de Volkskrant*, 8 June 1999.

16. For an industrial relations point of view, see the various contributions in Boyer (1988).

17. A fuller account of the origins of flexicurity, the implementation of this strategy in the Netherlands and the relevance to a theory of transitional labour markets is given in Wilthagen (1998).

18. Personal communication. This kind of analysis resembles the paradoxes and dilemmas discussed in Elster (1979).
19. Adriaansens, in an interview with Hikspoors (see Hikspoors, 1995). Flexicurity has to do with security or continuity of employment rather than with security of tenure in a particular job. It is not to be confused with the notion of 'employability', which has become a key concept in the renewed European Employment Strategy. See Auer in this volume.
20. Ministry of Social Affairs and Employment, information leaflet i 003 E, April 1997: Bill on Flexibility and Security.
21. In the preamble to this law, it is stated that legal regulation is deemed necessary 'in order also to create opportunties for combining work with caring and other responsibilities outside work'.
22. On this theme see among others (not specifically on the Dutch case) Neal *et al.* (1993), Lewis and Lewis (1996), Appelbaum (2000). A striking example of the Dutch policy approach, which has met with some cynicism, is the establishment on 4 November 1996 of a Committee on Daily Work Patterns, whose aim is 'to develop proposals for a daily work pattern for society that leaves more room for men's and women's choices in combining and balancing paid jobs and care activities'. The committee published its working plan, entitled 'Time for Work and Care' in March 1997. The committee has introduced the concept of 'task combiners' to denote people who combine work and care tasks.
23. Memorandum on 'Unpaid Leave and Social Insurance'.
24. Although no consensus has been reached yet on the issue of appeal in rescission cases.
25. It should be noted that by means of a collective agreement it is possible to deviate from a number of provisions of the law.
26. See *WSI Mitteilungen*, special issue on 'Flexicurity –Arbeitsmarkt und Sozialpolitik in Zeiten der Flexibilisierung', vol. 53, 5/2000.
27. For more examples of 'flexicurity in action' see Wilthagen (1998).
28. Cf. the white paper on *Our Competitive Future: Building the Knowledge Driven Economy* (Cm 411761), published in December 1998 by the British Department of Trade and Industry (DTI, 1998).
29. The following part of this section is to a large extent based on a current research project dealing with the regulation of training for flexible workers in the Netherlands and the US. Martijn van Velzen, Harm van Lieshout and Ton Wilthagen from the Hugo Sinzheimer Institute of the University of Amsterdam are involved in this project (see van Lieshout and van Liempt, 2000).
30. In practice, this is only partly the case, but the figures may be less negative than generally expected. In the Netherlands in 1997, a great number of temporary agency workers were indeed new entrants to the labour market (half the temporary agency workers were under 25 and 29 per cent had previously been unemployed) and more than a third (34 per cent) managed to find a permanent job within one year.
31. The negotiations on the collective agreement for the temp agency sector continued at the end of 1999, not on training issues but on the question of when the temp agency agreement applies and on wage issues. On 1 December 1999 it was agreed that the temp agency agreement applies when an agency earns more than 50 per cent of the wage sum due to temp agency work. However, if the agency earns more than 50 per cent of the wage sum in one specific sector (for example the metal industry) the agency is not considered a temp work agency. In that case the collective agreement of the particular sector applies. Furthermore, it has been decided that, having worked three months at a client firm, non-skilled workers will receive the wages that are stipulated in the collective agreement that applies to the particular sector they are deployed in; skilled workers will receive those wages from the first working day.
32. On the concept of job services see Schmid (2000).
33. See also the related discussion on the 'new social contract' in Europe. See Closa (1996), Jordan (1996), Macneil (1980); and in particular on gender relations: OECD (1991) and Ministry of Social Affairs and Employment (1998).
34. In an addendum to this chapter a selection of relevant provisions from the European Social Charter is included that might be of relevance for a discussion of transitions as envisaged in the TLM model.

35. One of the major legal and political problems in bringing about a legally binding European social 'basic law' is that the European Union is not a state itself and cannot therefore become a member of the Council of Europe as would be necessary if it were to adopt the European Social Charter. The most obvious solution would be to allow the EU to become a member of the Council of Europe. This is probably a long and winding road. A medium-term possibility advocated by the Dutch Socio-Economic Council (an advisory body to the Dutch government) is to change article 6 of the Amsterdam Treaty. This article now refers to the European Convention on Human Rights as the basis for European thinking on fundamental rights: it could be revised in order to refer also to the European Social Charter and the fundamental Conventions of the ILO (on anti-discrimination and so on). On 12 May 2000, the German Minister of Foreign Affairs, Joschka Fischer, in a speech on the future of European integration, delivered at the Berlin Humboldt University, made a plea for, among other things, a 'constitutional refounding of Europe' through the establishment of a European Basic Law with fundamental human and civil rights at its core.

36. It should be remembered that different institutional arrangements can produce similar outcomes and that similar institutional arrangements can produce different outcomes.

37. Article 13 of the EC Treaty represents a new basis for action to combat discrimination. A number of important initiatives based on this article have already been taken, including the non-discrimination package presented by the European Commission in 1999 (COM, 1999: 564–6), which, among other things, deals with discrimination in the labour market (COM, 1999: 565). See Barnard (2000: 284–7).

38. An example is the Dutch *Organisatiewet Sociale Verzekeringen*, which harmonizes and interconnects different laws in the area of social insurance and social security. One might strive for an 'organizational law on transitional employment'.

REFERENCES

Appelbaum, E. and P. Berg (2000), *Balancing Acts: Easing the Burdens and Improving the Options for Working Families*, Washington, DC: Economic Policy Institute.

Arbeidsinspectie (1999), *Deeltijdarbeid in cao's*, The Hague: Ministry of Social Affairs and Employment.

Arthurs, H. (1998), 'Landscape and Memory: Labour Law, Legal Pluralism and Globalization', in T. Wilthagen (ed.), *Advancing Theory in Labour Law and Industrial Relations in a Global Context*, Amsterdam: North-Holland, pp. 21–4.

Barnard, C. (2000), *EC Employment Law*, 2nd edn, Oxford: Oxford University Press.

Becker, G.S. (1964), *Human capital: A theoretical and empirical analysis, with special reference to education*, New York: Columbia University Press.

Blanpain, R. (ed.) (1997), *Law in Motion*, The Hague: Kluwer Law International.

Bottenburg, M. van (1995), *Aan den Arbeid! In de wandelgangen van de Stichting van de Arbeid, 1945–1995*, Amsterdam: Bert Bakker.

Boyer, R. (ed.) (1988), *The Search for Labour Market Flexibility*, Oxford: Clarendon Press.

Bruijn, J. and O. Verhaar (1999), 'Waar blijven de financiën voor een nieuwe zorginfrastructuur?', *Jaarboek Emancipatie 1999: Wie zorgt in de 21ste eeuw?*, The Hague: Elsevier, pp. 40–47.

CIETT (2000), *Orchestrating the evolution of private employment agencies toward a stronger society*, Brussels: CIETT.

Closa, C. (1996), 'A New Social Contract?', EUI Working Paper RSC No. 96/48, Florence.

Collins, H. (1999), *Regulating Contracts*, Oxford: Oxford University Press.

Commissie Arbeid en Niet-arbeid (1999), *Arbeid en Niet-arbeid. Naar een volwaardige participatie*, Leuven/Apeldoorn: Garant.

Crouch, C. (1997), 'Skill-based Full-Employment: the Latest Philosopher's Stone', *British Journal of Industrial Relations*, 35(3), 367–91.

Dickens, L. (1994), 'Deregulation of Employment Rights in Great Britain', in R. Rogowski and T. Wilthagen (eds), *Reflexive Labour Law: Studies in Industrial Relations and Employment Regulation*, Deventer: Kluwer Law and Taxation, pp. 225–47.

Dore, R. (1986), *Flexible Rigidities*, Palo Alto, CA: Stanford University Press.

DTI (1998), *White paper on 'Our Competitive Future: Building the Knowledge Driven Economy'* (Cm 41761), London: HMSO.

Eggertsson, T. (1990), *Economic Behaviour and Institutions*, Cambridge: Cambridge University Press.

Ehrenberg, R.G. and R.S. Smith (1997), *Modern Labor Economics*, Reading MA: Addison-Wesley.

Elster, J. (1979), *Ulysses and the Sirens: studies in rationality and irrationality*, Cambridge: Cambridge University Press.

Fölster, S. (1999), 'Social Insurance based on Personal Accounts' in M. Buti, D. Franco and L.R. Pench (eds), *The Welfare State in Europe: Challenges and Reforms*, Cheltenham: Edward Elgar, pp. 93–116.

Gendt, M.C.E. van (1980), *The Voucher Concept and the Publicness of Basic Education*, Meppel: Krips Repro.

Grijpstra, D.H., D.J. Klein Hesselink, P.M. de Klaver and E.P. Miedema (1999), *Eerste ervaringen met de wet Flexibiliteit en Zekerheid,* Leiden: Research voor Beleid/TNO Arbeid.

Heertum, A.H. van and A.C.J.M. Wilthagen (1996), *De doorwerking van aanbevelingen van de Stichting van de Arbeid*, Den Haag: Sdu.

Heijden, P.F. van der (1997), 'Een nieuwe rechtsorde van de arbeid', *NJB*, 7 November, 1837–44.

Herriot, P., W. Hirsh and P. Reilly (1998), *Trust and Transition: Managing Today's Employment Relationship*, Chichester: J. Wiley and Sons.

Hikspoors, F.J.H.G. (1995), 'Zekerheid door flexibiliteit', *Gids voor Personeelsmanagement*, 12, 44–5.

Hyde, A. (1998), 'Silicon Valley's High-Velocity Labour Market', *Journal for Applied Corporate Finance*, 11(2), 28–37.

Jordan, B. (1996), 'A New Social Contract?', EUI Working Paper 96/47, Florence.

Keeley, M. (1988), *A Social-Contract Theory of Organizations*, Notre Dame, IN: University of Notre Dame Press.

Klaver, de P.M., D.J. Klein Hesselink and E.P. Miedema (2000), *Ervaringen met en effecten van de Wet Flexibiliteit en Zekerheid. Tweede meting*, The Hague: Ministry of Social Affairs and Employment.

Levin, H. (1980), 'Educational Vouchers and Social Policy', in R. Haskins and J.J. Gallagher (eds), *Care and education of young children in America*, Norwood, NJ: Ablex Publishing Co.

Levin, H. (1983), 'Individual Entitlements', in H. Levin and H.G. Schutze (eds), *Financing Recurrent Education: strategies for increasing employment, job opportunities and productivity*, Beverley Hills, CA and London: Sage Publications.

Levin H. (1991), 'The Economics of Educational Choice', *Economics of Education Review*, 10, 137–58.

Lewis, S. and J. Lewis (1996), *The Work–Family Challenge: Re-thinking Employment*, London and Thousand Oaks, CA: Sage.

Lieshout, H.A.M. van and A.A.G. van Liempt (2000), 'Temporary employment agencies and Training in the Netherlands', in A.M.L. van Wieringen, M-van Dyck, B.W.M. Hövels and W.J. Nijhof (eds), *Nieuwe aansluitingen tussen onderwijs en arbeid*, Max Groote Kenniscentrum Jaarboek.

Luhmann, N. (1993), *Das Recht der Gesellschaft*, Frankfurt am Main: Suhrkamp.

Lyon-Caen, G. (1996), 'By way of conclusion: Labour law and employment transitions', *International Labour Review*, 135(6), 697–702.

Macneil, I.R. (1980), *The New Social Contract: An Inquiry into Modern Contractual Relations*, New Haven, CT: Yale University Press.

Madsen, P.K. (1998a), 'Working time policy and paid leave arrangements: the Danish experience in the 1990s', *Transfer – European Review of Labour and Research*, 8(4), 692–714.

Madsen, P.K. (1998b), 'A transitional labour market: the Danish paid leave arrangements', in H.U. Schwedler (ed.), *New Institutional Arrangements in the Labour Market: Transitional Labour Markets as a New Full Employment Concept*, Berlin: European Academy of the Urban Environment/WZB, pp. 68–73.

Meer, M. van der (ed.) (2000), *The trade-off between competitiveness and employment in collective bargaining*, Amsterdam: Amsterdam Institute for Advanced Labour Studies.

Ministry of Social Affairs and Employment, Directorate of Coordination of Emancipation Policy (1998), *Naar een nieuw 'sociaal contract' in de 21ste eeuw*, The Hague.

Ministry of Social Affairs and Employment, Directorate of Industrial Relations (1997), *Part-time work in the Netherlands*, The Hague.

Murray, J. (1999), *Social Justice for Women? The ILO's Convention on Part-time Work*, The Centre for Employment and Labour Relations Law, University of Melbourne.

Neal, M.B., N.J. Chapman, B. Ingersoll-Dayton and A.C. Emlen (1993), *Balancing Work and Caregiving for Children, Adults and Elders*, Newbury Park, CA and London: Sage.

OECD (1991), *Shaping Structural Change: the Role of Women*, Paris.

Oosterbeek, H. (1994), *Onderwijs op maat geknipt: een analyse van vouchers in het post-leerplichtig onderwijs*, Bunnik: Studie van Raad voor de Volwassenenducatie.

Osterman, P. (1994), 'Internal Labor Markets: Theory and Change', in C. Kerr and P.D. Staudohar (eds), *Labor Economics and Industrial Relations: Markets and Institutions*, Cambridge, MA and London: Harvard University Press, 303–39.

Pennings, F.J.L. (1996), *Flexibilisering van het sociaal recht*, Deventer: Kluwer.

Pfau-Effinger, B. (1998), 'Culture or structure as explanation for differences in part-time work in Germany, Finland and the Netherlands', in J. O'Reilly and C. Fagan (eds), *Part-time Prospects: an international comparison of part-time work in Europe, North-America and the Pacific Rim*, London and New York: Routledge, pp. 177–98.

Rogowski, R. (2000), 'Industrial Relations as a Social System', *Industrielle Beziehungen – The German Journal of Industrial Relations*, 7(1), 97–126.

Rogowski, R. and G. Schmid (1998), 'Reflexive Deregulierung. Ein Ansatz zur Dynamisierung des Arbeitsmarkts' in B. Keller and H. Seifert (eds), *Deregulierung am Arbeitsmarkt. Eine empirische Zwischenbilanz*, Hamburg: VSA, pp. 215–53.

Rogowski, R. and T. Wilthagen (eds) (1994), *Reflexive Labour Law: Studies in Industrial Relations and Employment Regulation*, Deventer: Kluwer Law and Taxation.

Rojer, M. (1995), 'Hoe meer zielen hoe meer vreugde?', *Tijdschrift voor Arbeidsvraagstukken*, 2/95, 173–87.

Schmid, G. (2000), 'Beyond Conventional Service Economics: Utility Services, Service-Product Chains and Job Services', (Discussion Paper FS 1 00–203) WZB-Berlin.

Schömann, K., R. Rogowski and T. Kruppe (1998), *Labour Market Efficiency in the European Union: Employment Protection and Fixed-term Contracts*, London: Routledge.

SCP (2000), *De kunst van het combineren*, The Hague: SCP.

Sels, L. and G. van Hootegem (1999), 'België-Nederland: strijd om de meeste flexibiliteit', in J. van Hoof and J. Mevissen (eds), *Nieuwe vormen van sturing op de arbeidsmarkt in België en Nederland*, Amsterdam: Elsevier/SISWO, pp. 159–84.

Simitis, S. (1994a), 'Denationalizing Labor Law: The Case of Age Discrimination', *Comparative Labor Law Journal*, 15(3), 321–39.

Simitis, S. (1994b), 'The Rediscovery of the Individual in Labour Law', in R. Rogowski and T. Wilthagen (eds), *Reflexive Labour Law: Studies in Industrial Relations and Employment Regulation*, Deventer: Kluwer Law and Taxation, pp. 183–205.

Solow, R. (1990), *The Labor Market as a Social Institution,* Cambridge, MA: Basil Blackwell.

Sousa Santos, B. de (1995), *Toward a New Common Sense: Law, Science and Politics in the Paradigmatic Transition*, London: Routledge.

Supiot, Alain (1999), 'The transformation of work and the future of labour law in Europe: A multidisciplinary perspective', *International Labour Review*, 138(1), 31–46.

Supiot, A., M.E. Casas, J. de Munk, P. Hanan, A.L. Johansson, P. Meadows, E. Mingione, R. Salais and P. van der Heijden (2001), *Beyond Employment: Changes in Work and the Future of Labour Law in Europe*, Oxford: Oxford University Press.

Teubner, G. (ed.) (1996), *Global Law without a State*, Aldershot: Dartmouth.

Toren, J.P. van den (1996), *Achter gesloten deuren? CAO-overleg in de jaren negentig*, Amsterdam: Welboom Pers.

Velzen, M. van (2000), 'The collective agreement of Stork Mobile', in M. van der Meer (ed.), *The trade-off between competitiveness and employment in collective bargaining*, Amsterdam: Amsterdam Institute for Advanced Labour Studies, 32–9.

Visser, J. and A. Hemerijck (1997), '*A Dutch Miracle': Job Growth, Welfare Reform and Corporatism in the Netherlands*, Amsterdam: Amsterdam University Press.

Weiss, M. (1996), *Fundamental Social Rights for the European Union* (Sinzheimer Lecture 1996), Amsterdam: Hugo Sinzheimer Institute.

Williamson, O.E. (1994), 'Transaction Cost Economics and Organization Theory', in N.J. Smelser and R. Swedberg (eds), *The Handbook of Economic Sociology*, Princeton, NJ: Princeton University Press, pp. 77–107.

Wilthagen, T. (1998), 'Flexicurity: A New Paradigm for Labour Market Policy Reform?', WZB Discussion Paper FS I 98–20X, Berlin.

Windmuller, J.P. (1969), *Labor Relations in the Netherlands*, Ithaca, NY: Cornell University Press.

PART III

Applications and Policy Strategies

E24 J24 M53
J68
J16

8. The dynamics of employment in the European Union: an exploratory analysis

Thomas Kruppe[1]

The introduction to the OECD *Employment Outlook* (1996: vii) evokes the theme of social exclusion and the measures to be taken to counter it. Important threats to social integration are cited. An inefficient labour market poses a threat to the social fabric, as the risk of falling into the 'unemployment trap' or remaining in poorly paid or precarious, fixed-term forms of employment is considerable. Possible escape routes from this difficult situation include such mobility processes as flows out of unemployment into full-time and part-time employment (O'Reilly *et al.*, 2000) or into fixed-term employment (Schömann *et al.*, 1998), lifelong learning within a company and changes of employer (Tuijnman and Schömann, 1996). These market-induced flows are increasingly being supplemented by participation in labour market policy measures, which already constitute a significant proportion of such transitions (Schmid, 1995; de Koning and Mosley, 2001).

The concept of transitional labour markets draws attention to the interaction between these flows which can be seen to some extent as 'communicating pipelines'. Increasing the dynamics of flows out of unemployment, for example through labour market measures, may be counteracted by increasing flows into unemployment, due either to the lower quality of matches or to the externalization of the transaction costs involved in employment contracts (Simon, 1951; Williamson *et al.*, 1975). Thus, if labour market policy focuses exclusively on unemployment outflows, it is unlikely to be successful in fighting unemployment since it may lead only to a simultaneous increase in the flows into unemployment. Policies in some European member states aimed at facilitating the outflow from unemployment by allowing more fixed-term employment (for instance in Germany, and especially in Spain) have met with only limited success because more fixed-term employment merely increases the flows into unemployment because of the greater number of short-term employment contracts constantly expiring (Schömann *et al.*, 1998).

However, even if such policies are not successful in lowering the overall level of unemployment in the short term, increasing labour turnover at a constant level of unemployment for some time may have positive side-effects. For instance, it may redistribute and equalize employment risks, thereby serving some of the social objectives that are also at the core of labour market policy. Higher labour turnover may also relieve the wage pressure exerted by insiders and lead in turn to an increase in employment and possibly also to a decrease in unemployment in the long term.[2]

Thus measuring labour market performance in terms solely of levels or flows of employment or unemployment will not capture the true dynamics of the labour market. If the interaction between flows and levels is to be captured, an integrative approach is required. This is, however, more easily said than done. Despite the move towards the 'information' or 'knowledge society', our statistical apparatus basically still relies on counting stocks and tracking their growth or decline over time. This information, valuable as it is, conceals complex and interrelated processes that are important for understanding the causal dynamics that would enable us to make reliable forecasts and sensible suggestions for policy intervention.

This chapter offers an integrative and comparative perspective on labour market transitions in Europe. Section 1 develops a systematic framework for a descriptive analysis based on transitional labour market theory. Section 2 sets down a benchmark for comparing the actual flow dynamics with a steady state and applies the analytical framework to 11 EU member states on the basis of the European Community Household Panel (ECHP). Section 3 concentrates on two key transitions, focusing on the status after leaving education or training and that after leaving unemployment. Section 4 concludes with suggestions for future research. Since methodologies and data sources for dynamic labour market studies are still underdeveloped, the following contribution has to be understood as a first but necessary step into a vast field of fascinating analytical possibilities.

1   A SYSTEMATIC FRAMEWORK OF TRANSITIONAL LABOUR MARKETS

Table 8.1 provides a synopsis of the various combinations of flows that are relevant in considering the employment dynamic. Most studies concentrate only on transitions between unemployment and employment, restricting their analysis therefore to the first four cells in the matrix (marked with a ① in Table 8.1). However, the interactive flow dynamic requires that all transitions into and out of employment be taken into account (②), and in assessing the impact of labour market policy on unemployment all movements into and out of unemployment have to be considered (③).

Taking the notion of transitional labour markets as a starting point (cf.

Table 8.1   Matrix of transitions from an initial status at time (t–1) to a final status at time (t)

t-1 \ t	Employment	Unemployment	Inactivity	Education	Retirement
Employment	① ② ③	① ② ③	②	②	②
Unemployment	① ② ③	① ③	③	③	③
Inactivity	②	③			
Education	②	③			
Retirement	②	③			

279

Schmid, 1995 and Chapter 5 in this volume), five types of labour market 'bridges' can be distinguished: (1) transitions between various employment statuses;[3] (2) transitions between unemployment and employment; (3) transitions between education or training and employment; (4) transitions between private and labour market activity; (5) transitions between employment and retirement. These employment bridges can be crossed in both directions and, in some cases, several times within one year.

Figure 8.1 shows the segments of the employment system and the possible flows, or labour market transitions, between these segments. Transitional labour markets are linked to the critical points of the life cycle where transitions

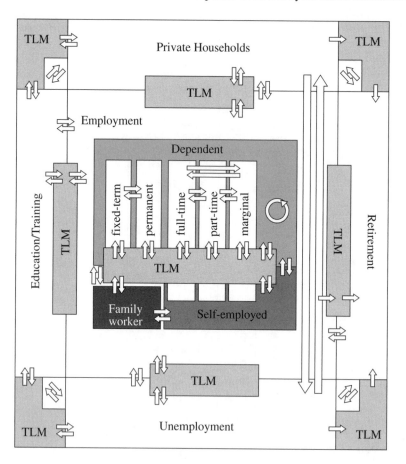

Note: TLM: Transitional labour markets; labour market transitions (flows) marked as ⇨.

Figure 8.1 Labour market transitions and transitional labour markets

can lead to labour market inclusion or exclusion. Labour market policy has traditionally focused mainly on transitions into and out of unemployment, although direct flows between employment and unemployment are only one subset of the flows into and out of employment. Yet the transitions between education and unemployment or those between paid work and retirement – the recent trend towards part-time retirement for elderly workers deserves a mention in this context – also constitute important flows.[4]

Every transition with its initial $(t - 1)$ and final (t) status can in turn be broken down into its various components. Depending on the objective of the analysis, distinctions can, for instance, be drawn between waged and salaried employment, self-employment and family workers. Again these kinds of employment could be broken down into full-time, part-time and marginal employment and, in addition, between permanent and fixed-term jobs. This means that transitions can take place into a specific subsegment as well as between these subsegments.

As far as the investigation of employment systems is concerned, the central point in Figure 8.1 is employment. Unemployment, education and training, retirement and private households are on the periphery. However, the figure draws attention to the various possibilities that exist to influence the employment dynamic. To date, labour market policy has often promoted flows in one direction only, for instance out of the labour market through (early) retirement, the aim being to reduce the labour supply. However, Figure 8.1 clearly suggests that, for instance, speeding up the process of entry from school to work (that is, increasing the inflow dynamics) or stabilizing employment relationships for women or men who have to combine family obligations with gainful work by institutionalizing flexible working-time arrangements (that is, increasing the duration of employment over the life course) could substantially increase the employment level.

However, a succession of transitions can also occur with or without the intervention of labour market policy. After a course of further vocational training followed by a period of unemployment, participation in a reintegration programme could lead back into employment. Any transition from $(t - 1)$ to (t) with an identical or a different initial and final dependent employment status could be interpreted as a change of job within a firm or as a change of employer.

2 TRANSITIONS IN THE EUROPEAN EMPLOYMENT SYSTEM

Before we attempt to identify and compare real patterns of labour market transitions, it might be useful to establish a benchmark from a steady state. What would the European labour market look like if there were no additional transitions during the life course except for entry into and exit from the active labour force?

Benchmarks for Transitional Labour Markets

Let us assume that people enter the active labour force at age 16, get a job immediately, remain in that job for the whole of their working lives and leave it at age 65. Since the level of labour force participation is the product of the inflow rate and the duration of employment, the natural labour turnover would be 1.4 per cent, assuming a fairly realistic labour force participation rate of 68 per cent and a wholly unrealistic job tenure of 50 years (see Table 8.2). In fact, however, labour turnover is much higher. Since no figures at the level of the European Union (EU) are available, the German figures have been adjusted to the EU15.

Table 8.3 also includes the flows into and out of unemployment, although without knowledge of the origin and the destination of the flows. In this more realistic scenario, the components of European labour force participation show an inflow rate of 16 per cent (of the working age population) and an average job tenure of 4.3 years. Accordingly, the 1998 unemployment rate of 10.1 per cent can be decomposed into the inflow rate of 18.1 per cent (of the active population) and an average of 0.6 years (6.6 months) duration for completed spells of unemployment.

These crude turnover rates give some idea of the true dynamic of real labour markets. However, they cover only a small part of the mobility processes. As Table 8.1 and Figure 8.1 show, many more transitions between

Table 8.2   The European employment system in steady state, 1998[1]

Population EU15 (1000s)			374 888	
Young <15	Working-age population		247 054	Old ≥65
	Inactive	Active population		
	3 359	167 961		3 359
	(1.4%)	(68%)		(1.4%)

Labour force participation rate $\quad = \quad$ Inflow rate $\quad \times \quad$ Duration

$$\frac{167\,961}{247\,054}(=68\%) \quad = \quad \frac{3\,359}{247\,054}(=1.4\%) \quad \times \quad \frac{167\,961}{3\,359}(=50)$$

Note: [1]Assumptions: continuous employment; that is, non-interrupted employment spells of 50 years.

Source: Employment in Europe, 1999; own calculations.

Table 8.3   The European employment system in transition, 1998[1]

Population EU15 (1000s)		374 888	
Young <15	Working-age population	247 054	Old ≥65

	Inactive	Active population	167 961 (68%)	

Employed   151 009 (89.9%)

30 401 (18.1%)

39 529

Unemployed
16 952 (10%)

31 675 (18.9%)

?

(16%)
?

?

Labour force participation rate	=	Inflow rate	× Duration

$$\frac{167\,961}{247\,054}\,(=68\%) \qquad = \qquad \frac{39\,529}{247\,054}\,(=16\%)\;\times\;\frac{167\,961}{39\,529}\,(=4.25\%)$$

Note: [1]Assumptions: Inflows (new hirings), average duration of employment spells, and inflows into as well as outflows from unemployment assessed according to German figures.

Source: *Employment in Europe*, 1999; own calculations.

various employment statuses are possible and indeed take place. Two questions arise. Firstly, what is the level of these transitions, and are there substantive differences among European member states? Secondly, what is the composition of these transitions?[5]

The Level of Labour Market Transitions in European Member States

The following figures are based on transitions counted between December 1994 ($t-1$) and December 1995 (t) by utilizing monthly information on changes in their labour force status (calendar variables) supplied by individuals from the European Community Household Panel (ECHP), waves two and three. Table 8.4 provides a comparative overview of the number and composition of transitions.[6] The number of individuals in each country who made at least one transition between December 1994 and December 1995 is given per million persons of the population aged 15 and over. The figures are also expressed as a percentage of the population aged 15 and over. Taking the EU11 average (16 per cent), most of the countries are – surprisingly – fairly close to this benchmark, with only Spain (29 per cent) and Luxembourg (11 per cent) as outliers.[7]

However, there is an interesting difference between men and women. First, although women make up only about 40 per cent of the active labour force, they account for 59 per cent of all persons who made at least one transition.

This clearly reflects the well-known fact that women are and have to be much more flexible than men in order to combine family and labour market work. In France (34 per cent), Luxembourg, Portugal and the United Kingdom (all 35 per cent), men obviously have much more secure labour market positions than women. Only Greece and Ireland display a relatively equal distribution of transitions between men and women, but this is probably due to the low employment share of women in these countries and therefore does not contradict the general pattern. Second, the last column of Table 8.4 indicates the percentage of persons who made more than one transition in the previous 12 months. While the EU11 average indicates that one-quarter of all persons changed their labour force status more than once, the variation between countries ranges from Luxembourg (15 per cent), Germany, Portugal and the United Kingdom (17 per cent) and Italy (18 per cent), via Belgium and Spain (25 per cent) and Greece (28 per cent) to Ireland (34 per cent) and Denmark (41 per cent).[8] At first glance there is no easy explanation for these differences. Only time series and information on the composition of transitions (see below) could reveal consistent patterns related to institutional employment regimes.

Individuals who had more than one transition naturally push up the overall number of changes in labour force status. This overall number is given in Table 8.5, again given per one million of the population over 15 years of age. Taking all transitions, the disproportionately high number of women who

Table 8.4   Number and composition of transitions (individuals)

	Individuals				
	Per million persons (16+)	Percentage of population (16+)	Male (%)	Female (%)	With more than one transition (%)
Belgium	173 625	17	37	63	25
Denmark	183 816	18	43	57	41
Germany	183 489	18	41	59	17
Greece	160 339	16	49	51	28
Spain	290 325	29	46	54	25
France	188 967	19	34	66	52
Ireland	190 851	19	47	53	34
Italy	164 507	16	43	57	18
Luxembourg	106 551	11	35	65	15
Portugal	194 438	19	35	65	17
United Kingdom	212 880	19	35	65	17
EU 11	197 807	16	41	59	26

Source: ECHP wave 2 and 3, own calculation

Table 8.5   Transitions by gender

	Transitions		
	Per million persons	Male (%)	Female (%)
Belgium	232 576	37	63
Denmark	278 097	45	55
Germany	221 545	43	57
Greece	215 207	49	51
Spain	399 874	50	50
France	322 846	35	65
Ireland	266 800	47	53
Italy	205 963	44	56
Luxembourg	128 587	37	63
Portugal	237 457	42	58
United Kingdom	287 725	42	58
EU11	269 827	43	57

Source: ECHP wave 2 and 3; own calculations.

(have to) change their labour force status remains but narrows a little compared to their share of all persons making transitions (cf. Table 8.4). In other words, many more women make or have to make transitions, but men who change status seem to have to do so several times. One way of explaining this narrowing gap is that men have a significantly higher probability of re-entering employment after a short phase of unemployment, while women have a higher probability of entering the 'unemployment trap'.

Composition of Transitions in European Member States

What is the composition of the high labour market dynamic just demonstrated in Tables 8.4 and 8.5? Table 8.6 shows the pattern of these transitions as a percentage of all transitions that occurred in 1995 and as an average across 11 EU member states.[9] Transitions were counted again between December 1994 (t–1) and December 1995 (t) using monthly data on individual changes in labour force status (calendar variables) from the ECHP, waves two and three.[10] The inner field of Table 8.6 shows that the main flows are – as expected – the transitions out of dependent employment into unemployment and the related counterflow from unemployment into dependent employment. However, what

Table 8.6 *Matrix of transitions from an initial status at time (t–1) to a final status at time (t), average of EU11 (as % of all transitions)*

t t–1	A	B	C	D	E	F	G	H	I	J	K	Total (out)
A	n.a.	–	2.0	–	1.9	**14.4**	2.2	2.6	–	1.6	1.0	**27.2**
B	1.0	n.a.	–	–	–	–	–	–	–	–	–	2.0
C	1.8	–	n.a.	–	–	1.0	1.2	–	–	–	–	5.9
D	–	–	–	n.a.	–	–	–	–	–	–	–	2.2
E	3.2	–	–	–	n.a.	3.1	–	–	–	–	–	**9.4**
F	**14.7**	–	1.4	–	1.3	n.a.	–	1.7	–	–	–	**22.3**
G	–	–	–	–	–	–	n.a.	2.1	–	1.4	–	4.9
H	2.7	–	–	–	–	1.6	2.1	n.a.	–	4.1	–	**12.1**
I	–	–	–	–	–	–	–	–	n.a.	–	–	1.4
J	1.6	–	–	–	–	1.0	1.8	3.4	–	n.a.	–	**9.0**
K	1.1	–	–	–	–	–	–	–	–	–	n.a.	3.6
Total (in)	**27.4**	**2.0**	**6.3**	**1.8**	**5.1**	**22.9**	**8.6**	**11.5**	**2.1**	**9.6**	**2.7**	**100.0**

Notes: A = dependent employment (inc. vocational training); B = paid apprenticeship or training under special schemes related to employment; C = self-employment; D = unpaid work in family enterprise; E = education or training; F = unemployment; G = retirement; H = inactivity (housework, looking after children or other persons); I = community or military service; J = other economic inactivity; K = missing calendar information; n.a. = not available; – = less than 1% of all transitions.

Source: ECHP wave 2 and 3; own calculations.

was not known yet, these transitions make up only about 29 per cent of all transitions between various labour force statuses – about 14.5 per cent for each direction of flow. In other words, 71 per cent of all status changes are not related to moves between dependent employment and unemployment!

More than 20 per cent of all transitions are exits from as well as entries into inactivity (or other economic inactivity). Those transitions out of inactivity (or other economic inactivity) that do not end up in dependent employment or unemployment constitute about 14 per cent[11] of all transitions. Those transitions into inactivity (or other economic inactivity) that are neither exits from dependent employment nor exits from unemployment account for about 15 per cent[12] of all transitions. In other words, about 30 per cent of transitions are not related to the labour market in the narrower sense. Nearly 10 per cent of all transitions are exits from education and training (excluding vocational training), while only 5.1 per cent are entries into education and training: the flows across the 'education and training bridge' are still predominantly one way, but this might change in the future.[13] About 5.9 per cent of transitions are exits from self-employment, with counterflows of 6.3 per cent; this obviously reflects a growing trend towards self-employment during the observation period.[14]

If we concentrate on the first row of Table 8.6 only, that is on *transitions from dependent employment to other statuses*, we see that 2 per cent of all transitions involve a change of status from dependent employment to self-employment and that 1.9 per cent represent moves into education or training. As already mentioned, 14.4 per cent of all transitions are entries into unemployment; in other words, slightly more than half (52.9 per cent) of transitions out of dependent employment end in unemployment and almost half end in another labour force status, such as inactivity, training or retirement. Entries into retirement account for 2.2 per cent of all transitions, 2.6 per cent are entries into 'inactivity' (housework, looking after children or other persons), 1.6 per cent are moves into other forms of economic inactivity, while 1 per cent of moves cannot be identified.[15] All together, these moves make up 27.2 per cent of all transitions.

Checking the other side of the coin, namely *transitions from other labour force statuses into (dependent) employment*, we see that 1 per cent (of all transitions) are exits from paid apprenticeship or special training schemes, 1.8 per cent from self-employment and 3.2 per cent from education or training; 14.7 per cent of all transitions (or 53.6 per cent of transitions into employment) are exits from unemployment, 2.7 per cent from 'inactivity' related to housework, looking after children or other persons and 1.6 per cent from other forms of economic inactivity. Taken together, transitions into dependent employment make up 27.4 per cent of all transitions.

Finally, one can look at the *balance of the transitions* in and out of (dependent) employment. Significant surpluses (inflows minus outflows) occur, first of all, in apprenticeships or training schemes. In other words (and as to be expected), substantially more people move from apprenticeship into employment than the other way round. Other surpluses can be found (again as expected) in education and training, in unemployment,[16] in inactivity related to housework and other forms of economic inactivity.[17] Significant deficits in 1994/5 occurred only in self-employment, implying a growing share of self-employment.

This informative description can be completed by checking the flows related to unemployment. Examination of the sixth row, namely *transitions from unemployment to other statuses*, shows that only a few transitions can be identified significantly. As already mentioned, 14.7 per cent of all transitions (or 65.9 per cent of all outflows from unemployment) represent moves into employment. In other words, about one-third of the unemployed do not end up in employment but in other labour force statuses! In addition, 1.4 per cent (of all transitions) are entries into self-employment, 1.3 per cent into education and training (probably supported to a large extent by active labour market policy) and 1.7 per cent into housework or family work. Taken all together, outflows from unemployment make up 22.3 per cent of all transitions.

Checking the other side of the coin, namely *transitions from other labour force statuses into unemployment*, we see that 14.4 per cent of all transitions (or 62.9 per cent of all inflows into unemployment) come from employment. In other words, more than one-third of inflows into unemployment in Europe come, on average, from other labour market statuses. One per cent (of all transitions) are entries into unemployment from self-employment, 3.1 per cent are moves from education or training in unemployment, 1.6 per cent are exits from housework or family work and 1.0 per cent are moves from other forms of economic inactivity. Taken together, 22.9 per cent of all transitions represent flows into unemployment.

Again, looking at the *balance of the transitions* into and out of unemployment, we see that (apart from the employment-related balance already mentioned) the only significant surplus is that related to self-employment; in other words, more people move from unemployment into self-employment than the other way round. The only significant deficit is related to education or training, with fewer people (1.3 per cent) moving from unemployment into education and training than the other way round (3.1 per cent). This is a problematic pattern from the point of view of active labour market policy.

Differentiating this flow analysis by gender, age and economic sector and enriching it with time series would allow us to identify country-specific patterns of employment regimes. Attention should also be paid to the sustainability of transitions. In the context of the debate on labour market flexibility in the EU, studies of flows into and out of fixed-term employment would be necessary as an additional yardstick for evaluating the quality and permanence of the transitions. In Spain, Ireland, France, Portugal and Denmark, for example, transitions from unemployment to fixed-term employment accounted for between 90 per cent (in Spain) and 46 per cent (in Denmark) of all transitions from unemployment to employment in 1994 (OECD, 1996: 16). This indicates that the new employment relationships for unemployed people may lack sustainability (Schömann *et al.*, 1998). In the following, the power of the transitional labour market approach is demonstrated by concentrating on mobility processes related to flows from unemployment to employment and to the education or training system.

3 TRANSITION PATTERNS IN KEY AREAS

Where do individuals end up after leaving the education and training system? What is the labour market status of individuals after they leave unemployment? What role are these transitions expected to play in a properly functioning employment system? Are there country-specific transition patterns? This section will provide answers to these questions, albeit in a very crude way.

Transitions related to education and training[18]

In a properly functioning employment system, one would expect the vast majority of people moving out of education or training to go directly into dependent employment or self-employment, or at least into an intermediate stage of employment such as apprenticeship, community or military service or another labour market programme intended to enhance employability. Table 8.7 presents data that will show whether this is so, albeit in a very crude way.[19]

There are considerable differences between the countries included here in the number of transitions out of education or training.[20] While the lowest level of transitions is found in Portugal, the ranking continues with Italy, the United Kingdom, Greece, Germany, France, Belgium, Spain, Denmark and Ireland. Further studies will have to be conducted in order to ascertain whether these differences reflect stable patterns and which factors might explain them (for example, age structure of the labour force, education system and regulatory framework). At first glance, for instance, the figures very clearly reflect the dual system in Germany, where there is a high number of transitions from initial education into apprenticeship.

In Belgium and France, the flow from education and training into dependent employment is nearly equal to that into unemployment. In Denmark, Germany, Ireland, Portugal and the United Kingdom, on the other hand, a far higher share of transitions are entries into dependent employment than into unemployment. In Greece,[21] Spain and Italy, the pattern is reversed, with those

Table 8.7 *The transition out of education and training, by country (%)*

Transition from education or training into:	Belgium	Denmark	Germany	Greece	Spain	France	Ireland	Italy	Portugal	UK
Dependent employment (inc. vocational training)	27	53	26	(13)	28	33	60	21	33	43
Paid apprenticeship or training under special schemes related to employment	–	(12)	34	–	(4)	–	(8)	(4)	–	–
Self-employment	(5)	–	–	–	–	–	–	–	–	–
Unpaid work in family enterprise	–	–	–	–	–	–	(3)	–	–	–
In community or military service	–	–	(10)	–	(3)	(4)	–	(3)	–	–
Subtotal	34.8	65.3	71.4	23.0	38.0	38.3	72.4	32.4	47.3	53.5
Unemployed	26	19	(13)	24	49	32	20	58	25	29
Retired	–	–	–	–	–	–	–	–	–	–
Inactive (housework, looking after children or other persons)	–	–	–	–	–	(3)	(3)	(4)	–	–
Other economically inactive	30	(10)	(7)	–	(4)	12	(4)	(4)	(21)	–
Subtotal	58.9	34.2	23.1	33.8	54.5	46.2	27.6	67.4	47.0	46.5
Missing	(6.3)	–	–	43	8	15	–	–	(6)	–
Total	100.0	100.0	100.0	100.0	100.0	100.0	100.0	100.0	100.0	100.0
Total number of transitions per million individuals	31 659	44 482	25 882	23 800	33 081	29 068	53 139	20 799	18 726	22 063

Notes: – = none or fewer than 10 observations in the unweighted sample; (n) = fewer than 30 observations in the unweighted sample.

Source: ECHP wave 2 and 3; own calculations.

290

leaving education and training ending up mainly in unemployment. Only in Belgium does a small percentage go straight into self-employment, while in several countries there are significant flows into inactivity of all kinds.

To return to the expectation outlined at the beginning of this section, we can state that only in Ireland (72.4 per cent), Germany (71.4 per cent), Denmark (65.3 per cent) and the United Kingdom (53.5 per cent) do more than half of those leaving education and training end up directly in dependent employment, self-employment or at least in an intermediate stage of employment such as apprenticeship or community or military service. In all the other countries, this share is lower than half of all exits from education or training and does not, therefore, meet the expectations of a properly functioning employment system.[22]

Transitions Related to Unemployment

One revealing result from the survey of 11 European member states was that about one-third of all flows out of unemployment ended, not in employment, but in other labour force statuses, such as inactivity or retirement. As in the case of the transition from education or training, it might be hypothesized that, in a properly functioning employment system, the large majority of transitions out of unemployment would end in 'active' forms of labour market statuses, such as dependent employment, self-employment or at least an intermediate stage of employment such as education or training, community or military service or another labour market programme intended to enhance employability. Table 8.8 presents data that will show whether this is so, albeit in a very crude way.

Once again, comparison of the number of transitions out of unemployment[23] reveals even greater differences between the countries than in the case of transitions from education or training. In Germany, the number of transitions per one million individuals over 15 years old is less than one third (31.7 per cent) of those in Spain, where the transition pattern is clearly related to the extensive use of fixed-term contracts (Schömann *et al.*, 1998).

As already noted, the average share of transitions from unemployment into dependent employment in EU11 is about two-thirds. Disaggregated by country, the share ranges from 57 per cent (Germany and Italy) to 75 per cent (Greece and France). To what destinations do the other transitions lead? Table 8.8 reveals certain country-specific patterns for these other destinations. In Ireland (12 per cent) and Germany (7 per cent), a substantial proportion of those leaving unemployment enter paid apprenticeship after a period of unemployment. This is also the case in the United Kingdom (4 per cent) and Italy (3 per cent). There is a significant flow from unemployment into self-employment in Italy (12 per cent), Greece (8 per cent), the United Kingdom (7 per

Table 8.8 The transition out of unemployment, by country (%)

Transition from unemployment into:	Belgium	Denmark	Germany	Greece	Spain	France	Ireland	Italy	Portugal	UK
Dependent employment (inc. vocational training)	61	66	57	75	68	75	59	57	66	65
Paid apprenticeship or training under special schemes related to employment	–	–	(7)	–	(1)	–	12	(3)	–	(4)
Self-employment	–	–	–	8	6	(2)	(3)	12	(5)	(7)
Unpaid work in family enterprise	–	–	–	(3)	–	–	–	(1)	–	–
Education or training	(6)	12	(6)	(4)	5	6	(9)	8	(4)	(5)
In community or military service	–	–	(3)	–	2	(2)	–	3	–	–
Subtotal	73.1	81.7	77.4	92.0	82.7	86.1	83.9	83.8	79.3	83.1
Retired	(9)	9	11	–	2	(2)	–	(1)	(5)	(4)
Inactive (housework, looking after children or other persons)	(11)	–	(8)	(4)	11	(2)	10	(11)	9	(6)
Other economically inactive	(5)	(8)	–	–	4	(3)	(4)	4	(7)	(7)
Subtotal	24.8	18.3	20.5	5.2	16.7	6.9	16.1	16.1	20.5	16.7
Missing	–	–	–	(3)	–	7	–	–	–	–
Total	100.0	100.0	100.0	100.0	100.0	100.0	100.0	100.0	100.0	100.0
Total number of transitions per millon individuals	39 414	75 466	36 360	48 278	114 671	67 938	58 303	44 858	43 356	50 045

Notes: – = none or fewer than 10 observations in the unweighted sample; (n) = fewer than 30 observations in the unweighted sample.

Source: ECHP wave 2 and 3; own calculations.

cent), Spain (6 per cent), Portugal (5 per cent), Ireland (3 per cent) and France (2 per cent). Only in Greece (3 per cent) and Italy (1 per cent) is the flow into family work of any significance.

Transitions from unemployment into education or training are significant in all the countries analysed here. The flows range from 4 per cent in Greece and Portugal to 12 per cent in Denmark. In some countries, they seem to constitute an important route back into regular employment. It would be interesting to know whether the use of this channel has a significant effect in terms of reducing the duration of unemployment and increasing sustainable new employment. In most countries, especially Belgium, Germany and Portugal, but also Denmark, there is still a considerable flow from unemployment into 'passive' statuses, such as retirement and various forms of inactivity. In this respect, Greece and France are outliers for which there is no immediate explanation.

Returning to the expectation outlined at the beginning of this section, we can say that in all the countries in question here more than three quarters of transitions out of unemployment lead to 'active' statuses, whether this be dependent employment, self-employment, apprenticeship, education, training or community or military service. The figures range from 73.1 per cent in Belgium to 92 per cent in Greece. Thus all the countries could be said broadly to meet the expectation of a properly functioning employment system. However, in some countries, especially Belgium, Germany, Italy and Ireland, where the share of transitions from unemployment into dependent employment is below two-thirds, we cannot say whether the intermediate stages between unemployment and employment serve ultimately as bridges or as traps. Moreover, the high share of transitions leading to retirement in Belgium, Denmark and Germany, as well as the high share of transitions into some form of inactivity in Belgium, Spain, Ireland, France, Italy and Portugal, raise some doubts as to the 'health' of these systems.

4   CONCLUSIONS AND OUTLOOK

This chapter has sought to demonstrate the utility of a dynamic view of labour market flows between different labour market statuses. It has developed a systematic framework for examining the interrelated complexity of transitions (the transition matrix) and has provided, for the first time, descriptive evidence on the size and composition of transitions for 11 EU member states. The database on which this chapter has drawn is the innovative material provided by the annual survey of the European Community Household Panel (ECHP), with monthly calendar information from waves 2 and 3 of 1994–5.

On average, 16 per cent of the European population aged 15 and over change labour force status at least once a year. Women make up 40 per cent of the active labour force but account for a disproportionately high 59 per cent of all persons undergoing at least one transition. This can be partially explained by the fact that only about 28 per cent of all transitions are related to dependent employment, while more than two-thirds of the transitions lead to unemployment (about 20 per cent), self-employment or to various 'inactive' statuses, such as education or training, household activities or (early) retirement. Examination of multiple transitions suggests that many more women make or have to make transitions but that men who change status seem to be more mobile. This could be partially explained by the higher probability of men re-entering employment after short phases of unemployment, while women, for their part, are more likely to enter the 'unemployment trap'.

The flow between dependent employment and unemployment, together with its counter flow, account for about 29 per cent of all transitions; in other words, 71 per cent of all transitions are not related to moves between unemployment and dependent employment. Moves in and out of dependent employment account for about 27 per cent of all transitions. Some 30 per cent of transitions are not related to the labour market in the strict sense of the term, since they lead into or out of inactivity but without entering or leaving dependent employment or unemployment.

Transitions out of education or training vary considerably across the countries. In Denmark, Germany, Ireland, Portugal and the United Kingdom, many more leavers end up in dependent employment than in unemployment; in Greece, Spain and Italy, on the other hand, the opposite is the case. Only in Ireland, Germany, Denmark and the United Kingdom do more than the half of all transitions out of education or training lead to an 'active' labour force status (dependent employment, self-employment, family work, apprenticeship or community or military service).

Transitions out of unemployment vary even more. In some countries, a substantial proportion of the unemployed (as many as 43 per cent in Germany, which is an extreme case) do not enter dependent employment directly but end up in other, intermediate, stages, such as inactivity or retirement. Taking into account the transitions from unemployment into other 'active' labour market statuses, however, more than three-quarters, in some countries up to 90 per cent, end up in one active status or another.

The utility of dynamic employment studies based on the transition matrix could be much improved if the data were structured in greater detail and collected more frequently. Such a monitoring system (Auer and Kruppe, 1996) would provide a basis for more penetrating analyses and also cover not only the flows discussed here but also other target group-specific transitions, such as the flows into and out of long-term unemployment, self-employment, education and industry or occupation-specific transitions. While the European Labour Force (ELFS) gives faster access to the data, the ECHP measures much more precisely direct transitions from one employment relationship to another and provides additional information on multiple transitions. However, future waves of this panel survey should emphasize more important dimensions of transitions, such as working-time mobility and transitions related to labour market programmes.

As more waves become available, the stability of transition patterns could be tested and compared systematically with institutional arrangements and performance measures, in accordance with the European employment strategy. Aggregate studies (like that embarked on here) could be complemented by comparative studies based on individual transitions in the respective employment systems. Finally, wages plus additional income sources connected with the current and previous employment relation should be determined, at least approximately, in order to assess whether employment mobility is associated with social integration or leads to social exclusion or new forms of labour market segmentation.

NOTES

1. I wish to thank Günther Schmid for his very helpful comments, fruitful discussions and support in the writing of this chapter. He also provided the idea of benchmarking transitions in section 2. Responsibility for the chapter remains, of course, with the author.
2. Spain's recent success might be interpreted in this way.
3. Possible transitions within employment are those between permanent and fixed-term employment, between part-time, full-time and marginal employment, between dependent employment, self-employment and family work or any combination of these.
4. The check for double states, which would be very important for part-time employed persons, is still a problem in the data sets available.
5. The most important question, namely whether different patterns of transitions make a difference to labour market or employment performance, lies outside the scope of this chapter. Any attempt to answer it would require information on the stability of transition patterns over time.
6. Unfortunately, the ECHP provides only restricted information on transitions. In particular, there is a lack of information on transitions between various working times (moves from part-time to full-time and vice versa) and transitions into and out of labour market programmes.
7. The Spanish result obviously reflects the excessive use of fixed-term contracts (Schömann *et al.*, 1998). We do not have a plausible explanation for the low figure for Luxembourg.
8. The figure for France (52 per cent) very likely reflects a statistical artefact produced by a high number of changes in the labour force status between 'inactivity' and 'other economic inactivity', which could be due to a change in the questionnaire or in the coding. Taking these transitions out of the calculation, France is no longer an outlier but close to the EU 11 average.
9. Belgium, Denmark, France, Germany, Greece, Ireland, Italy, Luxembourg, Portugal, Spain, United Kingdom; the missing countries are Austria, the Netherlands, Sweden and Finland.
10. Any number of transitions estimated at less than 1 per cent of all transitions appears as (–) in the following tables.
11. This is calculated from Table 8.6 as the sum of transitions out of inactivity and other economic inactivity minus the flow from inactivity as well as from other economic inactivity into dependent employment or unemployment (column/row):

$$(\text{Total H} + \text{Total J}) - (\text{HA}+\text{JA}) - (\text{HF}+\text{JF})$$
$$= (12.1 + 9.0) - (2.7 + 1.6) - (1.6 + 1.0) = 14.2\%.$$

12. This is calculated from Table 8.6 as the sum of transitions into inactivity and other economic inactivity minus the flow from dependent employment or unemployment into inactivity or into other economic inactivity (row/column):

$$(\text{Total H} + \text{Total J}) - (\text{HA}+\text{JA}) - (\text{HF}+\text{JF})$$
$$= (11.5 + 9.6) - (2.6 + 1.6) - (1.7 + 0) = 15.2\%.$$

13. In other words, we would expect a narrowing of the difference in future due to the trends towards lifelong learning.
14. About 10 per cent are entries into retirement while about 6 per cent of all transitions are exits from retirement, mainly into economic inactivity. The meaning of transitions from retirement into economic inactivity is not fully clear.
15. We just do not know, for there is no information available in the data set.
16. This does not indicate a general decline in unemployment for the year 1994/5. The sum of all transitions out of unemployment (22.3 per cent of all transitions) is definitely lower than the sum of all inflows into unemployment (22.9 per cent of all transitions); this clearly shows the importance of taking a systematic view of the composition of *all* transitions.
17. While there is an overall decline in inactivity (housework, looking after children or other persons), this is not found for 'other economically inactive' people. Putting both groups together we could state a higher outflow of about 1.1 per cent of all transitions, which means a shrinking of the so-called 'silent reserve'.
18. Due to the low number of cases, Luxembourg is not included in this or the following section.
19. Table 8.7 cannot clearly distinguish between the system of initial education or training and further training or retraining for adults; it would be preferable to include only adults (older than 30 years) in this table. Nor is there any information on the content of education and training.
20. Excluding paid apprenticeship and special employment-related training schemes, and calculated per one million individuals aged 16 and over; see last row.
21. In the case of Greece, interpretation is very crude, as there is no information on the final status of a huge number of those leaving education. This is also partially the case in France and Spain, Belgium and Portugal.
22. For Greece, cf. note 19.
23. Cf. note 18.

BIBLIOGRAPHY

Auer, P. and T. Kruppe (1996), 'Labour Market Monitoring in EU Countries', in G. Schmid, J. O'Reilly and K. Schömann (eds), *International Handbook of Labour Market Policy and Evaluation*, Cheltenham, UK and Brookfield, US: Edward Elgar.

European Commission (1997), *Employment in Europe*, Luxembourg.

Eurostat (1996), *The European Community Household Panel: Survey methodology and implementation*, Luxembourg.

de Koning, J. and H. Mosley (eds) (2001), *Labour Market Policy and Unemployment. Impact and Process Evaluations in Selected European Countries*, Cheltenham, UK and Northampton, US: Edward Elgar.

Kruppe, T (2000), 'The Dynamic of Dependent Employment and Unemployment – A Methodological Comparison', WZB Discussion paper FS I 00-206, Wissenschaftszentrum Berlin für Sozialforschung, Berlin.

OECD (1996), *Employment Outlook*, Paris.

O'Reilly, J., I. Cebrián and M. Lallement (eds) (2000), *Working Time Changes. Social Integration Through Transitional Labour Markets*, Cheltenham, UK and Northampton, US: Edward Elgar.

Schmid, G. (1995), 'Is Full Employment Still Possible? Transitional Labour Markets as a New Strategy of Labour Market Policy', *Economic and Industrial Policy*, 16, 429–56.

Schmid, G., J. O'Reilly and K. Schömann (eds) (1996), *International Handbook of Labour Market Policy and Evaluation*, Cheltenham, UK and Brookfield, US: Edward Elgar.

Schömann, K., R. Rogowski and T. Kruppe (1998), *Labour Market Efficiency in the European Union. Employment protection and fixed-term contracts*, London: Routledge.

Simon, H.A. (1951), 'A Formal Theory of the Employment Relationship', *Econometrica*, 19, 293–305.

Tuijnman, Albert C. and Klaus Schömann (1996), 'Life-long Learning and Skill Formation', in G. Schmid, J. O'Reilly and K. Schömann (eds), *International Handbook of Labour Market Policy and Evaluation*, Cheltenham, UK and Brookfield, US: Edward Elgar, pp. 462–88.

Williamson, O.E., M.L. Wachter and J.E. Harris (1975), 'Understanding the Employment Relation: The Analysis of Idiosyncratic Exchange', *Bell Journal of Economics*, 6(1), 250–80.

9. From salary workers to entrepreneurial workers?

Nigel Meager and Peter Bates

Much recent discussion in the academic and policy fields about the role of self-employment in labour market development incorporates two key elements. The first is the view that self-employment has become quantitatively more important in recent years and is likely to continue to increase its significance as a labour market phenomenon in many European countries (Kruppe *et al.*, 1998). The second is the growing acceptance of the view that self-employment is a 'good thing', associated with dynamism, 'entrepreneurism' and job creation in the economy and labour market. This view came to prominence in the 1980s (Meager, 1993), influenced by a belief that, on the one hand, new small firms were a major contributor to job growth in advanced economies and, on the other hand, self-employment entry could be an option for the unemployed faced with declining opportunities in wage employment.

Most European countries have, since the late 1970s, introduced active labour market policies to encourage and subsidize unemployed people who enter self-employment. The popularity of such measures has waxed and waned somewhat in the last 20 years, however, and it is notable that, faced with evaluation evidence of disappointing net effects on job growth,[1] the scale of such measures has been reduced in some countries which had the largest schemes. However the promotion of 'entrepreneurism' in general, and self-employment in particular, remains a key plank in the labour market strategies of many countries. Further, this notion has also been enshrined at a European level as part of the European Employment Strategy, following the 1997 Amsterdam Treaty. Under this strategy, member states sign up to annual employment guidelines, grouped under four 'pillars', one of which has the title 'entrepreneurship', and includes the specific objective of *making it easier to start up and run businesses* and to *encourage the development of self-employment.*

The time is ripe to review these assumptions and to ask what role can be played by self-employment and by transitions between self-employment and other labour market states in the development of 'transitional labour markets' (Schmid, 1998). This chapter draws on the wide-ranging nature of this concept and its focus on the full range of labour market 'transitions' experienced by individuals and, in particular, its dynamic emphasis on the importance of transitions over the life cycle. We start by briefly considering some of the evidence on the labour market significance of self-employment, looking at trends in stocks and flows of self-employment in European countries. We then look in more detail, from the perspective of transitional labour markets, at the changing composition and dynamics of self-employment. First, we examine the growing dynamism of the labour market in many countries and the increasing rate of transition between different labour market states, including self-employment. It is clear that, under a regime where 'transitional labour markets' become more important, for any given overall level or rate of self-employment an increasing proportion of the workforce will experience one or more spells of self-employment during their lifetime.

Second, this development is reinforced by evidence that traditional patterns of self-employment are breaking down. Self-employment now affects a wider range of people than those meeting the traditional picture of the 'entrepreneur' or small business person, with more women, young people and ex-unemployed people entering self-employment than was previously the case. If, increasingly, more people and different kinds of people experience self-employment during their working lives, this raises important questions about the longer-term and life cycle implications of these developments, in particular the following:

- What are the implications of self-employment experience for income potential, security and the effective transition between labour market states and life cycle periods?
- Is it possible to identify personal characteristics associated with 'positive' transition routes, involving self-employment as a vehicle of social integration and adaptation, on the one hand, and those associated with negative routes, reinforcing disadvantage and exclusion, on the other?
- What are the institutional frameworks and policy measures necessary to reinforce the role of self-employment in 'positive' transitions?

This chapter represents a first step towards exploring these questions. We draw on the UK as an example, since this is a country in which these developments have been most marked and which may, therefore, provide a pointer to the longer-term implications of the growing role of self-employment in transitional labour markets.

1 DEVELOPMENTS IN SELF-EMPLOYMENT IN THE EU

Overall Trends in the Stock of Self-employment

As previous commentators have observed (OECD 1992, 2000; Meager, 1993; Luber and Gangl, 1997), historical trends towards declining self-employment in most industrialized economies have, since the early 1980s, halted and in many cases reversed. While this chapter does not explore the reasons for such trends, it is worth noting some key points made in earlier literature. First, self-employment is a very heterogeneous category, encompassing independent 'entrepreneurs' and traditional small business owner-proprietors at one extreme, through professional own-account workers and freelancers, to relatively unskilled construction and service sector workers at the other. The latter are often highly dependent on large organizations for their livelihoods, and their 'self-employment', in many cases, differs from dependent or wage employment in name only. Growing numbers of self-employed in these latter groups reflect the growth of outsourcing, subcontracting and 'lean production' strategies amongst larger organizations (Meager, 1993; Dietrich, 1996). Second, it is clear that the overall explanations for any apparent upsurge in self-employment are as diverse as the category of self-employment itself and, moreover, appear to vary significantly between countries according to their institutional and policy environment, sectoral structure and overall stage of economic development (Acs *et al.*, 1992). As we have argued elsewhere (Meager *et al.*, 1996), this diversity of composition and the lack of a single explanatory theoretical framework make it difficult to model the development of self-employment as a single aggregate.

In this chapter, therefore, our aims are more modest. First, we examine briefly the extent to which self-employment has, in fact, become more important as a labour market phenomenon in European countries. Second, we examine some of the implications of growing self-employment, and particularly of the emergence of self-employment as a transition route for groups of people not traditionally part of the small business sector.

Figure 9.1 draws on data published by Eurostat for the 15 current member states of the EU to present recent trends in the overall self-employment rate (that is the proportion of paid employment accounted for by self-employment) in these states. The first point to note is that there has been no dramatic overall resurgence in self-employment. For the EU as a whole, the overall self-employment rate has changed little and remained slightly lower in the mid-1990s than it was in the mid-1970s. Individual country experience varies enormously, however. There is a group of (mainly southern) countries with high self-employment rates (over 20 per cent) which have typically experienced falling self-employment. There is another group of (mainly northern)

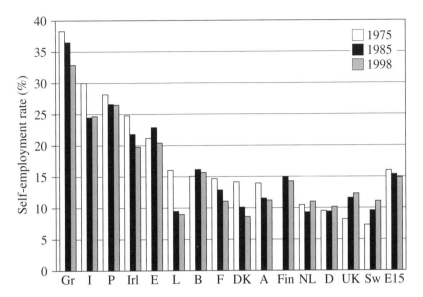

Figure 9.1   Self-employment rates in EU member states, 1975–98

countries with much lower self-employment rates, some of which (Denmark and France, for example) have recorded falling self-employment rates, while others have shown little change. In only two countries (the UK and Sweden) has the overall self-employment rate increased consistently over the period.

This picture is, however, strongly influenced by the inclusion of agriculture in the data. Self-employment rates are traditionally very high in agriculture (50 per cent or higher in nearly all EU member states). Countries with large agriculture sectors (particularly in the south) have, as a result, relatively large overall self-employment rates. The tendency in all countries for overall employment in agriculture to decline has the effect of reducing the overall self-employment rate in those countries with a large agricultural sector. For present purposes, therefore, it is of more interest to examine trends in non-agricultural self-employment rates, and these are presented (in indexed form) in Figure 9.2, using data from the Community Labour Force Survey (LFS) for the 12 countries that were member states of the EU prior to the accession of Austria, Sweden and Finland.

These data (which cover a shorter period than those in Figure 9.1), paint a more consistent picture. In all countries other than Denmark (where self-employment rates have fallen; although even here there is a slight increase between 1989 and 1996), France and Greece (where they have remained more or less constant), the non-agricultural self-employment rate was higher in 1996 than in 1983. These data give somewhat more support, therefore, to the notion

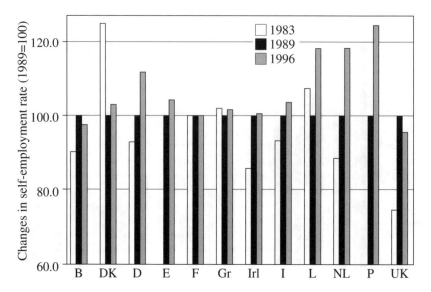

Source: Eurostat, Community Labour Force Survey (own calculations).

*Figure 9.2   Non-agricultural self-employment rates in EU member states,
1983–96*

that self-employment is generally increasing, although the increase is not in all
countries a dramatic or continuous one. Indeed, in the country that produced
the fastest and largest proportional increase in self-employment during the
1980s (the UK), the 1990s have seen a decline in self-employment (Meager,
1999).

For reasons discussed above, it is unlikely to be fruitful to attempt to forecast future trends in self-employment in these EU countries. While the
economic cycle clearly has an influence on self-employment levels and
rates, it is important to stress that there are several cyclical influences on
self-employment, which complicate any attempts to forecast aggregate self-
employment stocks. In particular, on the one hand, growing unemployment
and diminishing opportunities for wage employment (Bögenhold and Staber,
1991; Storey, 1991) act as a 'push' factor encouraging people to enter self-
employment. On the other hand, successful creation of and survival in a self-
employed enterprise are more likely in times of economic growth. These
influences act in opposite directions and their net effect on the level of self-
employment is not predictable a priori (Meager, 1992). As we have argued
elsewhere (Meager, 1993), the UK's exceptional experience in the 1980s,
when self-employment grew throughout the decade, appeared to involve

'unemployment push' during the early part of the decade (with high and growing rates of inflow to self-employment from unemployment). In contrast, the 'pull' effect of economic growth dominated during the late 1980s, reinforced by specific factors such as the effects of deregulation of the financial capital market and rapid house price inflation, both of which greatly eased access to capital for potential self-employed people during this period.

Similar country-specific factors have also been put forward to explain developments in self-employment in other countries (OECD, 1992 2000; Meager *et al.*, 1992; Luber and Gangl, 1997). Thus the relatively high benefit replacement ratio and long duration of unemployment benefits in Denmark (and the associated lack of incentive for the unemployed to consider self-employment) is argued to have contributed to the relative insensitivity of Danish self-employment to unemployment rates.[2] Similarly, the traditionally tight regulatory framework for business start-up and self-employment entry in Germany, as well as a more rigorous approach by financial institutions to business start-ups and a relatively undeveloped venture capital market, have been argued to inhibit self-employment entry among groups such as the unemployed.

Putting aside such country-specific and cyclical factors, however, and looking for common features encouraging self-employment, it is worth noting that many of the factors identified in the literature as contributing to recent self-employment growth remain a feature of the economic terrain in most European countries. These include, in particular:

- a continuing shift towards employment in the service sector, where self-employment rates are traditionally much higher than in manufacturing;
- changing contractual arrangements among larger organizations in the corporate and public sectors, with a greater emphasis on outsourcing and subcontracting arrangements;
- a policy stance at European and national level, which is broadly supportive of self-employment and business start-ups, and which includes a variety of specific initiatives to encourage self-employment, both through regulatory and taxation reform and through subsidies (especially for unemployed people);
- an increasing tendency for women to enter self-employment (which is observed in most EU member states – Luber and Leicht, 1998), coupled with growing female labour market participation rates, will contribute to a growth in overall self-employment rates.

Against this background, it is a reasonable working hypothesis that non-agricultural self-employment levels and rates will continue to increase and that self-employment will become a more prominent option in European labour markets of the future.

Self-employment Flows

Given our emphasis on transitional labour markets, however, our interest is also in inflows to and outflows from self-employment. What can be said about these flows, particularly in countries where self-employment has grown? To address these questions requires the use of panel data or retrospective work history data, and we make use of such data in subsequent sections of the chapter, where we focus on the UK.

To provide a wider context for the UK flows analysis, however, it is worth noting earlier research (Meager, 1993) that identified important differences between European countries in the volume and composition of flows to and from self-employment. Thus, for example, in the UK (compared with France and Germany), women and young people were significantly overrepresented in the inflow, as were people coming into self-employment from unemployment rather than from dependent employment or economic inactivity. The earlier research also looked at the activity of newly self-employed people and showed a disproportionate representation of self-employed inflows in the UK in certain, mainly low-margin, service sector activities.

This evidence makes it clear not only that the sources and composition of flows into and out of self-employment vary significantly between countries but also that the size of those flows relative to the stock of self-employment varies significantly. Transition matrices show, for example, that some countries (of which the UK is again a prime example) have relatively high rates of inflow to and outflow from the stock of self-employment[3] and, moreover, that these flow rates have been growing over time.[4]

These patterns of transitions, particularly in countries where self-employment has been growing, are, we would argue, consistent with a hypothesis that traditional models of self-employment may be breaking down. At the risk of simplification, such models have often seen self-employment as a largely distinct segment of the labour market, drawing on a *petit bourgeois* class in the small business and agricultural sector (and to some extent in the liberal professions). A key assumption of such models is that there is relatively little mobility between self-employment and dependent employment and, in so far as such mobility exists, it is commonly an event which occurs towards the middle or end of the working life, with individuals entering self-employment having accumulated financial and human capital in dependent employment and with the move into self-employment being a transition between wage employment and retirement. Thus self-employment was seen either as a state which people in certain occupations and sectors tended to occupy for most of their working lives or as a state into which people moved later in life for career or life style reasons. In countries such as the UK, however, it is clear that self-employment now plays a more dynamic role than is suggested by this kind of analysis, with high flow rates (in both directions) between self-employment, wage employment, unemployment and economic inactivity and high and growing inflow rates among young people and women particularly.

Crucially, we can no longer see self-employment as a discrete component of the labour market, affecting only a small minority of the workforce. The flow data suggest (see the UK evidence in this chapter) not only that a much higher proportion of the workforce experience self-employment spells during their working lives than is implied by the stock data alone but also that these spells often occur earlier in the working life than was previously the case.

National differences remain, however, and if we compare the position of the UK and Germany, for example, it appears that German self-employment remained (at least until the most recent period) closer to the traditional model than was the case in the UK. Inflows to self-employment are proportionately smaller in Germany and more concentrated among older age groups than is true for the UK. Further, compared with the UK, a much higher proportion of the inflows to self-employment in Germany come from dependent employment and a significant proportion of the outflows from self-employment in Germany are to retirement. There is recent evidence, however, that the traditional pattern is also breaking down in Germany, with a growth in self-employment flows (in and out) and a growth in inflows to self-employment among younger people. The dominant source of those inflows in Germany has, however, remained dependent employment (contrasting with the position in the UK and France, for example), reflecting perhaps the greater regulation of entry to self-employment occupations, the stricter capital requirements imposed by German financial institutions and the (until recently) relatively small scale of public subsidy for the unemployed to set up in self-employment in Germany.

To summarize, even if dramatic claims of an upsurge in European self-employment are not justified, there is nevertheless evidence of growth, with other countries following the earlier path of the UK in the 1980s. There is also evidence of a greater dynamism in self-employment, with more people experiencing self-employment spells during their working lives, with some people experiencing such spells earlier in their working lives and people entering self-employment whose characteristics do not fit the traditional picture of the self-employed. From a transitional labour markets perspective, if more and different kinds of people are experiencing self-employment and if such an extension of self-employment experience is increasingly an objective of public policy, what are the effects on the longer-term outcomes and economic well-being for such people?

2   RECENT EVIDENCE ON SELF-EMPLOYMENT TRANSITIONS IN THE UK

We begin our examination of the UK by analysing self-employment transitions, drawing on the British Household Panel Survey (BHPS), which is a nationally representative panel survey of over 10 000 individuals which began in 1990. The data were supplemented in waves 2 and 3 with retrospective information on respondents' employment history in previous decades and in some of the analysis that follows we use combined files linking the panel waves with the retrospective work history data (Halpin, 1997).

Modelling Transition Rates

We have used BHPS data to model the factors influencing the likelihood of individual transitions into and out of self-employment (see the statistical annex to this chapter). Key results from the models include the following.

1.   Men have a much higher risk of moving into self-employment than women but only a slightly lower risk of leaving self-employment than women, confirming that female self-employment, although less common than male self-employment, is almost as 'stable' as its male counterpart. This suggests that the emphasis by previous authors[5] on lower female survival rates[6] may be misplaced and that growing rates of entry to self-employment among women will, eventually, lead to a convergence of aggregate male and female self-employment rates.
2.   Educational level is an important influence on self-employment transitions. Better qualified people are more likely to enter self-employment (although the coefficient on the most highly qualified group is not significant). As far as transitions out of self-employment are concerned, the likelihood of making such a transition increases with qualification level. This suggests increasing 'dynamism' of self-employment flows with higher levels of qualification; that is, the least qualified are the least likely to become self-employed but once self-employed are the most likely to remain so.
3.   There are clear sectoral patterns in transition probabilities, which reflect sectoral differences in overall self-employment rates (Meager, 1993); thus the highest likelihoods of entry into self-employment (and the lowest likelihoods of exit) are in construction and agriculture and the lowest rates are in the extractive and manufacturing sectors.
4.   Occupational level is an influence on transition likelihoods. Those in managerial occupations are most likely to enter self-employment and those in clerical occupations least likely to enter self-employment (and

most likely to leave it), while self-employment in craft and skilled occupations is the most stable, in the sense that the self-employed in these
categories are least likely to make a transition out of self-employment.
5. Birth cohort is an important influence. Compared with those born in 1966
    or subsequently, older cohorts are more likely to enter self-employment
    (although the likelihood is highest in the middle-aged ranges). Stability
    in self-employment increases strongly with age: those in the youngest
    cohort are most likely and those in the oldest least likely to leave self-
    employment.

Cumulative Incidence of Self-employment Spells

We have argued above that the growing incidence of self-employment among
'non-traditional' groups (women, ex-unemployed and young people, for
example) and the greater dynamism of self-employment among some of these
groups imply increasingly that the self-employment rate underestimates the
proportion of the workforce likely to experience self-employment during their
lifetime. Evidence for this can be seen from Table 9.1, which looks at data
from the first four waves of the BHPS, identifying the number of spells of self-
employment that individuals have had (that is from 0 to 4) over the four-year
period. It shows that 13.5 per cent of the working age population have had at
least one self-employment spell over a four-year period. This means that even
over a relatively short space of time, the share of the population experiencing
self-employment is over half as large again as the self-employment stock at a
point of time (at wave 4, 8.7 per cent of the working age population were self-
employed). Even this is an underestimate, moreover, since some people may

Table 9.1   Incidence of self-employment spells over four waves of the BHPS

| | No. of self-employment spells (%) | | | | | | (%) self-employed wave 4 | |
	0	1	2	3	4	Total (n=100%)		Total (n=10)
All cases	86.5	3.9	2.0	1.9	5.7	5 216	8.7	5 481
Men	81.0	4.5	2.7	2.8	8.9	2 706	13.0	2 838
Women	92.5	3.3	1.3	0.8	2.2	2 509	4.0	2 643
16–24	95.2	2.2	1.6	0.6	0.4	702	2.0	965
25–34	89.1	3.7	1.5	1.6	4.0	1 395	7.3	1 396
35–44	83.8	4.5	2.8	2.2	6.6	1 233	10.5	1 234
45–54	83.1	4.3	2.3	2.2	8.1	1 207	11.9	1 208
55–64	83.2	4.3	1.6	2.4	8.5	679	11.8	679

Source: BHPS, waves 1–4.

have been self-employed between BHPS waves and not recorded in these data. The gender and age patterns in Table 9.1 are as expected, with the proportion of women with no recent spells of self-employment being considerably higher than the proportion of men. Note, however, that 7.5 per cent of women have had self-employment experience in a four-year period, which compares with only 4 per cent who are self-employed at wave 4. In other words, over four years, the proportion with self-employment experience is nearly twice as high as the stock, reflecting the more 'dynamic' nature of female than male self-employment. This point is reinforced when we look at the number of spells of self-employment that people have had during the previous four years: whereas women account for 40 per cent of all those who have had only one spell, they account for a mere 18 per cent of those who have been continuously self-employed.

As far as age is concerned, older people (in this case those aged 35 and above) are more likely to have had some recent self-employment experience than their younger counterparts, and the effects of age are even more marked when one looks at the number of self-employment spells in the four-year period. Thus people in the oldest (55–64) age group are more than 20 times as likely to have had four years' continuous self-employment experience than are those in the youngest group. Thus again we see not only that self-employment is rarer amongst younger people but also that it is more unstable.

3   SELF-EMPLOYMENT AND INCOME LEVELS OVER THE LIFETIME

Having examined the character of self-employment transitions, we turn to the central interest of the chapter, namely the impact of such transitions on the individuals involved and on their current and subsequent likelihood of social inclusion or exclusion. While recognizing that there are many ways of defining social inclusion/exclusion,[7] and that the notion of social exclusion may encompass a range of phenomena, it is clear that many of these are, in turn, associated with poverty. Indeed, a key reason underlying policy makers' concern with social exclusion is that it contributes to and results from poverty. In this light, we take the view, for present purposes, that income levels remain the best single indicator of the likelihood of social exclusion. We focus, therefore, on the income levels of the self-employed while they are self-employed as well as on the subsequent income levels of those who have previously made self-employment transitions. We have a particular interest in the cumulative impact on incomes in later life of job histories that include self-employment transitions during the working lifetime.

Issues of Measurement and Underreporting

UK evidence on the incomes of the self-employed is not extensive and has been bedevilled by the issue of underreporting. The self-employed are commonly believed, given the opportunity and the incentive to do so, to underreport their income levels in tax and social security data[8] and most commentators assume that this tendency carries over (albeit to a lesser extent) in their responses to anonymous social surveys.[9]

The issue of what counts as 'income' is also clearly more complex in the case of the self-employed than for employees, given the different ways of computing business profits and the opportunity to offset against tax a range of business expenses and capital expenditures. The fact that self-employment incomes typically fluctuate much more than those of employees also implies that the level of self-employment income for an individual or household may be very sensitive to the period over which it is measured.[10]

The few UK studies that include some consideration of self-employment incomes (for example, Brown, 1992; Curran and Burrows, 1988) acknowledge that these issues make comparison between employee and self-employed incomes difficult, but do not tackle them. Evidence from the USA, where there is a more extensive literature on self-employment incomes, confirms that underreporting is indeed an intractable problem, which is rarely tackled except through crude assumptions about the degree of underreporting (Aronson, 1991).

Notable exceptions to this pattern, in the UK, are found in the work of Pissarides and Weber (1989) and Baker (1993). Both studies use household expenditure data to estimate econometrically the extent to which the self-employed underrepresent their incomes. The methodology involves relating expenditure patterns to income levels for both employees and the self-employed and, subject to a number of (fairly strong) assumptions, drawing inferences about the extent to which the self-employed are likely to understate their incomes. The two studies yield broadly similar results. Pissarides and Weber find that self-employment incomes are underreported by about a third on average, while Baker's estimates suggest underreporting of between one-sixth and one-third, with no clear trend in the degree of underreporting over time. Both studies find that underreporting varies between occupational and sectoral groups.

The research reported here offers no significant methodological improvement on the previous work on underreporting. Indeed, our view is that the search for such improvement with secondary data sets would be in vain and that, in the absence of primary research focused on self-employment incomes per se, there is little likelihood of being able reliably to adjust incomes data for underreporting. We would argue, nevertheless, that the data sources most subject to underreporting will be official administrative data (taxation and social security data, for example). Governmental social surveys (for example, the LFS), in which data are anonymously collected and have no links with taxation compliance or means-testing, might be expected to exhibit lower degrees of underreporting, while social surveys that are independently conducted for academic and related purposes (for example, the British Household Panel Survey, used here) might be expected to generate even less underreporting of self-employed incomes.[11] Moreover, it is also worth noting that the data set used here to look at the lifetime impact of self-employment on economic well-being (the Survey of Retirement and Retirement Plans – SRRP) gives us even less reason to assume differential underreporting between the employed and self-employed. Crucially, a high proportion of respondents surveyed in SRRP were retired and it is unlikely that retirement income is subject to the same degree of underreporting as earned income in self-employment. Further, even among respondents who were not retired at the time of the survey, only a small minority (around 5 per cent) were *currently* self-employed. Our comparisons are primarily between the retirement experience and incomes of those who have been self-employed at some time and the experience and incomes of those who have not; and there is no a priori reason to anticipate that underreporting will be systematically greater among the former group than among the latter.

Current Self-employment and Income Levels

Table 9.2 presents BHPS data on average net monthly incomes for employees and the self-employed broken down by employment history. We can see that self-employed workers receive a mean monthly net labour income that is 7 per cent greater than employees. An important point to note, however, is that earned incomes among the self-employed are considerably more dispersed than those of employees, with a greater proportion of self-employed workers

Table 9.2   Distribution of monthly net labour income, by employment status

£ per month	Mean	Std dev.	Median	Ratio of 90th to 10th percentile	Cases
Total employment	831.3	655.4	732.9	7.08	4 790
Self-employed	884.0	1015.2	704.8	22.36	621
Employees	823.5	583.0	736.7	6.29	4 169

Source: BHPS, wave 5 and combined retrospectives.

recording labour incomes at the extremes of the distribution (note, in particular, the much greater difference between labour incomes at the 90th and 10th percentiles of the distribution in the case of the self-employed than in the case of employees). Thus the higher mean income among the self-employed is heavily influenced by a few very high earners; the difference between the median incomes of employees and self-employed is smaller and the median self-employed income is actually some 4 per cent less than that of employees.

It is, of course, possible that such differences between employees and the self-employed also reflect differences in working patterns and hours. It is, for example, already well-documented in most countries (Meager, 1993) that the distribution of weekly hours differs between the two groups, with the self-employed exhibiting a greater dispersion and including a larger proportion who work very long weekly hours. The UK is no exception, as shown in the LFS data in Table 9.3. Both self-employed men and women work significantly longer hours than their employee counterparts, although in the case of female self-employed there is also a relatively large group working very short hours.

To allow for the influence of working hours on earned income levels and returning to the BHPS data, Table 9.4 shows distributions of *hourly* net income, which exhibit broadly the same patterns for monthly net income, with a higher mean but lower median income for the self-employed compared with employees and a distribution with a much broader spread (as shown by the higher values for the standard deviation and the 90/10 ratio). Thus it would

Table 9.3   Distribution of working hours, by employment status and gender, Spring 1995

Usual weekly hours	Employees		Self-employed	
	Men	Women	Men	Women
10 or under	2.4	9.9	2.9	19.1
11–20	2.6	18.2	3.9	18.8
21–30	2.2	14.7	4.9	14.2
31–45	55.2	48.1	35.3	23.7
45–50	17.6	5.0	15.3	7.8
51–60	14.1	2.7	18.9	6.7
Over 60	5.1	1.0	17.3	8.3
Not known	0.8	0.4	1.5	1.4
Total (n = thousands)	11 599	10 588	2 544	811

Source: Labour Force Survey.

Table 9.4   Distribution of hourly net labour income, by employment status

£ per month	Mean	Std dev.	Median	Ratio of 90th to 10th percentile	Cases
Total employment	5.0	3.4	4.3	3.37	4 669
Self-employed	5.3	6.1	3.8	11.00	582
Employees	5.0	2.9	4.4	3.07	4 087

Source: BHPS, wave 5 and combined retrospectives.

seem that the high level of polarization in the distribution of self-employed incomes does not primarily stem from a similar polarization in the working hours of the self-employed. Rather, if anything, the difference between the two groups is accentuated in the comparison of hourly rather than monthly incomes, raising the possibility that the long hours worked by some self-employed may reflect necessity arising from their low effective hourly earnings. It is notable that nearly 20 per cent of self-employed workers record hourly net earnings of £2 or less (compared to 4 per cent of employees).

These overall patterns disguise very different situations for men and women. As shown in Table 9.5, again looking at hourly income (to control for the greater extent of part-time working among female self-employed), not only is the distribution of female self-employed income considerably more dispersed than that of males but the overrepresentation of women among the low-income self-employed is partly compensated for by a group of very high-earnings self-employed women. It is notable, for example, that although the median hourly income of self-employed women is less than that of their male counterparts (a similar pattern to that found among employees), the mean net hourly income of self-employed women is actually somewhat higher than that of males, owing to the influence of a small number of high-earning self-employed women.

Table 9.5   Average hourly net labour income, by gender

	Male				Female			
	Mean	Median	90/10 ratio	Base	Mean	Median	90/10 ratio	Base
Self-employed	5.28	3.8	9.4	441	5.34	3.4	31.4	131
Employees	5.38	4.8	3.1	2 052	4.52	4.0	2.8	2 035

Source: BHPS, wave 5 and combined retrospectives.

Nevertheless, it is clear that relatively fewer self-employed men are on very low incomes than is the case for self-employed women. Thus, for example, 24 per cent of self-employed men earn less than the lowest decile of the overall net hourly earned income distribution (that is, employees and self-employed taken together), while for self-employed women the corresponding figure is 36 per cent. The gender difference at the upper end of the distribution, however, is much smaller, with 16 per cent of self-employed males earning more than the highest decile of the overall net hourly earned income distribution, compared with 13 per cent of self-employed females.

The overall picture, therefore, is that the self-employed are more likely to be in the extremes of the labour income distribution than is the case for employees (and this polarization is greater when we account for differences in hours worked). This analysis does not, however, show that these differences are due to employment status per se (rather than, for example, other differences between the self-employed and employees, such as their gender or the type of work they do). In order to examine the influence of self-employed status itself, we need to hold such other characteristics constant through multivariate analysis.

In earlier work (Meager *et al.*, 1996) we undertook logit analysis using the cross-sectional data from the first wave of the BHPS, which examined the effect of being self-employed (controlling for characteristics such as sex, age, sector of occupation, working time and education) on an individual's likelihood of being in the bottom or the top decile of the overall net labour income distribution. The analysis showed that, relative to an employee, a self-employed person has over three times the odds of being in the lowest decile group of the overall labour income distribution. In other words, there is a distinct self-employment effect that cannot be reduced to the personal and occupational/business activity characteristics of people who happen to be self-employed. As far as the likelihood of falling into the highest income decile is concerned, the model showed that, although the self-employed are also over-represented in this 'rich' category, there is no statistically significant impact of being self-employed per se, once the effects of the other variables are controlled for. Rather, the key influences increasing the likelihood of being in this income group are being male, being older, being better qualified, being in a higher-level occupation and being in certain sectors, notably banking and finance.

In simple terms, therefore, this earlier analysis showed that personal characteristics (such as qualifications) are an important factor explaining or contributing to labour market 'success' (as measured by the likelihood of high incomes) and that, given these characteristics, current employment status (employment or self-employment) has little effect. At the other end of the spectrum, however, qualification and occupational level seem to be less important in contributing to the probability of a very low income but being self-employed significantly increases that probability.

The only factors that contribute consistently to an individual's probability of achieving both a very high income and a very low income are gender and working time. As already noted, however, there is a group of self-employed women that is strongly represented among the higher income levels. This latter finding raises the possibility that there may be some groups of women, in particular, for whom self-employment, perhaps on a part-time basis, and perhaps also in combination with part-time dependent employment, offers advantages in career terms. As has been noted elsewhere (Meager *et al.*, 1992), there is evidence from both the UK and Germany of significant growth in female self-employment among more highly qualified (managerial and professional) occupational groups. One hypothesis advanced for this is that it reflects recent growth in female penetration of these occupations and that women's expectations of career progression have also been raised. In practice, however, such expectations are often frustrated in the corporate sector and this may lead women to seek career development through self-employment, particularly where this also offers more scope for flexibility in terms of working time and the ability to combine domestic and family commitments with working life (this view is reinforced by case study evidence of the motivations of professional women setting up in self-employment: see OECD, 1990). Previous research (see also Carter and Cannon, 1988) reviewing the growth in female self-employment in the UK during the 1980s, argued that 'self-employment represents an attractive option (or in some cases the only viable option) for women who wish (or need) to combine participation in the labour market with domestic responsibilities' (Johnson, 1991: 8–9).

Strong support for this perspective, in the UK at least, comes from detailed analysis of the characteristics of self-employed women, from the LFS:

> In all age groups self-employment is more common among women with children, and more common among those with two or more than those with just one. It is also apparent that the younger those children are the greater the effect, with higher rates for those with children under 10. Moreover, there are differences in each age group, confirming that the presence of children is a more important influence than marital status. (Daly, 1991: 117)

What remains unclear from our research to date, however, is how far such trends are also reflected in other European countries (the low level of provision of state funding for childcare may be an important factor in the UK) and whether the beneficial use of self-employment as a transitional 'bridge' in the labour market is confined to well-qualified women. Are there other groups for whom it can play this role, and under what circumstances and with what support?

The Impact of Prior Self-employment on Current Incomes

So far, the observed relationship between employment status and the income distribution does not take account of previous work history. Of particular interest from our perspective of transitional labour markets, however, is the relationship between current income and previous transitions. In particular we are interested in the effect of previous spells of self-employment on current income levels: what effect does having been self-employed at various stages in the past have on an individual's current income potential? To examine this, we have used the wave 5 BHPS data set combined with retrospective work history information and undertaken a similar logit analysis, incorporating also variables relating to individuals' previous work history experience. The models are presented in the statistical annex below.

Looking first at the results relating to the likelihood of falling into the lowest net monthly income decile, it can be seen that some but not all of the variables relating to self-employment experience have large and statistically significant influences on this likelihood. Thus, compared with someone who has never had self-employment experience, someone who is currently self-employed has significantly higher odds of being in the lowest income decile, and the odds are similar whether or not the person has also had a self-employment spell or spells prior to the current one. For those who are not currently self-employed, however, the effects of having been self-employed in the past have much less impact on the odds of falling into this low-income group, and in this model the effect is not statistically significant. It would seem, therefore, that for those currently in the labour market, it is *current* self-employment which increases the risk of poverty, whether or not this has also been preceded by previous spells of self-employment. For those who have moved out of self-employment. For those who have moved out of self-employment altogether, however, previous self-employment has little or no impact on the risk of very low incomes. Another way of looking at this is that, for those still in the labour market, income levels can recover from the impact of prior spells of low-income self-employment. The impact of the other variables in the model on the risk of low incomes is largely in line with prior expectation and previous research (Meager *et al.*, 1996).

Turning to the analysis for the highest income decile, of particular interest is the finding that, just as the previous research showed that being self-employed did not in itself increase the risk of falling into the highest income decile, the same is true of previous experience of self-employment. Thus, compared with those who have never been self-employed, there is no statistically significant impact on the odds of being in the highest income decile associated with different degrees of prior and/or current self-employment experience. Once again, the impact of self-employment experience appears to occur at the lower rather than the higher end of the income distribution. It is other personal and employment characteristics that increase the likelihood of a very high income (gender, qualifications, occupation and prior workforce experience and so on).

Self-employment during the Lifetime and Incomes in Later Life

Having looked at cross-sectional relationships between employment states, on the one hand, and income levels and distribution, on the other, and having looked also at how current incomes may be influenced by prior experience of self-employment, we now turn to a longer-run perspective on work histories and incomes. The objective here is to understand the possible cumulative impact of spells of self-employment during the working life on outcomes in later life. For this, we need a sample of older people and information on current incomes and other indicators of economic well-being (savings, pensions and so on), as well as work history data. For this part of the analysis, we have made use of a unique UK data set, the Survey of Retirement and Retirement Plans (SRRP) conducted in the late 1980s on behalf of the UK Department of Social Security. This is a random national cross-sectional survey of older people (just over 3500 people, aged 55–69 at the time of the survey, were interviewed), with complete (post-education) retrospective work history data, allowing detailed analysis of the relationship between different career paths and subsequent outcomes.

Using the work history data from this data set, we created a lifetime work history variable to summarize whether or not individual work histories included spells of self-employment and whether the work history was continuous or included spells of unemployment or economic inactivity. At a general level, these data confirm that some of the patterns observed in cross-sectional data regarding the influence of self-employment experience on incomes are replicated in the longer term. Thus it is clear that some of the key aspects of the distribution of the incomes of the self-employed relative to employees are also found in the distribution of the incomes of those with self-employment experience in their history, relative to those with only dependent employment experience. In particular, the distribution of incomes of those in the former group is more polarized, with higher proportions in the upper and lower ends of the distribution than is the case for those in the latter group. Table 9.6 shows that for each of the eight categories defined by gender, retirement status and continuity of work history, net income inequality in old age, as measured by the Gini coefficient, is higher among those with periods of self-employment in their work histories than among those who have only been employees.

Among men, in particular, this greater dispersion primarily reflects an over-representation of the 'ex-self-employed' at the lower end of the distribution,

Table 9.6   *Gini coefficients (net weekly total income distributions) for*
55–69-year-olds, by work history pattern

	Work history pattern	
	Work history, employee only	Work history, including self-employment
Retired people		
Continuous work histories	0.35	0.41
Work histories including unemployment/inactivity	0.43	0.44
Still working		
Continuous work histories	0.32	0.52
Work histories including unemployment/inactivity	0.42	0.47
Men		
Continuous work histories	0.35	0.49
Work histories including unemployment/inactivity	0.32	0.44
Women		
Continuous work histories	0.42	0.52
Work histories including unemployment/inactivity	0.44	0.45

Source: Survey of Retirement and Retirement Plans (1988).

and to a lesser extent at the upper end. To see this latter point, consider Table 9.7. Taking all men in the sample together, some 24 per cent have self-employment experience. Among the (relatively few) men in the lowest decile group of the overall income distribution, however, this proportion rises to 57 per cent. Even among those in the lowest quartile group, the proportion with self-employment experience remains high (46 per cent). At the other end of the spectrum, self-employed men are indeed also overrepresented in the very rich (top decile) group, but only slightly (27 per cent), and their representation in the top quartile group is virtually the same as their representation in the sample as a whole. Among male ex-self-employed, the greater income dispersion than among ex-employees comes about primarily through overrepresentation at the lower end of the distribution, and to a lesser extent at the upper end.

Among women, however, the pattern is once again different. Women with self-employment experience are relatively rare, but there is no tendency for them to be disproportionately concentrated in the lower tails of the income

Table 9.7   Composition of income distribution tails, by work history and
            gender (per cent)

| Work history | Percentage in highest/lowest decile and quartile groups of distribution of usual net weekly income (whole sample), by work history pattern – men only | | | | |
	Lowest decile (<£19.25)	Lowest quartile (<£41.91)	Highest quartile (>£123.56)	Highest decile (>£185.23)	Whole sample
Men					
Employee only	43.1	54.0	76.6	73.3	76.2
Including self-					
employment	56.9	46.0	23.4	26.7	23.8
N (=100%)	65	124	739	307	1 887
Women					
Employee only	91.9	90.9	86.7	85.2	90.6
Including self-					
employment	8.1	9.1	13.3	14.8	9.4
N (=100%)	297	780	166	54	1 854

Source: Survey of Retirement and Retirement Plans (1988).

distribution. Indeed, the proportion of self-employed women in the lowest decile and quartile groups is lower than their proportion among women in the sample as a whole. At the other end of the distribution, however, there is a clear tendency for a higher than average proportion of ex-self-employed women to be found in the 'rich' categories. In simple terms, therefore, it seems that although (compared with men) women as a whole are considerably over-represented in the 'poor' categories and underrepresented in the 'rich' categories, ex-self-employed women (a small minority) are, if anything, slightly better off than their ex-employee counterparts.

Taken together, these results suggest that a growth in self-employment might be expected, other things being equal, to increase the size of the group who are 'poor' in old age but that any shift towards a growing share of female employment would not tend to exacerbate this trend. At first glance, this seems inconsistent with the BHPS findings in the earlier sections, where we observed that self-employed women were disproportionately likely to be found in the lowest income groups. It should, however, be noted that the Retirement and Retirement Plans data, collected as they were in late 1988, are unlikely to be picking up the full effect of the rapid growth in female self-employment in the 1980s, which would not yet have fed through into incomes in this older age group.

Once again, however, the key question for the current analysis is how to disentangle the effect of self-employment on incomes and economic well-being in later life from all the other various factors which may affect this, such as gender, periods of unemployment or inactivity, occupation, sector and so on. To explore this, we used the SRRP to conduct a very similar analysis to those undertaken with BHPS data above. The logit models can be found in the statistical annex below. The analysis looked at the influence of self-employment experience in the working life, alongside some of these other variables, on the likelihood of an individual being 'poor' or 'rich' in later life (that is in the 55–69 age range), the main difference being that this time we included income from all sources in the analysis rather than simply labour incomes, to allow for the possibility that self-employment experience also affects the ability to acquire pension entitlements, build up savings and so on.

The results show that, compared with a man, a woman has nearly five times the odds of being in the lowest income decile group. Similarly, a retired person in the 55–69-year-old age range is twice as likely as someone of the same age who is still working to be in the lowest income decile group. Turning to work history, those with work histories punctuated by unemployment or inactivity have 1.4 times the odds of being in the poorest group compared with those who have worked continuously. Of most significance for the present analysis, however, is the finding that those who have self-employment experience have nearly twice the odds of falling into this income group compared with those who have worked only as employees. Other points of interest are that an entitlement to an occupational pension (from one's former employer) significantly reduces the odds of being in the lowest income decile group, as does the possession of savings above £10 000.

Looking at the likelihood of falling into the highest decile group of the overall net income distribution, the results are generally the obverse of those above, with variables that increase the odds of being in the lowest decile group reducing the odds of being in the highest decile group, and vice versa. Thus being female, retired or having a broken work history significantly reduces the odds of being in the top decile, while having high levels of savings or an occupational pension entitlement significantly increases it. The most notable difference between the two models, however, relates to the 'self-employment' variable. It appears that experience of self-employment in the work history has, other things being equal, no significant effect on the odds of falling into the highest income decile group. It will be recalled that precisely the same finding emerged from our analyses of cross-section data, in which we looked at the influence of current self-employment (and of previous self-employment) on the likelihood of falling into the tails of the *current* labour income distribution.

So far we have conducted the analysis in terms of the total net incomes of people in the 55–69 age group. Also of interest, however, is the make-up of

Table 9.8   Income and savings, by work history (continuous work histories only)

Work history category	No. in category	With incomes less than £60 per week and savings less than £3000 (%)
Retired, employee only	572	24.4
Retired, incl. self-employment	108	32.4
Working, employee only	303	5.2
Working, incl. self-employment	139	18.0

Source: Survey of Retirement and Retirement Plans (1988).

those incomes. Thus, in so far as there is a significant group of older people with self-employment experience in low income groups, we can ask how far that is due to a lack of (non-state) pension entitlement, to low levels of savings/financial assets, or to a deficiency in other sources of income in later life. Table 9.8 looks at the relationship between low incomes in retirement and savings patterns, separating out, by work history category, those who have a usual net weekly income of less than £60 per week and who also have savings of less than £3000. These are expressed as percentages of all those in the work history category in question. Although caution needs to be exercised because of the small sample sizes, the data suggest that those with self-employment in their work histories (whether currently retired or working) are considerably more likely than their counterparts with employee work histories to have *both* low incomes *and* low savings levels in later life.

Table 9.9 presents a similar analysis of the relationship between low incomes (less than £60 net per week) and lack of occupational and private pension provision. Again, the data indicate that those with self-employment in their work histories are much more likely than their counterparts who have only been employees both to have low incomes and to have made no contributions to occupational and/or private pension schemes.

Finally, Table 9.10 looks at whether, among those with low savings, the lack of savings is compensated for by (non-state) pension entitlements, or vice versa. Once again, the data show a somewhat greater concentration of low savings levels and lack of pension entitlements among those with self-employment in their work histories than among those who have only ever been employees. This suggests that among the (ex-) self-employed there is a relatively larger group than among ex-employees whose lack of one key (non-state) source of finance in old age is not offset by their access to the other main source.

Table 9.9   Income and pensions, by work history (continuous work histories only)

Work history category	No. in cagetory	With incomes less than £60 per week and no occupational or private pension contributions (%)
Retired, employee only	610	13.0
Retired, incl. self-employment	121	22.3
Working, employee only	318	2.5
Working, incl. self-employment	148	10.0

Source: Survey of Retirement and Retirement Plans (1988).

Table 9.10   Savings levels and pensions, by work history (continuous work histories only)

Work history category (continuous work histories only)	Those in category with savings less than £3 000 and no occupational or personal pension contributions		
		As % of	
	No.	all in category	those with savings below £3000
Retired, employee only	74	12.9	26.0
Retired, incl. self-employment	20	18.5	40.0
Working, employee only	33	10.9	19.3
Working, incl. self-employment	22	15.8	28.2

Source: Survey of Retirement and Retirement Plans (1988).

4   CONCLUDING REMARKS: SELF-EMPLOYMENT AND TRANSITIONAL LABOUR MARKETS

We have seen that, while such growth is less dramatic than some have claimed, there is nevertheless evidence of an expansion in non-agricultural self-employment in many European countries in recent decades. It is also clear that many of the factors contributing to such growth (shifts to the service sector, growth in 'outsourcing strategies', an increased policy emphasis on encouraging self-employment and changing demographic structures) are likely to contribute to continued growth in self-employment. The evidence also suggests a shift in the composition of self-employment, with a breakdown in traditional patterns and growing numbers of people experiencing self-employment who do not fit the stereotypical pattern of the entrepreneur or small business person. In particular, in many countries, more women, more young people and more previously unemployed people are entering self-employment. We also noted evidence that self-employment is becoming more 'dynamic', with growing rates of transition between self-employment and other labour market states. The data from the UK confirm that, as a result of these changes, many more people are experiencing spells of self-employment during their working lives than would be suggested by an examination of stock data alone.

In the light of these findings, it is clearly of interest from the transitional labour market perspective to explore the implications of a labour market in which more people and different people are becoming self-employed for indicators of economic well-being. In this chapter, therefore, we have used the UK (where the recent growth in self-employment in the 1980s was particularly marked and preceded that in many other countries) as a 'case study' in order to examine the characteristics of the self-employed and of working lives that include self-employment, with a particular focus on the effects on income of self-employment experience, and transitions to and from self-employment. We have addressed these issues with a variety of data sets and empirical methodologies. The chapter represents only a starting point and there is more to be done to improve and extend the analysis and to refine the empirical models. Further work could, for example, be usefully done to bring in a greater comparative element through replication of the analysis in one or more other countries. At this stage, therefore, our conclusions remain tentative.

There are, however, some clear patterns emerging from the analysis which are consistent across the data sources used. These findings enable us to begin to paint a coherent picture and raise a number of policy-relevant issues about the role of self-employment in transitional labour markets.

Retirement Rights and Social Protection for 'Disadvantaged' Self-employed

In particular, the initial analysis of UK data suggests that the expansion of 'new self-employment' experienced since the early 1980s (especially among groups historically underrepresented among the self-employed) may have resulted in the growth of a labour market segment whose self-employment experience has been associated with low and unstable incomes, relative insecurity and low levels of income and wealth in later life (due to loss of pension entitlements and low savings potential during periods of self-employment).

This reinforces the evidence from previous research (Parker, 1997) that the principal cause of rising self-employment income inequality during the period 1976–91 was a substantial increase in the heterogeneity of the self-employed themselves.

It seems from the analysis so far conducted that being self-employed has a twofold influence on income levels and poverty. On the one hand, it appears that, other things being equal, being currently self-employed increases the risk of being poor. Similarly, from a longer-term perspective, having had periods of self-employment during one's working life appears to depress retirement income and asset levels. On the other hand, however, there appears to be no 'intermediate memory'. If those who remain in the labour market obtain wage employment following a self-employment spell, they can fully recover from any negative income effects due to that self-employment experience.

From a policy perspective, therefore, the key focus should perhaps not be on those people who make short-term transitions into self-employment and then into dependent employment and whose income chances do not appear to be detrimentally affected. Rather, it should be on those people who spend sufficient time in self-employment during their working lives for this to increase their chances of poverty in old age. Although there is evidence (again from the UK: see Knight and Mackay, 2000) that having been self-employed does not reduce the *average* level of income after retirement age, the problem is more one of the dispersion of incomes. As we have shown, the ex-self-employed contain a larger proportion of people in the lowest decile of incomes than does the group of people who have never been self-employed, and the chances of being in that decile are directly associated with having been self-employed, after controlling for other factors.

This poses the question of whether the social security system is well adjusted to the diversity of the self-employed, and in particular to this wider income dispersion and the significant group of low-income ex-self-employed. Given the composition of recent self-employment growth, it is also arguable that the latter group will increase in size in the future. In the UK at least, the role of the pension system may be critical here. It is clear that the existing system of state pensions is not well adjusted to the growing incidence of self-employment, particularly in so far as many of the 'new' self-employed are increasingly concentrated near the bottom of the income distribution. Such people are poorly placed to compensate for their lack of an occupational pension (provided by an employer) and their low level of entitlement to a state pension by making their own private provision. Essentially, although entitled to the minimum basic state pension, the self-employed in the UK have been excluded from the State Earnings Related Pension Scheme (SERPS), and it is clear that future reforms to pension systems should be aimed at ensuring a social security neutrality between those whose working lives remain dominated by traditional employment and the growing number who spend significant periods of their working life in various forms of self-employment.

A second dimension of the need for social protection for the self-employed relates to those who are self-employed in name only and whose self-employment could perhaps be regarded as a form of 'disguised wage employment'. We have noted the diversity of forms of self-employment, but one factor that seems clear is that part of the recent growth in self-employment reflects the trend towards subcontracting and outsourcing in many sectors and that many of the new self-employed are highly dependent on one firm or organization for their work, but do not have the working conditions and social protection which normally attach to waged employment. In particular, it is worth noting that the self-employed in the UK have generally been excluded from unemployment benefit, which was replaced by the Jobseekers' Allowance in 1996.[12] Indeed, a key motivation for the generation of such forms of self-employment may be that employers wish to avoid the 'burden' of social costs and regulations such as dismissal protection. This process was particularly marked in the UK in the construction sector (although similar trends have also been reported in Italian construction; cf. Cicconi, 1997), but the growth of 'pseudo self-employment' has not been confined to the UK, as the recent debate about *Scheinselbständigkeit* in Germany confirms (see Dietrich, 1996).[13]

From the perspective of policy development, it is not straightforward to design a regulatory regime which, on the one hand, protects the disadvantaged 'pseudo' self-employed but, on the other hand, does not inhibit the start-up potential of genuine small businesses. There has been, in the UK for example, considerable debate about new tax regulations introduced in 1999 aimed at the growth in 'personal service companies', essentially one-person businesses set up by specialist consultants or freelance workers, often selling services to companies for whom they were previously employed. As Freedman and Chamberlain (1997) note, such workers are present in significant numbers in the oil, construction and computer industries and among homeworkers and teleworkers, actors, television workers and journalists. The new regulations aim to treat such people, for tax purposes, as if they were employed (Peel, 1999). Again, however, there is a strong case not only for seeking neutrality or equity in the taxation of such people but also in aiming for social security neutrality; a first step in this direction can be seen in the recent regulations and laws introduced in several countries (OECD, 2000 notes such changes in Germany, Greece, Belgium and Italy, for example) to restrict the circumstances in which a person previously classified as an employee can become classified as self-employed for social security purposes. It is only a first step, however, in that it leaves untouched the position of those who are counted as 'genuine' self-employed, but are in a relatively poor position in the labour market, often in low-margin service-sector activities, and who are unable to invest in private insurances for themselves. Such people often remain outside the remit of many social security benefits.

Enhancing 'Positive' Self-employment Transitions

The evidence presented above also confirms the huge diversity of work history patterns and lifetime income potentials among the self-employed. It is clear from this evidence that growing self-employment is associated with growing heterogeneity and growing dispersion of incomes and experiences among the self-employed. A key issue for policy development in this area is not only to address the disadvantaged self-employed but also to be able to identify separately those groups of the self-employed and those types of self-employment which are associated with positive labour market transitions. Our research to date has only scratched the surface of this issue, but there are some interesting pointers for further examination.

Thus, as we have noted elsewhere (Meager *et al.*, 1996), for example, a further interesting feature of the recent UK experience has been a growth in the part-time self-employed population, which is overrepresented in the upper ends of the distribution of labour incomes (in comparison with part-time wage employees), in contrast to the full-time self-employed who are overrepresented in the lower end of the distribution (compared with full-time wage employees). This suggests that part-time work may have very different implications in the context of self-employment from those it has in the context of wage employment. The interaction between the growth of self-employment and the parallel growth in part-time work remains to be further explored.

A related point has been the growth in self-employment among women, particularly well-qualified women, and the data presented in this chapter are consistent with the notion that there is a group of women that are overrepresented, relative to their employee equivalents, in the higher income groups of the self-employed population. It is also of note that our transition rate analysis suggested that the difference between male and female survival chances in self-employment is much less than has often been assumed in the literature. A key possibility raised by all of this, and confirmed by some of the empirical literature on women entrepreneurs, is that self-employment is now beginning to offer, for certain groups of women, both career opportunities and flexibility in achieving a balance between work and domestic life that has been hard to achieve in dependent employment.

More generally, if policy development is also to focus on the reinforcement of positive self-employment transitions, an important avenue for further research is to attempt to identify more clearly the characteristics of individuals and activities that are associated with economic success in self-employment (in both the short and longer term) and those that are associated with less favourable outcomes. At this point it is worth referring to some findings from earnings models analysed by the authors (Meager and Bates, 1997), which begin to throw some light on the shorter-term factors affecting earnings among the self-employed.

- (General) educational level appears to be even more important for the self-employed than it is for employees in affecting earnings potential, as is the role played by specific work experience (although the role of vocational training is less clear – we discuss this further below).
- The kind of work undertaken by the self-employed is also relevant (those in professional occupations and in certain sectors earn more than the average, other factors being equal).
- The self-employed appear to exhibit greater satisfaction over given pay levels than do employees; but for the latter there appears to be a trade-off between pay levels and satisfaction with job security.
- As with dependent employment, stability (that is, duration in a given employment status/job) in self-employment is positively associated with earnings outcomes, and the evidence shows clearly that such stability is greater among men and among older people. The short-term flows evidence from inter-wave transitions in the BHPS presented in the 1997 paper suggests, however, that gender differentials in earnings are lower among people who have had recent self-employment experience (although the dispersion of women's incomes remains high). Again, this result is consistent with the notion that for some groups of women, at least, periods of self-employment may be a more effective route (compared, say with part-time dependent employment) of maintaining labour market activity during life cycle periods when flexibility is required.

Education and Human Capital

We have noted the strong role apparently played by education and specific work experience in influencing earnings in self-employment. Our transition rate analysis has also suggested that the dynamism of self-employment transitions appears to increase with education level: other things being equal, more highly qualified people are more likely to become self-employed and more likely to leave self-employment. Taken together, the two elements, earnings and transition flows, are consistent with the notion that it is particularly for the better-qualified that self-employment may constitute a positive transition route. Workforce experience may also be important, however, and a common explanation in the literature for the relatively low levels of self-employment among young people and their relatively low entry rates to self-employment lies in their relative lack not only of financial but also of human capital relevant to self-employment entry. This is despite a high and apparently increasing expressed preference for self-employment among young people in many countries (see the discussion in OECD, 2000).

What has yet to be explored in any significant way in the literature, however, is the role of human capital acquired *during* self-employment. There are at least two policy-relevant issues here. The first relates to whether, during relatively short transitional self-employment spells of, say, a year or two, individuals acquire experience and human capital which enhances their 'employability' and their chances of acquiring subsequent wage employment. The answer to this question is a critical one in assessing, for example, the value of state employment subsidies for the unemployed to enter self-employment. It is well documented that such schemes often have high levels of deadweight, unless they are focused on disadvantaged groups who would not otherwise enter self-employment. In the latter case, however, survival rates of the subsidized businesses are typically rather low (see Meager, 1996; Metcalf, 1998). Arguably, however, a high rate of leaving self-employment (often characterized as 'business failure' in the literature) matters less if the experience of a transitional spell of self-employment has enhanced the individual's future chances in the labour market. Thus we have the possibility that a negative evaluation of a self-employment scheme as an instrument for generating sustained self-employment among previously unemployed people[14] may, from a transitional labour market perspective, be converted to a more positive evaluation of the scheme as an instrument for enhancing general employability among the ex-unemployed. While this issue is underresearched, there is some relevant recent evidence in the UK literature.

Thus some earlier research argues that, if unemployed people who enter self-employment do so in response to labour market conditions which prevent them obtaining wage employment, they may lack the characteristics (such as the possession of financial and relevant human capital – the latter including certain attitudinal characteristics) necessary for success in self-employment. Some of the earlier empirical studies do indeed suggest lower survival rates for those entering self-employment from unemployment, or with a history of unemployment.[15] However, there are also more recent (and often more rigorous) studies (Cressy and Storey, 1995; Taylor, 2000) that challenge this evidence. Bryson and White (1996) have shown, moreover, using cohort data on the unemployed, that self-employed jobs obtained by the long-term unemployed are more stable than jobs in wage employment entered by the long-term unemployed. Over a longer-term period, this advantage is less evident, but their study nevertheless showed that the effect of a spell of self-employment after long-term unemployment on the time spent claiming unemployment benefits over a five-year period was as great as the effect of a spell of wage employment. Both groups were significantly better off in this respect than those who remained jobless.

Taylor (2000) has shown that those entering self-employment since 1991 have a longer 'survival' rate than those entering wage employment. This is equally true for men and women. Taylor's evidence also indicates that early exits from self-employment are nearly three times more likely to be voluntary shifts into better paid employment. This kind of evidence is consistent, therefore, with the notion that experience of self-employment may have similar effects on an individual's longer-term labour market changes to the effects of wage employment experience, and provides a much more optimistic perspective on the potential role of short periods of self-employment as a transitional route out of unemployment than emerges from the previous literature on self-employment schemes.

The second human capital-related policy issue, and one that also needs to be explored in further research, relates to the role of training and human capital acquisition during self-employment and the contribution that (lack of) ongoing training among certain groups of self-employed (particularly those who remain in self-employment for periods of significant length) may play in affecting their career and income prospects. It is well documented across nearly all EU countries for which data are available that the self-employed are less likely to receive work-related training in a given period than their counterparts in dependent employment (see Table 9.11 where, with the exception of Belgium and Germany, this pattern is generally confirmed).

This finding is not surprising, especially given the evidence from much previous research (see Meager, 1993; also Table 9.3 above) that many of the self-employed work much longer hours than their employee counterparts and often may not be able to spare the time to invest in ongoing training (even assuming they can finance it). The preliminary evidence from the earnings equations in our previous work (Meager and Bates, 1997) regarding the likely incentives for the self-employed to acquire training is mixed. On the one hand, as expected, the effects of academic qualifications (mostly acquired prior to labour market entry) are a strongly positive influence on self-employment earnings. On the other hand, the possession of vocational qualifications does not in itself show up as having an impact on potential earnings in self-employment. Further work is required on these issues and, given that our evidence suggests that a greater proportion of the workforce are experiencing self-employment during their working lives, a key question is whether their (in-)ability to obtain and finance work-related training on a continuing basis will disadvantage them in labour market terms vis-à-vis employees. It is not clear that public training structures and provision for in-work learning are always well adapted in terms of their timing, cost and content to the needs of the self-employed. If policy makers wish to enhance the likelihood of self-employment periods

Table 9.11   Proportion of employees and self-employed (30–59-year-olds) receiving job-related training in last four weeks, EU member states, 1995

Member states	Self-employed (with no employees) receiving training (%)	Employees receiving training (%)
Belgium	3.0	2.8
Denmark	6.6	16.3
Germany	4.6	3.8
Greece	n/a	0.7
Spain	1.0	3.0
France	1.1	2.0
Ireland	n/a	6.1
Italy	1.7	3.1
Luxembourg	n/a	2.9
Netherlands	8.8	12.9
Austria	3.8	7.6
Portugal	1.1	2.9
Finland	n/a	4.8
Sweden	4.0	18.7
UK	5.1	13.1
All 15 member states	2.7	5.7

Source: Eurostat, Labour Force Survey.

being 'positive' transition routes that enhance employability, they must identify those structures that must be put in place, in an environment in which 'lifelong learning' is becoming increasingly important, if the self-employed are to develop and update their vocational skills.

NOTES

1. The literature on such schemes and their evaluation in summarized in Meager (1996).
2. It is interesting to note that, following recent reforms in the unemployment benefit system, a slight upturn in Danish non-agricultural self-employment rates has occurred, after many years of continuous decline.
3. As shown in Meager (1993), for example, the greater 'dynamism' of UK self-employment compared with France and Germany throughout the 1980s resulted primarily from considerably higher rates of inflow into self-employment. Outflow rates were also higher in the UK, but to a smaller extent.
4. For more recent evidence on self-employment flows using LFS data, see Kruppe et al. (1988).

5. Including one of the present authors (see, for example, Meager, 1993).
6. Previous literature has posited lower self-employment survival rates for women as being due to women entering self-employment with less financial and human capital than men, or to their having different occupational/sectoral profiles and entering self-employed activities with poorer survival prospects, or to their entering self-employment (perhaps on a part-time basis) as a transitional phase, for example to cope with family and childcare responsibilities.
7. For a useful examination of the range of indicators available in the UK for monitoring poverty and social exclusion, see Howarth *et al.* (1998).
8. Smith (1986) argues that the 'black' or 'shadow' economy in the UK, defined in terms of the underreporting of taxable income, is concentrated among the self-employed.
9. In an exception to this common view, however, Hakim (1989) challenges estimates of the 'black economy' based on underreported self-employment incomes. She argues that there are large numbers of people, including many self-employed, earning low incomes and (legitimately) not paying tax and whose incomes are therefore omitted from many official statistical sources. As she points out: 'The implicit assumption is that there can be virtually no-one with earnings who does not need to declare them to some authority or other . . . The assumption is demonstrably wrong, yet survives to lend credibility to claims about the enormous size of the black economy.'
10. For a discussion of some of the conceptual and practical issues involved in defining and measuring self-employment incomes, see Boden and Corden (1994).
11. We have, however, undertaken some tests of the sensitivity of our conclusions to alternative assumptions about the degree of underreporting, and these suggest that applying the Pissarides/Baker estimates of underreporting to the BHPS self-employment income data used here does not change the main conclusions from the multivariate analyses below (for example, the conclusions regarding the influence of self-employment on the likelihood of an individual having an income level in the highest or lowest decile group).
12. For a discussion of self-employed people's benefit and social security situation in the UK, see Brown (1992).
13. For a wider discussion of these issues in a European context, see Shoukens (1998).
14. For a critical and differentiated assessment of the impact of the German 'bridging allowance' in these terms, see Pfeiffer and Reize (2000).
15. Some of this earlier literature is summarized in Bryson and White (1996).

REFERENCES

Acs, Z., D. Audretsch and D. Evans (1992), 'The determinants of variations in self-employment rates across countries and over time', Discussion Paper FS IV 92–3, Wissenschaftszentrum Berlin für Sozialforschung, Berlin.

Aronson, R. (1991), *Self-employment: A Labor Market Perspective*, Ithaca, NY: ILR Press.

Baker, P. (1993), 'Taxpayer compliance of the self-employed: estimates from household spending data', IFS Working Paper, no. W93/14, Institute of Fiscal Studies, London.

Boden, R. and A. Corden (1994), *Measuring Low Incomes: Self-employment and Family Credit*, London: HMSO.

Bögenhold, D. and U. Staber (1991), 'The decline and rise of self-employment', *Work, Employment and Society*, 5, 223–39.

Brown, J. (1992), *A Policy Vacuum: Social Security for the Self-employed*, York: Joseph Rowntree Foundation.

Bryson, A. and M. White (1996), *From Unemployment to Self-Employment*, London: Policy Studies Institute.

Carter, S. and T. Cannon (1988), 'Female Entrepreneurs: A study of female business owners; their motivations, experiences and strategies for success', research paper no. 65, Employment Department, London.

Cicconi, I. (1997), 'I paradossi della produzione postfordista nel comparto costruzioni', in S. Bologna and A. Fumagalli (eds), *Il lavoro autonomo di seconda generazione*, Milan: Feltrinelli, pp. 299–317.

Cressy, R. and D. Storey (1995), *New Firms and their Bank*, London: National Westminster Bank.

Curran, J. and R. Burrows (1988), *Enterprise in Britain: A National Profile of Small Business Owners and the Self-employed: an Analysis of General Household Survey Data*, London: Small Business Research Trust.

Daly, M. (1991), 'The 1980s – a decade of growth in enterprise: Self-employment data from the Labour Force Survey', *Employment Gazette*, March.

Dietrich, H. (1996), 'Neue Formen der Erwerbstätigkeit unter besonder Berücksichtigung der Scheinselbständigkeit', in A. Laszlo and M. Tessaring (eds), *Neue Qualifizierungs- und Beschaftigungsfelder. Dokumentation des BIBB/IAB Workshops am 13/14 November 1995*, Bielefeld: Bertelsmann, pp. 283–303.

Freedman, J. and E. Chamberlain (1997), 'Horizontal Equity and the Taxation of Employed and Self-Employed Workers', *Fiscal Studies*, 18 (1), 87–118.

Hakim, C. (1989), 'Workforce Restructuring, Social Insurance Coverage and the Black Economy', *Journal of Social Policy*, 18 (4), 471–503.

Halpin, B. (1997), 'Unified BHPS work-life histories: combining multiple sources into a user-friendly format', ESRC Research Centre on Micro-Social Change, University of Essex.

Howarth, C., P. Kenway, G. Palmer and C. Street (1998), *Monitoring Poverty and Social Exclusion*, York: Joseph Rowntree Foundation.

Johnson, S. (1991), 'Recent Trends in Self-employment in Britain', Policy Research Unit, Leeds Metropolitan University (mimeo).

Knight, G. and S. Mackay (2000), 'Lifetime Experiences of Self-Employment', Research Report no. 120, Department of Social Security, London.

Kruppe, T., H. Oschmiansky and K. Schöman (1998), 'Self-employment: employment dynamics in the European Union', *MISEP Policies no. 64*, Winter (European Commission, Employment Observatory).

Luber, S. and M. Gangl (1997), 'Die Entwicklung selbständiger Erwerbstätigkeit in Westeuropa und den USA 1960–1995', Arbeitspapier I/Nr 16, Mannheimer Zentrum für Europäische Sozialforschung.

Luber, S. and R. Leicht (1998), 'The Development of Self-employment in Western Europe: Patterns of Entrepreneurship and Labour Market Trends', paper presented at the XIV I.S.A. World Congress of Sociology, Research Committee on Economy and Society (RC02), Montreal, Canada, 27 July–1 August, 1998.

Meager, N. (1992), 'Does unemployment lead to self-employment?' *Small Business Economics*, 4, 87–103.

Meager, N. (1993), 'Self-employment and labour market policy in the European Community', Discussion Paper FSI 93–901, Wissenschaaftszentrum Berlin für Sozialforschung, Berlin.

Meager, N. (1996), 'Self-employment as an alternative to dependent employment for the unemployed', in G. Schmid, J. O'Reilly and K. Schömann (eds), *International Handbook of Labour Market Policy and Evaluation*, Cheltenham, UK and Brookfield, US: Edward Elgar.

Meager, N. (1999), 'Recent trends in self-employment in the UK', *SYSDEM Trends no. 31*, Spring (European Commission, Employment Observatory).

Meager, N. and P. Bates (1997), 'Transitions in employment contracts: the case of self-employment in the UK – an analysis of the BHPS and other data sets', paper presented to the 'Households and working time' meeting of the Translam Group, Paris, 23–4 October 1997.

Meager, N., G. Court and J. Moralee (1996), 'Self-employment and the distribution of income', in J. Hills (ed.), *New Inequalities: The changing distribution of income and wealth in the United Kingdom*, Cambridge: Cambridge University Press.

Meager, N., M. Kaiser and H. Dietrich (1992), *Self-employment in the United Kingdom and Germany*, London and Bonn: Anglo-German Foundation for the Study of Industrial Society.

Metcalf, H. (1998), 'Self-employment for the Unemployed: The Role of Public Policy', Research Report RR47, Department for Education and Employment, London.

OECD (1990), 'Enterprising Women, Local Initiatives for Job Creation', Organisation for Economic Co-operation and Development, Paris.

OECD (1992), 'Recent developments in self-employment', in *OECD Employment Outlook: July 1992*, Paris: Organisation for Economic Co-operation and Development.

OECD (2000), 'The Partial Renaissance of Self-employment', in *OECD Employment Outlook: July 2000*, Paris: Organisation for Economic Co-operation and Development.

Parker, S. (1997), 'The Distribution of Self-Employment Income in the United Kingdom, 1976–1991', *Economic Journal*, 107 (March), 455–66.

Peel, M. (1999), 'One-man bands may be forced to look for pastures new', *Financial Times*, 9 November.

Pfeiffer, F. and F. Reize (2000), 'From Unemployment to Self-Employment – Public Promotion and Selectivity', *International Journal of Sociology*, 30 (3), 71–99.

Pissarides, C. and G. Weber (1989), 'An Expenditure-Based Estimate of Britain's Black Economy', *Journal of Public Economics*, 39, 17–32.

Schmid, G. (1998), 'Transitional Labour Markets. A New European Employment Strategy', Discussion Paper FS I 98–206, Wissenschaftszentrum Berlin für Sozialforschung, Berlin.

Shoukens, P. (1998), 'Die Definition der selbständigen Erwerbstätigkeit aus einer vergleichenden europäischen Perspektive', in *Soziale Sicherheit und die Entwicklung der selbständigen Erwerbstätigkeit außerhalb der Landwirtschaft*, Geneva: International Social Security Association.

Smith, S. (1986), *Britain's Shadow Economy*, Oxford: Oxford University Press.

Storey, D. (1991), 'The birth of new firms – does unemployment matter? – a review of the evidence', *Small Business Economics*, 3, 167–78.

Taylor, M. (2000), *Self-employment in the UK: issues, controversies and evidence*, London: Routledge.

STATISTICAL ANNEX

Cox Regressions

In our analysis of self-employment transitions, the unit of analysis is a labour market episode or spell. Each individual will have experienced at least one episode, but may have experienced many more. Employment episodes are defined as the period in which the respondent is working for the same employer and carrying out the same job. Self-employment episodes are harder to define, since respondents were not asked directly about any changes to the nature of their work. However, in the aggregated panel sets 37 per cent of self-employment episodes were followed by an adjacent spell of self-employment. Our analysis of the variations in industrial and occupational characteristics between these adjacent episodes suggested that in the vast majority of the cases the nature of the work had indeed changed, and it therefore makes analytical sense to treat them as separate 'episodes' for the purposes of the analysis.

To model transitions into and out of self-employment, we have used a common multivariate method (Cox regression). The model assumes that the transition rate depends on a series of independent variables or covariates (X) and a separate function of time, or 'baseline transition rate', $r_0(t)$, such that

$$r(t) = [r_0(t)]e^{(bX)},$$

where $r(t)$ is the transition rate at time t, $r_0(t)$ is the baseline transition rate and X is a vector of covariates. We present in Table 9A.1 the results of Cox regressions for transitions into and out of self-employment, using data on job spells from the British Household Panel Survey. The model used is a 'competing risks' model, which assumes different transitions rates for exits, depending on whether they are moves to self-employment or employment. The impact of a variable on the transition rate can be assessed by examining $\{\exp(b)-1\}*100$. Thus, for example, looking at transitions into self-employment, being male increases the relative risk of moving into self-employment by 61 per cent but, once in self-employment, being male decreases the risk of transition to dependent employment by 4 per cent.

Logit Models

Table 9A.2 shows the results of estimating a logit model of the likelihood of being in the lowest or the highest monthly decile of net labour incomes,

Applications and policy strategies

Table 9A.1 *Transitions between employment and self-employment (Cox regressions)*

Covariate	Transitions to self-employment			Transitions from self-employment		
	Coefficient (b)	significance	exp.(b) – 1	Coefficient (b)	significance	exp.(b) – 1
Sex						
Male	0.48	0.00*	0.61	–0.04	0.05*	–0.04
Female						
Ethnic origin						
White	–0.31	0.25	–0.27	0.13	0.20	0.14
Black	–0.29	0.50	–0.25	–0.16	0.28	–0.15
Asian	0.24	0.46	0.27	–0.16	0.22	–0.15
Other						
Sector						
Agriculture	0.89	0.00*	1.43	–0.69	0.00*	–0.50
Energy	–1.20	0.00*	–0.70	0.06	0.33	0.07
Extraction	–0.35	0.15	–0.29	0.13	0.02*	0.14
Metal goods	–0.38	0.01*	–0.32	0.13	0.00*	0.13
Other manufacturing	0.15	0.28	0.16	0.01	0.88	0.01
Construction	1.30	0.00*	2.66	–0.50	0.00*	–0.39
Distribution/catering	0.42	0.00*	0.53	–0.03	0.43	–0.02
Transport	–0.33	0.08	–0.28	–0.07	0.13	–0.07
Banking/finance	0.71	0.00*	1.03	0.05	0.09	0.05
Other services						
Occupation						
Managerial	0.35	0.01*	0.42	0.08	0.10	0.08
Professional	0.09	0.60	0.09	–0.09	0.09	–0.09
Assoc. professional	0.24	0.11	0.28	0.00	0.97	0.00
Clerical/secretarial	–1.03	0.00*	–0.64	0.11	0.02*	0.11
Craft/skilled	0.24	0.08	0.27	–0.32	0.00*	–0.28
Personal/protective	0.00	1.00	0.00	–0.07	0.16	–0.07
Sales	0.08	0.63	0.09	–0.02	0.70	–0.02
Plant/machine ops	–0.25	0.14	–0.22	–0.05	0.34	–0.05
Other						
Education						
Degree or higher	0.18	0.08	0.20	0.30	0.00*	0.35
A level or equiv.	0.24	0.01*	0.28	0.12	0.00*	0.13
O level or equiv.	0.18	0.02*	0.20	0.12	0.00*	0.13
Other or no qual.						
Birth cohort						
Pre-1945	0.28	0.01*	0.32	–0.90	0.00*	–0.60
1946–55	0.36	0.00*	0.43	–0.40	0.00*	–0.33
1956–65	0.39	0.00*	0.47	–0.22	0.00*	–0.20
1996 or later						

Notes: * = significant at the 95% level.

Source: BHPS (combined panels).

Table 9A.2   Logit estimates of odds of being in lowest or highest net labour income decile

Independent variable		Lowest decile Exp(B)	Signif.	Highest decile Exp(B)	Signif.
Sex	Male	0.34	0.00*	2.86	0.00*
	Female	(1.00)	–	(1.00)	–
Age	16 to 25	0.53	0.26	0.24	0.04*
	26 to 35	0.76	0.53	1.28	0.49
	36 to 45	0.99	0.97	1.65	0.10
	46 to 55	1.30	0.41	1.40	0.18
	56+	(1.00)	–	(1.00)	–
Ethnic origin	White	1.11	0.82	1.17	0.62
	Non-White	(1.00)	–	(1.00)	–
Qualification level	Degree	0.45	0.02*	2.87	0.00*
	A level	0.61	0.07	1.61	0.03*
	O level	0.69	0.07	1.56	0.03*
	Below O level or none	(1.00)	–	(1.00)	–
Household status	Cohabiting	1.48	0.07	1.10	0.55
	Single	(1.00)	–	(1.00)	–
Hours worked per week	Up to 15 hours	19.99	0.00*	0.24	0.00*
	16–30 hours	0.84	0.60	0.13	0.00*
	31–45 hours	0.28	0.01*	0.79	0.21
	Over 45 hours	(1.00)	–	(1.00)	–
Industry	Agriculture	0.93	0.90	0.47	0.23
	Energy	0.02	0.74	3.02	0.00*
	Extraction	0.01	0.56	1.48	0.25
	Metal Goods	0.23	0.08	1.28	0.29
	Other	1.04	0.92	1.37	0.25
	Construction	0.78	0.62	1.53	0.15
	Distribution and catering	1.15	0.60	0.56	0.02*
	Transport	1.40	0.48	1.63	0.09
	Banking/Finance	0.91	0.78	2.15	0.00*
	Other services	(1.00)	–	(1.00)	–
Occupation	Managerial	0.37	0.01*	9.76	0.00*
	Professional	0.15	0.00*	8.48	0.00*
	Assoc. prof.	0.29	0.00*	4.36	0.01*
	Clerical	0.21	0.00*	1.19	0.78
	Crafts	0.58	0.21	1.93	0.27
	Personal/protective	1.21	0.53	1.76	0.39
	Sales occup.	0.60	0.14	2.56	0.17
	Plant/machine	0.52	0.18	1.43	0.55
	Other	(1.00)	–	(1.00)	–
Tenure in current job	Up to 1 year	1.59	0.18	1.10	0.69
	1–3 years	1.06	0.86	1.19	0.45
	3–5 years	0.65	0.31	1.63	0.05
	5–10 years	0.53	0.15	1.46	0.14
	10 years plus	(1.00)	–	(1.00)	–
Total employment	Up to 5 years	3.01	0.03*	0.25	0.02*
	6–10 years	1.49	0.35	0.54	0.09
	11–20 years	1.06	0.87	0.70	0.22
	21–30 years	0.96	0.90	0.96	0.84
	30 years plus	(1.00)	–	(1.00)	–

Table 9A.2 continued

Independent variable		Lowest decile		Highest decile	
		Exp(B)	Signif.	Exp(B)	Signif.
Total unemployment	At least one year	1.36	0.19	0.49	0.00*
	Less than one year	(1.00)	–	(1.00)	–
Self-employment experience	S/emp now and in the past	7.10	0.00*	1.06	0.79
	S/emp now but not in the past	7.43	0.00*	0.91	0.78
	S/emp in the past but not now	1.26	0.43	0.94	0.76
	Never s/emp	(1.00)	–	(1.00)	–
Region of residence	London	1.71	0.19	1.65	0.06
	South	1.56	0.25	1.13	0.62
	Midlands	2.08	0.07	0.51	0.02*
	North	1.33	0.47	1.01	0.97
	Wales	2.97	0.03*	0.83	0.63
	Scotland	(1.00)	–	(1.00)	–
Satisfaction with job	Not satisfied	1.26	0.32	1.01	0.93
	Satisfied or indifferent	(1.00)	–	(1.00)	–
Satisfaction with scope for initiative	Not satisfied	0.52	0.17	0.77	0.33
	Satisfied or indifferent	(1.00)	–	(1.00)	–
Satisfaction with work	Not satisfied	0.87	0.74	0.79	0.33
	Satisfied or indifferent	(1.00)	–	(1.00)	–
Satisfaction with hours	Not satisfied	0.90	0.70	1.21	0.19
	Satisfied or indifferent	(1.00)	–	(1.00)	–

Notes: * indicates satistical significance at the 5% level.

Source: BHPS wave 5 and combined retrospectives.

including various measures of previous labour market experience in the explanatory variables.

Table 9A.3 shows the results of a similar logit model of the likelihood of being in the lowest or highest total income decile in later life.

Table 9A.3 Logit estimates of odds of being in lowest or highest (total) income decile, 55–69-year-olds

Independent variable		Lowest decile		Highest decile	
		Exp(B)	Signif.	Exp(B)	Signif.
Sex	Male	(1.00)	–	(1.00)	–
	Female	4.96	0.000*	0.14	0.000*
Retirement status	Working	(1.00)	–	(1.00)	–
	Retired	2.25	0.000*	0.11	0.000*
Age	55–59	(1.00)	–	(1.00)	–
	60–64	0.42	0.000*	0.75	0.109
	65–69	0.07	0.000*	0.87	0.603
	70+	0.07	0.000*	0.81	0.581
Retirement age (anticipated/actual)	Before 55	(1.00)	–	(1.00)	–
	55–59	0.95	0.818	0.79	0.536
	60–64	0.75	0.225	0.44	0.033
	65+	1.22	0.447	0.33	0.007*
Work history (1)	Employee only	(1.00)	–	(1.00)	–
	Includes self-emp.	1.77	0.004*	0.90	0.569
Work history (2)	Continuous	(1.00)	–	(1.00)	–
	Broken	1.38	0.135	0.65	0.006*

337

Table 9A.3 continued

Independent variable		Lowest decile		Highest decile	
		Exp(B)	Signif.	Exp(B)	Signif.
Sector (sic)	Agriculture	(1.00)	–	(1.00)	–
	Production	0.42	0.072	4.61	0.013
	Construction	0.62	0.391	5.14	0.013
	Services	0.30	0.008*	5.88	0.003*
Occupation	Unskilled manual	(1.00)	–	(1.00)	–
	Semi-skilled manual	3.59	0.044	†	†
	Skilled manual	2.80	0.107	†	†
	Other non-manual	3.89	0.027	†	†
	Clerical/secretarial	3.22	0.060	†	†
	Manag./professional	2.88	0.084	†	†
Savings levels	None	(1.00)	–	(1.00)	–
	<£3K	1.05	0.750	1.59	0.108
	£3–10K	0.72	0.107	2.90	0.000*
	£10K plus	0.34	0.000*	10.87	0.000*
Occupational pension?	No	(1.00)	–	(1.00)	–
	Yes	0.45	0.000*	1.92	0.003*

Notes:
* statistical significance at the 1% level.
† estimate unreliable (high Wald statistic).

Source: Survey of Retirement and Retirement Plans (1988).

338

10. Working-time transitions and transitional labour markets

Dominique Anxo[1] and Jacqueline O'Reilly[2]

Modern industrial societies are currently faced by a number of fundamental problems, to which reforms to working-time practices are one policy response. In this chapter we intend to show how traditional reductions in standard working time were a policy used to adjust to unprecedented levels of post-war unemployment, in particular for workers in traditional industrial sectors. Since the use of these policies in the mid-1970s, there has been a further increase in both social and economic problems. These include demographic pressures on pension systems, the gradual decline of the male breadwinner employment model and the disintegration of traditional family structures, alongside even higher levels of unemployment and skill mismatches in the labour market. The broader impact of these problems would suggest that a more substantial and comprehensive policy reform is required than that initially implemented in the 1970s. Current reforms are addressing these policy areas in a piecemeal, incremental fashion. In this chapter we seek to show how the transitional labour market approach attempts to offer a more radical perspective on the nature of the reforms required in the area of working time.

Time allocation and working-time flexibility over the life cycle have been a key component in the development of transitional labour markets. Schmid (1995: 438; 1998: 4–5) has argued that a new concept of full employment is required, one based not on the traditional model of continuous employment but rather on a flexible organization of work averaging out at 30 hours a week over the life cycle. According to Schmid (1998), periods in the life cycle in which working time deviates substantially from this new standard are defined as phases of transitional employment, while the institutional arrangements facilitating such intermediate phases are understood as transitional labour markets. Thus the working life could be made up of a combination of working-time schedules that would enable people to move, at different stages in their employment trajectory, between a range of employment statuses. This might include a combination of full-time, part-time, overtime, short-time work or sabbatical leave arrangements. Thus time flexibility over the life cycle, and the institutional arrangements that favour such flexibility, appear to be at the core of the theory of transitional labour markets. However, as much of the research on these developments has shown, one of the major obstacles to such flexibility is the various forms of labour market segmentation that prevent such transitions.

This chapter concentrates on two major aspects of the introduction of working-time flexibility in Europe, namely trends towards a general reduction of full-time working hours and the development of non-standard employment. It will be argued that working-time reductions have been associated with attempts to develop universal solutions to working-time adjustment that cover all employees, or large sections of the workforce in a particular sector. Non-standard forms of employment, in contrast, are often seen as solutions for individuals seeking to adapt to particular circumstances and to resolve competing demands on their time, perhaps because they have to care for others or are involved in other activities, such as training or education. However, individuals' ability to make use of such options is highly contingent on the general regulation of working time in a given country and on the way employers use working-time flexibility.

Rubery (1998) has argued that standard and non-standard forms of employment need to be analysed together. This is because the conceptualization of non-standard employment implies the existence of a normative, often statutory, standard. Secondly, non-standard employment often involves inferior terms and conditions to those found in more protected and better paid standard employment relationships, usually found in internal labour markets (Rubery *et al.*, 2000; Grimshaw and Rubery, 1998). One of the fundamental barriers to the development of transitional labour markets lies in the differences between internal and external labour markets and the extent to which flexible working-time arrangements are associated only with employment in external labour markets.

The transitional labour markets framework laid out by Schmid in Chapter 5 of the present volume shows that flexible working-time arrangements can be found at various transition points, for example at the transitions from education and training to core employment, between household commitments and employment and between unemployment and paid work, and as part of the exit options prior to retirement. One of the key issues around these transition possibilities has been to ascertain whether part-time and temporary jobs can provide access to more stable forms of employment or are simply short-term measures for managing competing demands or employees' lifestyle preferences. Additionally, a fifth set of transitions includes movements between different working-time arrangements within the employment relationship (that is, between part-time and full-time employment).

On the basis of comparative empirical analyses published in this series (O'Reilly *et al.*, 2000), and in the context of our discussion of the relationship between standard and non-standard forms of employment, we propose in this chapter to examine three main areas. Firstly, we outline the different approaches to working-time regulation in a range of European Union countries, looking in particular at their effect on the actual duration and distribution of working time. Secondly, we examine the effects on employment and unemployment of policies for reducing standard working time. Thirdly, we focus on the development of non-standard employment, examining its potential for integrative transitions in the way suggested by the concept of transitional labour markets. By way of conclusion, we look at the broader policy options for the potential development of transitional labour markets.

1 THE DIVERSITY OF WORKING-TIME REGULATION IN EUROPE

The diversity of modes of working-time regulation in Europe reflects national differences in industrial relations, in bargaining systems (degree of centralization and coordination) and in the strategies adopted by the social partners with regard to the duration and organization of working time. These institutional and social differences may have a significant influence on the length and distribution of working time within the European Union and also on the employment effects of reduced working time.

Regulation can be conceived of as operating at five different levels: (a) the supranational level (through ILO standards and European Union directives), (b) the national level through statutory provisions and regulations, (c) the inter-industry or industry level through collective agreements, (d) the enterprise or establishment level through local agreements, and (e) the individual level through individual employment contracts. Of course the incidence, coexistence and/or prevalence of each of these levels of regulation varies considerably in Europe. In some countries, such as France and Spain, legislation plays a central role, while in others, such as Denmark, Sweden, Germany and the Netherlands, collective agreements at industry or enterprise level appear to be the determining factors. With the exception of the United Kingdom and Denmark, all the member states have legislation governing working time (see Table 10A.1).

Analysis of the relationship between the forms of regulation and the distribution of working time is likely to reveal three basic patterns. In those countries where statutory standards prevail or where there is a strong, centralized and coordinated collective bargaining system and high rates of union coverage, individual working times can be expected to cluster around the statutory and/or collective agreed working-time norm (Group 1). In a second group of countries, working time is governed by industry-level agreements. In this group, a wider spread of working time might be expected, the main cause of which is likely to be disparities in the collectively agreed norms between the various bargaining areas (Group 2). Finally, in those countries characterized by an absence of statutory or even contractual norms defining standard employment, and where the methods for regulating working time are basically laid down at enterprise or employment contract level, a very wide diversification and dispersion of working time can be expected (Group 3).

The contrasting working-time distribution profiles for France, Germany and the United Kingdom (cf. Figure 10.1) are a good illustration of the influence of national modes of working-time regulation on the distribution of working hours, although regulation is not the only determining factor (Rubery, 1994). Thus the prevalence of the statutory working-time norm in France, which reflects a certain weakness in regulation by collective agreement, is revealed in the high concentration of individual working times around the statutory standard. In turn, the wider distribution of working time in Germany reflects disparities between sectoral working-time agreements. Finally, the very wide dispersion of working hours in the United Kingdom reflects both the absence of a statutory standard and the weakness of agreement-based working-time regulation. Figure 10.1 also shows that the distribution of employees' working time remained relatively stable over the 10-year period in France and the United Kingdom, while the structure of working hours in Germany shows significant changes linked in particular to various collectively agreed working-time reductions in that country. The changing working-time profiles in Germany lead us, in the final part of this section, to enquire into the relationship between stated and actual working time.[3]

Advocates of work sharing assume that a *de jure* reduction in working hours results in a proportional reduction in the volume of hours actually worked. The relationships between the statutory/agreement-based standard and actual working time are crucial in evaluating the potential impact on employment of policies for reducing working time (Anxo, 1999). The essential question is whether a reduction in the published limit on working time (whether statutory or collectively agreed) will automatically be reflected in a proportional reduction in actual working time. The French example is revealing here and provides a good example. The Front Populaire reduced the statutory working week to 40 hours in 1936. However, it was not until the beginning of the 1980s (more than 40 years later) that the statutory working week in France tallied with the actual working week. This rather extreme case shows that there is a complex relationship between working time regulated by law or collective agreement and actual working time and that the public authorities can seldom take direct action on actual working time. There are, nevertheless, grounds for thinking that a reduction in working time at industry level is likely, by virtue of having been negotiated, to have a stronger impact on both the distribution of working time and the volume of hours actually worked. This appears to be borne out in the case of Germany. However, the reduction in actual working time at enterprise level may be less than that set out in the collective agreement negotiated at industry level, largely because of the different levels of coverage of collective agreements. A priori, therefore, there can be no guarantee that the actual reduction in working time will be proportional to the statutory or collectively agreed reduction which, in the short and medium term at least, reduces the potential effects on employment and unemployment of a policy of working-time reduction.

Changes in the structure and distribution of working hours are only a subset, albeit an important one, of recent changes affecting production methods and work organization. These new trends have generated changes in payment methods (monthly pay is now widespread) and a convergence of the status of different groups of workers (white-collar and blue-collar). There has been a marked shift away from the traditional methods of managing working hours towards more diverse and individualized working hours. These changes in work organization are also being reflected in a decentralization and delegation of responsibilities and decision making (increased autonomy, 'multi-skilling', teamwork). In a growing number of enterprises, strict control of working hours is being replaced by performance monitoring. These changes often give employees much more freedom in choosing their working hours. These new trends therefore reflect the transition from a relatively standardized work organization structure to more complex and more diversified structures (Fagan and Lallement, 2000). These new and innovative forms of work organization appear not to be confined solely to manufacturing but are also spreading to other sectors such as health care, retailing and banking (Anxo *et al.*, 2000; Rubery *et al.*, 2000; Grimshaw *et al.*, 2000). However, these new ways of organizing work and working hours are coming up against problems linked to inadequacies in the social infrastructure (accessibility and flexibility of institutional childcare arrangements, deficiencies in urban transport, and so on) and are also meeting a degree of resistance from employees.

Thus, despite the various types of working-time regulation and the differences in the working-time distribution profiles, there has been a marked trend since the 1980s towards the *diversification, decentralization and individualization* of working time. In the light of these profound changes and of clear trends towards the dispersion of working time, three types of flexibility strategy can be identified. In earlier research we distinguished between flexibility initiated by the state, as the main player in the changeover (France and Spain), negotiated flexibility (Germany, Denmark, Finland, Sweden, Austria and the Netherlands) and 'individual' or market-regulated flexibility, the most notable example being the United Kingdom and, to a lesser degree, Ireland (see Table 10.1).

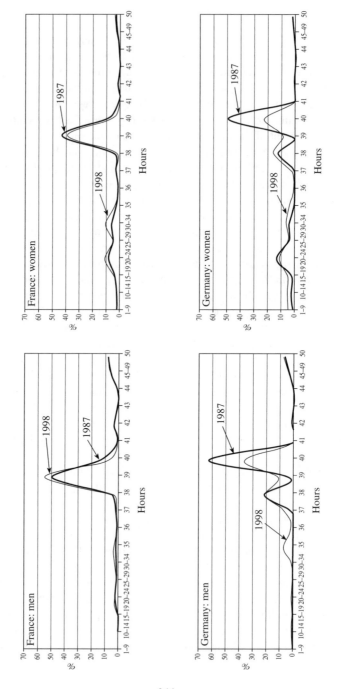

344

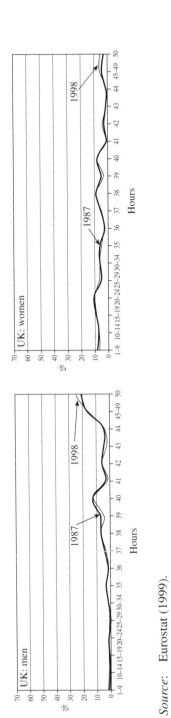

Source: Eurostat (1999).

Figure 10.1   Gender distribution of normal weekly working time, 1987 and 1998

Table 10.1   Regulation of working time and type of flexibility

Working time regulation/flexibility		Country
1. State-regulated flexibility	Relatively strong statutory regulation of working time. High concentration of individual working times around the statutory norm.	France, Spain
2. Negotiated flexibility	Weak statutory regulation. Wide scope for regulation of working time through collective agreements. Relatively high dispersion and diversification of working time due to disparities between bargaining areas.	Finland, Denmark, Germany, Austria, the Netherlands, Sweden
3. Individualized/ market-regulated flexibility	No statutory regulation until 1998. Wide dispersion and high gender polarization of working time: extensive use of part-time jobs (women) and of overtime (men).	UK, Ireland

Source: Anxo and O'Reilly (2000).

New requirements for flexibility/adaptability are reflected in diversified national strategies which, in turn, appear to be strongly affected by country-specific modes of labour market regulation, industrial relations systems and significant societal differences. The growth in flexible forms of working time means that enterprises now have a wider choice, enabling them to adapt their workforce needs to market requirements. From the employees' point of view, while it is true that diversified forms of flexible working hours might give them greater freedom of choice, it should also be borne in mind that the development of some forms of working time seems to be exacerbating the duality between different labour market segments and worsening gender segregation. Some forms of flexible working time are often associated with lower pay levels and with less stable employment relationships. Thus the increase in flexible forms of working time has been accompanied by an increase in fixed-term employment contracts and part-time work, although the level varies in the various member states (O'Reilly and Fagan, 1998; Schömann *et al.*, 1998). In general, national strategies on working-time policy are diversified, reflecting both the range of national priorities and different perceptions of the origin of imbalances. Nevertheless, these national strategies have certain dominant traits, which can be examined against the background of the transition patterns discussed earlier.

In some EU member states, improving employment prospects and combating unemployment are the priority for working-time policies. In terms of transitional labour markets, these policies seek to encourage transitions from unemployment to employment (job creation) and/or to reduce transitions from employment to unemployment (safeguarding jobs/employment maintenance). European countries that have implemented this type of strategy include Germany, Belgium, France and Italy. The second type of strategy seeks to encourage transitions from the domestic sphere to the labour market (integrative transitions). In particular, policies to encourage the development of part-time working (primarily by women) play a central role in this type of strategy. By virtue of the policies they have adopted over a period of 10 years, countries such as the Netherlands and, to a lesser extent, France and Ireland can be included in this category. The third type of strategy seeks to encourage smooth transitions over the life cycle. The Nordic countries, Sweden and Denmark in particular, belong in this category; they have developed statutory, flexible and innovative forms of legal absenteeism, such as parental leave, in order to help individuals strike a better balance between family commitments and paid work, introduced training leave as a means of improving individual skills over the life course and have even put in place phased retirement schemes. Such a working-time policy makes it easier to put in place higher-quality integration policies. The advantage of such job rotation schemes lies in the reallocation effect between generations and between insiders and outsiders where these leaves of absence lead to the recruitment of substitute labour. This type of comprehensive working-time and incomes policy is more in accordance with the transitional labour market approach.

Other working-time policies, those adopted in France, Germany and the Netherlands for example, have tried to reduce the duration of the working life by introducing subsidized pre-retirement systems, with significant effects on activity rates among older workers. A fifth and final group of countries, such as Spain and the United Kingdom, is characterized by a degree of indifference with regard to working-time policy. Having identified these different strategies for managing working time changes, we turn now to examine the effectiveness of policies aimed at preventing unemployment by reducing working time.

2 REDUCING STANDARD WORKING TIME

The issue of working-time reduction has been at the heart of political and social debates since the Industrial Revolution. However, the focus of the debate has changed over time (Fagan and Lallement, 2000). After the First World War, a number of legislative measures were introduced in order to regulate working time. The objective of these initial laws on working time, which introduced the eight-hour working day, was to combat the adverse effects of long working days on employees' mental and physical health, to reduce the high numbers of industrial accidents and to standardize employers' working-time practices. During the period of economic prosperity following the Second World War, as working conditions began to improve and incomes started to grow, the focus of the debate changed. There was a shift away from 'health' concerns towards more general welfare issues, that is the distribution of productivity gains and economic growth and the trade-off between increased income and leisure. In the context of full employment and sustained growth, most industrialized countries experienced a substantial reduction in actual working time.

The rising imbalances and weaker growth brought about by the first oil crisis led to a lively and polemical debate in a number of European countries on ways of reducing unemployment through a general reduction in working time. In some member states, as we have seen, trade union organizations took a favourable attitude towards the reduction of working time, hoping for net job creation or at least for a curb on rising unemployment. The economic impact of these reforms has varied. In some cases they have been supported by a set of legislative measures, as seen recently in France, or by agreement-based measures, as in Germany. The aim of this section is to discuss the effectiveness of general reductions in working time in creating employment and reducing unemployment.

Lessons From Macroeconomic Simulations

A critical review of macroeconomic simulations aimed at assessing the consequences for employment of a general reduction in working time has highlighted the strengths and weaknesses of the macroeconomic approach (cf. Anxo, 1999). Among these strengths, the possibility of modelling separate sets of scenarios makes it possible to assess the sensitivity of results to the results to the assumption adopted. In particular, these simulations emphasize the importance of the way the working time reduction is implemented. In particular, the assumptions adopted as to the level of wage compensation and the impact of the working-time reduction on labour productivity and capital operating time are crucial to the effectiveness in employment and economic terms of a general working-time reduction. A general reduction of working time with full wage compensation, limited labour productivity gains and a reduction of capital operating time will have a considerable negative effect on economic growth and a detrimental impact on employment prospects. Indeed, the various simulations show that, in order to be successful, a general working-time reduction must fulfil certain requirements. There must be only partial wage compensation, and productivity gains have to be achieved through a reorganization of the production process that maintains or increases operating time and raises labour productivity. Empirical evidence (see Anxo *et al.*, 1995) shows that these conditions are seldom fulfilled throughout the economy and require a high degree of flexibility in both the production system and the functioning of the labour market.

More generally, the deficiencies in the microeconomic foundations of these macroeconomic models, combined with the rudimentary nature or even absence of endogenous relationships reflecting, for instance, the impact of the reduction of working time on the labour supply, working-time distribution, wage setting and employers' recruitment strategies, constitute an obvious weakness. The microeconomic behaviour of economic actors appears extremely simplified as a result of the level of aggregation and therefore takes only very insufficient account of various adjustment mechanisms, which may substantially reduce the positive impacts of job-sharing policies. In this context, a critical review of the validity of the assumptions shows that the impacts of a general reduction of working time on employment and unemployment are frequently overestimated.

Lessons from Microeconomics and Company Case Studies

The Microeconomic approach is clearly of interest, as it makes it possible to identify a number of circumstantial factors that shape the work-sharing effect of a reduction in working time. A review of company case studies (see Anxo, 1999; Anxo *et al.*, 2000) reveals in particular the crucial role played by the implementation and bargaining processes surrounding the reduction of working time. The microeconomic approach confirms the role played by the re-organization of the production process, changes in work organization and the reorganization of working time in determining the employment effects of working-time reductions. However, even though some reduction of working time at enterprise level might have positive effects on employment and competitiveness, it may be questioned whether the best practices that have been identified can be reproduced and transferred to other enterprises, sectors or even other member states (especially when the institutional set-up in these member states means the negotiated compromises are harder to obtain). The unrepresentative nature of the sample selected should dissuade the reader from generalizing the sometimes beneficial employment effects to the economy as a whole.

The microeconomic approach also confirms that, in order to have a favourable effect on employment, a working-time reduction must be part and parcel of a wider context of change that includes production and work organization. Changes to working time seem to be one of a number of factors in the overall process of restructuring production methods and work organization. The transition from Taylorist methods of work organization and production management to post-Fordist methods paves the way for the introduction of innovation and diversified working-time patterns. It should be noted, however, that working-time flexibility is not enough on its own to produce a reduction in actual working time. While some changes to work organization may give rise to compromises leading, in some cases, to shorter working times, a review of empirical evidence gathered at firm level reveals also that adapting working hours does not necessarily lead to a reduction in actual working time. In other words, while changes in production organization usually involve a reorganization of hierarchical structures, internal mobility, increased 'multiskilling', an extension of capital operating time and opening hours, increased productivity through rationalization and therefore an overall improvement in firms' competitive position, the trade-off between income growth and leisure may vary from one enterprise or one sector to another. Even in the case of interest to us here, that is the choice in favour of a working-time reduction, it remains to be shown that such a reduction necessarily has positive employment effects.

Institutional and political factors may also limit the efficiency of collective working-time reductions. The efficiency of such measures is closely linked to the nature of industrial relations and relationships between the various social partners. It may well be that, in countries with centralized and coordinated bargaining systems and high union densities at firm level, the social partners will be better able to conclude agreements on working-time reductions likely to promote employment. However, while a high level of coordination and articulation of the various bargaining levels would seem to be necessary, this is not enough on its own to ensure the success of work-sharing policies. Consequently, in addition to the obvious problems of coordination between the various levels of social dialogue (both national and European), the emergence of compromises promoting employment is strongly conditioned by actors' behaviour and the objectives they are pursuing. It is therefore far from obvious that a collective reduction in working time will generate a convergence of interests that leads to increased employment.

While it is generally accepted that a reduction in working time improves the well-being of employees (*insiders*), it has yet to be proved that the methods by which this reduction in working time is implemented, in particular the level of wage compensation, improve the employment prospect of job seekers (*outsiders*). Most advocates of work sharing often neglect these conflicts of interest and implicitly assume a solidarity between 'insiders' and 'outsiders', an assumption which seems to be very restrictive when viewed against the growth and durability of mass unemployment. Uncertainties about the behaviour of the social actors in relation to wage compensation levels give rise to uncertain results in terms of employment. It is therefore crucial to take account of the conflicting objectives of the social actors and to look carefully at the circumstances that may pave the way for compromises that promote employment.[4]

The conditions required for a collective reduction in working time to have a long-term impact on employment and unemployment are very restrictive, because they are largely focused on the regulations that apply to standard core employees. A general and uniform reduction in working time has more to do with a Taylorist conception of work organization and production methods and no longer seems to meet either the new production constraints on firms or household preferences (Anxo *et al.*, 2000), as can be seen from the growing proportion of employees working non-standard hours (Fagan and Lallement, 2000). In contrast to general and undifferentiated, across the board reductions of working time, negotiated and decentralised reductions providing incentives for continuous training and education, job rotation and the use of time accounts may have more favourable impact on firms' competitiveness, employment growth and improve the efficiency of the matching process.

3   NON-STANDARD EMPLOYMENT

A considerable amount of research has been conducted on the development of non-standard forms of employment. This usually refers to working-time arrangements that differ from full-time working patterns, such as part-time and temporary employment. However, in some countries and sectors, such as retailing, these are becoming the norm. What much of this recent research has indicated is the need to distinguish these various types of non-standard employment from each other and to identify the ways in which they diverge from standard employment. In the case of part-time employment, for example, there needs to be greater awareness of the differences between those employed in 'long-hours' part-time jobs offering around 20–30 hours' work per week, which is closer to reduced-hours full-time employment, and those in more marginal forms of employment offering around 15 hours' work per week or less (Blossfeld and Hakim, 1997; Fagan and O'Reilly, 1998). Marginal part-time jobs are less likely to provide the same levels of employment protection or the same advantageous terms and conditions as 'long-hours' part-time jobs. The latter are more often associated with policies intended to facilitate leave arrangements, potential reintegration or partial labour market exits.

One of the issues central to the concerns of transitional labour markets is the potential integrative impact of such arrangements. Earlier quantitative and quali-tative empirical research focusing mainly on transitions through part-time work (O'Reilly *et al.*, 2000) identified three types of transitions: maintenance, integra-tive and exclusionary. Maintenance transitions were defined as a way of using working-time flexibility to sustain continuity of employment; that is, to prevent 'drop-outs' due to unemployment or withdrawal from paid work. Integrative tran-sitions involved those people outside paid work (the unemployed and the non-employed) who were able to gain access to the labour market through part-time or temporary employment. Exclusionary transitions, finally, were experienced by unemployed or non-employed people who had taken a flexible working-time contract, but shortly afterwards had dropped out of the labour market.

Using these three categories of transition, we found that the people who effected *integrative transitions* through part-time employment were more likely to come from the ranks of the non-employed than from the unemployed. This was largely the case for all countries except Spain, where unemployment levels are among the highest in Europe. Here, together with comparatively low levels of part-time work, there was less satisfaction amongst the unemployed who had taken these jobs because they were the least bad option. In general, the unemployed were more likely to be looking for a full-time job that could guarantee them an independent source of income. Only those who were seen as secondary earners or dependents could afford to take a part-time job and feel satisfied with it. Walwei's (1998) analysis of the potential for part-time employment to reduce unemployment as opposed to non-employment suggests that its impact is limited. He points out that most of the part-time jobs created since the 1970s have been taken by women or young people entering or re-entering the labour market, rather than the unemployed. In countries with low female participation rates, it is likely that the expansion of part-time employment will encourage women to enter the labour market but do little to help reduce the levels of overall unemployment.

Part-time work provides access to the labour market for people who cannot work full-time because they have caring responsibilities or are still in educa-tion. However, our research revealed a significant problem with transitions subsequent to a period of part-time employment, which was that only a very limited number of people were able to move on to full-time work. These find-ings were supported by analyses of several countries with both high and low levels of part-time employment, for example the UK, Spain, Ireland and Germany. In only a tiny minority of cases did part-time work form part of a continuous employment trajectory. It was more often the case that part-time work led to an exclusionary pattern of transitions and merely punctuated longer periods of non-employment. This research also revealed that *exclusionary tran-sitions* were more likely to be found amongst groups of people with lower-level skills and qualifications. Childcare and other caring responsibilities were also closely associated with significant patterns of labour market withdrawal or marginal forms of employment. Further support for this evidence for the European countries studied in the TRANSLAM project is to be found in studies conducted in the USA (Blank, 1998). Part-time work clearly acts as a form of integration for those outside the labour market, but it is rarely part of a maintenance transition, except for the young and more highly qualified, who have better prospects of moving on to full-time employment.

The potential for part-time work to integrate those outside employment is also dependent on the nature of the job growth and the volume of part-time jobs being generated in the economy. Bothfeld and O'Reilly (2000) show that there were significant differences in job growth and loss in the United Kingdom and Germany throughout the 1990s. While Germany has had a persistent and growing level of unemployment since 1992, in Spain, Ireland, the Netherlands and, more recently, the UK, there has been significant job growth (OECD, 1999). Clearly, increasing numbers of jobs help to integrate more people into paid work. However, job growth alone is not sufficient to guarantee successful transitions.

The quality of the jobs and working-time arrangements that can contribute to social integration is very much dependent on the nature of the collective agreements and employment regulations in different countries and sectors (Anxo and O'Reilly, 2000; Anxo *et al.*, 2000b). The relationship between the take-up of flexible and/or part-time employment and other institutional arrangements is central both to the nature of integration and to the whole concept of TLMs. This is clear, for example, from the evidence drawn from countries like Germany, where the link between education and part-time work is strong, particularly for men. British men, on the other hand, are more vulnerable to drop-out transitions preceded and followed by periods of unemployment. Men in all the countries studied tend only to spend very short periods of time in part-time work before moving on to something better.

Women, on the other hand, are likely to make more transitions over the life cycle than men, but are also likely to stay much longer in part-time employment. For women the tendency is more towards drop-out transition patterns. However, women in Sweden are less likely to drop out than those in the Netherlands (Anxo *et al.*, 2000a), a finding which is partly attributable to leave and parental arrangements. Such policies have clearly helped women develop *maintenance transitions* in Sweden. These we defined as ways of moving between different working-time regimes in order to enable employees to maintain continuity of employment. In many ways the traditional, conservative breadwinner model, which is more apparent in Germany, is also evident in the Netherlands.

The importance of employment continuity over the working life is closely related to the way welfare systems operate. Transitional labour markets require that career breaks or spells of non-employment do not lead to reduced pension rights or to the loss of entitlement to unemployment benefit over the working life. Wider access to childcare facilities, the earlier individualization of tax systems and a more generous and flexibly organized system of parental leave based on variable working-time patterns over the life cycle clearly help to promote integration as well as continuity of employment. Attempts to reform welfare systems to take account of more 'patchwork' careers can be seen, for example, in Germany and Sweden, where the child-rearing years are recognized for the purpose of calculating pension contributions, while in the Netherlands new legislation is being proposed that would facilitate individuals' working-time choices. Nevertheless, German women are likely to have more interrupted employment careers, taking longer times out of employment than is the case in the UK, and Dutch women are more likely to be found in very short-hour part-time jobs. This clearly indicates that a range of different policy measures have an impact on different working-time transition patterns. The diverse ways that working-time flexibility is being discussed and introduced in these societies suggest that the application of a TLM model will need to be sensitive to the different groupings of political actors within a given employment system.

4   CONCLUSIONS: WORKING-TIME TRANSITIONS AND TRANSITIONAL LABOUR MARKETS

This chapter has taken a summary of empirical evidence on changing national regulations on flexible working-time practices as a starting point for assessing the evolution of reductions in standard working time and of non-standard employment. The evidence shows that there remain significant national differences in this area. Firstly, we have identified differences in the distribution of working-time patterns and in the modes of working-time regulation. Secondly, we have focused on policies intended to bring about a universal reduction in working time and on assessments of their effectiveness in terms of employment protection and job creation. Thirdly, we have argued that the analysis of non-standard working time needs to be examined in relation to full-time employment. This can help us identify whether, and to what extent, it represents a distinct labour market segment, isolated from standard employment and more closely associated with exclusionary labour market transitions, or whether it can actually facilitate the integrative or employment maintenance transitions that are central to the concept of transitional labour markets.

Looking at the broader implications of these findings for the development of transitional labour markets, we return to the ideas advanced by Schmid (1998). The notion of promoting flexibility in working life is not new. In the early 1970s, G. Rehn (1972), a Swedish economist, proposed a comprehensive and innovative system of time allocation in order to cope with the major transformation individualized countries were undergoing. According to Rehn, the traditional Taylorist division of time between periods of education, paid employment and retirement reflects a social order and concept of work organization that does not seem to accord with the major features of post-industrial societies. In contrast to the prevailing piecemeal view of time allocation, he favoured a holistic approach, recommending the implementation of a single comprehensive and coordinated system for financing all periods of non-paid time. He proposed the introduction of general income insurance with access to individual drawing rights. Furthermore, in Rehn's view, this system should provide a high degree of interchangeability in the allocation of time over the life cycle. Thus, for Rehn, individual freedom of time allocation over the life cycle must be guaranteed through the introduction of a universal citizen's right supplemented by an integrated system of income transfer.[5] In other words, the financing of pensions, leave periods and training should be consolidated into an integrated social insurance system. In terms of social justice, the principle that contributions to the proposed financing system should be compulsory for all citizens and that drawing rights should be extended to all appears to be an equitable one, since it ensures that each individual is the main beneficiary of his or her own contribution.[6]

Irrespective of the social desirability of such a system, which has strong similarities to transitional labour markets, the current transformation of modern societies requires both a greater differentiation in working-time patterns and a system of income transfer between periods of directly productive paid work and other forms of activity over the course of each individual's life. The profound changes in household[7] and demographic structure that have taken place over the last two decades have created new needs, as well as posing new challenges to modern industrial societies. Globalization and the intensification of competition have had a great impact on production methods and work organization. Changes in consumer behaviour and product and service diversification have led an increasing number of enterprises gradually to abandon traditional methods of mass production. The introduction of these new methods (just-in-time, lean production and so on) has been reflected in the gradual abandonment of the traditional ways of adjusting employment and the establishment of much more flexible forms of work organization and working time. These changes often make the conventional weekly working time norm obsolete and are forcing enterprises to rethink the ways in which they regulate working time. In a growing number of enterprises, strict control of working hours is being replaced by performance monitoring. These modifications often give employees much more freedom in choosing their working hours. These new trends therefore reflect the transition from relatively standardized work organization structures and working-time patterns to more complex and more diversified structures.

The wide range of individual preferences as regards the reduction and flexibility of working time points in the direction of more flexible adaptations of working time over the life cycle. While general and uniform reductions in working time were undoubtedly necessary in the past, the flexibility required to accommodate a wide diversity of household situations and working conditions cannot be achieved solely through standardized forms of regulation that allow little scope for individual differentiation. Thus both economic efficiency and the heterogeneity of individual preferences require greater flexibility, that is more highly differentiated and variable working-time patterns. While most opinion polls show that people are generally in favour of a reduction of working time, they also show a considerable diversity of household preferences as regards the type of time reduction. In addition, while shorter working hours seem to be an aspiration shared by the majority of workers, most are unwilling to give up some form of wage compensation, which is an obvious *de facto* constraint on the work-sharing effect of a general working-time reduction. This diversity of individual preferences calls for greater flexibility of time choices over the life cycle. While general and uniform reductions of working time were undoubtedly necessary in the past, diversified methods of adapting and/or reducing working time over the life course are nowadays more in accordance with the transitional labour market approach.

These new trends coincide also with the emergence of the so-called 'information and knowledge-based economy', which requires both individuals and firms to reconstruct their competences more frequently than before. This new concept of accelerating changes calls for new strategies. The new information and knowledge-based economy increases the need for adaptability in terms of occupational mobility and continuing training. Thus transitional labour markets would appear to be wholly consonant with the major transformations modern post-industrial societies are currently undergoing. The transitional labour markets approach benefits not only individuals but also the economy as a whole, since the application of a universal citizen's right to recurrent periods of education or training enhances productivity throughout the economy by promoting investment in human capital and improving the efficiency of the matching process in the labour market. Our research on transitions indicates that low levels of education and training are more closely associated with exclusionary transitions. Lifelong learning policies, as discussed in more detail by Schömann and O'Connell (2002), need to identify effective labour market practices that can help the unemployed back to work, enhance employees' occupational mobility and make resource allocation more efficient.

While higher-level qualifications clearly improve integration patterns across many countries, the aggregate effect can vary depending on the distribution of qualifications in a given society. Improving qualifications per se will not necessarily get people into jobs. This is because, in some countries, highly skilled workers do not always fit into the existing skills structure; in other countries, the skills hierarchy effectively excludes those who do not gain a foothold through the standard entry system. Moreover, existing forms of training may be ill-adapted to the new demands of skilled employment and the new types of jobs being created in these countries (Crouch *et al.*, 1999; O'Connell and McGinnity, 1996). Further, qualification inflation can also lead to a relative polarization and the disadvantaging of those at the very bottom of the qualifications ladder, who are then left on the sideline. Nevertheless, a future policy and research agenda needs to identify those areas in which a combination of these policies on working time and training can improve social integration.

Another key element of the transitional labour markets approach has been to argue that policies need to focus not only on the sphere of production, but also on the organization of reproduction and the factors affecting the labour supply. Care responsibilities are one of the major factors associated with labour market withdrawal. The lack of care provision has a differential effect on the potential labour supply and on the terms and conditions under which employees with care responsibilities are available, if at all, for work. Future policy-oriented research needs to explore, from a comparative perspective, the range of different care options that are currently available or being discussed in a number of societies. These options range from publicly funded facilities to leave arrangements or tax incentives. While public provision, as in France or Sweden, offers the potential to create new forms of employment, parental leave schemes can create transition patterns of withdrawal, depending on the financial and organizational incentives associated with the take-up of such leave arrangements (cf. Germany and Sweden). A judicious combination of mutually reinforcing institutional arrangements, such as the permissive legal framework governing leave of absence and the decentralized decision-making processes on working time that exist in Sweden, can ensure relatively smooth working transitions over the life cycle. Nevertheless, the actual take-up of these various schemes varies under the influence of certain socioeconomic factors (age, gender, occupation and so on). This means that the provision of such leave entitlements needs to be examined in relation to the effects of tax and welfare systems.

The benefits system can create incentives for households to limit their labour supply or withdraw from paid employment. The complexity of these income effects is highlighted, for example, in Anxo and O'Reilly (2000), who show the relative impact of different working-time arrangements on household income for a number of countries. In Britain and Germany, social security contribution thresholds have created incentives in the past for both employers and employees to prefer short-hour part-time jobs. In Spain and Ireland, in different regulatory environments, part-timers would seem to benefit from somewhat higher wage levels, although here the growth of part-time work is more limited. A key issue for future research would be to examine how welfare policies can provide secure transitions in terms of both current and future income. These results indicate a field for future research that is central to the development of policies aimed at reform of the work–welfare relationship, which is currently undergoing such significant changes in a number of countries.

The idea of promoting flexibility in working life appears also to be a major concern at the European Union level. Enhancing working-time flexibility is a key element in efforts to improve the employment content of economic growth. Following the conclusions of the Extraordinary European Council on Employment in Luxembourg in 1997, the Council adopted a Resolution on guidelines for employment, intended to improve the adaptive capacities of both firms and workers. In order to promote more modern forms of work organization, the social partners are exhorted to negotiate, at the appropriate level, agreements on the introduction of flexible and innovative methods of work organization that reconcile firms' requirements as regards competitiveness and individual preferences as regards the division of time between work, leisure and education. This quest for new forms of negotiated flexibility could, for instance, take the form of agreements on working-time reduction, the annualization of working hours, the reduction of overtime, the development of part-time work, 'lifelong' education and career breaks. Even if these initiatives can be seen to be roughly consistent with the transitional labour market approach, they are still piecemeal measures and not part of an integrated strategy combining reforms of social insurance and of time allocation.

Irrespective of their social desirability and economic efficiency, transitional labour markets are also normative, in the same way as liberal economics, in the sense that the implementation of such a system depends on the political leanings and choices of the social actors and on the construction of a coalition of political interests. However, as our analysis indicates, there is a diversity of national responses to economic and social problems, while policy initiatives at the European level are attempting to create links between these various national approaches.

NOTES

1. CELMS, Gothenburg, Sweden (*Dominique.Anxo@economics.gu.se*).
2. WZB, Berlin, Germany (*jackie@medea.wz-berlin.de*).

3. In this context, the impact of the introduction in the United Kingdom of the European Directive on working time is an interesting subject for future research. Gender is another interesting dimension (cf., for example, Anxo and O'Reilly, 2000). As Figure 10.1 shows, working-time flexibility is greater among women, whose working hours are significantly more widely dispersed.
4. Recent theoretical developments (cf., for example, Cahuc and Granier, 1998) in the field of bargaining models shed some interesting light on the uncertain impact on employment of a reduction in working time. These models show, in particular, that inadequate representation of the interests of the unemployed (*outsiders*) in collective bargaining and the preference structure of people with jobs (*insiders*) in respect of the trade-off between income and free time both run counter to work sharing.
5. Income transfers between the various periods of paid employment and other social activities (leisure, education, training, retirement and so on) should be paid out of a general income insurance fund financed by social contributions.
6. Technically, the system of income insurance and drawing rights covering all periods of non-work, that is the current income financing of old-age and disability pensions and of various forms of leave of absence (parental and post-compulsory education/training leave, sabbaticals and so on), would be administered by a single central fund, with all payments being entered on individual computerized accounts. Each year, citizens could get access to their accounts, together with information about the current state of their rights and the conditions for their utilization, rather as the time accounts or time banks established by a number of leading companies are used.
7. In particular the increased feminization of the labour force and the related shift from the single male breadwinner household towards dual-earner households.

BIBLIOGRAPHY

Anxo, D. (1999), 'Working Time: Research and Development', Employment and Social Affairs, Industrial Relations & Industrial Change, European Commission, Brussels.

Anxo, D. and J. O'Reilly (2000), 'Working Time Regimes and Transitions in Comparative Perspective', in J. O'Reilly, I. Cebrián and M. Lallement (eds), *Working Time Changes: Social Integration through Transitional Labour Markets* Cheltenham, UK and Northampton, US: Edward Elgar, pp. 61–92.

Anxo, D., G. Bosch, D. Bosworth, G. Cette, T. Sterner and D. Taddei (eds) (1995), *Work Patterns and Capital Utilisation. An International Comparative Study*, Dordrecht, Boston and London: Kluwer Academic Publishers.

Anxo, D., J-Y. Boulin, M. Lallement, G. Lefevre and R. Silvera (2000a), 'Time, Lifestyles and Transitions in France and Sweden', in J. O'Reilly, I. Cebrián and M. Lallement (eds), *Working Time Changes: Social Integration through Transitional Labour Markets*, Cheltenham, UK and Northampton, US: Edward Elgar, pp. 251–88.

Anxo, D., E. Stancanelli and D. Storrie (2000b), 'Transitions Between Different Working Time Arrangements: A Comparison of Sweden and the Netherlands', in J. O'Reilly, I. Cebrián and M. Lallement (eds), *Working Time Changes: Social Integration through Transitional Labour Markets*, Cheltenham, UK and Northampton, US: Edward Elgar, pp. 93–131.

Blank, R. (1998), 'Labour Market Dynamics and Part-time Work', in S. W. Polacheck (ed.), Research in Labor Economics, Vol. 17, Greenwich, CN: JAI Press.

Blossfeld, H-P. and C. Hakim (1997), *Between Equalization and Marginalization: Women Working Part-time in Europe and the United States of America*, Oxford: Oxford University Press.

Bothfeld, S. and J. O'Reilly (2000), 'Moving up or moving out? Transitions through part-time work in Britain and Germany', in J. O'Reilly, I. Cebrián and M. Lallement (eds), *Working Time Changes: Social integration through working time transitions in Europe*, Cheltenham, UK and Northampton, US: Edward Elgar, pp. 132–72.

Cahuc P. and P. Granier (1998), 'La réduction du temps de travail: une solution pour l'emploi?', *Travail et Emploi*, 74 (1), 111–20.

Cebrián, I., M. Lallement and J. O'Reilly (2000), 'Introduction', in J. O'Reilly, I. Cebrián and M. Lallement (eds), *Working Time Changes: Social Integration through Transitional Labour Markets*, Cheltenham, UK and Northampton, US: Edward Elgar, pp. 1–21.

European Commission (1999), 'Employment Guidelines 2000', COM(99)441 of 8 September, Brussels.

Crouch, C., Sako M. and Finegold, D. (1999), *Are Skills the Answer?*, London: Routledge.

Fagan, C. and M. Lallement (2000), 'Working Time, Social Integration and Transitional Labour Markets', in J. O'Reilly, I. Cebrian and M. Lallement (eds), *Working Time Changes: Social Integration through Transitional Labour Markets*, Cheltenham, UK and Northampton, US: Edward Elgar, pp. 25–60.

Fagan, C. and J. O'Reilly (1998), 'Conceptualising part-time work: the value of an integrated comparative perspective', in J. O'Reilly and C. Fagan (eds), *Part-time Prospects: International Comparison of Part-time Work in Europe, North America and the Pacific Rim*, London: Routledge, pp. 1–31.

Gazier, B. (1998), 'Marchés du Travail et Inventions Institutionnelles', in B. Gazier, D. Marsden, and J-J. Silvestre (eds), *Repenser l'économie du travail. De l'effet d'entreprise à l'effet sociétal*, Toulouse: Editions Octares, pp. 175–85.

Gazier, B. (1999), 'Assurance Chômage, Employabilité et Marchés Transitionnels du Travail (mimeo).

Green Paper (1997), 'Partnership for a new organization of work', *Bulletin of the European Union*, supplement 4/97.

Grimshaw, D. and J. Rubery (1998), 'Integrating internal and external labour markets', *Cambridge Journal of Economics*, 22 (2) 199–220.

Grimshaw, D., F. Kers, G. Lefevre and T. Wilthagen (2000), 'Working-time transitions and employment status in the British, French and Dutch health care sectors', in J. O'Reilly, I. Cebrián and M. Lallement (eds), *Working Time Changes: Social Integration through Transitional Labour Markets*, Cheltenham, UK and Northampton, US: Edward Elgar, pp. 317–46.

O'Connell, P. and F. McGinnity (1996), 'What Works? Who Works? The Impact of Active Labour Market Programmes on the Employment Prospects of Young People in Ireland', Discussion Paper FS I 96–207, Berlin: Social Science Research Centre.

O'Reilly, J., I. Cebrián and M. Lallement (eds) (2000), *Working Time Changes: Social Integration through Transitional Labour Markets*, Cheltenham, UK and Northampton, US: Edward Elgar.

O'Reilly, J. and C. Fagan (eds) (1998), *Part-Time Prospects*, London: Routledge.

Rehn, G. (1972), 'Prospective View on Patterns of Working Time', Manpower and Social Affairs Directorate, OECD, Paris.

Rubery, J. (1994), 'The British Production Regime', *Economy and Society*, 23 (3), 335–54.

Rubery, J. (1998), 'Part-time work: a threat to labour standards?', in J. O'Reilly and C. Fagan (eds), *Part-Time Prospects*, London: Routledge, pp. 137–55.

Rubery, J., J. O'Reilly and S. Morschett (2000), 'Restructuring internal labour markets: integration and exclusion in the British and German banking sector', in J. O'Reilly, I. Cebrián and M. Lallement (eds), *Working Time Changes: Social Integration through Transitional Labour Markets*, Cheltenham, UK and Northampton, US: Edward Elgar, pp. 289–316.

Schmid, G. (1993), 'Übergänge in die Vollbeschäftigung: Formen und Finanzierung einer zukunftsgerechten Arbeitsmarktpolitik', WZB Discussion Paper FS I 93–208, WZB, Berlin (http://www.wz-berlin.de/amb/dp/amb93208.de.htm).

Schmid, G. (1995), 'Is Full Employment Still Possible? Transitional Labour Markets as a New Strategy of Labour Market Policy', *Economic and Industrial Policy*, 16, 429–56.

Schmid, G. (1998), 'Transitional Labour Markets: A New European Employment Strategy', WZB Discussion Paper FS I 98–206, WZB, Berlin (http://www.wz-berlin.de/ab/abstracts/ab-dp.de.htm#1998).

Schmid, G., J. O'Reilly and K. Schömann (eds) (1996), *International Handbook of Labour Market Policy and Evaluation*, Cheltenham, UK and Brookfield, US: Edward Elgar.

Schömann, K. and P.J. O'Connell (eds) (2002), *Education, Training and Employment Dynamics: Transitional Labour Markets in the European Union*, Cheltenham, UK and Northampton, US: Edward Elgar.

Schömann, K., R. Rogowski and T. Kruppe (1998), *Labour Market Efficiency in the European Union: Employment Protection and Fixed-term Contracts*, London: Routledge.

Walwei, U. (1988), 'Are part-time jobs better than no jobs?', in J. O'Reilly and C. Fagan (eds), *Part-time Prospects: International Comparison of Part-time Work in Europe, North America and the Pacific Rim*, London: Routledge, pp. 96–115.

Table 10A.1 Regulation of working time

Country	Statutory regulation	Collective agreements	Type of flexibility	Policy orientation	Type of transitions
France	Edict on Working Time (1982). Statutory max.: 39 hours/week, 10 hours/day, 552 hours over 12 weeks. Edict on Working Time, Loi Aubry (1998) (by year 2000 for firms with more than 20 employees and 2002 for all firms). Statutory max.: 35 hours/ week, 10 hours/day, 552 hours over 12 weeks.	Collective agreements at industry level enable firms to deviate from the statutory norm and also to introduce annual working time (1990).	Relatively strong statutory regulation due to weak links between the two sides of industry. Statist flexibility. Relatively high concentration of employees working around the statutory norm.	General reducation of working time in order to benefit employment. Governments encourage social partners to find negotiated compromises by statutory introduction of financial incentives for the conclusion of decentralized collective agreements. The aim has been to promote working-time reduction, foster more flexibile working-time patterns at firm level and improve employment prospects.	Favours transitions out of unemployment and increasing the inflow into employment. Favours the emergence of negotiated flexibility at firm level through financial incentives to facilitate employment maintenance and job creation.
Spain	Employment Act (1980). Statutory max.: 40 hours/ week, 9 hours/day. Employment Act (1995). Possibility of opting for annual working-time norm by collective agreement.	Deviations from the statutory norm and working-time flexibility over the year may be collectively negotiated.	Relatively strong statutory regulation. Statist flexibility. Relatively high concentration of employees working around the statutory norm.	Working time has not been a major issue on the political and bargaining agendas. Some recent trade union demands for a universal 35-hour week. Favours the introduction of annual working time.	Integrative transitions for women and young people, largely through the use of part-time work and temporary contracts. High level of segregation between work-poor and work-rich.

Sweden	Working Hours Act (1982). Statutory max.: 40 hours on average over 4 weeks. No statutory limitation on working day. Derogation possible to allow for the diversity and specific constraints of various production activities.	The two sides of industry are free to negotiate and conclude industry-wide and plant-level agreements on working time. Collective agreements may therefore partly or entirely replace legislation.	Flexible statutory regulation. Wide scope for regulation of working time through collective agreements. Negotiated flexibility. Relatively high concentration of employees working around the statutory norm owing to the lack of major agreements on working time at industry level(?).	Enhances working-time flexibility over the life cycle through universal leave arrangements. Favours the introduction of innovative working-time patterns at firm level. Gender equality dominates working-time policy.	Favours smooth transitions over the life cycle for different age groups.
Germany	Working Hours Act (1994). Max. of 48 hours/week, 8 hours/day. Daily working time can be extended to 10 hours/day if the daily average of 8 hours is respected over a period of 6 months.	Working time in Germany is essentially regulated by collective agreements. At the industry level these stipulate shorter weekly working hours.	Weak statutory regulation. Strong regulation of working time through collective agreements. Negotiated flexibility. Relatively high dispersion and diversification of working time owing to disparities between bargaining areas.	Negotiated reduction of working time in order to protect jobs. Favours the development of flexible working-time patterns and more efficient use of capital at firm level.	Favours integrative transitions for women taking up part-time jobs. Partial exit transitions for workers in traditional industries or employment-maintenance policies. Transition patterns in the former East tend to lead to higher levels of exclusion.

Country	Statutory regulation	Collective agreements	Type of flexibility	Policy orientation	Type of transitions
Netherlands	Working Hours Act (1996). *Standard regulation*: 9 hours/day, 45 hours/week, 520 hours over 13 weeks. *Consultation regulation*: 10 hours/day, no max. weekly working time, 200 hours over 4 weeks, 585 hours over 13 weeks.	If no agreement is reached, the standard regulations apply. Collective agreements stipulate shorter working hours.	Weak statutory regulation. Strong regulation of working time through collective agreements. Negotiated flexibility. Relatively high dispersion of working-time owing to disparities between bargaining areas.	Negotiated reduction of working time during the early 1980s. Favours the development of part-time and flexible working-time patterns at firm level. Labour supply-oriented working-time policy.	Favours integrative transitions from female inactivity to paid employment through part-time work.
Ireland	Conditions of Employment Acts (1936, 1944). 48 hours/week (average over a 4-month period), 9 hours/day.	Derogation and modification of the statutory norm can be achieved by collective agreement. National agreement in 1987 has resulted in a 39-hour normal working week for all employees.	Weak statutory regulation based on EU directives. Relatively high dispersion of working time owing to disparities between bargaining areas.	Not a major issue on the political agenda.	Growth of part-time work encourages integrative transitions for women. High percentage of work-poor households excluded.
United Kingdom	No working-time legislation apart from restrictions for youth workers aged under 16. New EU directive implemented in 1998.	Working-time regulation through individual employment contracts or collective bargaining at sector or firm level.	No national statutory regulation until the introduction of EU directive. Externally restricted flexibility. Weak regulatory environment. Wide dispersion of working time.	Working time has not been a major issue on the political and bargaining agendas. Development of flexibility at firm and sector level. Policies related to in-work benefits to address work-poor households and low-income groups.	Favours integrative transitions often through short-hour part-time jobs.

11. How can active policies be made more effective?

Jaap de Koning and Hugh Mosley

This chapter investigates how active labour market policy (ALMP) can be made more effective and contribute to the establishment of successful transitional labour markets. By 'active policies' we mean government-financed activities in the field of job placement, job search assistance, training and employment subsidies that seek to integrate or reintegrate unemployed and disabled people into the labour market. Active policies also include measures for those at risk of unemployment. The concept of 'transitional labour markets' as introduced by Schmid (1998) is a response in particular to the declining importance of the standard permanent, full-time job, the persistence of high unemployment and the increasing priority people attach to non-work activities, at least in some phases of their lives.

Both demand- and supply-driven forces seem to be at work here. Continuous technological change and turbulent product markets give rise to an increasing need for education and training during the working life. Firms face a great deal of uncertainty, which they want to transfer at least in part to workers. As a result, an increasing proportion of the population is engaged in flexible forms of work. The flexible element may lie in the duration of the employment contract, in the number of hours worked (per day, week or year) or in both. However, even employees with a permanent, full-time contract may find that their jobs disappear as a result of technological change, market shifts or insufficient investment in human capital. At the same time, workers are also developing a preference for more flexibility in their working lives. To some extent, their preferences may coincide with the employer's wishes. Training, for instance, will be considered important by both the firm and the worker. However, the worker's desire for flexibility is also determined by factors related to her or his private life (caretaking responsibilities and consumption patterns, for instance).

It seems unlikely that market forces alone can establish equilibrium between the wishes of firms and workers. A solution might exist in principle if workers were to become self-employed, selling their labour services in varying quantities to different employers. As yet, however, this option does not seem possible for many types of work that require stable teams of workers. Furthermore, workers will strongly prefer a stable income that reflects their average activity rate over time rather than at a specific point in time, while firms will stick to payment for actual performance.[1] Workers' preference for a stable income is presumably applicable to any type of flexible arrangement. Although workers could in principle transfer income during their lives by alternately borrowing and saving money, this seems feasible only for relatively few individuals. Imperfections in the capital market make it unlikely that, for instance, an adult person without much education could borrow the money needed to finance training.

The government, therefore, has to assume part of the risks inherent in a labour market of which flexibility is a major characteristic. It can help to establish arrangements to secure relatively stable incomes that go beyond the traditional social security regulations. Moreover, it can actively help people in making transitions such as that from unemployment to work which, for various reasons, they cannot achieve on their own. We would end up, then, with a labour market – the transitional labour market – characterized by greater flexibility and a higher volume of transitions than a traditional labour market but in which individuals have relatively stable incomes and are not involuntarily unemployed for long periods.

This chapter is structured as follows. Section 1 focuses in greater detail on the role active policies can play in transitional labour markets. Section 2 presents an overview of the evaluation literature on ALMP and concludes that the effectiveness of active policies has been disappointing to date. Section 3 considers how the effectiveness of ALMP might be improved, while Section 4 presents conclusions and recommendations.[2]

1   THE ROLE OF ACTIVE POLICIES IN TRANSITIONAL LABOUR MARKETS

Labour markets in Europe have undergone profound changes since the mid-1970s. There has been a secular increase in unemployment, which in many countries has reached levels unprecedented in post-war history. In the EU as a whole, 10.6 per cent of the labour force was unemployed in 1997 and about 50 per cent of the unemployed people had been out of work for more than one year. Although there was a cyclical decline in unemployment at the end of the decade and a number of countries (for example, Denmark, Ireland and the Netherlands) have had considerable success in reducing high levels of structural unemployment, it is unlikely that unemployment will return to the levels of the 1960s. The prolonged experience of persistently high unemployment, which has cast serious doubts on the feasibility of full employment as traditionally understood, has been an important driving force behind the transitional labour market approach (Schmid, 1998).

It is not only the level of unemployment that has changed: the underlying dynamics of the labour market are now quite different from the patterns of the past. Until recently, employment patterns were more stable and many employees even worked for the same employer for their entire working lives. This pattern is now breaking up under the influence of increased economic turbulence and uncertainty. Individuals are less sure of finding and keeping a job than in the past. The life cycle of companies tends to be shorter than it once was and employees may lose their jobs when companies go bankrupt. Initial education or training is likely to be no longer sufficient to keep individuals employable throughout their working lives and continuous training is needed to keep up with developments in many professions. Indeed, many occupations are at risk of disappearing as a result of technological change.

As a consequence of these trends, younger generations have experienced more unemployment than the older generations. This is documented, for example, in life history data on lifetime unemployment from the Netherlands and Germany. The difference in the incidence of unemployment is particularly significant for short- and medium-term unemployment. Thus the percentage of respondents who report never having been unemployed is markedly lower for the two youngest cohorts (58 and 66 per cent, respectively, for the Netherlands; 80 and 73 per cent for Germany), despite a shorter period of labour force participation.[3]

The probability of experiencing one or more spells of unemployment during the working life has increased considerably. Moreover, once individuals become unemployed, there is a risk of becoming long-term unemployed. This is particularly the case with the low-skilled, ethnic minorities and, to some extent, women.[4] On the other hand, people in employment may work more hours than they would actually like. They may not have enough time to invest in training for skills to be used in the current job or to develop a mobility strategy, even though, in a labour market characterized by continuous change, it is sensible to make timely transitions to other jobs ('get out before they throw you out'). Of course, individuals may also wish to have more time for household activities, hobbies or involvement in civic life.

Active labour market policy cannot reduce the higher level of risk inherent in a number of fundamental changes in the way the economy works (shifting consumer preferences, rapid technological change and globalization) but it might be able to prevent long-term unemployment, or at least to reduce its incidence. Increased insecurity for individuals who face a higher risk of unemployment, recurring unemployment or long-term unemployment implies a much greater need for active policies that maintain labour force attachment and bridge transitions to re-employment. Furthermore, ALMP can help to prevent unemployment among those at risk of losing their jobs. This is particularly important for older workers, who in most European countries have little chance of finding other jobs once they become unemployed. In view of the shrinking size of the age cohorts of younger workers entering the labour market, participation rates among older workers need to increase in order just to maintain current employment levels.

Transitional labour markets are institutional arrangements for enabling 'good' labour market transitions (see Chapter 5 'Towards a theory of Transitional Labour Markets' in this volume). If they function well, they can facilitate the match between individual preferences and employment and between labour market participation and other non-paid activities, on the one hand, and increase employment opportunities and reduce unemployment through a reduction in lifetime working time, on the other. Labour market programmes are an important but not the only element in transitional labour markets, which are also shaped, for example, by regulation and collective agreements. Like other labour market programmes, transitional labour market schemes also have to be assessed critically in the light of the individual and societal goals they are supposed to serve. Some designs are preferable to others on efficiency and equity grounds, while others may even be counterproductive. As in other policy areas, an initial case for public intervention due to 'market failure', broadly defined to include equitable considerations, needs to be made. Moreover, the expected benefits must justify the costs incurred.

For employed people, transitional labour markets may take the form of institutional bridges between full-time employment and periods of reduced working time, as well as career breaks for training, family or personal reasons. It is employed people with relatively secure positions in internal labour markets who can benefit most directly from this type of transitional labour market. Such arrangements, however, can also improve employment opportunities for the unemployed since public subsidies for such programmes are often explicitly tied to the hiring of a replacement from among the unemployed. The Scandinavian leave schemes are one example. Even where there is no such stipulation, the need to replace 'insiders' who temporarily interrupt their careers or reduce their working time creates additional employment opportunities for 'outsiders', that is the unemployed and new entrants.

What are the implications of the transitional labour market approach for active labour market policies? One is that the priority goal is clearly placement in regular employment and that job creation programmes should, therefore, offer only temporary employment under terms and conditions that are less attractive than regular employment. Measures should be implemented as close to the regular labour market as possible (in firms, for example) rather than in a specially subsidized job sector. Although active measures always entail some displacement of employment in competing firms or some substitution of programme participants for other employees, this is an acceptable risk if the overall effect is to reduce the average duration of unemployment. There is also an increased need for job search assistance and training since the pace of technological development and intensified competition means that individuals will increasingly have to deal with more or less involuntary transitions in their working lives. Since preventive measures will not always be successful, there is also an increased need for efforts to re-employ displaced workers and to prevent such involuntary transitions from culminating in long-term unemployment.

Active policies have to be pursued, not as an alternative to, but in conjunction with, other economic and structural policies to combat unemployment. As recent European 'success stories' in Denmark, Ireland and the Netherlands illustrate, policies such as wage moderation, deregulation, social security reform and the promotion of training can have a substantial impact on unemployment. Nevertheless, the remaining level of unemployment will still be too high and active policies will be needed to distribute the unemployment burden over more people and to promote 'good' transitions. This objective will be easier to achieve and to finance if the overall level of unemployment can be substantially lowered.

2   THE LIMITED EFFECTIVENESS OF ACTIVE POLICIES

During the last 20 years, there has been a proliferation of evaluation studies assessing the impact of active policies on labour market outcomes. Most studies investigate the effect of specific measures (such as training) on participants' probability of finding employment. A relatively small number of studies look at active policies from an aggregate point of view, examining, for example, the impact of a particular measure or ALMP as a whole on total unemployment or on long-term unemployment. In this section we summarize the main findings in the literature.

Micro Evaluations

Micro evaluation studies concentrate on the question of whether people improve their job entry chances by participating in a labour market programme. From a methodological point of view, this poses a difficult problem. People either enter a programme or not, and in each case it will never be known for certain what would have happened if the other option had been chosen. The substance of micro evaluations is a counterfactual analysis in which it is estimated, in so far as is possible, what would have happened if individuals had not participated in a programme, that is had not been 'treated'.

A random experiment is often believed to offer a better solution to the prob-lem. In such an experiment, a number of people are selected from the target group of the measure to be evaluated; some of this group are then randomly assigned to the participant group that receives the 'treatment' and the others to the control group. Both groups are monitored over a sufficiently long period to compare their labour market outcomes. If, on average, the participants perform better than the control group, it has to be concluded that the measure is a success. Success indicators often used are job entrance, job sustainability, job quality and pay.

Although a random experiment may seem a watertight method, it is in fact beset by difficulties (see also Heckman and Smith, 1996). We will discuss a few of the major ones. The first point is that it is impossible to be entirely certain that the people involved in an experiment are representative of the target group, since people cannot be forced to take part or to continue partici-pation until the end of the experiment. A second major problem is that, even if the experiment turns out to be successful and the measure is included in main-stream policy, there will still be a need to evaluate the measure as a generally applied ALMP instrument. At that stage, however, experimental evaluations are not very helpful.[5] They take so long to realize that the results, once avail-able, may have become irrelevant to policy makers because of changing labour market circumstances, for instance. Indeed, this could even be seen as a general drawback of experiments.

An alternative method often used is the so-called 'quasi-experimental' method. In this method, the control group is made up of people who were unemployed at the time the participants entered the programme and who did not subsequently participate in the programme. Different methods are used to ensure that the controls are good lookalikes. One possibility is individual matching: for each participant a non-participant is selected who closely re-sembles the participant in terms of individual characteristics and labour market history.[6] The main advantages of the quasi-experimental method are of a practical nature: it is relatively cheap and it does not take a long time. Its main weakness is that even a detailed matching procedure cannot exclude the possibility that the participant group and the control group differ in one or more unknown or unobserved factors that are relevant to the labour market outcomes. Econometric methods have been developed to deal with the prob-lem (see Heckman and Smith, 1996), but these methods do not offer a fully satisfactory solution.

Most studies, whether experimental or non-experimental, monitor the participants and the controls only over a limited period of time. In some cases, however, measures may improve the long-term prospects rather than the short-term outcomes. This may apply particularly to training programmes for young people. Youth wages are often relatively low and therefore most young people will find a job relatively easily, even when they have little in the way of formal qualifications. However, wage formation institutions usually provide for wage progression with age. In consequence, unskilled young people may have difficulties in developing a stable working career. Studies of the returns to education clearly show that a higher level of education pays off in terms of employment opportunities and income.[7] Of course, this applies only to forms of vocational training leading to recognized qualifications.

This critical discussion of evaluation methodology is not meant to suggest that evaluation results are not to be taken seriously. However, it is our view that policy making should not be guided by evaluation outcomes alone. This has to be borne in mind when the results of micro evaluation studies are being evaluated. What, then, are the main findings of these evaluations?

On the basis of various literature summaries of micro evaluations of active measures (OECD, 1993b, Fay, 1996; Friedlander *et al.*, 1997; Rabe, 2000) the following conclusions seem appropriate: (a) the outcomes of the studies vary considerably, (b) on average the net impact on job entry chances is low, and (c) the impacts are above average for disadvantaged groups. It is difficult to draw firm conclusions about the relative effectiveness of the different types of active measures. Until some years ago, training was generally seen as the most effective measure, but this view is not supported by the empirical evaluation literature (however, see our earlier remark).[8] More recently, job search assistance seems to have become the most preferred measure. However, there is little hard evidence to support this preference. The number of studies evaluating job search assistance is small. Although less in favour, wage subsidy schemes do not seem to perform so badly, particularly when aimed at specific groups of difficult-to-place people (Groevesteijn *et al.*, 1998; Stern *et al.*, 1995).

There is general agreement on the poor performance of job creation schemes. This type of scheme often prolongs unemployment rather than reducing its duration. Once in 'artificial' employment, people get used to it and begin to feel that they have the right to stay in it forever. However, that does not mean that job creation schemes are necessarily a waste of money. What it does mean is that this type of scheme must normally be preserved for people who, owing to a handicap, for instance, do not have any prospect of a normal job, even under relatively favourable labour market conditions. Only under special circumstances, such as a situation of mass unemployment, should this general rule be abandoned.

One significant drawback of micro evaluation studies is that they cannot take account of general equilibrium (or macro) effects.[9] However, according to some labour economists, it is precisely through the medium of general equilibrium effects that ALMP can reduce unemployment. Richard Layard is a prominent advocate of this view, which he recently expressed again during the OECD's 'Active Labour Market Policy and the Public Employment Service' conference held in Prague, in July 2000. The basic reasoning behind this view is that ALMP makes unemployed people 'employable' again and therefore enhances the actual labour supply. Through different mechanisms, such as the wage mechanism and the filling of latent vacancies, an increased supply will lead to more employment.[10] This argument reinforces the importance of aggregate impact studies, to which we now turn.

Aggregate Impact Studies

Aggregate impact studies analyse the relationship between aggregate ALMP indicators and aggregate labour market indicators. Aggregate ALMP indicators may refer to an individual measure (a specific training programme, for example), to a type of measure (all training programmes taken together, for example) or to ALMP as a whole. Since the objective of most programmes is to place unemployed people in work, active policies can be expected to reduce total unemployment or at least to have a redistributive effect in favour of the most disadvantaged among the unemployed population.

We have already discussed the possibility that ALMP can have a positive impact on total employment through its labour supply-enhancing effect. ALMP may also increase employment by reducing the friction between labour supply and labour demand; in other words, given levels of demand and supply will produce a higher number of jobs. It must be borne in mind, however, that when these effects occur the more disadvantaged groups do not automatically benefit from them.

Different types of aggregate analysis can be distinguished (De Koning, 2001).

1. Some use labour market disequilibrium functions such as u/v functions and more elaborate variants, which describe the friction between labour demand and labour supply. By providing labour market information, job placement services, counselling and training, governments can try to push the u/v curve back to the origin, which would reduce both unemployment and unfilled demand. Thus tests could be carried out to ascertain whether the location of the u/v curve is influenced by ALMP indicators (taking account of other factors, of course).
2. A second type analyses the influence of ALMP on the inflow into unemployment and the outflow from it. ALMP is supposed to increase the outflow from unemployment to work.[11] The impact on the inflow into unemployment is less obvious. ALMP participation may not only increase initial job entry chances but also reduce the chance of further spells of unemployment for those who manage to find a job after completing a programme. However, unsuccessful ALMP participants will re-enter unemployment.[12]

3. Time-series analyses relate an unemployment indicator directly to an ALMP indicator, with few restrictions on the dynamic specification. There are also more elaborate versions of this approach, in which one or two intervening variables are also taken into account. This method seeks to analyse causal relationships by 'letting the data speak'. The theoretical content is weak.

4. General equilibrium approaches study the impacts of ALMP in a macro-economic context. Some of these approaches use a more traditional macroeconomic framework, such as the Layard–Nickell approach (Layard and Nickell, 1986), while others are more micro-based (see for instance Jongen, 1999). General equilibrium models allow the effects of ALMP on wages, search behaviour and so on to be taken into account.

De Koning (2001) gives a summary of the literature in this field. Although there is again some variation in the results, the general picture is similar to that of the micro evaluation literature. Generally, there is little evidence that ALMP has a significant impact on labour market outcomes. However, there is even more reason to doubt the reliability of the results produced by the aggregate approach. Firstly, there are usually severe data limitations. The limitations may apply to the definitions of key variables, the quality of the data, the lack of data on relevant background variables and the length of the time series.[13] A second problem is that aggregate variables are often related in a complicated, two-sided way. Although econometric methods have been developed to deal with this type of problem, the results are seldom clear-cut.

On the whole, the evaluation literature on ALMP evaluation affords a rather disappointing picture. Micro and macro studies alike suggest that, although ALMP may have an impact, it is likely to be small. Although evaluation methodology has considerable weaknesses, studies that use more sophisticated methods and higher-quality data do not show more optimistic results. Thus it is unlikely that poor data quality and poor models give rise to a general bias in the results. We tend to accept the validity of the general conclusion that can be drawn from evaluations, namely that the effectiveness of ALMP has thus far been limited.[14]

The Impact of Organization and Implementation

We think that one major explanation for the low effectiveness of ALMP reported in evaluation studies may be the impact of variations in organization and implementation between countries, regions and sites. Relatively few studies have considered this aspect. Evaluation research in labour market policy has been predominantly programme-oriented, focusing on the impact of programme 'treatments' on individual participants. In our view, this type of micro evaluation has two major shortcomings. Firstly, it is based on a simplistic notion of the implementation process that underestimates the importance of programme variation in 'treatment'. Secondly, by focusing primarily on individual programme effects, it fails to address a range of other issues that are central to ALMP policy outcomes, and in particular those related to the organization of the labour market policy delivery system.

Labour market programmes provide complex services that are in practice very heterogeneous. In many countries, these services are in fact delivered under the umbrella of 'framework' regulations that permit a great deal of local variation in the organization, content and even the terms and conditions of participation. Even in highly structured national programmes, the quality of the 'treatment' provided may vary considerably. In sum, programme 'treatments' are seldom as standardized as the (misleading) analogy with medical research suggests and this needs to be taken into consideration even in impact analyses. When the overall impact of ALMP is found to be nil or weak, the effects may in fact be considerable in certain countries, regions or localities as a result of better organization or implementation. The overall performance of ALMP could then be improved if every country, region or site adopted these 'best practices'.

There are also a number of implementation issues that are neglected in traditional programme-oriented impact analysis. Of particular interest are structural issues related to the organization of the public employment service, for example, governance, management structures, interaction with other relevant actors, contracting out and privatization. These broader institutional features of the organization of labour market policy do not just pertain to individual programmes but may also cut across several programmes and indeed set overall priorities (Schmid, 1996).

Few evaluation studies account for variations in results between countries, regions or sites due to differing organization and implementation strategies. This shortcoming is due primarily to the general scarcity of good data on variation in programme delivery, which are seldom systematically collected by monitoring systems. Could it be that poor average results conceal successful local strategies and that there is an unrealized potential for improving the performance of ALMP? This is the question addressed in the next section.

3   HOW CAN ACTIVE POLICIES BE MADE MORE EFFECTIVE?

The conclusion thus far is that active policies have to date been generally rather ineffective. If these policies are to play a major role in transitional labour markets, they will have to become more effective. How this might be achieved is the main issue addressed in this section. Disappointment with the results has induced a number of countries to reform their implementation regimes for active policies. Traditional, bureaucratic public employment services (PES) are being transformed by innovative 'new public management' strategies such as management by objectives, contracting out, competition in quasi-markets even within government, customer focus and so on. Instead of being monopolistic providers of labour market services, PES organizations are increasingly expected to compete and cooperate with other private, public, and non-profit organizations involved in the same tasks. Several interrelated options and trends can be observed:

- optimization of PES resource allocation;
- modernization of PES management systems;
- network-based cooperative approaches to ALMP implementation;
- increased reliance on contracting out and other market mechanisms in service provision;
- performance-oriented financing;
- benchmarking of performance and dissemination of best practices;
- exploitation of new technologies and the Internet.

Optimizing the Allocation of ALMP Resources

An optimal allocation of ALMP funding depends not only on policy priorities but also on the efficiency and effectiveness of measures and on the labour market situation. Ideally, policy makers would establish goals and objectives for ALMP and professionals in the field of policy design and implementation would advise on the way the objectives might be achieved. However, the political need for a rapid response to labour market problems has often led to the use of ALMP instruments for purposes for which they are not suited. For instance, ALMP has been used – wrongly – to tackle mass unemployment. Active measures have also been applied to unemployed people with relatively good labour market prospects. It is no surprise, then, that net effectiveness has frequently been low. A more professional approach towards ALMP would be an important way of making it more effective.

The first step in such a process would be a sound analysis that addressed the following questions. Firstly, what are the problems in the labour market and what factors are causing them? Secondly, which labour market policies are most appropriate for solving the problems? Thirdly, for those cases in which ALMP seems to offer the best solution, and taking effectiveness and costs into consideration, which measures should be applied to which categories of unemployed? General employment services should be restricted to the provision of labour market information, access to vacancy and jobseeker databases and training in cases where there are shortages in certain segments of the labour market that can be solved only by training unemployed people. Even in the latter case, disadvantaged groups should receive priority. In other cases, it is difficult to see why active measures should be aimed at groups other than the disadvantaged or those in danger of becoming disadvantaged. This is a matter not only of social justice but also of economic efficiency. Selectivity, then, may be a powerful tool in improving ALMP performance. Different groups may need different measures.

Furthermore, the costs of the various measures, which may vary considerably, should also be taken into account in order that funding may be allocated optimally among different measures and groups. The problem can be defined formally as an optimization problem in which the objective function contains the objective variables (such as the level of employment and the standard deviation of the unemployment levels of various groups) and the restrictions are given by a model of the labour market in which ALMP measures influence the objective variables and by a budget restriction.[15] Even without an explicit optimization procedure, information on the reach of target groups' (net) effectiveness and costs of measures could help to improve the performance of ALMP. However, we know too little about what works for which groups. Furthermore, for many countries data on the reach and costs of measures are either unavailable or incomplete.

In transitional labour markets, the allocation of ALMP funding might differ from current practice. First of all, a shift may be needed from reactive to proactive measures. Reactive measures try to place those that have already become unemployed, while proactive measures seek to prevent long-term unemployment. Although highly appealing, a proactive strategy may be of limited use in practice (see OECD, 1998, and De Koning *et al.*, 1999, for a discussion). When not used properly, this form of proactive policy may even exacerbate the creaming problem.

What is really needed is proactive measures that prevent people from becoming unemployed in the first place. It is increasingly recognized that workers need to cultivate their employability in order to remain employed. Lifelong learning and job mobility strategies seem particularly relevant. Workers and firms have a joint responsibility in this area. However, the government can do several things to facilitate such strategies. Increased training provision means that more temporary replacements have to be found for those on training courses. This situation can be turned to good account by employing people who would otherwise be out of work. This in turn produces savings on unemployment benefits, some of which can be used to compensate workers and firms for the increased training and replacement costs. Similar schemes have been implemented in several countries, albeit with mixed results. There is also a need for advice on career planning and job mobility strategies, for job counselling and for information on training options (for training provided outside the company) and vacancies. The PES could carry out many of these tasks. Indeed, it could perhaps evolve into a general information centre for workers, unemployed people and firms, providing a specific package of services free of charge.

The change in focus from unemployed to employed is also important in view of the ageing of the population. Although unemployment rates among older workers are usually relatively low, unemployment duration is often very long. Furthermore, many older workers have left the workforce. They have either left the labour market on grounds of sickness or disability or taken early retirement. However, higher employment rates among the over-50s will be needed if the labour force is to be sufficiently large in coming decades to maintain production capacity at a high enough level. Bringing older workers back into the labour market is a difficult if not impossible task. For this group in particular, prevention of an early and irreversible withdrawal from the labour market is extremely important.

Young people lacking a proper education also need special attention. At present, they tend to drop out of the education and training system and subsequently slide into unemployment. Often the diagnosis is that they need vocational training. One option is to use the practically oriented training centres run by the PES in some countries to develop forms of initial education that better match the preferences and abilities of these young people.

Modernization of PES Management Systems

Management by objectives (MBO) is the common denominator in a range of performance management approaches intended to enhance the efficiency and effectiveness of public administration. In the field of labour market policy, Sweden and Norway are the countries with the greatest experience of MBO systems, which were introduced in the mid-1980s (Niklasson and Tomsmark, 1997). Finland, Denmark, the UK, the Netherlands and Austria also accumulated considerable experience with quantitative performance indicators during the 1990s (OECD, 1993b). In 1998, Germany also introduced a similar controlling system based on performance agreements between different levels of the PES.

Management by objectives (or management by results), controlling, benchmarking and quality management are the best-known performance management approaches. MBO is a management system based on quantified targets; its aim is continuous performance improvement. It emphasizes the ex ante formulation of explicit operational objectives and the ex post measurement of outputs and outcomes. The practical principles of MBO consist, in a nutshell, of target setting, decentralized operationalization and implementation, monitoring of

(current and final) results and practical conclusions based on a final performance assessment.

In management theory, controlling is the coordination of partial or separated management functions; such coordination replaces the guaranteed fulfilment of one particular management target. The aim of controlling is the
(continuous) maintenance of the information processing required for the entire
system to function effectively. Benchmarking, in contrast, is an evaluative
approach to analysis and management, in which empirical performance indicators for organizations are analysed and compared with the explicit aim of
improving performance through organizational learning (Schütz et al., 1998).
In practical terms, benchmarking entails (a) an analytical stocktaking to
explain performance gaps between organizational units and identify best practice, and (b) the translation of the results of this analysis into performance
targets (quantitative and/or qualitative benchmarks). Best practice benchmarking is the most celebrated variant of this approach.

Quality management is an important complementary component of performance management. Good performance management cannot be based
merely on measuring results; quality aspects have to be included. Customer
satisfaction usually serves as the measure of service quality. In practical terms,
the quality approaches adopted in the public sector are variants of three
approaches: quality control, quality assurance and total quality management
(TQM) (Bovaird, 1996; see Schütz et al., 1998: 9–12, for a brief overview).

MBO can enhance the efficiency and effectiveness of PES implementation
of ALMP because it

- helps to clarify priorities in labour market policies;
- sets clear standards by which PES performance can be fairly assessed;
- shifts emphasis from the inputs of ALMP to policy outputs and impacts.

Most countries with an MBO system reported that clarification of priorities
was the main benefit of using management by objectives. Public accountability
is enhanced because the PES is assessed on the basis of transparent and agreed
performance targets. The (continuous) comparison of results with targets is also
a powerful management tool for directing organizational activities. However,
the impact of the introduction of MBO-type management systems has never to
our knowledge been systematically evaluated; this is due primarily to the unresolved methodological problems of evaluating the impact of such a comprehensive change in the delivery system on the efficiency and effectiveness of
ALMP implementation. We also know that MBO-type systems can malfunction
or fail if improperly implemented (Mosley et al., 2001).

The use of MBO has to be based on principles of 'good practice' and the
avoidance of typical pitfalls. Good MBO practice includes

- use of a limited number of clear and understandable targets;
- developing and maintaining the commitment of regional and local PES staff to the performance management system;
- reduction in the density and complexity of administrative rules and directives;
- a reliable, flexible, and 'real-time' management information system for monitoring progress towards targets;
- establishing fair and transparent procedures for assessing and rewarding performance;
- complementary quality management approaches.

This list of 'good practices' is by no means exhaustive but highlights some of the most important ones. Use of a small number of goals directs PES activities by setting priorities; proclaiming too many goals dilutes priorities and deprives the organization of focus. Commitment to MBO at all organizational levels is essential to make it work and to avoid typical pitfalls, such as moral hazard. The reduction and simplification of administration rules is a crucial step in the introduction of MBO, and flexibility in implementation can decline again as a result of new programme regulations if not 'defended' by MBO protagonists.

A real-time and user-friendly management information system is an essential prerequisite for monitoring PES performance and for 'inter-unit benchmarking'. It should be emphasized, however, that the management information system derives its value primarily from its usefulness to users at all levels of the organization. Its usefulness depends in particular on the frequency of data reporting, the appropriateness and transparency of the performance indicators selected and the ready availability of the data at all PES levels. Data-based assessment of performance needs to be supplemented by personal exchange and dialogue in order to achieve the right combination of 'hard' and 'soft' information.

An important insight concerning fair and transparent performance assessment in benchmarking operating units is that target achievement should be only one element. Explanations for shortfalls in performance should be taken into account, without giving up the relevancy of target levels. In other words, reaching the quantitative targets has to be taken seriously, but the target level is not everything. The purpose of MBO is to direct organizational activities in a purposeful and quantifiable way and in the 'right direction', which is more important than achieving a particular numerical target. There are strong arguments for combining quality management and MBO approaches. First, the quality approaches correct for overemphasis of quantitative targets. Second, though useful as a first step, an exclusive reliance on the quality standards and certification (quality assurance) approach has to be rejected. TQM approaches, with their emphasis on continuous improvement, detection of cost drivers and self-assessment (involvement and empowerment) of staff, seem to be better suited to mastering dynamic goal and organizational development in European public employment services. Last but not least, the emphasis on service (customer) orientation as well as on the internal (personnel) development of quality management is a good supplement to the more 'traditional' output orientation of MBO (Mosley *et al.*, 2001).

Networks and cooperation[16]

The public employment service is only one actor in the implementation of active policies. There is good reason to think that the efficiency and effectiveness of ALMP can be increased by improving cooperation with other actors involved in ALMP implementation. There is currently a strong trend towards reforms in ALMP implementation regimes designed to improve horizontal coordination of the labour market between different policy domains. The situation differs from country to country depending on the specific institutional structures; in general, responsibility for unemployment benefits is often separate from responsibility for ALMP, and in a few countries responsibility for placement services and active measures are assigned to two or more separate institutions.

The primary cooperation needs are (OECD, 1997)

- coordination between placement and benefit administration in order to apply work tests effectively and hence fulfil one of the key preconditions for benefit entitlement;
- coordination between job placement services and ALMPs in order to ensure that the unemployed can acquire the skills necessary to fill available job vacancies;
- cooperation between benefit administration and referral to ALMPs in order to avoid long-term dependency.

The complexity of actor constellations in active labour market policy has been further complicated by the trend towards 'activation', that is, giving priority to reintegration of the unemployed versus 'passive' income maintenance benefits. In practice this means that institutions previously responsible only for administration of unemployment benefit and social assistance have now become involved in the provision of active programmes for their respective clienteles.

The implementation of labour market policy for the long-term unemployed and other disadvantaged groups has been further complicated by the fact that ALMP for social assistance recipients is in many countries not the responsibility of the PES, but of a separate agency, usually the local authorities. The stylized facts can be summarized as follows. The secular increase in unemployment in the last two decades has led in most EU countries to a tightening of eligibility conditions for unemployment benefit and the exclusion of more and more unemployed individuals, especially the long-term unemployed, from the PES's core clientele of unemployment benefit recipients. Parallel to this trend, there has been a rapid expansion of ALMP programmes sponsored by the local authorities responsible for social assistance. This has resulted in a fragmentation of the delivery systems for ALMP, with the PES and the local authorities each primarily acting separately to provide services to their respective clienteles. This results in specific coordination problems and presumably a loss of efficiency and effectiveness. In practice, this unfavourable division of labour also permits the public employment service to shift responsibility for disadvantaged groups onto the local authorities, whose ALMP activities are often less professionalized and as a rule less well resourced than those of the PES.

In the light of recent experience in Germany, the Netherlands, Sweden and the UK, there are at least three principal strategies for improving coordination between the PES and other agencies implementing ALMP for social assistance recipients. First, PES governance structures can be altered by giving more weight to representatives of the social assistance providers, who can be expected to represent the interests of 'their' clientele in PES policy making. Thus recent Swedish reforms of local ALMP implementation give representatives of the municipalities a majority on regional PES policy committees.

Second, in the Netherlands an alternative strategy has been adopted based on the introduction of a purchaser/provider model in which the PES becomes merely a labour market service provider (among others) for the local authorities responsible for social assistance and for the social insurance agencies. These organizations receive their own funds for purchasing services for their clienteles and PES priorities are shaped by the introduction of a quasi-market mechanism among the actors involved.

A third strategy is implemented through PES management systems and involves the introduction of programme eligibility requirements or performance indicators into active programmes that encourage or require local PES offices to give higher priority to the long-term unemployed and social assistance recipients. If such policies are enforced through adequate monitoring mechanisms and appropriate sanctions, PES offices will have sufficient incentive to seek cooperation with social assistance providers and to include their clientele in their programmes.

Finally, a unified and client-oriented agency can be created for the long-term unemployed and other disadvantaged groups, with no distinction being made between the type of benefit received (unemployment benefit, means-tested social assistance and so on). This is, for example, the thrust of the current reform of the PES in the UK.

These approaches are plausible because they promise not only to enhance efficiency by better bundling the resources of diverse ALMP actors but also to enhance effectiveness by increased focusing of ALMP on disadvantaged groups in the labour market. The actual effects of such organizational variables on the efficiency and effectiveness of programmes are, however, difficult to assess and few systematic evaluations have been undertaken. Two recent studies of the impact of forms of cooperation between the PES and local authorities on programme performance and on individual transitions to employment, respectively, showed ambiguous results. For the Netherlands, both a regression analysis and case studies showed no consistent relationship between forms of cooperation and programme performance (van Velzen, 2001). This result suggests that best practice in implementation has to be tailor-made to fit local circumstances and even specific programmes.

The Swedish study (Behrenz *et al.*, 2001) investigated whether 27 'model' municipalities perform better in terms of job entry rates than a comparison group of 27 other municipalities with similar characteristics. The findings did not show a strong impact of increased cooperation in the model municipalities on labour market outcomes for the unemployed. The weak evidence for a cooperation effect is due in part to the methodological problems that affect evaluation of organizational impacts. For example, the timeframe of the evaluation may have been too short for the effects that may occur to work themselves out, or other regions may have changed policies in a similar way to the 'model' regions.

Given the relatively small number of studies trying to assess the impact of implementation on results, our conclusions can only be of a provisional nature. There is certainly evidence of variation in performance between sites but we do not know much about the factors causing them. Therefore it is difficult to say how much overall ALMP performance can be improved by the general adoption of best practice implementation strategies. Clearly, simple general conclusions ('cooperation always leads to better results') cannot be drawn.

Contracting out Employment Services and Privatization

New public management strongly advocates contracting out, that is outsourcing employment services to external market providers, on the assumption that the market sector is more efficient that the public sector. The issue here, it should be noted, is not whether but how a public service should be provided: either 'in house' by its own employees or through external providers on a contract basis. Until a decade ago, allowing private agencies to engage in job brokerage activities was still a highly controversial issue in many countries.

Today, countries such as Australia and the Netherlands have largely privatized their PES by contracting out service provision to external providers. In both countries, the government is still funding active policies but implementation is left completely to private and semi-public organizations, which have to compete in a market for reintegration services. The expectation is that competition will improve service quality and the efficiency of the delivery process. Furthermore, by contracting implementation to non-government agencies the government does not have to maintain a large public employment service at times when there is less need for active measures. In principle, assessment and diagnostic activities to determine what type of treatment is appropriate for a given jobseeker could also be contracted out (but probably not to the agency implementing the treatment).

So far, no evaluations are available containing net impacts. However, some initial experiences with the new Dutch system point to a number of weaknesses. The most important one is the fact that agencies are paid solely on the basis of output (placements). This causes agencies to concentrate on short-term success and to underutilize the training instrument. Furthermore, there is no longer an institution that has an overall view of the labour market and can allocate the funding available for ALMP in such a way that the connection between supply and demand on the meso and macro levels is taken into account. In the Australian system, there is a mixture of input and output financing, which seems more promising. There is also still a PES-like institution that assesses the need for job search assistance and training for a particular unemployed person. Then the person receiving services is free to choose which agency provides the assistance. In the new Dutch system the unemployment benefit-paying agencies largely determine the type of assistance offered, and the PES plays only a limited role; the PES determines whether a newly unemployed person is to receive intensive employment services or only the basic service level (mainly the opportunity to use the PES information facilities, which are now located in the Centres for Work and Income). The Dutch system presupposes that unemployment benefit-paying organizations have a strong incentive to reduce the number of beneficiaries, apparently because this relieves the organizations' budget. However, it is not completely clear that this should be the case.[17]

Performance-oriented Financing

Organizations operating in a competitive market are more or less forced to supply services of good quality and to maintain the efficiency of their production process on a high level. In countries where the implementation of employment services is left to competing private agencies, payment is completely (in the Netherlands) or partly (in Australia) made on the basis of placement results.

However, in situations where government agencies are responsible for implementation, it is possible to create a quasi-market by making funding dependent on results. In Switzerland, the funding of individual employment offices depends partly on their relative performance (Ernst & Young, 1999). With the better performing agencies being rewarded, it is hoped that less well performing agencies will have incentives to improve their results. At first, there seems to be no basic difference between the situation in which implementation is privatized and that in which public agencies are responsible for implementation. There is an important difference, however. In a competitive market, badly performing providers of employment services can easily be replaced. In the Swiss case, clients are stuck with the PES and it is they who suffer if services are poor. Only if the budget cut stimulates the agency to improve its results are clients likely to be better off. However, it seems more logical that the PES staff or at the least the management should feel the consequences rather than the clients. Thus the Swiss system could be altered in such a way as to make PES staff salaries rather than the budget for active policies dependent on performance.

Benchmarking Performance and Disseminating Good Practice

Any attempts to measure output and to benchmark the performance of employment services providers within MBO-type PES management systems, as well as that of external providers in market or quasi-market systems, will be heavily dependent on the ability to measure the net output of service providers. Net output can be defined as the increase in total employment and in the equality of employment opportunities for the various groups in the labour market.[18] In principle this can be done as follows:

- one or more indicators are defined to measure output;
- each indicator is weighted, making it possible to construct a single output measure;
- cross-section analyses are used to determine for each indicator the relative performance of the different PES agencies after correction for the impact of factors outside a PES agency's control;
- the ranking of the agencies is determined on the basis of their overall performance (using the weightings).

This is more or less what the Swiss do (Ernst & Young, 1999). In this procedure, the error term in the regression is supposed to reflect an agency's efficiency. However, unobserved factors that are outside the agency's control may also account for part of the error term. Budgeting systems based on this type of analysis should therefore limit the size of the redistribution based on the estimated relative performance.

In the Australian case, the clients are supposed to choose the agency. Payment of the agency by the government is based partly on placement results. If the agencies had to publish their placement results, jobseekers could base their choice of agency on this information. However, placements are only a measure of gross output. An agency may show better placement results than its competitors because it is concentrating on the higher-profile jobseekers or because it is operating in a region with better employment opportunities.[19] In principle, it is possible to collect the information required for the government (or the researchers it commissions to do the job) to measure net impacts. However, the practical problems are numerous. A large number of agencies may be involved and the numbers of clients per agency for a specific type of measure in a region may be small. Not only will the data collection process be time-consuming, it will also be difficult to make inferences about effectiveness. Thus privatization may well mean that the government, which remains the paymaster, may know less about the effectiveness of ALMP than in a more traditional institutional set-up. However, when the effectiveness of ALMP cannot be properly assessed, the firms involved in implementation may in many cases be able to get away with providing ineffective services. Is it plausible, then, that privatization improves ALMP? It seems to us that privatization is advisable only when it is done in such a way that assessment of the net impacts remains possible. This may be easier to achieve in a quasi-market situation.

Dissemination of information about good practice will probably raise the average performance (although what is good in one situation may not be good in another). However, in a market or quasi-market situation dissemination may be impeded by the fact that the innovating agency has no incentive to share information with its competitors. Thus the government (or the organization operating on behalf of the government) should in some way compensate successful, innovating agencies for the diffusion of information on best practices.

The Application of Information Technologies in Employment Services

In recent years the use of information technologies (IT) has become widespread in employment services. The Internet is increasingly used by jobseekers and employers alike. Many companies include information on their vacancies in their website, making it possible for jobseekers to apply directly for jobs. The employer (through the information contained in his website) and the jobseeker (by attaching his CV) can exchange information in the process. The Internet is also used by a new type of employment services company which collects information on jobseekers and vacancies through the Internet and uses the information to match the two. The work (including the matching) is done almost wholly by computers. An important aspect of this type of activity is that set-up costs are relatively low. Furthermore, only a small number of employees are needed, mostly to do the marketing and the administrative work. This development may have far-reaching consequences. The costs of information on vacancies and jobseekers will be sharply reduced and labour market transparency increased, with positive impacts on employment.

However, if this type of private company is capable of matching demand and supply, will it still be necessary for governments (or the PES) to operate an information system in order to perform exactly the same task? Does the new technology not make job brokerage by public services obsolete rather than strengthening it? A number of issues are at stake here. Are Internet-based job search and recruitment services going to replace conventional job brokerage to a large extent? Do the disadvantaged have equal access to Internet services? As indicated, Internet services in job search and recruitment are growing rapidly, but how far will that growth go?

Representatives of the employment services industry in the Netherlands expressed the opinion that the new services will replace no more than about 20 per cent of the conventional services (Gelderblom, 1999). In their view, personal contacts between the employment agency, the jobseeker and the employer will remain necessary in most cases. People have to see each other, so they say, before they can trust each other. However, there is reason to doubt this assessment. First of all, most of the private agencies have now set up Internet services. Furthermore, further developments in technology may lead to acceptable substitutes for personal contact. Moreover, new generations will be more used to the idea of the Internet as a medium for communication.

However, is it not the case that disadvantaged groups do not have access to the Internet (they cannot afford to buy a computer or to surf the Internet) and that governments must therefore keep the traditional information system and job brokerage activities intact? This is certainly a matter for concern. Job search and recruitment through the Internet is still largely a matter for the more highly educated. On the other hand, the Internet agencies are reporting an increasing share of clients with only secondary education. It is not unlikely, given the increasing user-friendliness of computers and software, that Internet-based services will become firmly established. It is generally believed that in the next five years major breakthroughs in this field will be made. Given the already high penetration rate of personal computers and modern communication devices, it is not very likely that the less well educated will remain excluded from this development.

In our view, conventional job brokerage activities are still needed at the moment but will probably become outdated in the next decade. It is important that the government helps people to acquire the skills needed to handle the new technology and that it offers facilities to those who cannot afford to buy a computer or to use the Internet. Furthermore, it may still be useful for the PES to put information on vacancies and jobseekers from different sources together and offer clients a fairly complete picture in this respect. In countries such as Australia, Belgium and the Netherlands the PES is already moving in this direction. Thus we are inclined to conclude that in the long term the new technology will limit the role of the PES in job brokerage and force the PES to concentrate on its general information function.[20]

So far, we have discussed the PES's information and job brokerage function. Can information technology also play a role in other ALMP activities? That is certainly the case. Two applications can be mentioned. The first is the use of computer programs in early identification of long-term unemployment. The Dutch PES is developing software that should assist counsellors in assessing the need for early interventions among people that have just entered unemployment. The second is the use of IT in training. One possibility is website-based training. IT makes training more independent of time and place. Furthermore, the use of IT as a medium may reduce the costs of large-scale training programmes.[21] However, considerable investment is needed to develop, for instance, interactive forms of web-based training.[22] So far, little is known about the benefits of this type of training, particularly when applied to specific groups such as the unemployed. Given the uncertain returns, private enterprise may not be willing to invest without government support.

4 CONCLUSIONS

On the whole, active labour market policy has performed rather disappointingly to date. At the same time, there is no real alternative to active policies in terms of the functions they fulfil. Admittedly, social protection measures will probably increase unemployment. However, most people are prepared to accept higher unemployment as the price to be paid for procuring equity. Although there may be ways to make the social protection system more employment-friendly, this is unlikely to lead to zero long-term unemployment. Thus there is no real alternative to active policies if an attempt is to be made to push unemployment below the level generated in the labour market at the chosen level of social protection and with maximum use of other policies. It is understandable, therefore, that governments should persist with active policies, even when the results achieved so far look rather poor. As long as there are grounds for thinking that the results of active policies can be improved, this is probably the way to proceed.

Some countries have radically reformed their ALMP systems, sometimes choosing different options, while other countries have lagged behind. If we could conclude, on the basis of the experiences with reforms in a number of countries, that one system performs better than another, we would be in a position to make recommendations about 'how ALMP should be organized'. So far, there is little evidence to suggest that one particular country has a particularly effective ALMP. This does not necessarily mean, of course, that the reforms some countries have recently begun to introduce will not change the picture drastically.

Active policies seem to be of help in establishing a transitional labour market. In this type of labour market, unemployment turnover will tend to be higher. Once in unemployment, there is a risk that people will stay in it for a long time. Active policies can be used to prevent and cure long-term unemployment and may even be used to prevent unemployment. However, the evaluation literature on active policies is rather pessimistic about the effectiveness of these policies. This conclusion was reinforced by a number of recent impact assessments collected in De Koning and Mosley (2001). Thus, if active policies are to become an important tool in establishing transitional labour markets, we need to think about ways to improve the effectiveness of these policies.

So what can be done to improve ALMP performance? As a result of our considerations, the following possibilities are the most promising. First, the design, control and evaluation functions of ALMP could be separated from implementation, with competition or quasi-competition being introduced into the implementation process. However, this has to be done in a sensible way. Most importantly, the government (or the organization it chooses to act on its behalf) has to be able to monitor and evaluate the outcomes carefully.

Second, the allocation of ALMP funding could be improved by a careful selection strategy. ALMP should be designed in order not only to maximize the policy objective function, which should reflect policy goals and priorities, but also to take account of budget restrictions, the labour market situation and the effectiveness and costs of ALMP measures. This is to a large extent a technical matter, which should be left to a professional, publicly funded organization not closely linked to the government (probably the same organization responsible for the design, control and evaluation functions). The government should determine the general objectives of ALMP but not interfere too much with the daily operations.

Third, modern management techniques, especially management by objectives, should be introduced. Fourth, it matters how measures are implemented at the local level, although the results are not always clear-cut. Cooperation, for instance, does not necessarily improve results, contrary to what is often assumed. More needs to be known about the causes of variations in performance and whether general conclusions on this point can be drawn at all. Fifth, the opportunities offered by the new information technologies should be exploited. Finally, social security should be made more employment-friendly by introducing incentives for both workers and employers to prevent workers from entering the benefit system at all or – if this is not possible – by limiting benefit duration and channelling people into measures to enhance their employability.

NOTES

1. Although they will be prepared to take account of the consequences of cyclical output variations to some extent.
2. This chapter is based in part on the more comprehensive treatment of the role of ALMP in enhancing the employability and the job chances of the unemployed in De Koning and Mosley (2001) and on a paper presented at an OECD conference on active policies and the public employment service (De Koning, 2000).
3. See De Koning, Mosley and Schmid (2001), 'Active Labour Market Policies, Social Exclusion, and Transitonal Labour Markets', in De Koning and Mosley (2001), pp. 1–16, for a more detailed discussion of these studies.
4. The share of long-term unemployment among men in EU(15) was 47.4 per cent in 1997, 50.6 per cent among women (Employment in Europe, 1998: 149).
5. Experiments will also disrupt the daily operations of the implementing agencies.
6. For an extensive discussion and evaluation of this and other options, see Heckman *et al.* (1997).
7. This conclusion is underpinned by a large number of studies covering many countries. A good illustration is provided by an analysis based on survey data for seven countries (OECD, 1999). For each of the countries, educational attainment and at least one indicator of participation in continuing training are significant in wage regressions.
8. According to O'Connell and McGinnity (1996) training is more effective when the training content matches employers' requirements.
9. In the case of wage subsidy schemes, it is possible to assess side-effects such as substitution and displacement to some extent by using surveys of employers involved in the scheme (and perhaps also those not involved). Examples of this approach can be found in De Koning (1993).
10. The official unemployment figure may not decline if the 'activated' were not counted as unemployed because they were not actively seeking.
11. In the case of training, ALMP may initially stimulate the transition into education and improve job chances only in the longer term.
12. People engaging in ALMP will often not be counted as unemployed during participation. Unsuccessful participants will 'reappear' after completing the programme.
13. In many cases, long time series are not available. Under these circumstances, relatively short time series relating to different regions or countries are often pooled. However, in this approach it necessarily has to be assumed that the model is, with the exception of the constant term, the same for each region or country.
14. An exception may have to be made for vocational training leading to an officially recognized qualification. This type of training may have no or even negative effects in the short term but could have a positive impact in the long term. Evaluation studies do not usually monitor participants for more than a few years.
15. A simple version of such a model can be found in De Koning (forthcoming).
16. This section is based on Mosley and Sol (2001).
17. For example, it could even be argued that there is a disincentive because reducing the number of beneficiaries might put staff of these organizations out of work. Therefore the Australian system may provide stronger incentives to the implementing organizations than the Dutch system.

18. Perhaps more precisely: the increase in the objective function depending on total employment and its distribution over groups.
19. It is unclear whether agencies can refuse to 'treat' a client. If this is the case, creaming may be a problem, particularly in times of high unemployment.
20. This may consist of more than assembling existing information and providing it in a user-friendly way to the public. For instance, the PES could also support labour market forecasting.
21. Simulation programmes may partly replace real-life machines.
22. In a study by Gelderblom *et al.* (2000) it was found that, to date, ICT-based training as developed by private enterprise has been loss-making.

BIBLIOGRAPHY

Behrenz, L., L. Delander and H. Niklasson (2001), 'Towards Intensified Local Level Co-operation in the Design and Implementation of Labour Market Policies: An Evaluation of Some Swedish Experiments and Reforms', in J. de Koning and H. Mosley (eds), *Labour Market Policy and Unemployment: Impact and Process Evaluations in Selected European Countries*, Cheltenham, UK and Northampton, US: Edward Elgar.

Bovaird, T. (1996), 'Performance Assessment of Service Quality: Lessons from UK National Initiatives to Influence Local Government', in H. Hill, H. Klages and E. Löffler (eds), *Quality, Innovation and Measurement in the Public Sector*, Frankfurt a.M. and Berlin: Peter Lang, pp. 37–64.

Dercksen, W. and J. De Koning (1996), 'The New Public Employment Service in the Netherlands (1991–1994)', WZB Discussion Paper FS I 96–201, WZB, Berlin.

Ernst and Young (1999), 'Berechnung der Wirkungen der RAV unter Berücksichtigung exogener Einflussfaktoren', Berne: Ernst and Young.

Fay, R.G. (1996), 'Enhancing the Effectiveness of Active Labour Market Policies: Evidence from Programme Evaluations in OECD Countries', Labour Market and Social Policy Occasional Papers No. 18, Organisation for Economic Cooperation and Development, Paris.

Friedlander, D., D.H. Greenberg and Ph.K. Robins (1997), 'Evaluating Government Training Programmes for the Economically Disadvantaged', *Journal of Economic Literature*, XXXV, 1809–55.

Gelderblom, A. (1999), *De effecten van Internet voor de arbeidsmarkt*, Rotterdam: Institute for Labour Policy Research.

Gelderblom, A., R. Blanken and J. de Koning (2000), *Scholing and ICT*, Rotterdam: Institute for Labour Policy Research/SEOR.

Gravesteijn, J.H., M. Arents, K. Jonker, R. Olieman, J. De Koning and P.J. Van Nes (1998), *Wordt succes bepaald door de vorm?: onderzoek naar de doorstroom van gesubsidieerde naar reguliere arbeid*, The Hague: Elsevier.

Heckman, J.J. and J.A. Smith (1996), 'Experimental and Nonexperimental Evaluation', in G. Schmid, J. O'Reilly and K. Schömann (eds), *International Handbook of Labour Market Policy*, Cheltenham, UK and Brookfield, US: Edward Elgar.

Heckman, J.J., H. Ichimura and P.E. Todd (1997), 'Matching as an Econometric Evaluation Estimator: Evidence from a Job Training Programme', *The Review of Economic Studies*, 64(4), No. 221, 605–54 (Special Issue: Evaluation of Training and Other Social Programmes).

Jongen, E.L.W. (1999), 'What Can We Expect from Subsidies for the Long-term Unemployed?', *De Economist*, 147(2), 205–28.

De Koning, J. (1993), 'Measuring the Placement Effects of Two Wage-Subsidy Schemes for the Long-term Unemployed', *Empirical Economics*, 18, 447–68.

De Koning, J. (2000), 'How can we make active policies more effective? The role of organisation, implementation and optimal allocation in active labour market policy', revised and extended version of a paper presented during the conference on 'Labour Market Policies and the Public Employment Service', organized by the Czech Ministry of Labour and the OECD, Prague, July 2000.

De Koning, J. (2001), 'Models for Aggregate Impact Analysis of Active Labour Market Policy', in J. de Koning and H. Mosley (eds), *Labour Market Policy and Unemployment: Impact and Process Evaluations in Selected European Countries*, Cheltenham, UK and Northampton, US: Edward Elgar.

De Koning, J. (2002), 'Training for the Unemployed in the Netherlands: What do we know after more than 50 evaluation studies?', in K. Schömann and P.J. O'Connell (eds), *Training and Employment Dynamics. Transitional Labour Markets in the European Union*, Cheltenham, UK and Northampton, US: Edward Elgar.

De Koning, J. and H. Mosley (2001), *Labour Market Policy and Unemployment: Impact and Process Evaluations in Selected European Countries*, Cheltenham, UK and Northampton, US: Edward Elgar.

De Koning, J., H. Mosley and G. Schmid (2001), 'Active Labour Market Policies, Social Exclusion and Transitional Labour Markets', in J. de Koning and H. Mosley (eds), *Labour Market Policy and Unemployment: Impact and Process Evaluations in Selected European Countries*, Cheltenham, UK and Northampton, US: Edward Elgar, pp. 1–16.

De Koning, J., R. Olieman and C. van der Veen (1999), *The Chance Meter: Measuring an Individual's Chance of Long-term Unemployment*, Rotterdam: NEI.

Layard, R. and S.J. Nickell (1986), 'Unemployment in Britain', *Economica*, Supplement 53, 121–70.

Mosley, H. and E. Sol (2001), 'Process Evaluation of Active Labour Market Policies and Trends in Implementation Regimes', in J. de Koning and H. Mosley (eds), *Labour Market Policy and Unemployment: Impact and Process Evaluations in Selected European Countries*, Cheltenham, UK and Northampton, MA, USA: Edward Elgar, pp. 163–77.

Mosley, Hugh, Holger Schütz and Nicole Breyer (2001), 'Operational Objectives and Performance Indicators in European Public Employment Services. Research Report for the European Commission, Directorate General for Employment and Social Affairs', WZB discussion paper, FS I 01–203, WZB, Berlin.

Niklasson, H. and L. Tomsmark (1997), 'Zielsteuerung der Arbeitsmarktpolitik in Finland, Norwegen und Schweden', in C. Riegler and F. Naschold (eds), *Reformen des öffentlichen Sektors in Skandinavien*, Baden-Baden: Nomos Verlagsgesellschaft, pp. 197–248 (first published 1994 as 'Att malstyra arbetsmarknadspolitik', in *TemaNord*, 573, Copenhagen).

O'Connell, P. and F. McGinnity, 'What Works, Who Works? The Impact of Active Labour Market Programmes on the Employment Prospects of Young People in Ireland', WZB Discussion Paper FS I 96–207, WZB, Berlin.

OECD (1993), *Employment Outlook*, Paris: OECD.

OECD (1997), *Enhancing the Effectiveness of Active Labour Market Policies: a Streamlined Public Employment Service*, Paris: OECD.

OECD (1998), *Early Identification of Jobseekers at Risk of Long-term Unemployment: the Role of Profiling*, Paris: OECD.

OECD (1999), *Employment Outlook*, Paris: OECD.

Rabe, B. (2000), 'Wirkungen aktiver Arbeitsmarktpolitik. Evaluierungsergebnisse für Deutschland, Schweden, Dänemark und die Niederlande', WZB Discussion Paper FS I 00–208, WZB, Berlin.

Schmid, G. (1996), 'Process Evaluation: Policy Formation and Implementation', in G. Schmid, J. O'Reilly and K. Schömann (eds), *International Handbook of Labour Market Policy Evaluation*, Cheltenham, UK and Brookfield, USA: Edward Elgar.

Schmid, G. (1998), 'Transitional Labour Markets: A New European Employment Strategy', WZB Discussion Paper FS I 98–206, WZB, Berlin.

Schütz, H., S. Speckesser and G. Schmid (1998), 'Benchmarking Labour Market Performance and Labour Market Policies: Theoretical Foundations and Applications', WZB Discussion Paper FS I 98–204, WZB, Berlin.

Stern, J., C. Willis, N. Francis and R. Goodyer (1995), *OECD Wage Subsidy Evaluations: Lessons for WORKSTART*, London: NERA.

van Velzen, M. (2001), 'Activation through cooperation. A case study of the implementation of active measures in the Netherlands', in J. de Koning and H. Mosley (eds), *Labour Market Policy and Unemployment: Impact and Process Evaluations in Selected European Countries*, Cheltenham, UK and Northampton, US: Edward Elgar.

393-435

E24
J68
J24
J24
J65

12. Transitional labour markets and the European social model: towards a new employment compact

Günther Schmid

'The "social model" that many Europeans hold up as superior to the somewhat more limited welfare states elsewhere is not economically viable for the twenty-first century.' This harsh verdict by the Nobel Prize winner James Buchanan is shocking for Europeans who consider social protection to be both a productive factor and an effective buffer against the hardships of advanced capitalist societies. However, on reflection and further reading, that statement can be interpreted more optimistically. Buchanan proceeds: 'survival becomes possible only if generality is preserved. (. . .) The general welfare state may survive if it imposes a limit upon itself and does so generally; the discriminatory welfare-transfer state will not survive' (Buchanan, 1998: 14–15).

Buchanan's argument is based on two plausible assumptions. First, the actual 'rich' will not pay for the actual 'poor' if they cannot participate in the benefits as virtual victims of economic and social change. They will avoid taxes or contributions at any opportunity. Inclusiveness of social protection increases legitimacy and willingness to pay. The 'poor', on the other hand, can only ride along with others in the carriage; they cannot expect to ride alone, at least not in tolerable comfort. Second, the extensive general welfare state is incompatible with democracy because the 'natural logic' of majority rule implies differential or discriminatory treatment of those persons and groups that are in the minority. However, transfer entitlements enjoyed by the majority usually extend beyond any legislative period and are often not reversible even if the government changes. A ratchet effect is then set in motion and fiscal crisis takes root at the heart of an uncontrolled universal welfare democracy.[1]

If these assumptions are accepted, which they are in this chapter, albeit with some modification,[2] there are only two strategies that can avoid the risks inherent in social market democracies. The first is to include the 'rich' in social protection regulation and the corresponding employment policies; the second to invent self-regulatory rules governing the organization of social protection and employment policies that limit the scope for dismantlement by future generations. Thus the European social model has no future unless it succeeds in maintaining a universal and non-discriminatory system of social protection and employment policy. This suggests that the present trend towards a selective welfare state oriented only towards the so-called 'needy' is taking policy in the wrong direction. It further implies that employment policies aimed only at the so-called 'problem groups' in the labour market will be ineffective in the long run. The future of the European social model depends crucially on its remaining inclusive in social terms and containing the tendency towards discrimination. How can these principles be transformed into policy strategies?

It will be argued in this chapter that transitional labour markets can be part of the solution. They certainly do not replace conventional social or employment policy, but they can play an essential role in compensating for the increasing inadequacies of the established social protection system. Transitional labour markets are inclusive since they provide a set of mobility opportunities for all categories of workers, and they are self-containing since they require negotiation and cofinancing in the provision of social protection. Transitional labour markets emphasize the ex ante promotion of mobility instead of ex post redistribution through transfers. They transform social policy into joint risk management by encouraging people to accept more risks, with beneficial externalities for society. Examples of such risks might include starting a family or setting up a business enterprise, moving from uncompetitive to competitive sectors or locations, shifting from full-time to part-time work and vice versa, and investing in new human or social capital. The aim of risk management, therefore, is not to minimize risks but to make risk taking acceptable through the provision of new forms of intertemporal, intergenerational and interregional forms of solidarity.

This is what 'flexicurity' is about. More flexibility needs more not less security. This argument is developed in section 1. Section 2 provides examples of good practice related to the different types of risks on the labour market, while section 3 outlines the framework of a new employment compact required to implement the new European social model.

1   FROM SOCIAL POLICY TO RISK MANAGEMENT

The need to extend the scope of employment insurance stems from the changing nature of the risks[3] that have to be faced in the labour market during the life course:[4] the change of the family from a consumption unit to an investment unit (Carnoy, 1999), demographic changes, and in particular the ageing of the workforce, the so-called 'informational revolution' (Castells, 1996) and changes in the international division of labour, so-called 'globalization'.

On the labour *demand side*, work organization is changing in many respects: flattening of hierarchies, higher skill levels, extension of team and project work, increased delegation of responsibility to lower-level staff, improved communication throughout companies, flexible working hours and compensation regimes.[5] The organizational principle of large-scale, locally established enterprises will increasingly be replaced by loose networks of production or service units. Bureaucratic internal labour markets are mutating into network labour markets, with small and medium-sized enterprises or profit centres as their nodal points (Cappelli *et al.*, 1997). On the labour *supply side*, we observe an increasing interest in job or occupational mobility fed by pull factors (preferences for self-discovery and social status) and push factors (burn-out syndromes and regional mobility due to divorce, climate preferences or other idiosyncrasies). Both tendencies are interacting and fundamentally altering the employment relationship (see Chapter 5).

Transitional labour market theory (see Chapters 1, 5 and 6) suggests that risks should be classified according to the critical transitions that occur during the life course. A mutually supportive system of social protection and employ-ment policies, therefore, would have to find institutional responses for five main types of risks (Figure 12.1):

1. maintaining and enhancing *income capacity* during transitions between education or training and employment;
2. guaranteeing *income security* during critical transitions between various employment relationships, especially between part-time and full-time work and between dependent employment and self-employment;
3. providing *income support* during phases in the life course in which income capacity is restricted owing to social obligations, especially care of children;
4. securing *income maintenance* during transitions between employment and unemployment;
5. providing *income replacement* in the event of reduced or zero income capacity, due to disability or retirement, for example.

The characteristic feature of the future labour market will not be the risk of mass unemployment due to cyclical downturns, although this risk of course remains. A greater challenge will be the permanent risk of diminishing employability (Gazier, 1999) and the corresponding decline or volatility of income streams: the skill requirements of the 'informational revolution' can even turn formerly productive and healthy people into functionally disabled people. In addition, the feminization of the labour market will accentuate the risk of diminishing social protection due to discontinuous employment careers. Finally, in an era of individualization, growing income inequality and

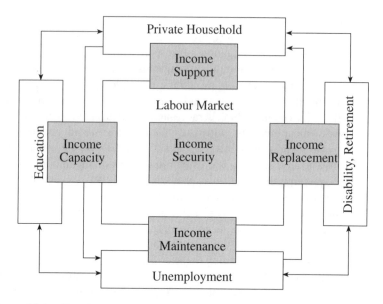

Figure 12.1   Typology of (new) labour market risks

chronic illnesses give rise to the risk of long-term dependency on collective forms of care or income subsidies.

Confronted by these new trends, the first crucial step in the transformation of ex post social and employment policy into ex ante risk management is the differentiation of social protection institutions according to the nature of the risks they are intended to cover. Such differentiation corresponds to the (positive) principle of 'requisite variety' in systems theory: 'only variety in institutions can meet varieties in problems'.[6] It also obeys the (normative) principle of 'cybern-ethics': 'act always in such a way that the number of possibilities increases'.[7] Secondly, flexibility is required to achieve growth in new markets, especially in the 'new economy'. Thus social policy and labour market policy have to provide not only work incentives but also flexibility incentives. To achieve flexibility, systems theory suggests loose linkages between (relatively autonomous) subsystems. This principle requires a decoupling of social security from specific jobs and its linkage with (flexible) life-time employment. Flexibility is endangered, for instance, when employees are unexpectedly laid off and have simultaneously to cope with changes in income, health insurance, challenges to their self-esteem and problems with childcare arrangements. Thirdly, the increased complexity produced by this differentiation and decoupling requires greater coordination between the various subsystems. Thus checks will have to be carried out to ensure that the interfaces of the various social security subsystems fulfil the principle of *complementarity* (see also Chapter 2).

Thus the reasons for extending the unemployment insurance (UI) system are straightforward. Classic UI responds only to external risks, such as cyclical fluctuations, seasonal influences in the product market or technological innovations. Extended employment insurance (EI) carries the idea of risk management one step further to cover 'manufactured' or internal risks in the labour market.[8] Paradoxically, therefore, one of the functions of EI is to encourage people to take responsibility for such risks themselves by providing institutional solutions to cover the related risks, for instance income support during sabbaticals or parental leave, enhancing employability through lifelong learning arrangements and income maintenance during changing working-time regimes (Figure 12.2).

The new institutions related to EI must be transparent and durable in order that their rules may become known and trusted, since perception of risks is important in employment decisions. Economists usually recognize the importance of risk in financial markets, but it is unusual to include it in analysis of the incentives for individuals to work or to assume responsibility for the risks of transitions between various employment statuses. It is especially relevant

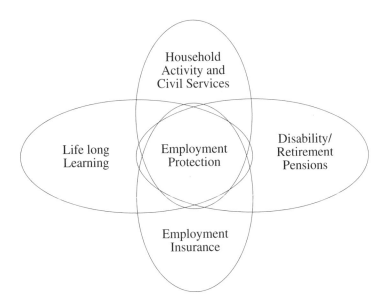

Source: Adapted from Schömann *et al.* (2000).

Figure 12.2 From unemployment insurance to employment insurance

for the decision to take on low-paid jobs combined with in-work benefits. The related risks often compare unfavourably with the (learned) certainty of pure benefit schemes. This makes it increasingly important to extend the UI system to cover the risks of employability, mobility and flexibility. Cofinancing more discontinuous employment trajectories in order to preserve and develop rights on an enlarged basis is a crucial element of a multifunctional EI. The future world of work requires not only 'making work pay' but also – and maybe even more crucially – *'making transitions pay'*. Other social protection systems that are closely related to the labour market, especially old age and disability insurance, should be scrutinized in order to ascertain whether they encourage people to undertake 'risky' transitions between various forms of employment, to combine various forms of productive activity or to move to another region.

Proponents of greater flexibility are often criticized for neglecting the related risks of social exclusion.[9] It is important, therefore, to formulate explicitly the criteria for sustainable flexibility and for managing the equality–efficiency trade-off.[10] Modern social choice theory[11] and new public management theory[12] suggest four criteria that institutional arrangements have to fulfil in order to support 'good transitions' and to prevent 'bad transitions'. First, individual *freedom* (or *autonomy*) has to be enhanced by empowering people and establishing entitlements not only to transfers but also to participation in employment decisions; in exchange, individual employees would accept greater risks, duties and obligations. Second, *solidarity* has to be promoted through generality and inclusiveness in risk sharing; the problem of adverse selection implies some ex ante redistribution through the inclusion of high-income groups, who usually have lower employment risks. Third, *effectiveness* has to be improved through specialization, coordination and cooperation; this usually requires a public–private mix in implementation. Fourth, *efficiency* has to be increased through the application to labour market policies of risk management techniques such as controlling, monitoring, evaluation and self-regulation through decentralization or management by objectives.[13]

2   RISK MANAGEMENT THROUGH MUTUALLY SUPPORTIVE SOCIAL PROTECTION AND EMPLOYMENT POLICIES

How can this model work in reality? To answer this question, I will now screen the five main types of transitions on the labour market and their related typical risks from the perspective of good practice. Evaluation of these practices according to the criteria formulated above will provide some clues about a feasible employment policy strategy within a new European social model.

Activating Transitions between Education, Training and Work

The most important change in risks related to human capital investment is the generalization of these risks over the life course. Both the transition from school to work and transitions between jobs over the life course bring with them the risk of uncertain returns on investment. In addition, the risk of skill obsolescence for adults is increasing, for various reasons.

Firstly, we are faced with a two-speed labour market. Each year, about 10 per cent of jobs are lost; the annual rate of job creation is also about 10 per cent, and most of these jobs have new skill requirements. However, the natural labour turnover (exchange of generations) is only between 2 and 3 per cent. New technologies and the consequent rapid depreciation of investments in human capital, together with the ageing of the labour force, are putting pressure on lifelong learning. It has been estimated that 80 per cent of the technology in use between 1995 and 2005 will be less than 10 years old, but that 80 per cent of the workforce will have been educated and trained 10 years previously.[14] The shortage of at least one million people competent in information technologies is already a serious handicap for Europe's competitiveness.[15] Competition between (highly) educated people is increasing because of the new information technology, which provides easy access both to price information (labour costs) and to specialized skills in any part of the world. Last but not least, women have significantly lower training expectations than men, due to less continuous employment patterns and high shares of part-time work with low training access rates. Thus gender-neutral risk sharing should become a top priority for social protection and employment policies, since good education and lifelong learning are increasingly decisive determinants of competitive labour markets. The tremendous gap in unemployment rates according to skill level clearly demonstrates the importance of income capacity and employability risks (Table 12.1).

Attempts to meet the education and training challenge of the informational labour market take three main institutional forms. The first involves the conversion of unemployment benefit entitlements into vouchers for training and education. In the second, income capacity risks are internalized by giving individuals new legal rights within the employment relationship to negotiate for paid or unpaid training or educational leave. In the third, continuous investment in human capital is given favourable tax treatment in order to enhance positive externalities or to overcome the 'prisoner's dilemma' that might be linked to this kind of investment. A good-practice case, explained in greater detail below, is the paid education or training leave scheme, also familiar under the name of 'job rotation', that has been implemented successfully in Sweden since 1991 and in Denmark since 1994. More and more countries

Applications and policy strategies

Table 12.1   Unemployment rates, by skill levels in selected countries, 1997

Country	Graduates (1)	Secondary II (2)	Primary I (3)	Ratio (3)/(1)	Total
Germany				.	
Women	7.0	10.9	15.9	2.3	10.9
Men	5.1	9.2	17.7	3.5	9.1
The Netherlands					
Women	4.0	5.6	10.1	2.5	6.4
Men	2.8	3.0	5.3	1.9	3.6
Austria					
Women	3.4	4.2	7.3	2.1	5.0
Men	2.2	4.3	7.9	3.6	4.7
Denmark					
Women	3.7	5.5	10.2	2.8	5.8
Men	3.2	4.0	6.1	1.9	4.1
United Kingdom					
Women	2.7	5.2	6.0	2.2	4.9
Men	3.4	6.3	9.7	2.9	6.8
France					
Women	7.3	12.3	16.9	2.3	12.8
Men	6.2	8.0	13.9	2.2	9.6
Sweden					
Women	3.3	9.8	12.1	3.7	8.2
Men	5.2	10.5	11.9	2.9	9.6

Source: Eurostat Labour Force Survey (1997); own calculations.

in the European Union are following this example and introducing their own education or training leave programmes.

According to the four criteria for good transitions, the design of such schemes should have the following ideal-type characteristics:

1. It should empower individuals by providing a legal entitlement to paid leave, during which time the employment relationship is protected and the income loss replaced to some extent. However, the right to training or education leaves would be conditional on negotiation with the employers. Entitlements to unemployment benefits are transformed into training subsidies and a progressive tax system subsidizes the reduced wage income during periods of training. In exchange, employees would partici-pate in financing such schemes, for instance through wage moderation combined with an investment component (wages or working time accounts linked to human resources investment). In some professions in

which adjustment to new technologies is crucial for proper performance and avoidance of damage (for instance doctors, teachers and engineers controlling or supervising complex technical facilities), it might even be necessary to make regular retraining an obligation.

2. Solidarity requires the inclusion of all incomes in financing public support of training and education. The solidarity element could also be enhanced by channelling public support towards target groups: the low-skilled, the elderly or women re-entering the labour market might receive preferential treatment, for example through higher subsidies.

3. Effectiveness would be enhanced through a rich infrastructure of specialized training institutions and local providers or agencies. Competition could be implicitly established by targeted regional budgets and quality standards which have to be met in applications for public support.

4. Efficiency of education or training leave schemes would be guaranteed through cofinancing arrangements between employers and employees. Negotiation between cofinancing partners (if there is a balanced power structure) will help to ensure the cost-containing principle of fiscal congruity (the equivalent balance of costs and benefits in the long run). Targeted regional budgets and a system of public fund allocation that took some account of performance would also provide incentives for local actors to use financial resources efficiently.

The Danish training and education leave schemes almost meet all four criteria for good transitions. Since 1994, workers with at least five years' labour market experience have been entitled to a generous period of educational or training leave of up to one year. Special public support is provided if those on leave are replaced by unemployed individuals; this is the so-called 'job rotation programme'. Experience with the scheme over recent years reveals some of the strengths and weaknesses that have to be considered in adopting and adjusting this model to specific national or regional circumstances. From the point of view of our theoretical framework, the most interesting observations to be derived from the Danish leave schemes are given below.[16]

First of all, it is important for employers that the replacement of those on leave by unemployed persons is not obligatory. Thus there is considerable flexibility in implementation and much discretion in the bargaining on cofinancing. Both employers and employees take a very positive view of such educational leaves. As the large share of public-sector employees taking leave indicates, small and medium-sized enterprises (SMEs) in the private sector often have great difficulties in implementing such a scheme. This imbalance also explains why 75 per cent of those taking training leave are women. If employment insurance (EI) in the form of training leaves or job rotation is to become firmly established within SMEs, which represent an increasingly important sector of employment, there is an obvious need for more sophisticated regulations and a rich network infrastructure in order to deal effectively with transaction costs. Risks that are unmanageable for small firms could be managed through job pools run, for example, by temporary work agencies. Furthermore, the long-term unemployed are underrepresented among the substitute workers, which means that the schemes have not influenced firms' recruitment behaviour in favour of 'outsiders'. In fact, it turns out that around 50 per cent of the substitutes are drawn from the 'extended internal labour market' (for instance, former employees or individuals well known to the employers in question). The chances of this target group participating in such measures might be enhanced if they were to receive preliminary training in the job pools.

There is some indication of a mobility chain fostered by the good economic climate in Denmark. One of the evaluations reported that 49 per cent of the substitute workers in the private sector and 34 per cent in the public sector continued in employment with the same employer; 10 per cent in the private sector and 4 per cent in the public sector remained in the same job. This means, in turn, that employed persons taking training leave probably obtained a better job, either with the same employer or in a new firm or organization. The short-term net costs to the public purse per participant in a leave scheme have been estimated at between 670 and 2670 Euro per person. Taking into account the social costs of unemployment and the potential long-term productivity gains, the cost–benefit ratio for society seems to be clearly positive.[17]

The European ADAPT programme has taken up the Danish idea of job rotation and sponsored various pilot projects for small or medium-sized firms and a network in order to acquire greater experience with this innovation. If the take-up level at its height in Denmark (1994–8) were replicated throughout the European Union, two million people, or 1.3 per cent of the employed population, would be involved in the scheme.[18] Other ideas for EI related to lifelong learning might include training vouchers, subsidized saving accounts for education and training and favourable tax treatment for expenditure on continuous human capital investment.

Activating Transitions between Various Working-time Regimes or Employment Statuses

The new employment insurance should also provide some cover for the risks related to the erosion of the standard employment relationship (see Chapter 7). Two hypotheses on managing the risks inherent in new employment relationships can be advanced. Firstly, there is a clear trend towards performance-oriented payment systems. As a consequence, income risks are being shifted from the firm to the worker. Moreover, policies aimed at strengthening individual 'employability' are also shifting a higher share of 'employment risks'

Table 12.2   Risk management and employment relationships

Risk of the service provision	Yi (individual)	$Y\alpha i + \beta c^*$ (mixed)	Yc (collective)
Work organization			
Xi (individual)	1 pure self-employment	4	7 insured self-employment
$X\alpha i + \beta c^*$ (mixed)	2	5 franchising	8
Xc (collective)	3 pseudo self-employment	6	9 pure dependent salaried work

Note: *The α and β coefficients ($\alpha + \beta = 1$) indicate that the proportions of the individual (i) and collective (c) dimensions are mixed and may vary according to the different cases.

Source: Adapted from Morin (1999), quoted in Gazier and Thevenot (2000: 248).

to workers. Secondly, this trend is not leading to unilateral changes in the employment relationship, because it can be combined with a variety of organizational choices. Risk management leads to very different work arrangements, even for the same task. It can be carried out within different organizational frameworks, with a different distribution of risks, duties and compensations. The following systematic table makes it possible to locate these hybrid arrangements at some point on a continuum between the standard salaried employed contract and self-employment (Table 12.2).

The transitions between various working-time regimes or employment statuses create new types of risk which are not yet covered properly by social protection systems or standard labour market policies. In general terms, and with respect to the increasing variability of employment contracts, the four criteria for good transitions would translate into the following requirements.

1. *Individual freedom* should be enhanced through new rights to make decisions or to bargain on working-time issues. In exchange, individuals will have to accept more flexibility in their employment contracts, for instance the accumulation and concomitant reduction of working time in accordance with operational requirements (flexible time accounts). The advantage to employers would be a reduction in overtime pay, while the advantage to insiders would be greater time sovereignty. For their part, outsiders would gain higher labour intensity.

2. The *solidarity* criterion requires the generalization of regulations on working-time issues and employment status. This implies, for instance,

the inclusion of the self-employed and other excluded groups in the general social protection scheme since these categories are also affected by the new risks. Social protection has also to be extended to cover the risks related to discontinuous income streams. Collective or individual agreements including performance-oriented payment systems could be more widespread if they were connected to specific insurance schemes. Alternatively, the established insurance schemes include elements of flexibility entitlements accumulated during the 'good times' of stable employment relationships.

3. The *effectiveness* criterion requires a rich network of local public–private partnerships to implement flexible working-time arrangements or transitions between various employment statuses; small and medium-sized enterprises with limited organizational capacities particularly need such support. Local and regional job pools jointly organized by temporary work agencies and the public employment service could enhance such a network infrastructure.

4. The *efficiency* criterion requires risk-sharing elements to guarantee *cost containment*. Collective agreements or individual contracts have to find ways of explicitly formulating such risk-sharing arrangements in order to strengthen self-regulation.

An example of the enhancing of individual freedom would be the entitlement to (negotiate on) an intermediate employment status between part-time and full-time work,[19] supported perhaps by a general part-time unemployment benefit scheme conditional on certain circumstances. To the best of my knowledge, only Finland has introduced a true part-time unemployment benefit scheme, which started in 1994.[20] Sweden provides benefits in cases of involuntary part-time work, that is when an unemployed person seeking full-time work takes up a part-time job. These part-timers have a legal right to be given priority in the allocation of full-time jobs if the firm's labour demand increases (Vidmar, 1999: 328). On the other hand, minimum standards are required to protect people in a weak bargaining position. For example, on-call work should be restricted by setting a minimum working time, as recently stipulated by the Dutch government. Another possibility for adjusting to new types of employment relationships would be to treat multiple employment relationships, usually a series of part-time jobs held simultaneously, as one regular employment relationship recognized as such in law. Germany has already introduced part-time benefits in cases of multiple employment relationships.[21]

Classic UI provides only income maintenance in the event of income loss through unemployment, whereas an extended employment insurance (EI) would also cover the risk of income volatility. A relatively old and well-known good practice example of EI related to transitions between various working-time regimes is the *short-time compensation scheme*. In functional terms, short-time benefits are part-time unemployment benefits that help employees to adjust for income loss due to business cycle demand fluctuations (Mosley and Kruppe, 1996). In most countries where it is applied, however, this scheme is in practice restricted to the manufacturing sector. This does not fulfil the inclusiveness and generality criterion. Since we are moving ever further towards the service society, the principle underlying this programme should be extended to volatile income streams in the service sector.

In addition, the cost-containment criteria would suggest that such instruments should be combined with investment in human capital to enhance future employability during periods of working-time adjustment.[22] Traditional lay-off schemes are the functional equivalent of short-time compensation schemes. They can be seen as a hybrid (some would say perverse) form of UI. Their function is to maintain relation-specific investments through the implicit contract, whereas UI takes over the income maintenance function. The objective of this instrument is not only to maintain income during shortened working hours but also to maintain the (firm-specific) skills and other investments in human capital, including social capital. Closer examination of the functioning of UI systems in Europe reveals that there are many more of those kinds of lay-offs than might be expected. In Denmark and in Austria, 'recall' of the unemployed by the previous employer is a widespread practice, which means that the UI system is already implicitly subsidizing or cross-subsidizing transitions for whatever reason: seasonal fluctuations in activity, internal restructuring, health problems or even implicit training leaves. A recent Swedish study surprisingly revealed that about 40 per cent of the unemployed return to their original employer.[23] If this observation is correct and foreshadows a growing tendency, this should be taken into account in the shift from UI to EI and attempts should be made to contain the costs of the (mostly hidden) subsidies through risk-related contributions.

Extending short-time work as a device for EI, however, is not enough. This is all the more true since this instrument is still closely linked to (old-fashioned) manufacturing industries and not yet adapted to the typical risks in the service or information society. A first example of these new risks is the increasing *mobility between dependent employment and self-employment*, or the blurring of the borderlines between the two. Some countries have recently incorporated into their UI systems insurance against the risk of failure for those of the unemployed population seeking to become self-employed. The programmes assisting the unemployed into self-employment usually contain regulations that maintain entitlement to unemployment benefit in the event of failure. On the other hand, as part of the fight against the spread of so-called 'pseudo self-employment', governments have introduced stricter regulations or mandatory social security contributions for the self-employed. However, few if any EU member states have yet found a satisfactory solution for managing the risks inherent in such imprecisely defined employment statuses.

Concession bargaining or efficient employment contracts[24] are interesting in this context because they reflect the emergence of new actors in risk management and the corresponding broader set of EI. The underlying principle of such contracts is that they combine wage goals with employment goals, for instance working-time flexibility or employability security. However, a further element would have to be added if they were to be subsumed under a true EI arrangement, namely some kind of insurance arrangement aimed at compensating to some extent for the associated loss of income or earnings capacity. In this kind of concession bargaining, trade unions typically concede a reduction of working time without (full) wage compensation in exchange for employment guarantees.

One prominent case is the Volkswagen agreement of 1994.[25] However, it is not so widely known that similar agreements were also adopted in other companies in the metal industry and indeed in other sectors in Western Germany, including the iron and steel and paper industries and retailing. However, most of the agreements were concluded at firm level and any employment guarantees related only to the workforce in post at the time of the agreement. To the best of my knowledge, no explicit solidary insurance arrangements have yet been put in place. Concession bargaining at industry level with a view to increasing the overall employment level raises the problem of how to control 'free riding' by individual firms. One interesting proposal in this context is the introduction of a licence system in which firms could buy licences to reduce employment below the agreed target from firms that increase employment above that level (Scharr, 1997). In the spirit of cooperative risk management, the state could step into this game and provide insurance by managing, supervising or supporting such arrangements.

Another kind of new risk management is related to *changing working time preferences*. If they reflect a desire to reduce working time, at least temporarily, the implementation of such preferences could be combined with measures to increase employment and to reduce unemployment. An interesting example is the recent initiative agreed between the social partners in the metal and electrical industry in the state of Lower Saxony in Germany. They agreed on a one-year pilot project (1999) and established an association to provide support for work-sharing arrangements among their 80 000 members. The association was endowed with capital of DM 10 million from the employers and DM 200 000 from the trade union, out of which employees reducing their working time were to be compensated for income forgone at a rate of between 70 and 90 per cent. The most important innovation compared with earlier work-sharing agreements is the intention to create additional jobs and not only to

prevent dismissals (as in the case of Volkswagen). Thus the partial compensation for income loss is paid only if unemployed persons are hired in proportion to the volume of working time cut. 'Unemployment has a name' is the
slogan used to promote employment-friendly work sharing.

Under this general rule, all kinds of work sharing are allowed. For instance,
six full-time workers could reduce their working time by one sixth, thereby
freeing enough hours for one new full-time job. In fact, the approach most
commonly adopted was for four employees each to reduce their working time
by seven hours (from 35 to 28 hours per week), with a fifth person being hired,
also on a part-time contract. After one year, the pilot project was considered
successful and extended for another year with the intention to extend it further.
A total of 550 people reduced their working time, and 120 jobs were created
during the first year. Two thirds of the newly recruited workers were women,
and at least 40 per cent of work sharers were men (Reinecke, 2000).

The programme, however, has four main shortcomings to overcome before
it can really take off. First, the time limit of the agreements reduces incentives
for newly recruited people to take up these jobs, while at the same time work
sharers may wish to reverse the arrangements. This trade-off is difficult to
resolve. Second, potential work sharers have to be capable of performing
broadly the same tasks. Such homogeneity of duties is usually associated with
low skills, large organizations and 'women's' work. Third, the compensation
payment gives rise to tax and social security obligations, which reduces the
level of resources available. Fourth, the unemployed individuals recruited to
fill the vacancies often need preparatory training; indeed, the skills required
may simply be unavailable locally. The social partners are still trying to
persuade the public employment service (with some success) and the government (so far without success) to join the association and to support the initiative by bearing the cost of any training required, exempting the compensation
payments from tax and social security contributions or contributing to the
association's capital. The exemption from taxes and contributions would be
justified by the savings to be made on unemployment benefits (see the principle of fiscal congruity referred to above).

Exemption of such compensation payments from at least part of the burden
of taxation and social security charges should be a realistic policy option in the
near future, since they are cost-neutral for the exchequer. However, the idea of
this initiative could even be generalized by expanding the present UI into an
EI by covering parts of the income loss related to explicit work-sharing
arrangements. The availability of part-time unemployment benefits could be
an incentive to negotiate work-sharing arrangements at the firm or industry
level that would lead to increases in the overall level of employment. The
concept could obviously be applied to three other employment bridges. It
would be possible to introduce provisions for combining part-time work with

training, family work or gradual retirement and compensating income losses during these phases with part-time unemployment benefits.

Activating Transitions between Private Households and Labour Market Work

Civil societies intent on increasing opportunities would provide many more bridges between unwaged and waged work in order to insure against the increasing number of 'manufactured risks' encountered over the life course. Such critical events often have little to do with the labour market and might include family formation, divorce, 'mid-life crises', the elderly becoming dependent on care, a partner's mobility, cultural or political ambitions and self-discovery experiments. The traditional insurance against these risks was the 'housewife', and in most European countries the problem of reconciling family responsibilities (and related critical events) with regular paid work is still solved largely by women withdrawing wholly or partially from the labour market.

With the steady increase in women's labour force participation, this traditional form of insurance is gradually being eroded. A good indicator for this is the declining gender gap in labour force participation in the core 25–54 age group. Although there are considerable differences between countries owing to differences in employment regimes, there is clearly a common and convergent trend towards equalization at least in quantitative terms (Figure 12.3). The increase in labour force participation is especially pronounced among families with children under the age of six. The immediate impact of the growing number of dual-earner families is the combined pressure of paid and unpaid working time, especially among women. This often leads to 'time famine' and a disjunction between husbands' and wives' preferred and actual weekly hours (Atkinson *et al.*, 1999; Appelbaum, 2000: 6). Research points to a growing need for flexible forms of work organization adapted to families' requirements (Pitt-Catsouphes, 2000). Furthermore, as a consequence of individualization, more and more transitions are voluntarily being sought by individuals wanting to have a break from demanding or monotonous jobs or to look for new career opportunities. Against this background, the four criteria for good transitions can be translated into practice as follows.

1. The *individual freedom (autonomy)* criterion calls for new social rights to contractual choices between paid work and unpaid social work. In addition, the set of choices should be great enough to allow for adjustment to widely differing individual or household situations. The further consequence of this criterion would be the rigorous individualization of entitlements to parental or other forms of leave and the provision of legal

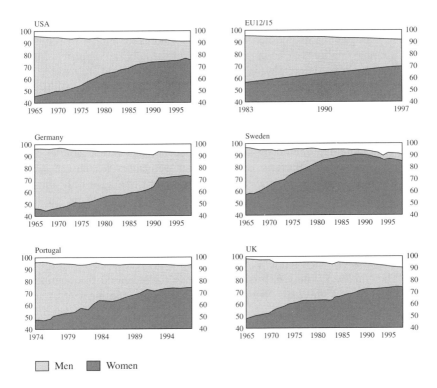

Men   Women

*Figure 12.3   The gender gap: labour force participation of men and women
(25–54) in Europe (E12/E15), United States, Germany,
Sweden, Portugal and United Kingdom, 1965–98*

protection for the bargaining partners through the introduction of fair
procedural rules or minimum standards.

2. The *solidarity* criterion requires that the new risks should be dealt with not
only as individual risks but also as collective risks, since they give rise to
positive or negative externalities. By analogy with unemployment benefit, this would mean, for instance, providing social protection during time
taken off for family reasons. In other words, parental leave has to be
handled as an income maintenance issue. The likely consequence would
be the participation of larger numbers of men, who have so far largely
failed in practice to share family risks because they still tend to have
higher and more continuous incomes.

3. The *effectiveness* criterion requires coordinated bargaining processes
between employees and employers at firm or sectoral level on the implementation of entitlements to family leave. In addition, public or

public/private support through full-time schools and kindergartens, as well as training institutions or community schools for adults, are required if employability is to be maintained during partially or completely inter-rupted careers. However, even institutions apparently unconnected to the work–life balance can make a difference. For example, the availability of dependable public transport can play a significant role in shaping a family-friendly environment. Research has shown that the availability of infrastructure services – publicly or privately provided at affordable prices – is a more important determinant of the rise in dual-earner families than tax structures.[26] Barriers on the labour demand side must also be removed. Since most small and medium-sized firms have only limited organizational capacities, their competitive position would be (further) diminished by increasing mobility options for their employees. Thus public or private employment services would have to cooperate in helping to replace workers on leave (or on substantially shortened working time) with suitably qualified jobseekers.

4. The *efficiency* criterion, finally, calls again for increased risk sharing in order to contain costs. Negotiated agreements are one element of self-regulatory efficiency. Cost–benefit analysis could help to determine roughly the limits of cofinancing through taxes. Since affordable house-hold services for the many well-educated women who still interrupt their careers would increase their employment opportunities, a gain in ef-ficiency at the macro level is quite likely. This gain will also probably exceed the original investment costs of providing the infrastructure or fostering the development of market services.

Good practice in the area of family leave is crucial for the shift from social policy to risk management. The impact of parental leave or parental part-time regulations on gender equality is to date ambivalent and the subject of some controversy.[27] Some experts see such arrangements as means of inducing mothers to reduce their labour supply in times of slack labour demand, thereby reducing competition for men, enhancing traditional role models and slowing down the career progression of highly skilled women in particular. Other experts stress that these measures improve the labour market attachment of those with young children as leave taking becomes legally established and may even contribute to a reduction of unemployment, as unemployed people can be taken on as substitutes and additional jobs are created as a result of increased demand for professional childcare. If this more positive argument is accepted, according to which the various forms of family leave (including sabbaticals) serve multiple employment objectives, we need to determine the preconditions for the non-discriminatory or gender-neutral take-up of such schemes.

My contention is that women would be in a much better bargaining position

in the labour market and within the household if all four criteria outlined above
were met. Freedom of choice for both partners would be maintained
completely, as even the traditional role model could be chosen under such a
regulatory framework. Sweden is probably the country that comes closest to
fulfilling all four criteria.[28] It has at least partly individualized the right to
parental leave by introducing a one-month 'father's sabbatical'. The 30 days of
the 225 days of joint parental leave that have to be taken by fathers will be
increased in 2002 to 60 days.[29] The regulations allow also for a flexible take-
up of entitlements to family time-off; the 225 days can be used until the children are eight years old. In contrast, until the year 2000, the German regulations
on parental leave stipulated that time-off had to be taken in a continuous three-
year block.[30] According to the empowerment criterion (enhancing individual
choice), this entitlement would have to be transformed into an entitlement to a
corresponding time account which could be used flexibly, for instance by both
parents working part-time for six years or by reducing both parents' working
time to six hours a day (30 hours a week) for 12 years.[31]

Sweden also has a rich cooperative infrastructure for individual empowerment. In contrast, West Germany in 1990 provided day nurseries for only 3 per
cent of children under three years of age. France (20 per cent), Belgium (25 per
cent) and Denmark (40 per cent) were much better equipped in this respect. These
countries also had a richer infrastructure for children aged three to six, providing
day nursery places for 80 to 100 per cent of this age group; the corresponding
figure for Germany was 79 per cent. Compared with many other OECD countries, Germany also lacks full-time schools. Sweden, finally, provides wage-
related benefits during parental leave. Treating childcare as an income
maintenance risk and not as an income support problem is a logical step in the
move from social policy to risk management. The present mainstream solution,
to compensate partly for childcare through a lump sum payment, can be questioned. Who can measure the productivity of this care? It seems to be more logical to compensate for the 'opportunity costs' related to earned income forgone.

In view of our normative criteria related to individual autonomy, freedom
and responsibility, it is worth mentioning that comparative surveys on preferences, norms and their realization corroborate my assumption. Some 71 per
cent of Germans believe that children of school age suffer if their mothers are
in paid employment; 31 per cent of German adults have the impression that the
presence of children restricts their autonomy. However, only 5 per cent of
Swedes believe that their quality of life is restricted by children (Thenner,
2000: 124). Unfortunately, hard information is not yet available to support the
plausible assumption that equality of opportunity for women in the labour
market is also efficient in terms of macroeconomic performance.

In most European countries, the proportion of men taking parental leave is
below 2 per cent. However, fulfilment of the above-mentioned criteria does

make a difference. In Denmark, where parental leave is an individual right but entitlement expires if not used by the father, about 8 per cent of those taking leave are fathers. In Sweden, the corresponding figure is 30 per cent, although men account for only 10 per cent of total days' leave taken. Recent statistics, however, show a slow but continuous increase in men's participation in parental leave in Sweden: on average, fathers now take 40 to 50 days during the first two years of their children's lives. In the Netherlands, parental leave is available only on a part-time basis and there is an individual right of half a year for each parent. However, eligibility is also conditional on applicants having worked at least 20 hours a week in advance of the leave period, which means that 40 per cent of those taking part-time leave are fathers. Belgium has integrated parental leave into a broader career break programme. The number of people taking such a break amounts to almost 2 per cent of all employed persons in Belgium. The take-up in the public sector is much higher than in the private sector, and 87 per cent of those taking a break are female (Thenner, 2000).

Finally, the old idea of a civil right to unconditional sabbaticals fits perfectly with the multifunctional concept of EI and should therefore be revitalized.[32] For instance, in purely arithmetic terms, entitlement to a total of one year's sabbatical during an average working life could increase the number of people in employment by some 5.5 million in the European Union (EU15). An interesting example is the 'teacher model' in Berlin, where teachers can take up a paid one-year sabbatical after 3, 4, 5 or 6 years on condition that they save up for their leave in advance by accepting a corresponding cut in their salary (by one-sixth, for example).[33] The favourite model in the late 1980s was six years' full-time work on six-sevenths of full salary and a sabbatical leave in the seventh year with the same salary. The idea of a sabbatical year was even recommended to farmers in the Old Testament! The reason given then was to prevent attrition of the soil, not a bad reason either for human bodies and souls. Such sabbaticals would also introduce a certain degree of 'creative disruption' into work organization systems and bring in useful experiences or networks from outside the firm. The 'teacher model' also shows that such sabbaticals would not necessarily incur additional costs. From a long-term perspective, many people can afford and would be willing to save income for this kind of privilege, which at the same time creates more employment opportunities for other potentially unemployed people, especially for women in the 'silent reserve army'. Banks or governments might support saving for sabbaticals through interest rate incentives or special tax deductions.

Activating Transitions between Employment and Unemployment

The relevant story here is briefly told. Despite the recent decline in overall unemployment, the problem of long-term unemployment in most EU member states has not been alleviated. On average, in 1998, 49 per cent of the unemployed had been out of work for a year or more, and in some countries this proportion even increased. Moreover, the share of the unemployed out of work for two years or more went up from 30 per cent in 1997 to almost 31 per cent in 1998; this group accounts for 62 per cent (almost two-thirds) of all long-term unemployed, a total of some 5.2 million people. This latter figure, in particular, emphasizes both the scale of the problem and the difficulty of resolving it (European Commission, 1999a: 9ff).

To what extent has social protection, in particular unemployment insurance, contributed to this gloomy situation? A look at two simple correlations suggests that this relationship is complex. First, if we correlate expenditures for unemployment benefits and other related items with expenditures for active labour market policy, we find two distinct classes of countries: high spenders and low spenders. That this is not just a reflection of the respective burden of unemployment is indicated by the fact that the high-spending and the low-spending group both contain 'model countries' with good employment performance. At the bottom are the USA and the UK (for a recent good performance) and at the top the Netherlands and Denmark (Figure 12.4). Low spending, therefore, is no guarantee of good employment performance. Conversely, high spending is not necessarily an obstacle to good employment performance. The second correlation (Figure 12.5), namely the relationship between normalized spending on 'passive labour market policy' (per person unemployed as a percentage of GDP per member of the labour force) and the evolution of unemployment in recent

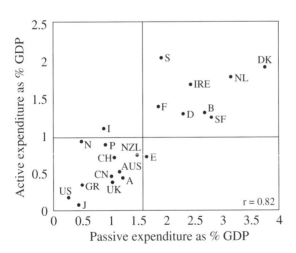

Figure 12.4   Spending on active and passive labour market policy as a percentage of GDP, 1997/8

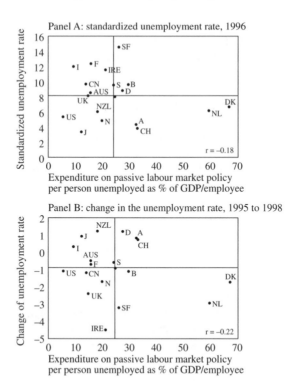

Figure 12.5   Spending on passive labour market policy per person
unemployed as a percentage of GDP per member of the
labour force

years, is almost zero. In other words, countries with high normalized spending
levels (a proxy for the overall replacement rate) actually have a slightly (but
not significantly) better unemployment performance than low-spending countries.[34] The lesson to be drawn from these two observations is that it obviously
depends on the kind of interaction whether social protection is supportive or
detrimental for employment performance. Under certain conditions, especially
if combined with activating measures, high social protection seems to be
compatible with or even supportive of a positive employment dynamic (see
also last section).

More sophisticated research, based on multiple regression models, supports
the now widespread consensus that social protection in the form of unemployment benefit plays only a minor role in explaining long-term unemployment.
However, most studies find that the length of entitlement to unemployment
benefit has a significant impact on the duration of unemployment, whereas

variations in the replacement rate have an ambivalent or no significant impact.[35] This finding clearly suggests that activating measures should replace long-term benefits as far as possible. This is not the place to present all the familiar examples of such employability-enhancing measures. I will confine myself to listing the main instruments: placement services, wage subsidies or in-work benefits (tax credits) to encourage the unemployed to accept lower paid jobs, re-employment bonuses to stimulate job search, wage-cost subsidies for employers to encourage recruitment among disadvantaged groups, service employment cheques to support low-wage sectors, and temporary public employment or relief work.

To what extent do present policies meet the four criteria for good transitions? To answer this question, we have again to translate the general principles into the specificities of unemployment transitions.

1. The individual *freedom (or autonomy)* criterion requires an extension of choice through the income maintenance provisions of labour market insurance schemes. Since new entitlements in this direction involve bargaining between employees and employer (or between the social partners), legal protection through fair procedural rules or minimum standards will also be necessary. An example of new entitlements would be part-time unemployment benefits in the event of a working-time reduction, payment of which would be contingent on recipients undertaking socially useful work (childcare, for example); making negotiated entitlements transferable to other firms would be an example of legal protection.

2. The *solidarity* criterion requires that all categories of workers be included in the extended labour market insurance, irrespective of employment status. Each hour of contracted gainful employment should be linked to an equivalent social protection. People unable to pay contributions could receive state support in line with government social policy.

3. The *effectiveness* criterion requires both specialized insurance and employment policy agencies (and the coordination between them) to allow for selection of programmes according to the nature of risks. Of special importance is the assessment of individual needs and capacities ('employabilities') and their match with available jobs. Owing to the increasing differentiation of supply and demand conditions, a quantum leap is probably required in the further professional specialization of placement services and their coordination.

4. The *efficiency* criterion calls for cost containment through self-regulation or control. In particular, the introduction of insurance schemes related to endogenous risks requires mechanisms for controlling moral hazard. Again, the introduction of risk-sharing elements will be one way to

enhance efficiency; negotiated cofinancing and competitive implementation of employment policies are two other promising routes. Rigorous follow-up (monitoring) of programme participants plus corresponding evaluations with proper control groups will also improve efficiency. Moral hazard related to participation in active labour market programmes will also be contained through the strict rule that such participation shall not give rise to claims to unemployment benefits.

Transforming entitlements to UI benefits into *vouchers*, either for in-work benefits (to encourage acceptance of lower reservation wages) or wage-cost subsidies (to encourage recruitment), comes closest to the idea of EI. Vouchers empower people to make choices. *Employment companies* providing effective local networks to assist with mass dismissals or with the reintegration of the very long-term unemployed are also close to this concept. One of the most prominent examples is the non-profit agency START in the Netherlands, which temporarily employs hard-to-place people, either loaning them to private employers (in order that they can gain work experience or find a permanent job) or training them if no temporary work is available. Other European countries have started to imitate this model, in particular through the establishment of 'transfer agencies' in Germany,[36] 'integration firms' in France and Belgium and 'job pools' in the Netherlands and in Denmark. The local employment agencies in Belgium should also be mentioned here, since they are new institutions that provide for greater mobility opportunities before people become unemployed.

The transformation of 'social plan measures' into cofinancing contributions for 'from-the-job placement' is also an important step towards the concept of EI because it prevents unemployment. The complete breaking of an employment relationship (that is, declared unemployment) reduces employability in various ways: stigmatization, loss of self-confidence and erosion of skills and competences. The new Employment Promotion Act in Germany opens up the possibility of a cofinancing arrangement involving at least four actors: (former or new) employers, employees in danger of getting unemployed, the regional employment office (UI agency) and a (private or semi-public) local training agency. Often the local municipality steps in as actor and cofinancing institution, with the receiver serving as mediator. The employment office can now offer a top-up grant equal to UI benefits. Three conditions must be met. Firstly, benefits paid to employees under the terms of the social plan[37] have to be used for training or other placement activities. Secondly, there has to be a likelihood that more than half of the employees affected would claim UI benefits from the employment office if there were no social plan. Thirdly, there has to be a worthwhile programme of training and other reintegration measures. The top-up grant is DM 16–17 000 DM employee, which equates to the average annual

UI benefit. The potentially unemployed workers (and this is important to people) retain the status of employees in an intermediate firm (or with the training or coaching agency) and the former or new employer can cut jobs and save wage costs without acquiring a reputation for dismissing employees at will.

A final interesting example is provided by the so-called *work foundations* in Austria, of which the Voest-Alpine-Stahlstiftung can be regarded as the prototype. This model has some very interesting features, which merit wider attention. It is noteworthy not so much for the introduction of individual new instruments but rather for its success in bringing together a number of different financial sources and fostering cooperation among key local actors. The aim of this model is to give redundant workers access to a well-endowed infrastructure designed to help them deal with the transition instead of being left to cope in isolation. The funding for the work foundations comes from four sources. First, those employees of the parent company forced to implement a mass redundancy programme who remain in their posts pay 0.25 per cent of their monthly wages as a solidarity contribution to the foundation. Second, the parent company provides the initial capital for the foundation, topped up with 50 per cent of the solidarity contributions. Third, the redundant workers themselves make a contribution by depositing 50 per cent of their redundancy payments into the foundation. Fourth, the public employment service guarantees the payment of UB for four years, which covers the majority of the costs. The foundation provides or organizes training and a wide range of other services helpful to those seeking new jobs in the regional labour market. Seventy-nine per cent of the redundant workers eventually found a new job. The average length of stay in the foundation was 18 months in the first half of the 1990s, with 45 per cent finding employment in the regular labour market during the first six months (Mühlböck, 1995). A rigorous evaluation at a later stage found very positive employment effects of participants in this programme, compared to a control group of non-participants (Winter-Ebmer, 2001).

The main message of all these good-practice examples is straightforward. Generous long-term benefits for the unemployed or for persons in immediate danger of becoming unemployed are compatible with the goal of increasing employment opportunities only if they are made conditional on activating measures that include a wide set of individual choices.

Activating Transitions between Work and Retirement

The traditional way of dealing with the risk of old age is to organize a full stop at a mandatory retirement age, usually 65 years, and to replace earnings with pensions. Women can retire in most EU member states as early as 60, a privilege thought to compensate for their family duties.[38] The actual age of retirement, however, has declined across the Union and is now around 60 for men in most member states; it has also declined in the OECD countries, from 66 (1960) to 62 (1995), and for women it is well below 60 in two-thirds of OECD countries.[39] Some countries within the EU, especially Belgium, Denmark, France and Germany, have used UI to relieve the labour market, thereby increasing the incidence of this sort of abrupt early retirement. Other countries, especially the Netherlands, adopted a similar strategy with disability insurance.[40] The combined effect of historical differences in retirement regulations and the increasing instrumentalization of social protection arrangements for the purposes of labour market policy has led to a declining overall trend in labour force participation rates among older men. Women's labour force participation in this age group is tending to rise, which further contributes to the narrowing of the gender gap. However, huge differences in activity rates persist in EU member states, and in some member states (and also in other OECD countries) the trend towards declining participation rates has already been successfully reversed (Figure 12.6).

Both the changing demographic structure (and the related problems of financing social security) and improved health conditions (and the related preferences to remain in work) help to create the conditions for a reversal of the actual retirement age and, in the long run, even for an abolishment of the mandatory retirement age. The notion of *active ageing*, which the European Commission rightly advocates, should lead to the development of a range of options for combined paid work with other useful activities or leisure (European Commission, 1999b). The increasing need for care in old age also provides a justification for gradual retirement schemes that allow both men and women to combine paid work with private care services. The removal of the (artificial) age limit would reduce age discrimination and help to justify human capital investment for older people. However, studies have repeatedly shown that the ideal of gradual or flexible retirement currently faces too many impediments to be realized (Delsen and Reday-Mulvey, 1995; OECD, 1998). Although there has been a slight increase in part-time work among the elderly, and although it has been shown that part-time work and participation rates among older people are positively correlated (European Commission 1999a: 123), there is still little systematic and comprehensive policy activity to enhance the variable opportunity set for older people.

Do good practices already exist that fulfil the criteria for good transitions and that may be taken as models for national or regional adaptation? The state of the art seems to suggest the following strategies.

1. First of all, *individual freedom* and empowerment require that financial disincentives for gradual retirement be removed and that employability be

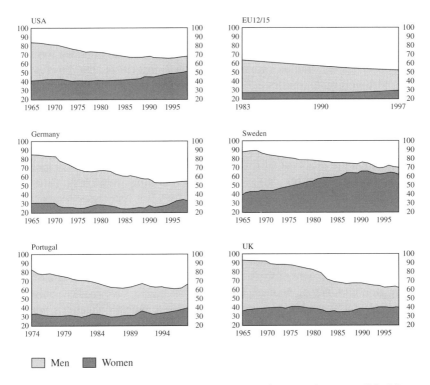

□ Men   ▓ Women

*Figure 12.6   Labour force participation rates of men and women (55–64)
in Europe (E12/E15), United States, Germany, Sweden,
Portugal and United Kingdom, 1965–98*

extended through training or income support in order to widen the range
of employment relationships suitable for older workers. Very often the
change from full-time to part-time work before retirement is connected
with a loss of status and income (a shift to less responsible jobs). Such a
downgrading may be the result of a lack of skills and competences. One
challenge, therefore, is to fight against the widespread age discrimination
in continuing education and training (Gelderbloom and de Koning,
2001). Secondly, the 'privilege' of an earlier retirement age that women
currently enjoy reflects the traditional 'male breadwinner model' and is
not consistent with gender equality. The same holds true for widows'
derived pension entitlements, which are completely dependent on the
husband's labour market career. If women are to be truly empowered, an
'individualized' old-age security system would have to be introduced, at
least in the long term, in which each adult partner in a family would

acquire independent pension entitlements. Third, if the problem is connected, not with inadequate skills or qualifications, but with declining physical capacities or a desire for more leisure time, an extended form of labour market insurance would support firms that create opportunities for older workers to transfer to tasks in which they remain highly productive. Studies show that suitable areas of employment for older workers might include retailing, care work, financial advice and counselling. In cases of declining productivity, a switch to easier (and less well-paid) jobs would be more realistic if firms were partially compensated for the loss of productivity (but continued to pay the same or a slightly lower wage) or if employees taking less well-paid or part-time jobs were partially compensated for their loss of income. There has been some experience with 'bridging jobs' or 'retirement jobs', especially in the USA and in Japan (OECD, 1998). There could even be tax exemptions for firms employing a majority of older workers.[41]

2. The *solidarity* principle means, first of all, that account should be taken of the changing nature of work, and especially of rising labour force participation rates among women. To date, career breaks have not been seen as a risk since such breaks were mostly related to family obligations, which were widely regarded as women's responsibility. This attribution of responsibility is no longer generally accepted. If it is accepted that such obligations should be equally distributed between men and women, career breaks due to family obligations become a risk. This holds true especially for family catastrophes, such as the onset of chronic illness or accidents leading to disability. Other circumstances also produce risks that might lead to career breaks. Chief among them are the volatile skill requirements associated with information technologies, but the 'internal risks' associated with new lifestyles and changing values (burn-out syndromes, divorce and so on) also have to be taken into account.

Most European pension schemes make little if any provision for the risks associated with discontinuous work histories, to say nothing of positive incentives to encourage people to assume greater responsibility for such risks in order to enhance overall labour market flexibility. One important impediment to flexible retirement, however, is the lack of coordination between old age insurance and flexible work histories. One way of building flexibility into the social protection system for the elderly would be to institutionalize *virtual entitlements*. The basic idea is to supplement each entitlement based on real contributions (from gross earnings) with a virtual entitlement that reflects the risk of fluctuating income streams that is (usually) associated with career breaks. These virtual entitlements would be activated in the event of a risk actually occurring (for example, reduced income as a result of parental leave or sabbatical, or an enforced change of occupation with a low starting salary). If no such risk occurs during an individual's lifetime (if he or she remains in a standard employment relationship throughout, for example), then that person will have redistributed some of the gains from such an untroubled career to those unfortunates who have had to face such risks, whether deliberately or involuntarily.[42] Accumulated virtual entitlements could also be used to compensate for loss of earnings during gradual retirement.

It should be self-evident from the previous discussion that regulations on gradual retirement should provide for a variety of different modes of implementation and not restrict gradual retirement to the old-fashioned part-time model of 20 hours a week. Moreover, many studies have shown that there are financial disincentives for older workers seeking to reduce their working time. Pension entitlements, for instance, are disproportionately reduced if the method of calculation is heavily biased towards the final wage or salary. This disincentive could be easily removed by changing the basis of calculation, for instance by taking average earnings over the life course,[43] or by partially offsetting losses of income incurred during spells of part-time work. The logic of an extended EI would even suggest that entitlements to UI benefits should include a voucher for in-work benefits or a wage-cost subsidy for gradual early retirement.

3. The *effectiveness* criterion raises questions about the organization of age-related social protection and employment policies. Flexible or gradual retirement programmes require individualized schedules and the cooperation of key local actors if they are to meet the tremendous variety of individual needs. For instance, 'new deals' at firm or industry level that promote part-time early retirement in exchange for maintaining or even increasing existing employment levels cannot be put into practice unless various potential cofinancers get together and come to mutual agreements after negotiations. There are also psychological barriers to be overcome because of the 'ghettoization' of part-time work. From a demand-side perspective, it has been noted that, as employers become more familiar with part-time work, the advantages have increasingly been seen to outweigh any possible disadvantages (Thurman and Trah, 1990: 25). And from a supply-side perspective, it has been recognized that 'men today . . . will not have any status problems with part-time work at the end of their working life if they have had variable working hours during their working period' (Schmähl and Gatter, 1994: 465).

4. For many years, the *efficiency* of social protection and employment policies for older workers has been discussed mainly in terms of the basic funding alternatives: should the risk of old age be financed through unfunded (pay-as-you-go) or funded systems? This is not the place to discuss this complicated and still very controversial issue.[44] However, it

is quite widely accepted that unfunded systems will have to remain a central pillar of pension systems in the future. This leaves unresolved the problem of cost containment stemming from generous pensions, ageing populations and increasing life expectancy. Once all the alternatives have been considered, gradual rises in (state) retirement ages are likely to be necessary, and indeed such measures are planned or have been implemented in some EU member states (Germany, UK and Italy) and in the USA. If this assumption is correct, it is all the more important to increase the opportunities for flexible employment relationships by establishing transitional labour markets. In view of the the correlation between disability and age, the measures required would include expanded rehabilitation programmes. A gradual increase in the retirement age would also enhance incentives on both the supply and the demand side to invest in the human capital of older workers.

We can now turn to a brief examination of some of the *good practices* that have developed recently in some of the member states. In Germany, the 1992 pension reform introduced the option of partial pensions; however, very few people availed themselves of this opportunity to enter gradual retirement. Even the introduction in 1996 of legislation on part-time work for older people has had little impact to date. Both employers and employees still prefer 'clean-break' early retirement. Firms want to shed jobs in order to reduce labour costs and (male) employees have not yet accepted the status of part-time worker. However, these preferences might change, if only because the fiscal crisis inhibits further exploitation of the UI systems of the past.

Recent reforms have improved conditions for older part-timers, or will do when they are fully enacted. In Germany, for example, the legislation on part-time work for older people opened up scope for negotiation of the following arrangement between the 'city state' of Bremen, the Federal Employment Agency (BA) and the social partners in the Public and Transport Services (ÖTV). If two older tram drivers go part-time (19 hours a week), one young unemployed person can be hired on a full-time contract. The part-timers' wages are topped up by the BA (that is by the UI system) to 70 per cent of their full-time pay, and the city of Bremen increases this up to 85 per cent. To complete the picture, the trade unions, as the third partner, agreed that the starting salary of young entrants should be slightly reduced. This agreement might serve as a prototype for many more regional solidarity pacts on employment.

The legislation on part-time work for older people also provided an opportunity to remove a seemingly small but fundamental barrier in social security regulations by redefining the employment relationship. The old legal definition of an employment relationship required the coexistence of a real labour service and remuneration for that service. This made it impossible to put in place a part-time scheme whereby an employee would work two years full-time on half pay before stopping work while continuing to draw half pay for a further two years. The old law required social security contributions to be paid for the first two years on the basis of part-time earnings only, while no contributions were required for the other two years because no formal employment relationship existed any more. The 1998 reform removed this barrier. This has also had a positive impact on other EI schemes, such as the reduced-salary sabbatical scheme (discussed earlier), or those based on working-time accounts, in which employers can accumulate any additional hours worked and use surpluses to take longer periods of leave or extended holidays. It is interesting to see that such complex arrangements also require complementary insurance arrangements to cover the new risks, such as company bankruptcy. Thus the new law requires the social partners to provide insurance against the risk of insolvency when they put in place part-time retirement arrangements.

The effectiveness and efficiency criteria suggest a two-tier process of negotiation. The general rules governing part-time work for older workers should be negotiated in broad outline by the social partners at the aggregate level, with legal reinforcement if required. The details could then be hammered out at firm level under the umbrella of collective agreements. One promising example is the collective agreement between the public employers and the Transport and Public Services trade union, which came into force in Germany in May 1998. When they reach the age of 60, employees now have the right to go part-time; employers can object only if they can prove that such a move would be detrimental to operations. The part-time arrangement can be implemented in the form of a period of full-time work and one of zero time; earnings have to be topped up to 83 per cent of previous earnings, and the employer pays additional contributions to the pension fund in order to maintain full social security coverage. Employees facing cuts in their pension entitlements if they take early retirement after the part-time arrangement are entitled to receive up to three months' salary as partial compensation. The social partners explicitly intend to use this agreement in order to create new jobs for the unemployed or for apprentices. The employment impact will be regularly monitored.

In 1985, so-called *career breaks* were introduced in Belgium (with modifications in 1991, 1997 and 1999). The aim here is to enable employees to adjust or reduce their work commitments from time to time. Those availing themselves of this scheme enjoy a dual guarantee: they both retain a certain share of their income and have a right to return to their jobs after the break period has expired. Because employees who take a career break have to be replaced by unemployed persons in order to gain public funding, the system also serves as a work-sharing device. Older workers (aged 50 and over) can take advantage of the scheme to work part-time up to their regular retirement age and receive partial compensation from the UI system. Experts recommend universal expansion of the scheme as an alternative to early retirement (on a voluntary basis for all employees) by increasing the financial incentives. Such a scheme would not only eliminate age discrimination but would also be three times more cost-effective (Denys and Simoens, 1999).

3 TOWARDS A NEW EMPLOYMENT COMPACT IN EUROPE

The industrial economy, starting in the 19th century and at its height during the 1920s and 1930s, attacked the risks of health, age, disability and, eventually, unemployment by establishing insurance systems. All these systems were closely linked with employment so that employment protection became a central and complementary element in the overall social protection system. Globalization, the rise of the information economy and individualization, however, give rise to new and increasingly differentiated risks in labour markets. The new risks relate especially to skill deficits and career breaks. The increasing differentiation of employment relationships calls for a correspond-ingly wide variety of social protection systems. The service and information economy, however, has not yet found proper institutional solutions either to these new risks or to the increasing diversity of risks. To conclude, we can now summarize the main findings and outline in broad terms the new employment compact that would be required to implement the new policy.

From Unemployment to Employment Insurance

The transformation of the time-honoured unemployment insurance system (UI) into a system of employment insurance (EI) would be an important step towards a solution. If such a system were to be established in a systematic way and coordinated properly with the other social protection systems (which would also have to be reformed and differentiated), it would be an effective functional equivalent to rigid employment protection systems and reduce the tremendous cost of UI expenditures. The shift from UI towards a multifunc-tional EI would not necessarily imply more public expenditure, as was dem-onstrated by many of the good practices that already exist. In many cases, legal entitlements to negotiate collectively or individually on various transitional arrangements would suffice. A multifunctional EI system would, for instance, include entitlements to negotiate unpaid leave and the income support required during such leaves would be financed essentially by employees themselves from savings already put aside for the purpose. However, and this is the trick, it would also be cofinanced through the EI system, since such leave creates positive externalities arising out of increased overall mobility. The share of cofinancing would depend on the nature of these externalities and would be a matter for negotiation. If those on leave, for instance, are replaced by unemployed people with the same skills and competences, the share of EI cofunding would be higher than in the case of a prolonged holiday.

EI could be enhanced by a general strategy of introducing voucher schemes. EI contributions could be divided into two parts, one covering the costs of classical UI (unconditional solidarity) and the other the costs of EI (negotiated solidarity). The latter could be used to establish voucher schemes to fund various kinds of transitional employment, as demonstrated in this chapter. Vouchers would enable workers legally and financially to engage in transitions and to manage their own transitions adequately. In this way, voucher schemes would help to empower workers. Furthermore, individual preferences could be enhanced even more strongly by allowing vouchers to be exchanged, within companies or perhaps in some sort of 'voucher exchange'. A voucher system might also halt the current legalization of the labour market, enhance labour market flexibility and allow for a 'reflexive deregulation' that does not neglect the fundamental need for social security during risky transitions.[45]

Thus the *first message* of our summing-up is that social protection systems are a support and promote employment only if they are structured according to the nature of the risks people face in the course of their lives. Conventional social protection insurance covers only standard income risks (unemployment, sickness, old age) and not those stemming from the new and variable employment forms. However, even the standard risks are changing as the world of work itself changes.

The *second message* is that employment policies are supportive of social protection only if they maintain and enhance individual employability, help to create sustainable market or public jobs and protect employees against unfair dismissal. High employment rates, high productivity and work that provides income security are the most reliable way of providing social protection. However, if employment rates are enhanced only through highly subsidized low-skill jobs, incentives to work or to invest in human capital will decline, competitiveness will be reduced and in the long run jobs will be endangered.

The *third message* is that UI has to be extended to create an EI system in order to activate the interfaces with other social protection systems. Improved coordination of the various social protection systems would expand the set of interactive responses to structural changes, with unemployment being used only as a last resort. Preventive social protection and employment policies would maintain employment relationships for as long as possible.

Employability is a necessary but not a sufficient condition for gainful employment. People need and want real jobs. The new dynamics of full employment demand, therefore, that all actors pull together to increase real employment opportunities and not just virtual ones. This requires a shift from an active to an activating labour market policy. How such a shift might be effected will be considered briefly below.

From Active to Activating Labour Market Policy

A new labour compact is emerging. This new regime of formal and informal agreements between the main actors in the labour market – the state, the social partners, firms and individuals – is already quite visible in countries that have succeeded in taming both unemployment and inflation (see Chapter 2). The basic feature of this new regime is that all actors playing the full employment game have refocused their efforts on their own specific capacities and capabilities and effectively coordinated their specialized activities. Let us consider this refocusing more specifically, actor by actor (see Table 12.3).

First, the state has shifted the focus of its attention from 'government' to 'governance', a change of direction that cannot be simply equated to the move from centralization to decentralization, from regulation to deregulation or from public to private provision.[46] These dichotomies do not adequately reflect the complex relationships that characterize the multilateral exchange mechanisms and bargaining processes in governance structures, which operate both 'horizontally' (between specialized actors in different policy fields) and 'vertically' (between different organizations at local, regional, national and

Table 12.3   Towards a new labour compact

		From active labour market policy	To activating labour market policy
State	Central	Conditional programmes, full cost compensation	Optional programmes, cofinancing
	Local	Employer of last resort	Policy networking, public–private mixes
	PES	Placement monopoly and transfer administration	Co-epetition, new public management, activating transfer entitlements
Social partners		Moderate wage policy	Flexible wage and working-time policy
Firms		Labour shedding, subsidized recruitment	Human resource management
Individuals		Passive benefit recipients, programme participants	Employability vouchers, activity contracts

transnational level). It is therefore more appropriate to see modern government as the joint management of risk by public and private actors at various levels of organization. Despite the neoliberal connotations of deregulation and privatization, the state remains strong in a 'governance regime'. There are three reasons for this. Firstly, its responsibilities are confined to its main function, that is the making and enforcing of binding rules. Secondly, it empowers collective and private actors to organize themselves within an effective regulatory framework, laid down by the state, that includes proper financial incentives and infrastructure. Thirdly, it guarantees social protection and security for the disadvantaged and for the actual or potential losers in structural change. If there is no social security, people will resist change; worse, they will also refuse to assume greater responsibility for risks as required by the new economy and the new civil society.

Emphasizing governance instead of government means a move at the *central level of the state* away from conditional to optional programmes. A typical conditional programme is one in which participation in labour market programmes is dependent on the length of a spell of unemployment. An employer may, for instance, receive wage cost subsidies for recruiting unemployed individuals only if they have already been unemployed for 12 months. Thus conditional programmes require the public employment officer to wait for 12 months instead of assessing the risk of long-term unemployment immediately and developing tailor-made measures for the individual in question right at the outset. The legal frameworks within which many public employment services in Europe operate still contain a lot of 'wait-and-see' rules instead of 'assess-and-do' options. This is rather like throwing the unemployed in at the deep end of a swimming pool and waiting to see whether they manage to get out unaided, instead of asking them beforehand whether and how well they can swim. Another feature of interventionist 'active labour market policy' is that the full costs of programmes are met if certain conditions are fulfilled. Such programmes provide no incentives for the service delivery agencies to be efficient. Indeed, efficient providers might even be punished if any money saved cannot be carried over to the next financial year or used to fund other projects. 'Governance regimes' either set tough budgetary constraints or provide cofinancing options requiring negotiation and adherence to quality standards.

In the old labour compact based on 'active labour market policy', local actors, especially the municipalities, were often used and abused as the employers of last resort. Typical examples are temporary public jobs and community work providing jobs for the hard-to-place. Evaluative evidence from OECD countries is not encouraging since re-employment rates are often low because of stigmatization, 'revolving door effects', substitution or displacement of regular public jobs (Martin, 2000). In the new employment compact, municipalities and communities become policy coordinators, whose role is to support private initiatives, social enterprises and temporary work agencies engaged in intensive placement services or case management. The Dutch job pools and services agencies (Start and Maatwerk) are models.

The public employment services (PES) have also changed their image as mere recorders of unemployment and conduits for dole money. The placement monopoly has been abolished in almost all countries, and although private placement agencies have still not gained much market share, they have at least pushed the PES further towards modernizing their service delivery.[47] Thus in the new employment compact the PES is developing into an important player at the local level in competition and cooperation with other emerging professional players. Its survival depends, however, on the successful application of modern management techniques and on its ability to convert transfer benefit entitlements into in-work or in-training benefits.

In the Keynesian labour compact, the role of the corporatist actors (the 'social partners') was restricted to managing wages policy at central or decentralized level. The objects of negotiation were wages and wage structures, and within the framework of these wage constraints employment decisions were left entirely to employers. The new labour compact extends the scope of the bargaining process in at least two respects. Firstly, successful employment regimes seem to be relying increasingly on a two-tier wage bargaining process: general agreements at the central level and special agreements at the decentralized level. This means that wage moderation is combined with the establishment of parameters within which wage bargaining can be conducted at firm, industry, region or even individual level. Secondly, network organization, project-oriented production processes and, last but not least, changing employee preferences require flexible working-time arrangements, including periods during which work can be combined with training, education or family care. Bargaining is increasingly focusing on these qualitative conditions and the related income risks are being internalized through collectively agreed risk management arrangements, for instance training or pension funds.

The old labour compact relieved employers to a large extent of the responsibility for investing in human capital. Only large firms with internal labour markets developed sophisticated human resource development programmes in order to enhance their competitiveness or reputation and thereby attract highly skilled workers in short supply. Labour market policy supported employers in this attitude by providing generous unemployment insurance schemes, subsidized recruitment and external training. In the new employment compact, firms seem to be assuming greater responsibility for human resource management, and some of the most promising new active labour market programmes require just such an attitude. The most prominent examples are training leave schemes ('job rotation') and internalized placement and counselling services in the event of large-scale restructuring or takeovers. There are also signs that successful countries, such as the Netherlands and Austria, design the funding of labour market policies in such a way as to reward employers who adopt preventive labour market policies, for instance by incorporating bonus–malus features into social security contributions.

At the individual level, finally, the new employment compact demands that recipients of passive benefits or programme participants adopt an entrepreneurial attitude towards their own employability. All successful employment regimes, notably those in the UK, Denmark, the Netherlands, Finland and Ireland, have made receipt of benefits strictly dependent on the acceptance of suitable job offers and on a willingness to enter into contracts requiring early assessment of employability and the implementation of individualized remedies. Other examples that might be cited are Canada and Switzerland, which have drastically reformed their UI systems in such a way as to create a more appropriate balance of rights and obligations, thereby starting the process of developing full-fledged EI systems. 'Making transitions pay' through optional programmes increases the opportunity set of individual adjustment. The other side of the coin, however, is the need to extend the corresponding *obligations*. This can be accepted if obligations are collectively controlled by quality standards and procedural rules governing negotiations between individuals and placement officers on objectives, specified measures, activities and timetables. Another type of obligation would be the mandatory contributions to specified funds, for instance wage investment funds, whether by collective agreement or by law. In occupations where it is essential to update skills and competences regularly because of rapid technological change and the potential damage that can be caused by incompetence, in the medical profession or teaching, for example, it may even be necessary to make further training mandatory.

To sum up, the European employment strategy still faces some significant challenges. There is still a wide diversity of national approaches in Europe, even within the framework provided by the 1997 (Luxembourg) and 2000 (Lisbon) summit guidelines. Specific problems of coordination arise in European labour market policies. Firstly, as preparations are made for the full introduction of the Euro, the main focus of European policy making is on budgetary and monetary matters. Somewhat paradoxically, the decisions being taken in these areas will put greater pressure on labour market adjustments, depending on the situation in each member state. Secondly, labour market policy remains a national competence. The guidelines were deliberately designed to overcome this constraint and to foster convergence by encouraging progress on priorities already agreed on. They constitute a balanced but scarcely systematic strategy for developing an activating labour market policy within the framework of a new labour compact. The strategy is balanced because concerns about individual employability are explicitly linked to a bargaining approach involving the social partners as well as to other 'pillars', such as promoting adaptability within firms, entrepreneurship and equal opportunities. It is not systematic because the approach adopted to date is additional and even incremental. Some priorities have already been fulfilled by some countries, while others are nowhere near being met. Only the future will show whether national perceptions and constraints will allow for generalized compliance with a new European labour compact.

NOTES

1. The crisis of the pension system in many European countries is a good example of the re-ality of this ratchet effect.
2. The modification concerns the real functioning of most European democracies, which already control some of the discrimination against minorities through several mechanisms that restrict the scope for dismantlement in the future: for instance proportional voting systems, federalism and 'sunset' legislation.
3. For simplicity's sake, I make no distinction here between 'risk' and 'uncertainty'. If not otherwise specified, 'risk' includes uncertainty; if necessary, I will make a clear distinction. For the classic reference, see Knight (1964 [1921]) and, for a popular and illuminating history of risk management from ancient times up to the turn of this millennium, see Bernstein (1996).
4. We use the term 'life course' instead of 'life cycle' in order to avoid biologist connotations and to emphasize the possibility of managing 'manufactured' risks during the life course (see also Chapter 5 for references).
5. See OECD (1999: 18–34 (part-time work), 133–67 (training of adult workers), 177–211 (new work organization practices)).
6. The 'law of requisite variety' was originally formulated by W.R. Ashby in his *Introduction to Cybernetics* and is expressed in the short version: 'Only variety can destroy variety' (Ashby, 1979 [1956]: 207).
7. By analogy with Kant's categorical imperative, Heinz von Foerster formulated the cybern-ethic imperative. The original quotation stems from an interview in German: 'Handle stets so, daß die Anzahl der Möglichkeiten wächst' (Heinz von Foerster, *Die Zeit*, 15.1.98, p. 42); for a collection of articles, see von Foerster (1993).
8. For the distinction between internal and manufactured risks see Giddens (1996 [1994]).
9. For an extended discussion of such criticisms, see Chapter 6 in this volume.
10. See the classic essay on this trade-off by Okun (1975); for a discussion of this alleged trade-off that specifically addresses labour market problems and demonstrates the possibility of creating virtuous circles between equality and efficiency, see Schmid (1994).
11. I refer especially to Sen (1995, 1999) and (for a labour market perspective) to Solow (1990). The basic distinction between modern (as distinct from traditional) social choice, rational choice and public choice rests, firstly, on the acknowledgement of 'social knowledge' (Arrow, 1994) and, secondly, on the emphasis on social consequences (for instance, inequal-ities in earning capacities or employability), without for all that neglecting the importance of certain procedural rules (individual liberties and rights) in the formation of social values or decisions.
12. New public management theories try to overcome the weaknesses of the first wave of public management approaches which, for instance, often championed results over administrative processes and imposed or substituted economic values for legal values such as accountabil-ity and fairness; for a critical overview, see Grey and Jenkins (1995).
13. One important mechanism for cost containment in the public sphere is fiscal congruity, which means the equivalence of cost and benefit streams; actors or organizations responsible for

financing adjustment measures should in principle and in the long run recoup the benefits from the investment (Schmid *et al.*, 1992: 205–9).

14. Europäische Kommission (1999: 6 and 7).

15. Europäische Kommission (1998). At the end of February 2000, the German chancellor Gerhard Schröder decided to fill this gap by introducing a 'green card' immigration scheme for some 30 000 specialists in IT from Eastern Europe and other, non-European, countries. A tenfold employment growth was expected to follow the removal of this bottleneck. At the European level (EU15), the shortage of highly skilled IT specialists is put at 140 000.

16. We draw here on Madsen (1998) and Kruhøffer (1999). Recently, with the shift of job rotation to the private sector, larger firms are being privileged and the proportion of women has declined as a result.

17. I am not discussing the long-run macroeconomic side-effects that might affect employment, for instance wage cost pressure due to the reduced labour force or the incentive for economically inactive people to enter the labour force; see Madsen (1998) and the bibliographical references given in this chapter.

18. The 'Job rotation' network reports that 13 EU member states have now implemented job rotation schemes involving 3 000 firms, some 100 000 employees and 25 000 unemployed individuals. Thus approximately one in every four employees on training leave is being replaced by an unemployed person.

19. As recently stipulated in the Netherlands (2000) and in Germany (2001).

20. The public employment service pays an income supplement of 50 per cent of the difference between the former full-time wage and the actual part-time wage for a maximum duration of 12 months, on condition that the resulting vacancy is filled in part by unemployed people. Thus the Finnish scheme is a kind of national job-sharing programme. In 1994, 390 people took advantage of the scheme; by 1997, the figure had risen to 6525 (about 0.3 per cent), most of them women. The trend is still upwards.

21. Another case is the Italian legal concept of 'para-subordination' whereby a person works (part-time) for several employers simultaneously, but is treated as continuously employed for the purposes of employment rights and social protection.

22. Recent changes in the German regulations have introduced training programmes during longer phases of short-time working.

23. Auer (2000) and in Chapter 3 of the present volume provides some evidence on this point.

24. In the literature, such arrangements are also know as 'efficient contracts', a notion that dates back to a model proposed originally by McDonald and Solow (1981).

25. In this model, there was an implicit insurance arrangement based on ingeniously designed wage cuts that preserved full social insurance entitlements.

26. See, for the United States, Appelbaum (2000); for Europe, CERC (1994), Gustafsson (1996), Dingeldey (2000).

27. See, among others, OECD (1995: 171–202), Thenner (2000), Fagan and Rubery (1996), O'Reilly and Fagan (1998).

28. The excellent comparative study by Janet Gornick (1997) on social policy supporting the employment of mothers reaches the same conclusion; she includes Denmark and France among the leading countries in this respect, thereby demonstrating that Esping-Andersen's welfare regime typology (Esping-Andersen, 1990) does not always accord with expectations; see also Thenner (2000).

29. Information communicated personally by Catharina Bäck, head of unit in the Ministry of Health and Social Affairs in Stockholm (Sweden).

30. Or six years if a second child is born within the three years. Within this period, however, men and women can take the leave alternately. They are also allowed to work part-time below the social security threshold of 18 hours.

31. Until 2000, the German regulation did not fulfil this condition. If both partners had reduced their working time to 20 hours in order to share childcare, they would not have been entitled to parental leave allowances. Since 2001, the German regulations have been more generous.

32. This idea probably goes back to Gösta Rehn (1988 [1944]), who saw regular sabbatical leaves as an effective work-sharing instrument in the fight against unemployment.

33. According to preliminary evidence, about 5 per cent of teachers took advantage of the scheme in the late 1980s, and the replacement rate was almost 100 per cent. Take-up declined in the 1990s and replacement was even forbidden because of budget deficits. But even in the worst case, the employment level is maintained. The German *Länder* of Bremen, Rhineland Palatinate, North Rhine-Westphalia and (most recently) Bavaria have introduced this programme and extended it to all salaried public-sector employees.

34. The expected significant positive correlation between unemployment and normalized expenditure does not even appear if the extremely high-spending countries, Denmark and the Netherlands, are excluded; the correlation changes to $r = -0.05$ (panel A) and $r = 0.09$ (panel B). The figures for the Netherlands and Denmark are to some extent a statistical artefact, since a certain number of elderly or disabled unemployed drop off the register and are thus counted in the expenditure but not as unemployed.

35. See Bellmann and Jackman (1996) and, especially, Nickell and Layard (1999).

36. On the German situation, especially in North Rhine-Westphalia, see Weinkopf (1996).

37. Firms going into liquidation or planning mass redundancies are required by German law to draw up a so-called 'social plan': management and the works council put in place measures to avoid redundancies or to provide compensation or alternative options (training and so on).

38. This holds also for the OECD; notable exceptions are France (where men and women can retire at 60) and Austria (where women can retire at 55 and men at 60).

39. The average figures conceal considerable differences. In Belgium, the average retirement age for men is around 57, in Iceland 69 and in Japan 67; for women, it is 54 in Belgium, 67 in Iceland and 64 in Japan (OECD, 1998).

40. See Casey (1996), OECD (1995, 1998), European Commission (1999a: 109–26).

41. The Danish labour minister, Ove Hygym, supported such a project.

42. A similar model has been proposed in Germany as part of an effort to develop 'flexible entitlements'; see Rabe and Langelüddeke (1999).

43. The 1997 pension reform in Austria did this for civil servants by adjusting their pension scheme to individual situations. Pensions are now calculated on the basis of the best 15 earning years in the working life (as happens in Sweden). From a transitional labour market point of view, however, average earnings over the whole of the working life would be the appropriate basis.

44. For an excellent overview and discussion, see Miles (1998).

45. On the legal aspects of transitional labour markets, see Wilthagen and Rogowski in this volume.

46. On the difference and interaction between 'government' and 'governance', see, for instance, Lallement (1999) and the related concept of 'embedded negotiation systems', in Scharpf (1997: 204–55, for example).

47. See de Koning and Mosley in this volume.

REFERENCES

Appelbaum, E. (ed.) (2000), *Balancing Acts. Easing the Burdens and Improving the Options for Working Families*, Washington, DC: Economic Policy Institute.

Arrow, K.J. (1994), 'Methodological Individualism and Social Knowledge', in *AEA Papers and Proceedings*, 84(2) May, 1–9.

Ashby, R.W. (1979 [1956]), *An Introduction to Cybernetics*, London, Chapman & Hall University Paperbacks.

Atkinson, J., H. Bielenski, G. Gasparini, J. Hartmann and F. Huijgen (1999), 'Employment Options of the Future. First Analyses of a Representative Survey in all 15 EU Member States and Norway on behalf of the European Foundation for the Improvement of Living and Working Conditions', Dublin and Munich (Infratest Burke), mimeo.

Auer, P. (2000), *Employment Revival in Europe. Labour Market Success in Austria, Denmark, Ireland and the Netherlands*, Geneva: International Labour Office.

Bellmann, L. and R. Jackman (1996), 'The Impact of Labour Market Policy on Wages, Employment and Labour Market Mismatch', in G. Schmid, J. O'Reilly and K. Schömann (eds), *International Handbook of Labour Market Policy and Evaluation*, Cheltenham, UK, and Brookfield, US: Edward Elgar, pp. 725–46.

Bernstein, P.L. (1996), *Against the Gods. The Remarkable Story of Risk*, New York: John Wiley & Sons.

Buchanan, J.M. (1998), 'The Fiscal Crises in Welfare Democracies: With Some Implications for Public Investment', in H. Shibata and T. Ihori (eds), *The Welfare State, Public Investment, and Growth. Selected Papers from the 53rd Congress of the International Institute of Public Finance*, Tokyo: Springer, pp. 3–16.

Cappelli, P., L. Bassie, H. Katz, D. Knoke, P. Osterman and M. Useem (1997), *Change in Work*, New York and Oxford: Oxford University Press.

Carnoy, M. (1999), 'The Family, Flexible Work and Social Cohesion at Risk', *International Labour Review*, 138(4), 411–29.

Casey, B. (1996), 'Exit Options From the Labour Force', in G. Schmid, J. O'Reilly and K. Schömann (eds), *International Handbook of Labour Market Policy and Evaluation*, Cheltenham, UK and Brookfield, US: Edward Elgar, pp. 379–401.

Castells, M. (1996), *The Rise of the Network Society* (Volume I: *The Information Age. Economy, Society and Culture*), Cambridge, MA and Oxford: Blackwell Publishers.

CERC (1994), *Social Welfare and Economic Activity of Women in Europe*, V/2184/94-EN, Brussels: European Commission.

Delsen, L. and G. Reday-Mulvey (1995), *Gradual Retirement in the OECD Countries. Macro and Micro Issues and Policies*, Aldershot: Dartmouth Publishing Company.

Denys, J. and P. Simoens (1999), 'Elderly on the Labour Market: Belgium', *Employment Observatory, SYSDEM-Trends*, 33, Winter, 9–15.

Dingeldey, I. (ed.) (2000), *Erwerbstätigkeit und Familie in Steuer- und Sozialversicherungssystemen. Begünstigungen und Belastungen verschiedener familialer Erwerbsmuster im Ländervergleich*, Opladen: Leske + Budrich.

Esping-Andersen, G. (1990), *The Three Worlds of Welfare Capitalism*, Princeton, NJ: Princeton University Press.

Europäische Kommission (1998), *Beschäftigungsmöglichkeiten in der Informationsgesellschaft*, Luxemburg: Amt für amtliche Veröffentlichungen der Europäischen Gemeinschaften.

Europäische Kommission (1999), 'Die Europäische Beschäftigungsstrategie. Europa geht wieder an die Arbeit', *ESF InfoRevue*, 9, September, 1–8.

European Commission (1999a), *Employment in Europe 1999*, Luxembourg: Office for Official Publications of the European Communities.

European Commission (1999b), *A Europe for all Ages*, Brussels, Com [1999] 221, valid from 21 May.

Fagan, C. and J. Rubery (1996), 'Transitions between Family Formation and Paid Employment', in G. Schmid, J. O'Reilly and K. Schömann (eds), *International Handbook of Labour Market Policy and Evaluation*, Cheltenham, UK and Brookfield, US: Edward Elgar, pp. 348–78.

Foerster, H. von (1993), *KybernEthik*, Berlin: Merve Verlag.

Gazier, B. (ed.) (1999), *Employability: Concepts and Policies*, 1998 Report of the Employment Observatory Research Network, Berlin: European Commission.

Gazier, B. and N. Thevenot (2000), 'Analysing Business Services Employment – some Theoretical and Methodological Remarks', in D. Anxo and D. Storrie (eds), *The Job*

Creation Potential of the Service Sector in Europe, Brussels: European Commission (Employment Observatory Research Network), pp. 243–66.

Gelderbloom, A. and J. de Koning (2002), 'Exclusion of Older Workers, Productivity and Training', in K. Schömann and P.J. O'Connell (eds), *Education, Training and Employment Dynamics: Transitional Labour Markets in the European Union*, Cheltenham, UK and Northampton, US: Edward Elgar, forthcoming.

Giddens, A. (1996 [1994]), *Beyond Left and Right. The Future of Radical Politics*, Cambridge and Oxford: Polity Press.

Gornick, J.C. (1997), 'Supporting the Employment of Mothers: Policy Variation Across Fourteen Welfare States', *Journal of European Social Policy*, 7(1), 45–70.

Grey, A. and B. Jenkins (1995), 'From Public Administration to Public Management: Reassessing A Revolution?', *Public Administration*, 73, 75–99.

Gustafsson, S. (1996), 'Tax Regimes and Labour Market Performance', in G. Schmid, J. O'Reilly and K. Schömann (eds), *International Handbook of Labour Market Policy and Evaluation*, Cheltenham, UK and Brookfield, US: Edward Elgar, pp. 811–42.

Knight, F. H. (1964 [1921]), *Risk, Uncertainty & Profit*, New York: Century Press.

Kruhøffer, J. (1999), 'Job Rotation in Denmark. Status and Problems', in G. Schmid and K. Schömann (eds), *Learning from Denmark*, Discussion Paper FS I 99–201, Berlin: Social Science Research Centre, pp. 17–23.

Lallement, M. (1999), *Les gouvernances de l'emploi. Relations professionnelles et marché du travail en France et en Allemagne*, Paris: Desclées de Brouwer.

Madsen, P.K. (1998), 'A transitional labour market: the Danish paid leave arrangements', in European Academy of the Urban Environment (ed.), *New institutional arrangements in the labour market. Transitional labour markets as a new full employment concept* (EA.UE ISSN 0949–5029), Berlin: European Academy of the Urban Environment, pp. 68–73.

Martin, J.P. (2000), 'What Works Among Active Labour Market Policies: Evidence from OECD Countries Experiences', *OECD Economic Studies*, no. 30, 2000/1, pp. 79–113.

McDonald, I.M. and R.M. Solow (1981), 'Wage Bargaining and Employment', *American Economic Review*, 71, 896–908.

Miles, D. (1998), 'The Implications of Switching from Unfunded to Funded Pension Systems', *National Institute Economic Review*, 163(1), 71–86.

Morin, M.L. (ed.) (1999), *Prestation de Travail et Activité de Service*, Paris: La Documentation Française.

Mosley, H. and Th. Kruppe (1996), 'Employment Stabilization through Short-time Work', in G. Schmid, J. O'Reilly and K. Schömann (eds), *International Handbook of Labour Market Policy and Evaluation*, Cheltenham, UK and Brookfield, US: Edward Elgar, pp. 594–622.

Mühlböck, B. (1995), 'Voest-Alpine-Stahlstiftung – Ein Modell der Zukunft', Vortragsmanuskript vom 29. September 1995, Linz.

Nickell, S. and R. Layard (1999), 'Labour Market Institutions and Economic Performance', in O. Ashenfelter and David Card (eds), *Handbook of Labor Economics*, vol. 3, Amsterdam: Elsevier Science, pp. 3029–84.

OECD (1995), *The Transition from Work to Retirement*, Paris: OECD Publications.

OECD (1998), *Maintaining Prosperity in an Ageing Society*, Paris: OECD Publications.

OECD (1999), *Employment Outlook*, Paris: OECD Publications.

Okun, A.M. (1975), *Equality and Efficiency. The Big Trade-off*, Washington, DC: The Brookings Institution.

O'Reilly, J. and C. Fagan (eds) (1998), *Part-time Prospects – An International Comparison of Part-time Work in Europe, North-America and the Pacific Rim*, London and New York: Routledge.

Pitt-Catsouphes, M. (2000), 'A Coming of Age: Work/Life and Flexibility', in E. Appelbaum (ed.), *Balancing Acts. Easing the Burdens and Improving the Options for Working Families,* Washington, DC: Economic Policy Institute, pp. 139–48.

Rabe, B. and A. Langelüddeke (1999), 'Flexible Anwartschaften als Element der Rentenreform', *Wirtschaftsdienst*, 4, 237–44.

Rehn, G. (1988 [1944]), '3 manaders semester som medel mot arbetslöshet', *Full sysselsättning utan inflation. Skrifter i urval*, Stockholm: Tidens Förlag, pp. 357–71.

Reinecke, K. (2000), 'Beschäftigungsförderung via Tarifvertrag', *Mitbestimmung*, 1–2, 66–8.

Scharpf, F.W. (1997), 'Games Real Actors Play. Actor-Centered Institutionalism', *Policy Research*, Boulder, CO and Oxford: Westview Press.

Scharr, F. (1997), 'Konzessionsverträge als Element einer beschäftigungsorientierten Tarifpolitik', *ifo Dresden Berichtet*, 1, 16–22.

Schmähl, W. and J. Gatter (1994), 'Options for Extending the Working Period and Flexibilisation in the Transition to Retirement in the German Insurance Industry: The Current Situation and Assessment for the Future', *Geneva Papers on Risk and Insurance (Issues and Practice)*, 73, 433–71.

Schmid, G. (1994), 'Equality and Efficiency in the Labor Market: Towards a Socioeconomic Theory of Cooperation', in G. Schmid (ed.), *Labor Market Institutions in Europe. A Socioeconomic Evaluation of Performance*, Armonk, NY: M.E. Sharpe, pp. 243–80.

Schmid, G., B. Reissert and G. Bruche (1992), *Unemployment Insurance and Active Labour Market Policy. Financing Systems in International Comparison*, Detroit, MI: Wayne State University Press.

Schömann, K., S. Flechtner, R. Mytzek and I. Schömann (2000), 'Moving towards Employment Insurance – Unemployment Insurance and Employment Protection in the OECD', Discussion Paper FS I 00–201, Social Science Research Centre Berlin.

Sen, A. (1995), 'Rationality and Social Choice', *The American Economic Review*, 85(1), March, 1–24.

Sen, A. (1999), 'The Possibility of Social Choice', *The American Economic Review*, 89(3), June, 349–78.

Solow, R.M. (1990), *The Labor Market as a Social Institution*, Oxford: Basil Blackwell.

Thenner, M. (2000), 'Familienpolitik als Politik zur Vereinbarkeit von Familie und Beruf', in Irene Dingeldey (ed.), *Erwerbstätigkeit und Familie in Steuer- und Sozialversicherungssystemen. Begünstigungen und Belastungen verschiedener familialer Erwerbsmuster im Ländervergleich*, Opladen: Leske + Budrich, pp. 95–129.

Thurman, J. and G. Trah (1990), 'Part-time Work in International Perspective', *International Labour Review*, 129(1), 23–40.

Vidmar, S. (1999), 'Atypische Beschäftigung in Schweden', in E. Tàlos (ed.), *Atypische Beschäftigung. Internationale Trends und sozialstaatliche Regelungen*, Vienna: Manzsche Verlags- und Universitätsbuchhandlung.

Weinkopf, C. (1996), *Arbeitskräftepools*, Munich and Meering: Rainer Hampp Verlag.

Winter-Ebmer, R. (2000), Evaluating an Innovative Redundancy-Retraining Project: The Austrian Steel Foundation', Discussion Paper No. 277, Bonn: Institut für die Zukunft der Arbeit (IZA).

Index